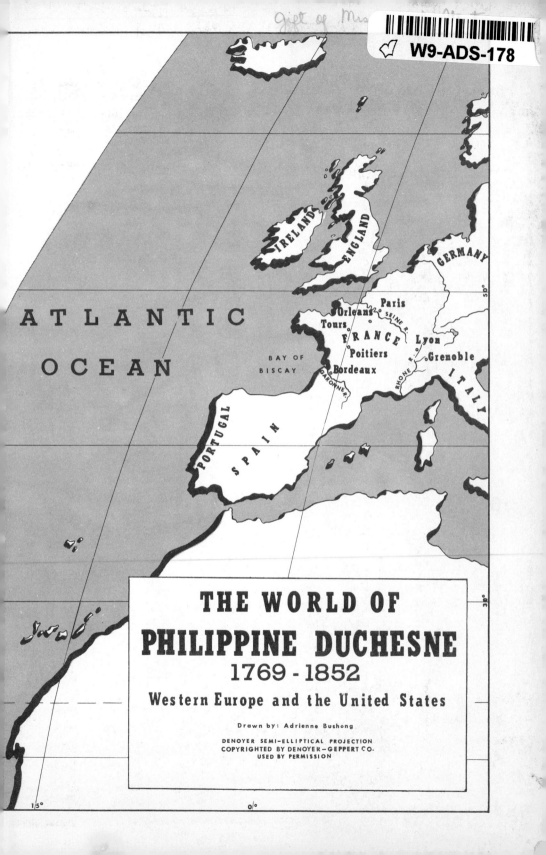

ATLANTIC

OCEAN

IRELAND

ENGLAND

GERMANY

Paris
SEINE R.
Orleans
Tours
FRANCE
Lyon
Poitiers
Grenoble
BAY OF
BISCAY
Bordeaux
GARONNE R.
RHONE R.
ITALY

PORTUGAL

SPAIN

THE WORLD OF
PHILIPPINE DUCHESNE
1769 - 1852
Western Europe and the United States

Drawn by: Adrienne Bushong

PHILIPPINE DUCHESNE

Frontier Missionary of the Sacred Heart

1769–1852

Portrait by the Austrian Artist Buvard.

PHILIPPINE DUCHESNE

✧✧

Frontier Missionary of the Sacred Heart

1769—1852

✧✧

by LOUISE CALLAN, R.S.C.J.

With an Introduction by
THE MOST REVEREND JOSEPH E. RITTER, S.T.D.
Archbishop of St. Louis

THE NEWMAN PRESS · WESTMINSTER, MARYLAND
1957

Dedicated

Through the Hands of Saint John Francis Regis, S.J.
to
THE SACRED HEART OF JESUS

Author's Note

A BOOK is always the fruit of an idea. The germinal idea for this book came from the Reverend Raymond Corrigan, S.J., Head of the History Department, St. Louis University, for many years. He suggested it in 1940, the year in which Philippine Duchesne was beatified. So slow was I in accepting the suggestion that the work had not even been undertaken when he died in 1943. But he left me with the inspiration and the ideal of "scholarship at the service of the Church and the Society of the Sacred Heart," which made possible the compilation of the book, for it is in largest part just that. The confidence he had expressed and the courage he had instilled have at last borne fruit. The book should, therefore, be *in piam memoriam* of that scholarly and saintly Jesuit, Father Ray Corrigan, who was also my loyal friend.

An itemized bibliography has seemed unnecessary, since the text is copiously documented. Interlibrary loans from the Library of Congress and Harvard University have enabled me to obtain authentic material for the European background of the life. Mother Mary Dowling, R.S.C.J., librarian of Maryville College of the Sacred Heart, St. Louis, was untiring in her efforts to procure the books I needed and to return them on time. I have turned for help and advice to Father Ralph Bayard, C.M., Kenrick Seminary, St. Louis, well-known expert in the field of pioneer Catholic development in the Mississippi Valley and Texas; to Father Joseph Donnelly, S.J., an authority on the history of St. Louis and its environs in frontier days, who allowed me the use of the St. Louis University library, particularly the files of *The Shepherd of the Valley;* also to Father Martin F. Hasting, S.J., of St. Louis University, for help with research; to Mr. Charles Van Ravenswaay,

Director of the Missouri Historical Society, St. Louis, who allowed me to use collections of precious documents housed in the archives of that Society, also the files of the *Missouri Gazette* and the *Missouri Republican*, gave me the freedom of the library, and let me draw information from his own note files on early St. Louis; he also discussed with me problems I encountered and furnished photostat copies of Duchesne originals and related documents. Through his kindness I gained the cordial assistance of several members of the staff at Missouri Historical Society's headquarters, and on them I made many calls for help and information. My niece, Mrs. Cecil Rogan Allen, of Nashville, Tennessee, procured for me a photograph of the rare print of St. Charles, c.1850, which was later acquired by the Missouri Historical Society. Mr. Paul Piaget of St. Louis and Mr. R. T. Steigemeier of St. Charles generously helped me prepare the illustrations for the book. I must also mention the courtesy of Longmans, Green and Company, New York, in allowing me to use excerpts from *The Society of the Sacred Heart in North America*, which they published for me in 1937. Mr. Clarence B. Odell, managing editor of Denoyer-Geppert Company, Chicago, directed the preparation of the map depicting "the World of Philippine Duchesne."

The bulk of the material incorporated in this volume comes from the archives of the Mother House of the Society of the Sacred Heart in Rome. The beatification of Mother Duchesne in 1940 made possible the release of her hitherto unpublished letters, which have been furnished to me in authenticated photostat, typescript, or long-hand copies. This meant an enormous amount of work on the part of many Religious of the Sacred Heart working in the General Secretariat of the Mother House, whose names are, for the most part, unknown to me, but to whom I am deeply grateful.

In editing these letters I have cited few of them full-length. I have generally omitted salutation and complimentary close, though these are often as revealing of character as the body of the letters, and I have corrected the spelling of proper names in order to avoid the repetition of [sic], which would otherwise appear in tiresome succession, for Mother Duchesne spelled proper names with an originality that is at times bewildering, as, for example, when *Monsieur Toquet* turns out to be Father Hilary Tucker. French names have in some instances been anglicized by omitting accents in accordance with American usage, for example, *Amelie* and *Adelaide*. The family name *Perier* is used without accent in the life of Mother Duchesne published in Paris in 1927. Where omissions in letters are indicated, the reason is usually that the material so omitted is repetitious or based on false information. My effort has been to make the book as largely autobiographical as possible, hence the incorporation of so many letters; for when Philippine Duchesne speaks for herself, we know we have the *real* Philippine Duchesne.

In the documentation I have acknowledged my indebtedness to many friends and to many of my Sisters in religion. Mother Anne Webster allowed me to make liberal use of her Master's thesis at St. Louis University, in which she translated and edited the Rosati-Duchesne correspondence. Mrs. William K. Holland (Dorothy Garesché), of the English Department, Maryville College, read the manuscript critically and gave helpful suggestions which I adopted. I owe very special thanks to Mother Marion Bascom, R.S.C.J., professor of English, Maryville College, who read each chapter of the manuscript as it was completed, and again when it was revised, to insure that the medium used for the portrait was pure, though as plain as Philippine herself. To enumerate the many other persons who have aided me over a period of nearly ten years would be a personal satisfaction to me, but too space-consuming to be practical. They all realize the sincerity of my gratitude. Three communities of the Sisters of the Visitation, however, must have special mention—Georgetown, St. Louis, and Wheeling, West Virginia, for from them I obtained invaluable material and help.

In the typing of the manuscript I was aided by many Maryville "Children of the Sacred Heart," above all by Celeste Michel Drain, Class of '53, on whom I also relied for some of the research needed for the background of the American period of Mother Duchesne's life. To her father, Mr. Charles Michel III, I am indebted for the photographs of the family portraits of General Bernard Pratte and his charming wife, of whom Mr. Michel is a lineal descendant.

In compiling the selective index of names, I have relied on the efficient help of Mother Corinne Happy, who had already spent long hours poring over old newspapers and checking steamboat lists, notices, and other items to lighten the task of research.

Special acknowledgment must be made of the editorial work on the manuscript done by Father Leonard J. Fick, Ph.D., of the Pontifical

College Josephinum, Worthington, Ohio, and of the devoted constancy which Mother Marion Bascom, M.A. (Oxon.), and Mother Mary O'Callaghan, Ph.D., brought to the tedious task of proof-reading. To Mr. John J. McHale of The Newman Press the Society of the Sacred Heart wishes to express its sincere thanks for the courage with which he undertook the publication of this monumental (the word is his own) volume, and for the unvarying kindness and courtesy he has shown since the day the manuscript was turned over to him.

To His Excellency, the Most Reverend Joseph E. Ritter, S.T.D., Archbishop of St. Louis and fourth successor of Mother Duchesne's best friend in America, Bishop Joseph Rosati, I am deeply, humbly, grateful for the beautiful paragraphs with which he so kindly introduces this work of love.

My filial gratitude for the privilege of making this study of the life of our great pioneer missionary goes first to Very Reverend Mother Marie-Thérèse de Lescure, Superior General of the Society of the Sacred Heart, then to Reverend Mother Ursula Benziger, Assistant General, through whom the primary source material and other information from the archives of the Mother House, as well as the data gathered by the Religious of the Sacred Heart at Boisfleury, near Grenoble, were transmitted to me. To Reverend Mother Angela McCabe, successor of Philippine Duchesne as Superior Vicar in the Mississippi Valley, my debt of gratitude surpasses expression here, not merely for the time and opportunity to compile the biography, but for encouragement, understanding, and sympathy, as well as enthusiastic interest and a rare appreciation of the character, career, and sanctity of Philippine Duchesne.

LOUISE CALLAN, R.S.C.J.

MARYVILLE COLLEGE OF THE SACRED HEART
ST. LOUIS, MISSOURI

Feast of St. John Francis Regis, June 16, 1957

contents

Part Two: IMMOLATION IN AMERICA

Introduction

IN THE FACE of the complexities of modern life, of the materialism and secularism that seem to engulf modern society, and especially in view of the world's forgetfulness of God, everyone today needs to be enlightened and encouraged and inspired to persevere in the gigantic struggle for salvation. The servants of God who have trod the rough road before us provide just that enlightenment, inspiration, and encouragement.

In this study of the life of Blessed Rose Philippine Duchesne, the gifted author has accurately and painstakingly traced the earthly career of an illustrious and saintly woman. More than that, however, she has penned a warm and inspiring story of the life, the labors, the struggle for holiness of a humble servant of God. From its pages, the very heart of Blessed Philippine speaks to the modern man and woman; her soul pours out its treasures for their enrichment; her labors eloquently beckon to them to follow.

Rose Philippine Duchesne was a pioneer apostle on American soil, and like a true apostle, her soul was literally on fire with an unquenchable zeal for souls and love for God. Her vigorous apostolic life was nourished by interior recollection and prayer that became almost habitual. Truly she was a "valiant woman" spoken of by the inspired writer, one whose name is held in benediction.

May this work of one of her devoted daughters open the way for her influence to enter more readily into a world that needs her inspiration.

MOST REVEREND JOSEPH E. RITTER
Archbishop of Saint Louis

May 1, 1956

PROLOGUE: | ## *Of the Frontier*

PHILIPPINE DUCHESNE was of the frontier in practically every aspect of her life. The rugged and beautiful province of her native Dauphiny was a frontier of old France which developed a vigorous genius for opposition and resistance, for initiative and independence. The men of Dauphiny, like all frontiersmen, were good at war and at trade, and many of them were expert in the law. Philippine's family belonged to that middle class of society which, during the closing decades of the eighteenth century, was making its influence felt all over France by hard work, increasing wealth, and a remarkable measure of wisdom. On her mother's side the Perier name was prominent in industrial circles before revolution swept the country in 1789; while her father, Pierre-François Duchesne, was to win distinction in both the provincial and the national life of France, becoming a political figure whom even Napoleon himself feared and against whom he used his dictatorial veto.

Philippine's home training was wholesome and without luxury. The growing girl mastered practical skills that stood her in good stead in later years—churning, baking, dipping candles, trimming wicks, making and mending clothes. She learned to nurse the sick and to care for little children. She was intense in her natural affections, yet sacrificed these with a spontaneity that was at times interpreted as selfishness. She sought religious life in an eighteenth-century cloister, from which revolution drove her. She knew then what it meant to risk her life in order to bring help to those who were in physical or spiritual need.

She became a pioneer member of an order in which a new type of religious life was tried out with remarkable success. As her patron saint she chose that "mountain man" beyond compare, John Francis Regis, missionary of the Society of Jesus. Long years of positive training stamped her with habits and loyalties that would endure through life, no matter how the grind of circumstances might wear down her strength. Her life-work brought her at middle age to the very fringe of migration on the American frontier for nearly thirty-five years of strenuous labor. Hers was the task of clearing the land, breaking the ground, preparing the soil, and garnering the first meager yield. The cion she planted was sprung from Old World roots. In the new environment it developed hardy and true to the parent stock, as one with it as the branch is one with the vine, yet bearing fruit whose flavor was unmistakably American.

She had little creative imagination or practical foresight, yet a vision lured her westward, always unfolding before her mind and heart vast opportunities for spreading the Kingdom of Christ along the American frontier and beyond it. She knew the isolation of remote regions, the primitive conditions of a one-room cabin with a loft overhead. She learned to live at peace with disappointment, yet eagerly to press forward, to extend a helping hand without discrimination to neighbors in need, especially to missionary priests whose exhausting labors she longed to share. Like many another pioneer woman, she was a strong, lonely soul, intimate with few in America, and those few usually much younger than herself—young women who spoke her language, to whom she revealed the beauty of the Master's face, the love of His Sacred Heart. This kind of intimacy was characteristic of her, for she was possessed of the spirit of youth even in the last decades of a long life of self-oblation. Never hardened by contact with an untamed environment, she was venturesome enough at three-score-and-ten to gamble with the uncertainties of the Indian frontier to win souls for Christ.

She shared life on both sides of that frontier, settling first in what she called almost desperately "the remotest village of the United States," pioneering in the Mississippi Valley among Creoles and Americans, and crossing the line to work among the Potawatomi. She journeyed over roads that had once been Indian traces or buffalo trails. She traveled in primitive fashion, on foot or on horseback, in springless carriage or two-wheeled cart, by pirogue or raft or steamboat. She knew the mighty Mississippi and the turbulent Missouri, knew their fog and fever, their treacherous current and unpredictable course, their seasons of freeze and flood. She experienced the changing fortunes of pioneer life, now heart-warming, now heart-breaking; its times of soaring hope alternating with spells of drab depression, for which only heroic faith and love could muster enough grim determination to carry on.

Her name has been associated through more than a century with strength, endurance, austerity, with burning zeal for souls and patience under trial and failure, with a certain severity of manner and outlook, and complete detachment from the things people generally cling to so tenaciously. Yet in this apostle of the Sacred Heart there was sweetness and sympathy, as well as strength; and hand in hand with endurance went a sensitiveness that made it all the more heroic. Her austerity was not born of any natural relish for suffering, nor was her patience the flowering of innate self-control. Hers was a vigorous personality, an intensely affectionate nature not ashamed to give expression to its inmost sentiments, a will fired with ambition to do big things and motivated from her 'teens by the single, dominating urge of love for the Sacred Heart. Her devotion to our Lady was as strong and tender as her own character, while her childlike trust in Divine Providence, her reliance on God, her Father, sustained her in courage and hope, no matter what difficulties she faced in her mission on the frontier.

She kept through life her gracious Old World charm, a gentle and reserved manner, a dignity that impressed mere acquaintances as somewhat aloof and out of touch with American ways of life. To a great extent her inability to express herself in English accounted for this impression. Let the conversation flow in French, and then the intensity and vivacity with which she spoke revealed her in a truer light. Her culture and refinement, as well as her education, which was of a rather high type for her day, made her respected and admired by the people who were privileged to know her, and she was loved with loyal affection by the young American and Creole girls who gathered around her in schoolroom or cloister and by the nuns who made up her religious family. The institutions she founded were all *firsts* on the religious and educational frontier of the Middle-West, and the name of Rose Philippine Duchesne heads the list of pioneer women of Missouri commemorated in bronze in St. Louis. She broke a trail that has led thousands of souls to Christ and has broadened into a highway of culture in the United States, Canada, and Latin America.

She had become, early in life, a settler on the spiritual frontier to which prayer draws the soul, that borderland of the supernatural which lies far beyond the ken and reach of mediocrity, but which was the constant dwelling-place of *Quah-kah-ka-num-ad*, the "Woman-Who-Prays-Always." That was the name the Potawatomi Indians gave her. That is the way they say it today. They were keenly observant of the white people who came amongst them. They singled her out from the rest. To the "good old lady," as they sometimes titled her with grateful affection, they brought the best of what they had—fresh meat, tender corn, or a newly-laid egg. And with intent gaze they watched her, hour on hour, as she knelt in prayer in the log church at Sugar Creek, where at long last in 1841 she reached the haven for which she had embarked on the *Rebecca* in 1818. She was old and broken in health. She was too weak to bear the hardships of the Indian frontier—almost too weak to throw the yarn over her knitting needle, yet feeling a need for that little natural activity, as she expressed it. But there was no faltering in her courage, no flagging in her prayer. That was her apostolate now. The ecstasy of night adoration, so frequent in her early years, may have passed long since, but the flame of love for the Sacred Heart burned with ever increasing ardor in her heart. In the August heat, in the December blizzard, "from the rising of the sun to the going down thereof," she was to be found almost continually in her little corner of the church, or lying exhausted on a hard pallet in the cabin-convent, rapt in communion with the God of her heart and the Heart of her God—*Quah-kah-ka-num-ad, Woman-Who-Prays-Always.*

PART ONE | *Preparation in France*

one

A Girl's Will
to Serve God

1. 1769—1788

> *I will go unto the altar of God:*
> *to God Who giveth joy to my youth.*
>
> Liturgy of the Mass

THE ROTTEN FABRIC of French political and social life was beginning to sag and tear and fall to pieces as the eighteenth century passed into its seventh decade. The ugly rent that had long divided Parisian from provincial life grew wider every year. Paris still imposed its will on many of the less resolute towns, but there were sections of the country where outmoded views were no longer current in discussion, where the warp and woof of life were not spun from servility to local conventions or to privilege in court or army or church. That intangible yet very real political force called "public opinion" was operating in all grades of French society, but with especially marked effect among the bourgeoisie. Tastes, fashions, aspirations, all were changing as the century progressed. The hardworking middle-class folk were coming into easy circumstances, improving their condition in many ways: better housing, better furnishings, better food and clothes, and better education; yet they were always economical in expenditure. There were few costly pleasures or amusements, but religious and family feasts were celebrated in a lively fashion. If strict economy prevailed in everyday life, even among the wealthy, this was offset by gaiety, kindliness of heart, and that careful attention to little things in which the French excel. Undoubtedly the great social event in France during the eighteenth century was the rise of these

9

very people, the bourgeoisie, whose power was to be revealed astonishingly in 1789.

In the provinces, where many a town was beginning to grow in importance, there were interesting middle-class people, not tailored to the Parisian pattern, but very much themselves—alert, intelligent, home-loving, and well-bred. The Duchesnes and Periers belonged to this class. Their native Dauphiny was, and is, a province so diversified in natural beauty that it is difficult to say of any one area, "Here we have the real Dauphiny." The people of this old frontier province were possessed of characteristics that identified them in the minds of their countrymen of the eighteenth century, characteristics which remain today wherever the true *Dauphinois* is to be found: love of independence, readiness for a struggle—whether military or civic or domestic—courage combined with a certain rashness which led frequently to adventure, if not to romance, and an attitude of caution which Stendhal has embodied in a telling phrase, *la peur d'être dupe,* a native dread of being "taken in." They were good talkers, these people of Dauphiny, but not loquacious. Their taste for political and philosophical discussions was well developed, though the lively and impertinent manner in which they spoke so lightly at times of the most serious things often surprised the outsider who failed to grasp the depth of thought hidden under the cloak of gaiety. They were practical in their way of life, tenacious of their rights, proud of the moral integrity which gave them self-respect, and conscious of the influence which won for many of them a place of honor in the history of France. There are Duchesnes and Periers on the list. Tradition has a proverb to the point: *Gens du Dauphiné sont fins, fidèles, et fiers.*[1]

There is a brisk and sunny atmosphere along the valley of the swift Isère that lends an indefinable charm to the lovely countryside. Ascending the river from its meeting with the Rhone, one passes the town of Romans and the wharf of Saint-Marcellin and reaches the old provincial capital, Grenoble, built on both sides of the stream. The city has perhaps the most impressive situation of any in France. Its background in the *massif de la Chartreuse* is unique, and the range of snow-clad Alps rising abruptly to north and east forms a picturesque screen that shelters it as a natural windbreak. It is a pleasant place, with bracing air and unrivaled scenic beauty, still glorying in its frontier history.

In the last quarter of the eighteenth century it was a small town, with narrow streets and massive old buildings so crowded within the ramparts that these protecting walls seemed to squeeze and stifle the twenty-five thousand people they were meant to guard. Though there were some attractive dwelling places, on the whole, gray façades and grated windows lined the crooked lanes that were paved with small cobblestones. Less crooked and more dignified than other streets was *Grande Rue*, which ran between the city's two most vital public squares, *Place Saint-André* and *Place Grenette*. At Place Saint-André all was usually serious and dignified exteriorly, a bit pompous, perhaps, for it was flanked by several imposing buildings—the town hall, the fine old Church of Saint-André, which gave the square its name, and the *Palais de Justice* or courthouse, a veritable legal beehive. At the other end of Grande Rue lay Place Grenette, the town's ancient market square, lively, bustling, surrounded with shops and cafés. A noisy town pump, a litter of refuse, and groups of talkative town and country folk constantly breaking up and constantly renewed made Grenette more typical of provincial France than Place Saint-André.

The city itself, with its vivid and turbulent past, had been a focal point in the development of France, for as the capital of an important province it was the scene of almost every great event in the history of Dauphiny, from the Roman conquest to the movement of 1788 when, leading the way, it was the first among the cities of France to formulate the program of the Revolution. And there were Duchesnes and Periers taking an active part in that formulation.

The Periers are an interesting family, native to Dauphiny. On the old feudal estate of Chatelard one hamlet grew up in a particularly rocky area, hence its name, from Low Latin, *Pererium* (rocky) or *Perier*, and the name of its principal tenants. From this stock came Jacques Perier, who was living there at the close of the seventeenth century with his wife and their large family. The son who bore his father's name arrived in Grenoble about 1720 and went into business with a relative whose shop and home were in a large rented building in Rue Portetraine, later called Grande Rue.[2] This Jacques Perier had ability and education and was successful from the start, not only as a merchant but as a citizen, respected for high principles and manly conduct. He was welcomed into the social life of the upper bourgeoisie and in 1741 married Marie-Elizabeth Dupuy, daughter of a city consul of Grenoble. Jacques took his bride to the big house in Grande Rue, which he had purchased. After the fashion of the day the ground floor was used as a place of business, the basement served as a warehouse, and the upper stories became the home of the Perier family. A covered passage from the street into a courtyard offered privacy and access to the home by a side door. It was very much like the other homes in the neighborhood, large and uncomfortable, perhaps, but it housed a family highly respected in the city and joyously satisfied with life.

For five successive years the household was increased each May by a new baby: Claude (1742), Jean (1743), who died in infancy, Jean-Antoine (1744), Helene-Elizabeth (1745), and Jacques-Augustin (1746). Then, as if to make up for a break in the sequence, twin girls came to complete the family circle on June 4, 1748. These were Marie-Elizabeth and Rose-Euphrosine.

It was a hard-working, fun-loving, ambitious, well-to-do family. Jacques Perier took into business with him his nephew François, a clever, enterprising young man, who became keenly interested in textile manufacturing and drew his uncle into that field of business. To distinguish his own branch from other branches of the family, François later added to his name that of an estate he purchased at Saint-Ismier and so came to be known as François Perier-Lagrange. His wife was "Tante Lagrange" to the children of three generations in the family.

Jacques Perier's income and civic importance seem to have increased as rapidly as his family, while his reputation for honesty in business and fidelity to Catholicism won for him a prestige of which his children were justly proud. The home at Number 4, Grande Rue, was well managed; the children were well educated. The girls were trained in the arts and skills that made home life attractive and bound the family into an intimate and loyal group. There was friction at times among the boys, for Claude, though gay and personable, was given to brusque self-assertion, and Jean-Antoine hid his sensitive nature behind a casual reserve, while Augustin was jealous and moody and apt to be rash in word and action. The girls were an attractive trio to whom tradition attributes charm of manner as well as beauty and all the "elegant accomplishments" that graced young womanhood in those formal days.

Helene had reached her nineteenth birthday when her father gave her in marriage to Esprit-Alexandre Gueymar, a lawyer from Die in southwest Dauphiny, who had taken his place in the courts of Grenoble in 1757, when Helene was only twelve years old. Later on Gueymar became a judge of high standing and vice-president of the court of appeals. He was, moreover, raised to noble rank as Gueymar de Salière.

In the municipal library of Grenoble there is a curious manuscript dated June 16, 1764, containing some verses "in praise of the Misses Perier, twin sisters and daughters of a rich and honorable merchant in Grenoble." The admirer who wrote the lines ascribes to the twins "identical charms: beautiful eyes, small feet, white teeth—in a word they are equally beautiful. Indeed they are so very attractive, it is hard to know which one a sincere admirer should choose. In this predicament and at a loss to decide which is the lovelier, the truest good fortune for a man would be to marry them both." [3] Here we have the badinage of an eighteenth-century wag, no doubt, but in it the Perier twins come to life and grow more interesting. They had just passed their sixteenth birthday, and the fortune that would make up their dowries was certainly a considerable attraction in itself. Suitors were numerous enough to be exciting—doctors, lawyers, merchants, and the handsomely uniformed military officers who brought much romance into the social life of Grenoble. Among all these it was Pierre Jordan, a merchant from Lyons, who won the hand of Marie-Elizabeth. They were married in October, 1765, and though they were to live in Lyons, their children spent much of their young lives at the home of their grandparents in Grenoble.

That very year, 1765, Jean-Antoine Perier came home from the University of Orange with his degree in civil and canon law. His friend, Pierre-François Duchesne, who had been admitted to the parliamentary bar of Grenoble just the year before, now became a frequent caller at the Perier home. Soon another trousseau was under way, and on October 1, 1766, Jacques Perier's third daughter, Rose-Euphrosine, became Madame Duchesne, with a dowry, like that of her twin, of one hundred thousand francs.[4] Her father also provided an apartment for the young couple on the third floor of the family home, where they began married life in a calm and comfort that gave little hint of the storms that were ahead.

The Duchesne family had lived for generations in Dauphiny—first in the northwestern part of the province and later at Romans on the Isère to the southwest of Grenoble. There they built up a reputation as textile manufacturers and carried on a large export business, finding wide sale for their goods both in France and in her colonies. As this trade was lucrative, the Duchesnes, like the Periers, had money. But there were other assets on which both families relied with greater confidence—religious faith, personal integrity, and strength of character.

Antoine Duchesne, head of the family in the mid-eighteenth century, married Marie-Louise Enfantin in 1737. Six of their twelve children grew to maturity, four daughters and two sons. Three of the girls became religious in the Visitation Monastery at Romans.[5] The older boy inherited his father's business ability and carried on the mercantile tradition of the family. The younger one devoted his remarkable talents to law. This was Pierre-François Duchesne, who was to distinguish himself in Grenoble along legal, political, and social lines. His marriage to Rose-Euphrosine Perier gave him as life companion a woman of poise and distinction, who managed her home and family with a firm hand and an affectionate heart. She was, moreover, so true to Christian faith and principle that she deserved to mother a great saint.

The first of her seven daughters was born in 1767. Marie-Adelaide was a frail child on whom Madame Duchesne lavished care during the little girl's short life. In the spring of that same year Claude Perier married Marie-Charlotte Pascal and moved into an apartment adjoining the Duchesnes. The sisters-in-law became close friends, and for twenty years they shared joys and sorrows and personal interests in an intimacy that gave strength and courage to both. Life was gay and interesting at Number 4, Grande Rue, and its momentum was increased almost every year by the great event of a new arrival in the family. Marie-Charlotte Perier was a woman of quiet wisdom and devoted love, who entered so heartily into her husband's commercial concerns that she became as keen a business woman as he could desire, yet family life was dearer to them than their unique economic partnership. Of their twelve children, ten grew to maturity. Their first baby was a boy, named Jacques for his delighted grandfather, but the year of his birth, 1768, was also that of his death: the first sorrow had come.

A second daughter was born to the Duchesnes on August 29, 1769, and placed under the protection of Rose of Lima, first saint of the Americas. Her maternal grandmother held her at the baptismal font and her uncle Jean-Antoine Perier acted as godfather. There in the Church of St. Louis of France on September 8 an apostolic patron was given her with the name Rose Philippine.

Philip the Apostle . . . Rose of the Americas . . . St. Louis of France . . . September 8 . . . 1769: the combination was prophetic rather than coincidental. Through the long life span that stretched before this child, she would repeat to countless souls St.

Philip's "Come and see," and experience joys akin to his when he heard that unexpected confidence from strangers, "Sir, we wish to see Jesus." And in that very September of 1769 a woodsman from Virginia, Daniel Boone, was edging westward to hunt in a new wilderness and spy out lands in the great meadow of Kaintuck; and a French-Canadian hunter, Louis Blanchette, was at work on his new frontier cabin some twenty-five miles northwest of the trading-post young Auguste Chouteau had set up just five years before on the Mississippi and called *St. Louis de France*. Blanchette was staking a claim on the west bank of the Missouri where sturdy bluffs would give a future village the unromantic name of *Les Petites Côtes* or *Little Hills*, which Spanish officials would change to *San Carlos* and Americans would speak of as *St. Charles*.

Philippine was just a few months old when in April, 1770, the Perier household rejoiced in the birth of a baby girl, christened Elizabeth-Josephine. These two children were to grow up together almost as twin sisters. Soon there were enough little Duchesnes and Periers to make things lively for many a year. Even in a double household, twenty babies in twenty years is something of a record.[6] Amelie Duchesne and Marine Perier were born in 1771, but the baby Marine died in infancy. In Lyons that same year the Jordans' first boy was born—Camille, who was to make a name for himself in the political and literary history of France, and a place for himself in the heart of his cousin Philippine. Euphrosine Duchesne was born in 1772, and in 1773 the Periers were delighted with the arrival of another son, called Augustin for his moody and impetuous uncle. Three more boys had been added to the Perier roster by 1777, when Pierre-François Duchesne became godfather to little Casimir-Pierre Perier, who would one day dominate the political life of France. The Duchesnes had lost their fifth girl, Agathe-Justine, some months before Casimir's birth.

The children of this big double family were greatly loved by their parents and grandparents, but never spoiled. The Duchesne in Philippine came to the fore early, revealing itself in a thousand wiles and wails of wilfulness and self-assertion, of stubbornness and independence, which called for more than ordinary handling on the part of her mother. Firmly but gently the child was trained to obedience and self-control, to courtesy and consideration for others. She had in her natural make-up strength and generosity, and a depth of affection that for all its seeming reserve was easily stirred to unselfish service. It was not a simple process to temper the iron in that character, but her mother found that this child responded quickly to motives of piety and grasped with more than ordinary intelligence the fundamental religious training that was given the children at home.

Philippine would grow up to be beautiful, her parents thought. That pleased Pierre-François Duchesne. The child's eyes were deep and luminous, her features well-proportioned, her forehead high, her mouth firm, if a trifle large, her smile direct and winning. As she grew older and learned the secret of bringing sunshine into the lives of others, her smile was an index of the sincerity with which she offered her services and accepted comradeship. But small-pox disfigured her face while she was still quite young—a rather common misfortune in those days in France. The scars softened and even disappeared to a great extent in later life, but Philippine suffered keenly from the comments of thoughtless grown-ups who contrasted her with her pretty cousins. Yet there was no petty jealousy in her, though she could be very stiff and uncompromising.

Philippine was still a child when her uncle Claude Perier purchased from the Duke of Villeroy one of the most magnificent estates in Dauphiny, the chateau and park of Vizille, some ten or twelve miles south of Grenoble on the Romanche, a mountain tributary of the Drac River.[7] In the early seventeenth century this famous old castle had been the feudal stronghold of the notorious Constable de Lesdiguières, and by a strange reversal of destinies it was to become the cradle of the revolution that would deal the final blow to feudalism in France. Claude Perier converted large sections of the building and its dependencies into a textile factory, reserving spacious apartments overlooking the park for a residence, though he and his family continued to live most of the time in Grenoble.

Grenoble was an exciting town to live in and grow up in, especially if one lived on the main thoroughfare and had many relatives in the magistracy and city council. Parliamentary opposition to royal authority amounted at times to a bold struggle for independence in Grenoble. Little local revolutions frequently upset the quiet tenor of provincial life. Edicts from Paris levying new taxes met with such sharp resistance in the 1760's that the next decade brought sterner measures. On November 7, 1771, the last of the local *parlements* of France—that of Dauphiny—was suppressed by command of the King.[8] That was a day to remember and to rehearse for many a year.

Another was May 2, 1775, which saw the re-establishment of

the *parlement*. When the edict was registered and the ancient courts functioned again, the whole town celebrated the local victory.[9] The grand illumination that night made a fairyland of public buildings and private homes. Laughter and dancing and horseplay gave evidence of the people's joy and satisfaction. Philippine and her sister Marie-Adelaide and Josephine Perier were old enough to watch the scene in Place Saint-André from the safe distance of a third-story balcony. But they did not understand how much the re-establishment of the courts meant to the several lawyers in the family, nor could they follow the conversation of their elders about Grandfather Perier's withdrawing from the post of city consul and being succeeded by his son Claude.

Uncle Claude was a great favorite with Philippine. Though a man of shrewd business acumen, he was the best of company at home. He had a gay, humorous manner with the children, and his stories were far better than any they found in books. It mattered little to them that he was a royal counselor, charged with the salt tax in Grenoble; that he was the leading business man in the town and drove, perhaps, the sharpest bargains. He was their personal banker, and they often had more spending money than other children in the neighborhood. Philippine used her money as she pleased —she gave it to beggars or to the poor whom she visited with her mother. No use arguing with her about it. "That's what I choose to do with it," she would say in a tone which the family came to recognize as final. She had a mind and a will of her own, but more —she had a heart that went out in sympathy to all who were in need, and she was not slow to answer affection with proofs of love.

It was but natural that these children would draw together in groups according to age and taste, that intimacies would form and affections deepen as the years passed. Philippine and Josephine became inseparable friends. When they were old enough to begin formal lessons, they were placed under the tutelage of "Mademoiselle Sophie," later Madame Luc, a capable governess for whom the girls had great affection. The Perier boys were studying under a tutor. Among them Augustin was best loved by Philippine and Josephine. He was younger than they, but he and Camille Jordan, who was nearer their age, became their playmates and intimate friends.

Dolls had no appeal for Philippine. She loved living things and enjoyed reading about real people. Her literary taste may seem a bit austere, but she probably had no opportunity to enjoy lighter books. Lives of the saints, preferably martyrs terribly done to death, gripped her imagination and roused in her a desire to imitate their heroism. She and Augustin spent long hours together, poring over these fascinating true stories and dreaming of similar exploits in some far-off land and time. Tales of antiquity also attracted her. At the age of nine she chose to entertain sick little Marie-Adelaide with selections from a volume of Roman history. This, however, was a very normal choice. Grenoble has antiquity, and childhood, alive to past and present, could bring Hannibal and his elephants on the scenes, or Caesar with his Roman legions, or the Emperor Gratian, for whom the village of Cularo was renamed Gratian-opolis, which in time was softened to Grenoble. Rollin's *Ancient History* was on a shelf in her father's library—long-winded and dull, perhaps, but full of heroes and heroics. Grande Rue was the oldest street in town, following the route of a Roman road that once ran through it. Traces of those far-off days were to be seen in near-by courtyards—an inscription here, a tower there, a terrace built on the very ramparts constructed by the Romans. Grande Rue was a place where history came alive from the past and where it would be made in the not-too-distant future.

The year 1778 was crowded with new experiences for Philippine. The death of her sister Marie-Adelaide brought real sorrow into her life for the first time. Soon she became aware of her position in the big family: she was the eldest of the children, and that was a maturing responsibility. There was much sickness and suffering in Grenoble that year as a result of the "Flood of Saint Crispin," which occurred on the night of October 26–27 and was one of the worst inundations the town ever experienced. The poor who lived along the river banks were homeless for days, while fetid slime covered floors and furniture in homes and merchandise in warehouses. The Duchesnes and Periers were active in helping the flood victims. While their fathers and uncles worked with the townsfolk in carts and boats to bring them aid, Philippine and Josephine helped their mothers prepare food and clothing for distribution. When the water subsided, a wretched condition prevailed along the water front: mud and ooze in houses, streets, and aqueducts; disease rife among the people, thieves at work, shortage of food in spite of the efforts made to supply the needs of those in want.[10] It was a season Philippine would not forget, an experience she would meet again on the banks of rivers whose names were as yet unknown to her, but never in after-years would she see generosity comparable to that of her own family toward the poor.[11]

Philippine did not enjoy romping, boisterous games, but she

loved the steep climb up Mount Rachais, the rambles along the Isère from the Porte de la Graille to the confluence of the Drac River, the happy give-and-take in the courtyards or the school-room, the sunny afternoons spent at Cousin François' home at Saint-Ismier or picking daisies in the meadow beyond the Church of Saint-André. Delightful holidays were spent at Vizille. Philippine loved the quiet of the woods and countryside, where she roamed about with Josephine, or played in the beautiful park, or lay in the shade of a spreading tree and watched the white clouds piling up on the horizon to the east. She was fond of wandering off by her-self, but this love of solitude was not an indication of morose introversion. She was a healthy, strong-minded child, serious for her age, who enjoyed being alone at times with her own thoughts and with God, who was already making known His claims upon her love and her life. There was, however, no isolating herself from the family. Her mother kept her busy with little household duties that developed in her a sense of responsibility which was to mark her in later years, but the lighthearted gaiety of childhood was not stifled by restraint.

In spite of the wealth which might have brought luxury to the home, Madame Duchesne reared her children in great simplicity. The cold of an Alpine morning was no excuse for lying snugly in bed. The presence of servants did not dispense the older girls from looking after the younger children. Lessons from books were followed by needlework or visits to the sick poor or a turn in the pantry or kitchen, though the mysteries of cooking always seemed to baffle Philippine. There was seldom an idle moment in the Duchesne-Perier home, though there were leisure hours for con-versation, discussion, and repetition of precious traditions inherited through generations. Family dinners were part of life in Dauphiny, and Philippine kept even in old age the happiest memories of these gatherings in the home of her maternal grandparents. At times Pierre-François Duchesne aired some of his increasingly rationalis-tic views. Then his wife's eyes grew troubled and imploring as she noted the impression made by such talk.

Philippine was still too young to realize that her father had drifted with the current of "liberal thought" away from Cathol-icism as a way of life.[12] He had long since followed that strange fashion of the day that confused faith with understanding and so rejected what it could not comprehend; that lost its hold on the supernatural in searching after the purely natural; that relegated religion to the underestimated level of children and women, especially nuns—and nuns had been numerous among the Duchesnes. The Visitation Monastery at Roman had drawn several members of its community from that family during the eighteenth century. Two of Monsieur Duchesne's sisters were now active and competent religious, and Philippine sometimes visited these cloistered aunts—Sister Françoise-Melanie, who was so fond of her irreligious brother, and Sister Claire-Euphrosine, who had entered the convent in 1766 and taken the name of her new sister-in-law.[13]

There was a monastery of the Visitation at Grenoble which claimed the distinction of having been founded by St. Francis de Sales and St. Jane de Chantal at the request of the citizens of the town. It was built on the left bank of the Isère, halfway up the side of Mount Rachais. Philippine and Josephine frequently climbed the steep winding street that led up to it. At a sort of alleyway between high walls they would turn and mount a few low platform-steps toward an arched entrance surmounted by an inscription which they learned by heart: *St. Francis de Sales chose this place for the foundation of the fourth monastery of his Order of the Visitation of Holy Mary. The first stone was laid in his presence on October 16, 1619.* High up the mountainside, remote from the town, cut off from worldly contacts and backed by the snow-capped Alps, this fourth monastery of the Order commanded a magnificent view of the valley below, where the sweeping torrent of the Isère had cut its bed in fantastic curves. It came to be known as *Sainte-Marie-d'en-Haut*, an almost untranslatable expression. It was "St. Mary's on the Heights," or "St. Mary's High-up-there," or "St. Mary's Up-High," or "High-up," to distinguish it from the Church of *Sainte-Marie-d'en-Bas*, in the town below. To Philippine it was always *Sainte Marie*, and so it shall be to us. She was well acquainted with the place when she and Josephine were placed there as boarding pupils in 1781 to be prepared for their first Holy Communion.

It was not easy for their mothers to give them up that year. Much had been happening of late in the double household. There was the arrival of two baby girls, one in each family, in 1779. In the following year Claude Perier purchased the house on the corner of Grande Rue and Place Saint-André, next door to Number 4. There was a doorway in the wall separating the courtyards of the two houses and this gave private access from one house to the other, so family news and chatter passed easily back and forth, and the voices of the children echoed gaily as they played together. The Duchesnes now had the two upper floors in Jacques Perier's home, while the old grandfather still lived downstairs with his sons, Jean Antoine and Augustin.

On February 27, 1781, the long awaited son was born to Pierre-François and Rose Perier Duchesne. He was christened Antoine-Louis-Hippolyte, carrying in a fourth generation a name familiar in the Duchesne family. In August a sixth son was added to the Perier family. So the older girls were really needed at home. But they were eager for boarding school and for the great spiritual event to which they looked forward with an ardor more mature than their years.

Mother Anne-Félicité de Murinais was then Superior of the community at Sainte Marie. Philippine became deeply attached to Sister Eugenie Latier de Bayanne, who was to influence her, not only during her brief years of formal education, but also in the training school of religious life. Faith had already struck deep roots in the girl's pure soul and prepared her for the religious instruction she was now to receive. Her piety was based on doctrine rather than on sentiment, and her devotion became more and more the aspiration of a soul that wills to give itself to God and so lifts itself up to Him in simple, direct prayer of faith, expressive of both reverent fear and ardent love. To offend God was Philippine's greatest dread; to love Him was her deepest joy and surest means of avoiding all offense.

There was a certain austerity in the training given at Sainte Marie. Character formation was the objective, and its motivation was drawn from faith and the tradition of womanly worth and dignity so carefully guarded in Dauphiny. Another and a far more powerful element entered into this motivation. Just a century before, devotion to the Sacred Heart had been confided by Christ Himself, in private revelation, to the humble Visitandine nun, Saint Margaret Mary Alacoque, and through her to the Order of the Visitation and the Society of Jesus. At Sainte Marie the devotion held a prominent place in the spiritual life of the community and throughout the church and cloister symbols of the Sacred Heart were to be seen on all sides. Soon "the Heart that has so loved men" became the center of Philippine's life and love, giving her courage to take herself in hand and determine to correct the asperities of her character.

Strength and weakness were blended in this girl just entering her teens. She was accustomed to leadership in a group of boys and girls who loved her and relied on her, no matter which way the wind of their childish fortunes might blow. They turned to her instinctively and she enjoyed this compliment. There was an imperiousness in her manner at times that got results in the home circle, but boded ill for the future if left unchecked. She had a will of her own, and what she willed she set herself to obtain or carry out, with high disdain for obstacles. Her impetuous impulses sometimes sent her headlong into trouble or involved her in difficulties that tried her patience almost beyond endurance. She could be petulant and uneven in manner, but never petty or selfish toward her school companions; and they loved her for her adventurous spirit and sincere friendliness.

That Philippine retained many of these defects in after-years is evident from letters of advice written by one who undertook her training in a very different school. "Strive to acquire gentleness, a more pleasant manner, evenness of disposition which produces patience" is a telling sentence.[14] Defects and faults were to bring many a humiliation to Philippine, but her honesty in facing the problem of a difficult character and the earnestness with which she tried to conquer her stubborn pride and sensitive reserve were evidences of the grace that was at work in her soul.

The idea of devoting her life to God did not come to her for the first time at Sainte Marie. Even as a little girl she had been thrilled by stories of heroic mission life in distant lands. From time to time missionaries appeared in Grenoble. They spoke in the churches, were welcomed in the homes of the townsfolk, gathered alms for the furtherance of their work. Among them were former Jesuits who had labored in the colonies of France and had been expelled from their missions even before the general suppression of the Society of Jesus in 1773. One of these, Father Jean-Baptiste Aubert, lived in Grenoble when Philippine was growing up. He had been in Louisiana and the Illinois country as a missionary to both the French settlers and the Indians. He told of places with the strangest names—Kaskaskia, where he had signed the parish register as late as 1764,[15] and Cahokia, just across the river from the site staked off that very year for a trading post to be called *St. Louis de France*, and Michigamea with its mission of St. Francis Xavier long since abandoned. Weird Indian names rolled smoothly from his tongue, but his eyes were wistful as he spoke of the work left undone among the forest folk of America and the heroism of the Jesuits who had given their blood in martyrdom in the great valley of the Mississippi. His stories of the wilderness held Philippine enthralled. An unquenchable desire to devote her life to missionary work was enkindled in her soul, and an ever deepening determination to do great things for God that would carry her in middle life to the farthest edge of Western civilization. She has left a sketchy paragraph about this earliest inspiration to follow Christ:

> My first enthusiasm for missionary life was roused by the tales of a good Jesuit Father who had been on the missions in Louisiana and who told us stories about the Indians. I was just eight or ten years old, but already I considered it a great privilege to be a missionary. I envied their labors without being frightened by the dangers to which they were exposed, for I was at this time reading stories of the martyrs, in which I was keenly interested. The same good Jesuit was extraordinary confessor at the convent in which I became a pupil. I went to confession to him several times, and I loved his simple, informal manner of speaking, a manner he had used with the savages. From that time the words *Propagation of the Faith* and *Foreign Missions* and the names of priests destined for them and of religious in far-away lands made my heart thrill.[16]

So Philippine cherished her desire and fostered it by prayer and acts of self-sacrifice and self-control. She seems not to have talked about it to her sisters or even to her mother. Josephine Perier had all her confidence and she kept the secret, especially from her Uncle Pierre, who would have had little patience with such pious dreams. Duchesne was a practical man who had no sympathy with those who would give all and apparently get nothing in return.

School life was simple and happy at Sainte-Marie-d'en-Haut. The curriculum included both the practical arts of living and subjects whose content required some studying and a good deal of writing. Along with religion there were arithmetic, history, geography, and the reading of selected classics of French literature, with plenty of needlework and the exercise of a variety of feminine skills. The small number of pupils—not more than twenty—made it possible for them to receive a good deal of individual attention. Philippine was serious and earnest about her studies and made steady progress, laying a good foundation for the more advanced work she would do under a tutor later on.

Reminiscing half a century later, she wrote to Josephine Perier:

> I find delight in recalling the simple pleasures of our childhood; our modesty in dress, the good times we had at the convent, eating salad with our fingers, the two of us with a single plate between us and sitting together on the same seat beside the fire—all

of which moved dear Sister Colombe to tears. She used to say: "How these two children love each other!" [17]

Sainte Marie was, in her own words to Josephine, "the home of our childhood . . . the cradle of our faith and of the intimacy that has united us." They received their first Holy Communion on the feast of Pentecost, May 19, 1782. With whole-hearted generosity Philippine responded to the call of grace in her soul and offered herself to God. She knew He wanted her to belong entirely to Him. She was a Duchesne, and the Duchesnes did nothing by halves, but she was also a Perier, whom family ties held fast in a web of intimate love. Religious life became the goal of her ambitions. Daily she prayed for light to know God's will in her regard and grace to accomplish all He expected of her. Confidently she placed her vocation under our Lady's protection, reciting the *Memorare* many times a day for guidance and strength. There were conflicts in her soul at times. Her love for her family seemed to gain an even greater hold on her. Then, too, the apostolic life of the missionary attracted her, while the prayer-life of the Visitation cloister grew more appealing, more personally satisfying, as she watched and imitated the nuns by whom she was being educated.

So she set herself to serious preparation for whatever God might ask of her. One of her companions at Sainte Marie gives us a picturesque account of her efforts:

> She was continually praying before the Blessed Sacrament, and her fervor now led her to get up every day at the same hour as the nuns, in order to be in the choir and make her meditation when they did. Sometimes in mid-winter she would hurry down half dressed rather than omit the practice or shorten her hour of prayer. Her companions, who did not realize the strength of her will, used to laugh at this great zeal and prophesy that it would slacken soon, but nothing ever turned her from the practice; as long as she remained at school, she was faithful to it. [18]

It was not long, however, before the Duchesnes were discussing with the Periers what Philippine's schoolmates related about her. Inquiries at Sainte Marie were answered truthfully: Philippine was thinking seriously of a religious vocation. Her parents were displeased at this, to put it mildly. Madame Duchesne was a very affectionate mother; she thought Philippine too young to give the matter serious consideration, and she dreaded the sacrifices such a vocation entailed. While a formal prohibition would never have come from her, she had not yet the courage to put Christ's claim on her daughter before her own. But Pierre-François Duchesne acted with swift decision, withdrawing Philippine from Sainte Marie and from the influence of the nuns after she had spent just two years there.[19] Both he and his wife expected a scene, with their daughter playing the lead. To their surprise she yielded with an obedience that was disarming and took up home life once more. The flame of her desire had not been quenched by her mother's affectionate outbursts or her father's vigorous wrath. She had but covered the fire until it seemed safe to let it leap up again.

At home some changes had taken place during the past two years. Her grandfather Perier had died in the summer of 1782. His fortune had been settled according to his will, Claude as eldest son receiving two-thirds, the other two sons one-sixth each. Jean-Antoine, Philippine's godfather, accepted the arrangement quite amicably and in 1783 left Grenoble for Paris, where he practiced law and remained unmarried. Augustin had from boyhood resented his position as youngest son in the family. He had recently married Marie-Charlotte Carrier and soon he too left Grenoble. He was not as keen a business man as were his father and his eldest brother and he lost most of his inheritance in ill-advised speculation.

So Philippine found her own family in possession of the entire household space of the old Perier home. She entered once more into comradeship with her sisters and grew more intimate with Josephine Perier. She gave much time to the little children of the family in order to relieve her mother and Tante Perier. Camille Jordan was living with them now, and he and the Perier boys were being tutored by a scholarly priest, Abbé Raillane, who kept them hard at work during school hours. He was a thin little man, very prim and neat, with sharp eyes and heavy eyebrows which gave him a severe appearance and helped him maintain strict discipline.[20] He loved poetry and history and communicated this taste to his pupils. He was austere and very priestly, and his way of life made a deep impression on his pupils and on Philippine, who now came under his tutelage with her cousins. Latin, history, French literature, along with Dante, St. Augustine, and the Psalms, were a part of the curriculum, and the abbé could not complain of the quality of his pupils. Yet love of books and study were not native to Dauphiny, and there was among its people far more cleverness than love of learning. They were, on the whole, quite honest in admitting the charm of idleness, and in his *Abridged History of Dauphiny* Augustin Perier asserted later on that this was the case in his day as well as in former times.[21] If Philippine Duchesne was not studious by nature, she had trained herself to the steady pursuit of learning and she made good use of the opportunities offered her. When problems in arithmetic proved too difficult, she turned for help to her younger cousins. Then Casimir Perier and Camille Jordan enjoyed a momentary superiority over the girl they loved and admired so whole-heartedly.

The historian, Alphonse Vernet, describes old Grenoble as a very gay place, and it is not difficult to picture Philippine watching with amusement the torchlight parades, the street illuminations, the fountains of wine flowing in the Place Saint-André, and the masked revelers on their way to the theatre for the Mardi Gras ball. She certainly attended balls and met the officers who were stationed at the garrison, and the young lawyers who were trying out their legal wit in the *Palais de Justice*, and many another young *bourgeois gentilhomme* wearing the scarlet coat with steel buttons and the three-cornered hat that was the fashion of the day. It was, on the whole, a full life, and she took part in it without argument. There were soirées, concerts, and dancing parties, all of which she thoroughly enjoyed.[22]

It was an age of graceful feminine styles and gay materials. Philippine wore full skirts and panniers, broad hats, fine gloves, and light stockings. Her manner was simple and gracious, her bearing dignified without stiffness. She liked to dance, though her sisters teased her about the seriousness with which she practiced the difficult steps. "This is not a problem in algebra, you know," and laughter followed at her expense. Details such as these come from the pen of her sister Euphrosine, who adds, "Later on, when she took me into her confidence, she assured me that even in the midst of these amusements she was thinking with joy of the time when she would be a nun, but in the meantime she applied herself quite willingly to her dancing lessons." [23]

Philippine also studied music and drawing. Her musical talent was nil, her artistic ability mediocre, but she would put this to practical use in later years. She had a flair for writing which Abbé Raillane encouraged her to cultivate. Her style was quick, natural, unadorned, with the strength and directness that were native to her character. She could write with precision and care for the niceties of language, but more frequently her sentences seemed to flow spontaneously from her quill with a sort of rough energy that sought only to record the outpourings of her soul. This ability for self-expression became an asset in later years when she needed an outlet and there was no one to whom she could talk confidentially. She was a good talker and loved to speak of spiritual and intellectual things, but she was never talkative and she learned early in life the value of silence as an aid to prayer.

While entering graciously into her parents' plans for her education at home and taking part in the social life of Grenoble, Philippine held inflexibly to a line of conduct that called for strength of will and courage of conviction. Her private devotional practices were never neglected for pleasure. Morning meditation had a place in every day. She braved the wide-eyed critics who with Jansenistic prejudice looked askance at her fortnightly confession and Holy Communion. Her love for the Blessed Sacrament increased through these years, as devotion to the Sacred Heart took fuller possession of her soul. The spirit of reparation inspired by this devotion was developing in her, and she gave herself to voluntary penance with a generosity unsuspected by her family. A little silver cross that had been given to her as an ornamental pendant became an effective instrument of penance when heated and pressed against her bare breast.

She sought out personal discomforts as well as fatiguing work about the house and relieved her mother of many household cares. Her small brother, whom all the family called "Duchesne," was just old enough to need watching, as he romped about with the youngest Perier boys. She listened with interest to her father and Uncle Claude as they talked of business and political affairs, of the needs of the General Hospital, of which Perier had become administrative director, or the development of the public library in which her father was interested. But she avoided all discussion of her vocation, dreading the clashes with her father which the mere mention of it brought on, and wishing to spare her mother pain. This attitude was interpreted by them as a sign that Philippine had accepted their views and was willing to have her future planned for her in the conventional manner of the day.

Pierre-François Duchesne had many plans. He had become prominent in Grenoble as a consistorial advocate in the *parlement*. He was director of the public library, which he had helped to found and organize. In 1785 he was elected president of the local bar association, an office he held by re-election several times.[24] He was irascible and self-assertive and often made himself unpleasant company, but his forthright manner and personal integrity commanded respect. He was an enthusiastic supporter of the new political and social ideas that were permeating all France in the last decade of the Old Regime, and he took an active part in spreading them in Grenoble. To the grief of his family he had by this time gone completely Voltairian, and his activities in radical clubs and Masonic groups brought anguish to Philippine and her mother.

The year 1786 was eventful in the family. There had been from time to time news from Uncle Augustin. In the spring of the previous year he had got into the service of the newly reorganized Company of the Indies which had an exclusive monopoly of trade in practically all countries beyond the Cape of Good Hope. This offered a wide expansion to the Perier business and Claude co-operated willingly. Augustin had been to India in the interests of the company and was back in Grenoble in the spring of 1786. On April 11 another baby girl was added to the Duchesne family and named Augustine-Melanie, with Uncle Augustin as her godfather. Success had come at last and Augustin Perier was director of the Company of the Indies, with his home at Lorient, the great port of shipment, handling millions of dollars worth of merchandise yearly and building a fortune which he hoped would match that of his brother Claude. Augustin was very busy and was growing very rich, yet he was restless and dissatisfied still.

Not so Pierre-François Duchesne, who was busy with plans for his several marriageable daughters. He and Claude Perier were in a position to judge the most suitable prospects, after deciding on dowry terms. Joseph Constans de Mauduit, Chevalier du Plessis, was an officer of the Royal Marine Infantry then stationed in Grenoble. He came of old Breton stock and had a promising future. In October, 1786, Amelie Duchesne became his bride. It was a satisfactory match, for Amelie—just entering her sixteenth year—was very attractive, but also very difficult to handle; and it was hoped that her alliance with de Mauduit would mature her character and soften its already hardening lines. The ceremony was a social event in Grenoble, and the marriage register of the Church of St. Louis bore the signature of thirty-nine witnesses, among them the bride's older sister, Philippine.

Within a year there was question of other weddings in the family, for Jean-Joseph Jouve, a young merchant of Lyons, was asking for the hand of Euphrosine Duchesne, while the Periers were discussing the prospect of Josephine's marriage to Jacques-Fortunat de Savoye-Rollin, advocate-general of the *parlement* of Grenoble since 1780. He was fourteen years older than Josephine, but that proved no obstacle to their happiness.

And what about Philippine? Her parents would have preferred

to marry off their daughters in the more conventional order. The eldest was now eighteen, so her father brought up the matter tactfully, with a suitable young man in the offing. Whoever he was, Philippine had no case against his suitability. Her arguments were positive: she wished to be a nun. She had heard the call of Christ; she had pledged to Him the full measure of her love and service; she felt she had a right to consecrate herself to God as many another Duchesne girl had done.

The pattern of life now changed for Philippine as she took her stand and held her ground. No more pretty clothes would she indulge in, except the really indispensable; no more parties, concerts, dances for her; in fact, no more social life than was strictly necessary, "and every time she was urged to do differently she showed the same fixed resolve." [25] But there was much more prayer now and a rule of life that she followed as faithfully as if she were back at Sainte Marie. The Duchesne in her was in the ascendancy, but it was to Tante Perier that she gave her confidence after Josephine had become Madame de Savoye-Rollin in January, 1788. Madame Perier understood the girl as no one else in the household did. She sympathized with her suffering and encouraged her resolution. Together they discussed the situation and agreed on the wisdom of waiting a little while. Soon they noted a gradual breakdown in the opposition, ascribable perhaps to Pierre-François Duchesne's satisfaction with his other daughters, but also to his stubborn but very intense affection for Philippine. Watching her alone now with the older Perier boys, or teaching the group not yet in their teens, or caring for the least ones, especially the baby sister Melanie, it seemed as if he could not part with her, yet he knew he could not keep her much longer.

One day in the spring of 1788 Philippine slipped through the inner door of the courtyard and made her way about the vast six-story home of the Periers until she found her aunt. She wanted help. She felt she must consult Mother de Murinais about her admission into the Visitation cloister and she begged Tante Perier to go with her to Sainte Marie. Though she was eighteen and a half years old, convention required a chaperone through the streets of the town. Besides, her aunt was such good company and such substantial support that Philippine had come to rely upon her in all circumstances. They went up the steep winding street, passed through the archway, lifted the knocker, and were quickly admitted to the monastery parlor. The interview with Mother de Murinais was informal. She had talked frequently with the girl about religious life. Philippine was eager, but restrained. Quite suddenly she announced a decision: she was at Sainte Marie; she was sure of God's will for her; she would remain now with the Visitandines if Mother de Murinais would accept her as a postulant. Tante Perier was not prepared for this. She pleaded with her niece, gently reproached her, argued for a return home. But Philippine had answered an inspiration of divine grace by an unshakable resolution which Mother de Murinais sanctioned.

Madame Perier returned alone to the double house in Grande Rue to break the news to the Duchesnes. Her sister-in-law, upset by this unexpected turn of events, was greatly distressed, but too reasonable to lay the blame where it did not belong. Supernatural views were dominant in Madame Duchesne, but even the deepest faith does not steel a mother's heart against poignant grief. There was still a slight hope that Philippine might yield to entreaties and return home, if only she could be made to realize how greatly she was needed, how deeply she was loved.

Madame Duchesne had recovered her poise and self-control to some extent when, a few days later, she went with her husband and little Melanie to call at Sainte Marie. The interview was stormy and the resulting pain felt as keenly by the unyielding daughter as by the pleading parents. True, Philippine was now in possession of what she had desired for several years, but her self-control hid a terrific conflict in her soul. Hers was a heart that loved intensely, that gripped its love tenaciously. Her family was a part of her very self. To break the external ties that bound her to them, to leave forever the dear old double home and the precious people it housed, called for detachment that only abundant supernatural graces could supply. But Philippine was in love with Christ and sure of His divine support, no matter what the trial of her faith might be. How often she had whispered in prayer, "*Introibo*—I will go unto the altar of God!" Now grace gave strength to her resolution. The Duchesnes went down Mount Rachais without her, not knowing that as they made the descent from Sainte Marie, Philippine was kneeling before the Blessed Sacrament, offering them all as her most costly sacrifice to God and thanking Him, in spite of the tears that ran unheeded down her cheeks, for the victory she had won in this battle of hearts and wills. Renewing her consecration to Christ through the intercession of St. Jane de Chantal, she left the chapel and went about her simple duties with peace in her soul, though pain still racked her heart.

2. 1788—1792

*That we may merit the grace of entering
into the holy of holies with pure hearts.*

Liturgy of the Mass

TURBULENT OLD GRENOBLE was seething with political disturbance when Philippine Duchesne entered as a postulant at Sainte Marie. The first phase of her religious life was spent in times when events were in the making whose repercussions have been felt ever since. The civic-minded Periers and Duchesnes were actively involved in the movement which set the opening scene of the French Revolution.[26] The *parlement* of Dauphiny was the first to protest against the royal edicts of May, 1788, in which Louis XVI announced the remodeling of the judicature throughout the country and the proroguing of all provincial *parlements* until the formation of new courts. A copy of the royal decrees was sent by courier to the Count of Clermont-Tonnerre, then Governor of Dauphiny, with special instructions regarding the suppression of offices and the reorganization of the judiciary.

When the Governor ordered the decrees registered, the magistrates of Grenoble protested. The General Council of the city then drew up a memorial expressing to the King the grievances of the people and representing the disastrous effects that might result from the enforcement of the decrees.[27] The royal reply came swiftly in the form of a *lettre de cachet* forbidding the City Council to assemble to discuss the edicts and warning the council members against attending meetings of a similar nature under penalty of severe punishment. The letter closed with a phrase characteristic of absolutism: "for such is our will in this matter." The will of the people, however, was at variance with that of the King, and opposition was strengthened by the determined efforts of men like Pierre-François Duchesne and his colleagues.

The situation was not improved when the *parlement* of Dauphiny threatened to withdraw the province from its allegiance to the Crown if the royal edicts were put into effect. The procurator-general summed up the situation when he wrote to Paris: "Consternation is general in the face of the complete annihilation of our privileges, which are one of the conditions essential to the union of Dauphiny with the Crown. Justice has ceased in the city, and the people refuse to pay the taxes." [28] The Count of Clermont-Tonnerre was under no illusions as to the danger, for he realized that people of all social ranks were now thoroughly aroused. Military measures seemed necessary and troops were called out, two companies encamping on Place Saint-André, in front of the *Palais de Justice*. Excitement must have run high in the Duchesne-Perier homes as the small boys watched the grenadiers drilling in the streets and the sentinels on guard day and night. One can picture members of the family going up to Sainte Marie to describe the situation to Philippine.

The precautions taken by the Governor were the prelude to a more drastic measure decreeing the arrest and exile of the magistrates of Grenoble. This act brought down on Clermont-Tonnerre the full wrath of the populace and ushered in what has been called "the first battle of the French Revolution." Excitement and tension mounted to a high pitch, and on the morning of June 7 the town presented an ominous scene: men and women milling around angrily in the streets, gates barricaded, church bells tolling. By noon the Governor found himself facing an angry mob demanding the convocation of the *parlement* of Dauphiny. The royal troops had been ordered to protect the Governor. In the rush on the palace fighting began. Soldiers fired. Then the populace let loose with paving stones and roofing tiles. A score of people were wounded, but the mob had won a victory on that "day of tiles," and the foremost citizens of Grenoble had supported them. Clermont-Tonnerre recalled the magistrates, who came in dignified procession to the *Palais de Justice* and used their influence to calm the populace.

A week later the notables of Grenoble, in consultation with members of the clergy and the third estate, decided to assemble the ancient Provincial Estates of Dauphiny, which had been suppressed in the days of Richelieu. Acting on their own authority, they agreed that the representation of the Third Estate should equal that of the other two groups and that all should deliberate and vote in common. This was indeed an innovation. The date set for the meeting was July 21; the place, Grenoble.

At the Court of Versailles all this was treated as rebellion, which it certainly was. Now the mild Clermont-Tonnerre was superseded by the more energetic Marshal de Vaux. With 20,000 soldiers at his disposal he was expected to restore the old order immediately. But he had scarcely reached Grenoble when he wrote laconically to Versailles, "It is too late." There seemed but one course open to him, that of granting permission for a meeting of the Provincial Estates on condition that it should not be held in Grenoble.

In the cloister at Sainte Marie the nuns were kept informed about the current of events that had begun to swirl and eddy through Dauphiny. Visitors to the parlor grille gave details of happenings that were creating disturbance, and the Duchesnes often called on Philippine to relate to her the incidents in which the family was most concerned. Anxiety about her father was keen when she learned that it was he who had called that extraordinary meeting of the Grenoble lawyers, in which they passed the resolution to plead no case in the courts until the unjust edicts had been withdrawn. On the "day of tiles" he had been in the delegation that went to the home of the first president of *parlement* to accompany him and the other magistrates to the *Palais de Justice*. On June 14 he had taken part in the meeting at the Town Hall, and even now he was preparing a *Mémoire* in the form of a *Remonstrance to the King*, embodying a protest against existing conditions and a statement of the reforms, financial and political, for which there was crying need throughout France. Duchesne intended to present this at the meeting projected for July 21, which Philippine soon learned was to be held at Vizille.[29]

Her Uncle Claude had placed his magnificent chateau at the disposal of the deputies of Dauphiny, and the offer had been accepted. More than two hundred cities, towns, and small communities sent representatives to the assembly. Through the mild summer night and early dawn the four hundred and sixty-three delegates made their way on foot, on horseback, in carts and carriages, along the country roads, paying little heed to the troops sent to intimidate them. Perier had spared neither trouble nor expense in preparing for the assembly. The vast indoor tennis court and *salle d'armes* of the old warrior-chateau were arranged to house the meeting that opened that Monday morning with the Count de Morges presiding and Jean-Joseph Mounier acting as secretary. After the formality of seating the deputies came the choice of a *Remonstrance to the King*, which occupied several hours.[30] Dinner followed, and some relaxation in the gardens of Vizille; then the men reassembled for deliberations which continued until long after midnight. By three o'clock in the morning of July 22 the final report had been signed, and all unknowingly this assembly had, with remarkably dispassionate wisdom, formulated the program of a mighty revolution.[31] Before the adjournment the Count de Morges expressed to "the honorable Claude Perier, lord of the marquisate of Vizille" the sincere appreciation of the entire body for his generous hospitality.[32]

Throughout the province of Dauphiny order seemed to have been restored, and the sessions of the assembly held in the autumn and winter at Romans carried forward its work in a less dramatic setting, but with determined independence. Pierre-François Duchesne did not attend the session of the Estates of Dauphiny that opened at Romans on September 10, 1788. On that day he was at Sainte Marie, witnessing the ceremony in which Philippine received the black habit and white veil and coif of a Visitandine novice. That her father was present at the ceremony and signed the convent register proved once more to Philippine how dear she was to him.

With characteristic fervor she entered upon the period of training that would prepare her for religious life and the vows by which she hoped to bind herself to Christ. Writing thirty years later, she gave a few details about her novitiate days:

> When I entered religious life at the age of eighteen and a half years, a desire to share in the apostolate made me choose the Visitation, where children were educated, in preference to Carmel, which I loved very much. My community was animated by the spirit of the Jesuits, from whose Constitutions they boasted their own had been drawn. The library was enriched with nearly all the works of Jesuit authors, because at the time of the suppression of the Society of Jesus three of its members found a refuge in our chaplain's house, and when they died they left their library to the convent. During two whole years of my novitiate I read only Rodriguez,[33] without ever tiring of it; and when we assembled after Vespers, I used to relate to my Sisters the lives of nearly all the saints of the Company of Jesus. That of St. Francis Xavier appealed most strongly to me. . . . I loved his touching appeals to the European schools to send him missionaries. How often have I not said to him since then, in my impatience, "Great Saint, why do you not call me? I would respond at once." He is the saint of my heart.[34]

He was, indeed, a great favorite with her always, but a rival patron came upon the scenes out of the same Company of Jesus, that mighty mountain-man of Vivarais, whose name she would carry halfway round the world and stamp on the first permanent Jesuit mission of midwestern America, as well as on her own first foundation there. If with Xavier she longed to share the apostolate of the foreign missions, with John Francis Regis she dreamed of devoting her life to the poor.[35] Her devotion to him began in a conversation with one of the Visitation nuns who had chosen him as her patron. A relic of the great "social crusader" was honored at Sainte Marie, and Philippine often prayed before it for the grace to follow his example in an apostolate far more obscure than that of Xavier.

Novitiate life is seldom eventful or romantic. There is an apparently monotonous routine to be followed, a fixed order of the day, spiritual duties, homely tasks, penitential practices, a whole new life to be learned, a life under rule and regulated to the least details. Wearing the holy habit, the novice must gradually be clothed in the spirit of Christ, growing in recollection as she concentrates her efforts lovingly on silence and prayer. The novelty of the life wears off quickly enough. The vitalizing spirit seems at times to die down to a mere flicker, and only a stout heart and a fixed resolve can weather the storms that may break over the soul of the novice. Philippine Duchesne was no exception to the rule, yet she seems to have been blessed with so lively a spirit of faith, such intense love of God and charity toward her Sisters, that the usual noviceship difficulties troubled her only slightly. She could write long afterwards: "The day I entered at Sainte-Marie-d'en-Haut I took the resolution never to fail on a single point of rule, and indeed I do not recall ever infringing a single one." [36] For a character so independent, so impetuous, and so mature, this unswerving fidelity must have been the result of heroic self-conquest. The continuous austerity of a completely regulated life rapidly developed in her that sensitiveness to grace which marks all sanctity.

The Visitation novitiate offered her countless opportunities for unselfish service in the little duties assigned to her and in the chance to help others by doing their work or replacing them in the various employments about the monastery. Her days, filled with activity motivated by love, were physically very tiring, yet fatigue seemed to drop from her easily when toward evening she went to the Mistress of Novices, Sister Eugenie de Bayanne, to beg permission for an extra hour of prayer before retiring. Those who lived with her at Sainte Marie always knew when she had obtained the permission, so radiant was her smile, so light her step, as she passed down the corridor to her favorite place in the choir before the tabernacle. There she found rest in prayer. Sometimes, forgetful of all but the divine Presence on the altar, she spent a great part of the night, even the whole of it, in silent adoration, kneeling motionless, truly lost in God. The spirit of St. Margaret Mary was already taking hold of her, and she was being prepared for an apostolate that would carry the knowledge and love of the Sacred Heart to mission lands she had dreamed of as a child.

The picture of those lands was being etched more realistically on her mind than she was aware by the reading of a seventeenth century biography—a book she pored over time and again. The *Life of the Venerable Mother Marie of the Incarnation* exercised a profound influence on her prayer life and missionary aspirations. The holy Ursuline's zeal thrilled her and inspired her with increasing ardor for the salvation of souls still groping in the shadows of paganism. The missions of Canada became the goal of Philippine's ambition even as she prepared for a life in the Visitation cloister. In spirit she traveled to that far corner of the world in search of souls redeemed by Christ. She loved to use the prayers of Mother Marie as she knelt before the tabernacle, and those prayers contained the very essence of true devotion to the Sacred Heart.[37]

Philippine had entered an order whose spirit and traditions were well defined. St. Francis de Sales had emphasized that "it is a spirit of profound humility toward God and of great gentleness with our neighbor." [38] Its contemplative life is modeled on Nazareth. No outward severity marks it, but complete inward self-renunciation is pivotal in the institute. Sweetness in strength, loving intentness in prayer, simple, unconditional self-surrender to God and His representatives, were instilled into it by the founder at the very beginning of its development.

Although Philippine was well acquainted with the community at Sainte Marie and quickly at home there, she still had much to learn about the little observances of common life, the practices of humility and penance, the words and phrases that formed a sort of family vocabulary intelligible only to its members. In joyous recreations, in hours of silent labor, in the quiet of prayer, in simplicity, kindliness, and fidelity to the little virtues which make great saints, she tasted the sweetness and experienced the charm of the fervent hidden life of the Visitation. She studied the crest of the order, bearing a heart crowned with thorns and surmounted by a cross, and came to realize how truly prophetic had been its choice by St. Francis de Sales. Devotion to the Sacred Heart was a precious heritage of the Visitandines from their founder, who called them "Daughters of the Sacred Heart of Jesus." [39]

The training given in the novitiate at Sainte Marie adhered faithfully to the Visitandine tradition, to which had been added the teaching of St. Margaret Mary. Love and fidelity to the Sacred Heart had been the burden of her divinely inspired message, from which followed reparation and self-sacrifice. In the fervor of her offering Philippine would naturally have gone to extremes in the matter of corporal austerities, had not the Visitation Rule and spirit checked her and shown her how prayer and recollection, charity and self-renunciation were to supply for the severities of Carmel. But moderation was to be a lifelong problem for her. She found, however, an outlet for her love of God in humility and prayer. To one of her disposition it was not easy to kneel humbly when asking permissions, acknowledging mistakes, receiving corrections, but the custom was accepted gladly for the sake of the inner meaning and motive that gave it spiritual value. Self-accusation may have cost her even more, but she made it a life-long habit, along with silence under rebuke, and the inevitable revelation of personal faults and weaknesses. All this combined to develop in her a deepening sense of her unworthiness of such a high vocation and her need of grace and direction. Under the guidance of Sister Eugenie she sought to acquire the habit of continual awareness of the presence of God, which St. Francis de Sales enjoins in his Constitutions; and it was evident from her fervor and recollection that her actions were animated by the realization of that divine presence. Prayer became her greatest joy, and from it sprang its inseparable complement, generosity in service and sacrifice.

So the happy novice was preparing to pronounce her vows of profession when the votes of the community in Chapter would admit her to that honor. It is customary at the Visitation for profession to take place a year and a day after the reception of the religious habit, unless for some reason the time of training is prolonged. Philippine's longing for this event increased with her realization of the dignity of a spouse of Jesus Christ. In spirit she advanced to the choir grille for the ceremony and rehearsed in her heart the words of the sacred promises. The community of Sainte Marie voted her acceptance in September, 1789, but Philippine Duchesne was to know a long agony of hope and disappointment and uncertainty before she was privileged to enter fully into the sanctuary of religious life.

The winter of 1788–1789 had been a time of great suffering in Dauphiny, as in nearly all France. Meager harvests caused a shortage of food. The weather was severe. Deaths from cold and starvation were numerous, in spite of generous alms from all who had money or supplies to give. Food riots occurred in the spring, and

Grenoble was saved from more serious disturbances only through the generosity of Claude Perier.[40] There followed a kind of panic that spread through France as summer came on.

It was a momentous summer. Exitement stirred Grenoble as news was received of the meeting of the Estates General in Paris, the division of opinion and delegation, the storming of the Bastille, fighting in the capital, brigands loose throughout the country. Such news was reported in the parlor at Sainte Marie. A reorganization of the local militia by the governor of the province seemed wise but ominous, and wealthy families began to leave the city, seeking refuge in country residences or secluded villages. This hurt trade, and a breakdown in economic life threatened.

The September of 1789 should have brought Philippine the joy of making her religious profession at Sainte Marie, but to her father this step seemed sheerest folly. He was too clearheaded not to realize that the revolution now under way threatened not only the monarchy but also the Church, with its clergy and religious orders. The confiscation and sale of ecclesiastical property had already begun. The suppression of religious orders would certainly follow. So Pierre-François Duchesne forbade his daughter to make her vows. He was willing for her to remain at Sainte Marie for the moment, but she must promise to make no religious vows before the age of twenty-five. This was a crushing blow to the novice, "the severest trial God could have sent me," she admitted later on. But a wise old priest to whom she confided her suffering counseled her: "Adore God, my child. He has His secret designs in what He allows to happen today. Later on you will understand." [41]

News that the suppression of religious orders was already being discussed in the National Assembly strengthened Monsieur Duchesne in his decision regarding Philippine. On February 13, 1790, a decree was passed secularizing the old monastic orders. Nuns were allowed to remain in their convents, those engaged in education and charity being especially favored. The religious women of France, remarks Lavisse, resisted both the decrees of the National Assembly and the urgent appeals of the patriots. Very few left their cloisters in the early days of the revolution, for neither attacks nor persuasion had any effect on them. Fear undermined the courage of very few; the vast majority resisted until they were actually forced to leave their convents in 1792.[42]

To the disappointment which Philippine experienced and the insecurity that now threatened the community at Sainte Marie there was added anxiety about her father. He had continued his political activities, though the revolution was making too great headway to suit him, and he had only contempt for the theatricals staged publicly in the name of liberty. He had represented the town of Gap in the assembly at Romans in November, 1788. When the Estates General had been convoked in 1789, a report on the happenings in Grenoble during the preceding year had been presented to the assembly. The leading lawyers of the city considered it a very garbled account, so they drew up a vehement protest. Duchesne was a signer of the document. Early in February, 1790, Philippine learned that her father had been elected to membership in the municipal council, an honor and office she knew he had hitherto refused. As councilman he was riding the crest of a great wave of popularity, but there was trouble ahead and he seemed to sense the danger. For some months he had been searching for a country home to which he might transfer his family. Now he settled on a place in southwest Dauphiny near the village of Grâne. After a last visit to Sainte Marie, Madame Duchesne moved there with Adelaide, Melanie, and young Duchesne.

Two months after his election to the municipal council, Monsieur Duchesne was requested to compose the formula for an oath which the newly federated National Guard would take in public ceremony. The formulation of this oath was his undoing, for into it he wrote the words: "Supreme power belongs to the King." The document became public property. A hue and cry was raised by revolutionary sympathizers and personal opponents of Duchesne, who accused him of attempting covertly to induce his fellow-citizens to swear away their own safety, or craftily to stifle their nascent liberty and re-establish the old abuses. Duchesne revised the oath to read: "Supreme power is vested in the King," and the men of Dauphiny were satisfied with the text, but not with its author, who now withdrew from public life to the home at Grâne.[43]

The shock of revolutionary changes was being felt in Grenoble that same year. Churches were still open; religious services were still allowed; but by mid-July the Civil Constitution of the Clergy had been completed and soon the priesthood of France would undergo an ordeal that had had no counterpart in the past. There was general uneasiness among the people and anxiety in the hearts of all who had regard for the religious welfare of the country. In October, Camille Teisseire, a man of sterling faith and principles, was appointed to the municipal council, to which Claude Perier also belonged. It was hoped at Sainte Marie that their influence might ward off the danger that was creeping nearer every day.

So far the religious institutions in Grenoble had been spared, but rumor had it that this state of affairs could not last. Gossip grew. Discussions were endless. Surely the *Grande Chartreuse* would not come under the ban, nor the long-established communities of religious women. The City Council had addressed a memorial to the National Assembly in Paris for the preservation of the *Grande Chartreuse*, the religious serving in hospitals, the two monasteries of the Visitation, and that of the Ursulines. Prayer grew more intense at Sainte Marie when it was learned that all religious in the city not mentioned in the memorial had been dispersed.[44] Dispersed! The very suggestion of such a course was heartbreaking, but the fact remained that the Visitandine nuns of Grenoble might share the fate of many another community. Philippine's aunts, Sisters Françoise-Melanie and Claire-Euphrosine, had already been forced to leave their monastery at Romans and find refuge at home.

In May, 1792, Philippine learned that the great cross that had stood for generations in the Place Saint-André had been torn down and the square itself renamed *Place de la Constitution*, while Grande Rue had become *Rue de la Regénération*. All this was a symbol of what lay ahead. In July a cryptic warning flashed from Paris to the remotest villages of France: "The Fatherland is in danger." The Legislative Assembly made way for the Convention, which deposed the King and sent the royal family to the Temple, but not before it had completed the temporary destruction of religious life throughout the country by two decrees. The first of these, dated August 4, 1792, suppressed all the religious orders of women which had up to that time been spared. Their crime was that of "making common cause with the refractory priests." The second, on August 18, abolished all congregations of men and women that had continued in existence since 1790 for work in schools and hospitals.[45]

Throughout the length and breadth of France the tempo of revolution was being speeded up. War and insurrection were heading the country toward the Terror. There was now no hope of saving Sainte Marie. In September, 1792, Philippine Duchesne was obliged to lay aside her religious habit and leave the cloister-home where she had spent four and a half years.[46] That was a short period, as religious training goes, yet during that time of grace she had laid hold of the supernatural ideas and ideals that were, in great part, to give impulse to the rest of her life. The heartache of the departure echoed in the cry that escaped her lips and pen: "Dear Sion, shall I never see thee again?" One ray of hope beckoned to her and she pleaded to be allowed to go to Italy, where Mother Eugenie de Bayanne was now Superior of a monastery. When her father refused this request, Philippine went down Mount Rachais to the Perier home. It was a descent she would repeat many a time in the years that lay ahead.

A sincere and hearty welcome greeted her, and the whole family vied in efforts to make her feel at home once more. They sympathized with the trial she had undergone, and their understanding made it easier for her to accept the new life. While she was with them, her days were very full. She renewed her friendship with Augustin, now in business with his father. He was showing marked ability for both banking and commerce, but he loved books of another sort, too, and talked with lively interest of those he was reading. Philippine read to Scipion, whose weak eye-sight was always such a handicap to him. She listened to Casimir's stories about boarding school life at the Oratorian college in Lyons, now closed. Casimir was a handsome lad. The family thought he looked like Philippine. She helped the younger boys with their lessons and played with the little ones. On Sundays, at least, she could attend Mass, if not in a church, then in the drawing-room of Dr. Gagnon's house just down the street, where Grande Rue met Place Grenette.

She spent many hours with Josephine in her beautiful apartments and shared the works of charity that were already gaining for Madame de Savoye-Rollin the title by which all Grenoble knew her for half a century—*"la Bienfaisance en poste,"* which might be translated as "kindliness personified." [47] There were many members of the family with whom she had not kept in touch and of whom Josephine could give her news. Before the political storm broke over France, Uncle Augustin, living at Lorient, had brought the Company of the Indies to full prosperity and had become a very wealthy man, but financial success had not given him contentment. In 1789 he had gone headlong into the Revolution. That year he had been elected commandant of the National Guard at Lorient and each succeeding year he had been re-elected. But Augustin Perier had enemies.

And Camille Jordan? He had been in favor of the Revolution at first, but Camille could not keep faith with a movement that broke faith with God. He was just twenty-two, but his adventurous spirit, his courage and influence had already given him remarkable power with the conservative element in Lyons. Euphrosine saw him frequently when he came to discuss affairs with her husband, Jean-Joseph Jouve, who held the same political views and whose mercantile interests were suffering greatly as a result of the economic dislocation throughout the country.

There was comparative quiet in Grenoble just now, but Philippine heard her Uncle Claude and Camille Teisseire, now a frequent visitor at the home, talking frequently with the older Perier boys and planning security for the town, economy in expenditures, and safety for the family. She missed her father's positive, often vehement, assertions of opinion and her mother's gentle restraining influence on him. She longed to be at Grâne for Christmas, though Tante Perier pleaded with her to stay with them. Soon there was a safe opportunity to travel, and she was off.

The road was not new to her, nor would Grâne be new. She loved the roomy chateau and the pleasant gardens and woods. The family had often gone there for the summer when she was a child, and two little Duchesne girls were buried there. From Grenoble Philippine could go down the familiar road to Vizille, then on southwest to Die, in the new department of the Drôme. From there the road followed the river to Crest, where a change was made from the regular stagecoach to a smaller vehicle that crossed the Drôme River by ferry or bridge and brought her safely to Grâne, a village that had grown up beside a little stream bearing the familiar name Grenette. In her childhood the approach to Crest was always signaled by the one who first sighted the great old feudal keep that stands on a rock high above the town. The castle had been destroyed, but the huge keep remained intact and was used as a prison. Silhouetted against the horizon, it was no longer a symbol of feudal domination to the closemouthed, reticent countryfolk of the neighborhood, but to children it was the setting for endless stories of fancy and adventure.

In this section of old Dauphiny low spurs of the mountains replaced the towering Alps, and wide pasture lands spread their grasses to feed large flocks of sheep. Vineyards and orchards covered the hillsides and plains along the Drôme and its small tributaries. Philippine had known it always in summertime. Now the mountains wore a thick winter covering of white. The fruit and nut trees were gaunt and bare. The piercing wind cut sharply at her as she sprang out of the carriage at the entrance of the chateau and ran to the door that was opened wide to her. She had come home, though all unwillingly, and she realized the strength of the love that welcomed her. But she had not come home to stay. Neither earthly affection nor human upheaval could shake the resolve of her total commitment to Christ.

two

Through Years
of Uncertainty

I. 1793—1801

*The thoughts of His Heart extend to
every generation.*

Introit, Mass of the Sacred Heart

PHILIPPINE FOUND AT GRANE not only her parents and the younger children of the family, but also her sister Amelie with her two little boys, who had sought shelter and safety in the country while her husband, Captain de Mauduit, was serving the fatherland with his regiment, the 58th Infantry.[1] They were joined almost immediately by a cousin, Julie Tranchand, a Visitandine from the monastery at Romans.[2] Philippine and Julie at once devised a way of life for themselves patterned as closely as possible on that of the cloisters they had left. Following the monastic order of the day, they rose early, made their morning meditation, recited Office, said the prayers and kept the fasts prescribed, and observed the Rule as far as they could. When members of the household found this manner of life too austere, Philippine accepted the criticism without irritation, but also without relaxing her efforts to live up to her vocation in altered circumstances. Her critics were, in fact, forced to admit that no selfish motive inspired her life of piety, nor did she allow her hours of prayer to interfere with any duty she owed her family. She helped irritable Amelie with her children, gave time and affection unstintingly to little Melanie, and did all in her power to relieve her mother of household cares. Cousins, friends, servants, all grew more attached to her than ever because of her unfailing thoughtfulness and kindness. She came to

43

know her father better and to realize the price he had paid in leaving Grenoble at a time like this.

Philippine has left few details about her life during this period. The following paragraphs, however, from her *Story of Sainte Marie*, written in 1805, are revealing:

> The decree which obliged all religious women [in France] to return to secular life obliged me to go back to my family. My heart was never attached to this sort of life and it was a land of exile for me, a foreign land, and Sion, my true country, remained the goal of my desires and of my costliest endeavors. The dwelling for which I longed was the sanctuary of religious life. Although I was very lovingly inclined toward the cloister in which I had received my vocation—and never for an instant did I feel a repugnance toward it—still, from the time of our dispersal several orders in different countries attracted my thoughts and became the object of my prayers, that I might know the Will of God in my regard. Several times I changed my mind about the place and the order, but never did I lose sight of my high ambition. I lived two years in a town of the Drôme which was in the vicinity of the tomb of St. Francis Regis. I had often heard one of my companions in the convent relate stories of the marvels worked by this saint, and there was a picture of him and one of St. Francis Xavier in the church of the town, where we prayed during the stormiest days of the revolution, but without Mass there. The popular devotion of the countryside to this great St. Francis Regis revived mine and I invoked his aid almost continually.
>
> In that neighborhood they always spoke of him as the *Holy Father*. Every house had a picture of him and a copy of his life. Nearly everyone who was given to piety made a visit to his tomb and some went every year. I went there in spirit frequently, but my family objected to the trip of twelve or fourteen leagues [perhaps thirty or forty miles] and I had to defer that pleasure. In this same neighborhood, however, I had the privilege of making the acquaintance of two former Jesuits, whom I consulted at different times about my vocation and who strengthened me in my resolve. One of them had been confessor to the Bishop of Grenoble, Monseigneur Dulau.[3]

There is far more of Philippine's character in these paragraphs than of her activities. The "two years in a town of the Drôme" must have been the years from 1795 to 1797. She gives only one hint regarding the worst period of the Revolution, which she spent at Grâne. During the first months of 1793 fugitive priests sometimes found their way to the Duchesne home. They ministered to the spiritual needs of the household, and there was the rare, tense joy of Holy Mass. This state of affairs was a sore trial to Philippine, who felt a great need for guidance. God answered her prayer for help by bringing into her home a man of marked holiness and learning.[4] Her father was planning to build a small textile factory, most probably in connection with the Perier industry. One day a stranger called on him to ask for employment as superintendent of the construction. The man was intelligent and reliable and before long was acting as overseer both of the estate and of the business enterprise, to the relief and satisfaction of Monsieur Duchesne.

The new overseer was a reserved man who kept in the background as much as possible, avoiding notice and seldom appearing when visitors came to the house. At the end of a few weeks he identified himself as the Abbé Poidebard, who had barely escaped the guillotine and for whom search was still hot. He resided with the Duchesnes through the greater part of the next two years, becoming tutor, friend, and confidant in the family. By day he was a conscientious, hard-working manager of affairs. In the evening he frequently gave religious instruction to the younger members of the household or held spiritual conferences with Philippine and Julie Tranchand. Before dawn he might offer the Holy Sacrifice of the Mass in a secluded room and give Holy Communion to those who were allowed to attend this secret service. That they did so at the risk of their lives made all the more precious the tryst they kept with Christ. The active part played by Pierre-François Duchesne in the early stages of the Revolution and his continued interest in all that happened in Grenoble seem to have shielded his family home from suspicion. His willingness to harbor a fugitive priest during the worst period of the upheaval points up his love for his family and his respect for their convictions.

At Grâne the Duchesnes were not cut off from contact with the members of the family who were living in Grenoble and Lyons. From time to time news came by letter or visitor or in a sheaf of printed pages bearing the marks of eager use by those who had already handled them. Toward the close of January came the shocking news of the execution of the King. Grenoble remained fairly quiet for two more months. The municipal council was composed of men of moderate views who hoped to save the city from excesses. There was want and misery, unemployment and the disorders that usually accompany it. Children ran undisciplined in the streets since the closing of schools and orphanages, and many lived like little animals, escaping the vigilance of the police and exulting in an unsavory freedom. Relief agencies were at work, and the need for charitable helpers was urgent.

Spring had come to Grenoble when the "people's representatives" began their activities. The town was too moderate to suit the revolutionary government. Now domiciliary visits became the order of the day. Priest-baiting was their special game. Nonjuring priests who were caught were thrown into prison. A decree for the arrest of citizens "notoriously suspect" of lack of patriotism brought about the arrest of many of the leading townsfolk. Sainte Marie became a prison in April, 1793, when the proscription lists were said to include hundreds of names.

When news of all this reached Grâne, along with snatches of information about the work Josephine de Savoye-Rollin was doing for the poor, Philippine could no longer endure the inaction of her sheltered life. With fine disregard for danger she set off for Grenoble to share in an apostolate of charity whose hazards must at times have satisfied her most venturesome inclinations. There were many homes open to her in Grenoble, but she determined to involve none of the family in her enterprises. She lived with a trusted companion in a section of the town where she would have the greatest freedom of action, though there is nothing to indicate that she refused altogether the hospitality of the Perier home or the joy of companionship with the Savoye-Rollins. The prominence of her uncle and the position of Savoye-Rollin afforded her a measure of safety.

Organization was needed. Philippine formed an association known as the Ladies of Mercy, whose primary purpose was to bring material and spiritual help to the priests who had stood courageously on the side of the Church and who were now either imprisoned at Sainte Marie or in disguise and hiding. This was, to be sure, a work of mercy after her own heart, but a second aspect of the work also appealed strongly to her. Public religious worship had ceased in Grenoble, but not sickness and death. At the risk of her life Philippine guided priests to those who needed their ministrations. She cared for the sick and dying and prepared the dead for burial. Sometimes a priest was among the pall-bearers on whose charity she called, for there was often as much safety in public risk as in private hiding.

At times Philippine went about her work with a heavy heart. It was hard to react against grief and anxiety about her loved ones. There was that terrible day in 1793 when she learned of the tragedy that had befallen Uncle Augustin and his family. He had failed to obtain re-election that year as commandant of the National Guard at Lorient. A violent reaction had set in against him. He was arrested as a suspect and hurried off to Paris for trial, but he did not reach the capital. On the way Augustin Perier was murdered at an inn. His wife and daughter were in Paris when they learned of his death. They set out at once by stagecoach for Lorient, but they were ambushed and murdered on the road by Breton insurgents.[5]

France was now at war with her neighbors, and Grenoble was once more a very important post of defense on the frontier. Detachments of troops arrived to strengthen the garrison; the local militia was increased; and a "regiment of hope" enlisted lads from eight to eighteen years of age. Even the youngest Perier boys were drilling on the square in front of the Town Hall. Then came news of the insurrection in Lyons against the terrorism of the Convention. Philippine knew that Camille Jordan was a leading spirit in the movement, that Jean-Joseph Jouve was an active sympathizer. Euphrosine was in Lyons with her husband and children.

The siege of Lyons lasted seven weeks. When the city surrendered in October, the Jouves escaped with their lives, but with little else. Philippine notes that Jouve "distinguished himself" during the siege. "In order to save life and fortune, he was obliged to take refuge with his family in the mountainous district after the surrender of the city. . . . Here he experienced great suffering and poverty in his efforts to bring up a growing family." [6] Camille Jordan also escaped, but he was obliged to go into exile until the fall of Robespierre.

And now it was another member of the family on whom the revolutionary government bore down severely. Captain Constans de Mauduit was dismissed from the French army in October, 1793. His noble Breton blood and name had made him suspect, but his connection with the Duchesnes and Periers saved him from forced emigration. He now joined his wife and family at Grâne, but Philippine remained in Grenoble.[7]

She had to be more on her guard as she went about her dangerous activities. She must remember to address her friends as *Citoyen* or *Citoyenne*, for the old courtesies of Monsieur, Madame, and Mademoiselle were banned in the new order of things. Churches were now deserted—even by the Constitutional clergy. The great bells of Saint-André were silent; the Cathedral of Notre Dame had been desecrated. With the streets renamed, she often found it difficult to give directions to those who helped her in her charities or to find the poor who were recommended to her care. There was dire poverty and distress in the city in the winter of 1793–1794. Food shortage brought on riots; troops were called out to maintain order. Claude Perier subscribed 24,000 *livres* to pay the troops, and Camille Teisseire, procurator of the commune, was sent to Paris to solicit aid. His efforts failed completely, but soon he was back in Grenoble, making more successful appeals for help for the prisoners who were being crowded, without pity or provision, into Sainte Marie and other places of confinement.[8]

The terror had come late to Grenoble and its form was rather mild. But at the beginning of June, 1794, the priest-hunt was renewed, and the city saw the guillotine at work in Place Grenette on June 26. The two priests executed that day were the only victims condemned to death. A great number of people, however, died in the prisons, where an epidemic of typhoid fever raged through the summer months and the work of charity reached its highest heroism. Philippine gave herself to the care of the prison victims with courage and competence. Though her association of mercy had been disbanded by the radical authorities, she was undaunted in her apostolate.

The record of her activities during this period is meager, but the details are characteristic:

> She was not afraid [wrote Madame de Coriolis] to enter the darkest dungeons in which prisoners were confined, in order to render them services of the most menial kind. . . . One day, when she was visiting some priests in prison, she held a long conversation with them about her Divine Spouse; and afterwards, whenever she spoke of that conversation, one could perceive what a flame of love had been enkindled in her heart.[9]

One of her sisters tells us:

> Every morning quite early, after fulfilling her accustomed spiritual duties, Philippine went to visit the sick, for whom it was very difficult to procure spiritual aid in those unhappy times. She knew the hiding places of faithful priests who had been proscribed. Hunting them out, she would guide them through a thousand dangers to the bedside of the dying. It would be impossible to give an idea of all the acts of charity she performed under these trying circumstances.[10]

One incident, however, she cites as characteristic: on her round of visits to the sick one morning, Philippine came upon a poor woman who was obviously very near death. Realizing that it would be too great a risk to bring a priest to that section of the city, she had the woman lifted on to a litter and carried to her own lodgings. There she put her in the bed which she herself shared with her companion, made her comfortable, and brought a priest to minister to her. When her companion came home that evening, she was somewhat taken aback at what she found there, but she was equal to the situation and could not help smiling at it. Philippine made no explanations, but begged her to watch with her through the night. Together they prayed by the woman, who was already in her agony and who died in the arms of *Citoyenne* Duchesne. "As a matter of fact," her sister continues, "nights like this were very frequent for Philippine, whether she spent them at the bedside of the sick or assisted at the Holy Sacrifice, which could be celebrated only furtively, under cover of darkness." [11]

Her relatives were in continual anxiety about her and frequently tried to check her perilous zeal by dwelling on the consequences that might so easily result from the risks she was taking. To these representations and to their pleadings that she return to live with some of her family she always gave the same answer: "Let me alone; it is my happiness and glory to serve my divine Saviour in the person of the unfortunate and the poor." [12] She was not, however, lacking in affection or interest where her family was concerned, and one event gave her much pleasure in the midst of the turmoil and terror. On July 31, 1794, Claude Perier gave his daughter Marine in marriage to Camille Teisseire. Camille was thirty years of age, a rich wine-merchant with a spacious home near Place Grenette; Marine was in her sixteenth year and "one of the prettiest women in the town," so Stendhal thought. Philippine had had no more loyal helper in the town than Camille Teisseire, and she always considered him a close personal friend.

The wedding had scarcely been announced when couriers rode into Grenoble with news of Robespierre's downfall. The city's reaction was true to form in Dauphiny, where the people had been disgusted with the extremes of terror, persecution, public crime, and godless life. At once the Ladies of Mercy were allowed to reorganize. A movement to ameliorate the condition of the prisoners gave them free scope for their charity. It was fortunate that municipal authorities with moderate ideas and a sense of justice had been retained, for the period of readjustment was critical. As the year 1795 opened, Dauphiny, if not the whole of France, was at peace.

Philippine was now free to return to Grâne. She had, most probably, visited her family at least once or twice during the past year and a half, for she wrote that she was there "during the stormiest days of the revolution." She found her mother in very poor health and her father active again in political life. Since her sister Amelie was expecting her third child, Adelaide was managing the household for her mother, though she was rather bored with life in the country, especially since Cousin Marine's wedding. Duchesne was now sent away to school, and Philippine devoted herself to nine-year-old Melanie's education. In February, 1795, the law of freedom of worship was proclaimed; but since church assemblies were still forbidden, the church at Grâne was without liturgical services.

There is no record of this period in Philippine's life. We know, however, that in the spring of 1797 Madame Duchesne's illness grew steadily worse. Her twin, Camille Jordan's mother, had died the previous December, worn out at the age of forty-eight by the terrible strain of the Revolution, but comforted by the knowledge that her sons were strongly Catholic in faith. The death of Marie-Elizabeth, the "Lise" of her childhood, seemed to drain from Madame Duchesne her last resistance. There were others who might have cared for her with constant attention, but from no one else would she have received the loving devotedness that Philippine lavished upon her. Madame Jouve wrote later on: "That daughter, who had formerly left her to follow God's call, was her most faithful nurse during her entire illness. Day and night she was at her bedside, caring for both body and soul; nor did she leave her until she had drawn her last breath." [13]

The absence of their father at this time was an added grief for the Duchesne sisters. Since his re-entrance into political life, he had first been named syndic at Crest, then chosen by the electors of the department of the Drôme as a member of the Council of Five Hundred in 1797. He had gone to Paris that spring with no premonition of the sorrow the summer would bring. Madame Duchesne would not allow the family to send for him, for she felt he was at his post of duty. She tried, however, to write him a farewell letter, but she could not finish it. After telling him of her condition and of having sent for her absent children, she gave a last expression to her love for him:

Death would have been too sweet if I had had the satisfaction of having you, my best friend, with me in my last moments. I die in sweet peace, leaving to my children the best of fathers, and to you affectionate and respectful children who will do all in their power to make up to you for my loss. The only anxiety I carry to the grave, my loving companion, is . . .[14]

Pierre-François Duchesne knew well what his beloved wife had left unsaid. Death came for her on June 30, 1797, and she was buried near the children she had lost in the early years of her motherhood. Euphrosine and Duchesne had not reached Grâne in time to kneel at her bedside; Amelie and Adelaide were elsewhere in the chateau when she died. It was Philippine who held her mother in her arms, and Melanie who knelt beside the bed. Two weeks later the little girl wrote to Euphrosine, pouring out her heart to the sister whose duties to her family had detained her in Lyons. It needs no stretch of the imagination to picture Philippine sitting beside her eleven-year-old sister and putting into words the sentiments that filled their hearts that Sunday afternoon of July 16, 1797:

It has cost me much, my very dear Euphrosine, not to be able to write to you sooner about our great sorrow. Since we could not have the consolation of being together in our grief, can we not be so in this way? Our Mother is gone, my poor dear Sister. No, I had never conceived an idea of what this loss would mean, but to lose a mother such as we had—one so affectionate, so kind, so virtuous! I have constantly in my memory the picture of her with that wonderfully calm, peaceful expression on her face, which was a sublime contrast to her state of physical exhaustion. She kept it even after death; the smile was still on her lips. . . . Philippine and I were in her room. I was kneeling at the foot of the bed and I heard the death rattle that was a sure sign she would not rally again.

I could never tell you what was happening in my heart, but it was still worse when I felt her cold cheeks. . . . What a sad and painful afternoon that was! We spent it in Amelie's room, weeping together. The night was also very hard, but the next day was worse, if that is possible. I never spent such a long day in my life. I rambled all through this immense house, and it seemed to me absolutely empty. My heart was empty too, though it was filled with sorrow. . . . But if ever there was a consoling death, it was our mother's. A few days before her death she said: "My soul enjoys perfect peace. I think of God only as a God full of goodness." . . .

O my dear Sister, you put it well in the letter I just received from you: there is a way in which we can prove our gratitude and constant remembrance of her, and that is by walking always in her footsteps. She has worn smooth a pathway of virtue, and we shall find it easy to follow because by doing so we shall become worthy children of our mother. And from heaven she will strengthen our courage and bless our efforts. . . .

I hope the closeness of our family union may bring some consolation to our poor father. He is as deeply grieved as we feared he would be. In the same mail with your letter came one from him, the first written since he had the news of our mother's death. You could not find more tender expressions of sorrow and love. . . . I realize I have not written you enough about mother, but now I must stop. I want to add just one more detail that will make you envy us all the more, and it is this: we go almost every day to pray at her grave, and we recite the Office of the Dead daily. I went yesterday. It was just two weeks since I had accompanied her body . . . and the memory renewed all my grief.[15]

In the property settlement after the death of Madame Duchesne, Philippine turned over to Amelie her own share in the estate at Grâne and gave to her other sisters and brother her portion of the property situated in Grenoble and elsewhere, in return for a yearly income which they agreed to pay her during her lifetime. This arrangement was made at her own suggestion, since it would free her from the care of real estate or commercial interests and would allow her to live independently wherever she chose and devote herself to works of charity.

The first of these charitable enterprises was no drain on her income, but a severe test of her virtue and a somewhat humiliating failure. At her father's suggestion she went to Romans to live for a time with her grandmother Duchesne. The old lady was not alone. The elder of her Visitandine daughters was still living with her, and there were tenants and servants on the place. Philippine seems, however, to have been concerned about her, feeling that some members of the family neglected her selfishly, exaggerating certain eccentricities that made companionship with her unpleasant. Philippine was to learn the truth, and quickly. Grandmother Duchesne was a character. Through a long life she had given free rein to a temper now ungovernable because seldom governed in the past. From morning till night she stormed at all who ventured near her, not excepting her elderly daughter or the faithful housemaid, Rose, who cared for her with docility and self-control inspired more by compassion than by fear. Philippine was in admiration of Rose. She herself was soon exhausted and was cogitating how she might withdraw from Romans without giving further offense, when Grandmother Duchesne dismissed her in words so clear and pointed as to free her from all hesitation about leaving. Meditating on these experiences, she drew a serious lesson for herself and for Amelie, to whom she wrote with charming frankness:

> I am still at Romans. It is not as easy to leave as I had thought it would be. I have let slip several opportunities, not wishing to leave Grandmother alone, and now I have no means of getting away. Julie is already rather surprised at my delay and seems put out with me for postponing my visit, but I have no wings on which to fly to her. Grandmother has expressed herself in no uncertain terms regarding my departure—it will make her quite happy. I had a pretty lively scene with her as a result of some representations I tried to make to her. I did not succeed in calming her wrath against either her tenants or her house-servants. From the conversation I gained only my own dismissal, and that in very pointed language.
>
> In seeing the changes which the years have wrought in our grandmothers, I cannot but make a few sad reflections. Their blood flows in our veins, and already we feel in ourselves flashes of their fiery impatience. Let us try to control ourselves now in the first stages of this defect, which increases with age and may become incorrigible. Let us try not to be exacting with others, but rather to pass over in silence those thousand little annoyances which tend to embitter us. For we know that no one is perfect in this life and we must put up with the defects of others.
>
> I marvel every day at Rose's self-control. No matter how indignant she gets, she never says more than: Poor woman, pity her. She is a good-natured lamb, a treasure of patience and peace in face of suffering from many sources. I encourage her in this patience and have made her promise never to quit her post. No one else would accept it, unless out of hidden and pliant self-interest.[16]

While Philippine may have felt in herself a tendency toward the defects that made her grandmother so unbearable, she had seen similar faults displayed by Amelie and knew that the household at Grâne was often shaken by her outbursts of temper. The forthrightness with which she speaks of their common failings is indicative, not only of the intimacy existing between them, but also of the fearlessness with which Philippine was accustomed to express her thoughts and the assurance she had that her remarks would be taken in good part. She also knew that her return to Grâne would give the family great pleasure; nevertheless, she did not return.

Instead, she set off for Saint-Marcellin, where Julie Tranchand was eagerly awaiting her. During the past few years the town had been the hiding place of many a confessor of the Faith and future martyr. The Church of St. Marcellin was still closed, but now and then a priest appeared in disguise and made his presence known to the faithful by a trusted underground. Then, too, the chateau of Murinais was in this vicinity, and Mother Anne-Félicité, Philippine's former Superior at Sainte Marie, was living there.

But Saint-Marcellin held an even greater attraction for Philippine. The town had had its monastery of the Visitation before the Revolution, and a group of fervent nuns had gathered there as early as 1795, still holding fast to their ideals and hopes, in spite of the price such fidelity entailed. At their head was Mother Claire-Euphrosine Duchesne. She had known a quarter-century of religious life at Romans before the Revolution drove her and her older sister from their cloister back to the family home, where Grandmother Duchesne made things so lively for all who came under her roof. Visitation annals speak of Mother Claire-Euphrosine as a woman of deep faith, selfless generosity, superb courage, and keen sense of humor. During the years spent at home (1791–1795) she carried on a remarkable apostolate,

> seizing every opportunity to glorify God and work for the salvation of her neighbor, to check acts of violence, to enlighten persons who had fallen into schism, and to save souls from sin. Human respect was no obstacle with her. Strong and courageous, she was never deterred by coldness, displeasure, sharp words, or insults. She just pretended not to notice such things and went about her holy enterprises, answering with a polite courtesy that frequently infuriated those who were questioning her. She was often able to procure the sacraments for the sick and to bring souls back to God.[17]

But living at home in relative security did not satisfy Mother Claire-Euphrosine: with her niece, Julie Tranchand, and another Visitandine, she moved to Saint-Marcellin. Taking up residence in what had been a boarding school, they carried on common life according to their Rule as far as possible. A few more companions joined them. The young girls who were their pupils often saw the priests who found refuge in the house, but no indiscretion or disloyalty ever betrayed their hiding place. Domiciliary visits were frequent, but no arrests were made, thanks to the presence of mind, the affable manner, and the gay disposition of Mother Claire-

Euphrosine. There were times when her family accused her of rashness, selfishness, lack of consideration for others, but she refused to compromise; and she was upheld in her resolution by Monseigneur d'Aviau, Archbishop of Vienne, who more than once found shelter at Saint-Marcellin.

This was the group Philippine now joined temporarily. There is no record of how long she was with them or why she was not content to remain. Two facts are known: she was not satisfied, and she made a spiritual retreat at Saint-Marcellin. During those days of solitude and prayer she came to a decision: she would return to Grenoble and devote herself to an apostolate of charity among the poor of the city and the victims of persecution who were still in prison or in hiding. She hoped, moreover, to see religious life reestablished in her own beloved monastery. The Visitandine stamp was imprinted deep in her soul, and Sainte Marie was the monastic home to which she was wholeheartedly attached.

Writing of this period some twenty years later she said:

> The time of trial, but not of indecision, seemed an eternity to me, and if, reflecting on its length, I wondered at times whether God meant me to remain in the world, He saw to it at once that some passage of the Gospel referring to detachment from one's family came to my attention and revived my courage. The separation from my father, who went to Paris, and the death of my mother, which occurred shortly after that, set me at liberty to leave home and return to Grenoble in order to associate myself with some women who wished to live under a religious rule. One of the Jesuits whom I had known was still living. As soon as he learned of my decision, he wrote to me, saying *that I had taken a step for which God would reward me.* At the same time he told me that public worship would soon be restored in France, according to a prediction of the Venerable Benedict Labre.[18]

The encouragement of this Jesuit was evidently a strong moral support for Philippine at a time when she needed it badly. She seems to have been misunderstood by both the religious at Saint-Marcellin and her family. When she informed the family of the decision she had reached, they made things unpleasant for her. Madame de Mauduit seems to have leveled at her the severest reproaches, with an insinuation of selfishness and weakness that cut to the quick. Amelie's pen could be as sharp as her tongue, and Philippine's reply is self-revealing. Addressing the letter to Citoyenne Mauduit at Crest, as Grâne was off the postal route, she wrote from a very full heart:

You know already, my loved Sister, that I have reached Grenoble, and you surely understand the motive of my trip. Certainly I would never have had the courage to undertake it for a few days of pleasure here. Do not suggest deception on my part toward you, my dearest friend. If on leaving the home where you are residing I did not state my ultimate intentions, then subject to a thousand uncertainties and to the duty I might have felt obliged to shoulder at Romans, I really had no fixed plan at the time. I simply left to Providence the care of lighting my path and showing me the divine will. It was easier, too, when leaving sisters whom I love so tenderly, not to consider the possibility of a long absence.

The reception I got from Grandmother and the dismissal she gave me were the first incitement to put my project into action. Far from being angry at the reception she gave me, I regard it as a real favor, for it wards off the reproaches Father might have made me for refusing to carry out his wishes, since she herself refused to have me around. Moreover, with three daughters near her —all quite as free as I—and two house-servants, there was not the least anxiety as to the manner in which she would be cared for.

My old desires were rekindled by the reflections that filled my mind during this period of leisure; and when I visited Saint-Marcellin, I really had no intention of remaining there. In the retreat I made there, I tried to strip myself of all overeagerness in desires, of all attachment to my own views, of all merely human sentiments. But how could human sentiments have part in a resolution that forced me to overcome those very sentiments and to lift myself above nature in order to correspond to a higher, stronger attraction? Stripped then of self, I sought to know the divine will, and I made up my mind. Few people understand what I am talking about, and few will refrain from blaming me. I excuse them because of their motives and beg them to act in the same way toward mine, if they cannot praise them.

My father especially, having no religion to fall back upon, will always be prejudiced against me, and I shall carry to my grave the sorrow of having caused him pain. . . . I know that I possess no power either to console him or to bring him peace. But in uniting myself to Him who directs all events and consoles all hearts, I can do more for my father than by seeking to please him by my attentions and constant companionship. Often I have prayed to God that the pain of this separation may be felt by me alone, that I may endure its full force, and that in return I may win for my family happiness, cordial union, and constant peace.

Can Father complain as long as you remain with him? You have almost taken our mother's place by managing the household; your children, whom he loves as his very own, increase the family circle and assure him years of happiness.[19] Take care of yourself for his sake, and for the sake of your husband, your sisters, and your children. . . . It was never my intention to abandon you without some compensation. You will be fair-minded enough to believe that one single motive has always guided me. My plan was laid long before I owned any property; and after a great misfortune brought me an inheritance, I planned to enjoy it by sacrificing it, keeping for myself only the hope of heavenly riches.[20]

Formerly I looked forward without imprudence to a life of security in religion. Now all is changed; my plans are no longer the same, for it seems impossible to follow my desires, as there is no religious order in existence in France. But I want this letter to bear witness against me if ever selfish interest comes between us, and if I am not ready to make all the arrangements that are most advantageous to you. I have found a companion somewhat older than I and free like myself. She has a little revenue which, with some work added, suffices for her own support and that of a very good young woman who has been in her service for ten years and whom we shall continue to keep. We are just about to rent an apartment; and as we must make the first payment at once, I need some money. Will you have the kindness to send me about 300 francs, if you can do so without inconvenience to yourself? I intend writing to Father to ask permission to take from among the things he has in storage the furniture I need most. . . .

Plead my cause with Father and do so at once, I beg of you. Do not let him worry lest events should bring failure to our plans; they are so limited, there really is no risk. We shall not undertake anything dangerous, but only some good works. We shall live in obscurity—this is our wish—so do not talk to anyone about me or what I am doing. Prudence requires this.[21]

"Prudence requires this." Conditions in Grenoble were far from normal, and Philippine realized how careful she and her companion must be, if they were to carry out their plan, which must have been sketchy enough at first. The rehabilitation of Catholic life and worship was necessarily a very slow process, but it was Philippine's ambition to share actively in this restoration. Mission work at home, the re-establishment of monastic life, the education of children, social work among the neglected poor, all of these were the object of her desires and prayers as she went about the city on her errands of mercy, nursing the sick, sewing for the poor, begging help for priests still in hiding, bringing comfort and encouragement wherever she went.

Sometimes she was at Tante Perier's house, where there was much to talk about. Casimir was conscripted that year, 1798, and Augustin had married Louise de Berckheim. He had taken over the direction of his father's business affairs in Dauphiny when Claude went to Paris in 1795 and was making a success of the big textile factories. Sometimes Philippine was at Marine Teisseire's home, where there was a baby boy about a year old. Marine was interested in the wedding that was being planned at Grâne, where Adelaide Duchesne became the bride of Henri Lebrument of Bourg in 1798. Philippine may have attended the ceremony and seen her father there. He was, as always, a very busy man, having been chosen secretary of the Council of Five Hundred in March of that year. He could give her news of the Savoye-Rollins, who were living in Paris now, as Jacques had accepted a position under the Directory.

This did not mean, however, that the men of Dauphiny to whom Philippine was related were in accord with all the policies and actions of the government they were serving. Outspoken Camille Jordan, who had been sent by Lyons to the Council of Five Hundred in 1797, had stood up so courageously for religious liberty and freedom of worship as to acquire the nickname of "Church-bell Jordan" (*Jordan cloche*) and be listed for deportation in the September Revolution. So the road to exile reopened for him. He would return to France in 1800 and be interned temporarily in Grenoble, where Philippine would enjoy his friendship again. She had great affection for this sincere and courageous cousin, whose finely balanced character drew admiration even from his severest opponents.

In 1798 the henchmen of Bonaparte laid violent hands on Pope Pius VI. The venerable old man had seen a stormy pontificate and had upheld the Church's rights in the face of revolutionary despotism in France, but he was powerless against armed force. Hustled unceremoniously from place to place, the sick pontiff was borne in a litter across the Alps into Dauphiny. A jolting cart carried him to Vizille, where a twenty-four-hour halt was allowed at the Perier chateau. Grenoble was reached early in July, and soon the invalid began the final lap of his earthly journey to Valence on the Rhone, where he died on August 29, 1799.[22] That was Philippine's thirtieth birthday, and also Napoleon Bonaparte's.

While the resurgence of France under the Directory gave partial satisfaction to those who had the best interests of the country at heart, the growing power of Bonaparte was viewed with concern by those who read aright the signs of the times.

Among these was Pierre-François Duchesne. With a fearlessness that scorned consequences he took his stand, and in November, 1799, distinguished himself by his opposition to the *coup d'état* by which the Corsican militarist overthrew the Directory. On that *journée de dupe*, at least one man from Dauphiny was not taken in, nor did he lose his seat in the Council of Five Hundred. So outstanding was Duchesne's legal ability that he was appointed to membership in the Tribunate after the Constitution of the Year VIII was inaugurated.[23]

Philippine, meanwhile, had begun to realize that she must center her energies on one project rather than scatter them on a dozen enterprises. The thing she longed for most was the re-establishment of religious life at Sainte Marie, and the vision of the old monastery as once more a house of prayer and cordial community life now became her dominant inspiration. The story of her efforts to accomplish this restoration and the final outcome of her striving is contained in the longest autobiographical record she has left us, a record compiled in 1805 at the suggestion of obedience.

In the spring of 1800 she risked another trip to Romans and, while there, decided to make the pilgrimage to the tomb of St. Francis Regis at La Louvesc. Travel was safe enough now, though its discomforts made it a penitential undertaking. The route took Philippine first to Valence, then across the Rhone and west to La Louvesc. She seems to have made no inquiries before setting out as to conditions at the shrine: her disappointment on arriving there was great. She writes:

> I was accompanied by one of my grandmother's servants who was very devoted to this saint because he owed to him his restoration to health. . . . The pilgrimage was on the feast of the Holy Cross, May 3, 1800. I learned afterwards that the Jesuit who had urged me to make the trip [in 1797] had died that very day. . . . As I had only two days for my trip to La Louvesc and back to Romans, I saw neither him nor the holy Archbishop of Vienne, Monseigneur d'Aviau, who in imitation of the apostolic life of the saint of Velay had hidden near his tomb during the worst persecution. They say he was still there [in 1800].[24]
>
> I did not go to La Louvesc in search of sensible consolation and I did not experience any, though I had expected to. Everything about the place had an air of desolation, resulting from the devastation of the church.[25] Mass could not be offered in the sanctuary, as one altar was smashed to pieces; several figures of angels which had supported [the statue or relic of] the saint were broken;

and one could have gathered up handfuls of dust on his altar. The Mass was offered in a miserable barn and I could not receive Communion on account of the crowd; but I had this happiness after the crowd had withdrawn.[26]

Philippine touches but briefly on the spiritual experience of that day of pilgrimage, yet it must have been filled with prayer and meditation on the heroic life of John Francis Regis—his missionary zeal, his apostolate among the poor of all categories in whom he saw only souls for whom Jesus Christ had died.

I left the shrine [Philippine continues] completely gripped by a desire to devote myself to the instruction of the poor in imitation of St. Francis Regis. Arriving again in Grenoble, where good schools for little girls were not lacking, I took charge of a few little boys who were entirely neglected and were living like animals. I dwell with pleasure on them for they were a real trial to my patience, and I really think that in a way we owe to them the house we now possess.[27] It was difficult to get hold of even three or four of them, but a few good meals and the promise of some clothes at last induced them to come for an hour a day. They brought along some of their playmates, so in this way I got together about fifteen or twenty boys, fairly well intentioned but so unbearably indolent and so noisy that they enraged everyone in the house against me. Their eagerness to greet me on the streets was also an embarrassment; it seemed as if I was acquainted with all the street-urchins in the town. They pointed me out to their parents, several of whom got on my track because I had told the boys not to work on Sundays. Really, if devotion to St. Francis Regis had not sustained me, I would many a time have abandoned my apostolate. I had, however, some consolations: several of these boys, who had never even heard of the Blessed Trinity, learned the entire catechism, their prayers, and some hymns, and taught all this to their parents. They all went to confession and several made their first Communion.

I got them to pray that God would enlighten me as to my vocation, and indeed the hour of His mercy was drawing near. On Pentecost Sunday, 1801, I went for a walk up to Sainte Marie, where I had lived two years as a pupil and four and a half years in the trials of the novitiate. I was with some former Carmelites and I talked of almost nothing but my love for that house and my desire to return there. I grew so enthusiastic in the conversation that I seemed already to see the place peopled with Visitation nuns, and the Carmelites installed in what had been formerly the chaplain's house.[28]

Philippine had with her that afternoon her sister Melanie, then fifteen years old, and her niece, Amelie de Mauduit, just six. The two girls were playing together on the terrace when suddenly small Amelie cried out, "Yes, I am coming here to school someday and I shall make my first Communion here." To Tante Philippine the child's words were a prophecy and she in turn prayed aloud, "My God, You have put these words on the lips of this child. Make them come true." [29]

2. 1801—1804

Lord, have mercy, Christ, have mercy,
Lord, have mercy.

Liturgy of the Mass

THAT FEAST OF PENTECOST, 1801, was a day of decision. Philippine determined to get possession of Sainte Marie and turned confidently to prayer. Her *Story of Sainte Marie* needs little annotation and is transcribed here almost full length because of its wealth of detail and character revelation.[30] She writes:

The feast of St. Francis Regis was drawing near and I felt an increase of confidence in him. Both before and after the feast I made novenas in his honor to know the will of God in my regard. It occurred to me one day that my return to Sainte Marie would be quite possible if it were reconverted into a religious institution, and I felt inspired to make a vow in honor of St. Regis in order to obtain that grace. I asked the permission of my confessor and worded my promise this way: "If within a year I am back at Sainte Marie in a manner conformable to my desires, I will: 1. send someone to La Louvesc to have a novena of Masses offered at the tomb of St. Regis, and also a novena of prayers; 2. receive Communion on the feast of St. Francis Regis every year and fast on the eve in his honor; and if I cannot do this, I will ask someone else to do so; 3. arrange in the convent an oratory in honor of St. Regis; 4. instruct twelve poor people in religion or have someone else do this.

With my intentions placed in such good hands I felt new courage and I began to take action. I consulted, or had others consult, the administrators of the diocese as to the proper course to take in order to get possession of Sainte Marie. They all thought it very desirable to do so, but they did not agree as to the wisdom of trying just then nor on the means that would succeed best. One of the vicars general was Father Brochier, a man of wide experience and animated by the spirit of God. I set great store by his approbation, foreseeing even then that many people would blame our enterprise and that it was wise to have the support of highly respected authorities. I was not then acquainted with Father Brochier, so I asked my confessor to consult him for me.

As he [Father Brochier] was not in favor of my purchasing the monastery, and as it was, after all, my own project, I wrote to him, hoping to influence his decision. I told him in detail my motives and my hopes and all that the vivacity of my desires put into my mind. My letter was long; so was his answer. It began with the words, *Digitus Dei est hic*, "The finger of God is here"; but he insisted that it was not wise to purchase the place yet, that the money could be better employed in other ways, and that to all appearances *that house would be given back to us some day*, but that we should try to get possession of it by some other means. I held to buying it, and I ended by going to see Father Brochier myself in order to obtain his consent, but he held firmly to his opinion and advice.

It was not enough to act with the consent and advice of my ecclesiastical superiors. I could not overlook the former Superior of the house on which I was building my hope for a re-establishment [of religious life], so I went to the country-place where she was living, in order to find out her intentions. She seemed quite pleased with the prospect of returning to her convent. I went a second time, and she wrote a letter in concert with the former confessor of Sainte Marie to Monsieur [Joseph] du Bouchage, who was then holding the position of prefect of Grenoble, to ask his help in this enterprise. I carried the letter myself and received his verbal answer to the effect that the time was not yet opportune for making such a request of the government and that we had better wait. This was also the opinion of Father Rey, one of the vicars general, who advised me to wait at least two months.

I waited longer than that, for my Father came home from Paris and asked me to spend the vacation with him, and I willingly did so. We went to Romans, and there I had the consolation of spending a few days in a convent of the Visitation which one of my aunts, a former religious of that monastery, had just rented in order to gather together her Sisters and establish a boarding school. We had conceived exactly the same idea at the very same time, but she had no need of contradictions, as I had, and in a short time her house was reorganized and the Rule was in full vigor.[31]

The vacation at Romans lasted about two months. It must have been a joy for Philippine to recall it, though her condensed record taxes the patience of her readers, while it calls up one of the happiest pictures of her that imagination can construct. She and her father were intimate comrades again. As he listened to her confidences, he cautioned her against impetuosity—a family failing, pointing to the mature experience that had enabled Sister Françoise-Melanie to accomplish so much for her monastery, and warning her that his income was not large enough to allow him to give her much help. Philippine, however, was not asking him for material aid, but for his approval of the plan she had conceived.

She always knew when she had pressed her point sufficiently. Then they would talk of her loved Uncle Claude, whose death had occurred so suddenly in Paris the previous winter. Fortunately his wife had come from Grenoble to the capital just a few days before he was stricken with pneumonia.[32] Philippine was eager for news of young Duchesne, who had become a congenial companion to his father and was following him in politics as well as the law. She asked many questions about Josephine and Augustin and the younger Perier brothers who were making a name for themselves in banking circles—a remarkably gifted set of men, these *Perier Frères,* as Paris was coming to know them. There were chats, too, about her sisters. Melanie was living with Amelie at Grâne, but she liked to get away to Lyons or Grenoble frequently. Euphrosine and Adelaide had growing families and very moderate means with which to care for their children. These children would need to be educated, and this brought the conversation back to Philippine's plan. The re-establishment of Sainte Marie would help take care of the education of her nieces. In the end she won her father's approval by arguments and promises and prayers. Now indeed she was free to return to her cloistered life. Recalling the joy of that victory, she wrote:

During that vacation with my father I confided my hopes to him and I enlisted the prayers of all the pious souls I knew and joined with several in a Forty Days' prayer for this intention. On the last day I was free to return to my holy cloister. No sooner was I back in Grenoble than Madame de Rollin, my cousin and most loyal friend, begged her husband to petition the prefect to let us have Sainte Marie, and he promised to rent it to us on favorable terms, though at a rather high price.[33] We had to address a petition to him, which I expected to have signed by the Superior of the house and the religious who would contribute to the establishment. Divine Providence allowed it to happen that the authorities were slow in drawing up that petition; and when at last they brought it to me, it was worded in the singular.

The anxiety which the delay had caused me, the need of secrecy to avoid a raise in the price, the distance of Mother de Murinais [from Grenoble], the complaints of some of her religious who had got wind of my visit to Monsieur du Bouchage, all were reasons which determined me to sign the petition myself in order to take advantage of the kind efforts of the people who were actively interested in our project.

The building was made over to me on December 10 [1801]. The prefect seemed to enjoy my happiness. I was to pay 800 francs in rent yearly and to be responsible for the repairs, which were rather extensive. My first impulse on leaving the prefecture was to go and thank God for His goodness at the bedside of a poor sick man whom I visited almost every day and in whose room I had often invoked St. Francis Regis, both for him and for my own intentions. He seemed to forget his suffering in the joy which my news gave him. I told him first because he represented my good Master by his sufferings.

From there I went to the home of Madame Faucherand [former Visitandine of Sainte Marie] who had shown the most enthusiasm about a reunion; but the agitation that was apparent in her whole person made me foresee her lack of perseverance. From her house I wrote to Mother de Murinais, offering to send a carriage for her and never dreaming that she would make the least delay [in taking possession of the house]. She sent me an answer, stating that she could not leave her present home without consulting her nephew, who was supporting her. I called again that same day on all the vicars general [in Grenoble], and they congratulated me and said I had certainly been inspired in my action.

Then I went home and began to pack my things and dispose of what I would not need. I remained indoors in order to avoid meeting the people who were displeased with me. All the former religious of the house were. They said I was rash in going to live in a building that was falling in ruins and from which I might be expelled again. They accused me of acting without consulting anyone and of sacrificing all to my own selfishness. "Has she the means on which to support the religious who have lost all their revenues? We do not want to starve to death. We have made a vow of poverty, but not of begging our living. We will not return to our convent until we can be sure of the same security as we had before." All these remarks were made with ill-temper and repeated in the same spirit, so I considered it useless to make any advances toward these women, as they were angered by the least suggestion of a return [to Sainte Marie]. It was enough for my peace of conscience that the door was now open to them and that both the ecclesiastical and the religious superiors had been consulted.

Father Rivet, whom I knew but slightly then, came to congratulate me, inspired by his zeal for the glory of God. His visit gave me great joy, for he knew about the signing of the concordat and encouraged me with the thought that I was not too far ahead of time in this work.[34]

On December 14 I returned to the house of the Lord. It would have been a consolation to have done so the previous day, anniversary of the death of St. Chantal, but I could not manage it. All the lads of my catechism class carried my bundles with remarkable alacrity in spite of the rain that poured all day. Not one of them stole a thing. I thought my only companion would be a poor girl of twelve whom I had instructed in religion, for Madame Faucherand had written me that she had had a slight hemorrhage and thought it only charity to wait until Easter in order to give her Sisters time to make up their minds. I replied that I was not going to put off for a single hour my return to that holy place for which I longed so earnestly, and that it was time to show the world that it had lied in daring to say that we had been kept in the cloister as victims of force and that we were glad to be back in secular life.

Then I hastened to leave my apartment. Late in the evening, in a storm of wind and rain, I reached Sainte Marie in the wake of my baggage, which the caretaker had put in safety. I was not as badly drenched as my poor little boys. Water streamed from their clothes, but every face beamed with pleasure, an indication, I took it, of our Lord's approval. Madame Faucherand, realizing that I was determined to carry out my plan, had got up courage and reached the house some hours sooner than I. In spite of my happiness at having a companion, I was a bit put out, for I had to sleep in the room with her to quiet her fears. My dearest wish had been to spend that night in the august sanctuary where for so many years the Name of the Lord had not been hallowed. I wanted to have the whole night for prayer, enjoying God's favors and giving Him my humble thanks.

The building was without lock and key, but I was not afraid, for I realized that as God had been my guide, so He would be my protector until I had had time to assure us of safety. I got to work on this at once, and my days were spent either with the workmen doing the repairs, or cooking meals for the community of two, or sweeping parts of the house that had not been cleaned for nearly ten years, or shoveling out snow and mopping up water, or trying to repair the window-panes—the most thankless task of all, for the paste froze immediately I put it on and would not stick and gave me plenty of occasions to exercise my patience.[35] With the exception of this one task, all the labor in the house was pleasure for me. I experienced all the consolations that St. Teresa had when sweeping her monastery. Never had the keenest worldly pleasure given me such satisfaction. We went for our spiritual duties to the church, where three windows and a door were missing. The cold was intense, but we did not feel it and neither one of us took cold.

At the end of two weeks we finally had the first Mass offered in the church. The outer door was still closed. As no priest could come for Mass on Christmas day, we went to assist at midnight Mass in the city, accompanied by a young girl who had been with us only a few days and a workman who had formerly been a brother at the *Grande Chartreuse* and who was always a kind friend of the house. We had made habits for ourselves, and they were blessed before Mass. We took them afterwards as a present from the Infant Jesus, and I had mine on two days later when we had a visit from Monseigneur Spina, Archbishop of Corinth, and Monseigneur Caselli, both of whom are cardinals today [1805].[36] They had finished their work on the concordat. Madame de Rollin, who was acquainted with the Archbishop, had told him about my returning to Sainte Marie, and he had had the kindness to ask Bounaparte [sic] to allow us to have the place rent free, but no reply had been forthcoming and his interest in us had not produced the desired effect. It was Father Rivet who had procured for us the honor of this visit. I thought it would help to lessen the ill-feeling; but, quite the contrary, it increased it.

Realizing now that if I was going to get companions at all they would have to come from different orders or be seculars contemplating religious life, I came to the conclusion that there should be a Rule we might propose to newcomers. The Visitandine Rule of Sainte Marie could not be observed strictly just then, but many parts of it could be put into practice. I gave a copy to Father Brochier, begging him to indicate the articles of the Rule that should be observed and those that might be modified for the present. He consented to do this and composed a Rule very wisely planned, which kept the interior spirit of Sainte Marie: seclusion, detachment, obedience, all things in common, but was outwardly less strict. He wished a superior to be elected for a year as soon as there were four in the group; then a superior elected for three years, according to the Rule, as soon as there were twelve of us and we could be more sure in our choice. This Rule was signed by all the vicars-general except one, the former spiritual Father of that convent, whom we had not asked to take up that position again because of his advanced age. Another of these priests insisted on adding this article: "Places must be reserved in the house for the religious to whom it belonged formerly." That was the dearest wish of my heart, and I persuaded Father Brochier to agree to it.

This Rule, from which I had hoped such great things, produced the worst effect. The religious criticized it loudly, especially the article on all things being held in common, which they found simply impossible. They had no scruple about retaining the ownership of their belongings, yet they raised an outcry about the overthrow of the Rule because the order of day was not exactly as it had been formerly and the election was slightly different. "Our former Superior is alive," they said; "why speak of electing another?" They did not consider the fact that there was no question of a superior for the religious who were still dispersed, but only for those who would come to the convent, which must have a head. Another article of the Rule answered all their objections, as it expressly stated that as soon as circumstances allowed, all the proposed changes would give way to strict observance of the former Rule. . . .

The majority [of the former Visitandines] did not come to celebrate the feast of St. Francis de Sales with us at Sainte Marie, but went instead to a private oratory, and after Mass assembled *to protest against what they called the measures taken by Madame Duchesne.* They then acquainted some of the vicars-general with that protest. I was in complete ignorance of what was going on and I enjoyed the greatest consolation on that feast of St. Francis de Sales [January 29]. Several priests of high standing came to offer the Mass for us with the joyous enthusiasm that holy souls experience at the sight of a work begun that may bring glory to God. The public entrance of the church was still closed, but the people came in crowds by the interior of the monastery, and our church was the first in Grenoble in which Catholic worship reappeared in all its splendor after the revolution.

Some days later I learned that I was considered an intruder. I said this jokingly to my companion [Madame Faucherand], who had been joined by a young girl and an out-sister. Her mind was somewhat unbalanced and in former days she had had some mental lapses. Her return to the monastery recalled these to her in a painful way. . . . She lost her mind for a time, but I had nothing to suffer as a result, except from her withdrawal. One morning, feeling ill, she told me she needed a change of environment; she left the house and did not return to live with me again. I felt this keenly, and all the more because it presaged further departures. The enemy had so disturbed the young girl who had come recently that she cried all day and longed for the time when I would find another companion; then she would depart without leaving me entirely alone. The out-sister did not hide from me the fact that her courage was failing, too, and she would stay but a short time. I went through some very bitter hours in view of all this, though I still counted a little on Mother de Murinais. She had told everyone that I had done nothing in the matter of recovering possession of the house without her consent and that she intended to keep her word and return to the monastery. Many people even told her that it was a point of honor for her to do so, especially since her letter to Monsieur du Bouchage [the prefect of Grenoble] was generally known. The former confessor of the house was of that opinion. He was her director, and I chose him, too, thinking that since the house was to be re-established, this was a point of rule for me. . . .

There were certain people who feared to have Mother de Murinais return to Sainte Marie. They persuaded a woman who was not a nun to pay me a visit and urge me strongly to write to her not to come and to say I would not be disappointed in view of the opposition of her family and her religious daughters. I was told I would endanger her life by this change of residence. I firmly refused to write such a letter, considering it contrary to the good of the institution and to general edification. It would, moreover, confirm the suspicions of those who said I wanted to dominate everything.

The gossip and criticism current in Grenoble through the winter of 1801–1802 were not the least part of the trial that Philippine was enduring. In a letter to her sister Euphrosine, written on February 14, 1802, she revealed her own reaction quite frankly, along with her affectionate interest in the Jouve family:

How relieved I am, my dear Sister, to learn that your children are recovering! Two days ago I had a letter from Mèlanie which left me little hope for the life of your Euphrosine. I have been thinking of you constantly and was about to write you a letter of sympathy when yours arrived, telling me that God has heard your tears and prayers and spared your daughter. Tell your husband how keenly I have shared his anxieties and how I now share his joy. My eagerness to write to you makes me put off my letter to Melanie, for I am so busy, I cannot write to her also today. So please give her my fond love, and also to Madame Jordan. Is Camille still in Lyons?

You are very kind to take an interest in the difficulties inseparable from an undertaking such as ours. What I feel most keenly is the opposition of some persons from whom I had expected gratitude. I have gotten myself talked about, both favorably and unfavorably; but as I did not act through worldly motives, I am not upset by blame nor elated by praise. I want that to come from

God alone and from the indescribable joy of finding myself once more in His House. . . .

As to the repairs needed, they are very extensive. But Providence, always so generous to us, has inspired some zealous people to contribute funds; and if we succeed, I know many others who will help us. My confidence increases when I reflect on the charity already shown me, for it reminds me of old times. It is a mistake to say that charity has grown cold among the faithful. Why, I have seen them, with tears in their eyes, offering me money with as much eagerness as others might show in begging when in urgent need. In return for their generosity may God see fit to bless our enterprise.

At present there are just four of us; but at Easter I expect Mother de Murinais and several religious who have reserved their rooms. We are making good use of our garden and hope to profit by what we raise. The church is charming, but Mass is still celebrated behind closed doors. We had six Masses on the feast of St. Francis de Sales and two sermons, one given by Father Brochier, who is greatly interested in our work and a counselor in both spiritual and temporal affairs. Adieu, my dear and loving friend.

Philippine had relied more on the presence of Mother de Murinais at Sainte Marie than on any other human factor. At one time this religious had been an excellent superior, firm and motherly, valiant in trial and persecution. She had kept in touch with many members of her dispersed community and had encouraged the project of rehabilitation. But she was past eighty years of age now, sickly, infirm, dependent in many ways on those around her and easily swayed by those who showed her personal attentions. Her arrival at Sainte Marie marked a short-lived triumph for Philippine, as she herself relates:

Finally Mother de Murinais decided to come during Passion Week, with a young nun who laid down the condition that she would have no employment but the care of the superior's health. She also brought with her two lay-sisters, one of whom was about eighty years of age, as was also Mother de Murinais. I had been joined a few days before by a new companion, an Ursuline nun, who was really only a boarder. The young girl had left at once.

At this time Father Rivet gave a retreat in our church. It was very well attended, though the public entrance was still closed. We made bold to open it on Holy Thursday, and it has remained open ever since, as has also that of the hospital, which was opened even before ours. It was a great joy for me to lead into our choir, in the presence of so many people, the venerable Mother for whom I had waited so long. It was a triumph. I had reasoned that her arrival would produce a very good effect on outsiders, would please my family, who really suffered because of my solitary position and the heavy [financial] burden of the house, and would edify the public who were gossiping about the indifference of religious who did not take advantage of the cloister opened to them. I hoped, too, that a boarding school would be established. I limited my hopes to that when Mother arrived.

Certainly things were better than before, but they in no way came up to my expectations of a religious institution. We had only Office in choir and meditation; there was no silence, no religious practices, no reading at meals, no *Benedicite* and grace in common, no cloister, no uniformity of dress, nothing. There was not even question of introducing these gradually. They all said they were just making a trial of it, for they had not made up their minds to persevere even in so easy a manner of life. What each one brought with her showed that; they had left their belongings elsewhere and had brought just about enough for a month in the country. In the depths of my heart I experienced much bitter anguish, realizing what all this augured for the near future. But while all this was in no way satisfactory, I was more distressed by the illness of the superior, which seemed to justify the predictions that a change of residence at her age would be fatal, and indeed they were already blaming me for her death. She recovered. I thought God intended to spare me, but He was really preparing me for a still greater affliction.

Two religious who had some pupils offered to join us, and Mother accepted them. In a conversation in which I took part and in which I insisted on the necessity of uniformity of dress, they said that *I wanted everything my way and did as I pleased, but that they also would do whatever they pleased.* The superior was present, but she had not a word to say. I withdrew, and I said afterwards to the confessor that I had wept bitterly when I realized with what intentions they had come, and that there was no hope that the government of the house would be firm enough to enforce the mildest rule, verging really on disorder. He shook his head and replied *that I had not wept enough, that I had but begun to weep, and that I must realize that it was enough for me to propose a thing to have it rejected, but that I must arm myself with courage.*

The spring and summer of 1802 brought to Philippine Duchesne some of the deepest anguish her soul was to experience. All she had hoped for, prayed for, worked for—all seemed utterly wasted. The fervent love that burned in her heart and urged her to a life of strict observance, penance, reparation, prayer, made the situation all the more unbearable. The inspiration she had interpreted as coming directly from the Heart of Christ seemed to mock her by the failure with which she was surrounded. Had she again misunderstood the designs of His Heart in her regard?

An agony of doubt and desolation pressed upon her at times as she went about her duties, silent, recollected, uncomplaining, where all about her murmured against the hardships inevitable in such an enterprise. And her very fervor, acting as a reproach to others, brought severe reprimands and sharp criticisms upon her. Had the situation been kept a community affair, there might have been some chance of its improving, but this was not the case. All Grenoble seems to have known what was happening at Sainte Marie.

It was also discussing the conduct of Pierre-François Duchesne that spring and summer. The republican element in Dauphiny admired him greatly for his political courage and acumen. He had escaped the purge of the Tribunate in 1801, but matters moved swiftly to a climax in the following year. In both the Council of Five Hundred and the Tribunate he steered a middle course on principle, now fighting a bill for the return of the *émigrés*, now upholding the right of former nobles to hold public office. He made a sensation on April 27, 1802, by attacking a projected law relative to public education, though he knew the First Consul himself had had a hand in its formulation, and by accusing the government of trying to keep the poorer classes in ignorance.[37] Two weeks later, on May 10, Napoleon proposed himself as consul for life. The Assembly resigned in a body. Three members of the legislative body, whose names are unrecorded, voted "no." In the Tribunate only Lazare Carnot and Pierre-François Duchesne dared to voice their opposition to the dictator. This vote marked the close of Duchesne's political career at the age of sixty years.

Resigning office almost immediately, he returned with his son to Grâne. The younger Duchesne was in perfect agreement with the stand his father had taken, though he realized that for them both it meant the sacrifice of careers which would have accorded with their tastes and for which they were excellently fitted. Later on, after his father's death, young Duchesne would again appear in political life. Even under the Empire the electoral college of the department of the Drôme honored Pierre-François Duchesne by choosing him for the Senate, but the Emperor Napoleon vetoed the choice on personal grounds and Duchesne remained for several years at Grâne.[38]

When he reached there in the summer of 1802, the news he received about Philippine must have caused him anxiety, for he had grown sympathetic with her holy ambitions and had even given her some financial aid, as the Periers and Savoye-Rollins were doing. Her description of life at Sainte Marie during these months continues:

> So the household was composed of a superior who, in order to attract subjects, accepted all types of character, or rather yielded in turn to each of several religious who were doing each as she pleased, and to some young girls who were boarding pupils. When the superior first came, I asked her what employment she assigned to me. She replied that I was to remain in charge of the repair work being done on the building, the sacristy, the portry, and of one pupil. Mother wanted to be treasurer herself and direct our household, along with that of her sister, who had remained at their country home and did not want that burden. This meant that we would have our accounts in common with a completely separate house, and we considered this an impossible arrangement. I had, moreover, told the superior that I would at the first opportunity give her an account of what I possessed and turn over to her my purse. But her illness made me postpone these explanations; afterwards I considered it more harmful than useful to do so. Since everyone was keeping what she had, I would only cause trouble without improving conditions generally. I even had in my possession 3,000 francs which a very generous person wished to give us, if the establishment succeeded. I asked the benefactor to lend us the money in the meantime and gave a receipt, with the consent of the superior. That money was to be used for repairs on the building, and the work was urgently needed.
>
> I realized that wills were unstable. Often there was such coldness toward me, I foresaw the breakup of the community. I did not want to have the least thing with which to reproach myself for having contributed to this, but everything tended that way. . . . It was pointed out to these women, and they realized it themselves, that discipline was absolutely necessary in the house, so they got together, both outside the convent and inside, to compose a rule, never having accepted that of Father Brochier. The superior showed me a copy, though they had asked her not to do so. I made a copy of it and showed it to Fathers Rey and Brochier, as it contained the vaguest kind of statements which gave not the slightest hope of making for stable union. There was no single purpose, no holding possessions in common, no cloister; one could

come and go at will. They both advised me to keep out of the
way as much as possible and to contribute to the upkeep of the
house only as much as each of the others did, and said that as a
result they might all move out and a better order of things be
established later on. I followed their advice. . . .

A few days later I learned that they were planning to leave, but
did not want me to know it. One of the Sisters who was loyal to
me came to tell me what she had learned. I hastened to throw myself at the feet of Mother de Murinais in an effort to keep her, but
as I could not do so without acting against my conscience by offering the same entreaties for the two people who were urging her
to leave, she held firmly to her resolution. The same Sister came to
tell me that I could get her to stay by promising to do all she required and by turning everything over to her. I found these conditions too hard. That complete self-surrender would have been a
joy to me, had I made it to anyone who was determined to observe a rule—no matter of what order. But what I saw around me
everyday convinced me that I would be making a useless sacrifice,
so I added nothing further to my entreaties to the superior.

On the feast of St. de Chantal I probed the depths of my soul to
determine whether some passion, some selfish interest, some resentment kept me from taking the steps necessary to prevent the
scandal of a rupture in the community. It seemed to me I could say
I would in all sincerity submit myself entirely even to the person
who had made me suffer most, if only she willed to enforce the
strict observance of the Rule, and I begged St. de Chantal to be
judge between me and her daughters. That thought occupied me
all during the High Mass, and I offered myself to God, being willing even to leave Sainte Marie if I was the obstacle to the good that
could be accomplished there. But I knew that if I left the cloister,
not a single person would remain, and so I resigned myself to being
practically alone again.

That very day I learned secretly that they were leaving me in
just four days, on August 26. And at just this very moment of bitterness God sent me a great consolation. Father Rivet, who knew
how matters stood in the house, suggested the possibility of some
of the *Dilette* coming to Sainte Marie.[39] At the first mention I was
strongly attracted to that recently founded order; and had it not
been for my agreement with the government and my desire to
prove to the world, in the very face of the collapse of our efforts,
that the yoke of Jesus Christ was my happiness in spite of so much
trouble, I would have asked to be allowed to go to Rome at once.

There are several circumstances I consider remarkable in all
these events. All the former religious of the Visitation [near
Grenoble] came for a reunion at Sainte Marie on July 2, the feast-

day of the order. I found the spirit so different from what I had formerly known, and the will to return to the cloister so undecided, that alone and prostrate before the Blessed Sacrament with the utmost agony of soul I said to Him that on that very feast of the Visitation I must make the sacrifice of the order. That agony was so intense it brought on a hemorrhage. When my handkerchief was saturated with blood, I could not remain in the church, and I had to leave our Lord all alone, though the house was filled with His spouses. It was, moreover, on the feast of St. de Chantal that I learned that the date of the departure was set. Furthermore, on the anniversary of her death, December 13, the vestments which had been made for the celebration of her canonization were carried off to be sold. August 26, the date fixed for the departure of Mother and her daughters, was the anniversary of the dedication of our church, and it was being abandoned by the very people for whom it had been blessed.

On the eve, August 25, feast of St. Louis of France, Mother de Murinais sent for me to tell me they were leaving the next morning. She was quite calm and spoke kindly to me. I have since thought that God took from her all regret in order that I might act more freely in a greater enterprise. I replied to Mother by tears rather than by words, and I expressed the hope of seeing her return, but she offered me not the least encouragement on that score, saying that she was too old for such undertakings and that they called for youth and courage like mine.[40]

On August 27 I found myself left with a select few—an Ursuline nun, Sister Giraud, then a boarding student, who had come to the school on the feast of St. Aloysius Gonzaga [June 21, 1802], a fact to which I called her attention that very day as an exceedingly good sign, and one lay sister, a former novitiate companion of mine, who got her sister to come and help her with the work, and six or eight pupils. I was crushed. I was a subject of scandal. Gossip had it that I had driven away the religious, that I would not yield in anything, that no one could bear to live with me, that Fathers Brochier and Rivet with their high-flown ideas were the only ones who took my part. The latter came to see me on that day of greatest affliction and pointed out to me that on just such a day St. Teresa had begun her reform and that all the city had risen up against her. He also wrote at once to Father Roger to inform him that the house was now free, if he could only induce Father Varin to send some religious. But that grace had to be merited by a long delay. Meanwhile God consoled me very much by the coming of Madame Rivet.[41] After making a retreat with us she decided to join our group and came on the feast of All Saints. Just before Christmas we were joined by Mademoiselle Balastron.[42]

As there were now four of us (the Ursuline still wanted to remain free), we begged Fathers Brochier and Rivet to form us into a little society, as there was no prospect that the ladies whom we were awaiting would come soon. Father Rivet had offered to take charge of the direction of the house and so I had no further contact with the former chaplain who, I learned, had been appointed to the care of a large parish. I let him know, moreover, that as we hoped to join the *Dilette*, the Fathers of the Faith would naturally become our spiritual directors.

I think these priests were not entirely convinced that I had a fear of being placed in authority; and as they knew I was not fit for such a position, they cast aside all my suggestions of union [with the *Dilette*]. It was useless for me to protest that we were not practicing any more virtue in the new order of things [than we had formerly]. They paid no attention to me. Worn out with these delays, I went at last to Father Brochier and got him to agree that we could have Madame Rivet for superior. He gave his approval and told me to wait just a few days. Then Father Brochier was named our ecclesiastical superior by the bishop.[43] He made some changes in his first Rule, gave us temporarily the name of *Daughters of the Propagation of the Faith,* and on March 3, 1803, received our simple vows of chastity and obedience at the moment of Communion, after having preached a very touching exhortation. After Mass, Madame Rivet was named superior and I had the tremendous consolation of seeing at last in that holy house a form of religious life and the practices customary in communities. We had not given up the recitation of Office, even when we were only two. Our boarding school increased to sixteen or eighteen and we spent several months in that uniform and peaceful life. Father Rivet obtained for us plenary indulgences for the feast of St. Ignatius, St. Xavier, and St. Francis Regis, whose feast we celebrated very solemnly with a sermon by Father Rivet.

Our peace was disturbed at times by the fear that the house would be taken for a seminary. . . . Kind relatives who had secured the good will of the prefect toward us also parried the blows and even succeeded in saving me from paying a single sou of rent for the house. Although we were quite happy together, we always aspired to join a larger religious society in which we could do more for God. So when Father Rivet was going to Belley to make a retreat, we begged him to plead with Father Varin to admit us into the order of the *Ladies of the Faith* [44] and to send us one of those religious as superior. Father Varin instructed Father Roger to come to Grenoble to examine the people and the place, and he gave us hope of a speedy accomplishment of our desires.[45] His heart, however, was really closed against us; something repelled him, and his attitude influenced Father Varin, who wrote to Madame Rivet that he could not yet reach a decision about us. So we were as far as ever from realizing our hopes. We even believed that they were entirely lost and that we would have to turn to the Visitation to increase our numbers and enlarge the work of the institution.

Among the religious of the Visitation in Grenoble I could see no one who desired or who was really able to direct the house. My mind and heart turned spontaneously toward my former Mistress of Novices, Mother de Bayanne, sister of the Cardinal.[46] She was then living in Naples, where she had sought refuge in a house of her order, having been driven successively by revolutions from the convents in Milan and Rome. Years before, her virtues had made so deep an impression on me that she was a continual inspiration to me. But she would have to be induced by some means to return to her native land. I got the Bishop to extend her an invitation to this effect, but she did not accept, giving as her reasons her age and the fact that the Cardinal Bishop of Naples would not consent to her departure unless she were returning to a strictly cloistered monastery, and we could not assure him of this. After the refusal of my dear Mistress of Novices, I applied to her sister in Milan and to another religious of eminent virtue who was in her monastery, but their answer was the same as that of Mother de Bayanne. So I had not the slightest doubt that since all my efforts to restore this house to the Visitation had failed, it was God Himself who had taken it from them, intending it for a different destiny.

As soon as I gave up my correspondence with Naples and Milan, the Holy Spirit made Father Varin understand *that He is opposed to delay*, and that a decision in our regard must be given, since the humble St. Francis Regis, who had become our protector, deserved that for love of him the Fathers of the Faith should not despise what was worth very little. After that inspiration Father Varin sent us word that he was coming to celebrate the feast of St. Ignatius with us. He and Father Roger arrived on the eve [July 30, 1804]. After Mass next morning they went through the whole house. I took my place directly behind Father Varin so I could hear all he might say and note any least sign he might give of satisfaction or disapproval. But there is no knowing the thoughts of these people who are so completely self-controlled, and I, who am not of this type, began to be not a little irritated.

When he came to the chapel of the Sacred Heart of Jesus, he exclaimed, "Ah, here we see what makes religious life at the Visitation appeal so sweetly to souls." That was not what I wanted at all. Father Roger gave me no more satisfaction than Father Varin did. When I asked him why they had made this trip [to Grenoble], he said, "We came to see Father Rivet." I thought to myself that for men so completely detached from all earthly things this was yielding a good deal to friendship. That evening at Benediction the Holy Spirit inspired Father Varin with a decision completely in our favor, but he kept that to himself. When Father Roger, however, suggested that I should note the fact that we had celebrated the feast of St. Ignatius together, his superior added that he was considering that augury.

They were leaving the following day and it seemed to me that the only outcome of the visit would be to confirm the statements of those who accused me of never desiring the return of the Visitation and of being the one and only cause of the departure of the religious. That opinion was already being strengthened because some inkling of our desires had got out, especially since the first visit of Father Roger.

Well, the morrow dawned. Madame Rivet and I went again to see the two priests after Mass. Father Varin spoke to me again of *Holy Indifference and of the slowness* with which the works of God are accomplished. I think I answered him that, on the contrary, Holy Scripture represents Him as *racing with giant strides*, and I followed this up with the statement that had St. Francis Xavier acted with such deliberation before undertaking good works he would never have accomplished them nor done so much in so short a time. The Father laughed at my vehemence and agreed that I was right and that he must send Madame Barat to found a convent for us as soon as possible. This consoling promise lifted at last from my heart that heavy mountain of uncertainty that had weighed me down for so long. That was a day of joyous happiness. In the afternoon I had a private interview with Father Varin which was very helpful, and on the following day, before leaving, he assured us that we could depend on his promises. He urged us to pray for the health of our future Mother, and we did so frequently with all our hearts.

He had been back in Lyons only a few days when I began to think he had forgotten us. So I wrote to him to express once more the intensity of my desires, and in order not to give offense I hinted that this was ordinarily regarded as a sign of vocation. I was getting impatient for a reply when I received a letter from one of my aunts in Romans informing me that by a decree of the Emperor she and her companions were again in possession of their former house and recognized as Visitandine teachers. Her letter caused me both joy and anxiety. On the one hand she encouraged me in the hope that I might one day share the same good fortune; on the other hand, I knew very well that once the decree was made public, it might arouse the religious who up to this time had held back through fear of opposition, and then I would be obliged to give refusals both painful and hard to explain on many counts, or to witness the collapse of the project we had formed on the feast of St. Ignatius.

At our request Father Rivet wrote to Father Varin, who was still in Lyons, to ask what line of conduct we should follow in these circumstances. Father Varin answered him and also sent me the following reply, dated August 15, 1804:

"Father Rivet has assuredly shared with you my answer to his letter putting before me the reasons for taking action with the government in favor of your house. Tomorrow I leave for Paris, where I hope to receive shortly the information I asked Father Rivet to procure. I do not need to repeat to you that I shall use all interest and zeal in co-operating with the plans of Divine Providence for your house. *I would sooner forget my right hand than the project about which we came to an agreement.* I shall write to you when I reach my destination and tell you when we shall be able to carry out that agreement. I shall hasten matters, inasmuch as they depend on me; help me by your prayers in the delicate business I have on hand. I count also on the prayers of Madame Rivet and your other companions. Every day I offer you and them in the Holy Sacrifice of the Mass."

Having arrived at Amiens, Father Varin wrote to Madame Rivet to tell her that Madame Barat, our dear Mother, would come to Grenoble sometime during October to make the foundation. Time passes very slowly when one is eager for things to happen; and before that letter reached us, I had written to our Father complaining of his silence. He replied:

"I am astonished that you have not received my letter from Amiens. I repeat the assurance that I gave you therein, that Madame Barat will leave early in October to fulfil the promise I made you. She will take two of her young companions with her. They will be accompanied by an ecclesiastic who, I assure you, is worthy of all your confidence. It is a great sacrifice for me to let him leave me, but I shall be repaid by the services he will render to your house, and I shall do my best to see for myself how things are going just as soon as possible. I read with great satisfaction the details you gave me about the first steps you have taken to obtain a favor similar to that secured by the Ladies of Romans. Follow the plan you submitted to me and give me news of its progress. When the moment comes, I shall do my part to help you."

We had, indeed, taken the first steps to secure the ownership of the house. Monsieur and Madame de Rollin, my cousins, to whom I already owed in part the first success in my undertaking, and likewise Monsieur Perier, brother of Madame de Rollin, were all in Grenoble just then.[47] All three consented to plead my cause, and Monsieur Perier agreed to use his influence with the prefect of the department of the Isère to secure his backing for our petition, which would greatly strengthen it, and also that of the municipal authorities. The Bishop refused to add his name because he did not want to make requests for anyone just then, as he was trying to get possession of a building for his seminary and was meeting with little success. In the petition we asked not only for ownership of the property but also recognition as teachers of girls of the well-to-do classes and of children of the poor whom we would instruct gratis. We addressed ourselves to Monsieur de Gérando, secretary-general to the Minister of the Interior in Paris. He is a friend of the family and with unflagging energy he saw the business through to a happy ending. Madame de Rollin and my father also recommended it to Monsieur Dédelay, a Senator and the avowed protector of the Ladies of Romans. He himself outlined the course we should follow and from the first assured us of success.

While we were busy with all this, two religious of the Visitation, but not of the community to which I had belonged, came in the name of their superior and twenty of their companions to propose to act in common with us to get government approval and possession of our house. I was deeply disturbed by this proposal. I had to give a refusal that was hard on members of a religious order to which I had belonged. They seemed to have no other hope for a re-establishment than our house, and while those who had belonged to my community and had at one time been kind to me did not put in an appearance, I felt that my refusal reflected on them and seemed to repay with ingratitude and injustice all the kindness I had received [in former days]. I was glad I did not have to make a decision and I told them in a sympathetic tone, but without hesitation, that we could not act in common, explaining that, since they had seemed to refuse a reunion [the year before], I was now bound to another group and could do nothing except in concert with those who desired to unite their interests with ours, and that I was already a dependent member. That statement caused exactly the result I had anticipated. All the old reproaches were hurled at me; I was again called a *usurper*. I had the courage to endure it as part of the price I must pay for the happiness to which I aspired.

But what was not my suffering when from a letter of Father Varin I was led to suspect that he had forgotten his promises and was leaving us without hope in a situation that was most painful in regard both to the public and to the religious who had just asked to reunite with us. He wrote that he had just seen the articles of the decree concerning the Ladies of Romans and he disapproved of several of them and he wished us to break off negotiations. I wrote at once, begging him to consider the fact that, at a time when so many religious were roused to activity, if we did not continue with our petition, it was to be feared that we would have to give up the house itself to those who might receive approbation ahead of us. For although through delicacy they had not demanded it, it might be offered to them [by the authorities]. At the time Father Varin was not impressed by my reasons and replied that, although he sympathized with the motives which made me desire to press the negotiations and considered them serious, the inconveniences which might result were also grave, and if we took our time, we might obtain more favorable conditions; so he wanted us to let the matter drop before he decided on the date of Madame Barat's visit. He added:

"Do not worry if the journey of your friend is postponed. I am concerned about it and so is she, but the greater good seems to require a little further delay. I am writing to her today, saying how much your house deserves her consideration. Pray to the Lord for the perfect accomplishment of His plans. Please send me at once a letter for Monsieur Gérando, authorizing me to confer with him about the affair you have entrusted to him." [48]

I did not delay in sending him a letter in which I begged Monsieur Gérando to do nothing about our petition without the consent of Father Varin, but to try to overcome the repugnance he felt toward pushing the matter. My letter to Father Varin was very pleading. My heart was experiencing a martyrdom in the fear that so much delay might result in a break with him and an end to his agreement with us, and that my own position in regard to the religious in the city would be more and more difficult. It began to look as if I had only wished to put them off and that my ties with another group were mere pretexts. I had, moreover, nothing to offer as proof to the parents of the children placed in our care nor to the people who were looking after our interests. Since no one came [to take over the institution], it looked as if we had put up a pretense in order to gain confidence and to reject the religious [who wished to join us], and several very worthy people who had asked to lodge in our house.

Father Varin wrote again on October 19, insisting on further delay and stressing in particular Madame Barat's repugnance for the articles to which he himself had raised objections. That was one of the most painful periods Madame Rivet and I ever endured. Two years and a half seemed already a very long time, and we were in continual fear about the future, yet there seemed no possibility of organizing our life any other way unless we were forced to give up the hope of finding a place in that holy society which was the object of our most ardent desires.

At last there was an end to the trial. A letter from Father Varin, written on October 25, gave us courage again. I will not omit a word of it for it was such a consolation:

"Madame, I wrote to you a few days ago and my letter—since it left still some uncertainty at least about the departure of those whom you so greatly desire—my letter, I say, could not have given you full satisfaction. *I do so love to give you some consolation that I am not waiting for your answer before telling you something positive.*

"Every day I feel urged to fulfil your hopes. I see by Madame Barat's last letter that she too shares these sentiments of mine, in spite of the repugnance she has to the articles about which I wrote to you. Your perseverance and that of your companions in the project of reunion which we decided upon is a sign to me that the dear Lord will bless its execution. I shall leave on Monday for Amiens, and I hope in a very short time to announce to you the day on which your friends will set out for Grenoble. Remember, I did not deceive you when I assured you that I took your interests as much to heart as if they were my own and that your religious family will be as dear to me as my own. Today I saw Monsieur de Gérando and handed him your letter. I had delayed doing so because he was away in the country. Seeing he was making a longer stay than I had anticipated, I went to see him. He told me your affair had met with no obstacle and that yesterday the petition had been granted, save for a final ratification, which should be obtained in the next week. My representations to Monsieur de Gérando came too late, for the case had been won. He told me he wrote to you yesterday and promised to let me know as soon as the ratification is given. I think I should tell you that if I desired a delay in the presentation of your petition, I had excellent reasons which you will know later on. Now that the thing is done, let us hope that the good God will gain glory from it. Write to me. I shall not be long at Amiens. From there, however, I hope to send you the date of departure of your friends. I commend myself to the prayers of all. In my own prayers I make no distinction between you and those who are most dear to me. Let us not belong to ourselves but to Jesus Christ."

Two days later I received another letter from our kind Father in which he said: "You should have received by now a letter from me which would have relieved the anxieties caused by previous ones. I leave for Amiens tomorrow and my first word to Madame Barat will be about her departure for Grenoble."

From the time I was twelve years and some months old, when

God bestowed upon me the grace of a religious vocation, I believe I never let pass a single day without praying to Him to enlighten me about it and make me faithful to it. From the beginning I put it under the protection of the Blessed Virgin, and the *Memorare* was my favorite and continual prayer to her. The many favors I received through the intercession of St. Francis Regis had inclined me to pray more directly to him. But during my retreat I read how the Carmelites of St. Denis, at a time when their monastery was about to be closed, were saved by the entrance of Madame Louise into their community as a result of a novena to the Blessed Virgin, in whose loving protection they had the utmost confidence. It seemed to me that I had in a way neglected this dear Mother of Mercy, so I begged her pardon, addressing her as mediatrix of all graces, and I begged her to obtain for us an end to our painful uncertainty. I asked Madame Rivet to have the entire household make a novena of fasts, Communions, and prayers in honor of our Lady. This was done, and before the close of the novena we received the assurance of at last being admitted into the Society [of the Sacred Heart] and of undisputed ownership of our house. This last piece of news came to me through Monsieur Perier, to whom Monsieur de Gérando wrote briefly: "My friend, I write to you from the office of Portalis to tell you with all speed that Madame Duchesne's petition has been fully and completely granted." [49]

But this statement was not really true. In the change of ministry a great number of papers got lost, ours among them; and had it not been for the vigilance of Madame de Rollin, we should have remained for a long time under this pleasant illusion. But she sent me word that we should have to begin negotiations all over again. At any other time this news would have crushed me, but Father Varin's letter had brought such joy to my soul that I really felt the weight of my happiness needed some counterbalance. And I had in the depths of my heart the hope that the house was assured to us by the will of Heaven.

The autumn of 1804 had brought Philippine another joy, a further proof of the love and confidence of her family, when her sister, Madame Jouve, entrusted to her the education of her eight-year-old daughter Euphrosine. The child was delicate and precocious. Her adjustment to strict discipline and formal school life was difficult, but in time she developed into one of Sainte Marie's outstanding pupils. Writing to Madame Jouve at the close of October, 1804, Philippine says:

I am sending you, my dear Sister, the first efforts of your little girl. She has taken the greatest pleasure in writing to you. She is very well, though she has a slight cold. Her studies go nicely, in spite of her great liveliness, which makes the study hour seem to her very long. I recognize her at a distance by the animation of her little figure. Tante Perier came to see her and took her out on Sunday. Tante Lagrange wanted her on Thursday, but that was too soon after the other outing.

Believe me, dear Sister, the news of the success of our petition was false. A letter yesterday from Monsieur de Rollin tells me that all his efforts have failed and that the case as such may not be reopened. We must begin all over again. This is all very tiresome and I do regret the trouble I have given my kind relatives. I am keeping the whole unpleasant business strictly secret so that we may not be forbidden to try again.

Adieu, dear Sister. How happy I am to have here at Sainte Marie a proof of your affection for me. In her I seem to see you again. . . .

Continuing her account of the correspondance with Father Varin, she wrote:

I answered Father Varin's letters with an outpouring of gratitude, telling him that even in the midst of the most crushing trials I had not mistrusted the paternal kindness, of which his recent letters had given a still more consoling proof. He replied on November 10:

"I received your letter of the 2nd. I congratulate you on having so generously resisted the sad impression which my first letter might have made on you and for having trusted *the sentiments of which I have given you assurance*. I am eager to share your letter with Madame Barat. I assure you that she is *yours*, and is as intimately united to you and your companions in mind and heart as to her religious family here at Amiens. She makes no distinction among you all. Her companions on their side are already so closely identified with you that they seem to forget all the heartaches the absence of Madame Barat will cause them, and to think only of the mutual joy that will result from this union. Madame Rivet should have received yesterday a letter from Madame Barat and one from me announcing the departure on the 22nd of this month, and certainly it will take place that day. I shall look forward with pleasure to the coming of spring, when I shall be able to see for myself the progress of your community in the service of God. Unite yourself very specially with the family of Madame Barat on the 21st of this month; that day is extremely dear to them, for it is the birthday of their Society. Some novices will have a spiritual birthday here that day. It will be spent in a holy joy which the thought of the morrow's sacrifice will increase rather than lessen."

Here is the letter of our Mother, Madame Barat, to Madame Rivet, written after the date of her trip had been decided upon. It was in answer to one Madame Rivet had sent in the name of us all, expressing the joy we felt in knowing we would soon be under her direction:

AMIENS, November 2, 1804

MADAME,

I received your letter of September 19 which expressed your sentiments and those of your companions in a way that fills me with joy because it shows me souls so well disposed and therefore ready to fulfil the designs of a loving Providence. Your dispositions make me regret keenly that God has chosen me to cultivate them; so many others would have been able to help you with far greater success than I ever can, or than I would ever dare to hope for, did I not trust entirely in God. But plants that grow in rich and fertile soil need less skill and care on the part of the gardener. Undoubtedly that is why the Lord has chosen me, poor, worthless, lacking all human means. But this is what fills me with consolation and assures me in advance that the Lord will bless you, and that by your prayers you will obtain for me the graces that are so necessary if I am to help you accomplish His designs. What a consolation it is for me to find souls who will to love our good God and make Him loved by others, souls ready to sacrifice all for His glory! How fortunate you are to have been called to such a sublime vocation! And happier still to be determined to spare nothing in order to make yourselves worthy of this grace.

I am very eager to be with you and to assure you personally of the great affection and interest I bear you. My two young companions beg me to express to you their sentiments of affection for you and to thank you for the opportunity you have procured for them of laboring in another center to spread the knowledge of Him whom alone they love.

Our departure is set for the 22nd of this month. It was impossible to arrange it sooner because of our transfer to another building. I send you and your companions affectionate greetings and beg a place in your prayers. Here we pray for you. Since we are soon to form but one community, we should already be one in the Lord.

That letter of Madame Barat was enclosed in one from Father Varin to Madame Rivet expressing the same kindly interest. On November 27 he wrote that Madame Barat was actually on the way:

"The friend for whom you have waited so long," he told me, "set out with her two young companions on the day fixed, the 22nd of this month. She stopped two days in Paris and is today at

Joigny, between Sens and Auxerre, where she will spend a week with her family. She will be in Lyons on the feast of the [Immaculate] Conception and will remain there three or four days to interview some persons who may very soon become members of your household. She is going to write to Madame Rivet from both Joigny and Lyons.

"She and I were both expecting to hear from you and your companions in answer to the letters we wrote on November 2. I am sharing your joy in anticipating the arrival of your friends. God will draw His own glory from a reunion that has Him alone for its purpose. I already experience real consolation in joining you in spirit, and I shall actually be with you in a few months. Let us hope all things from the generosity of our Lord, and let us be persuaded that the more we hope, the more we shall obtain. Open your hearts wide that He may be lavish in His mercies. I shall go to Paris in eight or ten days. Address your reply to me there. Your companions have become very dear to me in our Lord. Count on my entire devotedness."

It seemed to me that Father Varin had promised to come to see us before spring and I expressed to him the disappointment the delay caused me, thinking it would retard the organization of our community. He had the extreme kindness to answer me as follows:

"I wrote to you this morning, and this afternoon I received your letter of the 19th. I shall not repeat what I said about the arrival of Madame Barat, leaving on the 22nd with two companions, in Joigny today, at Lyons on December 8, and some days later with you. But I add that I could not possibly have promised to accompany these ladies, for at the time you realized, as well as I, that it was impossible for me to do so.

"If, however, by a false calculation you counted on my coming sooner, I shall try by serious consideration to fit my schedule to your calendar. I told you this morning I greatly desire it. Yes, I can say truly that your soul and the souls of your companions are very dear to me because I have realized that nothing will hinder them from belonging entirely to God. I understand your desire not to be bound to earth even by a thread. Strengthen that desire more and more. Keep on expecting me, and do not be put out with me if I am obliged to defer the day for which you are longing and on which I shall see for myself the progress you have made. . . ."

That is the last letter I received from Father Varin before Madame Barat's arrival amongst us, which took place on December 13 of that same year 1804. That day, blessed and never to be forgotten, was—I speak according to my own heart—the second Vespers of another day of grace for me, December 14, 1801, on which I had returned to this blessed house to work here at my own sanctification and for the salvation of souls. It is pointless to speak of the joy of that day; it belongs to our Lord who gave us this inestimable grace, and it is to Him we turn in prayer with sentiments of humble gratitude.

The community was then composed of the four persons of whom I have already spoken, along with Mademoiselle Second, who had joined us during the previous summer, two widows who resided with us, an Ursuline religious on the same footing, that is, following exteriorly the same spiritual exercises as we but not bound to dependence or to our Rule as far as personal conduct was concerned; there were also twenty boarding pupils and five girls helping with domestic work. The other Ursuline, my former companion, had left us two months before.

Besides our individual employments, all helped in the boarding school except Mademoiselle Second and the Ursuline, who conducted the free school for the poor of Jesus Christ. For more than two years Father Rivet had helped us with the boarding school; he said Mass for us daily and his zeal was untiring. He increased the solemnity of our liturgical feasts by inviting many priests to take part in them and to preach, and twice the Bishop honored us with his presence. . . . It is time for me to stop writing now. I must obey, saying with heartfelt gratitude: "I will sing the mercies of the Lord forever."

Some months later Philippine added a few lines to her account:

Since I wrote the above, the decree of the Emperor in our favor has come. It assures us possession of the house and recognizes us as an educational institution. It is dated from the Palace of the Tuilleries, *6 Pluviose, An 13.*

three

Under the Guidance
of a Saint

I. 1804—1805

> *The infinite wealth of God's love,*
> *bestowed on us in the Heart of His Son.*
>
> Collect, Mass of the Sacred Heart

THE RELIGIOUS ORDER to which Philippine Duchesne and her companions had asked admission was only four years old when its foundress arrived at Sainte Marie to organize her second community. She had been guided in her work by Father Joseph Varin, who had inherited from the saintly Léonor de Tournély a legacy of inspiration and obligation which he held as a sacred trust. Tournély had gathered about him a group of priests bearing at first the name of *Fathers of the Sacred Heart,* then the safer title of *Fathers of the Faith,* and ambitioning the resurgence of the Society of Jesus.[1] Before his death in 1797, he had confided to his followers a vivid inspiration received in prayer—the founding of a congregation of women to help in the regeneration of France by a comtemplative life, to which the activities of teaching and directing retreats would be added. His concept of the order was clear-cut and well defined:

> A Society whose members were destined to consecrate themselves to the Sacred Heart of Jesus, to endeavor to enkindle once more the love of Jesus in souls and to shed the light of His teaching in their minds; and for this end, to conform themselves to the interior sentiments and dispositions of this Divine Heart and to propagate this devotion by means of education.[2]

From a mustard-seed beginning in Paris in 1800—four members, only two of them persevering in the venture—the association had increased encouragingly at Amiens, where the first convent was opened in 1801. By the autumn of 1803, Father Varin was writing to the frail and timid young superior, who was known as Madame Barat: "It will soon be absolutely necessary to open a second house, for there are other postulants who are, or seem to be, fitted for you, and where shall we put them?" [3] When Father Roger visited Sainte Marie in the spring of 1804, he was completely noncommittal on the subject of merging the two communities. He gave good news, however, of Mother Barat's recovery from a serious illness and told of the progress made by the boarding and free schools her nuns were conducting. Their first house in Rue Martin Bleu-Dieu had proved too small to accommodate them, and now they were considering a move from the second in Rue Neuve to still larger quarters.

Returning to Lyons, he made so favorable a report to his superior that, in July, Father Varin decided to visit the old monastery and see things for himself. While rejoicing in the outcome of that visit, Philippine Duchesne little suspected the impression she had made, but within a week Father Varin was writing to Madame Barat: "On this trip I have made a fine acquisition for you, but it seems to require your presence. Can you cut yourself in four?" [4] Six days later he added:

Thank God, I have only good news for you. . . . There is no need, my dear Sister, to cut yourself in four, but only in two. I can hear you exclaiming, "My God, how can I? It is already so difficult to carry on this little establishment. And if the whole does so badly, what will a half do?" . . . O soul of little faith, why do you doubt? Our Lord will see to it that each half will equal the whole. Only have confidence. [5]

There was much to be done at Amiens before Madame Barat could undertake the trip to Grenoble, and she pleaded for delay. Faithful to his promise, however, Father Varin continued to urge the acceptance of Sainte Marie, writing from Paris on October 6:

Pray to the good Lord to give us light on the matter of your departure, for I foresee so many inconveniences that may result from it at Amiens that I believe the only way to make it succeed will be to make God Himself responsible for the undertaking, and in such a case we must be assured that He wills it. Pray and get others to pray. Bolster up your own courage with lively confidence, and in holy abandonment hurl yourself headlong into the arms of our Lord Jesus Christ. I wrote to Mademoiselle Duchesne today. Her letter gave me much pleasure. Oh, I am sadly mistaken if she is not a great and generous soul. . . . When you know her, you will say, "Now there is one, indeed." [6]

A few days later Father Varin was at Amiens. He found the little community quite at home in the Convent of the Oratory, to which they had transferred the previous September. He knew the place well, for the Fathers of the Faith had but recently vacated it. Assembling the household, he put before them his plan for the new establishment. There was hesitation on the part of the nuns. They argued their poverty and lack of personnel for such an undertaking.

"You could certainly spare two or three," the priest insisted. "You, for example," and he looked straight at Madame Barat, "and this novice," he indicated Rosalie Debrosse, "and you should take Sister Maillard along." He knew what a treasure she was. Ignoring the astonishment shown on every face, he continued earnestly: "You will find some companions there—especially one. Were she alone and at the remotest corner of the world, you should go after her." [7] Then he spoke with such enthusiastic admiration of Philippine Duchesne, with such supernatural conviction as to the designs of Almighty God in her regard, that all fear and hesitation vanished and the plan was courageously accepted. It was decided that Madame Baudemont would fill the post of superior during Madame Barat's absence, which would begin after the ceremony of first vows on November 21.

In the meanwhile the tempo of life had quickened considerably at Sainte Marie. There were preparations to be made, further repairs to be completed, school duties to be carried on, letters to be written, negotiations with the government to be pressed, hopes and fears and anxieties to be entrusted to the Sacred Heart. At recreation they rehearsed what they knew of Madame Barat: she was a peasant from a small place in Burgundy, the province just north of Dauphiny. Her priest-brother, Louis, several years older than she, had given her an education far above the ordinary level for girls in those days. He was one of the Fathers of the Faith, but he had been a professor at the seminary of Sens and had narrowly escaped the guillotine during the Terror. Madame Barat's name was Madeleine Louise Sophie—she had signed just "Sophie Barat" at the end of her letter to Madame Rivet. She had completed her studies under her brother's guidance in Paris after the Revolution—her mother had not wanted this, but Louis had his way—and she was planning to become a Carmelite when Father Varin met her. Her appearance was not very impressive, for she was slight and shy and plainly dressed; but he had recognized in her the person needed to carry out the inspiration of Léonor de Tournély and to found an order of religious women completely devoted to the Sacred Heart of Jesus and having the glory of this Divine Heart as their sole purpose in life.

It was always hard to get further than that point in the story: love for Jesus Christ, complete consecration to Him through love, no other motive but love for Him, no other purpose but the glory of His Sacred Heart. . . . It was well that prayer and silence always followed these recreations. Such thoughts and aspirations carried these ardent women out of themselves with joy. Even talkative Marie Balastron and lively little Emilie Giraud fell silent and drew deep breaths and longed more intensely for the day when Madame Barat would come.

Winter had set in and fires were blazing in a few wide chimney-places at Sainte Marie when the courier from Lyons rode up the steep street and turned in at the monastery with the letter from Amiens dated November 2 and addressed to Madame Rivet. It was the first greeting from Madame Barat, and reading it, the five women who awaited her felt that they knew her and belonged to her. They counted the days till November 21—then she would start on her journey. How long would it take her to reach Grenoble?

The fourth birthday of the Society of the Sacred Heart was celebrated at Amiens with mixed emotions. Catherine de Charbonnel, Marie du Terrail, and Rosalie Debrosse pronounced their first vows with joyous fervor in the presence of Father Varin and Madame Barat. The day brought an extra amount of work, for the final preparations had to be made for the departure next morning. Even short trips were not very common in France in those days, and it was something of a journey to go by public coach from Amiens in Picardy to Grenoble, six hundred miles away.

The party made it in four stages: to Paris first, where business kept them two days; then to Joigny, where they spent a week at the home in which Sophie Barat had been born and raised. The attic room, the vineyards on the hillside, the church of St. Thibaut in which she had been baptized, all were of interest to her companions. There were many relatives and friends to greet, and Sophie could have long talks with her parents and her sister, Madame Dusaussoy. There was a stopover in Lyons, with letters from Father Varin, one dwelling on the satisfactory conditions at Amiens, another on the central figure in the group at Sainte Marie:

> Have really lively faith [he wrote], faith that will pierce the heavens, that will open to you the Heart of our Lord and reveal to you what an abyss of goodness and mercy It is. That realization will fill you with wonder, and courage, and confidence. Then you will be that valiant woman who is so difficult to find. *Mulierem fortem quis inveniet? Procul.* . . . Who will find a valiant woman. . . . Afar off? . . . You will not need to go further than Grenoble to find her.[8]

Madame Barat had already found her when he wrote another eulogy of that valiant woman whom so many women had failed to appreciate, but whom holy priests and prelates of the Church recognized at her true worth in the midst of many an apparent failure: "I have not misled you by the way I have praised your future companion. I tell you again: *there* is a soul worthy to serve our Lord. Here in Paris I have met many people who have known her. All esteem her highly and no one speaks of her except with great admiration." [9]

The diligence from Lyons usually rumbled into Grenoble in the middle of the morning. The town, with its drab, slate-colored buildings grouped together in varied and curious heights and shapes, its labyrinth of narrow streets and squares and bridges over the swift Isère that divided it, was of interest to Madame Barat, who was seeing it for the first time. She was a woman on whom details were seldom lost. "There, *en haut*," a fellow passenger in the coach may have indicated, "is Sainte Marie," and the young superior would have got her first glimpse of the old monastery and church, a gaunt and forbidding pile. She felt very young. Just the day before she had passed her twenty-fifth birthday, and it was with the greatest self-diffidence that she was undertaking to mother this new group. She had, according to her own account, never seen a cloistered monastery until she rode into Grenoble that thirteenth day of December, 1804.

As the stagecoach ascended the narrow street leading up to and beyond Sainte Marie, she was astonished at the grandeur of the setting, the snow-covered Alps, and the view of the city and valley below. It was just eleven o'clock when she and her companions turned into the narrow passage between high walls that led up a terraced slope to the doorway opening into a deep vestibule. They entered a dimly lighted corridor that seemed more chilly and damp than the street outside. Suddenly a slender figure in black came swiftly toward them; and before Mother Barat realized what was happening, Philippine Duchesne was prostrate before her, kissing her feet and repeating the psalmist's words: "How lovely on the mountain are the feet of those who bring the gospel of peace!"

"I let her do it through pure stupefaction," Mother Barat used to say, as she told of their first meeting. "I was utterly dumbfounded at the sight of such faith and humility, and I did not know what to say or do." [10]

There are few scenes more touching in the lives of the saints than that of the frail little woman in her plain traveling bonnet and shawl, a satchel in one hand, a bundle or two under her arms, gazing down in wide-eyed amazement at the prostrate figure before her. It all happened so quickly that Philippine was on her feet again, giving a more conventional welcome to Father Roger and Abbé Coidy, to Rosalie Debrosse and Marguerite Maillard, before her companions reached the entrance door. It was all very simple and informal. Father Roger installed Mother Barat as superior and settled details with Abbé Coidy, who was to act as chaplain and confessor. There had been question of a retreat for the community before Christmas, but Mother Barat considered it wiser to postpone it for awhile, so that the members of the little family might learn to know one another and a cordial union of minds and hearts might be established from the very beginning. So Father Roger went back to Lyons, leaving Mother Barat to guide the foundation as best she could. He had no fear as to how she would accomplish her task.

Philippine and Madame Rivet were at home with her at once, and Marie Balastron was quickly won. Cecile Second was still somewhat ill at ease in her monastic surroundings, while Emilie Giraud avoided her new superior, allowing groundless fears to keep her at a distance for some time. The wisdom, tact, and maturity with which Mother Barat handled them all gave proof of the sanctity she brought to her work. She studied her new daughters as she came in contact with them in the cloister, at recreation, at household tasks or school duties, and as she knelt with them in the choir. She made them the subject of her prayer, holding each close to the Heart of Christ and begging for the grace that would enable her to develop in them the spirit and virtues that must characterize all who would be true members of her little society: prayer and interior life, generosity and cordial charity, along with boundless zeal in the service of the Sacred Heart. It was a sublime vocation, and she knew the heights to which Father Varin expected her to lead Philippine Duchesne.

The day after Mother Barat's arrival, Philippine wrote to her sister, Madame Jouve.[11] It was a hasty, happy note:

> What a joy it was, my dear Sister, to recognize your writing on one of the letters handed to me a few days ago. This was proof that you had recovered. I was waiting with keen impatience for this news. Before telling Euphrosine, I thought I would try out her feelings, so I asked her what news would give her the greatest pleasure in the world. Immediately she answered it would be to learn of the recovery of her beloved mother. The high color and anxious look in her eyes assured me that this wish came straight from her heart. She added that she had said her rosary many times for you.
>
> She is not writing to you today, as the schedule in the school is somewhat upset by the arrival of the three religious who have come to us from Amiens. Father Roger accompanied them from Lyons. It looks as if we have been most forutnate in getting them here. One of them is to be our superior. She has won the hearts of all the pupils by her cordial manner.
>
> I embrace you fondly,
>
> PHILIPPINE

The formal opening of the novitiate was deferred until Mother Barat had initiated the little group into some of the ways and customs already established in the new society. The season of Advent gave her an opportunity to stress silence, recollection, and detachment. At the age of thirty-five, Philippine found herself once more a "beginner" in a spiritual school whose lessons were based on the same fundamental teachings as those she had first learned from Sister Eugenie de Bayanne. The *Journal of Sainte—Marie* shows how the little community received these lessons from their new Mother:

> As the feast of Christmas drew near, the contemplation of Jesus in His manger-bed naturally occupied our thoughts at this time when we should reproduce in ourselves the virtues of His infancy. Our Mother put Him before us in all His attractive loveliness. At recreation she placed on her table a little figure of this Divine Saviour in order to teach us to center our love on Him as she did. She sug-

gested the practice of offering to Him whatever we were most attached to, whether it was a devotion that was mere natural sentiment, or something that was pleasant and convenient, or a too tender affection of friendship. Jesus received these first sacrifices through the hands of our superior and in her presence in order that, giving her our complete confidence, we might be more pleasing in the sight of Him who is the perfect model of religious dependence and detachment.[12]

The poverty and suffering of the Christ Child were reproduced at Sainte Marie in many ways. The stable at Bethlehem was scarcely more open to wind and weather than were some parts of the old monastery, in spite of all that had been done to make it habitable. The snow drifted in freely where doors and windows were still lacking. The cold was intense and there was no means of heating many parts of the building. In the community room an open fire-place gave a cheery glow as the nuns sat together at spiritual reading or at recreation, and small charcoal braziers were sometimes lighted in their sleeping quarters or hot bricks placed in the beds to insure warmth enough for sleep.

To Philippine all this seemed as nothing. She had become accustomed to it, and her fairly robust health was not affected then by such privations. In fact, she scarcely adverted to them at all. But to Mother Barat and the others in the community they were a source of suffering that supplied them many an hour of corporal penance and made disciplines and hair shirts easy in comparison. Yet all was accepted with joy and generous love.

The novitiate was formally opened on the last day of 1804. By that time Mother Barat had become well enough acquainted with her new community to begin the spiritual training which was the chief purpose of her coming to Sainte Marie. While the work of the two small schools had to be carried on—there were seventeen boarding pupils and twenty children in the free school—this was not allowed to absorb more time than necessary, and the daily schedule was so arranged as to give time for the instructions and conferences by which Mother Barat was to initiate her novices into the way of life and prayer already characteristic of the order. Before she began her work at Grenoble, Father Varin had written to her: "To gain souls for God or to train them for Him, one must have, not a little, ordinary soul, but one as great, as vast, as the ocean. Xavier undertook the conversion of the whole world just because he had a soul great enough to embrace the whole world." [13] On January 3, 1805, he sent her his New Year's greetings: "No compliments, but some wishes: that you may work and suffer for Jesus Christ, and never withhold from Him a single instant of your life; that you may die in His love and reign eternally with Him. Such are my wishes for you." [14]

The difficulties confronting Mother Barat in the first weeks of 1805 arose from several causes. She was having her first experience of founding a convent by adapting an old one to the new mode of religious life which seemed better suited to the times. She was also dealing with women of widely different ages, education, and spiritual training. Emilie Giraud and Marie Balastron were just past twenty-one, Jeanne-Cecile Second was not much older, while Marie Rivet and Philippine Duchesne were mature in age and experience. The young members of the group had had little formal schooling and not much religious instruction, while the two older novices were already leading deep interior lives based on solid religious formation. Yet all had to be initiated into the ways and methods accepted in the new society, and a fresh start made for each new postulant.[15]

In the matter of prayer the Ignatian methods of meditation and examen had been adopted. These differed somewhat from the forms prescribed by St. Benedict and St. Francis de Sales. While superficial critics have judged them formal, even mechanical, the intelligent application of the directions given by St. Ignatius leads to the development, in each individual soul, of a personal manner of prayer that allows the fullest flowering of the spiritual life in response to the attractions of grace. Hence, the hours of mental prayer, morning and afternoon, not in common, but in private, with each religious or novice responsible, under guidance, for her own material or "points" for prayer. Hence, too, the absence of prescribed or even suggested vocal prayers and aspirations accompanying the duties of the day, leaving the soul at liberty to commune with God in her own manner in prayer. And it was to prayer that Mother Barat directed her novices before all else. Faithful to Father Varin's teaching, she felt that a transformation could be effected only in the measure in which love of the Sacred Heart grew in the hearts of her daughters. To enkindle that love more ardently and to inspire them to feed its flame by prayer and sacrifice was her constant aim. The generosity with which they responded to her suggestions made her grateful to God and careful to guard against imprudence.

There were many things that had to be changed at Sainte Marie —traditional ways of acting, customs belonging to Visitandine life

—and this called for tactful handling on the part of the young superior. Old ties had to be broken, but in the breaking there could be no shock or irritation, no impression of substituting a better way, but only a more suitable method for the purpose and work in hand. If the novices had their duties assigned to them weekly and went about their daily routine without inquiring twice daily about the matter, as was the Visitation custom, it was not a mitigation of dependence in any sense; and they soon came to realize that at the Sacred Heart a "fixed order of day" is subject entirely to the will of the superior and to circumstances, and that in the course of an ordinary day one is liable to encounter the most unpredictable changes.

Mother Barat took as a guiding principle a sentence written to her by Father Varin a few days after her arrival at Sainte Marie: "Firmness when it is needed, harshness never, kindness and charity everywhere and always." [16] Keenly sensitive herself, she realized how costly for Philippine Duchesne would be the changes now being planned for the old monastery. The cloistered choir was to become an open chapel; the grilles would disappear entirely; the time-honored pronoun *our*, so expressive of dependent communal poverty, would drop from the community vocabulary; and many little formalities would drop from daily life. Mother Barat sympathized with the pain these sacrifices might inflict. Should they be imposed gradually or at once? Laying the problem before Father Varin, she received this wise advice: "Where a reform is undertaken, patience is needed more than ardor, prudence more than zeal. You must begin gently and so gain hearts. The rest will come in time and in detail, without protest or disturbance. Beware, then, of the desire to see everything improved immediately." [17]

On January 11 Father Roger opened the novices' retreat, giving the meditations and conferences in a little oratory above the sacristy, where the Blessed Sacrament was reserved. The house still bore all the exterior marks of a cloistered monastery, but he was acquainted with the remodeling that was planned to bring it into conformity with the type of life and work envisioned for members of the Society of the Sacred Heart. To achieve this purpose, he explained, the religious would present outwardly to the world far less poverty and austerity than had been the custom in monastic orders before the Revolution, but within the privacy of the cloister there would be the same severely simple furnishings, communal use of possessions, ascetic silence, and joyous obedience in the least details of life.

Father Roger seems to have feared that the decided taste of Philippine Duchesne for strict observance in all that pertained to cloistered life might make it difficult for her to accept the sacrifices that were to be imposed; hence, the keynote of his retreat was detachment. Every day he dwelt on the necessity of self-renunciation and the stripping off of every personal attachment. The generosity with which his retreatants responded to grace should have proved their will to belong unreservedly to the Sacred Heart of Jesus. The retreat-master, however, was not completely convinced and wished to make a final test of their virtue. On the last day of the retreat he ordered them to deposit in Mother Barat's room anything for which they felt the slightest attachment. Evening came and not an article of any kind had been brought to the superior. Father Roger was disappointed. When the community gathered for an informal conference with him, he questioned Philippine on the matter. "But, Father," she replied with a touch of vivacity so characteristic of her, "I could not deposit this house and its occupants in our Mother's room, and I am attached to nothing else in all the world." [18]

The routine of novitiate life began again, and Mother Barat had the joy of seeing her novices advance steadily in the path of religious perfection. Frequently she was obliged to check their ardor. This was particularly true in the case of Philippine. Her age and former position in the community seemed to inspire in her only a claim to the most menial tasks, the most inconvenient lodgings and assignments, the most supernatural obedience.

In the matter of corporal mortification she had many practices unsuspected by her sisters. One was to season her food with bitter herbs. Mother Barat forbade this, and Philippine obeyed. After a few weeks, however, she asked the permission again and was granted it "on condition," said Mother Barat, "that I do not see you do it." That seemed a sufficient safeguard against an overdose of penance, as Philippine sat beside her superior at table. She soon came to realize, however, that Mother Barat was usually too absorbed in the presence of God to take much notice of what was going on around her in the refectory. For several months Philippine had full liberty to indulge her taste for mortification. It was not until Mother Barat was about to return to Amiens at the close of 1805 that Philippine, whose austerity in no way damped her sense of humor and her enjoyment of a little family joke, placarded the superior's chair with a scroll bearing in large print these words from the Canticle of Canticles, "Wake not my beloved until she wishes it." [19]

While Mother Barat was training her novices so skilfully in prayer and in the spirit of the Society, she was also initiating them into the work of education as she understood it. In the boarding school she acted as mistress general, teaching the children and developing in them that ardent devotion to the Sacred Heart that stamped every soul that submitted to her influence. The school was increasing; the community was ideally happy; and all seemed well. But there were people in Grenoble who were bent on disturbing the peace of Sainte Marie. Curiosity asked questions; rumor answered them; and stories spread. Old gossip was revived; old sufferings were renewed. Why did these new nuns lead so penitential a life? Were they expiating former sins? And what kind of religious life could be carried on without choir and grille? What training had they for teaching? And had they really obtained the Emperor's approval? As a matter of fact, they had not, up to this time, though every day they hoped for the answer to their petition. Father Varin did not seem worried, for he wrote during the novices' retreat:

> I believe this new family of yours would be unworthy of you if it were not established on the same foundations as those laid by Our Lord for the one you left [at Amiens]. So in all that happens, you and your companions must constantly repeat: Sit nomen Domini benedictum, and that with the fullest confidence that all is for the best.[20]

Writing an account of these months in the *Journal of Sainte Marie*, Philippine gave vent to her feelings in regard to the unpleasant occurrences that were causing anxiety:

> People simply cannot leave this convent in peace. . . . They have repeated all the old accusations against the former inmates of Sainte Marie. Disgraceful jealousy and irreligion have dared to attack the stainless virtue of the courageous women who gave up the peace and happiness they were enjoying to take the risk of founding a new institution, having in view only the glory of God and the accomplishment of His Will.
>
> They have had the baseness to call them "penitents," to question their orthodoxy. They pretend to see mystery in a life completely hidden in God with Christ Jesus, and they imply that this life deserves reproach. Without going so far as this, many other people have taken the liberty to criticize the firmness with which

useless visiting has been checked and only young postulants capable of taking the training have been accepted. They also condemn the discarding of certain customs usual in old monasteries, but not suitable at the present time. And furthermore they question the teaching ability of the religious, making fun of their youth, especially that of the superior. . . . As if the gifts of God were limited to a certain age, as if the Holy Spirit depended on natural talent. . . . For myself, when I see our Mother acting always under the guidance of God, when I compare the sweetness and unction of her words with the sharp language of those who attack her, I have no difficulty in distinguishing between virtue and passion, and I laugh at the agitation which may check God's work for a time, but will never destroy it. They are making great efforts to withdraw some of our dear companions [in the novitiate] and to hinder the entrance of others who wish to join us, particularly Mademoiselle Henriette Girard, who lived in Lyons, for there, as well as in Grenoble, they censure our union with much animosity.

These are telling paragraphs and in them one can sense the workings of grace in the soul of Philippine Duchesne. There is, moreover, a depth of affection for Mother Barat that points quite clearly to the bond of intimate friendship that was drawing together these two gifted women. From the first they had understood each other. In spite of their difference in age and experience, the younger had become quite simply the mother and the guide, and the older, with a docility almost foreign to her natural character, had become a spiritual child again, eager to form her religious life on the pattern of sanctity that St. Madeleine Sophie had drawn from the Heart of Christ. There is vigor and vivacity, loyalty and indignation in the brief account and comment, and a sense of security, for Philippine can now laugh at criticism, ridicule and calumny, having learned to trust completely in the Sacred Heart.

She had need of such trust when, early in Lent, Mother Barat was obliged to make a trip to Lyons. Philippine had expected to accompany her, and in a letter to Madame Jouve she speaks quite simply of her disappointment and of the supernatural motives that brought joy into her sacrifice.[21]

My hopes of seeing you in Lyons, dear Sister, are vanishing. As the trip is not really necessary for me, it will probably not take place. This is not true in the case of the religious who will give you this letter. Business obliges her to leave us for about ten days, and she will not ask the hospitality you so kindly offered. As she is alone and unaccustomed to walking great distances, she would be too far from her center of business [if she lodged at the Jouve home]. I did not think it wise to send Euphrosine with her for so short a time, having arranged to give her this pleasure only if I myself was going to share it.

There is no need for me to tell you how much I should have enjoyed seeing you in the midst of your dear family, of whom I still know only one darling member. But you realize, dear Sister, that my vocation is a consecration to sacrifice and to privation of natural joys. So I am now making the exchange of the sweet pleasure of embracing you for that of keeping my promises and proving to God that His Will is always lovable, for there is joy in making sacrifices for anyone we love.

I did not mention to Euphrosine that she might have had the pleasure of a trip to Lyons. She is writing to you. You will get more satisfying details about her from Mother Barat, who will deliver my letter to you. She loves the child dearly.

I enclose your daughter's letter—a disgrace to her and to me! Remember me to your husband and to our cousins.

All yours,
PHILIPPINE

Mother Barat had hoped to meet Father Varin in Lyons, in order to consult him and interview some candidates he had proposed for admission to the novitiate, then to return with all speed to Grenoble. But her stay was prolonged, and it was by letter that she continued to direct her novices. Some of those she wrote to Philippine at this time have been preserved.

As character may be judged quite as much by the informal letters one receives as by those one writes, Mother Barat's letters to Philippine are precious as a sketch of her "eldest daughter," limned all unwittingly by the saint. One sees at a glance that she herself has come under the sweet influence of Philippine's Visitandine training, for she has adopted the *Vive Jésus et sa Croix* always associated with St. Francis de Sales and his religious family. Then, too, she has found in Philippine's spirituality an element already personal to her and so a close bond between their souls—a relish for the *Canticle of Canticles* not found in souls that walk the lower paths of prayer.[22] With Philippine she can climb to the "cleft in the rock" and enter in; to her she can speak, heart to heart, of the Beloved, the Spouse who makes His voice heard and draws the soul irresistibly to union with Himself. But she speaks always with a practical direction, a personal suggestion, revealing the close contact of friendship already existing between them, the depth of the Mother's holiness, and the height of the ideals she proposed to her mature novice. Buoyant, virile, she can make a quick transition and let the gaiety of her humor shine through the sprightly teasing she offers to this first close soul-companion she found in her little Society. Happily there is no need for analysis or comment on the text of the letters; unhappily none of Philippine's, written in 1805, are extant.

Lyons, March 27, 1805

Vive Jésus!

I wanted to be the first to write, my dear daughter, but I received your little note, which gave me a pleasure I had no scruple in dwelling upon for a minute. You see I do not blame you for the consolation you experienced Sunday evening, provided you were disposed to give it up willingly if your vexatious Mother had sent you to bed.[23] I hope you did not forget me before God, for just then I had little time for prayer. If I had not been away, I should have spent those three hours with you at the feet of our beloved Saviour. I hope to have that joy on Holy Thursday night, if I am back by that time. You see, I, too, am thwarted in my desires. No doubt the Lord wishes to make me feel what I put others through when I refuse their requests. As soon as I have had several conferences with Father Varin, I shall fly back to you all.

How different my life here is from our usual way! We spend two hours at dinner and have to keep up the conversation all that time. I wish I had you opposite me. What an expression you would wear! Admit now that your vexations are very small compared to these. But I see you smiling maliciously and saying: "At least our Mother is obliged, even forced, to regret Sainte Marie, and I am sure that more than once she has looked longingly in our direction." Yes, indeed, I constantly turn toward you, and I am continually united with you. . . .

Continue to keep yourself well in hand and to grow constantly in the love of Jesus Christ. May that love consume all in you that does not belong to Him. Your divine Spouse asks for your heart, undivided and without reserve. He says to you continually: *Surge, amica mea, et veni;* and the words that precede those in the Canticle of Canticles: *Tempus putationis advenit, flora apparuit in terra nostra, vox turturis audita est; propera, amica mea, et veni.*[24] But whither must the beloved go? To Thabor? No; *in forminibus petrae, in caverna maceriae.* Into solitude—a solitude dreaded by nature and the senses—complete self-renunciation, absolute detachment. . . . You realize, of course, that I am not referring to any new sacrifices you should make. You might think so and wear yourself out with uneasiness. . . . For you the "cleft in the rock" is this: to acquire the spirit of humility and meekness, the spirit of prayer. Set to work in confidence and peace.

I am longing to have news of your spiritual progress. Write to me about this rather than about the affairs of the house, though I am in no way indifferent to these. Tell Madame de Vaulserre that I do not think of her apart from you all and that she is in my heart quite as much as you are.[25]

What Philippine answered to this letter may be inferred to some extent from the following, written in quick response by Mother Barat on April 5:

I received your letter, my dear daughter, and you must realize how much pleasure it gave me. You know too well the loving interest I take in you not to have understood what a satisfaction I would find in this account of your dispositions and the resolutions you have taken. Realizing your own weakness, however, you fear you will fail to keep them and you beg me to promise to continue to help you to the end and not to weary of your slow progress. You know me very superficially if you need such a promise to count on. Our Lord, who gave you to us, has set no limits to this charge but that of death. Until then, if I can help you I shall do so with all my heart. I do not belong to myself but to you. Every day shows me this more clearly, so no more fears on that score. Read that sentence again, if you like, and never come back on the matter. . . .

Now I shall reply to a question to which you did not ask an answer. As to corporal penances, do on week days what I allowed you during the novenas, except on Fridays. During Easter week, nothing at all: you will put aside all penances, but to compensate for this, go to Holy Communion every day during the octave, if your confessor allows it.

Four days later:

I have just a few moments to tell you, my dear daughter, that I received the package, the money, and your letter. I am so grateful for all your kindness. Our Lord, for whom you have done all this, will reward you. You are the only one to whom I gave permission to spend the entire night before the Blessed Sacrament. You gave me to understand that our Lord would not be pleased if it were otherwise. But in turn I must tell you He will not be pleased with you if you sacrifice too much sleep. . . . I am sure that vigil will not pass without your renewing your resolutions, above all that of embracing the Cross. I would have you accept the crosses that are in store for you and that Jesus will send you as soon as you have made that act of generosity, for you realize that the Cross is the greatest of treasures! A large portion of it is reserved for you, but be courageous and ready to accept it willingly, without asking for it. You will have crosses that come from yourself, but there will be others that may seem more painful. You are going to tell me I make sad predictions—yes, sad for nature but precious for grace. I wish, however, to furnish you with subject-matter for prayer during that happy night of yours.

Above all, let your soul be penetrated with love for Jesus. Oh, if you could merit but one spark of that love, crosses would never seem heavy to bear. Like St. Francis Xavier you would exclaim, "Yet more, Lord, yet more!" But I only beg you to abandon yourself and say, *Paratum cor meum, Deus, paratum cor meum.* Pray for me during that night. My heart will be closely united with yours and my mind will travel there many times. . . .

A few days after Easter, Mother Barat wrote to announce her return to Grenoble the following week with a companion, and a very happy group of nuns and novices welcomed her back to Sainte Marie. They had been in good hands during her absence, for early in March Mother Genevieve Deshayes, one of the foundress's first companions at Amiens, had come to take temporary charge of the house, bringing with her a postulant, Virginie Piongaud. She had had some experience in the classroom and came with a generous spirit to share the training and the labor at Sainte Marie. The postulant whom Mother Barat brought from Lyons was Henriette Girard. She had already passed her fortieth birthday and had been somewhat prejudiced against the Society by misinformation regarding the trials and mortifications she would have to undergo in the novitiate. The gay, happy atmosphere in which she found herself, the cordial family spirit of the community, above all the lively discussions about the cross, its necessity, its advantages, its sweetness, all combined to mystify her, and she said to herself, "There is something underneath all this. They are hiding the truth from me. They talk about the cross and suffering, and I see only faces radiant with peace and joy. I must get to the bottom of this mystery."

The novices, discovering her perplexity, let her ask a thousand questions and gaily led her on until Mother Deshayes came to her rescue with the very simple answer: "Our cross? Why, it is realizing that we do not love God as much as we should and as much as we wish to; it is seeing that others do not love One who is so lovable; it is being unable to make Him known and loved by all mankind. That is our heaviest cross, the one that makes all others acceptable." [26] That was the spirit Mother Barat had inspired in her daughters; and as they gathered around her once more, each felt her own place secure in her Mother's affection, without pretense or patronage.

Once more they came under the charm of her strong and gentle personality, as she tried to satisfy their desire to know all that was tellable about the stay in Lyons. News about a projected foundation at Belley, about the work of Father Varin, the possibility of more postulants joining their ranks, and above all, and over and over again, the account of Mother Barat's audience with the Holy Father. Pope Pius VII was returning to Rome after the coronation of Napoleon, and his journey had been turned into a sort of triumph by the Catholics of France. Privileged to assist at his Mass, Mother Barat had knelt, tremulous with reverent joy, as the frail, saintly Pontiff gave her Communion. In the audience that followed she could appreciate his heart full of loving kindness, his mind free from bitterness and guile. Illumined by the light of the Holy Spirit, he gave close attention to this little woman kneeling so simply before him and telling him of an enterprise she had set on foot with a certain Father Joseph Varin, whom he knew, to glorify the Sacred Heart of Christ by a new religious order that would have this one and only purpose. Its members now counted about twenty-five, all told, and there were just two convents founded so far, but with the blessing of the Vicar of Jesus Christ they would surely prosper and expand, and by the holiness of their lives and the thoroughness of their teaching they would contribute in some small measure to the Catholic renaissance in France. "The many blessings he gave you are a happy pledge of the future lot of those for whom he gave them," wrote Father Varin, on learning of the audience, and the novices at Sainte Marie gloried, as novices do, feeling that the "happy pledge" was meant especially for them.

Mother Barat took up the training of the novices again. Living in her company, they came to realize that humility and truth are synonymous, and that simple disregard for self achieves liberty of spirit. She gave the impression of being constantly in the presence of God and of looking on herself merely as an instrument in His hands. This was a lesson she seemed always to be teaching: let yourself be used by Him for the glory of the Sacred Heart; this will lead to perfect confidence in His unfailing guidance.

The *Journal of Sainte Marie*, which Philippine Duchesne was charged to keep up to date, shows how much Mother Barat was helped in her work at times by the Fathers of the Faith who came to Grenoble on mission work. During the summer of 1805 the jubilee was preached there by Fathers Gloriot and Lambert with remarkable results. When Philippine noted that they had "changed the face of a guilty city, and brought the word of God home to hearts that had been estranged from Him for thirty, even fifty, years," she was not exaggerating their success.[27] Their visits to Sainte Marie always meant a conference or instruction for the novices. These men were deeply interested in the new order, which they considered, in a way, a part of their own religious family.

"On the feast of the Sacred Heart," noted Philippine in the *Journal*, "Father Gloriot spoke to us on devotion to the Sacred Heart, presenting it in all its sublimity and comprehensive beauty." The practical application of this doctrine was stressed by his companion in the ministry:

> On the feast of St. Ignatius, Father Lambert assembled us after Mass and spoke to us quite informally of the pleasure it gave him to find among us a happiness that was so supernatural and so evident that it had impressed him the moment he greeted us. He exhorted us to rise above the harsh criticisms current about us, stressed the advantages of the simple community life we have embraced, and congratulated us on being fools in the eyes of the world. He dwelt at length on the meaning of the divine folly, the folly of the Cross, which makes the soul so pleasing to Jesus Christ and so contemptible in the eyes of the world.

It is evident that gossip and accusations were constantly renewed by a talkative and hostile group in Grenoble. For two months that spring the rumor was current that Mother Barat had deserted the nuns at Sainte Marie. On her return from Lyons a new story was invented to deter parents from placing their children in the school. Even the approval of the Emperor, when finally it was given, did not satisfy the critics of this little institution which had been opened for the highest purpose conceivable. Many of the clergy of the city, and even the bishop himself, had been prejudiced to some extent by the stories they had heard, and it required no little effort on the part of Father Lambert to remove the false impression and instil into the minds of these ecclesiastics some appreciation of the little group of women—a dozen or more by this time—at work in the solitude at Sainte Marie.

Another entry in the *Journal* records the first visit of Father Louis Barat. Philippine had already heard much about him and was eager to make his acquaintance, but at first she was ill at ease with him. His austere virtue and scholarly conversation combined to repel her and inspire a kind of fear she could scarcely explain. Quite simply she admitted this, along with the change that soon took place as a result of his kindly interest in all that concerned the community over which his little sister Sophie presided as superior. In his instructions to the novices over a five-day period he dwelt in detail on union and conformity with the Heart of Christ as the very essence of their vocation.

> He showed us [wrote his most earnest listener] that the true lover of Jesus is so gripped with the desire to imitate her divine Model that she cannot live without experiencing the sword-thrust that must pierce the soul of every sincere follower of Christ. Nor can she resist that holy longing that springs from ardent love and finds satisfaction in no earthly thing, since creatures form a barrier to union with the Beloved.

Thoughts such as these were the spiritual element in which Philippine delighted. But when Father Barat took for the subject of a conference apostolic zeal, there stirred once more in her soul the inspiration, the driving ambition to become a missionary, to help establish the Kingdom of Christ in foreign lands, to carry the knowledge and love of the Sacred Heart to the uttermost ends of the earth. Reading again the life of Mother Marie of the Incarnation, she set her heart on Canada. Before the tabernacle she pleaded in the words of the great contemplative missionary:

> O Eternal Father, I come to You through the Heart of Jesus, my Way, my Truth, my Life. Through this Divine Heart I adore You for those who do not adore You, I love You for those who do not love You, I acknowledge You for those who in wilful blindness and contempt refuse this recognition of Your goodness. By this Divine Heart I desire to make satisfaction for the neglect of all mankind. In spirit I go through the world in search of every soul redeemed by the Precious Blood of Jesus, in order to make reparation for all through His Sacred Heart. I embrace them all in order to present them to You, O Eternal Father, through Him, and by Him I ask for their conversion.

Opening her heart to Father Barat, she confided to him her great desire, and from that time forward he encouraged her hopes and seconded her efforts, though he directed her thoughts toward lands less favored with missionaries than Canada.

When Father Varin came to Sainte Marie in August, he was delighted with the spirit and virtue he found among the nuns. A joyous mood and a glad generosity were traits he considered essential at the Sacred Heart, and these were in evidence, especially when the religious and novices gathered around him and Mother Barat for the evening recreation. There were no pious platitudes passed around with the darning cotton or the skeins of wool, no efforts at edification for the sake of the visitor amongst them, but there was that most charming element in the cloistered community life of the order, spirited and spiritual conversation. He was struck, too, by the dignity and recollection of these women whose life bore so markedly the stamp of austerity, but without a trace of rigidity.

Among the novices he noted particularly Philippine Duchesne, when a smile lit up her fine strong features with friendliness and vivacity, when a humorous notion danced in those eyes whose glance could be so penetrating, when the warmth of her words revealed the sincerity of her heart, when the rapt attention of her whole being betrayed the intensity of her prayer, or a quick response to a summons showed how steadfastly her will was set on God. The years of trial had in no way quenched her spontaneity, but the months of training had brought out her finest qualities, and Father Varin knew again with certainty that he had judged her correctly: this was a *great soul*.

Before going off to mission work again, Father Varin discussed with Mother Barat the possibility of allowing the novices to make their vows before the close of the year. This raised the problem of a rule and constitutions for the order. For months she had been urging him to put into writing a statement of what he considered essential for the guidance of the society they had established. Up to this time they had followed the Summary of the Constitutions of the Society of Jesus, along with its Common Rules and Rules of Modesty, but they were convinced that the Jesuit Rule would require much adaptation to make it acceptable for an order of women. It was agreed that the time had not come for the formulation of a complete religious code. The life must be lived over a longer period of trial and error, perhaps another decade, before accumulated experience would justify decisive legislation. But it was necessary to have at least a general plan of the institute to present to the Bishop of Grenoble before the novices at Sainte Marie could be admitted to religious vows. Father Varin would give the matter serious thought as he went about his work in

Lyons, in Paris, in Amiens, and he would return to Grenoble within three months.

Meanwhile the school work and the spiritual training went on side by side. Interest in the children was an apostolate Philippine loved, and she watched with guarded care the progress of her nieces, Amelie de Mauduit and Euphrosine Jouve. In the autumn Madame Jouve came from Lyons for a short visit with her sister. After her return home Philippine wrote in her warmly affectionate fashion:

GRENOBLE, November 17, 1805

> You are very lonely, my dear Sister, being separated from a child you love so tenderly; and I am very lonely since your departure. The joy of seeing you frequently for a few days makes me feel all the more keenly the sacrifice of living almost always at a distance from you. Although you warned me that you might not be able to write immediately on reaching home, I shall feel a little anxious until you announce your safe arrival. On reaching Lyons you will have learned that Adelaide is again a mother. Her husband has just informed me of the birth of their fifth daughter. He accepts the fact with resignation.[28]
>
> Your own daughter is such a joy to me. She brightens up my heaviest occupations. At catechism class she talks more than I do, corrects those who make mistakes, and prompts their answers. She always expresses herself correctly and with assurance, like a well informed person. She sends fondest love to you, to her father, and to her brothers and sisters.[29]
>
> Adieu, dear Sister. Being separated from you, I look with more pleasure than ever at your picture reflected in your child, and I love her all the more.

Philippine wrote this letter while in retreat. Fathers Varin and Roger had arrived on November 11 to prepare seven of the novices for their complete self-donation to the Sacred Heart. The community and several postulants who had recently arrived also followed the exercises of the retreat as well as they could while carrying on the school work. They were aided by Mother Henriette Grosier, who had come from Amiens some weeks before and would go on to Belley in December to found the third convent of the order. While the two priests worked also on an abridged plan of the institute, Mother Barat called on Philippine for help in composing a memorial that would serve as an introduction to the document. The purpose, the spirit, the means, the manner of life, the general rules—all that is essential to the Society of the Sacred Heart was contained in that first plan. Only the title was omitted through precaution. Mother Barat called her daughters *les Dames de l'Instruction Chrétienne* until it was safe to adopt publicly the name they cherished and aspired to bear, *les Dames du Sacré Coeur de Jésus.*[30]

Bishop Claude Simon approved verbally the document submitted to him and gave permission for the ceremony of vows at Sainte Marie, after naming Father Gaspard Rey, former vicar-general of the diocese and close friend of Philippine Duchesne, ecclesiastical superior of the convent. On November 21, 1805, in the old Visitandine chapel that had been the scene of so many life-consecrations on that same date in the years before the French Revolution, a very simple ritual was carried out when Philippine Duchesne, Marie Rivet, Marie Balastron, Jeanne-Cecile Second, Emilie Giraud, Virginie Piongaud, and Henriette Girard made their first vows. A second ceremony followed, as Mother Barat, with Mothers Grosier, Deshayes, Debrosse, and Maillard renewed the sacred promises they had made at Amiens. Father Rey presided, and in the sanctuary were Fathers Rivet and Rombaud, Varin and Roger. Taking as his text the words of Moses to the Israelites, "This day shall be celebrated amongst you," Father Varin preached from the fulness of his heart and in a vein far more prophetic than he knew.

It was not until the following Sunday that Father Varin announced that Mother Barat would leave for Amiens before the end of the week. This was not a surprise to Philippine and the older professed nuns, but it was a sacrifice calling for generosity from them all. Friday morning found them gathered at the entrance door to say *Au revoir*—for Mother Barat had promised to return in a few months. From the cloister they watched her and Mother Maillard climb into the coach, settle themselves with their bundles and satchels and the little basket of provisions, then wave gaily to them as they stood grouped around their new superior, Mother Genevieve Deshayes.

2. 1806—1812

> *May you be blessed by Him*
> *in whose honor you will be consumed.*

Blessing of incense at Mass

LESS THAN A WEEK LATER Philippine broke the seal on the following letter:

Vive Jésus   PARIS, December 10, 1805

Just a word, my dear daughter, about a draft I am sending you. It is payable in 30 days. If you can get your cousin [Perier] to cash it, you would render a great service to Madame de Luiset, who has promised to pay the workmen on the first of the year and has not a sou.[31] See that she gets the money as soon as possible. . . . Your brother gave it to me. Madame de Rollin has just left the city. I would have been so happy to see her. M. Jouve paid me a visit in Lyons. He was not satisfied with giving me some money; he came a second time with all possible kindness to offer me his services on the trip to Paris, if I needed him. I assure you I was deeply touched by such thoughtful kindness, and the family of my dear Philippine, which was already so dear to me, has become more so every day. For a moment I was somewhat put out with you for not telling me of your sister's condition. Pray for her, and thank her husband both for yourself and for me. . . .

I shall be expecting to receive a little note from you soon, assuring me that you continue to enjoy peace of soul, and that you are growing in union with our Lord, that union which I desire so ardently for you. Safeguard your peace of soul and sacrifice all else for it. In possessing it you possess all, for it conditions the soul for the reign of our beloved Jesus. Grow, then, in His love and you will have peace. That was the gift He left to His disciples. Daily I beg this grace for you from our Lord. Do the same for your friend, who is all yours in life and *in aeternum*.

SOPHIE BARAT

Philippine would stand in need of this gift of peace in the coming years. The Christmastide was a period of joy in the possession of that holy security which religious profession brings to a soul determined on the entire gift of self to God. It was a busy time in the school and the community, and more than ever Mother Duchesne claimed the heaviest share of the work. She knelt in adoration before the tabernacle as the Old Year slipped quietly into the past and the New Year took its place in the mysterious rhythm of time. She had more to offer to the Sacred Heart now than ever before—more love and gratitude, more submission and sacrifice, more prayer and high resolve, more joy and much more work. It was her way to bring everything to the feet of Christ, to lay before Him her duties and responsibilities, to talk over with Him her problems and anxieties, and then to lose herself in more selfless prayer. Now, as the year 1806 opened, she accepted from Him anew the multiple offices and employments that had been entrusted to her: assistant and secretary to Mother Deshayes, mistress general of the boarding school, procuratrix, instructor of the higher classes, infirmarian for both the community and the children. True, there were at first only thirty pupils, but Sainte Marie was also a novitiate, where comings and goings were more numerous than one might have expected.

In the life of Philippine Duchesne there is no single decade of years more important for her spiritual development than that which followed her first vows in the Society of the Sacred Heart. Nor is there a period in which her natural temperament and character are more clearly revealed. As a woman approaching forty, she undertook a life crowded with activities and responsibilities which left little time, according to her reckoning, for prayer. Yet prayer was the very breath of her soul. The expansion of the boarding school was a matter of importance, for education in this type of school was the principal external means by which the Society hoped to contribute to the glory of the Sacred Heart. The office of mistress general brought Mother Duchesne into contact with the parents and friends of the children attending the school and gave her the supervision of the educational work both in the classroom and in the cloister, for young nuns and novices alike were engaged in teaching, and some of them had scant preparation for this. To give them more time for study, she also took charge of one of the dormitories, along with much of the children's mending. It was indeed a crowded life.

As she prepared her simple points for meditation on the afternoon of January 5, the meaning of the morrow's feast came home to her with that vividness of insight which seems to have been a characteristic of her spiritual life. She herself said she found it difficult to reason in prayer, to follow out a prolonged train of thought and draw conclusions that would move the will. Instead, by an intuitive movement of the soul she reached the heart of the mystery proposed for consideration and rested at once in prayer. That was her way, though the "resting" might mean spiritual activity embracing every soul in all the world, or wrestling under the burden of personal faults and desires, under the urgency of grace or the trial of aridity and darkness that at times overwhelmed her. The sweetness of prayer was often lacking to her; the will to pray was a constant gift of the Holy Spirit.

On the feast of the Epiphany Dom Augustin de Lestrange paid a visit to Sainte Marie. He was on a begging tour through Europe, seeking funds and recruits to carry on the work of rebuilding Trappist life in France.[32] He had recently attended the opening of the convent of the Holy Will of God at Reidra, near Fribourg, Switzerland, where a group of Trappistines had reassembled to live their silent life of prayer, penance, and labor. He talked of them and also of the mission in America where, in September, 1802, twenty-five Trappists under Dom Urban Guillet had landed at Baltimore and soon after had made a settlement near Conewago in Pennsylvania. Letters from Dom Urban had given details about the migration of the Trappists to Kentucky, where settlers were numerous and land plentiful and cheap, but missionaries were lacking for work among the pioneers and Indians. Dom Urban had written quite simply about the grueling hardships that faced the missionaries and the desire that urged him to take his monks farther west into the lands that lay along the fringe of American settlement.

Dom Augustin spoke, too, of conditions in the United States, especially in the territory recently added by purchase from France. He dwelt on the spiritual needs of this vast land, the dearth of priests and churches, the missions fallen in ruins after the expulsion of the Jesuits, the neglected frontier settlements, the Indians roaming the fields and forests, some retaining a remnant of the Christianity taught them half a century before. America offered the missionary vast opportunities for spreading the Kingdom of Christ.

The abbot's words were deeply moving, and it seemed to Philippine that this visit was meant for her personally. Through it God had given her another holy friend whose name would be entered many a time in the *Journal of Sainte Marie* and later in the records of the first convent in Paris. Now, like the radiance of the star that led the Eastern wise men, his conversation lighted up her soul, recalling the enthusiasm of her childhood, when Father Aubert had told his tales of Louisiana and the Illinois Country, and the aspiration of her girlhood, when she had chosen to combine the active with the contemplative life. An overpowering desire to share in this tremendous apostolate gripped her soul with the strength of an inspiration coming from the Heart of Christ. Under the impression of this vivid call of grace she continued her daily meditation on the mystery of the Epiphany during the octave of the feast. Later on she wrote:

> On the tenth of January, while I was making my meditation in the children's dormitory on the detachment of the three Kings, I was moved by a desire to imitate them. Yielding to grace, I felt freed from my inordinate attachment for this house of Sainte Marie, which had cost me so many tears, and I resolved to offer myself for the foreign missions, to teach the pagans of China or any other distant land.[33]

For nearly two weeks this wholehearted offering of herself to God was the subject of her prayer, but she kept it to herself until she heard the outcome of a decisive meeting then being held at the convent in Amiens.

The touchstone of interior life is detachment. For Mother Barat the departure from Sainte Marie in December, 1805, meant the facing of an ordeal that would result, for her, in lifelong self-sacrifice, the total gift of self to God and to the work she had inaugurated for the glory of the Sacred Heart. The plan of the institute presented to the Bishop of Grenoble called for "an entire detachment from the world and from self" and a formal organization of government under a superior general holding office for life. Up to this time superiors had been appointed by Father Varin. The first, Mademoiselle Loquet, had withdrawn from the order, to be replaced in December, 1802, by Sophie Barat, though she was then just twenty-three years old.

During the year Mother Barat had spent at Sainte Marie, Madame Baudemont had governed the convent at Amiens. Exteriorly all had gone well. The regularity of the house was irreproachable, and there was an air of contentment in the community that might deceive a casual visitor. But to the foundress, returning in December, 1805, it was evident that a change had taken place. The spirit was no longer the same. She was received with marks of respect and deference, but there was lacking that warmth of cordiality and ease of companionship which from the beginning she knew must characterize community life in the Society of the Sacred Heart. Father Varin was worried, too, sensing the influence of a priest whom he had reason to mistrust, the Abbé de Saint-Estève, confessor at the Amiens convent for the past two years and close friend of Madame Baudemont.[34]

The guidance of the Holy Spirit in the events of this period is unmistakable. The plan of the institute approved by Bishop Simon of Grenoble was now to be submitted to the religious at Amiens, as it had been at Sainte Marie. This called for a general council composed of the professed nuns in that community, for there were only three houses in the Society at the time, the one at Belley having been opened about a month before. Fathers Varin and Roger presided at the council early in January, 1806. The conferences they gave left no doubt as to the spirit that must animate all who desired to embrace the life envisioned in the plan of the institute. Two decisions were reached: first, to add one article to this plan, namely, that the title of the Sacred Heart of Jesus would be assumed openly by the little Society as soon as prudence might permit; and second, to hold the election of a superior general on January 18, feast of the Chair of St. Peter, every professed member of the order having a vote.[35] The nuns at Grenoble and Belley were advised at once to send their sealed ballots to Father Varin who, with Father Roger, presided at the election. The Abbé de Sainte-Estève acted as witness to the casting and counting of the votes. By a majority of *one* Mother Barat was chosen for the office in which, more than in any other, "an entire detachment from the world and from self" would be required.

Two days after the election, which Father Varin had announced immediately to the communities at Grenoble and Belley, Mother Barat resumed her correspondence with Philippine. The dignity of her position was no barrier to their friendship, and the Mother General's letters are the only extant record of the workings of grace in the soul of her great religious daughter. Dating her letter from Amiens on January 20, 1806, she wrote:

> For several days I have been reproaching myself, my dear daughter, for my want of alacrity in answering your letters. Of course, we must be eager only for God, I know, but you might easily cite an authority to prove that we may be eager about things for God's sake, especially where charity is concerned. Besides, am I going to ward off the sentence I fancy you are quoting to me and fill up two pages just to silence you and spare your Latin, which you know how to quote so aptly?
>
> I cannot understand how you dare to cry for the wretched milk [of novitiate days] which has been taken from you. At your age, to seek such insipid food! Why, that is childish. Such weakness! . . . God forbid that you should have further need for a milk diet! That belongs to the past, both for you and for your

Mother. When she returns to Sainte Marie the present she intends giving her eldest daughter is the bouquet of which the Beloved speaks, *fasciculus myrrhae* [a bundle of myrrh] which will become in time *sicut malus inter ligna sylvarum* [as the apple tree among the trees of the forest].[36] You can complete the quotation, especially that beautiful word that thrills you with joy: *Sedi*. My dear daughter, to attain to this *Sedi*, milk is not sufficient nourishment. The tree that shades the resting-place of the Beloved is planted in the midst of a forest thick with brambles and underbrush, and to cut a path through it means uprooting these. But for that one needs courage and strength, which milk alone will never give. You understand me, my daughter. . . .

It is time I answered your questions. I had to interrupt this letter for several days. Much has happened to your Mother in this short interval. I have still to resign myself to it, and I can scarcely fix my attention on anything else. Pray for me and let's say no more about it.

After entering into such details as the arrangement of beds and cells, the cutting down of expenses, the doxology and hymn to be used at Office, the copying of report cards, and the weekly school conference, she concludes:

Adieu, my daughter. Continue to grow in the love of our beloved Jesus, and do not deprive yourself so often of the happiness of receiving Him in Holy Communion. I meant to tell you that I was displeased with you when you made this avowal to me. The way to repair this fault is to make up these Communions with the permission of your confessor.

Philippine now opened her heart to her spiritual mother. She knew that her missionary aspirations would be understood, but she never dreamed that her letter would, in turn, open to her the inmost secrets of a saint. Mother Barat's reply, dated February 3, 1806, is the beginning of a new phase in Philippine's spiritual life.

Your letter gave me great joy, my dear daughter, touching, as it did, a very tender chord in my heart. I felt that my prayers had been heard. Yes, I have been asking for this ever since our Lord entrusted you to my care, and I have often prayed for it ardently because I was convinced that He desired of you this devotedness, this complete sacrifice. But I had another motive that I can tell you now. This is just for yourself—it is one of my secrets. Even before I knew our little Society, the desire to carry the knowledge of God to the heathen was in the depths of my heart. When I became acquainted with the Fathers of the Faith, it increased very much, and St. Francis Xavier became my patron. The many graces I have obtained through his intercession made me hope that my prayer was granted and that he would lead me to the people who are buried "in the shadow of death." Once when I was urged more strongly than usual by this desire, I spoke of it to a holy soul who was inspired by a similar idea and from whom I hoped to receive encouragement. But what an answer I got, my dear daughter, after a few moments of recollection: "No, you are destined for France; you will never leave it. That is your battlefield."

I went away sad, but tried to resign myself, if such were really God's will. Time has shown me it is. . . . But have I given up my project? No. The same desire increases daily, and I pray that one of my companions may carry it out, and that the Holy Spirit Himself may prepare her and guide her. . . .

And now, my dear daughter, I seem to see you kneeling at the feet of our Lord and of your unworthy Mother, asking whether she destines you for the work, or rather, whether you are called to it by our Lord. You are awaiting the *yes* that you have sought and that seems so long in coming. Give me time; I cannot answer yet. But I say, instead: Hope on, foster these desires and sentiments, try to grow more worthy of the signal favor you long for. We will both pray most earnestly for this intention. How happy I should be if our Lord, who has so many reasons for refusing my services, were to accept yours. Ah, then it would be my turn to kneel before you and beg you to take me as your little servant. . . .

While awaiting this time, which we must hasten by the purity of our lives and the fervor of our prayers, I want you to know that there may soon be an opening for us. Father Varin and I were busy about it almost at the very time our Lord inspired you with these desires. You realize the importance of keeping this secret. No one must suspect it. I can say no more about it now; but when I come, I shall keep nothing from you. It will be a joy to talk to you about what is nearest to my heart. I have said enough to increase your love, if you are grateful, and to make you exclaim: *Quid retribuam Domino!* . . .

Pray much during Lent, and do no more penance than I have given you permission for. You also must begin to make your sacrifices. You are not to spend the nights in the chapel at Shrovetide. I am converted and I can no longer allow you all these devotions. I assure you I have a hard time making my conversion sincere, but if you only knew how I have been lectured on this score. I simply had to give in. . . .

Philippine's letter in response to this is the first one preserved for us by Mother Barat. The manuscript is undated, but there is no doubt as to where it belongs in the correspondence. It must have been written in March, 1806.

MY DEAR AND REVEREND MOTHER,

I have been longing to express to you my joy and gratitude to the divine Source of all good ever since I received your letter. So you allow me to foster this dearest wish! You do not deprive me of the hope that my desires will one day be fulfilled! In desire and in prayer I may visit the countries where someday I shall serve our Lord and have Him alone for my riches. What a spur to the work of self-reform is the fear of being unworthy of my high destiny! With what respect and deep emotion I shall hear from the lips of my loving Mother those thrilling words: "I send you . . . among wolves." Oh, if only you could add, "as a lamb"! With what transports of joy I would take your venerated hand and place it on my head, that you might bless me, saying: *Ab illo benedicaris in cuius honore cremaberis!*[37]

I often fancy myself at the decisive moment and oftener still in places where I hope one day to be. But would you believe this if you did not really know me? The more eagerly I look forward to the work ahead, the more conscious I am of my present cowardice. It is years since I spent such a weary Lent. I am not only merely natural, I am wholly immortified, wholly self-centered. . . .

Our Mother Superior will have told you that the affair of the rental for our first years here [1801-1805] has been settled in a manner most advantageous for us.[38] I am all the happier about it because it will now be possible for me to say my *Nunc Dimittis*, as I shall no longer be needed here. I hope you will write to us before Holy Thursday and retract that cruel injunction never again to spend the whole night in prayer. I beg you, let me. I have need of all that time to speak at leisure to our dear Master. . . .

The children are getting along fairly well. They wish to send you their respectful greetings. The lines in your last letter referring to them gave them much pleasure. I hope my dear Félicité does not forget me. My respects, please, to Madame Baudemont and her community.[39]

> I am your very unworthy
> PH. D.
> *Dieu Seul!*

In reply Mother Barat wrote from Amiens on March 28, 1806:

I was getting somewhat provoked at not hearing from you, my dear daughter, so you may judge with what pleasure I received your little letter, especially when I read there the continuation of your good desires and the ardor that animates you for the glory of our dear Master. What? Do you really wish me someday to give you that blessing: *Ab illo benedicaris in cuius honore crema-beris?* How ambitious you are! Yet quite lawfully so. But if you lay claim to that grace, if you really wish God to bestow it upon you, with what fervor you must serve Him now, and with what generosity you should offer Him at every moment the sacrifice He expects from a soul to whom He has been so lavish in His gifts and for whom He prepares such great graces! Yes, you must become a little lamb; otherwise could we venture to say, *In cuius honore?* Would any other victim be acceptable to our Lord? No, my dearest daughter, He wants a lamb. Try to train one for Him —begin at once. Desires would be a waste of time if they were spent only on a future perfection. You must concentrate your strength on the present; that is, you must be careful to follow all the inspirations our Lord gives you and be attentive to that interior voice which reproaches you so often for your infidelities. *Audiam quid loquatur in me Dominus Deus.*[40] Does He not frequently ask you to practice humility and meekness—in a word, to become a lamb? . . . This letter will, no doubt, reach you too late; if not, I give permission for night adoration. You may spend the night as you requested.

The coveted permission to spend the night of Holy Thursday in prayer reached Sainte Marie that very day, though it had been dispatched from Amiens only on the eve of Palm Sunday, and postal service was often very slow in stagecoach days. With her dearest devotion sanctioned once more, Philippine went directly after supper to her favorite place before the tabernacle. That night of prayer was one of purest joy. For twelve hours she knelt motionless, the incense of her adoration mingling with the myrrh of her sacrifice. It was a night of faith and hope and love. Not formal acts of prayer, but the entire being lifted up to God and surrendered to His grace through intense, living faith, boundless, assured confidence, ardent, generous love. It was the night of a contemplative at work on her great apostolate of saving souls for Christ. Impetuous and wholehearted, courageous and daring, Philippine gave herself to prayer in her own way: her prayer was her very self in action under the inspiration of the Holy Spirit.[41]

Her account of it, written with simple candor because she was so sure of being understood, reveals the activity of a soul immersed in God, carried out of herself by the intensity of love and the yearning to spend herself to the utmost in spreading the Kingdom of Christ.

My dear and revered Mother,

What happiness your letter gave me and how much good it did my soul! For three weeks my heart had been as hard as a rock, but when I read your words it melted like wax before a fire. My eyes were no longer dry, and my heart experienced a sweet joy that I seemed to taste all night, for your letter came before the night watch of Holy Thursday.

O blessed night! For a second time I believed my prayer had been granted. I am convinced of it, my dear Mother, because of the pure joy I feel and the firm confidence I have. Oh, if only I might go before the year is out! I have almost persuaded myself that I shall. All night long I was in the New World, and I traveled in good company. First of all I reverently gathered up all the Precious Blood from the Garden, the Praetorium, and Calvary. Then I took possession of our Lord in the Blessed Sacrament. Holding Him close to my heart, I went forth to scatter my treasure everywhere, without fear that it would be exhausted. St. Francis Xavier helped me to make this priceless seed bear fruit, and from his place before the throne of God he prayed that new lands might be opened to the light of truth. St. Francis Regis himself acted as our guide, with many other saints eager for the glory of God. All went well, and no sorrow, not even holy sorrow, could find place in my heart, for it seemed to me that the merits of Jesus were about to be applied in a wholly new manner.

The twelve hours of the night passed rapidly and without fatigue, though I knelt the whole time, and in the afternoon I had felt I could not hold out for one hour. I had all my sacrifices to offer: a Mother—and what a Mother!—Sisters, relatives, my mountain! And then I found myself alone with Jesus—alone, or surrounded by dark, uncouth children—and I was happier in the midst of my little court than any worldly prince.

Dear Mother, when you say to me, *Ecce ego mitto te*, I shall answer quickly, *Vadam.*[42] It is well that I must wait a while for the pleasure of talking to you about all this. There would be too much natural satisfaction in such an outlet. And besides, I would not like to have nuns knocking every instant at the door and wishing to speak to their Mother. I should want her all to myself.

I have tried to be sorrowful for the remainder of Good Friday, but I cannot rouse that sentiment within me—my hope has risen so high. Kneeling respectfully at your feet I am

Your humble and obedient daughter,
Phil. D.

Good Friday morning [April 4, 1806]

Easter came and went, and Mother Barat was detained at Amiens. As the Fathers of the Faith had come under the suspicion of the French government and persecution might strike them at any moment, Father Varin resigned the authority he had held up to this time as ecclesiastical superior of the society. He continued, however, to be Mother Barat's principal adviser during the years that followed, and his interest in the order remained unchanged for half a century.

St. Madeleine Sophie made her second trip from Amiens to Grenoble in May, 1806. During the following weeks Philippine learned the secrets which had so sharply piqued her curiosity through the spring, and they brought her pleasure and pain. The "opening" to which Mother Barat alluded in her letter of February 3 was a projected foundation at Bordeaux, the port of embarkation most frequented by missionaries on their way to foreign lands. A second foundation under consideration was at Poitiers. These would require the presence of the Superior General, and Sainte Marie would again be called upon to make the sacrifice of her. This arrangement had already been decided upon, but who would accompany her? Philippine might hope to be chosen, though she was given no encouragement when she expressed that hope.

Mother Deshayes was confirmed in the position of local superior, but Father Varin was uneasy about her mode of government. She was, he thought, too inclined to agree with Philippine in the matter of night vigils, penances, and other austerities, though they had not many character traits in common. "I beg you again," warned Father Varin, "to give Mother Deshayes a directive rule so clear and so specific that she cannot swerve from it, a rule, I mean, on the subject of moderation in the matter of night watches, etc. . . . Take care also that good Mother Duchesne is not over-burdened and does not overburden herself." [43]

To prepare for the work ahead of her, Mother Barat decided to make a retreat in the delightful solitude of Sainte Marie, but she had not got beyond the foundation exercises when a letter from Father Varin informed her that the project at Bordeaux had proved abortive and that her presence at Poitiers was needed at once. The will of God was very evident, and on July 10 she left Grenoble. There was suffering on both sides, and she admitted it quite frankly. She chose for her traveling companion Mother Henriette Girard, "whose age at least will command some respect for us," she said. Philippine did a little mental arithmetic, and the result showed that Henriette had merely a five-year advantage over her, but there was no arguing the point. There was wistful longing in her eyes as she watched them climb into the coach for Lyons. She would have so loved to go along. The Mother General knew all that was in the heart of her "eldest daughter," and with what generosity she would renew her sacrifice when she returned to the chapel after the good-byes.

Of the correspondence between them during the years that followed, only the letters of St. Madeleine Sophie have survived, but they are an illuminating record of the spiritual life of Philippine Duchesne from 1806 to 1812. Thoughtful reading of them throws interesting light on the character of their recipient in her early years as a religious of the Sacred Heart. It is evident that much of the spiritual training she had received as a Visitandine novice had stood her in good stead through the years of the Revolution and its aftermath. Her attraction for prayer and the interior life had not only been maintained, but had increased during the difficult period from 1792 to 1804. Under Mother Barat's guidance it had become more marked as the dominant trait of her spiritual life. At times her prayer reached a height far above the level to which souls can ordinarily lift themselves with the aid of grace. Her determination to give herself to God in the work of saving souls had never wavered. The motive of love for the Sacred Heart burned ever more brightly in her soul, and she was dauntless in her efforts to kindle this love in others.

Yet there is no escaping the conclusion that Philippine had climbed the path of contemplation before acquiring those habits of virtue which are needed to steady the soul on the lower walks of daily life and apostolic activity. Impatient, irritable, highly sensitive, she had now to face and recognize some of the acute spiritual losses she had sustained during her years outside the cloister. The gentleness, sweetness, humility which form so distinctive a part of the Visitandine spirit had suffered partial eclipse in her soul. The struggle against circumstances that were personally so trying, opposition that used every means to divert her from her purpose, and persecution that roused her combative daring, self-assertion, and independence, all this had tended to develop the irascible side of her character and to mark her more emphatically than before as blood-relative to the old grandmother who had been an Enfantin.

Recalling the influences that had been at work through the

decade before she came into contact with St. Madeleine Sophie
and the single year they had spent together at Sainte Marie, one
may read in the letters that follow a graphic revelation of Philippine's struggle during this period. They bring into relief the faults
and defects which she must constantly have regretted, repaired,
and resolved against, and they point the way to the acquisition of
those sterling virtues which were later on so much a part of her as
to appear quite naturally hers. She would never grow placid and
imperturbable, but the surge of native impulses would be calmed
to serenity through prayer and self-control. More than this, the
letters show Madeleine Sophie a saint unafraid to express the tender
affection she felt for the friend she was guiding to sanctity.

Saint Madeleine Sophie had placed the material management of
the convent, as well as the educational activities, in Mother Duchesne's hands. Repairs were still in progress throughout the old
monastery building, and the garden needed supervision. Now
house cleaning called for attention; now classes had to be reorganized; prizes awarded; retreats conducted.

The nuns had not yet dared to adopt a mode of dress that
would identify them publicly. Religious life in France had still a
very tenuous hold on existence, and Mother Barat thought it best
to retain a semisecular costume: a plain black dress with ample
skirt, close-fitting bodice, and soft white fichu, over which was
worn a triangular shawl of the dress material, held by a pin at the
breast. The head-dress was a white cap or bonnet such as women of
France had long been accustomed to wear both inside the house
and out-of-doors, with the hair parted and drawn back softly from
the forehead. At manual work the skirt was pinned up for greater
ease of movement, and a large blue apron was worn to protect the
dress. This lifting of the skirt reminded Philippine of her Visitandine days, as did many other customs retained, whether con-
sciously or not, in the pattern of life now established at Sainte
Marie.

Mother Barat had been gone from Grenoble almost a month
when Philippine received the following letter from her:

POITIERS, August 1, 1806
In the three weeks since I left you the Lord has given us many
proofs of His goodness and His love. Do you not agree with me,
my dear daughter? And have you not said more than once since
then: "Yes, Lord, You really had to deprive me of this friend
whom I love in all truth for You, but who is, I admit, a human

support. I must lean on You alone. Be, then, my one and only Friend. I want no other since You are so good as to choose me and even to seek so persistently the love of my poor heart."

Of course, you have believed up to now that my bits of advice helped you and that no one else, perhaps, would take so keen an interest in correcting your faults or would put up with you, seeing how much patience and courage this calls for at times! Now, thank God, you realize that this is not true, and that grace is not confined to a single channel, but flows more abundantly in proportion to your simplicity and trust, especially if you listen to your [present] superior as you would listen to our Lord Himself. . . .

After a detailed account of the trip to Poitiers, Mother Barat continues:

I open my heart to you, my very dear Philippine, but what I write is just for you, and for your superior, if you wish, but no one else. I have so great a desire that you should love our Jesus, that I disregard myself; I only long to enkindle in your soul the confidence and love I myself should have for Him, in order that you may love Him for me. . . . Pray for me, but do not let your mind dwell on me for any other reason but this act of charity.

The first letter I received from your superior told me something about you that was far from consoling. You wanted her to mention it to me, otherwise she would not have done so, desiring to spare me the pain. For I feel it keenly, my daughter, when I see you holding back from perfection to which you should aspire, instead of advancing by a faithful response to the love of God. But there—I promised not to be put out with you, but rather to forget the fault because of the avowal of it which you wished to make, and in the hope that you are now more obedient.

I realize, my dear Philippine, that for the moment our Lord seems to leave you to yourself, and this makes virtue more difficult to practice. You are without the sensible consolation that ordinarily accompanies a big sacrifice generously made, and you are forced to say with the spouse in the Canticle, "A bundle of myrrh is my Beloved to me." Oh, may you be able to add the rest of the verse, and with similar generosity! Yes, even if your Beloved offers Himself to you only on the cross, you should press Him to your heart with more eagerness than if He showed Himself to you in the radiance of Thabor. Now you will recall our little talk the evening before I left. Be convinced that the inestimable privilege of consecrating yourself to the Sacred Heart of Jesus was accorded you only on condition that you accept from His hand the myrrh with as much eagerness—I should say with more eagerness than if He fed you on the most delicious honey. The divine Spouse says, further on in the Canticle, "I have gathered myrrh with my aromatical spices." But you do not enjoy the pleasant taste of the mixture because you eat so reluctantly the myrrh with which the spices are mingled. You lack the courage to bite into it vigorously. You think only of the bitterness of the myrrh, forgetting the sweet spices. Yet the fragrance of these should counteract the bitterness and even produce another wonderful effect: soon they become so delightful that the soul desires no other nourishment but that very myrrh and is astonished that it ever feared so sweet a food. Then the soul cries out with St. Teresa, "To suffer or to die!" It would not live without suffering, and in its work for Jesus it asks only suffering as a recompense. How is it that we are so far removed from the age of such saints? May we not hope to see souls following in their footsteps?

I tell you, my dear daughter, when I reflect on the magnificent graces our Lord has bestowed on you from early childhood, I have the firmest confidence that with your responsive and grateful heart you will love Him after the manner of these great souls. You are placed in circumstances very much like theirs, and these very circumstances helped to make them great saints: a religious order still in its infancy, aided by men filled with the spirit of God and, above all, by the Heart of Jesus who urges you so persistently by His grace. I seem to hear you say, "All this is very true, and what about yourself?" There now, I do not want to push you too hard. Rouse your courage gently; clasp to your heart the bundle of myrrh. Renew your vow of consecration, and our Lord and His little servant will pardon all the past.

Adieu, my very dear—I do not know what to call you. My Sister? That is very flat. I cannot use it. My dear daughter? That is the name my heart gives you, and it always comes out spontaneously; but when I think of what I am and how unworthy to give myself the title of Mother, fulfilling its functions so wretchedly, I cannot write the word that is so dear to me, so I call myself

> Your little servant,
> SOPHIE BARAT

Shortly after her arrival in Poitiers, Mother Barat made a trip to Bordeaux to meet a group of young women who desired to enter the Society. On August 30 she wrote to Philippine from the seaport:

Some days ago I went to the wharf to see some of my companions off to Poitiers. As they were crossing the Garonne, I remained on the wharf watching them or rather looking at the vessels riding at anchor in the harbor—a great number from all parts of the world. Losing both sight and thought of my Bordeaux sisters, I was suddenly back on your mountain. Then it seemed to me that you and I were here on the wharf together, ready to embark on one of these ships for the land of your dreams. How I wished that you were sharing with me the sight of this beautiful port and all the thoughts it aroused in your Mother. Some days before that, Father Enfantin had given me a great many statistics about China —he even jotted them down—and I know the figures will interest you.[44]

After a page crowded with facts and figures relating to the success of the Catholic missionaries in one section of China, Mother Barat continues:

You will exclaim: "How good God is!" My dear daughter, that is not enough. You also must become good. Our Lord wishes to entrust His work to souls who prove their love for Him by earnest fidelity in acquiring the virtues of the saints. Now humility, meekness, charity, patience, these are the virtues which must characterize the apostles of this new Christendom. They must be filled with the spirit of our loving Saviour. Concentrate your efforts on acquiring this, and above all, while cherishing your desires, make acts of conformity to the will of God. Tell Him you are willing to sacrifice this joy if such is His good pleasure and if He wants only your generous offers of service. Then pray for those who are already working in the foreign mission fields.

Mother Barat remained at Poitiers, establishing a novitiate there and training the new candidates who were sent from various places by Father Varin and other Fathers of the Faith. Her letters to Mother Duchesne were not numerous, perhaps one every two months, but they were carefully treasured, read, and reread, and sometimes wept over before the tabernacle at Sainte Marie. The continual sufferings to which they allude form one of the most painful trials a strong soul must endure in its ascent to God.

Vive Jésus!   POITIERS, November 10, 1806

Every day I have to put off writing to you I regret it more keenly. The thought that I might be able to lessen your interior sufferings by a little advice urges me to write today. Believe me, I count it a real sacrifice not to be able to do so frequently. The details you gave me in your letter grieved me, both on your account and on account of those who share your anxieties. I hope, however, that the visit of one of our friends [one of the Fathers of the Faith] will cure, or at least partially heal, your heart-suffering. I earnestly desire this and I shall beg this grace for you continually.

The sufferings which try you so severely are the result of the many promises you have made to your divine Spouse. You should consider this a privilege, but there are many times when one has need of support and encouragement. The trial which your divine Master is now putting you through is one that calls for some help, and He will not refuse you what you need; but He requires of you more lively faith, more purity of intention, more simplicity and detachment from self. This will, I trust, be the fruit of your retreat and renovation of vows [on November 21]. If such are your dispositions, I give you permission to renew the last of your promises.[45] Do so for the year—I dare not say until I see you again, though that may be quite soon. No matter. Your constant desire always to suffer gives me joy in the midst of the trials I myself am experiencing, and I am glad my brother made that request for you.

Take advantage of the first free time you have to answer this letter. I hope you will be able to tell me a ray of heavenly peace has shone in your soul, announcing the coming of your divine Spouse. He is never far from you, but He hides Himself at times in order to make you appreciate more fully the happiness His presence brings and the care you should take to keep Him always in your heart. . . . I need say no more, except to recommend patience, if your state of spiritual abandonment remains, and to pray earnestly and often to God to cast a glance of mercy on you.

Dom Augustin de Lestrange paid a second visit to Sainte Marie on the feast of All Saints that year. This time he could tell of Trappist monks who had gone to re-enforce the American mission, among them Father Joseph-Marie Dunand. Neither the abbot nor Mother Duchesne could foresee that at some future date Father Dunand would be supervising the building of the first permanent convent of the Sacred Heart in the New World. Father Louis Barat came frequently to Sainte Marie. His stern asceticism appealed strongly to Philippine, and she opened her heart to him with great confidence. The encouragement he gave to her desires for mortification and prayer was often at variance with the views of his sister. When Mother Barat yielded to his representations in such matters, she never failed to let Philippine know it. Writing to her in February, 1807, on the subject of Lent, she warned:

Take care of your health and do not weaken yourself by fasting. I beg you to take six hours of sleep, otherwise I shall take from you that extra hour of nightly adoration and you will go to bed at the hour of rule. You understand I gave that permission only because my brother asked it for you. No, I will not allow you to take only five hours of sleep—with all the hard work you have to do. Be reasonable and be satisfied with what I have allowed. Must I tell you again that I have a scruple even about that? I dread a sojourn in Purgatory for having yielded too readily to your requests. Of course your charity reassures me on that point: you will pray for me! . . .

Now do endeavor to acquire the virtues so necessary for drawing hearts to Christ: meekness, humility, affability, evenness of manner, which is the fruit of patience, and above all that love of Jesus which I so desire to see in you. Oh, my dear Philippine, how earnestly I long to see you completely filled with this love! When will you be able to say and to experience the meaning of these sublime words of the great Apostle: "I live, no, not I, but Christ lives in me"? Endeavor each day to die to self in order that Jesus Christ may live more fully in you. Meditate frequently on these words of the *Imitation:* "My son, the more you renounce self, the more you shall find me." [46] . . . Again I recommend very specially to you a kind and gentle manner toward others, and I beg you to use it also in dealing with yourself. Be patient with yourself. Do not get downhearted about your faults, even if you commit a hundred a day. Draw from them, instead, an increase of humility and confidence.

During the Paschal season Mother Barat wrote:

I want news of you from time to time in the persistent hope that I may someday learn that your soul has broken its bonds and begun its upward flight. The thorns that irritate you so often simply prove that you have not that holy detachment; there is still too much self-will in what you wish to do for God.

I know one cannot always master weariness and disgust, but one can calm these feelings, even lessen them to a great extent; above all, one can turn them into a rich treasure of merit by surrendering oneself with entire resignation to God's will, and by accepting this kind of trial courageously. Remember, my dear daughter, our Lord calls you to carry His Cross. Have you forgotten these words He has so often whispered in the depths of your heart: *"You must become a victim, you must be immolated for love of Me"?* Have you forgotten the solemn promises you made to follow Him wherever He might lead you? I must recall them to you, for you have so frequently confided to me the inmost sentiments of your heart. This is the bond uniting our souls. Because we both want to love and to suffer, Jesus brought us together, though we were so far apart, that we might love Him alone and suffer for Him alone. Now He has parted us, given us employments so uncongenial to our natural attractions, and ardent desires that we cannot fulfill. . . . But did you take in the fact that by the Emperor's decree we are approved for the colonies as well as for France? Did that article not give you pleasure? Well, let us learn to wait, remembering that God's designs are accomplished slowly.[47]

The approval to which Mother Barat referred had not been lost on Philippine, as the following entry in the *Journal* shows:

We have received news that the Emperor, by a decree of March 10, 1807, has given his approval to our Society for France and for the colonies under the title of Ladies or Sisters of Christian Instruction. . . . This fresh mark of God's protection has given rise to lively gratitude among us. To prove this we have offered Communions of thanksgiving and a novena in honor of St. Francis Regis.

In the busy life at Sainte Marie her days were at times so crowded with duties and responsibilities, chores and charity, that Philippine often found herself at war with a repugnance that seemed beyond her strength to resist. One longing filled her soul —to have sufficient time for prayer in solitude. Happily she could pour out her heart to Mother Barat and be sure of understanding and sympathy, if not relief from her many distracting employments. When her pleading brought no change in conditions, she pressed her petition through Father Barat, hoping to obtain permission for greater freedom in the matter of night adoration. St. Madeleine Sophie replied in that soul-revealing fashion she so often used with Philippine:

I received your letter, my dear daughter, with one from my brother backing up your petition and counseling me to grant it if your health (about which he knows nothing) can stand these long night vigils for which you have such an attraction. Long ago I would have yielded to your pleading but for the well-grounded fear of ruining your health. Oh, dear! I have so often experienced the need we have for prayer, the pressing need to beg the Heart of Jesus to be favorable to us, and it is at night, I think, when so few souls are mindful of Him, that He listens most willingly to our prayers and grants the graces we ask. I should fulfil that office, for it is my duty to pray for you all, . . . but who would allow me to do it?

It will be a great solace and joy for your Mother to know she has a substitute, one of her dear daughters, who pays homage to the Heart of Jesus for her, for the Society, for the ungrateful world. Should it be necessary for my brother to plead with me for you? Does not Jesus Himself from His Sacred Heart urge me even more strongly? . . . Now here is a little plan I propose; it seems to me it would fit in with your employments, and I agree to it on conditions I shall state later on. If you take Mother Balastron and another religious into your secret, you can divide the night hours amongst you. . . . It will be very hard to keep it secret, yet you must do so . . . .

The condition of which I spoke is this: your superior must get permission from Father Varin. I do not think I can decide so important a matter without his consent, and knowing him as I do, I hardly believe he will give it. So I counsel you to beg our Lord to touch his heart, if such is the divine will. It would be wisest not to begin until you get his permission, unless you just want to give the plan a trial, so you could support your request by the fact that you find it quite possible to carry it out.

Another condition concerns you alone, my daughter, and it is this: if after some months of secret prayer with your divine Spouse you do not become more humble, more obedient, more patient, I shall withdraw the permission for night adoration. That will be the punishment for your infidelities. Ah, my dear Philippine, that will never happen, will it? [48]

Philippine was quick to try out the plan Mother Barat suggested. She took for granted the permission she hoped Mother Deshayes would obtain from Father Varin, not dreaming she would have to reckon with him in person very soon. The entry in the *Journal* describing his visit is full of charming candor, though one suspects it was written somewhat ruefully:

We had not counted on the favor of a visit from our Father Varin, but he gave us that agreeable surprise on August 8. . . . He gave us the greatest joy by promising in a tone of voice that really seemed inspired, that our work of educating young girls would not be confined to this one country, but that, perhaps even soon, we would establish houses in the colonies. . . .

The consolation which this visit brought us was somewhat lessened at its close when he forbade the continual adoration that Mother Barat had allowed us to try, while awaiting his approval. Since last winter we have had it every day, and since the feast of St. Magdalen [July 22] we have had it also at night. He based his refusal on such well-founded reasons, particularly the fact that we were withdrawing ourselves from the uniformity which must exist among all our houses, that we could only praise his motives in asking us to make so great a sacrifice.

It was easier for Philippine to write these generous sentiments than to put them into practice. One way still seemed open to her by which she might gain time for prayer, and that was freedom from responsibility: she would ask to be relieved of the several offices she held and to be allowed to hide herself in employments where only manual work was required. Mother Barat's reaction to this petition was written on September 7:

> You must hold on to your peace of soul by the practice of humility, meekness, obedience, and submission to your superior. Open your heart to her in all simplicity. Our Lord always blesses such straightforwardness. I am going to see to it that you have less to do by relieving you of the offices of mistress general and procuratrix, as you have been begging me to do for such a long time. Circumstances have made it impossible up to now. This is between us, however, until I can arrange with your superior.

In the autumn of 1807 Father Barat spent several weeks at Sainte Marie, a refugee in hiding from the imperial police. He gave a retreat of ten days to the community, then one of nine days to the pupils. Some of his conferences to the nuns impressed Mother Duchesne so forcibly that she made lengthy entries in the *Journal*. Regarding penance she noted: "Without corporal mortification there is no sanctity; and we must not go at it sparingly, nor fear to give our blood to Jesus Christ. . . . In the matter of penance we should not allow ourselves to be surpassed even by the most austere orders." This was certainly not the doctrine taught by Father Varin and Mother Barat, but just then it delighted the soul of Philippine Duchesne.

In another conference on the Rule, Father Barat lashed out at his listeners in a style that was calculated to inspire fear rather than love: "If a religious is not ready to give her fullest confidence to the superior, let her *leave*. If she is not ready to accept and to give up every kind of employment, let her *leave*. If she is not disposed to renounce all knowledge of what is going on outside the convent, let her *leave*. We should think of those we love only for an instant after Holy Communion in order to pray for them." It is small wonder that the novitiate lost several postulants shortly after this retreat. Nor does Mother Duchesne seem to have profited by such direction. Self-occupation resulted, along with an increasing desire to be transferred to Poitiers. Mother Barat chided her gently for this, writing on December 7:

> Your anxieties are not the least of my heart-suffering. I have given

you my full confidence. You are one of the friends with whom I am most intimately united. I assured you in my last letter that you have no grounds for worry. What more can I do to restore your peace of soul? Should you not, at this season, forget yourself and think of your friends? . . . My dear daughter, I do so ardently desire that you should become a saint. . . . Be faithful, then, and pray that I too may become one. . . .

The transfer of Mother Emilie Giraud to Poitiers in the spring of 1808 was a blow to Philippine's hope of being called there to live with Mother Barat. Her acceptance of this arrangement was not without struggle, and she wrote quite simply of it to the Mother General, who answered:

Emilie gave me your letter, my dear daughter, and told me something most consoling about you: at least, she assures me, you appear always the same exteriorly. The struggles in which your temperament involves you will end some day, and after so much resistance the victory will be yours. At times I rejoice in your suffering, recalling that you have often dedicated yourself to the Cross, and I realize that our Lord has accepted your offering. True, the bitterness that is at times mingled with the trials may come from a sense of your own shortcomings, but have confidence—you simply must be humbled. Rise after every fall, repair every infidelity, and as far as possible keep your peace of soul.

You are disappointed because I did not bring you to our solitude at Poitiers. I assure you we have often to sacrifice personal tastes for the general good. I give you a proof of that in leaving you so far away. . . . Six months here would do you much good. Of course you would enjoy it too much, and for you life should never be a time of pleasure. Our Lord wishes you to be *betrothed in blood*.[49] How fortunate you are in being called to follow Him so closely! Try to appreciate this precious destiny.[50]

Two letters written by Mother Barat in May, 1808, were called forth by impetuous outbursts on the part of Mother Duchesne. The first refers, evidently, to an urgent appeal for permission to set out at once for some distant mission.

I have taken twenty-four hours to think and pray over your letter, my dear daughter. I am answering with the hope that the Holy Spirit will guide me and speak to your heart. It is simply astonishing that a woman of upright intention and sane judgment like yourself could have concocted any such scheme, fixed her will on it, and then could believe it to be the will of God. What does it amount to? Simply abandoning a solid and lasting good to go in search of one that is uncertain, even almost impossible, considering the circumstances, of which you are, no doubt, completely ignorant. . . . While your letter pained me deeply, I would not hesitate to grant your request if I felt that God willed it—but everything is against you. I cannot explain all—I will do so later, I hope.

Meanwhile, I beg you, put aside promptly all thought on this subject. Take for your particular examen an utter abandonment of yourself into the hands of God and entire conformity to His will. Try to acquire this attitude of soul, which is the spirit of all the saints, and you will learn that we can sanctify ourselves only by following the will of our superiors. What seems to be a greater perfection is simply a snare and a delusion of the evil one to hinder your progress. What need you have, my dear Philippine, of spiritual direction! Without that, your imagination would simply run away with you. But I fear writing impulsively, so I will stop. . . . You may renew for another year your consecration to the Heart of Jesus. If I did not answer this question sooner, it was merely an oversight. I certainly intended to say *yes*. . . .

Two weeks later Mother Duchesne received from her Superior General a letter whose tone of severity must have brought her to her knees, humbled and contrite. A remark made by Mother Giraud had been repeated to her out of context. Piqued and very sensitive to criticism, Philippine had let her quick temper get the better of her. She had written to Emilie in a heat of self-love, and the letter, passing through Mother Barat's hands, called forth this reprimand:

Allow me, my dear daughter, to pay you a little compliment after the same fashion you employ in paying them to your sisters and, in my turn, to give you a lesson. I read your letter before giving it to Emilie, and as it would have been impossible for me to furnish her with such a well-conceived humiliation for an indiscretion of which she was not aware, according to her avowal, I gave her the letter, recommending her to read it with attention. You will have the consolation of knowing from her answer, which I in no way suggested, that the humiliation was not lost on her. Only you should have given it with a little more kindness.

You reproached her with pride. She has it; but it is easy to see that yours was wounded and that the pretext of defending others was used to give yourself more liberty to reproach her.

After a vigorous defense of Mother Giraud and an explanation of the remarks that had given offense:

> I assure you that all she says of you, and the attachment she has for you and inspires in her sisters, proves that she esteems you as well as loves you, and that her fault was due to a want of reflection. As she has accused herself of being more guilty than she is, I felt obliged to tell you this in passing, and hope that you will profit by it as well as she has. Remember that one must be more careful in giving reprimands in writing than by word of mouth. The spoken word passes, but the written word remains, and one is liable to give a great deal of pain that lasts a long time, if one is thoughtless.

Mother Barat left Poitiers in June, 1808, and went to Niort, some fifty miles away, where she founded a convent which she entrusted to the guidance of Mother Suzanne Geoffroy.[51] Two other houses were founded from Amiens this same year, at Ghent and at Cuignières, making a total of six in the Society. In July, Mother Barat traveled to Amiens with Mother Thérèse Maillucheau, her "sainte Thérèse," but conditions there under Mother Baudemont and the Abbé de Saint-Estève made it impossible for the foundress to remain without bringing about a conflict of authorities, and she preferred to withdraw to Grenoble. The *Journal of Sainte Marie* contains this entry:

> Mother Barat brought with her Mother Thérèse Maillucheau to train the novices. . . . She has also become mistress general of the boarding school, which counts about sixty pupils; and she was named consultor and admonitrix to Mother Deshayes. No matter what responsible offices she has had to fill, she bears the burden with easy grace, aided by our Lord, to whom she is united by a continual sense of His presence, by long hours of prayer, often six hours a day, and by daily Communion. Her conferences to the novices and her retreat meditations for the children flow from her union with Jesus Christ and inspire in souls a tender love for Him. She began her work here by a retreat of two weeks.

Before the middle of November Mother Barat decided to return to Amiens, leaving Mother Thérèse at Sainte Marie. Soon her correspondence with Mother Duchesne was resumed. The letters now are shorter on the whole, but not less vigorous, affectionate, and illuminating as regards the spiritual life of Philippine. On December 5, 1808, Mother Barat wrote from Amiens:

Your letter filled me with joy, my daughter. I could not desire a greater consolation than that of learning that your heart-suffering is over and that you are at peace. I have thanked our Lord, who gave this solace to the keen pain of our separation. I admit that it would still be very hard if I had learned that you were a prey to continued sufferings and anxieties, for my happiness is, in a way, bound up with yours. . . . Now as to the past—leave it entirely to the mercy of God. Repair it by great fidelity to the present moment and a complete abandonment of the future into His hands. . . .

I cannot help missing the friend whom I left with you, but I am happy in my sacrifice, knowing how you will benefit by her presence. . . . I do not forget your missionary desires. In the course of this month I shall see someone [Father Varin] and discuss matters with him, but it cannot be decided yet. You well know you could not leave me just at this time.

In the history of the Society of the Sacred Heart the name of Thérèse Maillucheau is linked inseparably with those of Madeleine Sophie Barat and Philippine Duchesne. She was born, like Sophie, in 1779, and was christened Elizabeth. When Father Enfantin first met her in Bordeaux, she had already developed into a charming young woman in whose eyes was reflected the heavenly union of her soul with God. She was well educated, adding Latin and Spanish to her native French. She loved poetry and could turn her quill to verse-making that at times reached a surprisingly high level. She was musical and played the harp well. She had faced the dangers of the Revolution with intrepidity and had been in the vanguard when the first lull in the storm allowed the rehabilitation of the parish church of St. Andrew in Cubzac, where the Maillucheau family had a summer home and took refuge during the days of peril.

In the solitude of Cubzac the girl gave herself to prayer and the study of St. Teresa. The call to religious life was accompanied by graces of interior recollection and prayer that became almost habitual. When Father Enfantin was in Bordeaux, Elizabeth assisted at a series of sermons he preached and placed herself under his direction. The flame of love already enkindled in her soul now gave its warmth and light to others, and she became the leading spirit in a group of young women who were determined to give themselves to God in a life of prayer and good works. Among these were the eight postulants from Bordeaux whom Mother Barat admitted to the novitiate at Poitiers in 1806.

Under the guidance of St. Madeleine Sophie, Elizabeth's spiritual progress was constant and rapid. Through devotion she took the name of Thérèse and concentrated her efforts on the development of the intense and loving interior life to which she was called by the Sacred Heart. The austerity of the novitiate offered no difficulty to Sister Thérèse. She had rather to be held in check by obedience, lest her generous fervor ruin her frail health. She brought a joyous note to the recreations, with her sweet voice, her merry laugh, her sense of humor that enjoyed nothing better than a joke on herself. And there were plenty of these, for at best Sister Thérèse was not highly endowed with practical judgment, and her absorption in prayer often took from her all sense of time and place.

Early in 1807 she was allowed to make her vows. Mother Barat's estimate of her at the time is eloquent: "She loves God with intense ardor and is always ready to sacrifice self in His service. In a word, she follows faithfully in the footsteps of her patron." [52] When the foundress decided to return to Amiens in the summer of 1808, she chose Thérèse as her traveling companion with the intention of soon carrying out her promise to relieve Mother Duchesne of part of her work by entrusting to Mother Maillucheau the office of mistress general, as well as that of mistress of novices. She had foreseen, moreover, the bond of friendship that would unite these two contemplative souls, and she hoped that the advice and example of Thérèse would be a powerful influence in the spiritual life of Philippine. She was not disappointed.

The Society of the Sacred Heart was still in its infancy when Mother Thérèse took charge of the novices at Sainte Marie. As the majority of the community had had only a year, some even less, of regular novitiate training, they gladly profited by the permission to assist at the conferences for the novices and to give their confidence to her in order to receive her advice and direction. The letters that follow can be understood only in the light of these circumstances. The foundress realized that the influence of Mother Thérèse was already at work when she wrote from Amiens on February 3, 1809:

> I have had two letters from you, my dear daughter, which I loved reading because in them you promise that once and for all you are resolved to love our Lord and to correct your faults of character in order to please Him and to draw souls to Him. We have a double purpose in our efforts: our personal perfection and

the salvation of souls. We must be saints. If you realized how ardently I desire this for you, I believe you would make the necessary efforts. But if you grasped how much more our Lord desires it, . . . then you would indeed be faithful to His call and you would cry out in a holy transport: *Trahe me post te; curremus in odorem unguentorum tuorum.*⁵³ But what am I saying? You might think I doubted the sincerity of your resolution, when your last two letters have been filled with desires to run in the ways of holy love, and regrets for the sloth of the past. You ask me earnestly to put you as a little child under the direction of one who will guide you in the path of perfection. When there is question of your progress, my dear daughter, have I ever refused you anything? . . . I hope that the help our Lord now provides for you through personal contact with a soul He loves so tenderly will break down your long resistance and enable you to rival her in virtue.

The winter of 1808–1809 was very severe in Dauphiny, and there was much illness at Sainte Marie. Postulants came and left; the children were difficult to handle; and life on the whole was very austere. Yet Mother Duchesne noted with satisfaction in the *Journal:* "Not an ounce of meat came into the house during Lent." She did the ordering, so she knew the facts.

There were dark days, spiritually, but Mother Barat's encouragement never failed her:

I always read your letters with pleasure [she wrote in March]. If I do not find in them all that I desire, my heart clings to its hope and I say to myself: My dear daughter is not yet all that she should be, but she desires that perfection and is working toward it. . . . If you make good use of the help afforded you, and if your heart is inflamed with love for Jesus, I shall be so glad I left her with you. . . .

Grasp this fact clearly: our Lord, in His goodness, wishes you to become a great saint. He brought you into this little Society just to give you the means of doing so. . . . Oh, you can do all things now, if only you are faithful. Success depends on your willing it. Do not fear, I shall never lose patience with you. Jesus has shown so much in waiting this long, and His love has offered you every means of sanctification. I know you cannot correct yourself suddenly. How could you become meek, stripped of all attachment to your own judgment, etc., when the contrary faults have been rooted in your character for so long? It will take a really good novitiate—and you will have plenty to do, even after that, but at least the virtues will have taken root, the soil will have been cultivated, and you will have only to keep up the habits formed. You can count on this time. As long as Mother Thérèse is at Sainte Marie, she is your guide. You must be her support and consolation.

The letters St. Madeleine Sophie wrote to Philippine during the next few months show to what extent Mother Mailucheau's direction influenced her. The saint's joy in the improvement she noted herself or learned from others mingles with the encouragement she offers and the spurs to greater perfection which she never fails to apply. All is not plain sailing at Sainte Marie; anxieties, heart-suffering, near-discouragement are still Philippine's portion at times, and she is forever straining toward the missionary goal:

> You seem to reproach me for not telling you about the departure of that group of missionaries whom you wish to imitate [wrote Mother Barat in July, 1810]. I knew nothing about them. The ones about whom I had information certainly were not suitable companions for you, and I could not let you set out on such a venture. Setting out is not the whole thing. You must know where you are going and what you are going to do when you get there. I still cannot understand how a woman with common sense can let her imagination run away with her to the extent of neglecting the means and yet hoping to attain the end. Happily you have Mothers to think for you and you are willing to accept their decisions. Otherwise, what a fool you would make of yourself! . . . But seriously, you may not be very far from your goal. Only keep your soul in peace, if that is possible, and desire the will of God in this as in all things else.

Mother Thérèse's sojourn at Sainte Marie lasted just fourteen months. Soon after her departure for Ghent, Mother Barat returned to Grenoble, and for a year Mother Duchesne had the joy and grace of her strengthening direction. The old intimacy was renewed, the old affection deepened, and the Mother General had the satisfaction of seeing how sincerely Philippine had profited by the care lavished upon her soul. In mid-November, 1810, Mother Barat was obliged to set out once more on her round of visitations, hoping by this means to insure union and uniformity among the convents under her care. On December 16 she wrote to Philippine from Paris:

> I find you much more sensible of late. . . . You know what joy

that gives me, you whose heart is so sensitive and so grateful. Continue to be docile and faithful, and even if you have not made great strides, go on trying without losing courage. Can you refuse these efforts to the Divine Infant who, in His little crib, preaches so eloquently, so persuasively the virtues of humility, meekness, obedience?

I will allow you to remain in adoration until midnight during the beautiful octave of Christmas. . . . Perhaps our Lord may inspire me to prolong that permission, but I cannot decide to let you have it indefinitely. In the long run it would certainly harm you. You are very well just now, but is that any reason for taking such a risk with regard to your health? God knows how much it costs me to be so far away from you! . . . Will of my God, how dear you are to the heart that loves You!

Traveling almost the whole of this year, Mother Barat continued to encourage Philippine in her upward striving for self-conquest and union with God. The hope that the missionary venture might soon be possible was never withdrawn, but the emphasis was always on the need for preparation by prayer and sacrifice. The tone and substance of the letters remain constant, and one feels the saint's contentment in her spiritual daughter, though there are still faults calling for reproof, and there is no hint that perfection had been attained along any line. From Poitiers she sent her this all-embracing little program in November, 1811:

Your letter is short, but it tells me much, accustomed as I am to read the thoughts and vexations of your heart. I answer: Courage and patience. Let God have His way. He will lead His servants to the goal of their desires. If we will only His holy will, I believe I can assure you He will do our will. Let us abandon ourselves to His good pleasure and lean securely on Him. I shall see you soon. I say soon, for the four months ahead will pass quickly.

They were long hard months for Philippine, for Sainte Marie was severely tried by sickness and sorrow. Mother Barat reached Grenoble again in May, 1812, and spent more than a year there. She had much to confide to Mother Duchesne, much to discuss with her. The Society was again involved in a situation that threatened disaster. The foundress had need of solitude for prayer and patient waiting. She knew that in five of her convents the true spirit of the Sacred Heart was in full vigor, but Amiens, the first house she had founded, was infected with a poison whose only antidote might be the cutting off of members who were still very dear to her. In this year of trial she came to know more intimately than ever the loyal heart of Philippine Duchesne.

four

The Outward
Apostolate

I. 1806—1812

Rooted in love, founded on love.

Epistle, Mass of the Sacred Heart

THERE HAVE BEEN FEW PERIODS in the history of France
less favorable to the development of new religious orders than that
of the Napoleonic empire, and there were few ecclesiastics more
continuously shadowed by the French imperial police during that
period than Father Joseph Varin. Even as early as 1801, all correspondence between him and the other Fathers of the Faith was
censored, and Father Varin had the unenviable honor of occupying
a good deal of the First Consul's, and later the Emperor's, attention.
When Napoleon wrote to Fouché in October, 1804, "My main
purpose is to hinder the re-establishment of the Jesuits in France.
They assume all sorts of guises. I want neither Heart of Jesus nor
Confraternity of the Blessed Sacrament nor anything that resembles
an organized religious group," [1] he was referring directly to orders
of men, but there was little desire in his imperial heart for the
resurgence of religious life among the women of France. Yet on
January 26, 1805, he restored the monastery of Sainte-Marie-d'en-
Haut to Mother Duchesne for the religious group with which she
had openly associated herself, and he did the same in countless
other cases.

Through the next two years, prudence required Mother Barat
and her nuns to have as little external connection with the Fathers
of the Faith as possible. The guarded tone of her letters gives proof
of this. Her correspondents knew to whom she referred when she

used the expression *nos amis* (our friends), and they were careful in turn to mention only the baptismal names of the Fathers with whom they might have contact. So cautiously did the foundress conduct her affairs that in the spring of 1807, when a petition was presented to Napoleon for the imperial authorization of the Society throughout France and its colonies under the title of *Dames de l'Instruction Chrétienne* (Ladies of Christian Education), Portalis himself supported it and the Emperor signed it on March 10, 1807, at Osterode in Prussia.

The news of this authorization reached Sainte Marie within a month, bringing to Mother Duchesne not only joy in the prospect of an increased and stable apostolate for the Society, but also personal relief from a situation which she found trying. Since the departure of Mother Barat the previous summer, Mother Deshayes had been superior within the community at Sainte Marie, but conditions in Grenoble were such that it had seemed advisable to keep Mother Duchesne at the head of the school as mistress general and procuratrix, and to have her assume the responsibility of administration whenever there was official contact with out-siders, especially with the local civil authorities. This arrangement was approved by the Bishop of Grenoble, and it was taken for granted in the community, as all the members understood the social and political influence of the Duchesnes and Periers in the city, and the need there was for prudence.

To Mother Duchesne, however, the arrangement was very try-ing, and more than once she begged Mother Barat to relieve her from a position that brought her into frequent contact with seculars and members of her family and was a source of personal annoyance and distraction in her life of prayer. In November, 1806, Mother Barat gave her the following answer:

> It is my intention that you continue to sign [all official papers] until my return, and this on our friend's advice. If, however, this is going to be a continual source of anxiety for you, write to him and tell him that I am willing to substitute the signature of R[ivet].

Philippine submitted for a while, but with the announcement of Napoleon's favor, she returned to the subject with some in-sistence. This time Mother Barat gave the assurance that on at least one point her plea would be granted, writing on May 31, 1807:

> Now about your signature. Have patience just a little longer and then your name will not appear again. Just as soon as the local

authorities receive copies of our decree [from the Emperor], the name of the superior will be given and Mother Deshayes will take her place as such. But mind you, you are to continue as mistress general until further orders. Greet the children affectionately for me.

While positions of authority were repugnant to her, Mother Duchesne realized the opportunity which the office of mistress General afforded her for spreading among the children the knowledge and love of the Sacred Heart and for training them to true Christian living. It was her duty to direct the work of the boarding school, not only in what concerned the studies, but also in all the activities that made up the life of the school, whether religious or social, recreational or disciplinary. The enrollment at Sainte Marie was gradually increasing as the reputation of the school was built up, and the children spent eleven out of the twelve months of the year at the convent. Although the Society of the Sacred Heart had as yet only the barest outlines of a rule for its members, a rule for the boarding schools had been drawn up, and Mother Duchesne found herself faced with the difficulty of enforcing it in opposition to the wishes of many parents. The formal schooling of the *ancien régime* had disappeared with the outbreak of the revolution in 1789, and it was not easy to establish strict discipline among the children of the new generation, especially in Dauphiny. Representing the situation to Mother Barat, Philippine received these lines as a directive:

> As to allowing the children to go on outings, we should hold to the regulations laid down. It would be to the greater glory of God if they went out as little as possible, but prudence must guide you in this matter, and there are some children for whom exceptions must be made. But let this be rare and hold to the general rule: once each trimester.[2]

The scholastic year was divided into three terms, with reviews and examinations held regularly each trimester, with prizes given informally in midwinter and in late spring, and quite formally at the close of the year, when the Bishop presided at the assembly known as the "distribution of prizes," and many an old custom of Visitation days was revived at Sainte Marie and incorporated into school life at the Sacred Heart. "The prizes" was one of the earliest expressions that went into the word-hoard that has come to be known as "Sacred Heart vocabulary," sharing a prestige quite as eminent as that of *primes, goûter, five-minutes, câche-câche, adjutrices,* and *ribbons.*

The responsibilities attached to the office of mistress general were often the theme of Mother Barat's letters to Philippine. There was, the foundress knew, no better training ground than this for the soul she was guiding to sanctity, and the ideal she set before her was always illumined by love. Writing in February, 1807, she says:

> How are all the pupils? Do you try to rouse their fervor by your example and by your instructions? Your zeal for their welfare should be constantly increasing, my daughter, when you think that our Divine Master has entrusted this little flock to you. There is no better way of proving your love for Him than by taking care of the children for whom He has shed all His Blood. Strive earnestly to acquire the virtues that are so necessary for you if you are to win their hearts: gentleness, affability, evenness of temper which insures patience with them, and the love of Jesus which I desire for you more than all else. Oh, my dear Philippine, how I wish you were on fire with this love!

Mother Duchesne's zeal for the welfare of the children involved her in a multitude of necessary activities, yet she was ready to undertake extra work whenever there was question of a spiritual advantage for them. In January, 1807, she conceived the idea of publishing a prayerbook for their use and wrote eagerly about it to St. Madeleine Sophie. The reply was a gentle refusal on the grounds that "the work may have already been undertaken elsewhere and so . . . you had better wait." Undaunted, Philippine set to work on a new project and sent off the copy to the Mother General. But the saint was obliged to inform her that a competent critic had found many mistakes in this collection of prayers, and added: "I regret that you spent so much time copying it. That time could have been put into a more useful work of which I stand in great need—I mean a very accurate copy of all the Regulations of the Boarding School, following the latest revision. . . . I really need a good copy that I can keep." [3] Not many weeks passed before she was thanking for that "good copy."

Mother Duchesne was relieved of the position of mistress general when Mother Thérèse Maillucheau came to Sainte Marie in the autumn of 1808, but in less than two years the management of the school was again in her hands. The enrollment had increased; the scholastic level had been raised; the critics in Grenoble had been silenced or won to a more sympathetic attitude. In the school Mother Duchesne was loved with sincere devotion by the children. They would have died for her, they said, but they also helped her die to self at times by their mischievous conduct. Euphrosine Jouve and Louise de Vidaud were gifted children in whom Mother Duchesne soon discerned the grace of religious vocation, but with prudence born of the Holy Spirit she watched and prayed for years, seconding the work of grace and waiting silently for each soul to make its own offer of confidence.

From the pen of Mother Louise de Vidaud comes a charming and lively picture of Philippine Duchesne in her apostolate among the children at Sainte Marie:

> Among the sweetest memories of childhood, I treasure the lasting impression made upon me by the strong, pure virtues of that holy Mother, so humble, so fervent, so generous in her devotedness . . . that it led her to take upon herself the whole burden of responsibility for the school. She taught the higher classes, the upper section of Christian Doctrine and Geography. She presided at meals in the children's refectory and sometimes ate with them [as was then customary]. We could never understand how she did it all, but we found out that her working hours stretched far into the night, and sometimes she was so weary, she napped a little while presiding at our study period. She must certainly have possessed a robust constitution to have endured the fatigues of such a life.
>
> But that was not all. When it was decided to separate the younger and more troublesome children from the older ones, in order to insure discipline in the school, Mother Duchesne took almost entire charge of the younger group of ten or twelve, acting as a true mother to them. As her many other employments could not be neglected, she often made these children her little helpers. One morning she would take them out to weed the garden while she discussed the real business on hand with the gardener. Another time they would go with her to the storeroom to cut eyes from potatoes. These impromptu occupations were far more attractive to us than study was, and we got much practical knowledge in this way. When our good Mother had to make an inventory of the sacristy, she gave her small charges a day of retreat, with prayers and spiritual reading, then let us help her with some vestments, while one of the most serious amongst us climbed up to investigate the contents of the top shelves of the big closets. It was on one of these adventures that we discovered some precious relics of St. Jane de Chantal, which must have been lying on that shelf for many a year.

Of course, study was not entirely neglected, but in those days education had a more spacious meaning than it has today and there was time for all sorts of things besides the formal class instruction she gave us. Later on, when we were so fortunate as to have her as mistress of the higher classes, we found her manner of teaching very clear and interesting, but woe to the girl who was inattentive to her explanations. Mother Duchesne passed right on to the next topic, and the idler could only plead for help at the next study period, sometimes without much success. Sometimes, after inspecting our penmanship books, she would read to us from the Iliad or the Odyssey, by way of relieving the tedium of the writing exercise, I suspect.

Our dear Mother Duchesne took a keen interest in all we did, even our sewing and our recreations. Frequently she spoke about her ardent missionary desires. One day, while we were playing blindman's buff, one of us caught her and guessed at once who it was. Now she was "it"—but how could we blindfold her, we asked. Quite simply she took off her bonnet [the little house bonnet worn then by the nuns] and let us bind the handkerchief over her eyes. We were tremendously impressed by her gray hair, her direct simplicity, and her complete confidence in us, her troublesome set. We were impressed still more when at the end of the game, she gaily adjusted her bonnet, then turned toward us with radiant enthusiasm and said, "Now, children, which of you wants to go with me to America to convert the Illinois? Let anyone who is willing make a pact and give me her hand as a pledge." Every child in the group held out her hand, and indeed many of us would have followed her to the end of the world. Only one amongst us could ever keep that rather hasty promise,[4] but many religious vocations germinated there and saw a happy development. . . .

If a child was sick, Mother Duchesne became her nurse. How often we met her, wearing an apron and carrying a pot of tea to the dormitory or the infirmary. She put so much heart into her care of us, yet it was marked also with an austere simplicity. A little unsweetened tea, a day in bed on a meager diet, easily cured our colds. Who would have dared to complain, knowing the pattern of her religious life? Fasting, eating the food we would have wasted, working far into the night to catch up with her duties as treasurer or secretary. . . . If a child was attacked by a repulsive disease, Mother Duchesne took complete charge and gave her the greatest care. . . . She took every precaution to prevent the spread of contagion in the school and used all her skill to bring about the complete cure of these sick children. . . .

But it is not only in the development of our minds and the care of our bodies that she showed her motherly interest in us. Our souls were far more precious to her. Her corrections were often severe and often met with stubborn ill-humor on our part; but when we finally came around, she pointed out our faults and mistakes in such a kindly way that we gave in and made reparation—especially to God by a sincere act of contrition. I recall with lively gratitude the gentle, persuasive manner in which she reached down, as it were, into the depths of our souls to root out evil tendencies and plant a little good in their place.

She taught us to offer all our actions to God, suggesting that we learn to use the prayers composed by Mother Marie of the Incarnation, and by this means she gradually led us to devotion to the Sacred Heart. Her words had all the more influence with us because they were accompanied by such great virtue. An angel in adoration in the church would not have impressed us more, so reverent and recollected was she at prayer. Kneeling on the floor, upright and without support, hands clasped, she remained motionless for hours. One felt the presence of God in her. Besides the holy hours of prayer at night, which were the ordinary thing with her, each year she spent the entire night of Holy Thursday to Good Friday rapt in adoration before the Blessed Sacrament. Aloysia Rambaud, who often noticed her in the chapel as late as ten o'clock in the evening, and found her in the same place next morning, cut tiny bits of paper one Thursday night and dropped them on the skirt of Mother Duchesne's dress before retiring. "If she moves," the little imp remarked covertly, "the papers will tell me so." Hurrying to the chapel early Friday morning to gather evidence, she found the good Mother in the same posture, the papers undisturbed, so the whole night had been spent motionless. It is easy to understand why we considered her a saint!

And that impression engendered another—a sincere and respectful affection. But how could we ever show her how we loved her? It was difficult because she was so humble. When her feast-day came, however, we tried to put into words our gratitude, but she in turn tried to hinder our every effort. One year, on the eve of the feast of St. Philip, our white dresses were spread out on our beds, ready to be worn the following day. Passing through the dormitory, Mother Duchesne spied them, carried them all off, and threw the fancy sleeves into a bucket of water, so we could not possibly dress up for her feast. Another year she hid so successfully that for three-quarters of an hour we waited while search was made for her. Finally they found her in the cellar behind a large case where she thought she could escape from our joyous demonstrations of affection. Oh, how lovingly we crowded around her! The more she tried to hide herself, the more she revealed to us the extent of her virtue and the rare qualities of her character. We knew the reserved and austere manner she assumed was only a disguise, for her character was tender and sympathetic, her heart sensitive and affectionate, and we counted on her love.[5]

At times it took an order from St. Madeleine Sophie to secure for the children the opportunity of celebrating the feast of St. Philip at Sainte Marie. Early in the spring of 1811 Mother Duchesne was pleading to be spared the customary good wishes offered to the mistress general. The mother general answered from Ghent with gentle and sympathetic firmness: "You will have your feast in the school. Submit to this and act for the good of the house, no matter what it may cost you personally. Have patience— a little while and your sufferings will be eased. Your Mother is working in your favor, though you may not believe it."

Mother Duchesne's interest in the children followed them after they left school. Two letters remain to show us how simple and friendly she was with them, how earnest she was in her efforts to help them and to keep them informed about the activities of their former companions. Her use of the family names of the girls about whom she writes may have been a mannerism of her own or one picked up from Mother Barat, who was fond of using this form in letters to some of her nuns. Writing in the autumn of 1810 to Julie Pinet, whose home was at Veynes in the Upper Alps, she says:

> You should have received a letter from me in return for the one you wrote me for my feast. Your dear mother passed through here in such haste on her way home from Lyons, she did not give us time to fulfil your desires. On her first stop she told us, to our regret, that you and Adele would not return to us. God willed it, so we must not complain about that sacrifice. I am very anxious to have Adele well prepared for her first Communion. For her, more than for others, this period will either strengthen her character or leave her a slave to her defects. Then pray, exhort, urge that this act be accomplished in a worthy manner. But preach by the example of your fervor rather than by words. That is the very best sermon.
>
> As to a method for tutoring your sister in grammar—you know how we teach it. It needs constant repetition and the use of good models and the dictionary, along with aptitude and application. The last two factors are indispensable.
>
> Chauvert's death is distressing and a very great sorrow. You realize that such blows prove the inconstancy of fortune and

worldly happiness, and force us to look to the future life and to convince ourselves of the need of making good use of the present.

I have had no details about the death of Jenny. Sophie is so stunned by this loss and still more by the loss of her mother, she is, as it were, in a stupor. For more than a month she did not write at all, then in so confused a fashion as to tell us nothing except that for the present she is alone with Rosalie, and that her younger sisters are in the academy at Chambery, near their guardian. Rosalie is quite brokenhearted. Tell Lesbros to pray for that grief-stricken family that is so dear to her, and to serve God with fervor, since we carry to the future life only the merits of such service.

Jouve has just been godmother to a little sister.[6] The family has moved out of the city to live in the Chartreux quarter; this gave her a great deal of work. They told her a tale about your being married and taking a trip to Lyons. It was the result of confusing you with Lambert. I have had news from Lise. She inquired about you, for her friendship for you is very cordial. I seldom see Durand.[7]

Do pray for Mother Deshayes; she is suffering a great deal. She has great affection for you and so have all in this household, and I share their sentiments sincerely. . . .

Your friend,
PHILIPPINE

To another of her pupils who had recently married and was living at Gap, some fifty miles from Grenoble, she wrote in that friendly yet serious style that characterizes so many of her letters:

GRENOBLE, December 6, 1812

MADAME AND VERY DEAR FRIEND,

I should much prefer the pleasure of seeing you, but since Divine Providence has upset your plans and my enjoyment of them, I am glad I can still chat by letter with one of our dearest friends, one whose friendship we hope to keep always. I have prayed most fervently that the divine will may be accomplished in you and that you may be happy, and I seem to have been answered, judging by your good dispositions and your happiness. And I shall think this true always, even when suffering comes to you, for what state of life is without it? Is any life completely free from suffering? We must struggle here in order to reign there. We must bear up bravely if we are to be soldiers of a Leader who entered glory only by enduring the cross. Your own future crosses will seem slight if you hold on to these thoughts; or at least instead of surprising you, they will give you the assurance that when God gives you a share in the chalice of His Son, He will also give you a share in His kingdom.

You asked my advice and you see I begin with that, for I am convinced that a young matron on whom everything has smiled may think at the time of her wedding that that condition of things will last a long time. She does not yet foresee the suffering that comes with bearing and rearing children, or with the loss or diminishing of fortune. Now I do not want you to be surprised at anything, but rather always disposed to regard happiness and home duties as God's design for you, without wavering in His service, without neglecting to pray regularly, to frequent the sacraments, and to avoid too great pleasure-seeking. You will have satisfying friendship in the company of Madame Gautier and Madame Callandré. Remember me to them cordially and tell them we do not forget them.

Mother Barat, who is still with us, and Mother Deshayes both wish to be remembered to you. . . . I have no news of Walter. Jouve and Mauduit are in good health and very well behaved.[8] Desplagnes is coming back to school, having obtained the permission from her guardian. We also expect Henriette and another niece of Mother Barat.[9] I am teaching the same class, but I never forget the pupils I taught in former years. Tell them all this for me and believe me,

Your very devoted friend,
PHILIPPINE.

During these years at Sainte Marie Mother Duchesne was in constant contact with her family. Several of her nieces and cousins were in the boarding school. Her sisters came occasionally to visit her, Amelie from Grâne, Euphrosine from Lyons, and Adelaide from Bourg. Melanie and Duchesne were with their father at Grâne for some years after 1802; then the men returned to Grenoble and lived at Number 5, Grande Rue, where family gatherings brought together old aunts Gueymar and Lagrange, the Periers and Teisseires, and often the Jordans from Lyons and the Savoye-Rollins on their way to or from Paris. Philippine kept in touch with them all, for the family ties were close and intimate, and she knew that all had need of spiritual help. God had blessed many of them with material wealth, but the treasure of faith had been lost by nearly all the men in the family.

In her letters to her sister, Madame Jouve, her personal interest in all that concerned the family is revealed. She was warmly affectionate and did not hesitate to express the sentiments that welled up from her heart as she wrote to one whom she loved tenderly and by whom she knew she was sure to be understood. The presence of her nieces in the school at Sainte Marie was a joy and a responsibility. She studied them, trained them, wrote of them in her simple, forthright manner. Health, diet, and clothing, progress in classwork and piety and character formation were carefully watched over and reported on with discernment and sincerity. The names of these nieces are rarely entered in the *Journal of Sainte Marie*, but the personalities of some of them are deftly portrayed in the charming letters that are still treasured in their families. At times the duplication of names must have caused some confusion even within the family circle, for there were Amelie de Mauduit, Amelie de Mauduit II, who married Henri Bergasse, Amelie Jouve, and Amelie Teisseire; and the mention of "Camille" might raise a similar problem.

Mother Duchesne followed a somewhat formal style in writing to and about members of her family, using *Madame* and *Monsieur* in preference to their baptismal names. Her fondness for the colloquial *amie* (friend) as a term of endearment to her sisters must be understood in its true significance. Throughout the pages that follow it is seldom translated literally lest it create a false impression. That many of the letters contain nothing of real importance in the life-story of Philippine Duchesne has not seemed a reason for discarding them. Their importance lies in the fact that they allow her to speak for herself, and this self-revelation is far more valuable than any secondhand sketch of her could be. The letters cited in this chapter were all written to her sister Euphrosine, Madame Jouve, and addressed now to the Jouve home in Lyons, now to the country place at Grâne, where the Jouves went each year for a visit of several weeks.

In the autumn of 1806, Philippine was doing what nuns seem to do in every generation and in all parts of the world—she was sending letters and parcels "by opportunity." This became a life-long habit with her, and she enjoyed the inward thrill of saving postage, though the carrying costs may sometimes have inconvenienced the friendly "opportunity."

> Madame de Vaulserre's maid is going to enter with us [she wrote], but first she wants to go to Lyons to see her son, whom her former mistress is educating at *l'Argentière*.[10] So I am taking advantage of this opportunity to send you some of your daughter's drawings and her first geographical map, with which I am quite pleased. She

does give promise. Tell me what you think of her work, and also of her résumé of the *Iliad*.

I am making use of the liberty you gave me about her clothes and am making her a new dress, as she will need it soon. As to the knitted petticoat, she will make that herself. She is very clever and skillful with her needles when she puts her mind to the work, but you know her vivacity.

You complain about the brevity of my letters, and I really feel I cannot reform on that point, as I have so few free moments. I can tell you in a line that I am daily more and more content with the good fortune that has come to me, and my companions are also. I am very well, and the time just flies by.

For several years Philippine had been watching the development of a religious vocation in her sister Melanie. She had hoped to see her enter the novitiate at Sainte Marie, for Melanie had felt a strong attraction to the new institute which, she knew, would one day bear the title of Society of the Sacred Heart. She was called, however, to the Visitation and at the age of twenty-one entered the monastery at Romans, where her aunts and a cousin were members of the community. Philippine wrote briefly about it to Euphrosine:

Madame de Vaulserre offered me the chance to put a few lines in her letter to you, so I am taking the opportunity with much pleasure. It will be delivered to you by Father Roger, who has spread a feast of kindness and spiritual nourishment for us during his stay at Sainte Marie.

Such helps are really necessary to make up for the privations life brings. Melanie's departure is a great sacrifice for me, but she has so much joy in being at Romans that her own sacrifice is greatly lessened. I received a letter from her yesterday. She was simply carried out of herself with happiness. . . .

Melanie received the habit at the Visitation on May 24, 1807, with the name of Sister Marie-Xavier. Shortly after her departure from Grenoble, Adelaide came with some of her children to visit Philippine. Meanwhile Madame Jouve was begging to have Euphrosine come home for a few weeks. A minor conflict ensued between duty and affection, and loving Tante Philippine was happy over its outcome when she wrote on April 9:

To satisfy your desires, my dear Sister, we are allowing Euphrosine to go home for 10 days, or two weeks at most. I do not like the arrangement, for she is the first pupil for whom this exemption from the rule has been made, and others will take advantage of this fact or will complain. However costly it is for the parents, I cannot change the rule nor find fault with it, realizing as I do that the children are quite noticeably more contented and studious when their heads are not full of outings and trips. Last year's trip was certainly detrimental to your daughter, as far as docility is concerned. I beg you, ward off the undesirable effects of her father's excessive praise. I know how well founded this may be, for Euphrosine is quite advanced for her age and full of ambition. But of what use is fruitless knowledge without the more desirable traits of modesty, piety, docility? On these three points she has a long way to go.

After giving you this little sermon, it is only fair to tell you that I am so glad you and Euphrosine will have this happy time together and that I really helped to secure it by pointing out how sad you would be at a refusal.

I am losing my dear Adelaide this evening. How happy I was to see her again with her darling family! It is evident that she has them well in hand. They sing the praises of your little Amelie. I send her my love without knowing her and I am so glad you have such a dear, good little companion at home.

Euphrosine is taking home with her a chronology to study. She should also read over the history of the emperors in order to keep up with her class. You will find in her satchel two heads she has sketched, two geography maps, and her most recent exercise in church history.

Our other nieces [Amelie de Mauduit and Caroline Lebrument] are very well and send you their respectful greetings. Give me news of Jordan. Tell him I am praying earnestly for his health. Special regards to Camille, also.[11]

I love you tenderly.
PHILIPPINE

Little Amelie Jouve was about ten years old when she joined her sister at Sainte Marie in the autumn of 1807. Her cousins, Henriette Lebrument and Amelie Teisseire, were somewhat younger than she and soon became her close friends. Philippine wrote of Amelie's first days at school:

In spite of my precise instructions and efforts I could not get Amelie here until Sunday evening. Camille and Augustin did not want to give her up, and our very obedient commissionaire, being unaccustomed to resistance, came to me and said quite calmly, "I was not able to bring her." In the evening Marine Teisseire brought her. She had heard that she would be in a low class with her cousins. This, joined to the memory of you, which causes much homesickness, made her weep bitterly when the older cousins left. In order to console her, I tried to find out what class she wanted to be in, and to her great joy she was put in the second, where she is very happy. I think Henriette and Amelie Teisseire will soon join her there. We shall pay special attention to her diet and expend still greater care in preparing her for her first Communion. . . .

All yours—love the children for me.

In the busy life she was leading there was little time for long letters. At times, however, Philippine expressed herself at some length, as on November 19, 1807:

Believe me, my dear Sister, it is as hard for me to have to write briefly as it is for you to receive letters that give you insufficient details about your daughters. But forgive me because of my many occupations. I am responsible, in part at least, for 38 children. I have to order meals for sixty people. There are days when I should have quite enough to do if I only answered the door and went over the children's mail, yet I must also teach my classes and secure time for my prayer and other spiritual duties. I only wish Euphrosine could supply for what I leave undone, but it is as impossible for her to write at any length as it is for others to put their ideas into words. She has a brief, concise way of expressing herself, very laconic, that shows little feeling, though she is intensely affectionate. But she will never excel in self-expression.

She has not been confirmed. She was considered wanting in piety and self-control. I think she has improved a little. At least she has faith, and I find her much more easily handled. As she is ready for anything, she is never embarrassed. As to manners, let us not mention the subject. You realize that being put out of the confirmation class, and for that to happen after having been to confession in preparation for the sacrament, was a severe humiliation. So she would not have been in a hurry to tell you about it. She has argued that in refusing her this source of strength, they have taken from her all means of resisting temptation.

She is making great progress in her studies and is now learning a little Latin and Italian (but not more than I know, as you may realize). I hope, however, that she will soon surpass the little I know. She can understand the prayers in Latin and read Italian easily; to speak it is quite another thing. And all this is no burden to her. Generally speaking, she likes study. I do hope she will develop more lively piety, more modest deportment, and more gentleness. These are essential.

Amélie has become very negligent about her little personal affairs, but she promises much as to piety and good conduct, and also as to study. She has composed and written out a rule of piety for herself and her little companions—you can just imagine what it is like. Both girls are well, and I shall take the precautions against chilblains which you suggest. They will both need new dresses soon, so authorize me to have them made. Euphrosine is already making hers under the direction of one of our religious who cuts out and makes garments very well.

The event of which you wrote is certainly of importance to religion. Those on whom its rigor has fallen hardest will accept it with the most perfect resignation and even the deepest peace, I am sure.[12] Now I embrace you tenderly, also your children and our nieces. A thousand affectionate messages to your husband and a little reminder about our business affair.

In the letters of the next few years there is an interesting character study of Euphrosine and Amelie Jouve as their devoted aunt saw them. Both were to become members of the Society of the Sacred Heart, the younger entering on a long religious career as the older was finishing her short life of suffering and sanctity. On May 2, 1808, Philippine wrote to her sister:

Ma Bonne Amie,
I put off sending Amelie's letter until today so as not to make overweight the letters you will receive from Euphrosine and from Mother Deshayes, with the report cards. A second reason was that Euphrosine had an attack of fever the very day she wrote, and I wanted to know how it would develop before telling you about it, for we have had some cases of scarlet fever. Fortunately Euphrosine's illness lasted only a day. She had energy enough to learn and act a part in a little play given on my feast [May 1]. She and her sister did very well. The latter is now quite hoarse from singing too much. The prize Euphrosine received and her first *accessit* to the ribbon of merit have gone to her head and she has again assumed her haughty and imperious manner. . . . I embrace you and your little baby [Constance]. Give my affectionate respects to Father. Mother Thérèse sends you a thousand messages of affection.

Not long after this she was writing:

Ma chère Amie,
By now you should be reassured about your husband. I was surprised to see him, and the time we spent together seemed very short. I received him in the parlor, for since about the time

Madame Lebrument [Adelaide] was here, we have become stricter about cloister, and we do not have to make any mystery about the fact since we received our decree [of approval from Napoleon]. I should have been very proud to show him our terrace at sunset, and I feel that he would have been enthusiastic about it. The children were wild with joy on seeing him. Happily he was not too demonstrative and did not make too much over Euphrosine. She is already well aware of her own merits. But at least she is improving; her manner is calmer; she is more affable and pious. If this continues, she will be allowed to make her first Communion on the feast of the Assumption of the Blessed Virgin. As to the trip you want her to take, that is quite impossible. We are refusing that permission to all who ask it. She can be godmother to the baby by proxy. . . .

Your husband was very generous about offering me some money; but as we shall need to purchase many things during the year at Lyons, it would be more convenient, if it suits you, to be able to draw on you for the money there.

I did not know Melanie had been ill until your husband spoke of it. Amelie did not seem so anxious about it. Melanie's sight seems to be impaired. If she becomes blind, the good Lord will have given her a double grace in calling her to religious life. They love her very much in her convent.[13]

August came and went, and there was no ceremony of first Communion at Sainte Marie. To Madame Jouve's inquiries Philippine replied:

I see you are impatient to know when the children's first Communion will take place. It has been retarded for them all. I hope it will be before Christmas, between All Saints and the feast of the [Immaculate] Conception. Euphrosine is preparing for it rather coldly; still I think she will merit this privilege. Her character simply lacks the effusive tenderness of more demonstrative souls. She will serve God generously, but she will not enjoy much sensible fervor. The stiffness that marks all her conduct gives her a proud and disdainful air. She has a real need of all the help grace can give her for working on her character. She is not one from whom you can expect much now in the way of helpfulness. Only convictions and experience of the trials of life will make her realize, and sympathize in, the needs of others. So in spite of the fact that you seem to want her at home, I think she needs another year here very badly. If you are too hard pressed by the tuition fees for the two girls, besides all the incidental expenses, go back to what I begged you to do in the beginning: stop worrying. You have only to pay for Amelie as long as Euphrosine remains here. The latter is not doing as well in art as she could, because of her restlessness and lack of patience. In everything else she succeeds perfectly. Amelie is very good, except for a little stubbornness when corrected for her faults. . . .

Euphrosine made her first Communion with seven of her companions on November 13, 1808. St. Madeleine Sophie was there at the time and took a special interest in this gifted, difficult girl who would one day be the perfect religious of the Sacred Heart, the one of whom the foundress said, "Such was my dream for all of them." From the day of her first meeting with Jesus in the Blessed Sacrament, Euphrosine began her steady climb toward sanctity. In a fragment of a letter written on Christmas Eve, 1808, Philippine noted the fact:

Euphrosine is improving steadily in character and piety, but not much in politeness and thoughtfulness. In this matter she still consults her own inclinations, with little regard for respect and duty. She is always first in studies and is very skilful at needle work, though she gives little time to this on account of classwork and secular teachers. The drawing has been a bit neglected these holidays because the drawing master has not yet commenced his lessons, and the same was true during her retreat and preparation for first Communion.

Amelie will have skilful fingers, too, but she is less gifted than Euphrosine. I am busier than ever just now and so I am forced to cut this short and tell you very briefly but with all possible tenderness that I am always devotedly yours,

PHILIPPINE.

Early in 1809 she was answering enquiries of a different kind:

MY LOVED SISTER,

It is a pleasure to add some lines to your daughter's letter, not to praise her sentiments, as you know them well, but her heart. She is really beginning to realize all she owes you. You know she has appeared wanting in feeling, but this, I believe, has come from a want of reflection, a fault so common to her age, rather than from any unpardonable hardness of heart toward her good parents. She now speaks more often of you both with an expression of real gratitude, and one day she said *she would gladly spend her life in a dungeon*, provided she was with you. But this increase in affection does not lessen her love for Sainte Marie. She seems satisfied; so does Amelie. That little air of sadness is simply affected, the outcome, perhaps, of a prejudice against us because we are opposed to the ways of the world, or the result of her own personal appearance, so lively and attractive. I have questioned her and have had several others do so, among them her mistresses and companions, and she has always replied that she is very happy and has no desire to leave school. It would not surprise me at all, however, if she cries sometimes when she thinks of her parents, for she is very sensitive. . . .

Amelie is not lively like Euphrosine, and they are not very congenial. Euphrosine is eager to take drawing lessons, but she has not begun yet, as I am expecting some other pupils to join the drawing class at the end of the month. The drawing master is very good. He teaches at the Lycée and at three of the best institutions in the city. The hope that our school will increase has induced him to come to us for a very reasonable fee.

Accompanying a letter written by Euphrosine to her mother in May, 1809, is a brief but very telling note:

I fear, *ma chère Amie,* that the report on your daughters may cause you some anxiety. As to Euphrosine, her health is perfect at present. I would have told you sooner about her illness if I had not thought it best to have her examined before raising any painful fears about her. Some baths and sedatives have sufficed to put her on her feet again. Euphrosine has been better as to conduct this month, and her studies go well. The sewing progresses slowly, but do judge her leniently. I do not push her. She must not be pressed to fatigue, as this might bring on a fresh case of irritation of the nerves. The withdrawal of one of her companions who had the ribbon of merit has procured the ribbon for her, as she had the second *accessit* at the last distribution of prizes. This is a much coveted honor in the boarding school, but no one is envious of her.

Amelie is very good, but not high ranking. A note from Madame de Mauduit yesterday told me that you had returned home [from Grâne] and how charming your family is. Do not be put out if your daughters did not write to their father during your absence. It is partly my fault and partly Jouve's. The bell is ringing for Office. I give you an embrace as I stop.

While life at Sainte Marie seemed to be moving at a normal pace, all France was seething under the impact of the military campaigns by which Napoleon was striving to increase and consolidate his imperial position. Grenoble on the French frontier was often astir. War in Italy, revolt in the Tyrol, troop movements through Dauphiny, and the threat of Austrian invasion, all disturbed the peace of the old fortress town. From time to time Philippine got news of the members of her family who had thrown in their lot with Napoleon or had been drawn into his army. Prominent among these were Josephine Perier's husband, Jacques-Fortunat de Savoye-Rollin, whose services were rewarded by a baronate in 1809, and Camille Perier, a financial genius, who had held the post of auditor in the Council of State. Even closer to her heart was her young nephew, Amédée de Mauduit, who had left Saint-Cyr as a sub-lieutenant of infantry in 1808, taken part in the Spanish campaign, and been wounded at Regensburg.

News of another kind was now filtering into Grenoble. The very month Philippine wrote the last letter cited above, the papal states were incorporated into the French Empire. Soon the French flag was hoisted over St. Angelo and a new bull of excommunication against all who had violated the rights of the Church was affixed to the walls of Rome's great basilicas. Early on a morning in July of that year 1809, Pope Pius VII and Cardinal Pacca were arrested. Though weak and ill, the Pontiff had still the moral courage to defy the brute force of the emperor's soldiers. Five years of exile and suffering lay ahead, but through it all the saintly bearing of the august prisoner awakened religious fervor as well as sincere sympathy among the people of France. Packed off hurriedly to the French frontier, he reached Grenoble in a pitiable condition.

In the *Journal of Sainte Marie* Mother Duchesne wrote an account of the stay of this lonely and defenseless old man in the prefecture of the town—a building she had so often visited in what now seemed a distant past:

> The most thrilling event of this whole year was the stay of the Pope in Grenoble, and it procured many blessings for our house. Pope Pius VII has occupied the Chair of St. Peter in very difficult times. He was arrested in Rome during the night by order of Napoleon, Emperor of France, not being given time to take anything with him nor liberty to choose a companion on his journey. By the goodness of Divine Providence and without a direct order from the Emperor, the captain in charge brought him to Grenoble by an almost uninterrupted journey and without seeing even Cardinal Pacca, who was a prisoner with him, but kept entirely separated from him. He arrived at four o'clock on the afternoon of July 21, 1809. As he was lodged in the prefecture directly opposite our windows, but on the opposite bank of the Isère, we could see his carriage arriving, escorted by soldiers. His very

meager suite followed in miserable vehicles. . . . We saw the Cardinal kept at a distance from him and conducted to a different lodging place. Next morning we had the joy of loaning a missal and cruets for the Pope's Mass.

A tenant of this house . . . obtained the captain's permission to bring our Superior, Mother Deshayes, the next day. She went at the hour announced for the Pope's Mass, but it was already over. She was not wearing her ordinary religious costume, but a black silk dress such as a widow might wear. . . . The guards thought our Mother Superior was Madame de Vaulx, and this was a lucky mistake. The Pope gave her the warmest welcome, allowed her to kiss his ring as well as his feet. But Mother Deshayes revealed her identity by asking the papal blessing for her spiritual mother [St. Madeleine Sophie Barat], her religious sisters, and the 400 children being taught by them. Suddenly the Pope assumed a troubled air, either out of compassion for religious in such unhappy times, or because he feared the outcome of this visit, since neither priests nor religious were supposed to enter the prefecture while he was lodged there without express permission. But this mistake could have occurred only on one of the first days. The Bishop of Grenoble was in Lyons for an ordination ceremony. He hurried back, but could not obtain permission to see the Pope. . . .

But to come back to Mother Deshayes's visit: God certainly disposed the captain's heart in favor of her and her companion, Madame de Vaulserre. When the latter asked him to point out our convent to the Holy Father sometime when he was walking in the garden, so that he might bless it and the boarding school, the captain said, "Why don't you bring the children here? I would not want the young ladies mingling with the crowd that gathers to see the Holy Father. Perhaps they could see him in a separate room. I will get them in tomorrow at 10 o'clock. They will have a special place."

This was an exciting occasion for the children. Sixty of them, dressed in white, bareheaded, with their black veils on their shoulders ready to be donned for the audience, waved goodbye to Mother Duchesne and filed down from Sainte Marie to the prefecture, accompanied by Mother Deshayes and Madame de Vaulserre. When they arrived there, the captain had gone out, so they went to a nearby church to pray and await his return. Happily his friendliness was unchanged; and when the children had assembled in the room assigned to them, he brought the Pope in. With gentle kindliness the Holy Father laid his hand on the head of each child and gave her his ring to kiss. Then he blessed them all, after telling them what a pleasure it was for him to see "such well-behaved children."

The other members of the household who could not go to the prefecture received the Holy Father's blessing each evening at the windows, for he gave it to the immense crowd that tried to see him when he took his walk between 6 and 7 o'clock. . . . In spite of our distance from the prefecture and the slope of the mountain, we could see him clearly; and we noticed that he looked attentively at our house and seemed to bless it very particularly. . . .

As the laundress for the prefecture is also ours, she brought us a rochet belonging to the Holy Father. We had the consolation of darning the lace, mending the garment, and changing the taffeta lining the cuffs. We have kept the old silk as a precious relic which really touched the Holy Father's chains, for he had worn this garment on the whole trip from Rome. . . . On August 1, feast of St. Peter in Chains, the Pope was obliged to leave at 3 o'clock in the morning with only a few moments' notice. . . . In the bustle of this hurried departure the Pope retained his perfect outward calm, spoke kindly to all, and praised the welcome given him in Grenoble.

The Pope was to be held as a captive at Savona. Going by Valence and Avignon, the little cortege reached there on August 15. That day Philippine wrote to her sister:

I received your letter, *ma bonne Amie*, and put off writing until after Adelaide's departure, also awaiting a good opportunity for sending a letter. You can just imagine what a pleasure it was to see this sister of mine after more than two years of separation from her. And how I enjoyed seeing her happiness in being able to be with her children whom she loves so much! She came on Friday night and stayed with her two little girls; she spent Tuesday and Wednesday at Vizille, then left us on Thursday after dinner. The news she gave me of Augustine was both consoling and disappointing. The main thing is that she is doing well and that both she and her baby are safe. Please give her and her husband my regards and say how happy I am for them.

Camille was kind enough to come to see me yesterday and give me news of you. He repeated what I have so often heard about the zeal, piety, and talents of his brother Noël,[14] and the remarkable merits of Father Rauzan. Do take advantage of his presence in your vicinity. I do want Euphrosine to appreciate him and to stand firm when she leaves school. Her character is so well grounded on principle, I can hope for this; but she has not improved much in thoughtfulness, kindness, and courtesy. I trust we shall easily find a traveling companion for her at the end of September.

No doubt you have heard all the details of the Pope's visit here, his trip to Nice, and the extraordinary welcome they gave him, especially in that city. Everywhere that visit of the Pope has had the effect of a mission. Wherever he went, there was a return to the sacrament of penance and a great demonstration of faith. God has drawn good out of evil. The long experience we have had of His goodness makes us hope He will withhold the arm of His justice and not punish us to the very end.

We are very grateful to you for your solicitude about us, but we are remaining quite calm, just living from day to day. We are children of Divine Providence; God has given an increase to the works of this house without visible means. If He destroys it, He is the Master; so we live in security.

Answering her sister's greeting for the New Year, Philippine wrote on January 10, 1810:

I received your letter, *ma bien bonne Amie*, containing your New Year's wishes. I had hoped to be ahead of you this time, but my position here forces me to set aside my own personal pleasures in order to fulfil duties and obligations much less pleasant but of such a nature that they must come first, since they touch upon the general good of the house. So I trust your heart completely, knowing that it will always welcome the outpourings of my own, since the friendship that unites us is without suspicion and without reserve. Being powerless to give you all I wish for you, I beg God to bless you and your children very particularly, so that the seeds we are sowing in their hearts may bear fruit in His good time and so give you much consolation. This will be your reward for all the care you have lavished, and are still lavishing, on them.

Euphrosine is too strong a character ever to waver in her principles. She does not possess great personal charm, but that is so dangerous, I do not desire it for her. If she is faithful to duty, that is the main thing. With fewer personal attractions she will have more peace. You simply have to be content with what contents God. He did not make all the good people lovable, but He loves them just the same, and He does not change them. I am just giving you a word of warning, lest you expect a great many courtesies and attentions from your daughter. She simply is not observant. One has to suggest things to her, and there is no use expecting from her both the little joys of this life and the great hopes of eternity. When one has the essential, one must be content. Children are entrusted to you in this world just to be prepared for the next. I still prefer Euphrosine, stiff and positive in character, to Amelie, who is often too soft and lazy and who does not work to develop her character, dreading to make the least effort. Euphrosine is meant for great things. Amelie will merely ornament a household, and not without shadows here and there, for she is rather temperamental.

While her judgment about Euphrosine was correct, Mother Duchesne was quite mistaken with regard to Amelie. There was fine stuff in the child, and happily her aunt would see its development. The older girl was finishing her formal schooling that year and leaving Sainte Marie to take her place in the home where she was particularly needed just then. Her departure took place shortly after the following letter was written to her mother by Tante Philippine:

I am so grateful to your husband for giving me news of the baby and also of the godparents chosen. . . . Euphrosine will not be able to take part in the prizes, as they have been retarded six weeks. I do not yet know a good traveling companion for her. I hope she will be a big help to you, relieving you of part of your work and so repaying the care we have bestowed on her. That care has always been lavished on her with earnest affection. Amelie will suffer because of her departure. Although her character is gentler than that of her older sister, I doubt that she would be as helpful to you: she is indolent and not very generous about overcoming this defect. I hope that after she makes her first Communion, and especially after she is confirmed, she will develop more energy. Strength certainly is needed to face life in the world and to stand by right principles, especially in the age in which we live. People seem to be losing all taste for the true joys of mind and heart. Vice is clever at disguising itself. It would be more easily avoided if it showed its real ugliness. I am glad Euphrosine is called to a quiet, laborious life.

In the spring of 1811, Euphrosine fell dangerously ill, and Philippine wrote to Madame Jouve:

Your letter, my dear one, has brought grief to me and to all who know dear Euphrosine, especially Mother Deshayes. She has begun a novena with the entire household for this sick child whom we all love. I rely on prayer for her cure. She will be more fervent than ever after her illness, and you will be doubly indebted for her to the Giver of all gifts. He is making you realize just now that He has only loaned you your children and that they really belong to Him. I beg Him to give you strength in this hard trial. I appreciate your feelings all the more because I have always shared intimately in all your sufferings. . . .

For several years Mother Duchesne had watched eagerly for some sign of a vocation in this favorite niece of hers. Euphrosine had kept her counsel and given no direct hint as to the working of divine grace in her soul, but her secret had been divined by her devoted aunt, who wrote to her mother in May, 1811:

I was waiting for Amelie's home-letter in order to enclose mine in it, but she sent hers off without telling me. Of course, that delayed my answer to you and I would have found this disappointing, had I been obliged to send it by post. Joseph Arbranchand, who is going to carry it, has not quieted all my fears regarding dear Euphrosine. How intimately I share your anxieties and how I desire to ease your suffering! At least I try to do so by praying to God with all the fervor that the sincerest love and interest can inspire. Mother Thérèse shares this interest and presses me for news of your daughter. I know that Mother Barat saw her, but according to my cousin she is not yet in a condition to feel anything but suffering.

When you were so near to losing her, did you not think of offering her to God, even in this world, since human means were powerless to save her for you? Euphrosine has never given me her secret confidences, but I have reason to suspect that she has some idea of the cloister. One day when they were speaking of chastity, she let fall this remark: *That is the virtue I love above all others.* Without letting her realize, you can find out whether my ideas are right and sound out her courage in this matter. Who knows but what some interior struggle may be the cause of this illness.

Amelie is good, but not very pious. I am as eager as you to see her obtain her great desire [of making her first Communion]. The ceremony has been postponed a few days, however, at the urgent request of Monsieur de la Vallette, whose daughter is dying at Avignon. His son-in-law, Monsieur de Vidaud, cannot leave there for some days, but he wants to be present at the first Communion of his own daughter here. Tell Camille how much I shared his anxiety and now share his joy in the recovery of his wife and her mother.

Again in a short note written on New Year's Day, 1812, Philip-

pine expressed the ever deepening affection she felt for her family.
Madame Jouve had paid her a visit shortly before she wrote:

> I have not yet had news of your safe arrival in Lyons, my dear
> Sister, but I like to tell myself that the trip was pleasant and above
> all that the baby did not suffer from the traveling. You are very
> dear to form such wishes for me. One of the wishes I find the
> greatest joy in is that God may let me be helpful to my dear ones,
> and that Euphrosine may fulfill my desire to see her worthy of
> you and a real help in the laborious life you seem destined to
> lead for many a day. Her intellectual development is sufficiently
> advanced. May God grant her that kindliness and cordiality of
> manner which make for happiness both in our own private lives
> and in the social group in which we live.
>
> I have received a letter from Paris which seems to have been
> left at Lyons by Monsieur de Mauduit. I am impatient for news of
> his arrival at Grâne, and still more, of the manner in which he
> takes up his rural occupations again. The thought of that house,
> sheltering so many people and things that are dear to me, is con-
> stantly in my mind, since I know my loved ones there are suffering
> and I can do nothing to ease the pain. . . .

Characteristic of the letters Mother Duchesne wrote to her
family is her silence regarding matters that pertained to her life
within the cloister. There is never any emphasis on the personal.
There is no hint at the difficulties that gave battle daily in her
soul, no selfish enumeration of the fatiguing activities that filled
her days and nights, no mention of the continual round of charities
she performed. She wrote with a simple disregard for self and a
liberty of spirit that sprang from a sense of being an instrument in
God's hands. Buoyant, virile, conscious of her responsibility
toward the children she taught and the family she loved, Philippine
wrote as she was learning to live, with singleness of purpose and
little thought of self. She was learning her lessons the hard way,
but that was of the pattern of her life. St. Madeleine Sophie had
still to urge her to "join recollection, gentleness, humility, and
obedience" to her Lenten fast in 1812.[15] When Philippine found
herself groping her way once more through a fog of interior trials
and personal difficulties and crying out for help,

> Suffer in peace and if possible with love [wrote the Mother
> General]. Oh, if at least the highest part of your soul remained in
> the clear sunlight, as the peak of Mount St. Bernard so often does.
> But courage and confidence! This difficult period will pass, I assure

you. . . . Try to advance along the path of holy detachment. Become gentle, humble, obedient. What risk is there in obeying? It is always the surest way, and you know the other path is not.[16]

She had suggested affectionately some weeks earlier: "If you want to put off your retreat until I reach Sainte Marie, I should be very glad. If, however, your soul is more disposed to solitude during Lent and you can secure the time, then make it. We shall have much work to do when I arrive." [17]

2. 1812—1817

The Lord is compassionate and merciful;
patient and plenteous in mercy.

Gradual, Mass of the Sacred Heart

DURING THE OPENING MONTHS OF 1812 the convent of Sainte Marie was severely tried by illness. The cold was intense, and the old building was damp and drafty. Nuns and children alike suffered from heavy colds, rheumatism, pneumonia, tuberculosis. Entries in the *Journal* show the number whom Mother Duchesne cared for that winter. From January to May the infirmaries were always occupied. When death came for the Countess de Vaulserre on February 12, Mother Duchesne wrote into the *Journal* a eulogy of her charities and her virtues which tells why this woman of fifty-three years, so distinguished by birth, education, and social position, was the admiration of the whole community, whose "watchdog" she had constituted herself in 1804.

In April the convent was in grief again at the death of Marie Julie Pont, just twenty-two years old, who made her vows on her deathbed. It was hard for Mother Duchesne to lose this novice who had been her pupil and had given promise of a fervent religious life. As Mother Deshayes was often ailing, the responsibility for the entire household fell to Philippine. "Courage and confidence," she repeated, as she read Mother Barat's letter over and over again. "This difficult period will pass, I assure you." And it did pass with the arrival of the Mother General in May for a stay of sixteen months at Sainte Marie.

"We shall have much work to do when I arrive," she had written, and Philippine had wondered what the foundress meant by that sentence. She knew that the Society was faced with serious problems, but she became aware of the gravity of the situation only when Mother Barat confided to her the tangled details and asked her help.

The Society was still without rules and constitutions of its own. Mother Barat had worked on these with Mother Duchesne on former visits to Grenoble and with Fathers Varin and Barat at Amiens recently, striving to combine in them the apostolic ardor of Ignatius with the contemplative spirit of Teresa. But the Abbé de Saint-Estève had presented a fantastic compilation of his own, drawn from divergent sources. Copies of this weird document had been sent by Madame Baudemont to the several houses of the Society, and the Mother General, journeying from one to another, watched the reaction when it was read to the professed nuns.

In the community at Sainte Marie there was disappointment, repugnance, near-bewilderment. Where was that precious thing they all desired—that spirit of ardent love, adoration, consecration, and total sacrifice that flowed from devotion to the Sacred Heart? Above all, where was devotion to the Sacred Heart? St. Madeleine Sophie assured them that this was but a tentative draft and begged them to trust a little longer and to pray much more. With Mother Duchesne she discussed the matter more freely and explained the reasons for delay. The Abbé de Saint-Estève was both dangerous and determined. He had already caused such trouble to Mother Julie Billiart and the Congregation of Notre Dame as to force the new order to leave Amiens for Namur in Belgium, in order to escape his domination. Mother Barat hoped to save her religious family from a similar fate by retiring into obscurity. Father Varin approved this course, but advised her to continue her work on the constitutions and rule while at Grenoble. This was the work the foundress hinted at to Philippine.

An unexpected turn of events occurred shortly after Mother Barat reached Sainte Marie. The Abbé de Saint-Estève was arrested in Amiens and carried off to prison in Paris. He had run foul of episcopal authority, and the imperial police were glad to put one more priest in confinement. But to his friends and followers all this added the glory of a "confessor of the faith" to the abbé's reputation and strengthened Madame Baudemont's resolution to have his rule accepted by the Society or to withdraw the order from Mother Barat's jurisdiction. To keep the Society intact and to preserve in full vigor the true spirit of the Sacred Heart was the object of all the prayers and efforts of the foundress during the sixteen months she spent at Sainte Marie. And it was to Mother Duchesne she turned for help and support in this trying situation.

Her presence was a tremendous joy to Philippine. The old intimacy was renewed; the things that could never be put into writing were so easily expressed in conversation, talked over, laughed over—for the tragedies of daily life are often comedies in retrospect. The project of the foreign mission was often broached by Philippine, but the answer was always the same, "Not yet," and the reasons against it were numerous enough to form a litany. One of these reasons was Philippine's health. Mother Barat had cause to worry at times about that. She had frequently warned her not to overtax her strength. Writing from Paris in July, 1811, she had begged Emilie Giraud to "pray for your dear Mother Duchesne. She is not at all well," adding that she might even change her plans and go at once to Grenoble on that account. Seeing her going about her multiple duties, tall, straight, resilient even under the pressure of the heaviest work, few in the community suspected that physical suffering was becoming a companion with whom she would travel through many years of her life. Yet rheumatism was at work in her strong active body, affecting her hands particularly, as she admitted to her sister, Madame Jouve, by way of excuse: "It is a long time since I wrote to you, as I have had a very painful condition in the fingers of my right hand." [18] And Mother Barat lamented later on: "Our Philippine is unable to write."

Sometimes Philippine enjoyed a moment of satisfaction during this year, when she could have her own way in caring for the Mother General, and sometimes she was firmly checked. The saint wrote in November, 1812, to Mother Giraud:

> If you want to know where I am lodged just now, it is in the little room adjoining the novitiate. Mother Duchesne, who must be obeyed sometimes, has had a fireplace made in it and has had the wall knocked down that separated it from the room on the other side. . . . I am quite alone in this part of the house. Mother Duchesne did not like to leave me alone this way, but she had no choice about that.

There were days when Philippine's heart was heavy with anxiety about members of her family who were in the Russian campaign. André Perier in the quartermaster's department was less exposed to danger than young Amédée de Mauduit in the artillery. For four months there had been no direct word from him, while all France knew that tragedy had stalked Napoleon's line of march.

Good news came in November, when a letter from Amédée himself reached Grâne, telling the family with just a little swagger that he had come safely through the battle of Smolensk and the siege of Moscow, where he had "commanded the artillery and bombarded the enemy for several hours *avec une vivacité sans égale.*" [19] Tante Philippine was grateful to the Sacred Heart for this report and for the bravery of the lad who so distinguished himself as to gain his captaincy at the age of twenty-two.

In December Mother Josephine Bigeu was called to Grenoble to take charge of the novitiate, which the Mother General herself had been directing for some months, for illness had now incapacitated Mother Deshayes. Among the postulants who entered in 1813 were Lucille Mathevon, a former pupil of Sainte Marie, and Hélène Dutour, a young woman from Savoy. These are names to remember, for they are linked inseparably with Philippine Duchesne's. As novices they learned to know her well, to see her as St. Madeleine Sophie described her at this very time to Mother Giraud:

> We have had the blessing of the cross, too. Several of the children ill; eight, I believe, in the infirmary now. Your dear Mother Duchesne spends her days and nights there, teaches her classes, manages the house without constraint and almost without being overburdened. What a valiant woman! . . . No, she will not leave the mountain—we just could not get along without her. If anyone is transferred, it will be Mother Deshayes.[20]

Philippine's continued residence at Sainte Marie was both a comfort and a solace to her father. He had returned to Grenoble with Duchesne soon after Melanie's entrance at the Visitation in Romans and taken up residence at the Perier home. With the reorganization of the local barristers' association in December, 1810, he was again chosen as its president and reappointed in 1812.[21] He became once more a familiar figure at the *Palais de Justice*, on the Grande Rue, and Place Grenette. But age was beginning to tell on him, though his white hair and careful gait added dignity to his appearance. He was still the forceful, outspoken legal expert, but he had mellowed so noticeably that Philippine could recognize the stirring of faith that had lain dormant in his soul for half a century. From the tall windows of his rooms at Number 5, Place Saint-André, he could look out across the river and see Sainte Marie perched high up on the mountain side. Sometimes he climbed the steep ascent to visit his daughter and give her news of the scattered family. They were concerned about Madame Jouve when Philippine wrote to her in the summer of 1813:

I have learned from several people who have seen you that you are much thinner and seem to be pregnant again, and I realize that this condition is a new cross for you. For no matter how much one loves the children God sends, still there is fear at their coming, a certain right and natural dread of suffering and of the burden which a large family entails. I sincerely sympathize with you in this, and I do so want to lighten your cross in every way I can. Here is a thought that occurred to me: I can arrange my business affairs in such a way as to increase my income a little.[22] Then after this spring I can take care of the tuition of Constance, if you will put her here at school with us, or of Amélie's, if you think Constance is too young to leave you. You know with what sincerity my superiors allow me to make this offer. We realize that a mother who raises such a large family and directs a household can have very little time left for the many lessons necessary for boys and girls of different ages. We are only sorry that your little boys cannot also become a part of our family at Sainte Marie.

And again, a few weeks later:

Yesterday I received a letter and package from Adelaide; but as I wrote to her not so long ago, I shall devote these free moments to you. My heart must tell you how I share in all your sufferings. I trust that God, who gives you little rest in this life, will make up generously to you in the next.

Adelaide consoled me by telling me how good your children are, how much less troublesome to you. I hope the one you are now carrying may be a *Joseph* or a *Bernard*.[23] God blesses large families; and when He does great things, it is often one of the youngest in a family that He chooses, because His ways are often just the opposite of ours: He chooses the weak and the little to confound the strong. If at this very moment you bear within you a saint, how fully you will be repaid for the additional hardships!

Yesterday I had the pleasant surprise of a visit from Father. I found him looking as young as ever, but I noticed that his legs are becoming stiff and it is difficult for him to go down the stairs. Still I just cannot believe that he is growing old. His kindness makes me wish he would never die, but unhappily there is no earthly joy untroubled by the thought of death. I have no time to write to the girls. I received their letters. Give them and their father many affectionate messages for me.

In September Mother Barat left Sainte Marie with Mother Deshayes and traveled north to Besançon, then on to the chateau of Chevroz, where Father Varin was awaiting them at the home of his sister. The time had come for the final drafting of the constitutions and rules over which they had prayed and labored intermittently for nearly ten years. For many weeks founder and foundress worked steadily in the solitude of that lovely country place, while news of military disaster echoed through France and defeat at Leipzig opened the way to invasion by Napoleon's enemies.

Philippine had no news from the Mother General through the autumn months. She bore the responsibility, but not the name, of superior at Sainte Marie and prepared as best she could for any emergency that might arise as a consequence of invasion. Grenoble was exposed to attack and poorly prepared to resist. Austrians, Bavarians, and troops from Italy were reported massing on the frontier. And in the midst of this anxiety there came a tremendous personal joy. Young Euphrosine Jouve confided to Tante Philippine her desire to enter the novitiate at Sainte Marie and begged her help in overcoming the objections of her idolizing parents. Praying for guidance and self-restraint, Philippine began on October 29, 1813, a spiritual campaign that would cover the next twelve months.

> My beloved Sister,
>
> I sent you a letter by Adelaide and have had no news from you since she left. I hope you will answer me regarding Constance, whom I asked you to send us in Henriette's place.[24] Certainly she is well cared for at home and better off there than elsewhere. But realizing that you are so burdened with cares, I wanted to help you, as a devoted sister, and if possible to do more than ever for you.
>
> For a long time I have suspected the secret yearnings of your eldest daughter, though she tried to keep them well hidden from me. And this was the subject of a suggestion I made to you when she was so ill—a suggestion which, I was told, caused you much pain. Yet what I merely guessed then is a reality today. Euphrosine wishes to leave you, not for a human husband and an earthly home, but to give herself to God, who has given her everything she has. Only recently did she confide to me her desire. Knowing her love for Mother Deshayes, I told her that dear Mother is no longer superior of this house. That fact, however, did not alter her desire to enter here. She has but one obstacle to overcome—her love for you and the pain she feels in trying to speak to you of this matter.

I have promised to do so for her, knowing, of course, that I speak to a loving mother, but still more to a Christian mother who is accustomed to the most heroic acts of resignation. I am not going to preach to you. I prefer to let grace plead—that grace which is active in the generous hearts of both mother and child. If the uncertainty of political conditions frightens you, you must realize that in such a contingency we have the understanding that we shall be free in case of a catastrophe. [Fragment missing] And how many events in the meantime may happen to assure more stability! Besides, is there real stability in anything under the sun?

Forgive my straightforwardness if it wounds you. Accustomed as I am to see God as the only end of all things, I did not think it would offend you to suggest Him as the one end for which your beloved daughter was created. I must stop hurriedly and embrace you tenderly.

Madame Jouve was evidently wounded. Her reply gave Philippine small satisfaction. In fact, the mention of Euphrosine's vocation called forth an unexpected threat, which Philippine parried with some hard facts about young Amelie Jouve:

I received your letter and I am really vexed that you refuse to send us Constance. If you withdraw Amelie in the spring, I fear she will not be much help to you because of her character, which is often sullen, peevish, and intractable. Her piety is undeveloped, and it is very difficult to influence her as she does not give anyone an opening and sets a standard for herself that is very comfortable.

One cannot reproach her for not studying; she has great facility in that line, but she does her work carelessly, as you can see by her writing and spelling, though she could do much better. She would like to neglect everything for reading, which is an easy occupation. I was obliged to put a limit on that and forbid her teachers to give her as many books as she desired, for I have seen the bad effects of immoderate taste for reading. Nothing dries up the unction of piety as this does.

This will take the place of a report. All yours,

PHILIPPINE

Meanwhile at Sainte Marie a change had taken place. The work at Chevroz had been completed, and St. Madeleine Sophie, on her way to Amiens, paid a brief visit to her family at Joigny. From there she wrote to tell Mother Duchesne that Mother Deshayes would not return to Grenoble and that Mother Bigeu would replace her as superior. Mother Duchesne was authorized to install her in her new office and accompany her when she went to call on

Father Rey, who was then acting as ecclesiastical superior of the convent.

> This new Mother Superior [wrote Mother Barat] will find in you, my dear Daughter, what I have always found—a support that will lighten the burden our Lord lays on her and help her carry it. [As assistant] be cordial and active in your watchfulness within the community. Inform your superior faithfully of any abuse you perceive, in order that she may check it.
>
> During the course of the coming year we shall have the joy of being together again. I shall then bring you the results of the work we have completed, which will, I trust, be for your greater good. Meanwhile, pray for me, as I do for you with all the power I possess.[25]

Following the instructions she had received, Mother Duchesne assembled the community on the morning of November 21. After the customary prayer to the Holy Spirit she read them a letter from Mother Barat announcing the appointment of Mother Bigeu as superior of Sainte Marie. A member of the community noted:

> During the afternoon recreation, without any other ceremony, the Mother Assistant came into the room and knelt before the Superior, kissing her hand in token of respect and submission. We all followed her example. Mother Bigeu received us with that sweet cordiality that is so natural to her. Then the recreation went on joyously. There was no more ceremony than that. But in the evening we had a little assembly in the refectory in honor of the renovation of vows that day.

As the year 1814 opened, Philippine was still pleading with Madame Jouve to give Euphrosine at least a chance to try out her vocation under Mother Bigeu's direction. Her letter of January 2 comes straight from a heart that has supernaturalized its deepest affections, yet lost none of its human tenderness.

> MY VERY DEAR SISTER,
> Through the sorrow that appears in your letter, I see the same virtue that shone out in the one you wrote me when it seemed as if God were taking your daughter from you in a much harder way than He is asking her today. I marveled at the fulness of your resignation in that sacrifice, though I have never mothered a child. God seems eager to increase your merits by facing you with this sacrifice a second time and so doubling your reward.
> I will not dwell on the words of a father who was so keenly

afflicted in his children, friends, goods, and personal health: "The Lord gave; the Lord took away; blessed be His holy Name. If we have received good things from Him, shall we not also receive evil things?" If a loving mother was offered the most attractive prince in the world as a fiancé for her daughter, but one who would take her far away, the mother would forget the pain of separation and think only of the illustrious alliance and speak of it with joy. Why is Jesus Christ the only one to whom it is so terrible to give oneself? Where is our faith? Where is the fruit of all our experience? . . .

You speak of her health—but that broke under the strain of hiding from you her great desire. And if God gives you the strength to be generous in offering Him your daughter, you will see her soon restored to health. When leaving here, she had a nervous spell which I thought was the result of excessive emotion.

Still, while I plead for her, I put myself in your place, as far as natural sentiments are concerned, and I realize what a weight of sorrow this project must cause you, especially in the case of that one of your children from whom you expected so much help. You can be sure, however, that this trial comes straight from God. Euphrosine is not the kind of person to be influenced—she decides for herself. God Himself gave her a vocation; she kept it secret. If I surmised it, that was the result of my observations of her character and the tastes I perceived in her. I knew that if she put no obstacles to the inspiration of grace, all this would lead her to choose the cloister, with freedom from marriage and the opportunity of helping save souls. Do you think she has made a poor choice in preferring Jesus Christ to any man? the riches of heaven to those of earth? occupations that draw us upward to those that fasten us to earth?

There is nothing low or human in Euphrosine's views, and there is no outside force urging her on. Her desires come from God, who makes us realize that He directs hearts as He wills. Is she not fortunate to have been found worthier than others to be united to Him, to have been given such a privilege?

Far from being displeased with you, I share your suffering, while at the same time I rejoice in a vocation whose value I realize. I hope that when you and your husband have recovered your composure, you will consider the fact that your children belong to God before they belong to you. You would have given Him Henri, so your husband told me, and He asks for Euphrosine. Don't earthly sovereigns take your children without consulting you? The mystery of the necessity of suffering in this world is hard to understand, but it is inevitable.

Within a few weeks Philippine was able to discuss the matter with her sister personally. Their father's health had been causing anxiety. Early in February Madame de Mauduit came from Grâne and Madame Jouve from Lyons to care for him. Philippine, too, was allowed to visit him and help with the nursing, as the rule of cloister had not yet been made binding in the Society. One little note of hers tells what was in her heart as she ministered to him, knelt beside him, prayed for him, and brought him back to God. Addressing her note to Madame Jouve, "at her father's apartment, Grenoble," on March 2, she wrote:

> The news I received today of Father's condition grieves me. I think one of us should spend the night at his bedside. You watched last night, Amelie is sick; so it is my turn. I can do it, as I have Mother Bigeu's permission. If you foresee that he is going to have a bad night or that he should receive Holy Viaticum, send for me before 8:30, for I shall have no companion this evening. Send me word whether the priest visited him this morning, and do not defer the sacramental helps of the Church. That is our principal duty, and also say a word about God from time to time. Even the most pious sick persons need this help, for illness exhausts them and the devil prowls around, seeking his prey.

Pierre-François Duchesne lingered through the month of March—that last month of Napoleon's empire. Madame Jouve was obliged to return home, lest she be caught in Grenoble by invading troops. All France was in turmoil, with Napoleon fighting a coalition now sure of victory, with the English in Bordeaux by March 12, and the Austrians, victorious in Italy, pushing through Switzerland into old Dauphiny. The courageous defense directed by General Marchand was broken down before the close of the month. The enemy moved forward to take Voreppe on April 2 and to enter Grenoble ten days later. The empire had already collapsed in defeat at the battle of Paris, which was begun the very day Pierre-François Duchesne was buried. A loyal, upright figure had passed from the scene, leaving a void in many hearts, but greatest in the heart of his eldest daughter.

A relative calm was soon restored in Grenoble. The municipal council drew up its declaration of allegiance to the Bourbon Louis XVIII on April 13, 1814, and among its signers was Augustin Perier.[26] His presence had been a support for Philippine and her sisters through these weeks of personal sorrow and civic upheaval, and she had hoped that both Augustin and her brother might be influenced by a realization of the grace given to Pierre-François Duchesne. Her father's conversion was a triumph of faith and trust and prayer made powerful by the complete sacrifice of self, but Philippine wrote of it to Madame Jouve with quiet restraint on April 18:

> I do not want to keep you waiting longer for news, so I shall write. Our brother leaves next week for Paris. He will give you all the details you desire. Amelie was detained by God's snow and by the troops that barricaded the other route, so she left only today. She and I were together at Father's side when he died. His agony was long and painful; for several days he did not speak, his body no longer functioned, yet his soul was at times a prey to fears. He had received extreme unction in good time and had a second and a third absolution with the plenary indulgence. The funeral was very simple in view of conditions here and the prohibition against the ringing of bells that day. It was March 29. I trust he is with God.
>
> Now that all is quiet again, I repeat my request for Constance. I think M. Durand, who is certainly coming to see his daughter, would be glad to bring her. He is a very nice gentleman. No one expressed more sincere sympathy to me than he at the time of Father's death. If you are generous enough to let Euphrosine come with Constance, you will have the merit of mothers who willingly offer their children to God. But I leave this to God's grace. I shall write at length and send it by our brother.

The casual mention of M. Durand is interesting. His daughter Caroline was a pupil at Sainte Marie at this time, and her older sister Coralie had been at school there with Euphrosine Jouve and Louise de Vidaud. Had Hippolyte Duchesne met her in the convent parlor on one of his rare visits to his sister Philippine, or at the Jouve home in Lyons? Evidently M. Durand considered Duchesne a suitable match for Coralie, in spite of the fact that the young lawyer had no practical religious faith.

With the settlement of her father's estate Philippine found herself again in possession of an inheritance which she was free to use at will, for the Society to which she belonged was not yet a fully constituted religious order. Her first impulse, however, was to consult the Mother General on the subject. The advice she received was characteristic of the saint:

> If I were in your place, I would save the money in order to use it later on for the greater good of your family. For example, if

Euphrosine becomes a religious, why not assure a life annuity to her? Then, too, it would be astonishing if, out of the eight Lebrument girls, not one of them had a religious vocation. It would be a good thing to dower any of them, and your family would certainly applaud this use of your inheritance. Suppose none of them became nuns, they would get married, and you could help those who needed it. I assure you that helping young couples who desire to establish homes for themselves is a better work than many people realize.[27]

Saint Madeleine Sophie wrote these lines at Amiens where for some months she had been watching and praying for the Society, for France, and for the Church. The fall of Napoleon had put an end to both the captivity of the Pope and the dispersion of the Fathers of the Faith. Father Varin went quickly into action, visiting the convents he had helped to found. Ten years had passed since he had paid his first visit to Sainte Marie. Now he was experiencing some of the same eager anxiety he had roused in the soul of Philippine Duchesne when he teased her impatience by his casual deliberation. He had hoped the Holy Father would act promptly, once he reached Rome. Two months passed. Then on August 7, octave day of the feast of St. Ignatius Loyola, Pope Pius VII promulgated the bull *Sollicitudo omnium ecclesiarum*, revoking the brief of Clement XIV and re-establishing the Society of Jesus throughout the Church and the world. The venerable Pierre Joseph Picot de Clorivière was named superior of the order in France. For forty years he had kept intact the Jesuit tradition. Now within two months he admitted nearly seventy novices into the Society. The greater number of these were former Fathers of the Faith, including Fathers Varin, Roger, Barat, and many others who had befriended the little group of women who were struggling to become the Society of the Sacred Heart.

The re-establishment of the Jesuits had far-reaching consequences for the Society. Up to this time they had lived under the rule of St. Ignatius, as far as this rule could be adapted to their vocation. Their spiritual life had been built on Ignatian principles. They were to experience continued guidance from the faithful friends who had entered the Ignatian company and to enjoy the spiritual help and direction of a countless number of fervent Jesuits who became their staunch supporters. There was not one among them who admired the Society of Jesus more than Mother Duchesne, and her admiration would only increase when she saw them at work on the American frontier. But foreign missions seemed a very remote possibility in the autumn of 1814. Conditions within the little order were strained. Through the influence of the Abbé de Saint-Estève the convent at Ghent withdrew from the general government. Some of the religious stationed there set up an independent institution, while the majority returned to Amiens. Following this unhappy episode Mother Barat was critically ill, but the five loyal convents carried on their work with courage and fidelity, knowing little of the danger that threatened them. At Sainte Marie all went on as usual in peace and charity and plenty of hard work.

There was some social excitement in Grenoble that autumn of 1814. Plans for Coralie Durand's marriage to young Duchesne had taken shape. Relatives from far and near gathered at the Perier home in Grande Rue or at the Teisseire house in the Rue des Vieux Jesuites, where there was a new baby girl, Louise-Philippine. Singly or in groups they came to call at Sainte Marie and inform Philippine of the least details of the event. When she learned that Jean-Joseph Jouve was coming from Lyons, she made bold to suggest that he should bring Euphrosine and little Constance with him, and he did so. Philippine appreciated what a sacrifice her sister had made and wrote encouragingly:

MY LOVED SISTER,

The pleasure of seeing Euphrosine has not kept me from realizing and sharing the pain you have felt in giving her up. We can only trust that it is all for the greater glory of God, and that the Master who repays a hundredfold will shower His graces upon you and your whole family. Euphrosine still seems rather strained. She says she is quite happy and I believe her character is free from pretense. I had been told that she had got over her stiff manner, but she has not. I notice it particularly with people she knows only slightly. This defect is hidden by so many other good qualities, I feel she is a subject of great promise. Her sister Constance is very happy; she gazes at her lovingly and is kept on her best behavior all the time.

The wedding took place this morning, and since then I have seen your husband only for a moment to hear about it. I very much fear that on one side God had not reason to be pleased in the matter of religious duties. I had hinted at this in letters, but I got no reply, so I do not know the result of my efforts. We can only trust that the future may bring an improvement in this matter.[28]

Mother Bigeu sends you her regards. She learned that Euphrosine wrote you that she [Mother Bigeu] did not want her to go to the wedding. She simply said she thought it better for her not to go; and besides, Euphrosine was not invited. Duchesne had told me two days beforehand, with regard to Caroline Durand, that the young girls were not invited to the wedding. I am sure your daughter has told you all about her visits [to the relatives in Grenoble].

In spite of her generosity in sacrifice, Euphrosine's mother was most unhappy about her daughter's entrance at Sainte Marie and wrote quite frankly, even perhaps harshly about it. Philippine tried to console and strengthen her with all the love and sympathy her heart felt and her pen could express:

Never worry about my sentiments in your regard, my beloved Sister. Though I attributed your silence to heart-suffering rather than to your many occupations, I really was neither surprised nor put out. For while as a religious I marvel at the work of grace in your daughter and the faith that gave you courage enough to consent to her departure, yet as sister and close friend I share your suffering and beg God to pour healing balm on the wound He Himself has inflicted by asking this sacrifice. Your entire family will gain grace and merit from it.

When Euphrosine left school, I knew that many people thought she would not persevere [in her religious vocation], but that was because of the cordial manner I begged her to cultivate, especially with our kind relatives. I had been distressed by the stiff and abrupt way she acted with Madame de Rollin. I urged her to improve, not only for her own sake but for the honor of religious life. So many people believe that a nun cannot be her frank and affable self with her family.

Euphrosine is getting along nicely; she has a lively manner. She wanted to keep secret her intended entrance into the novitiate, but everybody knows about it now, thanks to the industry of Duchesne and M. Durand [his father-in-law]. That added to the gossip that spread the rumor that she was either hesitating—because she did not want to explain why she was waiting—or that she was too fitted for the world to give herself to God. All this gossip made no impression on me, and I find Euphrosine, just as I expected, firm in her resolve, but without that enthusiasm which is often the effect of nature rather than of grace.

As to her tender love for you, have no doubt of it. She may have had strength and courage enough to hide it from you, but the tears she has shed over your letters—and these she cannot simulate—show the depth of her affection for you, her beloved mother. As to her singing in the coach, I neither saw nor heard that—but people do put such mean interpretations on actions.

Do realize this, that neither Father Fauvet [29] nor any of us made up that vocation; but I surmised it a long time ago, as you yourself could have understood from the letter I wrote you when she recovered from that dangerous illness. She never gave me the slightest confidence in the matter, but judging from things she said and preferences she expressed when she was a pupil here, I drew this conclusion. God always gives natural inclinations toward the things for which He destines a soul. She has great strength of character and she needed this in order to leave such loving parents. She had no attraction for married life. Several times she said, "The virtue I love most of all to hear about is virginity." At times she aspired to teaching the poor and even to martyrdom. . . . If you never heard her speak of her vocation, do not be astonished. When the desires of one's heart call for separation from a dearly loved family, it is not easy to speak of them. The heart suffers, knowing it must cause suffering. . . .

Will you not have the courage to change your decision about not allowing her to take the religious costume for a long time? . . . She will not be any more bound to us by wearing the habit, and with us the time of probation is longer than at the Visitation. Tell me your wish in this matter.

Euphrosine entered the novitiate at Sainte Marie on Christmas day, 1814, with Louise Rambaud, Octavie Berthold, and Josephine Meneyrond. Louise, be it recalled, was the imp who had strewn the bits of paper on Mother Duchesne's skirt to secure evidence of her nightlong prayer. Octavie and Josephine would both come to the American mission, but in very different roles. Together they received the habit on Easter Sunday, 1815, Euphrosine changing her name to Aloysia out of devotion to the young Jesuit saint, Aloysius Gonzaga. Soon the new novices began to help in the boarding school, as was the custom then. Mother Duchesne watched with satisfaction the ease with which "Madame Aloysia" took up her work.[30] These were happy months.

There was sharp anxiety, however, when Napoleon returned to France with his heroics and showmanship. Landing in Provence, he took the Alpine route that brought him through Vizille and into Grenoble in triumph. The people of Dauphiny had, to a great extent, been taken in by fair words and the promise of a resurgence of liberty. The road to Paris lay open, and by the middle of April not a Bourbon could be found in France.

Turmoil again, and the call to arms! Mid-June saw the French troops cross the Belgian frontier. The Hundred Days were drawing to a close at Waterloo. By June 18 all was over, and Napoleon was back in Paris three days later. In the Representative Assembly there, it was a deputy from Isère, one Antoine-Louis-Hippolyte Duchesne, who made the formal proposal that the Emperor be asked to abdicate.[31] Strange turning of the tables this. But peace was not yet won. The Austrians, coming in from Switzerland, were threatening Grenoble when Philippine wrote to Madame Jouve on July 4:

> I received your letter and was considering it quite unnecessary, for at the moment there was talk of nothing but peace terms and arrangements. Now a proclamation has been made by the general, who exhorts all to aid in the defense and says the enemy is at hand. They are trying to convince him that without troops and with only a handful of national guards, resistance is impossible; and it seems as if the best we can hope for is favorable conditions from the enemy. I have tried, however, to plan for the departure of your children, while other people are asking a safe refuge with us; and their departure will take place, if that is at all possible. But without coach, without horses, and perhaps with the city gates closed—I do not know whether the project will succeed. And even if there is a coach, what traveling companions your children will have! It would be equally futile for you to attempt to come for them, as you could not get through. But try not to worry, if possible. Very soon you will have news of us either at Lyons or at Valence.

Happily the nuns were not obliged to evacuate Sainte Marie. After a courageous attempt to withstand the attacking forces, the city capitulated on July 9. Although the terms imposed by the enemy were not easy, this second occupation of Dauphiny by the Allies was of short duration. Before the winter snows blocked the roads again, the foreign troops had been withdrawn. But the returning Bourbons were not popular, nor did they bring real peace to France. The Church, however, could now enjoy a certain measure of freedom, and this meant renewed activity among the many groups that were working to restore Christian life and worship to the country and establish the schools that were so sadly needed.

The constitutions and rules of the Society, elaborated at Chevroz, had not yet been adopted, but the influence of Mother Barat's sanctity was working silently. The collapse of Saint-Estève's scheme to control the order gave the foundress an opportunity to convoke the Second General Council to meet in Paris in November, 1815. Two professed religious from each of the five houses were invited to form the deliberative group. Mothers Bigeu and Duchesne traveled from Grenoble in late October by way of Lyons. At last Philippine was to visit her sister's home for a day or two and meet the little nephews and nieces she had not seen before. She set out on short notice, as nuns so frequently do. Madame Jouve was at Grâne with the younger children, but she came home as quickly as the diligence would carry her. Meanwhile Josephine de Savoye-Rollin was welcoming Philippine with warm affection, and there was too little time for all they had to tell each other. The nuns were soon on their way to Paris. From there Philippine sent her sister a delightful letter on November 2, crowded with love and gratitude, comments on persons and things, and a few afterthoughts, as was her way in letters:

> Through your care, my dear Sister, and that of my kind brother I made the trip without inconvenience. I left my first traveling companions with transports of delight, those of the boat with great joy, and those of the stagecoach without regret. The officer of the engineer corps was the best of the lot; people with education respect the outward conventions, at least. Here I am in Paris, I am sorry to say. With what difficulty the love of solitude adjusts itself to the noise and bustle of a great city! The soul finds itself under a kind of tyranny. Try to rejoice with Euphrosine in the happiness she is experiencing. The joys of the spirit are as far above other pleasures as heaven is above earth. You have done more for her in giving your consent to her reception of the habit than if you had made her a queen.
>
> I was worn out by my first ventures into the world during my short stay at your home. But I was so happy to know your charming family, and it was a great pleasure for me to see you. I do not know when that will happen again, but I do not want to give you so much trouble. It pained me when I realized how much inconvenience I had caused you. I think I left a little combination knife and corkscrew at your house. Do save it for me. . . .
> P.S. Madame de Rollin came to see me before you arrived. A thousand affectionate messages to your kind husband and the children. The lunch you provided was sufficient for the entire trip to Paris, and your warm shawl gave the cold no chance to reach me. I did not take it off the whole way. May I keep it until the return journey? Without it I certainly would have suffered.

"The return journey?" For Philippine Duchesne there would

be no return to Lyons, and Grenoble, and her loved Sainte Marie. Her life was to be a forward course until she reached the Indian frontier in midwestern America.

In Paris Philippine, seeing St. Madeleine Sophie for the first time in two years, marked the effect of trial and strain and illness on her, and marveled at her energy and gaiety. She also met old friends among the council members—Emilie Giraud, her first pupil at Sainte Marie after the Revolution, Henriette Girard, who had been such a delightfully gullible postulant in 1805, Mothers Grosier and Deshayes, who both shared her love for Sainte Marie. Philippine's greeting to Mother Giraud gave the whole group a good laugh: "Well, Emilie, we certainly are going on the foreign missions, and you are one of the group." Emilie, taken aback, shifted her position a little and said something about "wanting only the will of God."

"What?" questioned Mother Duchesne with vivacity. "Is this all that is left of your courageous ardor of long ago? What has become of your glowing zeal for the salvation of the savages?" And after a pause, "There, now, I understand. You are too fond of your little house at Niort and of Mother Geoffroy." [32] Mother Geoffroy herself was present, and others whose names were as familiar to Philippine as hers was to them—Mothers Desmarquest, de Charbonnel, and Eugenie de Gramont. Her intense love for the Society made it a delight for her to share the friendship and labor of these women who were, like herself, the foundation stones of the order.

The council opened on the feast of All Saints, with Mass in the chapel of the Jesuit house in the Rue des Postes and a sermon on devotion to the Sacred Heart by Father de Clorivière. The meetings were held at the convent of St. Thomas of Villanova, where the religious had found hospitality. Mother Barat presided. Father Varin proposed, one by one, the statutes drawn up at Chevroz. The members of the council examined, discussed, and at length adopted all unanimously. The result of these conferences gave the order a rule that breathes the spirit of Christ's own Heart, a way of life by which successive generations of Religious of the Sacred Heart have lived for nearly a century and a half.

The all-pervading thought and purpose is stated in the opening sentence of that rule: "This little Society is wholly consecrated to the glory of the Sacred Heart of Jesus and to the propagation of Its worship." The means of personal perfection proposed to the members are union and conformity with this Divine Heart by prayer and the imitation of Its virtues. The work of education and all other zealous activities must be fed from the deep springs of interior life. Action and contemplation must be so mingled that the one is but the external manifestation of the other, the work being enriched and glorified by the prayer which directs the simplest and most ordinary actions to the glory of the Sacred Heart. By the *Constitutions* the authority of the Superior General was established once and for always; the name and spirit of the Sacred Heart came to reign throughout "this little Society," as Mother Barat ever called it.

With the adoption of the new rules and regulations, the obligations of religious poverty had to be examined by each member of the council before the formal renewal of vows closing the assembly. Mother Duchesne turned again to St. Madeleine Sophie for advice. She knew that, with the exception of Mother Eugénie de Gramont, she was the only one of the group who had any wealth to contribute to the order, as the others all came from families completely impoverished by the French Revolution. For the sake of the Society she resolved to sacrifice the satisfaction of giving further financial help to her family. On December 14 she wrote to Madame Jouve:

> As I am about to renew my vows and hope to do so with more peace and security under a stable constitution, I want to regulate my temporal affairs in such a manner as to preclude all anxiety of conscience. It would have been a great satisfaction for me, in breaking completely with the world, to have left my sisters in easier circumstances. But Divine Providence, which does all things well, has willed to detach you from worldly goods that are of little real value, and allowed that I, who have few personal needs, should not be at liberty to strip myself entirely of my possessions because of those who are associated with me. I have only been able to arrange matters in such a way that if nothing unforeseen happens to the Society, Constance and Josephine can complete their education at Sainte Marie during my lifetime. Wishing to give my godson [Henri Jouve] a little mark of affection, I am going to ask my brother to send you a note for a thousand francs from me. He will address it to your husband without knowing its purpose, and you will be careful to keep this secret from him and also from Henri. It is best that way; then no one will talk about it.
>
> If, against all probability, Tante Gueymar dies without a will, I shall make no claim against her estate, and you will receive my share. You may be surprised at my foreseeing such a case, but what I mean is that I am renouncing the right to this inherit-

ance, and if the case should occur, then my three married sisters would take my place.

I received the bill of exchange which your husband sent me and cashed it. I beg you to tell him so and thank him again for all his kindness. If there is any money left over after our purchases are made, he could put it into a little sealed packet and give it to the Misses Fonsala, who will in turn give it to the first one of our nuns who passes through Lyons. I do not know yet whether it will be Mother Bigeu or I, nor whether we shall stop, owing to the feasts and the bad weather. What detains us, and may continue to do so, is the foundation of a convent of the Sacred Heart in Paris. It cannot be made just now, but we must secure a house, and that has not been done yet. In any case, do not write to me again before hearing from me. If I do not see you before New Year's Day, find here my greetings and good wishes for the coming year.

I am all yours, and I embrace the children.

PHILIPPINE DUCHESNE

On the day after this letter was written, elections were held within the council. The votes gave Mother Barat three Assistants General: Mothers Bigeu, de Charbonnel, and Grosier. The office of Secretary General fell to Mother Duchesne. The council's decision to found a convent in Paris as a residence for the Superior General and a central novitiate sent the nuns on a hunt for property. A suitable house was found at Number 40, Rue des Postes. It was small, but had some attractive features, and could be enlarged. The work of preparing and organizing the new convent was entrusted to Mother Duchesne.

The council closed on Saturday, December 16, with Mass in the chapel of the Franciscan Sisters in Rue de Grenvelle. At the Communion, the eleven religious of the Sacred Heart went to the altar rail, each carrying a lighted candle, and renewed their vows aloud before receiving the sacred host. Mother Duchesne called this little ceremony "the rebirth of the Society" that had always desired "the glory of belonging in name as well as in fact to the Sacred Heart of Jesus." "The day," she added, "was spent in holy joy." [33] Soon the other council members left for the houses from which they had come, and Mother Barat went to Amiens before the close of January. Mother Duchesne was left in Paris with plans and a little money and just two helpers, a young choir nun and a reliable coadjutrix Sister.

Mother Bigeu returned to Grenoble to install Mother Thérèse Maillucheau as superior at Sainte Marie. She traveled with Mothers

Victoire Paranque and Adrienne Michel [34] and carried with her a letter for the community from Philippine.

SS.C.J. et M.   PARIS, January 8, 1816

MY VERY DEAR SISTERS,

As I am not going to see you again, I should pause at the beginning of my letter to think seriously of the meaning of these words which ought to be placed at the beginning of all our letters now: *Sacratissimi Cordi Jesu et Mariae.*[35] All we do is for the Divine Heart, and it is in the Heart of Jesus that we bring all to a close. So we cannot withdraw from the Heart of Jesus, either in beginning or in ending our actions; and even if we are entirely separated from each other, we declare that we shall always be united closely in this lovable center of all our affections, the Divine Heart of Jesus.

I am so grateful for all your New Year's wishes, and if I put off answering your letters until the departure of Mother Bigeu, I did not fail to say how much I appreciate them, for I spoke of them to God in prayer the very moment I received them, and in His presence I formed special wishes for your perfection. I shall rejoice in the thought that God will be glorified in that house which is so dear to me and in which I have often taken too keen a personal interest. But God watches over it far better than I can. You know this very well, and so you must live in peace under the sheltering care of Divine Providence. . . .

It is really not my fault that our absence has been prolonged, for I am very tired of my worldly life. All the beauties of St. Sulpice are of less value to me than the quiet of our own chapels. I long for the day when we can secure a little corner for lodgings in our own little convent and I shall see no more of the streets of Paris.

Mother Bigeu will tell you that the street on which our house will be situated has many other religious institutions on it. So has the one where we are now. The area of the city called the Faubourg St. Germain is the section of religious establishments, the pious quarter of Paris. I see many people at Mass and Communion, but very few at confession. On the eve of Kings' Day I went after supper to the parish church. There was not a single person near the confessional.

I am so glad to know that you are all keeping well. I have learned that a good means of avoiding colds is to go out often in the fresh air. We have had to go out in all kinds of weather, but not one of us has had a cold. Mother Bigeu had sore throat and fever some days and was in that weak, languid condition she sometimes experienced in Grenoble. She said to me at such times: "You see, they cannot blame my illness on the house of Sainte Marie."

She will have many interesting things to tell you. Those that rouse your curiosity the most—and rightly so—concern our holy Rules. And, indeed, nothing is more satisfying for us than to be able to know well our obligations, in order to be more faithful to them. Let us beg God's pardon for the past and make all things new again within our souls.

Mother Duchesne and her two companions continued to live at the convent of St. Thomas. Each morning they rose very early, the older nun giving the newly adopted call, "*Ave Cor Jesu et Mariae*," and the others answering with alacrity, "*Vobis cor nostrum offerimus*." [36] After prayer, Mass, and breakfast, they went to Number 40, Rue des Postes, to spend the day in heavy manual labor. As usual, Mother Duchesne took the hardest work on herself, scrubbing and polishing floors, cleaning walls and windows, and occasionally inserting a missing pane of glass. While directing the workmen who were remodeling the house, she frequently picked up a trowel to speed a mason's job, or a brush to finish up some painting or whitewashing.[37] She was a tireless worker, yet a considerate superior, careful to safeguard both the physical strength and the spiritual life of her companions. At recreation in the evening she often entertained them with stories of Sainte Marie, as they sewed on caps and veils and habits fashioned after the new pattern adopted at the council. When she admitted that she was "always there in spirit," she gave the measure of the sacrifice she had made when asked to remain in Paris to prepare and organize the new convent. Sundays gave time for more prayer, some rest, and the accomplishment of the many little things they had put aside during the week. There were also visits to the well-known churches of Paris, and Mother Duchesne became acquainted with a great many places of pilgrimage before the cloister regulations were enforced.

In the midst of all the heavy work the foreign missions were constantly in her thoughts. On February 26 she sent Mother Thérèse copies of "a little account of the planting of religion in Korea," asking her to have them distributed to the community at Sainte Marie and to a number of priests in Grenoble and Chambéry. And in a postscript she adds: "I beg you, Mother, have the promises [to honor St. Francis Regis] kept at Sainte Marie, and be very exact in saying the prayer to St. Regis, or substitute something else if that promise is not carried out." He was the patron on whom she still relied for the opportunity to carry devotion to the Sacred Heart to foreign lands.

Easter Sunday fell on April 7 in 1816. Philippine seems to have expected visitors that day. Duchesne and his wife were in Paris, as were also Camille Jordan and three of the Perier men—Augustin, Scipion, and Casimir—who made frequent trips between the capital and Grenoble. With this in mind she used her leisure on Holy Saturday to give Madame Jouve some information about things of special interest to her:

> With the hope of having a chance to send you a letter, dearest Sister, I am hastening to write it today—to tell you that if you have any commissions for me, there will be some young people from Grenoble at the home of the Misses Fonsala en route here. They can bring your messages.
>
> Euphrosine's tendency to brevity in letters makes her overlook the fact that you love us too much not to want details about us. I am going to give you some: we now bear the name of Religious of the Sacred Heart. Our costume is a thin veil over a plain bonnet fastened under the chin. The novices wear white veils; the others wear black. The habit is of black material, cut *à la vièrge* [high-waisted with full flowing skirt]; we wear a silver cross and a gold ring. The work of the institute is the education of young girls and also of poor children; we also offer to seculars the opportunity of making closed eight-day retreats.
>
> The general novitiate is at Paris. Candidates have from three to six months' trial in the different convents [at which they apply]; then they go to Paris for two years of novitiate. After that they make vows for five years and are employed in the different houses of the Society. At the end of five years, if they persevere, they make perpetual vows. There is no fixed dowry: that depends on the means of each one. The ample resources of some make up for the penury of others. You know that I have provided for Euphrosine, and it would have been a joy for me to have done more, but we are without income, and our houses are at greater expense than other religious institutions because of the retreats, so all my income is used up.

On April 15—it was a Monday morning—the three religious of the Sacred Heart moved into the habitable rooms of the new convent. Gradually the entire house was furnished and made ready for the community that was soon to assemble there. As Madame Jouve had written during May, asking for some further information and giving some news that delighted Philippine, the latter answered on June 1, and for the first time the name of Monseigneur Du Bourg flowed from her quill.[38] She knew his visit to Lyons had aroused great enthusiasm and his appeals had met with generous response. Many priests had volunteered for the distant mission in Louisiana, and some large donations in money and church equipment had been made. A movement had been set on foot, moreover, that would result in the formation of the Society for the Propagation of the Faith, one of the most remarkable charities ever organized. Philippine was eager to know more about Bishop Du Bourg, but she wrote with circumspection:

You gave me much pleasure in writing about Monseigneur Du Bourg. I also heard a great eulogy of him from Augustin. We hoped he would come to Paris, but troubles arising in his diocese have, perhaps, delayed his journey. I am told, however, that the government of the United States wishes to reach an understanding with the Pope, and that the faith is making great progress in that part of America. At Georgetown there is a fine Jesuit college and a monastery of the Visitation, no doubt the first in the New World. Monseigneur de Neale [sic] is the Catholic bishop of that place.

Since you wish to know exactly all that regards the financial arrangements of those who enter our Society, here is our plan: 1. No fixed dowry: this matter is arranged according to the means of the parents and the usefulness that may be expected of the candidate, her health, etc. 2. The novitiate lasts two years and is preceded by a trial of three months; after these two years and three months the novice makes her first vows for five years; at the end of that period perpetual vows are taken—we call this profession, and it is only then that we give up the right to dispose of our property—and even this will not be obligatory on us until we receive the approbation of the Holy See, which may be long in coming, as all is done at Rome with great deliberation. . . .

When I made over to Euphrosine the life-annuity of 450 francs, it was with a view to relieving you of a financial burden that might have been difficult for you to meet in these hard times. You have until her profession, five years from now, to consider what arrangement you will make with regard to her right [to a share in the family estate]. By that time, I trust, we shall be in a more stable condition. Even in the old orders they still make use of the power they received from the Pope and the laws of the state to inherit, even with the vow of poverty.

Our house is still in foundation. The community will gather here on the 21st: I hope that will be the day of our installation and the solemn blessing of the chapel, which is not yet completed. We are in a quiet quarter of the city, surrounded by gardens, near a supply of fresh water, in the most elevated part of Paris, near St.

Etienne du Mont, formerly Ste Geneviève. At her tomb and in the other places of devotion, I have not failed to pray for you, your husband, and all your little children, especially for Henri, my dear godchild, and your three daughters, who are also mine by the affection and interest I bear them.

Meanwhile at Sainte Marie young Aloysia Jouve was writing again to ask Tante Philippine to act as go-between for her, this time with the Mother General. She had expected to make her vows at Eastertide after a single year of noviceship, but the new constitutions called for two years of training, so she begged her aunt to use her influence to gain an exemption for her. As Mother Barat stopped at the Paris convent on her way from Amiens to Poitiers early in May, Philippine had an opportunity to speak for Aloysia. Though the answer was indefinite, she was optimistic and sent off a letter to her niece toward the close of June. Written in a warm, appealing mood, it is bright with the glow of her devotional fervor:

My dear Euphrosine, or my Sister Aloysia,

This letter will reach you only after the feast of the Sacred Heart. I do not know whether you will have obtained the happiness you were longing for. When I was petitioning it for you and making the request, our Mother [General] wished to have time to think about it, and she left [Paris] without giving me an answer. Whatever happened, you are sure that the will of God is being accomplished, and we must bless His will, whether it consoles us or makes us suffer. We all have our troubles just now, and the Heart of Jesus lets us experience what our title requires of us: a consecration to the sufferings which pierced that Heart.

It was not without emotion that I thought of you celebrating the feast of St. Francis Regis without me. Do not fail to tell me how it was solemnized at Sainte Marie, and whether you keep up your devotion to him. You have real need of his continual protection. As the 16th of June fell on Sunday, I had no work to do, so I told myself no one would see me here that day. In fact I was here only for dinner. First I had five Masses said in honor of St. Regis by the Fathers at the Visitation monastery. At nine o'clock I went to Ste Geneviève, where the procession of the Blessed Sacrament was just coming out of the church. There I assisted at four more Masses, the last being solemn high, after the procession re-entered the church, and ending at one-thirty. Immediately after dinner I went to the Church of the Blessed Sacrament, where Father Varin preached, and I finished my day at Ste Geneviève, where, after the Office had been chanted, they had another proces-

sion of the Blessed Sacrament inside the church. There were two
repositories, so in all I had six benedictions. . . .

I leave you now to go and make a visit in a church where the
dear Lord is very much neglected and where one can truly call
Him at certain hours the *Unknown God.* Remember me to all my
Sisters and to the pupils, especially to my class and to yours. Do
not fail to give a cordial welcome to Madame de Rollin. She does
all sorts of kind things for me.

St. Madeleine Sophie's answer to Aloysia was not the permission she had asked, but only that of consecrating herself to the
Sacred Heart by vows of devotion. Philippine assumed that this
would entitle her niece to the black veil. The old missionary long-
ings were to the fore again in her thoughts and prayers, and she
shared with Aloysia the items of mission news that came to her,
whenever there was an opportunity to send letters to Grenoble by
travelers. Early in August Dom Augustin de Lestrange stopped at
the Paris convent to pick up mail for Lyons and Grenoble. The
letters Philippine sent to Madame Jouve and Aloysia show two
facets of her character. Her sister may have smiled as she read the
one addressed to her and wished she could have heard the lively
discussion it reflected:

They tell me, my dear Sister, that the abbot of La Trappe is leaving for Lyons, so I am taking advantage of the opportunity to
write to you and tell you I received your letters of June 11 and
July 9. I would have answered them sooner, but the arrival of our
religious from several places, the arrangement of our convent, and
our religious ceremonies have taken all my time. We are at last
living in community with the dear Lord at home with us. Father
d'Astros, the vicar-general, who was kept so long in prison by
Bonaparte, and Father Perreau, one of the almoners of the King
and also a confessor of the faith, performed the ceremony of blessing our chapel. There was question of making it an elaborate
affair, but in the end the simplicity which I do so love was decided
upon . . . so I was very happy about the whole thing.

You are curious to know my position in the convent here: it is
just the same as at Sainte Marie.[39] Mother Bigeu is Mistress of our
general novitiate, and Mother Eugenie de Gramont is Mistress
General of the boarding school, which is not yet organized, as
there are very few children; but we must have patience.

I know that Augustin Jordan expressed surprise at the slow
development of our establishment, and that he does not like the
variety and multiplicity of religious institutions. I have tried per-

sonally and without success to alter that opinion of his and a good many others, which characterize the man of the world and which grieve me, revealing as they do how seculars judge their fathers in the faith and meddle in ecclesiastical affairs. As to ourselves, does he think such a complex foundation can be made and developed favorably in three months? We got possession of the house only on the first of April and the community was assembled only on the first of July. Has he succeeded in all his enterprises on schedule time? Let him refrain from criticizing us.[40] We must see that our work strikes deep roots of humility and patience, so that it may enjoy success without danger. I continue to hear many things in praise of Euphrosine. Constance is now more easily handled by her teachers. . . .

To Aloysia she wrote that same day:

I have been very slow about congratulating you on your happiness. I hope you are wearing its exterior sign, the black veil, as hereafter there are to be no novices in the individual houses. So you have passed from childhood in the spiritual life, and I trust you will act like a strong and generous soul. You have, no doubt, read the life of St. Ignatius. Nothing is better calculated to stir up one's courage and increase the love of one's vocation. Father Varin is a striking example of what this reading does for the soul. He has broken with us as completely as the saint did with Dame Roser. Recently he has appeared once or twice on the horizon, but with great circumspection. We had Mass offered by Father Janson on July 31, but he would not preach. He had astonishing success at Nantes with Father Rauzan.[41] They are going to Bordeaux and spoke of an invitation from the Bishop of Grenoble.

On Friday the Benediction was given by the Superior of the Foreign Missions. He has just received a letter from China, in which they gave him details of the martyrdom of the last bishop of that country, who had been there forty years and whom the Superior himself had known.

There follows a long and graphic description of the bishop's imprisonment and death, then information about mission work in India, Senegal, Cayenne, and Louisiana. The concluding sentences flow straight from her apostolic heart: "Many affectionate messages to the children. Tell them to pray for the missions."

Among the novices whom St. Madeleine Sophie had called to Paris to form the nucleus of a general novitiate there were two with marked attraction for the foreign missions—Octavie Berthold and Eugenie Audé. When Mother Duchesne presided at their recreations, she often told the novices stories she had heard from visiting priests, for missionaries came frequently to the *Sacré-Coeur* in Paris, asking for hospitality and aid. Her position as assistant gave Mother Duchesne the pleasure of welcoming them, offering them refreshment, and pleading their cause with the Mother General, whose fund of alms was kept replenished by generous gifts from charitable friends. Philippine's heart beat high with eagerness as she listened to stories of work and trial and suffering and success in pagan lands. She was encouraged in her desire by Father Barat. Living in Bordeaux, he frequently met missionaries on their way to and from America and other foreign lands. He had talked with Monseigneur Du Bourg sometime during 1816 and had assured him that Mother Duchesne was just the person to work in his diocese. The type of work was vague enough in Father Barat's mind; the type of religious order to which she belonged was not investigated by the bishop at the time, as its reputation was already well established in France. Father Barat had written to his sister and to Philippine about the Bishop of *la Louisiane* and the mission field in his diocese. Mother Barat felt the urgency of grace in his letters and wrote to Mother Thérèse in October:

> Can you believe it—Philippine is always thinking about her mission overseas, and my brother has almost smoothed the way for her. In spite of the terror such a venture causes me, we shall, perhaps, see it carried out. I tremble to think of it. Pray about it, but do not talk about it, lest people get excited and lose their heads. We live in an age in which it does not take much to upset people.[42]

Philippine had reason for excitement when she received a letter from Father Barat in mid-November, telling her of an interview he had had with Bishop Du Bourg:

> On the eve of his departure for Provence [he wrote] I had a long conference with the Bishop, during which we talked seriously about the Louisiana mission and you. Your superiors have recognized the supernatural character of your vocation, and Monseigneur wants you to help with the work in his vast diocese. You desire it sincerely and steadfastly, so the matter is arranged. There remains only to decide on the time of your departure and the means of accomplishing the project.

It seemed as simple as that to Louis Barat. Having no authority in the matter, he counted on his influence as the Mother General's brother and even began to direct proceedings with a bit of dry humor:

> Now [he continued] you will need three generous religious to accompany you. But they must be great souls, and among women great souls are very rare. That thought may discourage you, but you have sighed so long a time for your savages and with such constancy, it is probable that God will make an exception in your case and not require you to be a wholly great soul.[43]

This letter sent Philippine into a transport of joy, hope, and prayer. The way was really opening before her.

> On December 3, feast of St. Francis Xavier [she wrote in her *Mémoire* of February, 1818] I went to Mass at the Church of the Missions. These words of the Epistle sank deep into my soul: "How will they ever know the truth if no one instructs them, if no one is sent to them?" I wept in spite of myself. I did not know where to hide. To avoid a recurrence of this, I resolved not to return to that church in the afternoon. But on arriving at our house in the Rue des Postes I found all the doors locked. I do not know how that happened, so I went back to the same church. My devotion led me to the place where the relic of St. Francis Xavier was kept. There near it and near the Blessed Sacrament, which had been brought to his chapel, my hopes soared high—as they had soared all during the novena before the feast, which I had made solely for the intention of knowing the will of God.

She was trying to keep these hopes a secret for the present, but Madame Jouve seems to have got wind of Father Barat's plans for Philippine, and she was upset by the idea of this dearly loved sister leaving France. Her heart was torn with anguish, too, because Euphrosine's health was giving much concern at Sainte Marie, though she had been allowed to make her first vows on November 21. A note dated January 9 shows by its brevity and restraint that Philippine was determined to keep from her family the joyous expectations that were surging through her soul. She was, however, very sincere in expressing anxiety about her niece and lovingly sympathetic with Madame Jouve when she wrote:

> I am most grateful to your husband, my dearest Sister, for the service he has rendered us and to you for your gift and for all the good wishes you express for my happiness. I shall find it always in the accomplishment of God's will in my regard, so a change of residence will make no difference. When I came to Paris, I neither

expected nor desired to remain here. I love far more the simplicity of small towns. Wherever I may be, I shall always find a way to give you news of myself and to receive news from you. As yet nothing has been decided, so I must wait and tell you later what is going to happen.

If you wish to give me a very acceptable New Year's present, have a Mass offered for me at Fourvière. Euphrosine writes me that she is drinking ass's milk for the fifth month—which tells me she is not free from the lung trouble. God is sending us a great trial in her illness. The more I reflect on conditions here in our little Paris convent, which is not large enough to house us, the more I realize that she is much better off at Grenoble than she would be here. *Fiat* in all. Believe, dear Sister, in my inviolable attachment.

Eleven years had passed since she had first revealed to Mother Barat her inspiration to sacrifice all for the sake of souls in some distant corner of the world. During those years she had done invaluable service for the Society. She had proved her worth, her loyalty, her fidelity to trust. She was one of the group to whom Saint Madeleine Sophie gave her confidence in matters of gravest import to the order. And the influence of the saint had been at work in her soul, softening the rugged energy of her character, curbing the vehement impulses that shook her whole being, guiding, restraining, helping her to cooperate with divine grace and so become a fit instrument for whatever work God had in store for her. To her pleading to be off on the enterprise beyond the seas Mother Barat always answered: "Wait and pray. Later, perhaps, we may think of it. It is out of the question now."

So matters stood [Mother Barat related in after years], when on January 14, 1817, [a Tuesday afternoon, just five days after Philippine had written her cautious note to her sister], Monseigneur Du Bourg, Bishop of Louisiana, arrived from America and had the kindness to call on me. Mother Duchesne knew of the visit, for she was acting as portress just when he arrived. When she came to tell me he was there, she implored me not to let such an opportunity slip. God's hour had come, she assured me, and I had only to say the word. I did not let her see that I shared her conviction, but only answered that if the Bishop brought up the subject, I might discuss it, but that I should want a year or eighteen months to prepare.

On the following day the Bishop offered Mass in our chapel and I sat and talked with him while he took his breakfast. He told me he wanted to establish religious orders in his vast diocese and was eager to have the religious of the Sacred Heart there. As he urged me to consent to this, I said to myself, "Things are certainly looking well for Mother Duchesne." To him I replied that if the plan were feasible, I should have someone quite ready for the work. Then I told him about Mother Duchesne and her vocation. Monseigneur Du Bourg was delighted and asked to meet this future member of his diocese. When she came in, she threw herself on her knees for his blessing. It is easy to imagine her joy, and the rapturous way she showed it, and the gratitude she poured out in prayer to her divine Master.[44]

Monseigneur Du Bourg continued his European tour in search of missionaries and financial aid for his diocese. In May he was in Paris again. To his dismay he learned that opposition was being raised by people who had a right to advise the Mother General. Although Father Varin had allowed Philippine to make a vow to devote herself, under obedience, to the foreign missions, he was very much averse to her leaving Mother Barat at a time when she seemed so necessary in the Paris convent. Father Perreau, who was acting as ecclesiastical superior of the order in the name of Cardinal Tallyrand-Perigord, considered that the interests of the Society required Mother Duchesne nearer home. Yielding to the opinion of her chief advisers, the Mother General had decided to postpone the departure of her missionaries.

On May 16 the Bishop came to pay a last call at the *Sacré-Coeur*. He was a keenly sensitive man who knew how to use to advantage both the gifts and the defects of his temperament. That Friday afternoon he was sad, disappointed, displeased. He had set his heart on the project; and as he walked slowly toward the outer door with Mother Barat, he made little effort to conceal the chagrin which opposition always aroused in him. Suddenly from a doorway Mother Duchesne appeared. She knew what was happening and could no longer restrain her pent-up ardor and anxiety. Now she was kneeling with clasped hands on the threshold the Bishop was about to cross and pleading with the Mother General: "Your consent, Mother! Give your consent." A moment of silent prayer in three dedicated hearts, then St. Madeleine Sophie spoke with all the deep affection she felt for this, her "eldest daughter," —"Yes, my dear Philippine, I consent, and I shall begin at once to look for companions for you."[45]

Father Barat learned of the decision from Bishop Du Bourg, who arrived in Bordeaux in the middle of June to take ship for

America, and he wrote at once to Philippine, disclosing no little ignorance about American Indians, but also much fine zeal:

> At last, my very dear Sister, at last the matter is decided, and you are to set out for the mission to the Illinois. Long ago you dreamed of the Iroquois, but you have had to come a few hundred miles south. You were not holy enough to be eaten by Hurons and Algonquins. Now, God be praised, you will not be devoured by any savages. Instead, you must allow yourself to be consumed by the fire of love for God and zeal for the salvation of souls. . . . Now beg the dear Lord to choose as a missionary to this same region the one who writes you this letter. He would be very pleased to go, as his superiors know. You can tell them this, if you have a chance.[46]

Bishop Du Bourg sailed for America on June 17, 1817, on a small vessel of the royal marine, *la Caravane*, that had been put at his disposal by Louis XVIII. Four months later he wrote to Mother Duchesne from Baltimore, giving her a guarded warning that the transatlantic voyage offered many difficulties, but adding that every day women and children, as well as men, crossed the ocean to travel to the Mississippi Valley for the sake of temporal advantages. "And shall we not do the same with much greater zeal for the glory of our good Master and for the salvation of souls that have been redeemed by His blood?" [47]

One missionary companion Mother Duchesne had hoped for was her niece, Aloysia Jouve. Not, perhaps, in the pioneer group, but after she had completed the training required in the Society before final vows. But Aloysia's health was by this time seriously impaired. What at first was an apparently insignificant sore on her foot had carried a vicious infection into the blood stream, and there was no curing the disease. The best doctors in Dauphiny were called in on the case. Then Madame Jouve begged to be allowed to bring her daughter home for treatment. Aloysia was opposed to the plan and Mother Duchesne tried to dissuade her sister from pushing the request, but soon she had the joy of writing for the Mother General a letter that brought consolation to the Jouve family in the first week of July:

> Our Mother General, sympathizing with your tender mother-love, wants to satisfy you, to safeguard our rule, and to respect Euphrosine's resolution not to leave Sainte Marie. She has made a plan that harmonizes these three. She told me that there is a certain latitude

still allowed as to our going out for reasons of health, and that in this circumstance your request presents fewer inconveniences than might be expected and is made in a very urgent case. So, my dear Sister, she grants you permission to take your daughter home to see and consult any doctors you choose. But when they have diagnosed the trouble and prescribed the treatment, she wants you to take her back to Grenoble at once. . . .[48]

The young nun spent some weeks at home, but there was no improvement in her health. The suggestion of a trip to Paris gave Philippine the hope of seeing her once more, but that was beyond the invalid's strength. Aloysia returned to Sainte Marie to face a protracted agony with courage and love, while her aunt made preparations for the venture to America.

She began the study of English with strong resolve. Happily she could not foresee how thoroughly that language would elude her. She began to draw in as much money as possible from the several investments she had made through her cousins, the *Perier Frères*, and from property which she still held in common with her sister Amelie. The Paris convent was in need of funds, and she felt bound to aid it as far as possible, knowing that in turn she would be aided in her mission. Two letters to Amelie, written in the summer of 1817, contain no mention of her American project, but they show a very determined resolution on Philippine's part to settle the business in a friendly fashion. In July she wrote:

MY VERY DEAR SISTER,

As the last letter I wrote you was delayed at Lyons, I grew anxious about your silence, and so to relieve my own anxiety and because I thought Monsieur de Mauduit would be as interested as you in the proposition I made you, I wrote directly to him to get news of you and to repeat the offer. He answered that you had talked to him about it and that he agreed to the reimbursement of 10,000 francs, but that he had not that sum just now at his disposal. It is for you to decide now, and I cannot help thinking it would be to your advantage to accept, for if I live an ordinary lifetime, it will cost you far more. To make things easier for you, here is my last proposition: give me 10,000 francs now by promissory note, and we will cancel the six months' arrears due me. This will be an easement that you can make use of for Amelie. When you send me the promissory note, I will burn our written agreements or put them in the hands of a third person. You can ask Scipion to keep your copies, for they would be too bulky for the post.[49] . . .

As to the observations you felt it your duty to make to me, I understand their practical sense, but they have no weight with me. I have never regretted the money I put into Sainte Marie, and if I had not done so, would I now be able to help Adelaide [educate her daughters]? . . .

I am convinced that I shall never be in want. Divine Providence is admirable in caring for us and has furnished us with means in circumstances far more difficult during those unhappy years when there was even danger of starving to death. And even if I should suffer privations, I shall simply be practicing my vow of poverty. . . .

Adrien's poor health grieves me. You wished to make a priest of him; perhaps God will call him to heaven. But no! Pray to our good doctor, St. Francis Regis, and he will obtain health for this interesting child.[50] They write me from Grenoble that Euphrosine's condition is not improving. How little we can count on health! At one time she seemed so robust. Several promises have been made for her at Fourvière and at the shrine of St. Francis Regis to obtain her cure, but God seems deaf to our prayers.

In a few days the benefactress who founded our house at Quimper, Mademoiselle de St. Pern, cousin of Mademoiselle de Verges, is going to receive the habit here at Paris. She came here just recently. She has spoken to me several times of you and Augustin. She is a model of detachment and virtue.[51]

Madame de Mauduit still demurred about the terms of the settlement. The fortune Philippine had spent on Sainte Marie seemed a sufficient sum for her to contribute to the order, and she had said so bluntly, but without effect. Philippine had some arguments of her own—she had argued before with Amelie—and when she stated them, she took it for granted that Amelie would acquiesce, and Amelie did.

I am using a letter to Monsieur Jouve [she wrote on August 8] to save you the postage on a letter. I had scarcely sent off my letter to you when yours arrived. I tell you again that I hold to 10,000 francs and I think you are the gainer, since the income represented a capital of 15,000 francs at 8 per cent a year. Our Society is not accustomed to insist on its rights [financially], and in the bottom of my heart I prefer the interest of my own family before those that concern me personally. It has always been gratifying for me to be able to make sacrifices. But we are now in real need ourselves. It is surprising that our Paris foundation, made in such unhappy times, has not suffered more.

This mark of Divine Providence and all that I saw in the establishment of Sainte Marie assure me that if you entrust all your interests and anxieties to the goodness of God, He will take care of you. . . . So, while sharing and feeling deeply the full extent of your suffering, I want you to carry heroism even so far as to face in silence the gradual diminishing of your income, as so many of the saints have done, and God, who is never outdone in generosity, will bless your harvests along all lines. Wearied as you are with the management of the farm, could you not turn it over to Amelie and follow in the world that attraction for solitude of which you spoke to me in one of your letters? But above all, my beloved Sister, suffer in silence after the example of our Lord Jesus Christ. I, too, long for the time when I shall be freed from temporal cares. The soul loses much from this contact, and Clement XIV was right when he said: *Among earthly cares one's very heart grows earthly*.

The condition of Adrien's health grieves me. Consecrate him to St. Regis. Euphrosine's health is wretched. How much poor mother-hearts must suffer! I have all the sentiments of a mother for your children and regret that you do not tell me whether or not Amelie gives you consolation. Seek this solely in the meek and humble Heart of Jesus Christ, and you will find it in its lasting form. . . .

Although Mother Duchesne was determined to hide from her sisters her hopes and plans regarding the American mission, she had already given her confidence on this subject to her *best*, her *most beloved*, her *dearest* friend and cousin, the Baroness de Savoye-Rollin. Josephine always went to see her when she was in Paris, and the two women talked with the same affectionate confidence as when they were girls together at Sainte Marie. While Philippine aspired to the difficult life of a foreign missionary, Josephine found an outlet for her zeal in generosity toward the poor. With her, charity was not so much a kindly habit as an innate quality of soul. In the several cities where her husband had been prefect during the Napoleonic decade she had a brilliant reputation for wit, gentleness, and charity. In the evenings she did the honors at the prefecture after having worked all day to make the poor happy and in some degree less uncomfortable. During the siege of Antwerp she showed fine courage and energy, working constantly in the ambulances and hospitals while her husband was ably seconding Carnot in the defense of the city. "Wherever she went," writes Choulet, "her presence was considered an honor." She possessed great wealth, but never lived in luxury; and she honored her wealth by the use she made of it.[52] At times she shared the secret of her charities with Philippine or told her of experiences of the past years when visits to Grenoble had been rare.

On her forty-eighth birthday Philippine sat down to write to Josephine. She was already trying to cultivate that characteristic that seems essential to all missionaries—the begging habit. It was always a difficult habit for her to practice, and she was never very successful at it, though she wrote with ease to Josephine that twenty-ninth day of August, 1817:

MY VERY DEAR COUSIN,

I am taking advantage of an opportunity to write to you. I am also very much interested in writing to you, and I am not ashamed to use the word "interested" because the matter is not personal, but regards the service of God and our fellowmen. Since you left [Paris], my desires for the American mission have not diminished, and God seems to be listening to my prayers. I saw the Bishop of Louisiana on the eve of his departure. He must be in America now. Our Mother General promised him six of our nuns for next spring, and I am one of them. So we must prepare what is needed for a sacristy. Furthermore, the vicar-general [of Bishop Du Bourg], who is remaining at Bordeaux as agent for the mission, writes to our Mother General, begging her to procure material, muslin, linen, galloon, all that can be used to make vestments and all that can impress the savages in the pomp of liturgical ceremonies. You are so sympathetic toward physical miseries; I know you will be even more interested in the conversion of souls, since their eternity depends on this.

You told me once that you had in Grenoble a quantity of things which would be useful to us. Look them up, my dearest friend, or beg contributions. God will bless you. But do not mention me in connection with this matter. I am so unworthy of sharing in this inspiring work that I always fear it will escape me. Not a word about me, then, but speak in general about a distant diocese where everyone is poor.

You have learned through my cousin [Augustin Perier] that we have drawn a part of the money you had deposited, and you know why we did so. . . . Remember me, please, to Monsieur de Rollin, to my aunt [Tante Perier], and to all my cousins, especially Madame Teisseire.

I am, in the Heart of Jesus,

Your devoted cousin,

PHILIPPINE.

This is the first of Philippine's letters that Josephine saved. For years they wrote to each other—not very frequently, it is true, but often enough to make the extant letters one of the surest and most illuminating sources from which to study the character of Mother Duchesne.

five

"To St. Louis in the Illinois Country"

1. February—May, 1818

*One of the soldiers
opened His side with a lance.*

Gospel, Mass of the Sacred Heart

JOSEPHINE WAS IN PARIS just when Philippine needed her most. She was at home in the capital; she had entree and influence; and she was at the service of her cousin. The maturity of their friendship and the sympathetic understanding with which each shared the other's interests, joys, reverses, drew them closer than ever in the face of a separation they knew would in all probability be lifelong.

There were many other members of the big double family in Paris that winter, as a wedding was scheduled for January. Marine Teisseire's eldest daughter, Amelie, was betrothed to Louis Bergasse, a merchant from Marseille. Since the marriage ceremony was to take place in Paris, Philippine had the opportunity of seeing many dearly loved relatives. A wealthy, well-dressed, well-mannered group gathered at times in the parlor of the convent in the Rue des Postes to visit her and talk, not about her and her plans for the future mission, but about the wedding and, still more, about Casimir Perier and the stir he was making in the capital.

For fifteen years he had been prominent in financial circles. As director of *Perier Frères*, he had worked with his brother Scipion, the administrator of the firm, in a remarkable combination, and their banking house had attained European renown. Now they

202

were among the top bankers of Paris, the younger brother being more active because he was in better health. In 1815, Casimir had published the first of the pamphlets with which he made his debut in political life. He was a recognized genius at finance, and no matter how severe his criticisms of the government might be—it was the policy of obtaining secret foreign loans to pay the heavy penalties imposed by the Allies in the peace treaty of 1815 he denounced—his patriotism and loyalty could never be questioned. The dignity of his character and the uprightness of his life eliminated all suspicion of personal selfishness in his fight against the methods used by the minister of finance.

In the September elections of 1817 he was voted a seat for Paris in the Chamber of Deputies. At the royal séance opening the session in November he was the youngest member of the Chamber, having reached his fortieth birthday on October 12, between election and seating. For the rest of his life he was to be in public office. All Paris was talking about Casimir Perier after his first speech on December 13, 1817; for that speech, with its brief, incisive style, its perfect phrasing and dynamic delivery, placed him among the finest orators of his day, and gave him a claim to the position he held for a dozen years as a leader of the opposition in the Chamber of Deputies.[1]

Philippine loved this handsome cousin, who had groaned as a lad over her lack of talent for arithmetic; and she was proud of the high principles he was defending. And there was his sister, Marine Teisseire, mother of the bride-to-be, prettier than ever and always doing thoughtful things for Cousin Philippine. Augustin and his family were in Paris, too.[2] The Periers shared the mission secret before Mother Duchesne wrote it to her sisters, though the date of departure was actually set before she had the courage to tell anyone but Josephine that she was leaving France.

Preparations for the voyage were, however, under way. News of the Superior General's promise to Bishop Du Bourg had traveled to Amiens, Poitiers, Grenoble, Niort, and Quimper. In all the convents contributions for the mission were being collected and packed for shipment. Many nuns who shared Mother Duchesne's aspirations offered for the venture to America, but Mother Barat was slow in announcing her choice. The Paris convent had been through a serious epidemic in the autumn of 1817. "For three months we had much illness in the house," wrote the annalist, "and we lost several religious and children. Mother Duchesne was on duty day and night, sometimes spending entire nights by the bed-side of the sick, never giving a thought to herself." [3]

The New Year dawned—1818—and ran its course quietly enough for nearly three weeks. Then a letter from Father Bertrand Martial, vicar-general of Bishop Du Bourg, announced that he was sailing for America in mid-February and expected to take with him the Religious of the Sacred Heart destined for St. Louis. [4] This advance in the schedule delighted Mother Duchesne, though it complicated life for her family. An eyewitness of those last days in Paris gives an affectionate account of what took place:

> Mother Duchesne would have forgotten all that concerned the temporal side of the preparations, had not our Mother General strictly charged her with the whole affair. She set to work vigorously, and God certainly blessed her efforts. What an influx of merchants, tradesmen, workmen of different types! People coming and going, all wanting to see Mother Duchesne! And how joyous she was in the midst of it all! It was a calm, thoughtful, deep joy, that forgot nothing but self. She packed the trunks, cases, satchels, without the least anxiety or trouble. Everything ran smoothly; everything was ready on time. Seeing her joy, we could not be sad at her going; and I fancied to myself the emotion she would experience on setting foot in that land she has longed for so ardently and embracing the first little Indian girl.
>
> The passports gave most anxiety, for it was feared they would not be obtained in time. But a relative of Mother Duchesne took the matter in hand, battled with the difficulties, and brought the papers a few hours before the party left us. All was arranged with so much speed and success that even those most opposed to the enterprise as an extraordinary adventure just at this time, recognized the finger of God in all and His plans for making the adorable Heart of Jesus known in the New World by means of our little Society. [5]

Josephine's part in the battle to secure the necessary papers shows up in a few notes and letters she saved. Acting as chaperone and messenger, she had a busy time during those last two weeks her best friend was in Paris. The menfolk, too, were busy with notes and bills of exchange amounting to nearly 20,000 francs—their own money or Philippine's—to finance the missionary venture of this middle-aged cousin whom they loved so sincerely. Josephine was living at the Perier home in Rue St. Honoré. On Saturday morning, January 24, Philippine sent her a hurried note:

MY DEAREST COUSIN,

Since I last had the pleasure of seeing you, I have had a visit from Augustin and his charming family. He offered me the money Monsieur de Mauduit had asked him to transfer to me, and I begged him to remain my banker still. But the next day I learned that our departure will be advanced and all the money we shall take with us must be at Bordeaux by February 10 or 11. So I beg you to give me what remains, and also ask Cousin Augustin and Cousins Scipion and Casimir to send me what they have by letters of exchange on Bordeaux, dated as I have indicated. My brother sent me a note for 7000 francs, which I am not eager to cash until there is actual need. But I do not want the several sums of money to be decreased by the rate of exchange or by delay.

The religious who are going with me have nothing to contribute except their good will. The Bishop warned us not to count on him for financial aid. The expense of the voyage and the necessity of providing a dwelling place will use up all the money. That is why I must collect as much as possible. I shall await your reply regarding my notes. Tell Augustin about my project, but do not let it reach my sisters.

In order to expedite the financial arrangements that seemed to be getting a bit tangled, Josephine offered to take this business in hand also. Philippine was relieved and wrote again on Wednesday, putting her letter under the protection of St. Anthony of Padua:

MY DEAREST FRIEND,

Taking advantage of your offer, I am sending you all our notes. There is one with my Perier cousins that is not due, but I hope they will kindly advance the payment, since we have not accepted interest on sums payable within a few months. I could not make out a receipt for what Cousin Augustin was to give me in the name of Madame de Mauduit because I could not recall the exact amount. I shall send the receipt as soon as I check on the amount.

I want my Perier cousins to give me a letter of exchange for 600 francs to pay what we owe Monsieur Jouve, and all the rest is to be in letters of exchange on Bordeaux, payable on February 12 or 13, and made out to me. If my cousin cannot conveniently give me the full amount at once, there is a banker in Paris who handles business for the Society; we can apply to him confidentially.

I have already told you it is useless to solicit help from the minister of Marine, unless he would retract the refusal he already gave. Our arrangements must be made with the captain of the vessel on which we are to sail; and you realize that, once the contract is made, we must pay. Nearly all our money will be used up on the trip, but God, who has willed the work, will sustain it. As it is part of His plan, however, that we should help ourselves by every possible means, I earnestly recommend this work to you, and I beg you to contribute to it as long as you live. You will have the consolation of helping in the salvation of souls who might be lost if they were not given spiritual food and also material food in order to draw them to Christ. You will do this, not so much because of the friendship that unites us—and its bonds are so dear to me—but because of the blood of Jesus Christ which frequently cannot do its redemptive work because of our lack of zeal in supporting enterprises that are set on foot to save souls.

Let me know at once if you can do something about the black vestment. There is not time to have it dyed. I think I already asked you to inform my cousins, especially Augustin and Camille, of what is happening to me, but I stress the fact that my sisters should not be told before I write to them myself. Tell Madame Teisseire also that the departure has been advanced. If you know of an opportunity for Valence, please send Madame de Mauduit the notarized statement which I am sending you, and according to which all that she owes me is canceled in view of the sums she has already paid me. Adieu, my dear Cousin. I shall love you always, no matter where I may be.[6]

On Sunday, February 1, she found time and courage to write to her sisters. The letters to Melanie and Adelaide are missing. A fragment remains of the one Madame Jouve received, while the letter to Amelie is intact:

MY VERY DEAR SISTER,

I received from Cousin Augustin the sum of 1514 francs, for which I enclose the receipt. I have entrusted to Madame de Rollin the contract made between us. I see her rather frequently. The wedding has taken place and everyone is happy.[7] I also see Madame Teisseire, who is kindness personified.

I have confided to these two dear cousins news of a project which I also want to share with you. For a long time a very strong and definite attraction has drawn me to the teaching of the infidels. I even thought of going to China, but that is not practicable, as women cannot appear in public there. God has listened to my prayers and has let me find nearer home and at less financial cost the happiness for which I prayed. In Paris I met the Bishop of Louisiana, and it is in his diocese that I shall work to instruct the savages and found a house of the Society. The departure was at first set for May, but other missionaries are going this month on a vessel that is well known and has a good captain, so it has been decided that we shall go with them. I leave Paris next Sunday. Only five of us will sail this time, but in September others will embark.

I hope you will write and give me news of yourself. I wish you would send me a supply of seed of all the kinds you have, labeled and marked with the time for sowing. The land is so fertile in the area where we shall live that the cattle are entirely hidden in the prairie grass. If you can send this little shipment by wagon, address it to Monsieur Caseaux, c/o M. Jhonoton, Facade des Chartreux, Bordeaux, for the Bishop of Louisiana. Put a letter inside the package indicating that it is for me.

Believe me, my beloved Sister, I shall always be closely united to you. You and your daughters, your husband and your son will be continually in my prayers. Tell Amelie to recall the days of her first fervor and never forget the *one thing necessary*.

Adieu, my dearest Sister. Have a Mass offered in honor of St. Regis.

PHILIPPINE

The fragment preserved by the Jouve family makes the same announcement and adds some affectionate personal touches:

. . . I am leaving Paris, perhaps within a week. Bordeaux will be my first halting place; and if God raises no obstacle, Louisiana will be the last. Here in Paris I had the opportunity of meeting Monseigneur Du Bourg, Bishop of Louisiana. For a long time I have wanted to do so in order to open my heart to him about my desire to instruct the infidels—a desire long combatted by my superiors and confessors. But at last Providence has arranged everything for the accomplishment of this very desire.

Monseigneur Du Bourg showed me much kindness. We shall live in his episcopal city [St. Louis].[8] It had been arranged that six of us should leave in May, but the earlier sailing of a vessel whose captain is well known and which is carrying one of the vicars-general and other missionaries, made us leave sooner than expected. So, unless untoward circumstances arise, I shall leave France this month. But in doing so, I carry with me my memories and my affection for my dear sisters and their children. You will pray for me, as I shall for you. At the moment when I am leaving all to work for the salvation of souls, I pray most earnestly that you will cling to the *one thing necessary*. Say this above all to Henri and to my Amelie, to whom I shall not have time to write. One does not make a change like this, and so hastily, without having much to do.

I am, and I shall always be, closely united to you in the Sacred Heart of Jesus.

PHILIPPINE DUCHESNE

It was not an easy matter to leave France hurriedly. Official red tape fettered the missionaries, and in the excitement Philippine was getting confused. Josephine's address escaped her mind completely, so on Monday she sent a note to Madame Teisseire at the home of Madame Bergasse, begging that it be delivered, *s.v.p.*, to Madame de Rollin:

> MY DEARLY LOVED COUSIN,
>
> My two trips to the police commissioner made me realize more keenly than ever how much I am obligated to you for all the long trips you have been making for me in this continually bad weather. I owed to you my return to Sainte Marie, and I feel that I owe everything to you just now.
>
> I thought there would be three of us to go to the police agent, but our Sister from Amiens will arrive here only on Thursday. There will not be sufficient time to secure her passport here, so she will have to join the two at Bordeaux. They tell me the consuls at Bayonne and Bordeaux constantly issue passports for Spain. This will be the solution to the problem if we do not obtain here in Paris assured permission for them to leave the kingdom—a favor I beg you to try to secure.
>
> If it is necessary to go to the office of the prefect of police, I think we could manage without the help of my kind relatives. It may be inconvenient for them. Send me some word tonight or tomorrow morning—or even send me back our papers. You could entrust them to Monsieur Ricolet, the grocer, who lives in the same building as Madame Bergasse, to have them sent to us.
>
> Tell me honestly, did you not suffer greatly from the cold yesterday? I was so preoccupied, I did not notice that you were unprotected, and you always take such care of me. Affectionate messages to Madame Teisseire and her daughter.

And now it was time to write a farewell to Sainte Marie. The letter to the community there is both an act of reparation for the past as it appeared in her eyes and an expression of humble gratitude for the grace that was at hand. In it appears that tone of self-depreciation which is so difficult for most people to understand, but which was the sincere expression of Philippine's opinion of herself, and that opinion was according to her Rule. Her days of self-sufficiency were over; her natural independence was giving place gradually to complete reliance on God, and humility was becoming a settled habit.

MY VERY DEAR MOTHERS AND SISTERS [she wrote],

When I look into my own soul, I cannot find any reason for expecting you to remember me. I know full well that I deserve to be forgotten, and I really ought to desire this very thing. For if you remember me, you must inevitably recall all the faults I committed—faults that were prejudical to an institution for which I would willingly give my life, faults I repent of most sincerely. But when I think about the charity which is the bond of union in our holy Society, I am not surprised at your thoughtfulness, and I beg you to add this kindness—pardon for all my past faults and prayers that I may avoid such conduct in the future. You must be as merciful to me as God Himself is.

Ordinarily He gives one outstanding grace to a soul, and this becomes the source of many others. In my case that signal grace was my return to Sainte Marie [after the Revolution] and membership in the blessed Society of the Sacred Heart. This was far beyond anything I had hoped for. And still—in spite of the fact that I have profited so poorly by all the instructions and the examples of solid and sublime virtue I have received—still God in His goodness is opening to me a new career that calls forth all my gratitude and overwhelms me with confusion when I think of it.

Several distinguished prelates have already praised our voyage overseas and sent or given us their blessing. Among these was Monseigneur d'Astros. . . . Our Mother presented me to him, along with Octavie, my future companion. He was very encouraging. But what need we both have of your prayers! An infidelity might hinder the flow of grace, and we commit countless faults. The happy opportunity is promised us, the graces are offered, but they are not yet our very own. What motives this gives us for fear and vigilance! I hope you will not cease praying to the Blessed Virgin and St. Regis for this great enterprise. I have poured out many tears and prayers for America at the shrine of our Lady where St. Francis de Sales was freed from his temptation. That statue is now at the convent of St. Thomas, where I lived for several months. I believe I gained much grace at that shrine and at Montmartre. I beg you again to pray very specially to them for us. We should be on fire with zeal. . . .

It was harder to write to her beloved niece, and the note enclosed to her in the letter to Sainte Marie tells by its rather incoherent style the strain under which it was written:

I am leaving Paris, my dear Aloysia, and soon I shall be leaving France. We shall meet in heaven at least, I hope, if we never have that consolation again here on earth. Offer your sufferings for us and we shall pray for you.

Yesterday we made a pilgrimage with Octavie to obtain new protectors in heaven. We visited the shrine of our Lady at St. Sulpice and that of St. Francis de Sales. We went to the Church of the Foreign Mission Society to hear Mass at the altar of St. Xavier and received Communion from the hands of the Bishop of China. From there we went to Montmartre. Our Mother General is better.

I hear that you are ill again. Let your sufferings be your prayers for me and for my poor charges. I shall offer for you the eloquent prayers of the poor. Envy my happiness and relish your own. God wishes us to be separated on this earth and reunited in His Heart. Affectionate messages to Mothers, Sisters, and children at Sainte Marie. I have announced my departure to my sisters and my brother.

The six months' journey to St. Louis began on Sunday, February 8.

On the eve of the departure [wrote a member of the Paris community] our Mother General assembled us all and gave Mother Duchesne her obedience as superior of the mission band. She dreaded this office and believed she would never be able to bear it. She certainly had not foreseen, when begging for the foundation, that she would be placed at its head. She submitted to the burden, however, realizing, no doubt, that it would offer her more opportunities for suffering. Our Mother General recommended, above all, union among themselves and inviolable attachment to the Society in France as the surest safeguards in their efforts to glorify God. And she told them to send us news of themselves as frequently as possible.[9]

Next morning Father Perreau offered the holy sacrifice of the Mass, at which Eugenie Audé made her vows. Then the Blessed Sacrament was exposed for adoration all day, for this was a great day in the history of the Society. There were many visitors that morning, among them Fathers Varin and Druilhet and Father Roger, now master of novices at the Jesuit house of Montrouge. The Periers were there—Augustin, Josephine, Marine—and Camille Jordan, all adding to the provisions already prepared for the trip. Hippolyte and Coralie Duchesne may also have been there, for they had been in Paris for the wedding, and Duchesne had contributed a generous sum toward the expense of the journey. Subdued excitement and the sound of many footsteps were audible as novices hurried through the halls, carrying baggage. Joy and heart-suffering struggled in Philippine's soul.

The missionary group was summoned to lunch. It was a hasty meal, for in the midst of it Mother Bigeu came in to say the carriage was waiting. Philippine rose from the table immediately for her final goodbye to Mother Barat and the community. Then she went quickly to the parlor for a last word with the family she loved so dearly. The nuns had gathered near the outer door, and one of them noted briefly afterwards:

> The moment of separation was very painful for us all. As for Mother Duchesne, she did not shed a tear, though we know how deeply she felt it all; for she is naturally so affectionate. Seeing Mother Octavie crying as she said goodbye, . . . Mother Duchesne took her gently by the arm and led her out of the house. The carriage was waiting and there was no time to lose.[10]

In the emotional crisis of the departure Mother Duchesne's response was one of fine controlled maturity. She would admit later on how costly the sacrifice had been, but at the moment she gave no outward sign. Happily she could not see the length of the way that stretched ahead nor the circumstances in which she would be called upon to sustain that generosity. Her gift for sustained effort was one of the splendid natural endowments of her character.

A crowd of curious onlookers gathered around the stagecoach before the nuns climbed in with their satchels and packages. The trunks and packing cases had gone ahead in a wagon. With a smile and a last wave of her hand to friends who had come to see them off, with *bon voyage* outside answered by *adieu* from within, Philippine took her place in the coach with her companions. The reins were lifted over the horses, the whip cracked sharply in the chill air, the crowd shouted a noisy send-off, and the coach headed south on the road to Orleans. The nuns prayed silently. An army officer, soon bored with the journey, sang lustily to while away the time. Evremond Harrissart, a seminarian bound for the American missions, intoned psalms and hymns to drown the words of the drinking songs he feared might shock the nuns.[11] He was a tall, spare, ascetic-looking young man, grave in manner, deliberate and earnest in speech. Sister Lamarre would have liked to join him as he sang, for she had a very good voice and enjoyed using it.

Mothers Berthold and Audé had dried their tears even before they boarded the coach and were alive to the changing scenes through which they were passing. Like Mother Duchesne they had been born and reared in mountain lands. Octavie Berthold was from Geneva. A well-educated Swiss convert, her beauty might have attracted attention, but her reserved manner and religious bearing impressed all who saw her. Eugenie Audé's home was at Moutiers in Savoy, some fifty miles northeast of Grenoble. She had lived in Italy, had been presented at the court of Napoleon, then under the impulse of grace had chosen the cloistered life at Sainte Marie.

A new world was already opening up to Philippine and her companions. This was for them a new part of France, a section in sharp contrast with their Alpine country, and they were interested in every feature of the countryside and towns along the way: Orleans, with its memories of Jeanne d'Arc; Tours, with its tower of Charlemagne and the ruins of St. Martin's ancient church and the River Loire that she found so beautiful, but the town was especially appealing to her as the birthplace of Marie Guyart, who as Mother Marie of the Incarnation had set out from here on her journey to Canada in 1639. A halt at Blois gave an opportunity to send letters back to Paris, and every morning there was Holy Communion in a different place. At Poitiers the travelers were at home again for just two hours, and Philippine saw for the first and only time the old monastery of the Feuillants that Mother Thérèse had so often described to her. Here, too, she met Sister Marguerite Manteau, fifth member of the missionary band. Then on to Angoulême, and into Bordeaux, the fine old seaport on the Garonne, with its beautiful thirteenth-century Cathedral of St. Andrew looking out over wharves and ships and commerce from the four corners of the world.

Father Barat was on hand to greet them, with Father Boyer, vicar-general of Archbishop d'Aviau, who drove with them to the convent of Notre Dame, where Madame Vincent, the superior, welcomed them and gave them hospitality until the embarkation.[12] They had expected to board the vessel immediately, but in this matter the weather had its way, and the waiting seemed very long. The first few days were filled with the business of material preparations that were necessary in the days of ocean travel by sailing vessels. The arrival of mail from Paris and Grenoble helped to keep up the morale of the nuns at a time when there was danger of spiritual depression after the excitement of the departure and the novelty of the trip had worn off. Letters from Lyons and Grâne tore at Philippine's heartstrings, adding a measure of suffering she had tried to ward off.

Before leaving Paris, Mother Duchesne had given Father Perreau a lengthy *Mémoire* in the form of a letter addressed to Mother Barat. In it she had tried to outline the history of her missionary vocation, the encouragement she had received at various times from her spiritual directors and from the Mother General herself, and the signs by which Divine Providence had marked the way for her toward this goal. One of her consolations in Bordeaux was a letter from Father Perreau.

> I am happy to be able to tell you [he wrote] that the document I handed to your dear Mother Barat was gladly received by her. As for myself, the more I reflect on it, the more I see that God has called you to this mission. In order to stamp your holy enterprise with the symbol characteristic of all that is done solely for His glory, He has allowed it to go through trials of many kinds . . . Continue with the same perseverance and the same abandonment to God's will the work you have begun so nobly. He will always be with you to uphold you. I dare to say more: you should count on our Lord's very special protection, for with the apostles you can say in all truth: *Domine, ecce reliquimus omnia et secuti sumus te; quid ergo erit nobis?* [Lord, we have left all things and followed you; what shall we receive?] The reward He will give you for this great act of renunciation is His own Divine Heart for your refuge, His Spirit to guide you, and some drops from His own chalice of bitterness to purify, to detach you from self, and to teach you to rely on Him alone.[13]

Mother Barat's first letter gave Philippine further assurance, bringing sunshine into her soul at a time when she had great need of it.

> It is not without emotion, dear Mother [wrote the saint on February 12], that I write you this first letter since you were given the task of leading a little group so far away from us. It was very hard to part with you! When the anticipation of it cost me so much, what must the reality have been! Our Lord did sweeten it wonderfully by the thought that you would be happy in doing His most holy will in the midst of labors and privations. Your example strengthened me, and I could not help envying your lot

. . . At least pray for me; you owe me this for the tender love I bear you, which distance will only increase.

I did not need your letter to be convinced that your high vocation is from God. The persistency of your desires, the ease with which the plan, apparently so beset with difficulties, was carried out when God's time had come, the way everything concurred to bring about the departure that cost us so much, the strength God gave you to overcome obstacles, all proves to me that in spite of the arguments of human prudence our Lord has called you to found a convent of the Sacred Heart in *la Louisiane*.[14]

Now, my dear daughter, enter more and more fully into the designs of our loving Lord. Try to grow each day more worthy of His work by laying a deeper foundation of humility in your soul, for out of this will spring gentleness and forbearance with the souls entrusted to you. I am happy about your love for them, and I know you will do all in your power to lessen the sacrifice they have made. . . . Take care of your health. The hard penance of the position of superior, which you have always dreaded so much, must replace all other penances . . . Everyone here sends most affectionate greetings. We are praying for you. Pray for me. . . .

In the first letter she wrote to her family from Bordeaux the influence of Father Perreau's encouragement is apparent, for Philippine repeated the quotation he had used. In it, too, she shows once more the kind of work she expected to do on reaching America.

BORDEAUX, February 15, 1818
MY VERY GOOD FRIENDS AND DEAR CHILDREN,

In this hour when I am giving up everything almost as if I were going to die, since it is practically certain I shall never see you again, nor my many Mothers and Sisters in religion, my relatives and friends, I believe I have a right to ask great things of God, with the same confidence as St. Peter when he said to Jesus Christ: We have left all for You; what shall be our reward?

Oh, the reward I ask of Him is the great, the ineffable consolation of learning that you are all fervent in loving Him, that you show that love by good works, and that by this means you tend toward that solid piety whose outcome will be the enjoyment of God, in this world by grace and in the other world by the state of glory. Yes, across the enormous distance that will soon separate us, my heart will always be seeking you and praying for your happiness. If I can contribute to this by obtaining prayers for you from the interesting children who will become the flock of Jesus

Christ, I shall not neglect a means that is so strongly according to my heart. When I see myself in the midst of a crowd of simple, innocent souls, I shall say: "Pray for the children I left in France, for every dear memory of them adds value to my sacrifice. Pray for your very first benefactors. They did not know you, yet they prayed for your conversion and helped procure it by the gifts they contributed for you. Nothing selfish or human tarnished their offerings. They knew only that the religious, their friends, would distribute the gifts and would acknowledge them. Everything is done for God, all for the salvation of your souls." Then certainly they will be inspired to pray for you.

I hope to give you details about our establishment in the New World, if God places no obstacle in the way of its foundation. I was to have sailed today with my companions, but a few days' delay gives me time to write to you and suggest that you put aside any objects that might be used as rewards or means to attract the little savages we shall instruct. I hope to be in their midst in two or three months. Our trip by way of New Orleans will be longer than the route by way of Baltimore, but also less dangerous. We shall ascend the Mississippi on a steamboat. These boats are built like sailing vessels and have rooms with beds in them. The trip takes 20 or 25 days. The boats are run by steam. As there is great uncertainty as to the success and outcome of our voyage, pray earnestly for us.

That same day she wrote more intimately to Mother Thérèse:

I was deeply moved by the tenderness of your recent letters, as I am moved also by the mercy of God in my regard. I am impatient to board the vessel that will carry me to the goal of my desires. I may set sail any day now—and I may also have to wait. It all depends on the weather. I leave in France so many people I hold dear and shall always cling to by the strongest bonds of love. These bonds will tighten continually when I think of all I owe to the Society. I am going to have the joy of helping to extend it in the New World and to see devotion to the Sacred Heart flourish there. You would like to share this joy—but God makes use of you right where you are. As I am good for nothing here, He is giving me a chance to do something useful elsewhere, like the nuns who are changed from one house to another frequently in the hope of finding them useful somewhere. Pray that I may not always be unfaithful.

My companions are very courageous and people envy them, even Father Boyer, the vicar-general. He says he would set out too, if he were younger. He is very kind to us, and so is the

Archbishop. We called on him and he returned our call. Today
we attended Mass he offered for us. Of course the [Jesuit] Fathers
are kind, too. Father Debrosse is quite willing to receive and forward our letters; and when vessels are sailing for New Orleans,
you could send letters to him, by occasion, of course, but do not
give his address to anyone else, for fear of imprudence or indiscretion. The two trunks, the little case, and the vine-slips for
planting have reached us. The freight charges came to about 170
francs. When you send the picture by wagon, do not address it as
I first directed, but to Monsieur Fournier, care of Monsieur
Caseau, Rue de l'Eglise near St. Turin, Number 7. Father Debrosse
lives too far from the wharves, but small packages can always be
sent to him at the minor seminary.

I was hoping to get a letter from Father Rambaud. I wrote to
him from Paris. I have waited in vain. Tell him so and beg him
to pray for me. I am filled with gratitude for all the prayers you
have obtained for me. You will have all the merit of our mission,
and we, all the dangers to soul and body.

Monsieur Morange has been so thoughtful as to supply us with
wine for the sea voyage. I owe this to you. After waiting several
days I had the pleasure of greeting Madame Morange and
Mademoiselle Emiline. They are wonderfully kind.[15] I have never
had a more cordial welcome. Eliza could not come, but she sent me
a charming letter. They are going to supply us with preserves
and apples—they say apples are the best fruit to quench thirst. In
so much kindness and cordiality I recognize the heart of my
Mother Thérèse. I shall see them again.

As the sailing was delayed rather indefinitely, the nuns made a
retreat. This was quite to Philippine's liking, but she could not look
back to it with very happy memories. It was made at a difficult time
and under such trying circumstances that even the spiritual direction of Father Barat did not call forth much enthusiasm or consolation. There was time for letter writing, and Philippine used it to
advantage. She had already given details about their five-day trip
and safe arrival in Bordeaux when she wrote to Mother Barat on
February 18:

We are in retreat. I have seen no one about the sailing and know
no more about the date of departure than when I wrote my last
letter. Please have the goodness to write to us at once, for I hope
to receive another letter from you. You must have had several
from me, and I sent one to Mother Bigeu. Please answer my question about day pupils—may we receive them? [16] And may we
recite the Office of the Dead every month?

How grateful we are for all the proofs we have had of your maternal love for us and for Mother Bigeu's remembrance for each one! I delivered her letter to Father Barat. We see him almost every day. He hears our confession on alternate days, but he is not giving us any sermons. He says he is exhausted every night because he has so much work to do. But he gave two instructions this week to some kind of very fervent Carmelite nuns who have just established a convent near where he lives. Father Wrindts is giving them a retreat. I was struck by the emaciated appearance of this priest. He is nothing but a skeleton topped by a fiery head. I fear he has some very serious disease of the nose. Father Jennesseau barely stopped on his way through the city.[17]

I have been to the home of Madame Fournier, Bishop Du Bourg's sister. She had rented a lodging for us and also got us a servant and a person to attend to our meals—all near the *Reunion*, where she really wanted to take us. I declined her arrangements because of the retreat. She has reserved our sleeping quarters on shipboard and is now talking about *comforts*, that is, things to take with us for the sake of the body—mostly food. As to the wine, Monsieur Morange has kindly taken care of that.

Father Boyer paid us a long visit yesterday, showing great interest and speaking of the consolation we shall enjoy. He is going to give me some relics. I am not sure he is the one most opposed to the union [of Madame Vincent's community with that of the Sacred Heart]. I suspect it is Madame Vincent herself. She holds to all her customs and thinks her order is more like the Jesuits than we are. She has a mother, a sister, a brother, and a niece. If a revolution in the government should occur, she would be worried about their welfare.

It would be impossible to show more cordiality and charity than she has shown us. And the same is true of her Sisters. They are very edifying. But all this kindness surrounding us is not you or my own Sisters; and although God sustains my courage and even the intensity of my desires, still, when I arrived here, my soul was in a state of anguish, hard and dark. Going into the Church of St. Andrew, I dwelt insistently on the words: *O bona Crux, diu desiderata, et iam concupiscenti animo praeparata!* [O good Cross, so long desired and at last prepared for my longing soul!]

My companions, too, have had their moments of weakness. I realized this and tried to be of help to them, knowing full well my own wretchedness. All this only makes it seem more astonishing that God in His goodness should have made choice of us. Your brother gives a good push forward on the pathway of perfection to souls who lag behind. . . .

The precautions I took to avoid receiving letters from my

family were all useless. Love finds a way, and I needed that extra little cross. I have not written to Madame de Rollin yet. I wanted to do so, but your brother did not like the idea of my going to the prefecture, and I do not know how to tell her I have not used the letters she wrote. Later on I shall arrange matters. Tell her I shall write after my retreat, when I know the date of departure. Your second letter has just come, and it filled us with joy.

Philippine answered that second letter with details of many kinds:

I have received the packet of letters and the recommendations, and I am writing at once to Madame de Rollin, as she is a dear friend to me and I am sure she will never forget me. . . . Like her, Madame Fournier, whom we have met here, is very zealous and active. As she has made a sea voyage like ours six times, she knows exactly what to do. Only I find her too bent on precautions. I should prefer the way of St. Francis Xavier, whose poverty I envy, and I would entrust our health to St. Francis Regis. But you do not want us to neglect human means, so all will be taken care of, and I am very sure of doing God's will in obeying you and following the advice of your brother, our kind Father Barat. I submit everything to him, and he enters into all the details (even with regard to the sugar!) I have seen no more of Madame Fournier's box of sweets. She will come some day with more for us, so your maternal solicitude will be satisfied.

I have more need of being reassured about your health. You did not say a word on the subject. It is always a great help to receive letters from you. They will form the second volume of my collection, and I shall be in greater need of them at the enormous distance that is going to separate us. We are all steadfast in our resolutions, but God has begun sending us trials. The retreat goes rather badly. I am hard as flint. My head is in a whirl. You can have no idea of the many details and anxieties connected with a trip of this kind—they never end.

Our baggage, sent off from Paris on Quinquagesima Sunday [February 1], has not reached us yet. We have written to Monsieur Menglar. Madame Vincent continues to take the kindest care of us. Still we know we are a burden and an embarrassment, and that makes us the more eager to sail. She counts on Divine Providence, but she told me no one gives her any help. She says food has cost 3,000 francs more this year, and the pupils have paid 3,000 less! I admire her virtue and that of her community. She has six novices and four postulants in very good form. Night adoration is kept up by seven nuns who sleep in a dormitory near the tribune where they pray, so the one in adoration is not fearful because alone, and she has just a step to take in order to call the one whose turn is next. They replace one another every hour.

Their life is austere: coarse bread at almost every meal, with sea food, rice, and peas. But all seem in good health except Madame Vincent herself, who coughs and takes no care of herself. I have already made a great advance in changing my diet. I had never eaten sea food before. . . . My companions are well, only Octavie has her usual stomach complaint and so is not fasting. Our most affectionate messages to our Mothers and Sisters.

That same day Philippine wrote to Josephine and her sister. Again the old address in Rue St. Honoré escaped her mind, and she sent the letter to Madame Bergasse, asking her to deliver it.

My very dear Cousins,

It would have been a great satisfaction for me to have written to you as soon as we reached Bordeaux, to try to express my undying love for you and all the gratitude I feel. How much these sentiments have increased during the past weeks, if increase was possible, seeing all the trouble you went to for me, all the important services you rendered, all your tender solicitude. When my thoughts revert to what I am leaving in France—all that is dear to me—I put them aside, being intimately convinced that, as I have desired only one thing—to answer God's call and abandon myself to His Providence—so the voyage and the trials ahead will never be as great as the help I may confidently expect from Him.

So far our journey has been pleasant. As the vessel is not yet ready to sail, we are making a retreat for a few days. I have gone out only to call on the Archbishop and the sister of my future Bishop. She has made this ocean voyage six times, so she knows exactly all that we need. As she is very zealous about her brother's mission, she has arranged about the making up of our berths and is directing our embarkation, conjointly with her brother.

I learned from them that the *piastre* is now very high, being the medium of exchange most used in the India trade. So they will draw only a small sum for us and convert our notes into bills of exchange on Baltimore and New Orleans. They assure me that navigation on the Mississippi becomes easier every day. There are always about a dozen steamboats traveling up and down, and they are almost as large and convenient as a seagoing vessel. They have informed the Ursulines in New Orleans of our coming, and we shall lodge with them or relatives of our Bishop.

The letters to the French consul will be very necessary for us in order to get our luggage through the customs office, if we are leaving New Orleans at once, and will also be a very good protection in that land where we shall be far from any kind of safeguard. I just received the two additional letters of recommendation to the French ambassador and the consul, and I at once put aside the first one to the Ambassador in order to avoid any mistake. For this last attention on the part of Madame de Rollin I can only say that, as she already deserved my lifelong gratitude, so in piling up so many kindnesses in our behalf, she is accumulating for herself an inexhaustible treasure of pure joys in this life and of the merits of charity in the next.

The letters from my sisters are a weight on my heart which I beg God to lighten, as I also pray that He may alleviate the hard things in their lives. But we must all carry the cross, and only those who know *how* to carry it are happy.

Remember me very specially to all my loved relatives and particularly to my dear Amelie and Henriette. The vessel leaves Bordeaux Tuesday to go to Pauillac, but I do not know what day we shall go aboard. It cannot be long now. Respectful greetings from all my companions. As I cannot recall Madame de Rollin's address, I beg Madame Bergasse to pardon the liberty I have taken [in using hers].

A letter to her sister Amelie, written on February 18, is more intimate, more alive with human interest and tender affection, as these paragraphs will show:

The Bishop of Louisiana, in whose care you addressed your letter to me, is in his distant diocese, while I am still in Bordeaux, where the vessel on which we are to travel has been delayed for some days. I know your heart well enough to realize that my going would cause you sorrow, but I was also sure enough of your courage and faith and of the judgment you would pass on the motives that inspire me. These motives have overcome the opposition of my superiors. I also knew that my decision to go to America would not alter in the least the tender intimacy with you that has been a joy in my life and now adds to the costliness of my sacrifice. Surely, exposing oneself to danger is nothing in comparison with giving up a tender and holy friendship. But no—that friendship will continue, will even grow stronger and increase just because of the detachment, and God, who is always generous, will give us graces that will make its value infinite. My prayers will be with you always, and if God blesses my efforts, you and your family will have a large share in the work of our inspiring mission. God has drawn me to it through years of attraction and has granted me this great grace after many, many prayers. In bringing it about, the guidance of Divine Providence is evident in so admirable a manner that all holy souls see in it the finger of God.

The Bishop of Louisiana has manifested a very fatherly interest in me, and I found myself quite at home with him, as if I had known him all my life. He thought it best to set out ahead of us in order to look after our interests as his very own. . . . We are going to live in the same place as the holy Lazarist, Father de Andreis. He may be our confessor. He is at the head of the seminary and so is stationed in one place. The trip up the Mississippi has been made much easier by the invention of steamboats, which are run by steam made by a continual fire, and which offer the same space and convenience as a sailing vessel.

I am so grateful for the Mass in honor of St. Regis. Nothing could give me more pleasure. I went to call on the Archbishop of Bordeaux. I ought to become a saint, being so much in the company of saints.

Now good-bye, my dear Sister. Our friendship is too strong to be affected by distance. I shall always love you tenderly, my beloved Sister, and your husband and his sister and your children. Give my regards to them all and have them pray for me. I shall do the same constantly for you in the generous Heart of Jesus Christ.

March came in with the westerly winds still blowing a fierce gale from the sea and keeping the *Rebecca* at her mooring in the Garonne, but a change in the weather was predicted, so Philippine wrote her promised farewell to Madame Jouve:

MY VERY DEAR SISTER,

As my departure has been delayed, I received your letter here at Bordeaux, which we leave perhaps tomorrow, if the weather permits. I knew very well your sentiments toward me, and the thought of giving up such dear sisters has added much to the general sacrifice I have made to God in order to fulfil His designs. If He accepts and blesses our work, I shall dare to ask Him in return the most abundant blessings for you and your family, to whom I remain intimately united. And I shall maintain the bonds between us by giving you news of our work. I have already written to Madame de Mauduit, and I beg you to share this letter with Madame Lebrument.

There are five religious of our Society leaving to found a convent of the Sacred Heart in the diocese of Monseigneur Du Bourg at St. Louis in Louisbourg [*sic*] in Upper Louisiana. We go by way of New Orleans, where we shall lodge with an Ursuline community that was established there a long time ago. Here we are staying with a very edifying community. I went once to call on the Archbishop and another time to assist at the Mass he offered for us in his chapel. I hope that since so many holy people are praying for us, we too may one day become saints. That is the one and only reward I ask in return for a sacrifice for which God alone can make compensation. Everything seems to show me that we shall have a very holy Bishop. They compare him with St. Francis de Sales. Everyone praises him. Do not forget to give affectionate messages to my brother-in-law and to your children.

Adieu, dearest Sister. I shall never forget you.

The wind had changed by March 2, and the *Rebecca* nosed away from the city wharf and sailed downstream to Pauillac on the west shore, where the passengers would embark. That day Philippine wrote hopefully to Mother Thérèse:

There was time enough for me to receive your letter. It came the very day I had written to tell you I had seen Madame Morange and Mlle. Emiline. . . . Today the vessel sailed down to Pauillac, where we shall board it in two days. Father Martial, the vicar general, will be the only priest on board, and if he is ill—and even now he is not very well—we shall be deprived of Mass. But how can I worry when you are so generous with prayer and help!

You have my sincerest gratitude; my heart can never express all it feels. I have little hope of ever seeing you again. You are doing good in France; if Aloysia is called to do good elsewhere, then you two will also be separated. Perhaps God is waiting for that sacrifice before He restores her to health and employs her for His glory . . . How grateful I am to you for all the care you give her and for all your kindness to the Lebrument children. My sister [Adelaide] is in admiration of it and sees in it only Christian charity, which can do what friendship alone would not attempt.

I saw your dear sister and your attractive niece again this morning. You must be patient, but I hope God, who is working in her soul, will draw her to His service. I leave France overwhelmed by their kindness and deeply moved by yours. The Heart of Jesus alone can know all. The picture you are sending to Paris can come on another vessel. One sails every month.

But there was a further delay, which gave Philippine time for another letter to Josephine containing much that she had written to her sisters, but adding a few details straight from her sensitive heart:

The vicar-general with whom we are traveling is not very happy about this arrangement; we add so much to his responsibility. That will help toward my perfection, for I suffer when I see I am causing trouble. No one but you, my dear Cousin, has the art of taking the weight out of gratitude and leaving only the sweetness. . . . Everything seems to promise us a pleasant voyage. A multitude of prayers are rising to heaven for us; even the holy Archbishop of Bordeaux has offered Mass for us. So I leave in peace about all things. If the enterprise ends in misfortune, God will have allowed the efforts for a better purpose than the one we envisaged as His will. May He be blessed in all that happens.

A thousand affectionate messages to the Teisseires and the Periers and all my dear relatives. Farewell, dear Cousin. This carries the sincere and tender expression of my eternal devotedness to you.

In a postscript to this letter of March 5, Philippine adds: "We did not sail today; a contrary wind detained us." Five weeks had passed since the nuns had left Paris, and only on March 14—a Saturday, they noted—did they go from Bordeaux to Pauillac. Sister Lamarre's account of the stay there is a charming bit of narrative, introducing her lively personality which blended courage and ability with the intense affection of a keenly sensitive nature. She had taught in the free school at Cuignières and in the orphanage at St. Pezenne nearby, and had shown there the virtue and power of adaptability that made her a valuable member in any community. She was active and independent by nature, a bit headstrong at times, and inclined to chafe under restraint. Her letter, dated from Royan at the mouth of the Garonne on March 16, is addressed to Mother Prevost, superior of the house at Amiens, where Sister Lamarre had been living when called to join the mission band.

MY DEAR MOTHER,

As you see, we are not yet dead. One needs great patience and resignation, however, to go through all that the Heart of Jesus has willed for us and allowed to happen. We thought we were on the point of sailing when I wrote you last, but bad weather made its appearance again and detained us longer in Bordeaux. . . . Fair weather seemed to reappear on Monday of Passion Week, along with a favorable wind. The captain notified us that we must be on board at ten in the morning, and we obeyed. . . .

Kind Father Barat gave us his blessing before we went down to the wharf, where we were to take a small boat carrying the passengers to the ocean vessel, which was at Pauillac, some twenty miles from Bordeaux. During that short navigation the weather changed. After spending a night on the *Rebecca*, we were obliged to land again by means of a little boat that seemed about to be submerged at any moment. There was reason enough for fear. The wind was terrific, but God was good to us, and what confidence I ought to have in Him. . . . We had expected to find lodgings near the pastor's house, and what was not our surprise on learning that we would have to separate into three groups. We have with us a lady from Bordeaux who is none too wealthy and who was glad to share the charity offered us, and of course it fell to my lot to be named with her. So here I am with her. I leave the rest to your imagination. . . .

I meant to tell you about the first night on the vessel. When the time came to retire, I did not know just how to manage in the narrow berths. Of course there was a good deal of laughter among us, but I finally managed with patience and some pain. My berth was the top one. When at last I got into it I found I had very little covering, but I could not get out and down again. When I tried to turn over I bumped first against one thing, then against another. I got settled, but there was no sleep, and there was not room even to raise my head. But it is all for the love of the Heart of Jesus that we endure this and much else, . . . the more the better, and God be praised for all. And now fair weather has come. The captain has just sent for us, saying we embark at 7 in the morning, Holy Thursday. God grant we reach America alive.

The *Rebecca* was piloted through the last channel, and on Holy Saturday put out to sea. For a whole week she tossed in rough weather on the Bay of Biscay, and her passengers experienced the desperate helplessness of seasickness. Then things improved and they were able to take some interest in life again, to note the progress of the boat: March 30 they reached the latitude of Lisbon, nearly identical with that of St. Louis; April 2 they rounded the Azores. Then came the long stretch of unbroken ocean, when there were pleasant days on deck and they could think more coherently, pray more peacefully, listen more attentively to Father Martial's little spiritual talks and to the English lessons they all found so difficult. They chatted with subdued gaiety—Father Martial was very firm about its being subdued—each telling of her vocation and the houses of the Society she had known. Three of them had known and loved Sainte Marie, and Mother Duchesne had much to tell them about its history and her own experiences there and in Paris.

Sometimes she sat a little apart from them and meditated on the contents of a creased sheet which she guarded carefully from the wind and ocean spray. Her companions recognized the handwriting and knew it was the document the Mother General had given to her when she named her superior of the mission. It was the supreme mark of trust on the part of St. Madeleine Sophie toward her "eldest daughter," bestowing on her the exceptional authority which alone would enable her to carry on the Society's work in America, "clothing her," as the document stated, with powers which normally only the Mother General herself could exercise. The admission, retention, and dismissal of subjects, temporary changes in the religious costume, the disposal of funds, the acquisition of property, the foundation of convents, nomination to offices in the community, changes of employment, dispensation from cloister during the day for the sake of teaching in free schools and for hearing Mass on Sundays and feast days in the absence of a chaplain—such were the powers delegated to her who was to bear the responsibility of a mission undertaken, as the letter of obedience stated, entirely for the honor and glory of the Sacred Hearts of Jesus and Mary.

On this transatlantic crossing the *Rebecca* encountered as many tribulations as a caravel of fiction might have to its credit in a fantastic tale of the sea. Teriffic storms that threatened to drive the vessel on rocky islands, torrential rains and violent headwinds, excessive heat and calms that kept the helpless boat drifting idly in the doldrums, an encounter with a pirate ship from Buenos Aires, manned with one hundred and twenty sailors and armed with eleven cannon. "They forced us to stop," noted Mother Duchesne, "but on being informed that this was an American vessel, they allowed it to pass unmolested." [18] The stench of the hold came up sickeningly when wine casks burst and food was rotting; the water was contaminated and the ship-biscuits were moulding. Superstition was stirring among the sailors: who could interpret the double sign of a partial eclipse of the moon, followed shortly by a comet that was visible for several nights? And then a fire on the deck, with Sister Catherine giving the alarm and the passengers extinguishing the blaze.

But the voyage was not all of that pattern. There were stretches of beautiful weather, when a good stiff wind filled the sails. There was Holy Mass at four or four-thirty in the morning whenever Father Martial was well enough, and Communion for the nuns followed by a long thanksgiving, before the ship's bell sounded for breakfast. Often in the late afternoon the nuns stood together in the bow of the boat, their full skirts rippling out in the breeze, their thin veils waving in the fading twilight. Then the captain called for "the hymn," and the sweet strains of the *Ave Maris Stella* floated over the waters. As her nuns sang, Mother Duchesne's intent gaze studied the sky, the waters, and the western horizon. The long weeks of the voyage, the stench, the nausea, the still tender memories of separation from loved ones, laughter, news about people and things that were part of her life—all seemed to drop away as she stood there, looking westward toward the sunset and her promised land.

When the evenings lengthened and were fair, they remained on deck "as late as nine o'clock," Father Martial sitting quietly near them as they talked of France and the friends they had left so willingly, yet so reluctantly, or of the events that had broken the monotony of the day: a ship sighted and signaled to—"bound for Granada," they learned through the *porte-voix*; a porpoise caught —"so big it took several men to haul it in, and when served at table it tasted like beef, but the fat was like pork"; latitude reckonings and islands coming in sight, and "the trail of light behind the vessel when it made good speed." That phosphorescence was a phenomenon they gazed at with astonishment and delight.

While the nuns suffered a good deal from their crowded and stuffy sleeping quarters, they had no complaint to make about the meals served on the *Rebecca*. Mother Duchesne said only that the food was nourishing and abundant, though she found cabbage soup disgusting when she was seasick. Mother Audé, however, praised the menu, remarking that:

> Dinner was usually an affair of six or seven courses—soup, fresh roasted chicken, ham, vegetables, fish or eggs, dessert, dried fruits, liqueur. At breakfast there was omelet, herring, anchovy, ham, sausage, fruit, tea or *café-au-lait* three times a week, preserves. Once a week a sheep or a pig was slaughtered, so there was very little dried meat served. Fresh fish was caught frequently, and there was plenty of excellent wine.
>
> The captain [she continues] was very nice to us; but after four passengers left the vessel, he was much nicer. The sailors of the crew were as meek as lambs, working quietly and without any objectionable language. The second-in-command was a very intelligent man, silent and reserved, whom the sailors obeyed without a word of objection to orders. As for the passengers, they were all bound for New Orleans to rejoin their families. They were

polite and friendly on the whole. One lady [Sister Lamarre's partner at Pauillac] stayed close to us during the whole voyage.

A little feast was celebrated privately on Ascension evening. It fell on April 30, and the nuns surprised Mother Duchesne by offering their good wishes for her feast on the following day, May 1, St. Philip the Apostle. She took it all quite simply and embraced each of her daughters with that tender affection they knew so well, though they saw it frequently masked with gravity under the burden of responsibility. That day they began the devotions for the month of May and the novena in honor of the Holy Spirit. At sundown on Pentecost, May 10, the watch in the crow's nest thought he sighted land. But a terrific storm struck them toward evening, and the captain decided to lie to for the night. On the twelfth they passed Great Inagua. Two days later they were sailing in superb weather through the channel between Cuba and the Bahama Bank.

Nearing Havana on May 16 the ship was becalmed, and Mother Duchesne took out her writing materials, knowing there would soon be an opportunity to send a letter back to France, the letter she yearned most to speed across the Atlantic. As she sharpened a quill, her mind went back through the last twelve months, and she smiled as memory pictures flashed clear-cut to her mind. For a moment quiet peace enveloped her as she wrote to Mother Barat:

A year ago today at this very hour we received the visit of the Bishop of Louisiana, and you gave your consent regarding our mission to the New World. Happy as I was then, I did not dream that the anniversary of that day would find us so near the holy goal of our journey, for what are 180 leagues as compared with the 2,200 we have traversed in fair weather and foul, since we sailed from Royan! An officer who was detained by some irregularity in his passport boarded our vessel by a small boat last night and told us there were reports of trouble in Paris and Bordeaux. The very thought that you may be suffering, along with so many people who are dear to us, is the severest trial I have had so far, for if we had been lost at sea, only a single branch of the tree would have perished, a branch that so far has produced no fruit, but if the trunk of the tree was endangered! How impatient we are for news from you! We live in the hope of finding letters awaiting us in New Orleans, for the vessel that was to sail soon after we did may have made better time than ours did, and it is sure to have on board letters from you.

We are nearing the end of our journey in fairly good health. As it is summer, we are able to sail the whole length of the coast of Cuba, a passage not usually chosen because of the currents, but shortening the trip by 400 leagues. The other route lies between Martinique and Guadaloupe. After avoiding this detour, we became so becalmed south of the Tropic of Cancer that there was question of passing between San Domingo and Porto Rico, or of taking a northerly course and then coming south through the Bahama Channel which separates Florida from the Great Bank of Cay near the United States.

For fifty-two days we saw only sea and sky. It was May 11 before we actually caught sight of land in the distance, the island of Caicos, one of the Lucayas belonging to England. Between it and Mayaguana we ran on to a Bahama sandbank one day, but the water covering it was deep enough to float the vessel. There was great rejoicing on board at the sight of that Lucaya island, for land is far more attractive than the sea.

The ocean holds such terrors at times that I was more than once on the verge of writing to beg you not to send another person out here until you received assurance that all is well with us and that such a sacrifice would be of real worth. I should keenly regret missing the opportunity of our nuns traveling with Monsieur Velay and the Ursulines in September, but even at best you can scarcely hope to hear before October that we have reached St. Louis or know our needs with any measure of certainty. It may even be later than that. So if you are able to send us the help, I shall not count on their coming before next spring, and I earnestly entreat you to send only persons of solid virtue, who are not conceited and in whom you see a marked vocation from God rather than desires expressed only in words. I am thoroughly convinced now that people who have been to Louisiana generally speak only of what is attractive, lest they should discourage anyone from going there, and that is Father Martial's line of conduct. But I owe you the truth, and I shall not hide from you either the perils of the sea or my own cowardice.

A storm at sea is really a terrifying sight. The roaring of the deep mingled with the crash of the tempest would drown both thunder and the booming of cannon. Add to this ear-splitting din the rolling of the vessel in the midst of great waves. The shouting of the sailors as they encourage themselves at their work has a tragic, a lugubrious effect. But their silence is even more dismal, and still worse is the sight of the captain pacing the deck in deep thought. A vessel tossed violently in an angry sea gives one some idea of the confusion of Judgment Day. The sky and the stars seem to disappear suddenly behind mountains of water. The sea, nearly black during the storm, gapes wide, revealing its bottomless depths, then suddenly closes. The waves sweep over the deck and are hurled out to sea with a new rolling of the boat. Twice during the night the high waves burst open the portholes and flooded our berths. The bending masts, the sails furled or torn, the steering wheel abandoned, lest the boat be too strained—all this is very terrifying unless one sees God in the storm.

The odor that permeates the whole ship is another trial, the confinement, the stench from the hold that is so nauseating and that can be avoided only by going on deck for fresh air—and one cannot always go there, especially in bad weather or when the sun is very hot. At night men sleep there; in the morning they are getting up. Besides, we cannot leave our little holes too early because people dress in the common room.

But if I have realized regretfully that many of our nuns could not endure the terrors of the sea, I have lamented still more over the great number who could not survive the stifling atmosphere of the cabins, the hard, narrow berths, the continual noise. In addition to the handling of the rigging and cordage, which often goes on at night, there is loud talking as if it were daytime. Eating and drinking go on in the common room, where two of us sleep and which adjoins the cabin occupied by the other three.

Seasickness is a wretched malady, affecting both stomach and head. One is utterly good for nothing; connected thought is impossible. One can scarcely drag from one's dull heart the least little prayer of love. I could only repeat the *"Ita, Pater,"* and "My God, I have left all things for You." And if in this condition one asks for a little water to drink or a cup of tea, it is often brought five or six hours later. If one can take only broth, what they bring is made from cabbage and is covered with grease, and sometimes it is made from spoiled meat. It is a mistake to say one should eat when one is seasick. For several days I could take only a little broth once or twice in twenty-four hours, and this only if I remained flat on my back, but I was quite well after that. Eugenie and Marguerite were either more courageous or in better condition for the trip, for they have suffered less from this illness. For two or three days we were all so ill, we could not help each other at all, and the steward had to take care of us. Either he or the captain's boy served us tea or broth through the opened curtains. As for Father Martial, we did not see him at all those days, for he was very ill. . . .

The *Rebecca* had been two months at sea when this letter was written, and ten more days were ahead of her before she reached the mouth of the Mississippi. Mother Duchesne and Sister Marguerite bunked in an alcove of the ship's lounge—the "common room"—for seventy days. It was Philippine's way to take the less desirable place and to keep close to her the Sister who was finding it so difficult to adjust herself to change. Already Marguerite was showing more nervousness and inadaptability than had been expected. Anxious and restless, she found calm security only in Mother Duchesne's company. Of the whole group, however, Father Martial had formed a very high opinion, for he wrote to the Superior General:

> I leave to good Mother Duchesne the telling of the tale of our voyage; you will get from her a very correct account. I reserve to myself the right to tell you what is in my heart with regard to the interior life of your religious. I shall begin by reproaching Monseigneur Du Bourg and you for having humiliated me for seventy days by putting under my guidance women whose virtue surpasses my power of expression. You will both have to answer to God for having chosen for them a director whose capacity and virtue were in no way proportioned to the souls confided to him. You can rejoice, however, in having furnished me with means for a renewal of interior spirit by the example I witnessed daily, for I feel obliged to tell you that not one of your Sisters was ever guilty of the least shortcoming. The passengers, the whole crew, all were in admiration. I had only to moderate their zeal—and this for my own sake: the contrast between my easygoing ways and their constantly increasing fervor would have been too noticeable.[19]

The value of this tribute is enhanced in the case of Mother Duchesne by the fact that for her the whole voyage was a period of spiritual desolation. With remarkable fortitude she showed unvaryingly for nearly three months the same joyous courage, the same thoughtful consideration for others, the same uncomplaining acceptance of circumstances and events that tried her soul at times almost beyond endurance. Yet she admitted, once the trip was over, that throughout it all she had known only darkness and disgust that were unrelieved by sentiments of hope or love. Physical debility was in part at least a cause of this: she had left Paris fatigued to the point of exhaustion. The responsibility laid upon her by Mother Barat had added to the depression. The retreat at Bordeaux had left her in spiritual dusk that deepened into a night of darkness. As yet the vision was far off. She sought relief in prayer, remembering Xavier's terrible description of the desolation that drove him to write, "I cannot go on"; yet he persevered. So she fought resolutely, concealing the struggle as far as possible, with that heroism which is the only antidote to this spiritual malady. If Father Martial knew about her suffering, he made no allusion to it in his letter to the Mother General.

The *Rebecca's* passage through the Gulf of Mexico was fairly smooth, and the nuns used this opportunity to write letters announcing their safe arrival, in the hope that these might catch a vessel leaving port soon after they docked in New Orleans. Mothers Berthold and Audé had kept a diary of the voyage, as had Mother Duchesne. Their account of the landing in America is more detailed than hers and better than any secondhand description could ever be, though repetition has made it something of a classic in the literature of the Society of the Sacred Heart:

May 25. We have reached the point where the waters of the Mississippi mingle with those of the sea, forming a distinctly different color. Today the pilot from New Orleans boarded our vessel to guide it through the difficult channel. The customs officer also came on board to talk with the captain. We entrusted to him letters we had written to St. Louis, to Madame Vincent at Bordeaux, and to the Mother House and our families.[20]

From this point on we were directed entirely by soundings, which diminished as we advanced up the river. Once the vessel touched bottom. Passing Balize, we saw huge rocks in the channel which only a skilful pilot could have avoided. The view is becoming more and more interesting. Dense shrubbery lines both sides of the river, and at night fireflies twinkle here and there, much brighter than our glowworms of France. We saw several crocodiles at a distance. The sailors caught a small one measuring about an arm's length. It looked like a lizard, black skin mottled with yellow, scaly and rough. . . .

Every day things grow more interesting. There are plantations with big houses, Negroes large and small on the banks of the river, herds of cattle, beautiful groves. We anchored so close to the bank several times that some passengers got off for a stroll, bringing back for our benefit anything curious they found. We have seen the kind of straw from which they make hats, sycamore trees like those of France, other trees that produce enormous thorns, and still others from which hang huge masses of green hairy stuff which they say is used effectively for making mattresses both by the poor people in the country and by the townsfolk in New Orleans. As to the birds, the only one that sings well is the *mocker*, but there are cardinals, blackbeaks, and one they call the green pope, interesting because of his name and his plumage. . . .

May 28. Four of the passengers left for the city in a little pirogue. This same evening the mosquitoes attacked us for the first time, and in spite of our nets they gave us no chance to sleep with their continual *bourdonnement* and their stings, which get very badly inflamed. . . .

May 29. The great Feast of the Sacred Heart of Jesus. Father Martial gave us a little sermon, and we renewed our vows at Holy Mass.[21] All day we crept slowly up the river. The country along the banks is becoming ever more smiling and open. Wide fields of cotton and corn under cultivation bespeak the industry of the inhabitants. While we were gazing at these new sights, came a message that a carriage awaited Father Martial on the river bank to take him and us to the city, for we were still some twenty miles downstream. Actually there were two carriages and it was about seven o'clock. By eight our satchels were packed and we were being let down into a small boat by means of the famous armchair which we had eyed so often with fear and envy during the crossing. . . .

It was with the deepest emotion [continued Mother Audé in the diary on the following day] that we set foot on this soil which is for us, in the eyes of faith and the designs of God, the Promised Land. Mother Duchesne's heart could not contain its sentiments of gratitude. In spite of the marshy ground she knelt and kissed the very soil. Her eyes were wet with tears, tears of joy, the kind Father Varin desired for us. "No one is looking," she whispered to us. "You kiss it, too." If only you could have seen her face! It was radiant with joy that only the Heart of Jesus could inspire in a soul filled with His grace and bent on glorifying His Sacred Heart.

It was a glorious night. The stars that studded the deep blue heavens were mirrored in the silvery waters of the stream. Fireflies sparkled in the low bushes. . . . At a plantation we bought some fresh bread, which we had not tasted for seventy days. Father Martial had sent a letter to the Ursuline religious announcing our arrival. Two priests who were at the convent when the letter was opened did not wait to hear it through, but went off immediately to engage the carriages, which came for us with a cordial invitation from the Ursulines to hasten the pleasure they anticipated in welcoming us. It was about two-thirty in the morning when we reached New Orleans, so we went to the priests' house to await the dawn. As the *Angelus* was ringing, we reached the Ursuline convent. The religious received us with a charity of which every moment has given us new proofs. . . .

2. June—August, 1818

CREDO—I believe . . .

Liturgy of the Mass

THE GRACIOUS WELCOME extended to them by the Ursuline nuns made the travelers from France feel at home immediately. Their very first day in New Orleans was filled with experiences they would record and long remember: the joy of Mass and Holy Communion in the convent chapel after eleven weeks out of cloister; the visit of Mr. Du Bourg, the Bishop's brother, and the French consul; Mother Duchesne's first sight of Indians—two of them begging near the convent grille—"sad-faced but vigorous," she thought, and she gave them an alms; a brisk tour of inspection through the convent and its adjacent buildings; news about the house that was being prepared for them in St. Louis—false report, they learned later on—but no news from Bishop Du Bourg. That was rather disconcerting, but this was only the first day. The nuns were fascinated by all the works they saw conducted so efficiently by the Ursulines, and they began to write glowing letters to France. As the weeks passed, however, and still no word came from the Bishop, anxiety clouded the eager eyes of Philippine Duchesne. She was, moreover, very sick, though at first she tried to conceal this fact, hoping she could be her own physician.

She became acquainted with the Ursuline community so quickly that on May 30, her first day in their convent, she was writing about them to Mother Bigeu:

> Here I am in New Orleans since two o'clock this morning. Yesterday we renewed our vows on board the vessel in union with you and all our loved ones in the Society, and the Heart of our good Master seemed to carry on a little rivalry with the heart of His Mother in answering our prayers after that holy ceremony. At eight o'clock in the evening of the feast of the Sacred Heart I set foot on land, which I had not touched since Holy Thursday. I kissed the ground reverently under cover of the darkness—this land that has been the object of so many prayers.[22] All the vivacity of my desires had surged up again as we drew near to it.
>
> The Ursuline religious, whose kind welcome simply overwhelms us, had gotten word of our arrival, so they sent carriages a distance of seven leagues to the place where the vessel had stopped for lack

of wind. We rode in procession and arrived at two o'clock in the morning on the last Saturday of May. So you see why I say there was some rivalry with her Divine Son to favor us. . . .

I am very eager to receive the blessing of the Holy Father. He himself wrote to the superior of this house while she was still at Montpellier. She had written to him, without the knowledge of her confessor or her bishop, to get a decision about coming out here. The answer was prompt and favorable, and Monseigneur Fournier told her it was a unique case for a pope to answer an individual's letter without first consulting with her bishop.

In this hospitable community there are several Creole nuns, one of them the daughter of a very early settler in the city. Two came from Pont-Saint-Esprit thirty-two years ago,[23] and I had the fun of repeating to them all I remembered from the account of their trip. Their third companion is dead. Eight of the community came from Montpellier with their superior eight years ago by way of Philadelphia and Baltimore.[24] In the latter town they were much discouraged, but a holy man told them that a lay-sister had predicted that the Mississippi River would one day have many religious institutions along its banks. That encouraged them. The other members of the community are the religious whom Monseigneur Du Bourg chose in France. Ours will be the second institution [on the Mississippi], at a place 500 leagues higher up the river—but when will it deserve to be called an institution? . . . For undertakings like ours it is important to choose silent, mortified people with good judgment. Americans are not soft in their ways, nor do they seek delicacies. They admire culture as much as the French do, but they do not like the French. . . .

The Ursuline convent is the haven of religion in this city. Besides the five of us, the nuns are now housing six ecclesiastics. Ordinarily they board and lodge two priests, who live here and have no source of income. In this country there are no revenues set aside for ecclesiastics. If they band together, they come under the law and their apostolic efforts are censured. . . . Cotton, linen, black material, and bread are medium-priced here, also crockery, but food and lodging are very dear.

This paper ends too soon. Get many blessings for us from our Mother General and from the [Jesuit] Fathers. Many affectionate messages to our Mothers and Sisters. We are all writing, and the consul will dispatch our letters.

To her brother and sisters she sent a long letter on June 2, addressing it to the eldest, Madame de Mauduit, at Grâne:

I am sure the love that unites us has caused you some anxiety as to the outcome of my voyage, anxiety increased, perhaps, by the length of time we were at sea. But here I am on land and in a city where the language and customs make one think one is in France, and the convent in which we are given hospitality is so like our own. Nowhere could we have received greater proofs of affection or more attentions. As our vessel was becalmed about six leagues below the city, the Ursuline nuns, to whom we had been recommended by our Bishop, sent a carriage for us that must have cost them at least fifty *écus*, and they thought nothing of it. Once we reached their convent, we were given a touching example of all the virtues of hospitality, along with every kind of care: medicine to forestall the effects of the change of climate, baths, refreshing drinks, the best of food, all kinds of clothing, and our own clothes taken away and washed the same day by the Negro women. Mothers could not have done more for their children. They even talk of giving us many more things for the rest of our journey, for we have to ascend the Mississippi some 400 or 500 leagues on a steamboat—a wonderful invention that makes the trip in twenty days, whereas settlers two years ago spent at least six months on it. There are now forty of these boats in operation. Commerce on the Mississippi is becoming more important every day, and Upper Louisiana, where we are going, is making daily progress in civilization. . . .

I want Melanie to know that on reaching New Orleans I wrote to the superior of the Visitation at Georgetown, begging her prayers. Here I met one of their former pupils. . . . She promised to tell my aunts, my cousins, and Reverend Mother how much I rely on their prayers. A French merchant of Havana who boarded the boat near Cuba was so interested in our work that of his own accord he gave us, in the most modest way, more than 200 francs, desiring, as he put it, to co-operate in our work.

I would like to write to the two Amelies, to my godson, and to the oldest Lebrument girls, but I have many letters to write and we may be leaving here at once, so I beg them to read all that is in my heart; if they want details of the trip, let them get our Journal from Constance. I hope one day to see some of my nephews or nieces in this country, coming either like ourselves to work for the salvation of souls or to make a fortune for life in a few years out here. I beg Madame de Mauduit to have nine Masses offered for me at La Louvesc. Mother Barat will give the stipend if Amelie does not want to make me this present.

In the midst of brave, chatty letters like these, one comes upon a cry of anguish welling up from Philippine's heart to Aloysia Jouve and enclosed in a letter to Mother Thérèse on June 3:

I have entrusted myself and all my dear ones to the Sacred Hearts of Jesus and Mary, but I do not know what you are doing or where you are—in His Hands always, I hope, and disposed to do His will. I submit beforehand to all He arranges, and still I feel that I cling to you. Even in sleep I seem to hear you calling to me, urging me, saying I shall be too late. I seemed to run; but just as I thought I had reached you, I awakened to realize that I am many hundreds of leagues from you. I renewed my sacrifice. . . .

Remember me to your dear parents, to Constance, to the Lebruments. Add the names of my nieces to the address of my letter for the children of the boarding school; it will reach you from Paris. . . .

The letter to the children in France is a charming description of the new world that was opening up to her. No shadow of heart-suffering crosses it, no hint that she was in physical pain. She was always the interesting *raconteuse*, and she enjoyed exercising this talent to give pleasure to others. So she sent this account of a variety of things that had attracted her attention since she bade them goodbye, writing at long length in her delightfully informal fashion.[25]

There was, however, a very disturbing side to life in New Orleans; and as Mother Duchesne became aware of it, she was puzzled, grieved, disillusioned to some extent. It was not long before she learned exactly why Bishop Du Bourg had chosen to travel by way of Baltimore and to establish his residence in St. Louis. When he had first come to New Orleans as Apostolic Administrator in 1812, he had been dismayed by the conditions prevailing in the city: the laxity of morals, the lack of religious practice, the neglect of religious instruction—a very sickening state of affairs. Still worse, he found himself opposed by Père Antoine de Sedella, a Capuchin friar of enigmatic character and baleful influence, and his backers, the trustees of the cathedral. Though somewhat timid in handling the situation, Father Du Bourg had suspended Père Antoine, as he had authority to do, and laid an interdict on the Cathedral of St. Louis of France. But he had fled to St. James Cabahanoce, to escape the mob violence aroused by this exercise of authority.

The Apostolic Administrator had regained prestige by his conduct after the British attack on New Orleans in January, 1815. He had carried out the ceremonies of thanksgiving for victory with imposing dignity and had delivered an eloquent address, for he was a masterful speaker. But in September of that same year he had gone to Rome to lay before the Pope the difficulties under which he was trying to administer the diocese, leaving Father Louis Sibourd as vicar-general to manage as best he could. Even after his consecration as Bishop of Louisiana and the Floridas, Monseigneur Du Bourg did not return to face the situation in New Orleans, but obtained from the Sacred Congregation *de Propaganda Fide* permission to establish his see temporarily at St. Louis in Upper Louisiana.[26] Such a step did not gain popularity for him in New Orleans.

Father Sibourd was acting as chaplain at the Ursuline convent on Chartres Street when Father Martial, Evremond Harrissart, and the Religious of the Sacred Heart arrived. Even as vicar-general he could not officiate in the cathedral nor claim the least pittance of a revenue on which to support himself. His efforts to carry on under such trying circumstances had proved his patience, loyalty, and devotion to the Church, but they had also undermined his health. Father Martial's arrival was a great relief to Father Sibourd, for he knew the tact and prudence of this priest, as well as his ability, and with Bishop Du Bourg's consent he persuaded him to remain in New Orleans.

Mother Duchesne learned all this and more from Mother St. Michel, the Ursuline superior, and the details were heart-sickening. She had had to admit, moreover, that she was ill, so ill, it turned out, that she had been put to bed soon after her arrival. The doctor recognized at once the disease so frequently contracted on shipboard in the days of sailing vessels. Mother Duchesne had scurvy. Her physical discomfort did not worry her, but to be a guest in such a busy convent and to need so much care caused her real embarrassment. In a letter to Father Barat, written on June 4, she mentions the doctor casually, for she had other things on her mind and heart. Happily her soul had at last shaken off the "desert dryness" of the long voyage, and hope and love were again in command as she initialed the letter paper *SS.C.J.etM.*, and wrote:

> Here we are, almost at the end of our journey, for four or five hundred leagues are very little when one has traveled thousands. And a trip on a gentle and beautiful river is a pleasure after one has seen the ocean and its storms. The Mississippi is not very formidable except at its mouth. It will soon be as heavily navigated as our rivers of France, so greatly is commerce progressing on its shores.

The doctor who attends the convent where we are staying has pictured New Orleans to us, perhaps too optimistically, as becoming very soon the equal of Bordeaux, and St. Louis becoming like New Orleans, and all Upper Louisiana transformed in a few years into another France, as far as climate, fertility, commerce, and civilization are concerned. The idea of so much progress in so little time has sent my thoughts flying after my heart. They have raced to the far northwest and across the South Sea [the Pacific] to Korea or Japan to gain the martyr's palm. That is the way with ambition in this world—never satisfied. But I can assure you that would satisfy me. I aspire to nothing more than martyrdom. Before attaining this happiness, which may still be far away, I let myself form other wishes concerning our mission, and the most important for it and for us will certainly be to see some of your sons out here. If only you would work to bring this about!

How much there is pent up in my soul—expecting to find here only saints and meeting almost immediately a priest (not the one who has caused the schism, but another) who holds opinions bordering on heresy, who has no love for the august name which it is such an honor for us to bear, and who makes trouble for a convent which, after God, is the main support of religion in this city. . . .

The closer I approach it, the more clearly I realize how very difficult our work is going to be and how meager are our means for getting started. But God is in the work; His will was manifest; and far from feeling an increase of that dryness of heart which was such a trial for me at Bordeaux and on the ocean voyage, I feel my heart expand now with hope. I am the more blameworthy for not being more virtuous, since I have to recognize the fact that so many graces have been poured out on us. Help me by your prayers, and recommend me, I beg you, to the prayers of all your sons. I beg the same favor from Fathers Roger and Druilhet, to whom I offer respectful regards. . . .

Mother Duchesne was spared a very severe case of scurvy, thanks to the competent nursing of the Ursuline infirmarian, Mother Gerard. The illness did not interrupt her letter writing, that happy gift by which she herself preserved for us the true Philippine Duchesne. A letter to Mother Eugenie de Gramont on the First Friday of June shows her in a bright mood, in spite of discomfort from fever, insects, heat, and some personal disappointments:

I wrote to you from Bordeaux. I do not know what happened to my letter, as I had no answer, though the time we spent in that city was long enough to have brought us that consolation. I realize, even from the anticipation of the joy which a reply from our Mother General will bring us, with what eyes and heart we shall devour it. We are upheld in this trial of lack of mail from her and from you by the thought of the great merit attached to our sacrifices and by the protection of Divine Providence, which shows us the goodness of God in our regard. We have been received by the Ursuline religious with the greatest charity and kindness. . . . They have expressed the wish that we should spend the summer here with them, so as to give time for our house to be completed. They refrain from insisting only because of the illness that often occurs in the month of August here and affects nearly all new-comers. They say I shall be immune, as I have had a severe fever along with mosquito bites that set me on fire; they also think I had scurvy. I was dreadfully embarrassed in this condition, especially being a guest in the Ursuline convent. They have pushed charity so far as to express pleasure over the fact that I was quite safe and that it was better to be sick at their convent, where we would have what we needed. Then they took my hand and offered me some tobacco [after the manner of the Indians and Negroes], just to show me they were not afraid of contagion.

The mosquitoes are nothing in comparison with the creatures that appear by the millions at sunset, swarm on people's heads, even get in their mouths. At night the only thing to do is fan oneself or stay under a mosquito bar. The heat is very moderate this year, and this is the more remarkable since there is no rain. Just at present there is no refreshing fruit to be had. The boarding pupils and the community have *café-au-lait* and butter every morning for breakfast, and so do even the Negro women in the kitchen. They also have milk at dinner and at goûter.

Mother Gerard has laughed a good deal every morning on see-ing me take, not a little coffee without sugar, and that covertly, but a big cup of *café-au-lait* sugared to syrup. As I did not want to take any breakfast when we first arrived, the superior had the doctor order me to do so. He said it is absolutely necessary in this country, and it would be better to omit supper, so I obey his order. All my companions are well, except for mosquito bites. How much our poor Mother General would suffer from this! They say there are no mosquitoes in St. Louis. The milk there is also more wholesome and delicious, the fruit more abundant, especially the apples. But best of all, we shall find kindness more general, and more piety and innocence. They speak English rather than French, so we continue to study it with a postulant, a pupil of the Visitation at Georgetown. There are already 36 religious in that monastery. We have not the glory of being the first to bring devotion to the Sacred Heart to the United States. I saw a book printed in this city, full of prayers to the Sacred Heart. In the convent here they have a beautiful picture of the Sacred Heart that was painted in Rome. I beg you earnestly to give me news about my niece and the children.

On Sunday, June 7, she wrote at greater length to Mother Barat:

The longer I am away from you by God's will, the more keenly I long for news from you and from our Fathers, Mothers, and Sisters. Not knowing whether you received the letters we sent at the middle of May when we were near Cuba, or the one I sent Mother Bigeu from here by way of Georgetown, I shall repeat a little of what I said in those two letters. It is the fashion to repeat when one sends letters across the ocean. The French consul has promised to dispatch our letters by a boat sailing for Havre in a few days. Those we want to send to Bordeaux can wait for the *Rebecca*, as she sails again before the end of this month.

Perhaps we shall hear something from St. Louis before I finish this letter. The Bishop has not written and that is not encouraging. Three days ago I met a rich man [Mr. John Mullanphy] from the North, who told us there is a great demand for both a college for boys and a boarding school for girls. The college is to be located in St. Louis; our school is to be seventeen miles from there, at Florissant (or St. Ferdinand), a village situated in one of the loveliest and most fertile parts of the country. It seems there is no suitable house in good condition. The inhabitants build quickly but not solidly. There is no question of stone; only wood or brick is used there, as also here in New Orleans.[27] In the convent where we are living now all the dividing walls between small rooms or large apartments are of wood. So are the roofs. I have never seen anything so nice.

Every day they grow kinder to us here. They even want to keep us here, as they fear illness [from river travel in summer]. These religious have had us purchase many things and want to pay for everything, saying, "We shall take care of that. We are so frequently given ten-dollar bills in alms." The superior told me today that her house will always be our stopping-place, and whenever more of our nuns come, they must choose a season of the year when they can stay here for a longer time. She has also offered to take care of any business for us or shipments for St. Louis. I hope that in time we may have many houses in this country. But it will be necessary to train nuns who can speak English and Spanish. St. Louis, they say, is more English than

French as far as language goes. Here English is as common as French. Nearly all the children speak both languages, and many of the parents speak only English.

I have never met more manner and charm than these Creoles possess. On the plantations the education of the girls may be somewhat neglected, but among the Americans in the cities much care is expended on it. I saw a little ten-year-old girl today whose schooling will be completed when she is twelve. To keep her busy at her books they are teaching her Latin. Her brother, now twelve years old, speaks French and English, writes these and also Latin, and is studying Greek. He is going to St. Louis with Father Martial. . . .

The merchant from St. Louis, whom I mentioned, is on his way to Philadelphia, whence he will take four of his daughters to France to put them in boarding school. They were all here at school at one time. The eldest, now about twenty years of age, wants to become a religious, but her father will not allow her to enter here. He insists that she spend two years in France. I spoke to him about our house at Poitiers, without making any definite arrangements. He seemed pleased with the idea. Mother Grosier would do well to accept them if they apply for admission to the boarding school, as they are very nice girls. . . . The Ursulines also spoke to me about another pair of sisters who are going to France for their education.[28]

The religious who come to join us out here should have very light clothing for the tropical part of the ocean voyage and the river trip, with long-sleeved linen undergarments. They ought to bring along bouillon tablets or a bottle of powdered consommé. it can be purchased for three francs in Bordeaux—to make broth with hot water when they are seasick; and a small kettle that can be heated with a lamp and so supply hot water for the broth; also some peppermint lozenges, sweet wine, lemons, and vinegar. One gets so thirsty. I laughed at all the provisions they made us take when we set sail, but nothing was superfluous. . . .

They say we may have to remain here a good while longer, so Father Martial has gone to the country for two weeks. I am giving an order at Lyons for our charitable benefactresses, the Ursulines. Their kindness really overwhelms me. They expect a priest and three more nuns to sail from France in September. If you could have them bring as a gift to this convent a very pretty embroidered flounce for an alb, I should be most grateful. They have none here. They have lavished a hundred times its value on us, and with a delicacy I cannot express in words. Here is the end of this sheet of paper. Another vessel is sailing in three weeks. . . .

Not a word about her illness, a single remark about the strange silence on the part of the Bishop which was causing her such anxiety, paragraphs of praise for the Ursulines, information picked up from John Mullanphy or the nuns—she filled the large sheets with thoughts of everyone except herself. She regained her strength as the weeks passed. She discussed with her companions this unexpected situation—they had been so sure the Bishop would send them some directive regarding their trip up the river to St. Louis. Now the news that the convent of the Sacred Heart was not to be located in St. Louis drew earnest pleading from many people that they remain in New Orleans. Responsibility for the decision lay with Mother Duchesne, and there seemed to be but one answer —to go on to St. Louis. Her letter of June 12 to St. Madeleine Sophie is more personal in tone than many others:

MY VERY REVEREND MOTHER,

The Captain of the *Rebecca* has reported sooner than the date set for his departure. I am taking advantage of his offer of service to send you some handiwork of the Indians, which I believe you will treasure as I do. The note attached to the package explains the various articles. . . . This is my fourth letter to you. I have repeated things in them all and have even contradicted myself several times, for I wrote as things happened and quoted different opinions. And more than this, the heart suffers from sacrifices whose value is known only to faith and love. But even in distress love cries out bravely, *"Deus meus, laetus obtuli omnia."* [My God, gladly have I offered Thee all things.]

I experienced this sentiment quite definitely when the doctor declared with a sinister air that I had scurvy. The questions he asked showed how astonished he was that the physician who visited our vessel at the mouth of the river had not noticed it. Other people asked me why I ever left France. . . . I was not worried, but I was very serious when I thought that God had no further work for me; that Eugenie could steer the boat, which would only gain by the change; that, more fortunate than Moses, I had entered the Promised Land and had brought here a colony destined to struggle for the glory of the Sacred Heart, and that I had sacrificed more than the great Lawgiver did, for he gave up only captivity, and I was giving up the Promised Land itself. I assure you death held every attraction for me, since I have every reason to fear I may spoil the work of our foundation; but God has shown me only His divine attractions.

My limbs were badly swollen, inflamed, and spotted with sores. After a treatment lasting several days, they returned almost to their normal condition. I really believe the doctor was mistaken. During the sea voyage my hands were not rough and blotched, as they so often are, and I did not have any soreness in my gums. It was only after I landed that I developed the welts and sores, and I attribute them much more to insect bites than to scurvy. My teeth and gums were nothing to boast about in France, so they could not be considered a basis for diagnosis. But now I am recovering. Catherine had almost the same thing. I did not mention scurvy to her, but I made her share the treatment. We have both been thoroughly dosed with medicines. Octavie has suffered from her palpitations, but her eyes have not troubled her. Eugenie is not sleeping and eating well, and Marguerite has her ups and downs.

I do not know how to describe the touching kindness shown me by the superior during this illness. It is quite inexpressible. We are the object of her continual attentions and also those of her community. After having cared for us in our distressing illness, she now wants to help defray the expense of our river trip, calling the 500 francs she offers us a "widow's mite." I scrupled to accept it, fearing she thought us worse off than we are. So I was perfectly frank with her and told her about the 10,000 francs sent by way of Philadelphia. At the same time I expressed the fear that, when we reach St. Louis, we shall find that this sum has been spent. She shared my fears on this score and advised me to write to the Bishop. She approved of what I wrote and asked me not to mention the 10,000 francs to the members of her community, in order not to lessen their sympathetic interest in our affairs, for they decide everything in Chapter here. We shall certainly never be the losers in dealing with these religious, so I beg you to pay Monsieur Jouve in Lyons the amount necessary to cover an order they have sent him through me. They like Octavie and Eugenie very much, and they want to keep us here in the city. They promise us all success, assuring us of their help with a disinterestedness that is admirable. However, while they wish to help on our work, they see as we do that it is more for the glory of God that we go on to St. Louis in the Illinois Country.

The kind merchant from Havana has been here to see us. He would like us to go to his country, but makes no promise of aid. . . . We are finding English very difficult. Even Octavie, who succeeds best among us, is not yet able to converse with the children's parents. In St. Louis they will be chiefly Americans, and these will not be satisfied with mediocrity. They can go a long way intellectually, and nothing in Europe is beyond their ability. The Creoles, who are in the majority in New Orleans, are softer, lighter, and more pleasure-loving. They marry at twelve or fifteen and consider sixteen too late. One of them, after taking music for a month, was able to compose. They are like those trees that grow quickly and die early. Their appearance is charming in every detail.

I beg you not to forget our novena at La Louvesc. I asked my sister, Madame de Mauduit, to have it made. I should have done this in fulfilment of my promise before I left France. . . . I wrote you that the French consul here is willing that letters for us be addressed to him; in that way they come gratis. He will also dispatch our letters to France, and he will take care of small packets of mail that may be sent to us. Large parcels must be sent to the customs' warehouse. The Ursulines will get them through without duty, if possible, and will give hospitality to any of our nuns who come from France. School equipment, such as books, instruments, etc., which are declared accurately and addressed to the educational institution [of the Sacred Heart] in St. Louis will pass the customs' office duty-free. The duty collected here is so high that it has brought the government as much as 40,000,000 francs in a single year. Commerce is becoming very important. We do not know yet what we shall have to pay on our baggage, etc. One thing is sure—all we brought with us is here at the convent in good condition, except the wine, part of which was lost by leakage. Through the good offices of the consul nothing was opened by the customs' officers; they were satisfied with the declaration. That was fortunate, for it is very important that the cases and luggage should not be unpacked before we embark on our second navigation.

We have been told that the trip up the river is not dangerous and that the captain, who has already been informed about our passage, is a very trustworthy man. The steamboats operate under very strict regulations. The men's quarters are entirely separate from the women's, so during the entire trip we shall be able to have neither Mass and Communion nor confession. We do not know yet when we shall leave. Not a word from the Bishop. Travelers tell us we are much wanted in St. Louis, that we shall lack nothing, and that all success will be ours. We need an English-speaking postulant. One who wanted to join us here is too delicate.

The priest whom we have seen most often here is a Benedictine from Florence [Father Moni].[29] He wanted to be a Jesuit and loves that Society dearly. He looks upon us as sisters and daughters, and we are able to appreciate him in spite of his difficulty in speaking our language. He was delighted when Eugenie and Octavie understood what he said in Italian. The priest whose opinions so appalled me when we first arrived here has taken his departure after being shown up in his true colors. He has done much harm here, and an effort is being made to repair this.

Going back to the Ursulines, it was Louis XV who had their convent built, and everything needed for it was sent over from France free of charge. The Jesuits procured the foundation, and the Jesuit missionary who visited Sainte Marie when I was a child got Ursuline recruits to keep the work going. He was the first Jesuit I knew. I have been very much struck by the details of the trials endured in this convent and by the loving intervention of Divine Providence in sustaining it. One of the stories centers about a statue of the Blessed Virgin and is much like that connected with my picture of St. Francis Regis.[30]

You will see from the letters of my companions that they are suffering. Fortunately they are kept very busy by the Ursuline nuns. All are longing for a letter from you. This long silence is not your fault but that of the vessels—they are all delayed this year. While we offer to God this privation of news from you or advice and directions, we find some consolation in telling you how we long to hear from you. Pray and have others pray for us. I kneel in spirit at your feet.

This letter and others had been sealed and packeted, and the samples of Indian handicraft carefully wrapped for the voyage to France, when the *Rebecca*, true to form, it would seem, was again delayed. The *Gustave* had been in port nearly three weeks when at last its mail bags were released and letters were brought to the convent for Mother Duchesne and her companions. After carrying them to the chapel, they sat down together to read or to listen, to laugh or to cry with joy, to talk things over once more and by so doing to strengthen their determination to carry out the original plan of their journey.

The letter Mother Duchesne received from St. Madeleine Sophie in New Orleans is missing from the collection she treasured and guarded so carefully to the end of her life. But her own letter of June 24, 1818, is preserved:

God, who loves to console His own [she wrote], has permitted a delay in the departure of the *Rebecca*, in order to allow us time to receive and answer your letters, along with those of Mother Bigeu and your brother. They came on the *Gustave*, but had not been released. We have not gotten the picture of the Sacred Heart yet, but Mr. Fournier says it was taken on board by the captain. I shall not repeat what I wrote in my last letter. We carried yours to the foot of the altar before reading it—we wanted to thank God for this great joy. You can understand the sentiments of our hearts. The superior of the Ursulines brought the mail herself and asked quite graciously that we give you her regards and say she would love to know you. She is really a great-souled religious. . . .

Please forgive my letter from Bordeaux, as you have done with regard to so many faults you have put up with so patiently in the past. It was only natural for me to express my fears regarding the office I hold, and I am every day more fully convinced that I have no ability whatsoever for guiding souls. But God is doing the work for Himself, and my Sisters are happy. They will tell you so.

Father Martial is remaining in New Orleans longer than we are. Since I finished my last letter, everybody is telling me encouraging things about our venture in St. Louis, and here, too, if we made such a foundation. Mother Rivet would not be too old for this work. Ursuline religious have come out at the age of fifty-two. But one must be steadfast, especially on the sea trip, and ready to face death.

The *Rebecca* also carried a letter to Father Barat. Philippine dated it on the feast of St. Aloysius Gonzaga, June 21, and wrote from the fulness of her heart:

My very, very dear Father,

I have already written to you, but I do not know the fate of my letter, and it would be so helpful to have an answer to it. . . . At the beginning and during the greater part of our ocean trip I experienced that aridity which caused me such suffering at Bordeaux. My soul rejoiced, however, as we drew near to this land I have so desired. But this was in order to give me grace to bear a heavy trial—that of hearing a priest who had been highly praised to us speak of the affairs of this diocese, of the schools, etc., in a manner that greatly astonished me, as I had imagined I would find only saints out here. He almost gave himself away in a sermon I heard. Afterwards someone had the courage to say to him, "If you had preached that way in Italy, you would have been forbidden to appear again in the pulpit." He realized quickly enough that he had displeased the religious in particular, and he went off, leaving them in great privation, as Father Sibourd had just left for Philadelphia, where he is going to have a very bad growth removed from his nose. He seems lost to this mission.

A very excellent priest, Father Moni, has left his parish, which is eight leagues from here and where he is greatly loved, to give spiritual help in this city. But his meager command of French hinders him from doing the good he might accomplish. He spoke to me about you with great praise, and he loves the Society of

Jesus. He hopes you will come out here. What a harvest you would find, and how few the laborers are! The condition of the parish is heart-breaking. The partisans of Père Antoine bought him a mitre and brought it to him, telling him they wanted him to be their bishop. Happily he answered that bishops are not made that way. They gave some signs of submission, just to prevent actual schism.

Up North, they say, good progresses slowly but surely. Protestants stop *preaching* in order to go on Sundays to hear the holy Pastor [Bishop Du Bourg] who preaches in English. They love him as much as the Catholics do. In general, people speak encouragingly about our prospects. I foresee many difficulties, but I face them with great peace of soul. I have never been more at peace, though I am without any consolation. I have broken my ties—spiritual and human—without any promise of success. I recognize my incompetence in the work of guiding souls. I fear being an obstacle to good, and yet I cannot regret what I have done. I always feel that God wants this work.

It seems that we are not going to be stationed in St. Louis. Many people want us to stay here, especially the charitable Ursulines who are taking such care of us. They want to retain Father Martial, too, and I would like that for their sake, for they have become very dear to me. He listens to all this with only one ear, but he works willingly with the religious. We do not yet know where we belong; but wherever it is, God is there. My companions are well, especially since we reached the cloister, which is so necessary for Octavie's happiness. Catherine talks too much. They will tell you much more than I have. We are in a rather trying situation. How we long to be living our Rule! I am sending you a packet of letters for our Mother General. Kindly forward them to her by an opportunity or by the diligence, and distribute the other letters, after examining the interesting handiwork of the Indians and reading the note accompanying them.

For nearly three more weeks the five Religious of the Sacred Heart remained in New Orleans. Though they were within the cloister most of the time, they became acquainted with many features of the old colonial town. In the convent garden or on the galleries overlooking it, they heard the cry of the vendors mingling with thin strains of street music, the shouts of teamsters and the peculiar drawl of Negro voices, the quick staccato of Creole women calling to neighbors, the banter of boys playing on the banquettes, and a hundred other sounds combining to make a din that contrasted sharply with the noises of Paris or the silence of

Sainte Marie. The garden air was heavy with the scent of flowers—
a lovely place in which to walk and pray or to sit and write in the
early morning or late afternoon, though one would need to keep a
fan at hand to ward off the mosquitoes.

Sometimes Mother Duchesne and a companion went on business to shops or offices, passing attractive houses in Spanish or
French style, with their paved courtyards, wide grilled gateways,
and shops fronting on the streets. Flowering vines and oleanders
growing against the brick and plaster walls added color and
fragrance, though they encountered less pleasant odors at times as
they walked along the banquettes and made their way down the
Street of the Levee. There on the waterfront a babel of voices
greeted them, and Philippine was more convinced than ever that
the gift of tongues was a requisite for the missionary in the Mississippi Valley. Often, as she rested at night on her moss-filled
mattress while the breeze from Lake Ponchartrain stirred the
protecting mosquito bar above her, she listened to the street sounds
die away. Then she would realize how tired she was—not from
any bodily exertion, but from her effort to conquer physical weakness and from anxiety. She could not kneel through the night hours
in the Ursuline chapel, but she could pray in the quiet sanctuary of
her own soul, laying down the burden of her responsibility in
simple faith and trust.

These were difficult weeks for Mother Duchesne because of
the increased pressure brought to bear on her by the Ursulines
and other friends who wished to keep the Religious of the Sacred
Heart in New Orleans permanently. Zeal and charity motivated
the urgent appeals and arguments, and the reasoning was always
plausible enough. Then, too, Bishop Du Bourg's silence was so
hard to explain and to accept. Mother Duchesne turned more than
ever to prayer, spending long hours each day before the Blessed
Sacrament, begging for divine assistance and guidance, for courage
to cling to the original plan, and making fervent acts of faith in the
grace of obedience. She discussed the matter again and again with
her companions, and they agreed with her that they should go to
St. Louis on the first available steamboat.

The *Franklin* was booked to leave on Sunday, July 12. The
nuns began to pack their valises and to make the rounds of the
Ursuline convent, saying goodbye to each member of the com-
munity, to the children they had learned to know, and to the
Negro women who had served them so cheerfully and so well.
Many friends came to call on them, insisting that this was just

au revoir. Mother Duchesne's last letter from New Orleans was begun on July 9 and written at several sittings during the next two days. It is a crowded epistle, very characteristic of its writer, summarizing conversations, abounding in faith and humility, in ardor and gratitude, in fear of self and childlike dependence on the fatherly protection of Divine Providence.

My very reverend Mother,

This is the fifth letter I have written you since we reached here, and I realize with sorrow that it may be a long time before I receive any answer. The letters that came on the *Gustave* were pretty old. Our picture of the Sacred Heart is held in the customs office because Madame Fournier fastened under the wrapping paper a little packet for the Bishop unstamped. We hope to get the picture by Sunday, the day set for our departure from New Orleans. It was to have been tomorrow, and our boxes and baggage are already on board the steamboat for St. Louis. We did not unpack anything, as we used only what we had in our valises. The Ursulines had our clothes laundered every week, and we have bought cotton dresses of light material for the trip up the river. They are black with a single white thread running through the goods. The Sisters have dark purple dresses. Both the doctor and the Ursuline nuns insisted on our doing this. We wore our religious costume on the ocean vessel, and no one thought it out of place. On the contrary, they commented that it was a well-chosen habit, having nothing singular about it. The Ursulines, even those who have come out during the last thirty years, have traveled in secular dress, and we shall have to do so on the steamboat. We shall also be deprived of Mass and confession.

Father Martial would like to be going with us to St. Louis. I asked him to write you a few lines. I do not know whether he did so or not. He did not relish the idea. He said he had no complaint to make; and that if he wrote in our praise, you would see that he had been asked to do so. He reproved me for having written you any unpleasant impressions about C. When I told him it was my duty to give you an account of things, he answered, "Yes, but not so soon. Later on you would be able to mingle good reports along with bad ones. It is a mistake to put on paper and send such a distance unfavorable impressions that cannot be easily removed." I tell you this so that you may disregard anything in my expressions that you think comes from my harshness of character.

Father Martial has been very kind to us and has continued to direct us fervently in the confessional. I have skipped him, however, three or four times and taken advantage of the presence of an Italian priest [Father Moni], who is much like Father Perreau. He is a man of deep piety who loves the Society of Jesus. His soul is great and noble, like the family to which he belongs. He has taken a very kind interest in us.

After a repetition of many of the difficulties confronting her, she continues:

But why should I worry about the future? When the time comes for action, Divine Providence is always on our side and on that of the missions. For the last one hundred years no boat carrying missionaries has been wrecked, though so many accidents occur. The *Peterson*, which sailed soon after we did, was wrecked off the Windward Islands. Fortunately the passengers bound for Georgetown were saved, but we do not know all the details. The *Rebecca*, in spite of bad weather, a fire, and an encounter with a dangerous pirate ship, was safe while we were on board, but as she was going down the river she was pillaged by pirates. I do not know what happened to our letters—there was quite a number of them—and the package containing the little handiwork of the Indians which I had sent to your brother for you. Not knowing whether you have received the letter containing my several requests, I shall repeat them here. . . . Vessels come here frequently from Havre. If Madame de Rollin would give you an address there for sending and receiving mail, it might be better than sending through Bordeaux. . . .

They say a foundation here is indispensable, as it would be the center of all the houses we may one day have in America, and that this is a suitable place for our novitiate, as the city is large and cosmopolitan. They think, too, that we should have a house here for those whose health is too delicate to stand the cold in St. Louis. Those who cannot bear the heat here could go up there. Finally, they have impressed on us how glad they would be to have us and all the religious who will join us later on. But they stress the fact that later on there may be no opening for us.[31]

I saw the wisdom of the inducements held out to us, but I answered consistently that it is God's will for us to go on to St. Louis. . . . We know the will of God. But I am so impressed by their arguments that I beg you to make a foundation here next spring. I shall talk to Monseigneur about it, and to the French consul here, if I can see him before we leave. . . . I am so glad to have come out here, I shall willingly make sacrifices in order to procure foundations. I think I should be ready for anything, even to face again the terrors of the sea or to cross uninhabited wilderness.

One thing that excites my jealousy is to see Father Martial

already overworked, while we remain idle. There is so much to be done in New Orleans, for the city is growing fast and we have seen as many as twenty vessels come up the river in two days. . . . Again I beg you for a foundation here. Mother Rivet is very willing to come, and at her age she would be more easily acclimated than if she were younger. Mother Thevenin is also eager to come. This country would just suit her, and her sweetness, her culture and facility for languages would make her very useful. One does not need great learning here; perhaps more is needed for the Americans in St. Louis, as they are deeper in character than the Creoles. You can count on Eugenie as a future superior. She has religious maturity and always acts wisely and in the presence of God. . . .

The *Franklin* pulled away from the landing and headed upstream as scheduled on July 12, with just fourteen passengers on board, but with a heavy lading in the hold. It was a new boat in its second season, and Captain Reed was flattered by the lively interest of the French nuns in everything he showed them. The machinery occupied almost the entire length of the first deck, leaving only a small space in the rear for "deck passengers." The domain of the cabin passengers was the second deck, where the ladies' parlor was well to the rear for the sake of safety in case of a boiler explosion. The pilot house and officers' quarters were on the top, or "hurricane," deck.

It was all novel and interesting, but it was a very expensive trip, costing perhaps five hundred dollars for the five nuns. When Mother Duchesne had tried to offer Mother St. Michel and her community a little gift in return for their cordial hospitality, the Ursulines would not hear of such a thing. Instead, they pressed on their departing guests another three hundred dollars to help defray the expense of the river trip. And through the decades that followed, their charity continued with a generosity that is beyond all counting.

The nuns had been assured that the river trip was not at all dangerous. But the fact that it took the *Franklin* forty days of navigation to reach St. Louis shows that perils abounded, for the Mississippi was so notoriously dangerous that travel by night was rarely attempted in the early decades of steamboating. Shallows and sand bars, planters and sawyers were practically everywhere and difficult to avoid. A snag could rip such a rent in the wooden hull that the boat would sink in a few minutes. In summer and autumn when the river was low, shifting sand bars changed the channel continually and built up hidden traps on which boats ran aground and listed perilously, if not disastrously. Spring floods, carrying great loads of debris from upstream, occasioned troubles of another kind.

There were man-made dangers, too, on the river trip. Mechanical inefficiencies abounded, for the steamboat was still in a trial-and-error stage. Faulty boilers sometimes burst under high pressure of steam. Wood used for fuel threw off showers of sparks that often set fire to the highly combustible boats. Crude sanitary conditions added danger to discomfort, for the steamboats became carriers of the dreaded epidemics that ravaged cities and towns along the river for nearly a century. Mother Duchesne would experience the rougher side of river travel in the years to come, but both the *Franklin* and the Mississippi were on their good behavior during the summer of 1818.

From the time the boat was loosed from its moorings and headed out into the stream, the nuns were engrossed in the beauty of this new phase of their new world. Three of them had known the grandeur of Alpine country, the placid beauty of its high valleys, the clear current of its swift rivers that raced between narrow banks and were bridged by a span or two of arching. Here was a mighty expanse of mud-yellow water, so wide that its fearful swiftness was almost unperceived, yet holding unpredictable destruction in its treacherous current. Gulls soared or sailed overhead or skimmed the surface of the water. On either side, beyond the lavish tangle of rushes and sedges, stretched flat land without so much as a hill to break the monotonous vista to the horizon. As the *Franklin* moved up the great waterway, the nuns noticed how the dense growth on the shoreline was first a mingling of palm and willow and cane, then changed to brakes of cypress, live oak, and cottonwood. Here and there along the continually winding stream appeared wide plantations of corn and cane and flooded rice fields. Cattle grazed in the moist green meadows, but the grass, Mother Duchesne noted, was *not* so tall as to hide the animals from view. Now and then on the lower stretches of the river, substantial plantation houses could be seen, gleaming white or creamy yellow in the sunshine, with stately avenues of trees leading from the river landing to the pillared gallery, with sugar houses and slave quarters, stables and carriage houses scattered at no great distance from the big house.

In the swampy bayous, once a part of the river's channel, alligators floundered or swam or crawled about, and pelicans fished with awkward dignity. Tall, moss-draped cypress trees rose from swampy land sunk in brown ooze and formed an impenetrable forest wall. Sometimes the *Franklin* plowed along in their deep shade and the passengers found relief from the midsummer sun. Herons rose from the tangled thickets, startled by the splash of the paddle wheel that left a choppy white wake on the water. Swarms of mosquitoes attacked the passengers, and their stings were like sparks of fire, Mother Audé thought.

As the steamboat took its zigzag course up the highway of the valley, it stopped now on one shore, now on the other, to take on passengers or freight or fuel wood. At the Donaldsonville landing Father Benedict Richard came aboard with two seminarians, Evremond Harrissart, whom the nuns knew quite well, and Michael Portier.[32] Heading upstream again, Captain Reed pointed out the entrance to Bayou Lafourche, a steady, languorous stream that had broken away from the river long ago and taken an independent course through rich lands that attracted early plantation settlement. Mother Duchesne and Mother Audé would know that bayou and Assumption Parish, through which it found its way to the gulf. Now it was only a name.

There was high ground on the shore to the east before the boat reached Baton Rouge. *"Baton Rouge?"* Once the domain of the Houma Indians, someone explained, and marked by the warning red stick.

When the river was lashed by summer storms, the angry waters were dark under the gray sky, but the *Franklin* rode them sturdily, and the nuns were unafraid, for they had weathered ocean storms far worse than those that struck the river in 1818. Fair weather meant oppressive heat, but sundown brought relief and the soft, still night, when a million stars hung low in the rich, dark sky above, or the golden moon rode behind the giant trees or shone in splendor on the rippling water, hiding its murkiness under a lustrous sheen. Then a mocking bird, perched high, would pour forth its sweet melody, and all else was still save the swish of disturbed waters.

In their diary the nuns kept an almost day-by-day account of incidents and accidents. Nineteen hours aground on a sand bank was worth noting, also a sudden halt and reversal of the boat, when a great drift of tree trunks and other water-logged debris barred the channel where the river had torn away a vast stretch of its eastern shore. A bread shortage gave a new topic for talk but caused little inconvenience, for there was plenty of corn meal on hand. At the frequent stops for refueling, the boat hands chopped in the forest while passengers hunted wild turkeys, ducks, and rabbits to add to the dinner menu. Sometimes they also brought back specimens of the rich vegetation that lined the shores, and the nuns were introduced to new varieties of plants—the lovely magnolia, the tulip tree, cypress, pawpaws, water lilies in delicate shades, and many others unknown in Dauphiny.

The high, green bluffs of Natchez came into view on July 17, and the *Franklin* drew in to the landing. During the day some drunken Indians on horseback rode down to the river bank, the men bedecked in native finery of skins and bright-hued feathers, the women wearing red calico and shining ornaments. The sight of them attracted and repelled Mother Duchesne, and she was relieved when they rode off, swaying and sagging on their mounts. In the sunset at Natchez the river was tawny gold, reflecting the glory of the horizon beyond the flat green of the western shore. As she gazed across the water at the crimson sky, Philippine did not suspect the agonies she would endure on that shore one day, nor the charity with which she would be received into one of the many beautiful homes that had already been built in and around Natchez.

The river was gradually narrowing as it led into the heart of the wilderness. The landscape was changing to gently rolling country, but it was not a gentle country they were heading toward. Here and there appeared a pioneer's clearing, a log cabin, a patch of cultivated ground. Further on, tilled fields, small orchards, and fenced pasture lands marked the outskirts of settlements and the industry of the pioneers. Early in August the *Franklin* passed the Arkansas border, and Missouri lay on the left bank. Mother Duchesne noted the course of the boat in her *Journal:* "We met with many accidents," she wrote, "because of snags and sand bars, but we saw other steamboats treated much worse than ours." After mentioning stops at several small river towns, she dwells at some length on Kaskaskia, where

> the boat was to remain for twenty-four hours, so the Religious of the Sacred Heart, knowing that a priest resided there, hoped to find an end to their long spiritual privation. . . . They were disappointed in their hope, for the pastor was just leaving and took Father Richard with him.[33] But a half-civilized Indian chief of the Illinois tribe came to the river bank with his wife and many followers.

On August 19 the boat stopped at Ste Genevieve and the

pastor, Father Henri Pratte, came to see the religious.[34] Mother Duchesne was so impressed by this young priest and all he told her about the town and its people, that when she found herself in what seemed to be a situation impossible of acceptance in St. Louis, her thoughts turned eagerly to Father Pratte and his parish, but she was not allowed to found her first convent in that fervent Catholic community.

The long river trip was drawing to a close. As the limestone cliffs grew higher along the west shore the travelers strained to catch a glimpse of the spreading group of houses that was the town. From the river St. Louis presented a charming sight—white buildings high on the bluffs against a backdrop of green. With more than half a century of quiet annals to record, it was still just a frontier trading post, but its unique geographical position as the center of the fur trade and western commerce gave it promise of a splendid future. Pierre Laclede Liguest had chosen well when he marked the site in the winter of 1763 at a spot where an abrupt wall of limestone rose from the river bank. On the level, well-drained tract of land fronting the bluffs a plan was laid out for the village which Laclede himself declared would someday become "one of the most beautiful cities in America." [35]

The growth of the village was slow. Small groups of settlers came from the Illinois Country just across the river, which had fallen into English hands, and from Lower Louisiana, Canada, and France. The place was distinctively French. Fur trade, traffic in assorted merchandise, and agriculture in common fields made up the bulk of the livelihood among the inhabitants. They were honest, hospitable folk on the whole; they were happy and not too hard-working. They loved their traditional way of life, and in spite of the cession of the region to Spain and the infiltration of Spanish and American settlers, the village remained decidedly French in manners and customs, language and law until 1804, when the western flow of American population began to stream across the Mississippi. By 1818 the population of the area of which St. Louis was the chief town totaled more than sixty-five thousand and raised a national crisis when Missouri asked admission to the Union as a state in which slavery was allowed by law. All this the nuns on board the *Franklin* had learned when the steamboat anchored for the night a mile below the foot of the Market Street landing on the evening of August 21, the feast of St. Jane Frances de Chantal. The boat had been expected for several days and its cargo of merchandise had been advertised in the *Missouri Gazette* that very day, but the presence of the nuns on board was not presented as a news item.

They were expected, however, by Bishop Du Bourg, and he had made arrangements for their coming. General Bernard Pratte and his wife gave hospitality to these first nuns who ever crossed a threshold in St. Louis. Their home stood at the corner of Main and Market Streets, a French colonial structure of the best frontier type, built of upright posts set on a stone foundation, two stories high, with a gallery extending around the four sides. There was the usual detached kitchen to the rear, and a roomy garden and orchard were neatly fenced in. Bernard Pratte and his wife had lived there since 1797. For twenty years the lower floor was used as a general store, where dry goods, groceries, liquors, hardware, and sundries were sold, the common medium of exchange being furs, which were usually stored in the small warehouse that stood on the southeast corner of the property facing the river. In 1817 General Pratte remodeled the home and added a two-story brick building, which fronted on Main Street, as did the home, and housed the general store on the first floor.[36]

So Mother Duchesne and her companions were welcomed to the newly renovated home, and there they remained for three weeks in the midst of kindness and consideration that rivaled even the charity of the Ursulines. The Prattes were a happy French Catholic family, presided over by a charming Creole mother, who had been Emilie Labbadie, and including two sons and five daughters. They were related to "almost everybody in town," as their maternal grandmother was Pelagie Chouteau, sister of the co-founder of St. Louis, and intermarriage had been frequent among the best Creole group in the town.

Neither the sultry August heat nor the fatigue of travel and first acquaintance with so many people deterred Mother Duchesne from writing to her Superior General on the night of August 22 to give an account of much that had happened on the trip up the river and much that she had learned during her first day in St. Louis:

MY VERY REVEREND MOTHER,

We are now nearly 3000 leagues from you, but the farther I go, the closer I try to keep to you by my desire to act according to your intentions and to carry out your instructions. But at such a distance I can at times only groan inwardly as events happen and situations arise and I am unable to ask your advice. Here we are

at our third halting-place since we left Paris. Bordeaux and New
Orleans were unpleasant only because they retarded the joy we
were anticipating. We had our hearts set on St. Louis, and it turns
out to be another camping place. We are lodged in a comfortable
home, where we are getting acquainted with the children who will
be the first pupils in our boarding school. In a week we shall leave
for St. Charles, where we are to begin our work in a rented house.
Monseigneur is going to accompany us there and remain a few
days to help us get settled.

He is very kind to us. He heard our confessions today and says
he regrets that he cannot keep us in St. Louis, but there is not a
single room for rent in the town. He puts before us the great advantages St. Charles possesses. He thinks it will become one of the
most important cities of North America, as it is situated on the
Missouri River, along which the population is growing daily and
which is about to give its name to a new state of the Union. No
day passes without the arrival of four or five families with their
belongings, who come to settle in a country which is making
astonishing progress. If they carry out the project of opening a
canal which will give a water route from the Mississippi and the
Ohio to New York, then letters from France will come that way
more quickly than by New Orleans.

We left there on the steamboat *Franklin,* July 12, and arrived
here only today, August 22—that is, the steamboat did. But last
night when we stopped just a mile below the town, I disembarked
with Octavie, and the captain escorted us to the Bishop's residence.
He greeted us graciously and brought us to the home in which he
had so kindly procured lodgings for us. He is going to give us as
chaplain Father [Benedict] Richard, who knows your brother,
Father Barat, and who was for a time with the Jesuits, they say.
The Bishop says he will visit us often at St. Charles, which can be
reached from here in a morning's drive. Although Ste Genevieve
is a little further away from St. Louis, I asked him to send us there
instead. . . . Father Pratte told us he had asked the Bishop to
allow us to settle in his parish, for he loves nuns and he was
cared for by them in Canada. He said there were more than forty
girls who would have hurried down to the steamboat to see us,
had they known we were there. That visit was very consoling, for
we realized we were listening to a true father and apostle. . . .

This section of the country is becoming more and more English
in language, and it will become Protestant in religion if the Catholics are not given more help, for it is being settled by people from
cities on the eastern coast, among them Swiss, Germans, and
others. Monseigneur says there can be no question of a foundation
in New Orleans at present. . . . As to Ste Genevieve, he says it is

gradually being ruined, as the Mississippi is slowly eating away its land and it is losing its commerce without hope of regaining it. But the land along the Missouri is steadily developing into a rich country.

As a matter of fact, you will see by our Journal, which we are sending you by way of New Orleans, that between Natchez, which is about one hundred leagues above New Orleans, and the mouth of the Ohio River, not far from Ste Genevieve, there is on the east bank only a forest inhabited by Indians, and on the west, woods broken here and there by a clearing on which there are some miserable cabins. There is no stone for building on either side of the river, and there are no men to chop down the trees. On nearing the Ohio one sees Kentucky on the east and several villages on the west. The scenery has changed completely. Instead of the uniform green curtain formed by impenetrable forests, there are houses, herds of animals, cultivated fields, rocks, and a pleasant rolling country.

There are many Indians in the vicinity of Kaskaskia and many of them are Catholic. They work in the fields, live in the village, and attend the church we visited. The chief of the Illinois and his *princesses* came to the river bank to see the steamboat we were on—the first to enter the Kaskaskia River to unload merchandise. These Indians were on horseback and dressed in beaded garments, and other Indians formed their suite. Seen from a distance, they presented a spectacle not at all ridiculous, but rather imposing and full of interest. Our Journal will tell you other things. I beg you not to worry about us. You expected us to have something to suffer, and the example of our holy Bishop, who might have had a brilliant career in Paris and who chose poverty, labor, and suffering instead, is an inspiration to us. . . .

During the next three weeks Mother Duchesne became fairly well acquainted with St. Louis, a town of four long streets, with farms beginning just beyond and extending over the hills and out on to the prairie. In the freshness of the early morning the nuns went each day to assist at Mass in the old church that was falling into ruins. No wonder the Bishop was so insistent about the construction of a cathedral! After the first day or two, they noticed a young girl waiting each morning at the street corner near the church—a slight figure in a cotton dress and sunbonnet. Her large blue eyes were fixed on the nuns with a devouring gaze, but she kept aloof as she followed them into the church and knelt where she could watch them. When Mother Duchesne inquired who she might be, Mrs. Pratte recognized at once a protégée of hers, little Mary Ann Summers. She was just about twelve years of age, but she was doing a woman's work, keeping house for her family—a sickly mother and an older brother who worked on the waterfront. When Mrs. Pratte sent for Mary Ann one day, the girl was at first speechless with joy and could only hold out shyly the apples she had brought as a gift for the nuns. Mother Duchesne put her at her ease very quickly and they talked together for a little while, for Mary Ann spoke French as well as English. She had just one desire —to go with the nuns wherever they might open their convent. But that was out of the question now; her sick mother needed her care.

The nuns went on foot through the town with General Pratte, inspecting first one place, then another. Mother Duchesne drove to Florissant with the Bishop to look at a house. It was a delightful drive through one of Missouri's most beautiful stretches of country —virgin country almost uninhabited—but the house proved to be as unsuitable as the locality itself. There were lengthy discussions —in French, to Mother Duchesne's great relief—regarding the prospects of a convent at Ste Genevieve, but St. Charles had been decided on, long before the nuns reached St. Louis, and after their arrival the Bishop gave no serious consideration to any alternative. He listened to the arguments, suggestions, and generous offers of General Pratte, who doubted the wisdom of placing the nuns in an outlying district and was willing to put at their disposal a house in St. Louis. He admitted the need for an educational institution in the town and the desire which many prominent Catholics had expressed with regard to the Religious of the Sacred Heart. Yet he held to his first decision, and Mother Duchesne knew that soon she would have to say goodbye to St. Louis with its pleasant homes and gardens behind high picket fences of rough saplings, its narrow streets bustling with activity, its river-front crowded with boats of many kinds and shapes, and the wagons lined up on the Illinois shore and waiting to be ferried across to the "promised land." On her birthday she wrote several letters to France. Thinking of her sisters and their families, of Josephine and her brothers, she gave them a few details about her new world:

My very dear Sisters,

I wrote to Madame de Rollin today by way of Washington. But I could send only one letter that way, so I shall take advantage of the return trip of the steamboat that brought us here, to give you news of myself. The river trip from New Orleans to St. Louis took 40 days and was pleasant. In a few more days we shall set out for St. Charles on the Missouri, where we shall reside for the present.

This section of the country is going to be organized into a state, which will enter the Confederation of the United States, of which it is now only a territory. St. Louis will be the capital, and its population is increasing every day. They are building on all sides, yet it is impossible to find lodgings. Rents are higher here than in Paris and so is the price of food. Luxury is a strange thing. It has penetrated even into the midst of some savage tribes that are partly civilized. Since the coming of Monseigneur [Du Bourg], religion has begun to take some hold, and it has been established in Kentucky by the zeal of Monseigneur Flaget, who is the bishop there. Before he came, the people really had no religion. He has had several churches built. The only churches I have seen here are made of wood.

I am eager for letters from France that will tell me how you all are. I am well. Our holy Bishop survives, in spite of his strenuous labors. If you want details of my trip, our nieces at Grenoble can get you the loan of our Journal. It will reach there later, going first to Paris. Be assured, my dear Sisters, that my prayers include you all and that my heart was never more concerned about your happiness. I embrace all your children.

The presence of the nuns at church on Sunday, August 30, caused more than a little stir. Visitors had been calling on them frequently—pretty, intelligent Creole women who compared quite favorably with those whom they had met in New Orleans. They carried themselves with easy grace, were lighthearted and impulsive and just a trifle curious. Their conversation, spiced with gay repartee, reminded Philippine of happy gatherings she had known in distant Grenoble, but their French, though quite correct, was spoken with a somewhat languid drawl and often interspersed with expressions borrowed from Spanish or English, which she did not always understand. But their esteem for culture and their desire to give their children opportunities for education she did understand, along with their regret that the Bishop intended relegating the nuns to a village—and such a village—beyond the Missouri. Monseigneur Du Bourg's decision regarding their place of residence had aroused opposition, as his decisions so frequently did during his years in St. Louis, and many of the prominent Catholic men of the town had offered suggestions on the subject. They were serious and sincere; they had daughters to be educated. A group met after Mass that Sunday morning to discuss tuition fees as well as ways and means of helping Mother Duchesne. After reaching an agreement on several points, they decided to call on the Bishop the next day.

General Pratte was the most active friend the religious had, and Mother Duchesne seems to have relied on his influence with Bishop Du Bourg, even though the prelate gave her no grounds for hoping he might yield to representations or entreaties. On Monday she gave St. Madeleine Sophie an account of what had been happening and what had been suggested:

It is a real suffering to have no news from you and to be so cut off by distance from the means of hearing from you when I am in such need of guidance. We reached here on the 21st, and I wrote to you at once by way of Georgetown. Since then I also sent a letter to Madame de Rollin in care of the French consul in Washington. In spite of having written these letters and five others since we passed Havana, I have so many things to tell you that expressions of sentiment must give way to business and details about our trip. My letters are disgustingly dry, and still I ought to write more concisely in order to give you more information. If you received my letter of July 11 from New Orleans and the one I wrote from here on August 22, you know that our trip up the Mississippi took 40 days. It was very pleasant for us, though nearly all the other passengers were ill—several seriously—owing to the heat. We had only slight indispositions.

Bishop Du Bourg's episcopal palace resembles a little barn in France, and his church is a wooden structure that is falling into ruins. He is having another built at the expense of the Catholics in St. Louis, who feel that they are already overtaxed. He was not able to rent a house for us anywhere except in St. Charles, a village twelve leagues from here. . . . I refused to open our school at Florissant. The country is beautiful, but very sparsely settled, and we should be obliged to build there. St. Louis seems out of the question, for it has grown so quickly in the last two years that a piece of land now sells for five times what it did before.

The brother of the parish priest at Ste Geneviève, Mr. Bernard Pratte, in whose home we are living while we go about house-hunting, is so eager to keep us in St. Louis that he simply refused to hire a vehicle to take us to St. Charles. He was willing to buy a house here, such as would cost 36,000 francs to build, and then rent it to us. I visited the house. It is very well situated and quite new, but it would need changes which we could make only if we owned it. . . . The lot which the Bishop offers is not large enough to afford us a garden, whereas the land around this house would suffice, and we could pay for it on time. I proposed to buy it from

Mr. Pratte, and I do not think my proposal was rash, for at least 7,000 francs must be left from what you sent the Bishop for us.

Mr. Pratte may also offer us some aid. He is going to entrust to us his five daughters in succession. He deserves already the title I have given him of "temporal father." He owns a well-equipped store where prices are moderate, and he has promised us credit for as long as we need. His wife is the most highly esteemed person in the city. Her five little girls, though dreadfully spoiled, have taken such a fancy to us that they want to come to our school, wherever it may be. When we go out, they are distressed lest we should not return. In season and out of season Celeste torments her parents at least four or five times a day to send her to school sooner than they planned. These five interesting children have the happiest dispositions and such charming voices. They seem to be related to almost everyone in St. Louis. A great number of their cousins, all delightfully well-mannered, have come to see us and want to be our pupils. One of them could not sleep for joy the night we arrived. I attribute this eagerness to the inspiration of their guardian angels. . . .

We cannot hope for large institutions at first in this country. During the next few years we must be satisfied with houses on the same footing as Cuignières. The houses here are like the shelters in the vineyards of France or like our country cottages. It may be best for us to divide our number and so do more good by carrying on our work in smaller groups. . . . See how I reach out to many activities when I have not even a firm foothold yet; but desires are unruly when one realizes what needs there are out here. . . . Monseigneur says English is as necessary here as bread, and that at fifty years of age one cannot learn it. That is something to consider.

Philippine was interrupted in her writing. General Pratte wished to talk to her again, as there was still some possibility, he thought, of overcoming the Bishop's opposition to the pleas of many Catholic families. Later she continued her letter:

Mr. Pratte just called me for a little conference. He is working hard to get us a house and a number of pupils with whom to begin our work. The parents themselves have fixed the tuition at 225 dollars, that is 1125 francs, including laundry. If I do not hear the outcome of their efforts before the *Franklin* leaves for New Orleans, I shall write to you by way of one of the eastern seaports, and perhaps that second letter will reach you before this one.

The Bishop is not opposed to the monitorial method of teaching and regrets that the Jesuits have not taken it up. He will not force it upon us here, however. His kindness does not prevent him from being very firm. He knows me already and tells me the truth. Eugenie and Octavie please both him and the children's parents. He reproved me for showing more affection for Eugenie. I had not been aware of doing so, but I told him, as I have told you, that she has more depth than the others. I am not pleased, however, with two things she has done, though she has not held to her own way in these things: first of all, without saying a word to me, she suggested to the Bishop that she be placed alone in a home where only English is spoken, so as to be forced to converse in that language; and secondly, when I held fast to founding our house in St. Louis and said St. Charles seemed to me a tomb in which our enterprise for the Society would be buried, she insisted that all details should be carried out as in France. Now this is simply impossible, and conditions must be taken into account. We must be satisfied with making our houses as nearly like those of France as we can. We shall not even be able to have beds such as you have; on account of lack of space they will have to be taken down every day. Enclosure will be difficult to arrange until we have money enough to pay for it.

There is a Madame de Perdroville [sic] here with her two very attractive and talented daughters. She wants to open a boarding school.[37] Although Mr. Pratte is in some way connected with her husband, he prefers to entrust his two eldest daughters to us right away. That will be an inducement to others. He just returned home, having been at the Bishop's house with several other fathers of families. He refused Florissant positively, saying a house there large enough to lodge twenty-five children would cost, not 40,000, but 80,000 francs. As things stand now, we shall certainly be obliged to go to St. Charles. . . .

For another week the religious enjoyed the hospitality of the Pratte household. Mrs. Pratte continued to "overwhelm them with kindness," as Mother Duchesne recorded in her *Journal*. She and the General, however, had lost the campaign for residence in St. Louis, so the nuns sadly packed their valises again. And again Philippine said her *Credo* in the midst of doubts. She could go forward courageously, knowing in Whom she believed. The children were heartbroken at losing the nuns and spread the unhappy news among their cousins and friends. This brought more visitors, but they were always welcome. Emilie and Therese Pratte had obtained their father's solemn promise that they would be the first pupils of the boarding school, once Mother Duchesne and her companions were settled in their new home. The General reluctantly ordered a charette for the baggage, a carriage for the nuns, and saddle horses for the Bishop and Father Richard, to be ready early on Monday morning, September 7.

The *if's* of history furnish fascinating material for speculation. If General Pratte had had his way, the American life-story of Philippine Duchesne might have been quite different in many respects from the tale of struggle with poverty, anxiety, hardship, isolation, and suffering that stamped her thirty-four years on the frontier.

PART TWO | *Immolation in America*

six

First Year
at St. Charles

1818—1819

> *To do Thy Will, O my God,*
> *is all my desire.*
>
> Offertory, Votive Mass of the Sacred Heart

"BUT YOU DID NOT EXPECT TO LIVE IN ST. LOUIS, did you?" The Bishop's question stirred again in her memory, rousing the tumult of emotions Philippine had been struggling for days to control. The carriage, with its clerical outriders, was moving up the Market Street hill toward the old fort. The charette lumbered heavily behind. Philippine prayed. The little procession crossed the "common fields" to the prairie beyond. They were now on the "King's Highway," a worn dirt road, rutted with the traffic of rough carts, and the carriage offered little comfort to its occupants.

Yes, she *had* expected to live in St. Louis. Mother Barat had expected it, too. The Bishop had promised the Mother General exactly that when she yielded to his plea for missionaries. Philippine had expected to begin her work among Indians, not among the children of Creoles and Americans, whether rich or poor. She had had no thought of opening schools for them when she talked so eagerly with the Bishop in Paris—how long ago? It seemed much more than fifteen months. The Bishop had stressed the need of missionaries to bring the light of the Gospel to the savage natives of America. She had built her dream around *les sauvages*. In New Orleans she had begun to suspect the type of work Monseigneur Du Bourg really intended her to inaugurate. Still she had clung to

267

the hope of fulfilling her ambition and the vow she and her companions had made before leaving Paris. She had not allowed herself to dwell at length on her disappointment while in St. Louis. Now as they headed toward St. Charles, the truth was borne in on her with almost sickening realization.

As she prayed, she recalled some other words the Bishop said he had written in the letter that had not reached her in New Orleans. He had written on June 24. How had that letter gone astray? [1] "You say you have come seeking the Cross. Well, you have taken exactly the right road to find it." She had indeed taken the *King's Highway*, and now it was leading west-northwest through stretches of rolling country and meadow land, broken here and there by little streams and groves of oak and walnut, hickory and sycamore, and wild fruit trees. The persimmon trees bore their hard, bitter fruit that only sharp frost in late autumn would mellow to sweet succulence. Dense thickets of wild berry bushes sometimes lined the roadside that was bright with tall blue sage and sunflowers, goldenrod and rose and blue asters in rank profusion, and clumps of scarlet sumac blending with yellowing cottonwood trees. The road was dusty; the day was uncomfortably warm; yet autumn's mark was already on the countryside.

There were some signs of human habitation along the road: here a log cabin near a field of withered cornstalks drying for fodder, with orange pumpkins and striped squash scattered on the ground; there a cleared plot where a woodsman was lopping off branches from newly felled trees and preparing them for a house-raising. A thin wisp of smoke at a little distance indicated the camping place where a pioneer mother was bravely making a home in a shelter of boughs. These were American settlers. What had the Bishop said about English? "As necessary as bread out here. . . . No one could learn that language at the age of fifty." Philippine had begun her fiftieth year just a few days ago. But Divine Providence might aid her in that as well as in other matters. The road led uphill for a last time, and the Bishop explained that they were nearing the bluffs along the south side of the Missouri River. These stood far back from the stream, leaving wide bottom-lands that made good farms, but were exposed to damaging floods. St. Charles had a well-protected site, resembling St. Louis in several ways. The Bishop always stressed these advantages.

It had been a long drive, but now they were descending the gently sloping approach to the river. Looking across to the opposite shore, where the bluffs rose sharply one above another, the

Bishop pointed out an opening in the trees that gave a glimpse of a house with smoke rising from a chimney. But Philippine had caught sight of a band of Indians near the ferry landing, and they absorbed her interest. They were from the Upper Missouri and had come down to see General William Clark, then Governor of the territory, "the Redhead" whom they respected and trusted. Trade and friendship were their purposes; and when they caught sight of the nuns, they expressed reverence and friendliness by gestures of courtesy they had learned from the white man.

Lafrenière Chauvin was in charge of a ferry at St. Charles. He advertised good crafts, experienced watermen, and a crossing made with safety and dispatch.[2] As he operated from both sides of the stream, he assured his passengers they would not have to wait, "if the crossing is safe."[3] It took some time, however, to unload the charette. Since the vehicles were returning that same day to St. Louis, they were not taken across, but the seven passengers, the saddle horses, and the baggage gave the ferrymen plenty of work. On the opposite bank another cart was procured and loaded with the trunks and cases and the precious picture of the Sacred Heart. The Bishop entrusted the horses to a man on the waterfront, and the little party went on foot to the house up on the hillside.

St. Charles began as a trade center for white men and Indians on the north bank of the Missouri, some twenty miles from its confluence with the Mississippi, at a spot where the river's almost due north-south course gave the trail along its shore a fairly straight direction. The first streets of the village lay parallel to the stream, but the steep bluffs rising in a first and second gradient taxed the endurance of those who made the ascent and offered a dangerous downward trail to riders or drivers of heavy carts: Blanchette Chasseur, a French Canadian, had been shrewd in his choice of the site in 1769. The town and Philippine were the same age. For some twenty years or more he acted as civil and military governor of *Les Petites Côtes*, as he called it. He had not thought of a town with streets carefully laid out, a public square in front of the church, a government house and all that went with Spanish town-planning. The first huts and houses were built well back from the river's edge where the bluffs dropped down on the north to a sheltered cove. A belt of good timber crested the bluffs, and the prairie land gave open fields for farms and pastures.

When the English colonies on the Atlantic coast were declaring their independence, Blanchette the Hunter was directing the construction of a log church for the village, and missionaries were beginning to visit there, finding hospitality in the founder's log house and served by his Pawnee Indian wife. The French name of *Les Petites Côtes* (Village of the Little Hills) had given place to the Spanish *San Carlos del Misuri* when Blanchette died in 1793, but French customs and language prevailed for many a year. Each villager had his lot of land in the town, a share in the "common fields" to cultivate, and a right to cut wood and to pasture cattle on the "commons." Indian dangers may have been an influence in all this, for there were Osages on the Missouri near the mouth of the Kansas River, and Sioux on the Mississippi above the Des Moines, and Kickapoos in the neighborhood of San Carlos, where in the earliest decades of its existence the bulk of the population was made up of Indians and Canadians.

Another French Canadian who left his mark on the town was François Duquette. He had come into Upper Louisiana as a young man, lived for a time at Ste Genevieve, then moved to St. Charles, where he obtained a grant of land at a short distance south of the village. There he built a frontier home, roomy and substantial enough to be called a "mansion" in those days. It was constructed in true French pioneer fashion, of upright white oak posts, with slant roof of pegged shingles and a five-foot gallery around the house. The dimensions given in the contract are thirty-five by twenty-five French feet, with three partitions.⁴ Duquette married Marie Louise Beauvais of Ste Genevieve and brought her to this new home while the Revolution was in full swing in France, and religion was proscribed there under a rule of tyranny. The Duquette house became a religious center for the Catholics at St. Charles, for priests were seldom able to visit the town. Devotions were held there on Sundays and during Lent, with François Duquette reading the prayers and passages from the Gospels. He was a merchant, trading peltries and merchandise, not always successfully, but he and his wife lived comfortably and were highly respected in the town.⁵

In 1816, François Duquette died at the age of forty-two. His widow then opened her home to boarders, and in September of that same year the Reverend Timothy Flint and his family came to occupy half of this "peaceful and pleasant residence," which stood "between the first and second bluffs, a little distance from the village, in a situation delightfully sheltered by fruit trees and shrubbery." ⁶ Flint seems to have found the house comfortable enough, but he described its setting rather than its interior arrangement.

The town [he wrote] is partly visible from this retirement, although the noise is not heard. The river spreads out below it in a wide and beautiful bay adorned with an island thick set with those regular cotton[wood] trees which so much resemble trees that have been planted for a pleasure ground. The trees about the house were literally bending under their load of apples, pears, and the yellow Osage plums. Above the house and on the summit of the bluff is a fine tract of high and level plain covered with hazel bushes and wild hops, a great abundance of grapes, and the red prairie plums.[7]

This was the home to which Bishop Du Bourg led the religious of the Sacred Heart. Madame Duquette received the party kindly and turned over to Mother Duchesne the house with its furniture, reserving for herself temporarily the use of one small room, but she did not occupy it after the nuns arrived. When Mother Duchesne described their lodgings as "five small rooms and one that is larger," she was referring to the parts of the house the nuns were occupying during the first weeks in the Duquette "mansion." On another occasion she stated that the house had seven rooms. Mother Lucille Mathevon, who lived there later on, gave the dimensions of these seven rooms: the large central room extended twenty-eight feet across the front of the house and was almost square; the six little rooms, three on each side of the big room, were eight feet by five, with three doors and two windows each. So one could enter the house by either the front door or the back door of the central room, or one could come in from the gallery by any one of the small rooms, and these also had communicating doors in all contiguous walls, and windows looking out on the gallery. It was a house with eight outer doors, ten inner doors, and fourteen windows, none of which could be locked securely. And there was a loft over the central room which could be reached by a ladder against one wall. Two chimneys gave fireplaces in the central room and in one of the small rooms on each side of the house.

Tradition has placed the first chapel of the St. Charles convent in the large room of the Duquette house, but a close study of the documents relating to the foundation seems to indicate a different arrangement. In her *Journal* Mother Duchesne wrote:

Madame Duquette welcomed us kindly on September 7. The next day, September 8, we arranged an altar hastily and the Bishop said the first Mass for us. While he paid a visit to Portage des Sioux, we prepared a little chapel in the house, which has just five little rooms and one that is larger. The Bishop said Mass there on September 11 and left us the Blessed Sacrament, our greatest Treasure. He took his departure on the 12th, after naming Father Richard pastor here. The latter will lodge near us, will say one Mass on Sundays in our chapel and also on week days.

The nuns had been very busy while the Bishop was installing Father John Acquaroni as pastor at Portage des Sioux.[8] Unpacking the furnishings they had gathered in Paris nearly a year before, they found them all in good condition and placed them where they would show to best advantage. Mother Duchesne was pleased with the effect and noted one detail in her *Journal:*

> We placed in the chapel a picture of St. Regis before which prayers for the American mission had so often been said. He has been chosen as special patron of the house in accordance with a promise made in Paris, with our Mother General's permission, on condition that he obtain this favor for us. We also promised to erect a shrine in his honor and celebrate his feast as the patronal feast of the house. Monseigneur Du Bourg has agreed to this.

In her first letter from St. Charles, Mother Duchesne speaks of the "tiny chapel" (*très petite*), and compares it in size to the sanctuary of the provisional chapel she had helped to arrange in the Paris convent of the Rue des Postes. To have placed the chapel in the central room, which was the general passageway, not only in and out of the house but also in and out of each of the small rooms, would have been a very inconvenient arrangement and one lacking in reverence for the Blessed Sacrament, whereas a little corner room would offer greater opportunity for silence and devotion. Mother Duchesne compared the size of the central room to that of the parlor of the Paris convent. It was a schoolroom by day, a recreation and study room after school hours, and a dormitory at night. When a few boarding pupils arrived in October, they slept on mattresses in this room, as did Mothers Duchesne, Berthold, and Audé, and Sister Lamarre, while Sister Manteau put down her pallet on the kitchen floor.

Mother Duchesne's first letter from the little frontier convent was written to Mother Barat on September 12 and sent to St. Louis for mailing by the Bishop himself. It is a brave, loyal letter, without a suggestion of the intense personal disappointment that was weighing her down. The Bishop is the central figure. His views, his activities, his remarks are recounted, and his troubles hinted at sympathetically. Some of the problems and needs of the nuns are touched upon, and some of their hopes, though the sense of the impending failure of their mission at St. Charles is already felt. The Bishop had evidently tried to encourage them by the suggestion of some property at Florissant, but he had no intention of giving them the "large tract" he owned there. Certainly Philippine must have made a tremendous effort to restrain the outpouring of her heart and soul to the saint, who always understood her and who would read much between the guarded written lines.

SS.C.J.et M.   St. Charles on the Missouri
                                                               September 12, 1818

My very reverend Mother,

Having made the rounds, either in spirit or in person, of St. Louis, Ste Genevieve, Florissant, and St. Charles, we are now settling down in the last named place, which seems to put us as far away from you as is possible in America, because of the many halts and detours one must make in order to get here. Monseigneur Du Bourg, who looks very far into the future, considers this place quite important, as it is the largest village on the Missouri, about 20 miles from its junction with the Mississippi. American settlers from the eastern states are constantly pouring into this section of the country—restless people, who hope St. Charles will become a great commercial link between the United States and China, for the Upper Missouri rises not far from another river [the Columbia] that pours its waters into the Pacific Ocean at a place where the crossing to Asia takes just two weeks.[9] Hence everything is very scarce and very expensive here. We cannot get a workman even for ten francs a day. We are renting a house, but it is too small; and the rent is exorbitant. The village is willing to give the Bishop a plot of ground for us, 180 feet by 300 feet, but two Presbyterians are withholding their signatures and so preventing the donation. The Bishop is going to take up the matter with them. The parish would build for us near the center of the lot and close to the church, as the pastor will also be our chaplain, and he will offer the Holy Sacrifice of the Mass twice on Sundays. If we do not succeed in St. Charles, we shall be able to count on a large tract of land at Florissant.

As for St. Louis, there is not the slightest chance of our going there. The Bishop has troubles enough in that quarter. On the trip to St. Charles he was extremely friendly, riding close to our carriage, seeing us safely on and off the ferry boat, and bringing us to this house, where he has visited us several times. He leaves St. Charles today, and I do not know when we shall see him again. He spoke of writing to you. He did not have time to read our

Constitutions, but he bade us be faithful to them and said we would merit a severe penance if we failed to do so without necessity. There is no difficulty about wearing the religious habit, but cloister is less marked here than at Cuignières and St. Pezenne. We have a tiny chapel in one room, and we hope to open our school for the children of the poor the day after tomorrow. For the boarding school we have only two or three pupils promised, and no Indians at all. Those who live around here are less well disposed than the Canadian Indians, who are good Catholics. Still, the seed is being sown for a future harvest.

A company has been established in St. Louis to carry on trade with the Indians who live along the river. They are growing more friendly with the white people and come down the river at times. We met quite a band who were going to make a treaty with representatives of the United States at St. Louis. They followed us as far as the river, kissed the Sisters' hands, and watched us until we reached the other side of the stream.

Monseigneur is appointing to the Missouri mission some of the priests who are coming here from Rome. The Holy Father takes a great interest in this part of the country. It is no longer called Upper Louisiana, but the Territory of Missouri, and soon it will be a state of the Union.

The men who ferried us across and those who brought our baggage up to the house in a cart would not accept a penny, saying that we represented our Lord Jesus Christ. The Bishop wants us to accept Protestant children, though many of these people say that girls educated by nuns never want to leave them. He inspires us by his example and says that we are the mustard seed and that great good will come of all this labor. He is quite pleased with our sacristy equipment and still more so with Eugenie and Octavie. Seeing them laughing as they helped arrange our poor little house, he said to me, "Look at those two young women who might have shone elsewhere, and who are so gay in this situation! Oh, that is splendid, splendid! As for you and me, we are just *old sinners*." Another time he told me that they are all well disposed and that several are making strides in perfection. He was afraid we might waste the priest's time, but he was the first to mention confession.

I wrote to you from St. Louis. It is hard to have no news from France. They say we must allow six months for letters to come to us and three or four months for ours to reach you. I asked for some English books. Here everything is in English—prospectus, newspapers, bills, addresses. Monseigneur is sending us an American postulant.

I am anxious about your health, also about Mothers Bigeu, de Gramont, and de Charbonnel. Only when one is as far away as I am can one realize how strong are the bonds of respect, gratitude, and love that attach us to the best of mothers. . . .

On September 14 Mother Duchesne opened at St. Charles the first free school for girls west of the Mississippi. The children whom Father Richard had gathered throughout the village came to learn the elements of the Christian religion, along with an introduction to reading, writing, and counting. In them Philippine saw a living counterpart of one class of children for whose instruction St. Madeleine Sophie had provided in her Rule, and soon that section of the Rule was being admirably applied: "Their poverty, which makes them so closely resemble Jesus Christ, their ignorance and roughness of manner, everything [about them] will only give them additional claims to the tenderness and zeal" of the Religious of the Sacred Heart.[10] They were impetuous, undisciplined children, a rather motley group, to whom Mother Duchesne devoted herself wholeheartedly, delighting to find that many of them spoke French. Gradually they responded to the efforts of the nuns, and an atmosphere of affectionate respect was created, which made the schoolroom a homelike place where devotion to the Sacred Heart could develop.

In St. Louis that fourteenth day of September, Bishop Du Bourg was writing Mother Duchesne a letter of approbation of the Society of the Sacred Heart for his entire diocese. He added some encouraging words after the grand manner in which he was accustomed to write and speak, but Mother Duchesne does not seem to have been deeply impressed by them. An increase in the number of children attending the free school, however, was very gratifying, and soon there was a separate class of day pupils who could pay a nominal tuition fee. This was a small group of girls—Creoles, half-breeds, mulattoes—whose program of studies was quite as elementary as that of the free school. When the weather was pleasant, they had class on the gallery with one of the nuns, while Mother Duchesne and the others taught in the central room. The house looked out across the rolling waters of the Missouri to the meadowlands beyond. There were small boats on the river frequently, and these were at times far more interesting to the girls than were catechism and the alphabet and the mysteries of arithmetic. One period of the day brought all the children together for prayers and the singing of hymns. This assembly was held in the big central room with the chapel door open.

On Saturday, October 3, the boarding school opened, when

General Pratte redeemed his promise to Emilie and Therese and brought them, with their cousin, Pelagie Chouteau, to St. Charles. The girls were delighted to be with the nuns again, no matter what inconveniences they had to put up with. Pelagie's affection for Mother Duchesne had begun in St. Louis, and it went on increasing until her death in 1823. This happy trio of cousins came under the special care of Mother Octavie, though all five nuns helped at times with all the children under their care.

General Pratte also brought with him on that first Saturday of October mail from France—letters from the Mother General, Fathers Barat and Perreau, and copies of letters from Cardinals Litta and Fontana which had accompanied the blessing of Pope Pius VII for the American mission. The letters were six months old, but that did not lessen their value. One can fancy General Pratte and the girls left to entertain themselves while the nuns ran hurriedly through the three packets of mail and then came to tell the General about the Holy Father's blessing. On Sunday morning a Mass of Thanksgiving was offered in the tiny chapel, and there was some extra recreation after the *Te Deum* had been chanted. Mother Duchesne read again and again the lines written by Mother Barat on April 21: "You see, our Holy Father the Pope has approved your mission; it was, then, God's will and that is why all circumstances converged so remarkably to make it succeed. . . . How happy we shall be to learn that you have reached the end of your journey safely."

A few days later Philippine began a long letter in answer to this, first giving free rein to the joy that filled her heart, then describing sketchily both the work the little pioneer community was engaged in and the living conditions in which they were trying to carry on:

> After we had languished with desire for news from our dear Society, three packets of mail arrived at the same time, two addressed by Father Barat and one by Mother Girard. No doubt they came on different boats as far as New Orleans, but the same steamboat brought them to St. Louis, where they were again delayed. We received all this dear news from France last Saturday, when our three boarding pupils arrived. So our Lady, on this day dedicated to her, added to the many graces we owe her that of the foundation of our first American boarding school and the arrival of the letters from Rome. We are invoking her under the title of Our Lady of Prompt Succor, as we promised the kind Ursulines we should do.

We shed happy tears on learning that the Sovereign Pontiff has added his approbation and blessing to the many signs that our mission is God's will. Tomorrow we shall chant the *Te Deum* and have a Mass of Thanksgiving offered. Fancy our joy in looking forward to the coming of two more religious to help with this foundation. It was good to hear about the progress of our schools in France, your trip to La Louvesc, . . . and to have news about all our dear ones. . . . My companions and I intend to answer all these letters by way of New Orleans. This one must be less voluminous as it will go by way of Washington. That is the way I sent the last letters I wrote from St. Louis and the first from St. Charles.

From them you have learned that Divine Providence has brought us to the remotest village in the United States. It is situated on the Missouri, which is frequented only by those trading with the Indians who live not very far away from here, but I have not seen any little Indian girls since we came here, only a *half-breed* who is promised to us as a domestic or postulant, according to her aptitudes. [Against this race there is not the same prejudice as there is against *Negroes* and *mulattoes*.[11] Monseigneur Du Bourg has said positively that we may not admit them to either of our schools, and he has appointed one day a week for the instruction of the colored people; otherwise, he says, we should not hold the white children in school. He told us of an experience he had in the college in Baltimore, which shows how difficult it is to overcome race-prejudice in this country. He consulted the Archbishop of Baltimore on the matter and was told that this attitude would have to be maintained as the last safeguard of morality and manners in this country.]

omit

I am sending you Monseigneur's approbation of the Society in his diocese—such as it is, for he had no time to read the Constitutions. He is now at The Barrens, or *Bois Brulé*, not far from Ste Genevieve. The seminary is being built there at the expense of a congregation made up of Americans from Kentucky. These people were instructed by Bishop Flaget[12] and the Trappists, and they live like the first Christians of Jerusalem or the Guarani in Paraguay.

In St. Charles things are very different from this, though there are some signs of improvement. A few years ago, however, one might have witnessed conduct comparable to pagan bacchanalia: girls scantily clad, holding a bottle of whisky in one hand and a man with the other, dancing every day of the year and never doing any work.[13] Now there is more exterior decency, but these people are as ignorant of morality as the Indians are. In our free school we now have twenty-two children, and in proportion to the population this equals a school of one hundred in France. These children have never heard of our Lord, of His birth or His death, nor of hell, and they listen open-mouthed to our instructions. I have to say to them continually, "Yes, this is really true." All except two are learning the alphabet. Among the children who pay a little fee there is the same ignorance. When we complain to the Bishop that we have no savages, he replies: "Indeed you have, and your work among these children will be wider and more lasting because of the influence of the rich over the poor." We have to combat worldliness as well as ignorance. Some of the boarding pupils have more dresses than underclothes or handkerchiefs; they have embroidered dresses of gaily colored silk, with lace trimmings and fancy sleeves of net or lace. The day pupils who pay tuition dress on Sundays like our boarding pupils in Paris. They scorn black shoes and must have pink or blue, yellow or green ones, and the rest to match, but they do not use handkerchiefs. We have had to require them to do so at school.

We are very inconveniently lodged and shall have to go elsewhere at the end of a year, for we are paying nearly 2,000 francs for seven small rooms badly in need of repair, a large garden and orchard left uncultivated, and we have no one to work them. We need a French gardener. Our baker and carpenter are French. As we cannot find a larger house, we shall be obliged to build. There are in this neighborhood more English-speaking people than there are French or Creoles, but, as both languages are fairly well understood and the children are accustomed to hear both, Mother Octavie can take care of the English part of the school just now, as all these children are very ignorant. . . . Everyone likes Mother Eugenie. The most marked characteristic of the Americans is scorn for anyone and anything that is not American. Since they are not given to flattery, I think Eugenie will not be harmed by their kindness.

Our furnishings arrived in good condition. Monseigneur was very well pleased with all the chapel equipment. The statue of our Lady over the tabernacle touches the ceiling of our tiny chapel, which is about the size of the sanctuary of our chapel in Paris, but all is very devotional in this little corner. There is a beautiful picture of the Sacred Heart with more than fifty figures. This came from Rome. The picture of our Lord showing His Sacred Heart is also from the Eternal City. The paintings of the Nativity and of the Adoration of the Magi are ravishing.[14] There is a reliquary containing small fragments of the True Cross, . . . relics of many saints, including St. Ignatius and St. Francis Regis—more, all told, than you have, and finally that picture of St. Regis which I found in the garret of the church in Grenoble, and which I promised to have honored if he should bring us to America. We placed it above the tabernacle the day it was framed, and the Mass in honor of St. Regis was said.[15]

Winter came on, and the religious at St. Charles were exposed to new hardships. First there was a bread shortage, with not even corn meal for sale in the village. As the Missouri was blocked by floating ice, no supplies could be obtained from St. Louis. But there were quantities of apples stored in the cellar under the front of the house, or still on the trees in the orchard, for Divine Providence had sent a fine crop that matured quite late that year. A more serious shortage occurred when the Duquette well went dry; the little springs nearby were muddied by animals or icebound, and no regular supply of water could be obtained from the river. But worst of all physical hardships was the cold. There was no "central heating" in the Duquette mansion. There may have been four open fireplaces, certainly not more than that, but at times fuel was lacking for these. With little money to buy food, the nuns were often hungry, and this added to their sensitiveness to the cold. Mother Duchesne felt her strength diminishing to such an extent that she believed death was at hand. Hunger blurred the brain of this usually clearheaded woman. She sat dazed before the tabernacle in the tiny chapel. The cold was beginning to send little knife-blades of pain through her joints as rheumatism again set in. She tried to conceal her suffering from her companions in order to deprive herself still further for their sake, and she found courage for this in prayer and in reading again and again the letters of Mother Barat which she had saved through the past twelve years.

Bishop Du Bourg spent a few days at St. Charles in November, offering the Holy Sacrifice of the Mass in the convent chapel on November 21, when the nuns renewed their vows in union with the Society in France. Although he had in his possession more than 7,000 francs belonging to them, he gave them no financial assistance, and Mother Duchesne was left to her own resources for the support of the community and schools. Whatever she may have thought of the Bishop's attitude, she made no comment on it in her letters. His name does not even appear in the long account she wrote to Mother Barat and asked him to post in St. Louis, along with a letter to the nuns and children in France. The serious tone of her letter, however, is indicative of the anxieties that weighed upon her mind and heart:

Living in this remote corner of the world, cut off by the Mississippi and the Missouri rivers, I do not know whether you have received a single one of the letters we have written, but I have had the inexpressible consolation of receiving several from you, Mother Bigeu, and Father Barat, written before you had news from us, but your kind brother knew that the *Rebecca* had arrived at New Orleans. . . . This is the tenth letter I have written you. I shall not repeat what I said in any of the others about the different situations we have experienced and the things that have been said and retracted. What interests you most is our present condition: it is what we should have desired, thorny and difficult, but it is made easier by the unction of grace and alleviated by an all-kind Providence whose help is never withdrawn and whose protection is felt at every moment. I have found the greatest consolation in the letters of the Cardinals, the blessing of the Holy Father, news of the two projected foundations in France, and the decision to keep the novitiate in Paris, even though the school has increased so much, also your trip to La Louvesc and my dear Sainte Marie. The kindness of your dear brother follows us, even at such a great distance, and is a sign of God's protection. . . .

Among all the things we shall need and those I have already asked for, the essential are such as may keep us alive, as here on earth the soul depends on the body. . . . We look on potatoes and cabbage as you in France regard rare delicacies. There is no market. The gift of a pound of butter and a dozen eggs is like a fortune received. In spite of our desire to fast, we have had to avail ourselves of permission to eat meat on all Saturdays of the year. During the hunting season, which we are in now, we can procure venison and ducks, but in the spring and summer one can get only salted fish and meat. Many of the cows are almost dry. . . . If we have to buy milk, it costs twelve cents a bottle, and fifteen cents in winter. And with all the salt diet we lack water. The well in our garden is dry and it costs twelve cents every time we send someone to the Missouri to get us two little buckets of water.

So many difficulties make us dream of building elsewhere, but the townsfolk have had a meeting and named a committee with a chairman. They are getting the signatures of all the inhabitants who are willing to chop trees in the common woods and prepare them, so as to erect and roof a house for us. We should have only to finish it off inside and put up the partitions. They plan to make it 36 feet long and 25 feet wide—and that is considered large out here, where there are only log houses plastered with mud, which comes off easily and so lets in light through the chinks.

Sister Manteau sleeps in the kitchen; the other religious and I sleep in the large classroom of the free school with the boarding pupils. We can never accept more than ten in that group; there are just three now, but others have reserved places. We also have six day pupils who pay fifteen francs a month and twenty-four children in the separate free school. We must be careful not to call this a "poor school," for that hurts the feelings of the parents and keeps the children away.[16]

We are learning by experience what faith teaches—that those who are lost have only themselves to blame. The Indians have respect for the priests; why, then, do they not go to them for instruction with the same eagerness they show in begging for whisky on which to get drunk, though they realize the fury it brings on them when they drink it? We sweetly dream of instructing docile and innocent savages, whereas the women as well as the men are afflicted with indolence and drunkenness. Jesuits are needed to make men of them before we attempt to make them Christians. So far we have dealt only with half-breeds—born of one Indian and one white parent; there are many such in the vicinity of St. Charles.

I am persuaded, however, that God had His designs in bringing us here. Already pictures of the Sacred Heart adorn several churches, for I have revived my old talent for painting and making paper flowers, and we have made decorations for several tabernacles. At St. Charles no one knew when to answer *Amen* at church. Now our day pupils sing at Benediction, and they have learned some of Father Barat's hymns, particularly one to the Sacred Heart. They are eager to learn and they learn easily. . . .

The pastors of the neighboring villages have been very kind to us, especially the Trappist at Florissant, who is urging the people of St. Charles to build a house for us in order to keep us here. We cannot stay where we are, but it will cost a good deal to finish and furnish a house. I am already hard pressed to provide for our household on what comes in from the tuition of three boarding pupils, for the cost of living is exorbitant. We must live from day to day and stint even drinking water. But there is consolation in this poverty and daily dependence on the help of Providence, which is quite evident. My strength is diminishing in both body and soul. This humbles me before God and warns me that death may be near. I see with pleasure that the other nuns are liked better than I am; I really only help them. Octavie is in charge of the boarders; Eugenie helps her with the day pupils; and God blesses their work.

As we are making many friends with our painting and paper flowers, we shall need a great deal of carmine and rose coloring, needles, pins, thread. We are trying to cook without pot-hangers, pots, kitchen stove, a spit for meat, a warmer, etc. . . . If the vocations we hear about are true ones, we shall need a separate house for a novitiate. I had this idea: by the end of the year the new convent here at St. Charles will be built and ready for use, and the two younger nuns, who are successful and have gained the confidence of outsiders, could conduct this school, and I could open a novitiate at Florissant. The pastor at Ste Genevieve, who is such a distinguished priest, is training some good postulants, and there are some in the free school here.[17]

The letter she addressed "To my Mothers, Sisters, and Children of the Society of the Sacred Heart" and dated November 20,[18] is filled with information and stories she had picked up in conversation with the chaplain, the missionary priests who called at the convent when passing through the village, especially Father John Acquaroni and Father Marie-Joseph Dunand, and with local visitors who came to bring a small gift or pass the time of day with her and lingered a bit curiously, perhaps, to talk to the nuns who always stayed at home and whom the school children spoke of so affectionately. Philippine was by instinct friendly, as those who spoke her language readily understood, and to this friendliness the community and children often owed their meal of venison or wild turkey, the butter that made dry corn bread more palatable, or the homemade wild grape wine and cherry bounce that cured their colds and added cheer to their meager meals. Her geographical misinformation may cause her readers to smile, but it will not astonish anyone who has delved into the writings of her frontier contemporaries.

On December 15 Mother Duchesne noted in her *Journal:* "Today we received a postulant, Mary Mullen, who speaks English. Monseigneur sent her to us. He realizes, as we do, our need of an English teacher. Fortunately all our children speak French, so Mother Octavie can handle their classes, helped by Mother Eugenie. . . . Letters have come directly from Grenoble, where our Mother General and Mother Bigeu are just now." Mother Barat had been in Grenoble during the previous summer, and for Philippine time suddenly folded back and she was in spirit at Sainte Marie. As she read, a change came over her features—they softened, glowed, and her deep eyes grew wistful with remembrance.

Ever since I came to your dear mountain [wrote St. Madeleine Sophie on July 6], my mind and heart have been filled with sweet and heartbreaking thoughts and memories of the past, which struggle for the upper hand in my soul. Once more I seem to see you receiving me for the first time, turning over to me this house, this religious family. I recall what pleasure I used to experience when I came back after my journeys and found you here in this peaceful solititude. How keenly I suffered this time when not only you were not here to greet me, but also I knew you were so far away from me! Of course, faith comes to my aid; and when I forget my own pain, I realize your good fortune. . . .

I suppose you are having your dose of trials and hardships. I am so anxious to know how you stood the trip, whether you have reached St. Louis, how your health is, and how your companions are. I must be patient. Not a line from you since Easter. It is such a long time. My love to your dear daughters. You know how we all pray for you. Do the same for us, and receive the assurance of my tender and inviolable attachment in C.J.M.

Your Mother and friend,
SOPHIE BARAT

It was only on August 21, the day Philippine reached St. Louis, that Mother Barat received letters from New Orleans announcing the safe arrival of the nuns. Now in mid-December there was an opportunity to send letters to St. Louis with the friends who had brought Miss Mullen out to the convent, and Mother Duchesne availed herself of it. Only the letter to Mother Thérèse Maillucheau is extant. It was written after a long, hard day, when the other occupants of the little house were asleep. Gusts of cold wind coming in through chinks in the walls threatened the tenuous life of the candle-flame as Philippine gripped her quill with aching fingers and wrote:

All the news from France fills us with joy and lightens the pain of separation. Thank you for Aloysia's journal and, above all, for the details about the two new foundations. God is good in thus bringing about the growth of this little Society. You see, Upper Louisiana will not be your rival; *we* were suited only to a land still in a half-civilized state. I do not know how to describe the place in which we live. Its population is made up of a mixture of American emigrants from the East, French and Canadian Creoles, German, Irish, and Flemish settlers, along with half-breeds who seem to inherit the worst faults of both Indian and white parents. As for real Indians, we never see them because the Americans from the East are pushing them out and making war with them. They are withdrawing further away. We would need Jesuits to bring them to us, as they brought them to Mother Marie of the Incarnation. We would attract them more quickly with liquor than with sermons. They will give anything they have in exchange for that.

But in conscience no one should give it to them, seeing what a state it puts them in and how dangerous it makes them. God allows some faint light of religion to shine amongst them and bring about conversions, but these are very rare. Degradation is almost general amongst them, and the diversity of languages, the enormous distances in this country, the difficulty of travel, all combine to make it impossible for us to help them yet.

God, who willed that we should come here, has allowed us to come in contact with Indians but rarely. He sends us, instead, people who have the same needs and whose instruction can procure a greater good. He also seems to offer us some vocations, and there would be none among the Indian girls. Their laziness, the freedom of their way of life, which is a barrier to all self-restraint, their slowness in acquiring even a mediocre degree of instruction, point to the most distant hope of ever having them amongst us. In the class for day pupils we have several half-breed and mulatto girls; the others are Creoles or Americans. In the free school all speak French; some speak both French and English.

We have just received our first postulant, Mary Mullen. She was educated by religious in Baltimore and in Kentucky. She understands only English, and I despair of ever speaking to her or of really understanding her. To read English and understand what one reads is not so difficult, but the pronunciation staggers me. Mother Octavie is quite successful, Eugenie less so.

We have had the privilege of doing without bread and water. I had expected the former privation, but I never dreamed that on the banks of the Missouri we should lack water with such an abundant flow of it in sight. We may not go down to the river, and no one is willing to go there for us. Sister Marguerite came back today from the two springs nearby, carrying her buckets, one only half full of water and the other filled with ice. The Missouri is almost frozen over, and it is so cold that the water freezes beside the fire, as does the laundered linen hung there to dry. Neither doors nor windows close tight, and no one here knows how to make a foot warmer; besides, it would cost at least 25 or 30 francs. A little stove cost us 250 francs. We have logs, but they are too large, and there is no one to chop them for us and no saw with which we might cut them ourselves. Laziness is the vice of this region; it belongs to the way of life. People work only when obliged to do so, and pride keeps many from working for wages. For food we have corn, pork, and potatoes, but no eggs, butter, oil, fruit, vegetables. So, dear Mother, the things that could be bought more cheaply in France than here and that we are most in need of are seeds of fruit trees, vegetables of all kinds, grain, even shrubs that might be planted to form our enclosure, the tools

John Francis packed for us,[19] a small iron stove with a jointed pipe that would save space, some English books on religious life and sacred history, etc. These books can be got in Bordeaux. We should also value a case of altar wine and one of olive oil—the only edible oil to be had here is bear grease, which is disgusting—but if you do send us some, please make sure that the casks will not leak on the way out here. I do not see how we shall survive Lent with only fish cooked without either butter or oil, and not an egg to be had till spring. But we are willing and glad to be in want. Not a single thing we brought from France or New Orleans has proved useless.

I scarcely know what I am writing. It is late at night, but tomorrow will be too late to write. I cannot reply to all the dear letters I received. Please make up for me, especially to Mother Bigeu, who should have heard from me more often. I fear that several letters sent by way of the Jesuits at Washington have been lost, as I was given the wrong address. *Fiat!* The Sisters here are well. I have spoken of them more in detail to our Mother General. I am undoubtedly the one of least worth here. Octavie and Eugenie are well. Au revoir in C.J.,

PHILIPPINE

The Christmas season brought little relaxation from regular work, as only the great liturgical feasts were school holidays then, both in France and America. The girls who had already made their first Communion were invited to spend Christmas Eve at the convent with the boarding pupils. They arrived with their blankets or buffalo robes, each prepared to make her own shakedown for the night in the schoolroom. After supper they gathered around the log fire that lighted the rough, low-ceilinged room with its bright glow, and enjoyed a story hour. The wonders of the Christ Child's first coming to earth held their minds and hearts in rapt attention, then gay *Noëls* were sung, and Mother Duchesne told them of Christmases in France and of the children she had known and loved at Sainte Marie. While the nuns prayed or completed preparations, the children slept for a couple of hours. At the sound of the bell all assembled in the chapel or its adjoining rooms for midnight Mass. The Christ Child was reborn on the altar and in the hearts of the twenty nuns and children, who welcomed Him with love and gratitude.[20] Then silence enveloped the little convent, and the children slept until the nuns called them to breakfast. The Christmas dinner was a festive affair, thanks to the kind Prattes, for Emilie was twelve years old that day, and her family had sent bountiful provisions for the celebration.

Bishop Du Bourg's greetings reached St. Charles on December 28. He wrote "with paternal affection" and added some flourishes about his desire "to see his diocese covered with convents of the Sacred Heart." [21] With the punctilious courtesy of the cultured French, Mother Duchesne returned New Year's greetings from the community and children, and followed this up with a letter setting before him the major problems and anxieties that beset her and a plan by which she hoped to work more effectively in the diocese. Four months in St. Charles had demonstrated beyond doubt the unsuitability of the place at that time for a boarding school. But Mother Duchesne loved the children of the free school. She realized how great was their need of schooling and how well they were responding to the training now being given. She loved this remote village on the Missouri and knew it was the river that had proved the greatest obstacle to the development of the boarding school, her only source of revenue. The Bishop had offered only one alternative to St. Charles, and that was Florissant. She had visited Florissant and had refused to consider a foundation there. What was she to do? Had she been able to consult the Mother General and take a stand with the support of her advice and directives, she might have been able to bring the Bishop to a more reasonable and practical decision. But she had no more chance of doing so now than she had had in the previous August.

The idea of dividing the community into two groups had come to her even then. She felt that, given the conditions in which they found themselves and for which they were so unprepared, she and her companions might accomplish more by such a division. Now that they had made friends in St. Charles and were offered some definite help by the people of the village, the idea of division recurred to her more strongly, and she wrote of this and much else to Bishop Du Bourg. His reply is dated January 29, 1819:

I heartily approve the plan of dividing the community and leaving only a free school at St. Charles under Mother Eugenie, Sister Marguerite, and Miss Mullen. The boarding school will be far better situated at Florissant. There the property is assured you. I will give you the greater part of the money needed for the construction; day-labor is cheap in that locality. To oversee the work you will have the Prior [Father Dunand], a man more experienced and more active than any in St. Charles. Material is abundant and not too expensive; firewood will cost you almost nothing; and you cannot fail to draw a large number of pupils for the boarding school, which is a more important work than you seem to realize, for it is from the education of the upper levels of society that reform must come, and they are just as ignorant as the lower classes. This seems the time to consolidate your establishment. For my part, I am quite decided on this point. If you are determined to follow *my advice* (I give no *orders* in this matter), then we must get to work and lose no more time. What you tell me of Miss Mullen remaining with Mother Eugenie makes me think you count on her. God grant that she will prove suited to religious life. I believe that in the little school she will do her part as well as anyone else. . . .[22]

The generosity with which Bishop Du Bourg volunteered to provide the greater part of the money needed for the construction of the new convent must have surprised Mother Duchesne, who was well acquainted with the financial difficulties he was facing in St. Louis. Evidently she did not rely much on this promise. Had the Bishop not promised Mother Barat that the Religious of the Sacred Heart would found their first American convent in St. Louis? She wondered what Mother Barat had thought when she heard of the foundation at St. Charles. How long would it be before she heard from her again?

Early in February came a packet of mail containing a letter from Father Martial, along with the letter Bishop Du Bourg had written on June 24, 1818, and sent to New Orleans. Then on the fourteenth of the month letters from France arrived—but none from the Mother General. Father Perreau's long letter of spiritual direction was in answer to the one she had written to him eight months before. Alluding to the desire for martyrdom she had then expressed to him, he replied:

It would be very consoling for a soul that really loves God to finish off this mortal life by such a sacrifice. But always bear in mind the fact that you are not worthy of so glorious a death, and so live with the firm resolution to give yourself unreservedly to your divine Spouse and always to make generously the sacrifice of all He may ask of you.[23]

With renewed courage Philippine wrote to her Superior General on February 15:

Just a few days ago I received from New Orleans a letter from Father Martial, four months old. He is coming to St. Louis. And there was one from Monseigneur Du Bourg, written six months ago, but it depicts so well what one can expect to find in this country that I thought it might interest you. A second, and quite recent, one from him concerns our transfer to Florissant. The experience of a winter here, and that a very mild one, has made us realize that at present we would only vegetate in this place, without accomplishing even the little good we might do elsewhere. But it is hard to abandon so many interesting children, several of whom desire to belong to the Sacred Heart of Jesus, and it seemed to me advisable to arrange temporarily to leave Mother Eugenie here with Sister Marguerite to help her. She would be able to run this day school for a while with the help of some young people.

They tell us of several [who wish to enter as postulants]; meanwhile the postulant we have is being trained and she can teach English and be an interpreter. She still has six months to get accustomed to the French, and the study of this language is developing her mind. Mother Eugenie is loved by the whole school. She just finished her retreat, and she was welcomed with tears of joy that caused her own to flow. They all cried; and since they have heard that we may leave here, several of the older ones are saying, "I'll be packing my things soon, too." And the youngest beg to be taken along, declaring they will obtain this favor from the Heart of Jesus.

If we were not so short of funds, we could do much good by educating several of these children at our own expense. But what can we do, with neither lodging nor provisions? We cannot remain in this house, where one room the size of the parlor in the Paris convent and six small rooms cost almost 2,000 francs. Monseigneur was badly mistaken when he thought we could house twenty-five boarding students here. We cannot lodge ten, even with rolling up the beds every morning. The section north of the Missouri River can never send us boarding pupils who will pay tuition. The best we can do here is a day school run by a few of us, and it will not support the nuns. Pride tries to hide misery, but we see these poor, hungry children coming barefooted often in the coldest weather and wearing a single cotton garment—a very thin one, too—and nothing under it.

You see, my dear Mother, that though we are forced to give up the boarding school here, it is heartbreaking to leave no help at all for these children, who could be nicely trained. In four months many have learned to read, to write, to know the whole of the little catechism, a number of hymns, and the prayers at Benediction. They do all the singing [in the church] now, and formerly the priest could not get a single person to say *Amen.* I hope you will approve what Monseigneur desires so earnestly.

Father De La Croix, a young Flemish priest and our extraordinary confessor, recently returned from the country of the

Upper Missouri. No priest had ever been there before. There are two settlements, one at Côte-sans-Dessein, which he dedicated to St. Paul the Apostle—twenty-two families live there; the other at Franklin, which he placed under the patronage of St. Francis de Sales. He gave a mission there; all the Catholics profited well by it, and the Protestants came to listen to the sermons.[24] That field of labor is immense, but the population is sparse and poor. I would let my desires run in that direction if English were not the only language they can speak.

I come back to February 14, when I received four letters. . . . We had much joy in reading them. It seems to me that in binding us more closely to the whole Society, these dear letters also bind us closer to one another, reminding us of the grace God gives us in the Society of His Heart. Father Perreau shows by his letter that he is ever a father and I am always his spiritual daughter, and in truth I find no one here to fill his place, nor do I hope to. This solitude of the heart, which finds nothing on earth that answers to its desires, forces the soul to throw itself into the Heart of Jesus. Thank this kind Father for his letter and for the joy which he procured for us by that third blessing of the Holy Father and by the promise of the brief for the Confraternity of the Sacred Heart, which will be precious to us. . . .

As to cloister, in the whole country for 500 leagues around us there is not a single wall around property. They put up wooden fences that keep out animals better than human beings. Our cloister consists in staying at home, but people come in as often as they please. They make openings for themselves anywhere. We shall have to be in our own house in order to regularize our life. In this house it is impossible. In spite of the fact that we are living in an almost wholly uncultivated section, we own not an inch of land. It is all held in common or owned by Congress, which has as yet made no definite land laws. One can build only on land purchased from individual owners, and the price is high. So we do not need the people Father Perreau has suggested sending us.

If our Sisters in France imagine us surrounded by savages, they are quite mistaken. I have seen only a few old ones who made their first Communion at fifty or sixty years of age, when temptations to passions had passed. But to compensate for our disappointment we have new employments: we dig in the garden, carry out the manure, water the cow, clean out her little stable—the only one in this place, for all the animals wander at large. And we do all this with as much joy as we would have if we were teaching Indians, for God wills it this way, and our poverty, along with the false pride of the settlers, prevents us from getting servants. . . . The letters of Mother Marie of the Incarnation can give you some idea of our country, which has been settled only within the last forty years by Canadians, so the first settlers all speak French.

The weather has been very clear, on the whole, since we came here, but they tell me there are often furious windstorms and loud thunder. We have had a few slight earthquakes. As the country is not well organized and it is easy to get away by stealth, it is also easy to set fires deliberately. . . . People sometimes set fire to the woods and to the wide prairies where the tall grass is very dry. One night the Americans in St. Charles had to keep watch lest the fire spread into the village, for it spreads like a whirlwind. In the autumn we saw fires on all sides and in the woods opposite us on the other side of the Missouri.

The money in use here is another inconvenience. Gold and silver abound in New Orleans, but are lacking up here. They use bank notes issued by individual states or even by individual people, and these notes decrease in value while you handle them. You think you have paid a debt, and the creditor comes back to say the money is no good. Almost every day one must consult a new list of the reliable banks.[25] The land is very fertile here, but it is almost entirely uncultivated because of the laziness of the settlers. The half-breeds in the population share the hatred of the savages for work, and also their love of drink. In some villages, in practically all of them, every household has its drunkards. The girls are crazy about dancing—balls every week. This passion will be controlled only in the coming generation.

It takes saints to work on hearts so poorly prepared. And it is all the greater a sorrow for me that I am not one, when I see that our two Sisters are losing instead of gaining spiritually. This is my own fault. As to Octavie and Eugenie, they are running in the way of perfection, and the little good we accomplish is due to them. In them you will have two superiors, and if you cannot replace me by an English-speaking religious, Octavie could take my place. We shall soon have more American children than French-speaking Creoles. What good am I without a fluent use of English? I feel this with our postulant. For her good and that of the others I would gladly see myself in the lowest employment in the house. What is more, you know me. The nuns are afraid of me, and a superior should put everyone completely at her ease. . . .

On February 20 Mothers Duchesne and Berthold drove to Florissant to meet the Bishop there and inspect the property he offered as a gift to the Society. It was not a part of the farm he had purchased, but a separate plot in the village, intended originally as a church site, and for this purpose the Bishop was retaining a portion of it. He showed the nuns plans that had been drawn for the convent and for a church to be erected contiguous to it, but he was very vague about ways and means to finance the construction of these buildings. Mother Duchesne noted in her *Journal* next day: "Fear of expense which building at St. Ferdinand entails terrifies us, and we have begged the Bishop to let us remain at St. Charles in the house the townspeople wish to build for us on the property they are willing to give us."

Fear of expense in the matter of building gave Mother Duchesne long hours of anxiety. She had known trials of this kind before—at Sainte Marie and in Paris, but she had had money at her disposal in those days and had also been able to enlist the aid of her relatives. Letters had come recently from her sister Euphrosine and from Josephine de Savoye-Rollin. It had been months since she had written to them. Now she did so. To the Jouves she barely hinted at the anxieties confronting her, though she did mention the rheumatism in her hands that made writing very difficult. To Josephine she expressed herself more freely, repeating many details she had already written to France, details she knew would appeal to her *très chère Cousine*, and asking help in her usual straightforward manner. The letter is undated, but it was written before Lent, 1819, when the nuns still had only one cow:

> Having reached the end of our journey, I counted securely on your tender friendship following me here. It is as precious to me now as when I tasted all its sweetness in the days when every circumstance drew us together in our childhood, and I shall never forget my first, my most intimate friend.
>
> We are perfectly happy here, for we have found the cross which we looked for; but since the truest crosses are those we do not choose ourselves, God has prepared for us many trials we did not expect. We thought we would find innocence and ignorance combined, and we meet with children whose fathers are given to drunkenness and laziness, and whose mothers are consumed with a love for fancy clothes and dancing, and quite indifferent as to whether their children ever learn any more than they themselves know. But the children are attracted irresistibly to us. Some beg to come to school; some even cry in order to get leave to do so. We cannot teach them to sew, for they have no material at all. A hank of cotton for knitting costs five francs; thimbles, thread, needles are very expensive. So even if we had room enough to house them from all danger, we could not furnish them with occupation. Here where everyone is so poor, each one makes her own chemise, her dress, even her shoes, and one must speak of

these articles of clothing in the singular, so poverty-stricken are these people.

We are paying nearly 2,000 francs for the only house that could be found for us. As this section of the country is newly settled, houses have not been built. The expenses of the trip were simply enormous, and we have on hand just 5,000 francs with which to build a little house that will cost 15,000, without a basement, everything being so costly, especially the hire of laborers. The Bishop is giving us the ground for the house and garden, with a small cabin to use for a free school. Minds are very favorably inclined toward us in St. Louis, and we shall be nearer there when we leave St. Charles.

Since you ask me to confide in you and tell you my troubles, these are the anxieties that weigh upon me, but do not discourage me. For since the general attitude toward us in St. Louis is becoming more favorable, we shall have enough pupils to enable us to pay back what we borrow. See if you can procure a loan for us. I shall pay it back as soon as possible. I gave Mother Barat the address of a banker in Philadelphia who has an agent in St. Charles. This agent has done us a thousand services, and the quickest and safest way to send us money would be through him.

The winter was mild for this climate, but there was a shortage of bread in this little village. We were without it at times, and we suffered from a lack of water on our property. We had to send down to the Missouri to get it. But the white people do not want to work as servants here, and we are not rich enough to buy slaves. So we take care of the cow ourselves and also of our chickens. We dig in the garden and fetch the water when the spring near our house is running; otherwise we have to pay for it.

Do not think that all this costs us; the thing that hurts is not being able to get in contact with the little savages, the objects of all our desires. . . . If a boarding school brings in a revenue, we shall get the Indians to let us raise their little girls. The only way to instruct them is to take entire charge of them and give them a home with us. Would you believe it, in the Creole class, no matter what the nationality, there is, proportionally speaking, more luxury and corruption than in Paris.

I am so grateful for the detailed news you gave me of your family and mine. Give affectionate messages to all, especially Tante Perier, your husband, Augustin and Madame Perier, my brother and his wife. When I was leaving Paris I sent my brother my life-certificate so he could collect my entire annuity for 1817. Now I am having another sent for 1818. I do not know whether they will be accepted. I shall know in a year from now. Ask my brother if he got the two certificates and assure him at the same time of my tender affection. You know how sincerely I love you, my dear Cousin. Everything here at St. Charles recalls your generosity. Our chapel, above all, is decorated entirely by you. All yours in our Lord Jesus Christ. . . .

Lent came, and with it some help that gave the nuns courage and hope. Divine Providence was "very wonderful" in their regard, Mother Duchesne recorded gratefully, but she had added anxieties. The Bishop was very fond of talking, and on occasions he had spoken to Sister Lamarre about her work in France when she lived at Cuignières. That convent had been opened by Madame Baudemont in the spring of 1808 as a place of refuge during Napoleon's persecution of the Fathers of the Faith, when it was feared that a similar fate might befall the little order founded by Mother Barat. The convent was situated in the diocese of Beauvais, deep in the heart of the country, remote and isolated. For a time there were only three nuns in the community, one of them a coadjutrix Sister, who visited the sick in the nearby village and did much good among the people. Gradually a free school was established, then a Sunday school, a small boarding school, and an orphanage at some distance from the convent, under the patronage of St. Pezenne. This work, however, had been inaugurated before the Society had adopted its final Rules and Constitutions and only as a temporary establishment.

The Bishop was interested in all this, remarked how suitable the arrangement would be on the Missouri frontier, and gave Sister Lamarre to understand that he wanted her to help inaugurate a free school in St. Louis. She was zealous, earnest, capable, but she was talkative and gave the impression of wanting to act independently at a time when Mother Duchesne was expending prayer and energy on the solution of the problem of their future home and work, which, as superior, she felt she must handle in concert with the Bishop and in conformity with the Society's usual manner of acting. Mother Eugenie Audé was also causing her some anxiety. Tense and high-strung, Eugenie was sometimes upset emotionally. The idea of being in charge of a little school at St. Charles after Mother Duchesne moved to Florissant created fears which were difficult to control. In a large community this condition might have passed unnoticed, but in so small a group it was disturbing. Moreover, Mary Mullen had grown dissatisfied and was asking to return to St. Louis. So there was friction. Mother Duchesne touched on it very lightly when she wrote to Mother Barat on March 5:

I do not fear the reproach of silence, but rather that of indiscretion. I think I have written to you about twelve or fourteen times, and I count on being able to write every month regularly, either by New Orleans or by one of the Eastern cities when someone we know is traveling that way. For 600 or 700 leagues is considered no distance at all in this country; it is like 50 to 100 in France, though it is much more dangerous. The steamboat *Franklin*, on which we came up the river, was stuck for three months on a sand bar at about one-fourth the way up the river on the trip following ours. It was floated off, however, and continued its trip, only to be pierced by one of those tree-trunks that are such an obstacle to navigation on the Mississippi. The *Franklin* sank. No lives were lost, but all the cargo of merchandise is at the bottom of the river in the very deepest water.[26] Why did that accident not occur when we were aboard? Here is a new proof of God's care of us and of His will that we should be here. And what is more, they told us the *Franklin* carried a shipment for us, but I just learned that it is aboard the *Washington*, which fortunately has made a run from New Orleans to St. Louis in thirty days.

We are awaiting impatiently the case Father Barat says is coming to us and your long delayed letters, for a recent one from Mother Bigeu refers to previous letters, and they will be the first written by you since you had news of us from New Orleans. Our benefactresses in that city seemed by their silence to have forgotten us, but a letter from them proves quite the contrary. They have put on the steamboat, prepaid to us, four copper kettles, soap, bluing, candles, a case of dried raisins, one of codfish—all this for the boarding school; a barrel of cane syrup and several other cases whose contents I do not know, as the invoice is with the shipment. The syrup alone is a considerable gift. Maple syrup sells at 25¢ for 14 French ounces, and is very ugly. The other kind went as high as five francs a pound during the winter. We use a good deal, for at breakfast here we have to give the children coffee nearly all the time—there is nothing else [to give them to drink].

Providence is very wonderful in our regard. One day, not knowing how to pay the baker, the washerwoman, the salt bill, etc., we began a novena to Divine Providence and Our Lady of Prompt Succor. The next day Father Richard, our pastor and chaplain, told us he was determined to pay his board, having received a stipend for his services. In spite of my resistance he fixed the price at 600 francs for the year and then gave us 350 francs, which took us out of debt. So we resolved to continue saying daily the Litany of Divine Providence, and at once we received news of the charitable gifts of the Ursuline religious. Now we are asking them for a loan of 1,500 francs, on the advice of Monseigneur, who assures us they will oblige us. Undoubtedly he knows their desire to help with our building. Moreover, the people of St. Charles are very active about our convent here. They have already hauled to the spot huge logs forty feet long to build the house. It will look out over the Missouri, as Ste Marie dominates the Isère, and the view would be just as beautiful if the country were as well cultivated. . . .

Since I last wrote to you, the Bishop asked us to meet him at Florissant. I went there with Mother Octavie the Monday before Lent began. He arrived an hour later at the pastor's house. He showed us the property he offers to give us and the plan of the house, of which just one third will be built this year, thirty-six by thirty-two feet in dimensions. It will stand on good ground between a small stream that never runs dry and a creek that dries up in the summertime. The house will be of brick and cost 15,000 francs. We have only 5,800 francs at most in the Bishop's keeping. Besides, we shall need 300 or 400 francs to furnish the house at St. Charles. The townsfolk have promised only to build and roof it. . . .

Mother Eugenie has weathered her storm and goes forward now in the way of perfection. She could do any work assigned to her. She seems to be in the prayer of quiet. I beg you to tell me how to guide her in this. Mother Octavie is also very fervent and gains in self-assurance. The children love her very much and she will go with them willingly to Florissant, without envying the independence Mother Eugenie will have here. Marguerite is out of her element in this foreign country. Catherine is doing fairly well, but her conduct is influenced by her state of health, which is not strong enough for a life like ours, which is so fatiguing. . . .

A great kindness of Divine Providence since our novena—we were able to buy a second cow. She will pay for herself in a month and a half and will help solve the problem of our fasting all during Lent. Only the boarding pupils will have meat four days a week, as is the custom throughout the United States. People told us these cows would be frenzied if we tethered them in our grounds, but they are behaving nicely and follow us around like two big dogs; they even try to follow us into the house. . . .

The departure of the postulant, Mary Mullen, relieved Mother Duchesne of one anxiety. Her place was taken almost immediately by Mary Ann Summers of St. Louis. She was too young to become a postulant at once, and at first she chafed under confinement and discipline, but she became a reliable and helpful member of the household, finding in Philippine Duchesne a second mother and loving the life of prayer and work and family joys. She had been through sorrow in the past months; she was an orphan now, be-friended chiefly by Mrs. Pratte, the first of many orphans to whom Mother Duchesne gave a home.

The slight friction perceptible in the community that spring was aggravated by the Bishop's criticism of some points of the Rule which he considered incompatible with pioneer conditions, particularly cloister and the distinction between choir and coadjutrix nuns, though this distinction has held a place in communal religious life almost from its very inception. Mother Duchesne mentions the matter almost casually in a letter of March 15 to Father Barat:

> As we are in a time of trial, God has allowed that all I wrote about our situation here has changed, and for a new convent we have no resource but the good will of the people of St. Charles, who show some interest in building a skeleton of a house for us. I understand their eagerness is diminishing. Instead of a month, they say it will take them until next autumn. God knows what will happen; let us leave it all to Him. As to the project at Florissant, everything is delayed for several reasons. . . . When I saw the contractor's plans and estimate for a convent there, I realized it was simply extortion—excessive expenditures that would bring ruin on us. I wrote to the Bishop, refusing the services of the contractor and telling him that we had no other funds than those we had placed in his keeping. He replied that he had weighed the matter well and, being unable to assist us, he thought it best to drop the undertaking at Florissant. . . . You can form no idea of the problem we have here to maintain order and regularity. Nothing can be locked, and we are taken unawares by outsiders at any time of the day. The important thing is to get a house of our own. . . .
>
> An inspiration of Providence of which I cannot yet see the outcome is the fact that the young girl who always followed us to church in St. Louis and who brought us the apples, lost her mother at Christmas; and her brother was drowned while trying to bring aid to the *Franklin*. Monseigneur sent her out to help us. We gave her a home, not knowing at the time that this was the same child who was so instinctively drawn to us. She can read and write, and she speaks both languages. So she will be very useful, for the first postulant had no vocation and was very indolent. This girl is intelligent, and we are going to train her to help in the free school. . . . Orphans are really our only hope in the way of domestic help, as we have no slaves and can hire no white servants. Now is the time to face the problems raised by the Bishop. People say that two different religious costumes create a bad impression.

After comparing the customs of the Ursulines in New Orleans with those of the Society of the Sacred Heart in regard to distinctions within the religious community, Mother Duchesne drops the matter and turns to more personal affairs:

> During the winter I thought I had lost my health, but it is quite restored and I have no pain at all now. But I shall have much to expiate, for in that improvement in my condition the measure of consolation outweighs the suffering. What a joy it was to hear again that the Holy Father approved of our voyage! Realizing from this fact that it was the will of God takes away the cruel anguish caused by the thought that under the pretext of following an inspiration I was merely doing my own will. . . . So now my prayer is just an outpouring of gratitude for the assurance of that most completely desired will of God, which will seem all the more desirable in all that is ahead. Then the Society of the Sacred Heart and its members will spread the reign of Jesus Christ in these new lands. . . .
>
> The dear Lord is trying us in another way. Our first boarding pupil, a ribbon of merit, is ill. She is the eldest daughter of the lady who gave us such a kind welcome in St. Louis. If she dies, it will be a severe blow to us, humanly speaking. But God is all-powerful.

Emilie Pratte's illness was so serious that Mother Duchesne sent for her mother. Mrs. Pratte arrived with the family nurse, a competent Negro woman who had cared for all the little Prattes and who loved "Miss Emilie" as her own child. Madame Duquette's room was used as the school infirmary, and Mrs. Pratte was lodged there with her sick daughter. There was great excitement in the little house one evening when the nurse made too hot a blaze in the stove in the infirmary and the chimney, a stone and wood structure, caught fire. Nuns and children were badly frightened, "having no man to help them and almost no water." But the blaze was extinguished and no serious damage resulted. Emilie soon recovered and life returned to its normal routine. This trial united the little community by a closer bond of love, for all had shared the anxiety and prayed with increased fervor, and there is no more efficacious means of union than shared responsibility and prayer. All was going fairly well now, and Mary Ann Summers was proving a far more willing helper than Miss Mullen had been.

Bishop Du Bourg visited St. Charles before the close of the month, and Mother Duchesne recorded:

Monseigneur came to make his retreat at Father Richard's house. He spent one whole day upsetting all our plans, as well as the desires of Fathers Richard and Acquaroni, who have simply exhausted themselves in their efforts to get us firmly established here at St. Charles. The Bishop has in his keeping the sum of $2,000, which was sent to him from France by Mother Barat for us at the time of our departure for America. He declares he will use it only at St. Ferdinand's and that he will borrow the rest of the money needed for the erection of the new building. He says we shall not have to worry about the details of the construction, as he will have the pastor there superintend the work. This priest [Father Dunand] is a Trappist and has had experience, having built a convent for nuns at Fribourg in Switzerland. He is also eager to have us in his parish. Bishop Du Bourg added that he does not want us to divide, as our number is too small.

In the midst of all this trouble he has shown us more kindness and interest than ever before. He has read our Constitutions, found them full of wisdom, thanked us for having acquainted him with them, and said he preferred this Rule to that of any other order he knew. Finally, on leaving, he said graciously that he left his heart with us, that he had come here seeking rest for mind and heart and had found both. In the beginning he wished to change some of our rules, to adapt them to American ideas. He tried to win us over to his views, talking to us individually. But on receiving from each one the same answer—that we would change nothing without permission of our Superior General, he said that we were five heads in one bonnet. And now he has admitted that there is nothing to change.

So a compromise had been reached. The Bishop had had his way about the change of residence, though this meant a sad disappointment to the people in St. Charles who had already begun to build the new log convent, and the nuns, with Mother Duchesne as their guide, had stood loyally for strict observance of the Rule and customs of the Society, as they had promised to do on leaving France. They had set a precedent, and all the Religious of the Sacred Heart who have followed them in missionary ventures for the glory of that Divine Heart have clung with unswerving fidelity to it and preserved intact the precious union of mind and heart that makes possible the central government of so large a religious organization.

Holy Week was approaching, and Father Richard had expressed his intention of performing the liturgical services in the convent chapel, as the villagers seldom came to Mass except on

Sundays and other days of obligation. Mother Duchesne's joy in this "favor of Divine Providence" was intense, and she was looking forward to Holy Thursday and a night of prayer like those she had spent at Sainte Marie, though her frontier vigils of adoration had been as prolonged as her strength would permit. Mother Audé and the children prepared the repository, decorating it with fresh white muslin and artificial flowers. It was pretty, they thought, and very devotional.

After Mass on Holy Thursday the little convent was more silent and prayerful than usual, as the day pupils had no classes and the boarding pupils followed the example of the nuns. Toward evening, while three of the nuns were praying in the chapel, a gust of wind through a chink in the wall blew a corner of the cotton drapery across a candle flame. In an instant the altar was ablaze. The religious pulled away whatever furnishings they could reach as the flames licked upward along the wall. Cries of alarm brought Mother Duchesne to the scene. Mary Ann and the other girls ran for buckets, dipped them into the rain barrel, which had been filled providentially by an April downpour, and passed them up the ladder to Mother Duchesne who had climbed to the attic ahead of all the others. Balanced against an upright post, she threw the water on the dry beams and up to the shingled roof to prevent the spread of the fire. How she succeeded in doing this was a matter of astonishment to all. By prayer and self-control and intelligent direction the little group extinguished the flames and saved the house, and not a person in the village saw the fire or came to their assistance. Describing the accident to Mother Barat, Philippine wrote:

> Fire broke out in our chapel while Mother Octavie and Sisters Catherine and Marguerite were praying there. They could not extinguish the blaze and in an instant the whole chapel was in flames. They ran to tell me the Blessed Sacrament was destroyed. I had them throw water on the fire and pull out whatever furnishings they could reach. Mother Eugenie went in courageously and got her cap and hair and eyebrows burned. I hurried up to the attic to pour water on the beams above the chapel; for if the roof had caught fire, no human means could have saved the house and all the belongings we had stored in the attic, which is reached by a kind of ladder. . . .
>
> When at last I made my way into the chapel where the altar stands, everything on it had been burned. I saw a black square in the midst of the debris. I lifted it—it was the pall that had covered

the paten which was resting on the chalice. The paten had fallen from the chalice, but the Sacred Host had not slipped from it, and there it was, white and intact under the charred pall. I lifted It on the paten and placed It in the tabernacle, which was just slightly damaged. The statue of our Lady was not harmed, but St. Francis Regis had preferred to let his own picture get burned in two places rather than prevent that fire. And now that dear picture I brought from France is gone.

Two weeks previous to all this I had had a fright. It happened that during the night, when we had no water and no man on the place, and one of the boarding pupils was very ill, they came to tell me the chimney in the large room was on fire. I ran to the spot and saw that the flames were coming from a stove in an adjoining room. So I had that fire put out and there was no damage done.[27]

Through the spring and summer Mother Duchesne and her nuns worked steadily with the children, trying to give them all the training they could crowd into the few months that remained. May and June were celebrated with the same devotional practices in the convent on the Missouri as in those on the Seine and the Isère, and the feasts of St. Francis Regis and of the Sacred Heart were days the children would remember for many a year.

There was plenty of food now for nuns and children, as the garden yielded an ample supply of vegetables and the fruit trees bore an abundant crop. Looking back over the last months at St. Charles, Mother Duchesne noted:

It would be very wrong for us ever to lack confidence in Divine Providence or to complain, after all the proofs we have had of God's care of us: a small sack of rice—about 20 pounds—sufficed for the entire year, and we ate rice frequently. We did not have to buy coffee or much sweetening. These were supplied by the kind Ursulines in New Orleans. The apples that matured last year in October were ripe this year at the beginning of August, and we had far more vegetables than we needed. We were swimming in an abundance of fresh food, and we sold enough to pay for bread for two whole months.

She would not have the pleasure of recording material abundance very often in her life on the frontier, and even now a less agreeable episode flashed through her memory as she added:

I am, however, opposed to laying in large provisions. The children did not like the salt fish we had last winter and would not eat it. As a result, part of the supply spoiled. In order to get rid of it, we had a little burial service one morning very early. But the village dogs tore up all our work, burrowed into the ground, and scattered large pieces of spoiled fish around the house and on the road. Passers-by saw the mess and ridiculed us, saying we certainly were going to have sick children on our hands if we fed them on rotten fish.

The long, hot summer days were relieved now and then by hours of relaxation, when the children played under the spreading trees or waded in the creek that flowed through the south meadow or gathered fruit for their goûter in the orchard. On July 22 they celebrated in honor of the Mother General in far-off France, nuns and children enjoying a gay holiday. But Philippine was heartsick with disappointment when she wrote to Mother Barat a week later:

Following the recommendation you made to us, I have begun numbering my letters. The first was to Father Barat. We have never been so long a time without writing to and receiving letters from France. The last that came to us was from Sophie Lacroix and told us only what we already knew from former letters about your journeys. Our delay is due to the fact that the steamboats we expected daily were held downstream by low water. At our distance from St. Louis, moreover, we miss many opportunities of sending mail. We do not complain among ourselves about these privations in order to express regrets, but to add fuel to the fire of our sacrifice and so renew it. . . .

The most recent letters from you arrived last January. Mother Girard wrote then about foundations at Lyons and Nîmes. Since then the dear Lord has favored us with a share of His cross. The greatest and undoubtedly the hardest to bear is the lack of success in our work here. If a saint had been in charge, all would have gone well. That thought makes the burden of my office all the heavier. Every day I see more clearly that I do not possess the qualities necessary in a superior.

The new house at Florissant is progressing. They say we can move into it by December 1. Monseigneur may not be back from Bois Brulé by that time. Some business affairs concerning the seminary have detained him there. They tell me Father Martial has joined him there. I am trusting in Divine Providence with regard to the debt that house has brought on us and the transfer to Florissant. One day recently I was down to almost nothing. The paper money I had on hand all proved worthless at the same time, but that is the only kind of money people pay us. God will be our refuge. I am more and more convinced that He wants us here, and it consoles me greatly to know that the other four nuns feel as I do, even the one whose perseverance seemed somewhat doubtful. If at times we feel the thorns that press upon us from all sides, still we know we are your daughters, we have Fathers, Mothers, Sisters, and children all praying for us, and so our courage cannot fail.

There is little hope of our working among the Indians. In the days of Marie of the Incarnation the Jesuits went everywhere among them, gathered the children together, appeased the parents, interpreted their diverse languages and skilfully reduced them to writing in the dictionaries and books they composed. This kind of work is far beyond the ability of a few isolated missionaries, as we who are on the spot well realize. But my desire to devote myself to these poor souls has not diminished, if only God opens the way for me. . . .[28]

August was a very busy time. The First Communion ceremony was set for the fifteenth of the month, and this meant material and spiritual preparations before the retreat, which Father Richard gave the children. Then the "closing exercises" were planned and practiced, for the Bishop had promised to come for this event. Packing, too, was under way, but Philippine found time to write to Mother Barat on August 28:

It is a real suffering when we count the months and realize that we have had no word from France since January, and even then I had only five or six lines from you on a letter from Mother Girard. . . . I did not write any letters from April to July, as I had no way of sending them. . . . This is Number 4, which I shall send to your usual address.

I allow myself the pleasure of reading again and again the letters I have received from you and others in France. They console and encourage me. I do not say they bind me more closely to you all; the ties between us could hardly be drawn tighter. That is why it gave me such joy to hear Monseigneur say one day in commenting on us: *Ah, c'est bien de la race.* [Ah, that is a family trait of the Society.] However, dear Mother, I am beginning to realize that there will be differences because of national character and climate. The summer heat has been as prostrating here as it was in New Orleans last year. It is impossible to sleep with the windows closed at night. The children will not endure even their curtains closed in a dormitory. Out here they draw the beds in front of open windows and doors and fireplaces, and no one pays any attention to drafts. . . .

We are going to have the distribution of prizes soon. From the difficulty we have had in assigning these on the basis of a review of the year's work, you could realize how hard it is to teach classes out here. Some children came for three months, and they could not read when they first came. The mistresses have simply exhausted themselves teaching them the catechism and other elementary things and have made little progress. Some read English, but not French; others have a knowledge of the two languages; still others know only French. The same is true for the grammar, geography, and arithmetic classes. Many cannot afford to buy books, pens, paper, or sewing materials; they lack scissors, needles, thread, etc. As an excuse they say, "Mother has none at home," and they get none for school.

Knowledge of English is bringing Mother Octavie forward. The Americans are quite proud of her. Their national pride seems to make them scorn those who do not speak their language, so English is a real necessity. I simply despair of ever speaking it. Eugenie hesitates, too, but she has enough to do with the French-speaking children. She is venerated by them. From all this you will realize that God has not bestowed on us the gift of tongues. Perhaps He wants His missionary nuns to sanctify themselves on failure. That is what I conclude when I see young priests preaching fluently in English at the end of a few months. . . . Our Bishop also has all kinds of crosses to bear, but now he wants two of us to go into St. Louis to open a little day school. How can we ask you for more nuns just now? . . .

I had just finished my letter to you when I received yours of April 18, which mentions one of the previous month that I did not receive. . . . I am so grateful for your generosity at a time when you are in want yourself. I share all your anxieties; do not give any more thought to ours. Suffering brings its own sweetness, for Providence never fails us. . . .

On Sunday, August 29, Philippine found time for a last letter from St. Charles. Her heart was full of memories of August 29 in former years—in Grenoble, at Vizille, at Grâne, at Sainte Marie—and of those who had always made it such a joyous day for her by their constant love and devoted friendship. And so she wrote to Josephine. She had had no news from her in more than six months, but she had learned the way of the mail on the frontier and she was schooling herself to accept this circumstance, which she found so trying. Her interest in the dear ones she had left in France was as keen as ever, her love as tender and grateful as she wrote:

A year ago today I was writing to you from St. Louis just after our arrival there. Since then our situation, though always precarious, has presented few variations. We have had very few boarding pupils, as both St. Charles and the section of the country north of the Missouri are too poor to send any. Then, too, the river separates us from St. Louis and is subject to terrible floods, storms, and ice, so the mothers have considered all this an insurmountable obstacle to putting their children in school here.

A house is being built for us at Florissant, which is nearer St. Louis. We shall pay for it little by little and we shall leave St. Charles next month with keen regret. This place is better populated than Florissant; the day pupils are so well disposed; and the site of the town is much more desirable. It will be an important place some day, for trade on the Missouri with the Indians or the new American settlements at Franklin and Boonlick and on the Upper Missouri is growing every day. To aid and encourage this, the government is putting troops and cannon on the steamboats, which were not seen hitherto on the Missouri. Someone told me recently about a steamboat that went from New York to New Orleans with steam and paddle-wheels in ten days. At New Orleans it discarded its sails and came up the Mississippi just as other steamboats do. It was the first trial of such a voyage.[29] With regard to boats on the Missouri, we saw the first four that ever attempted the navigation of that stream.[30]

I am fifty years old today, my dear friend. That age makes me realize my unfitness for the venture I have undertaken, but it does not lessen the tender affection that has bound me to you, to Augustin, and to Camille for so many, many years. You were my dearest friends in all the world; and though I left the world, my love for you has survived a sacrifice that was akin to death. Thank you so much for your tender interest in my work. Your letter touched the deepest chords of my heart. My companions are greatly loved here and do much good. They want to be remembered to you. You heard about our accident by fire on Holy Thursday, when we had all your gifts displayed in our chapel. Your generosity made it possible for us to see other gifts from your hand used as decorations on Easter Sunday. Many other things in this sanctuary remind me of Josephine and her tender and solicitous love.

Our greatest problem has been to get a house. Monseigneur, the Bishop, is having one built, but at our expense. Where shall we find 30,000 francs, when we have only 5,000? I shall know the actual cost of the house only when we are in it. I dread it, yet I trust it all to Divine Providence. I grasped at a means offered me in a proposition you made in the letter you enclosed with one from Father Dumolard.[31] I explained to you our situation and asked a little loan to help us; but if this is not possible, rest assured it will not lessen my gratitude to you, my remembrance of you in prayer before God, and my eternal friendship. Affectionate regards to my aunt and her family. . . .

Bishop Du Bourg arrived at St. Charles with Fathers Martial and De La Croix on August 30. Presiding at the distribution of prizes next day, he congratulated Miss Odile DeLassus on winning highest honors and complimented the children on their good manners as well as on their recitations and singing. He was sincere in his praise and expressed great satisfaction at all that had been accomplished in the classes. Then he spoke with regret of the necessity that forced the nuns to leave St. Charles. The evening before, he had told the community that the convent at Florissant, which not even Mother Duchesne had seen yet, was not ready for occupancy and that, since their lease on the Duquette house expired on September 6, the best arrangement he could suggest was for them to use the log cabin on his farm a mile from Florissant. True, Father De La Croix was living there at present—and was also listening to this conversation—but he could move elsewhere for a few weeks. No one asked where "elsewhere" might be, and no more was said on the subject. The Bishop's optimism was equaled only by his vivid imagination, which always bypassed the difficulties involved in the arrangements he proposed. He rode off on horseback next morning, the priests following with two gentlemen in the carriage that had conveyed them from St. Louis, and the nuns were left to face an unhappy task.

It was easier to close the school than it was to dismiss the children. They wanted to spend at least part of the First Friday of September at the convent. On the eve they came to rehearse the hymns they had sung at the first Communion ceremony in August. On Friday morning all who had made their first Communion then or earlier in the year came for Mass and breakfast. "Father Richard was as deeply moved as we were," noted Mother Duchesne, and after a very touching little sermon "he went off without taking his breakfast."

So the first long, laborious year in the frontier mission field came to a close. In Mother Duchesne's eyes it was a failure, and failure, whether real or apparent, was one of the severest trials that could come to her. She belonged to a family that had been eminently successful and to a religious order whose steady growth and development were remarkable. She had been put in charge of an apostolic enterprise which seemed to offer high hopes of success and which now had every appearance of failure. In spite of the very evident material factors that had conditioned the failure, she felt that its primary cause had been herself. She was not blind to patent facts nor to the almost hopeless circumstances in which she had worked for twelve months, but she was blind to the courageous leadership, the unswerving loyalty, the selfless devotion with which she had carried on that work. The struggle had been constant, even heroic, yet she was so alive to a sense of her own incapacity that she simply could not see things in any other light. This very conviction of incapacity was a forward movement in the contemplative life which was her true element. Self-pity and resentment had no place in her soul. Her close intimacy with God, her absorbing devotion to the Sacred Heart kept her in quiet self-control and made possible a growth in detachment and a surrender to God's will incomparably more generous than any she had known in the past. She was ready and willing for whatever lay ahead in the Flowering Valley on the other side of the turbulent Missouri.

Palais de Justice

Place St. Andre, Genoble, France

Statue of Bayard
Home of Claude Perier

Pierre-François Duchesne

Amelie Duchesne de Mauduit

The Chateau
at Grâne,
the Duchesne
country home

Claude Perier

Charlotte Pascal Perier

Casimir Perier

The Chateau of Vizille, the Perier country home

The Choir of the Visitation
monastery of Sainte Marie

Church of Sainte Marie as Mother
Duchesne knew it

The Chapter room of the monastery
of Sainte Marie

Courtyard of the monastery of Sainte-Marie-d'en-Haut, Grenoble, France

Mother Aloysia Jouve in the
habit first worn by Religious
of the Sacred Heart

Father Joseph Varin, S.J.

General and Mrs. Bernard Pratte, Senior

Ursuline convent, New Orleans, where Mother Duchesne and companions
were given hospitality on reaching America in 1818.

View of St. Charles Missouri, 1841, showing at extreme right Jesuit Church, brick convent built in 1834–35, and "Duquette Mansion" (1794), which was the first convent of the Sacred Heart in America (1818).

—*Courtesy of Missouri Historical Society*

Convent built at Florissant in 1819 by Mother Duchesne. The church (contiguous) was built in 1821.

Stairway in Florissant convent showing door opening on closet used as sleeping room by Mother Duchesne.

Bishop Joseph Rosati

Bishop Louis William Du Bourg

Plan of the city of St. Louis (1824) showing
the original property of the foundation
and the location of the City House.

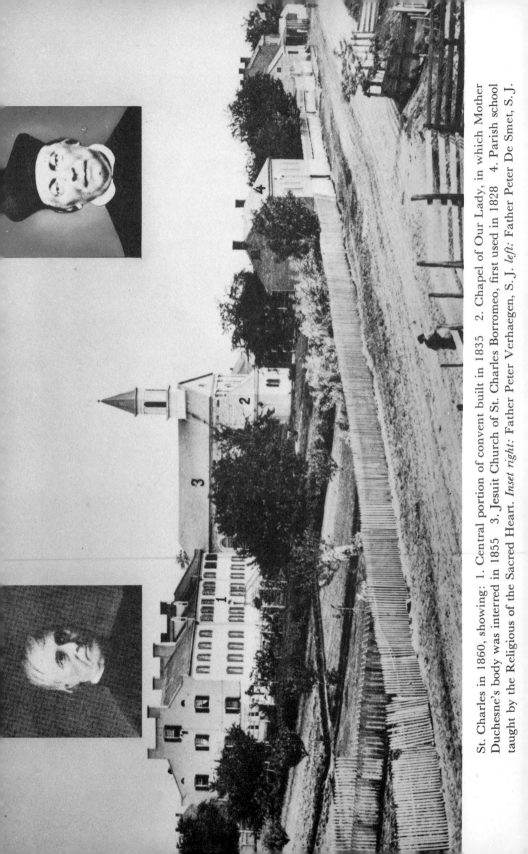

St. Charles in 1860, showing: 1. Central portion of convent built in 1835 2. Chapel of Our Lady, in which Mother Duchesne's body was interred in 1855 3. Jesuit Church of St. Charles Borromeo, first used in 1828 4. Parish school taught by the Religious of the Sacred Heart. *Inset right*: Father Peter Verhaegen, S.J. *left*: Father Peter De Smet, S.J.

St. Madeleine Sophie Barat
1779–1865
Portrait sketched from picture taken after death

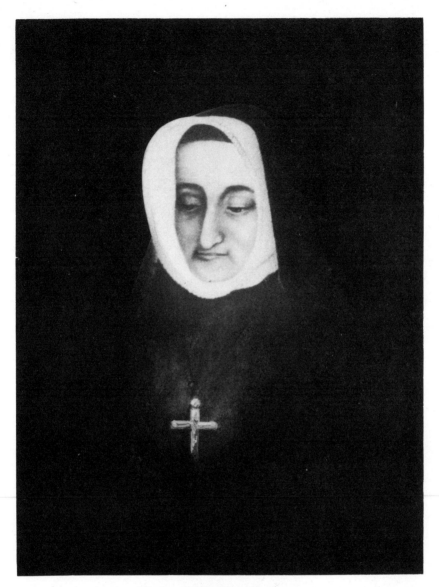

Mother Philippine Duchesne
1769–1852
Portrait sketched from picture taken after death

Unfinished memorial church of Blessed Philippine Duchesne, St. Charles Missouri

Tomb of Blessed Philippine Duchesne in Memorial Church

seven

Building
on the Frontier

I. 1819—1821

> *Lord, I have loved the beauty of Thy house.*
>
> Liturgy of the Mass

THE TREK TO FLORISSANT was true to frontier pattern, and no one could describe it better than Philippine did. She seemed to enjoy her own narrative, for she wrote it with the quiet humor and directness that characterize so many of the little accounts she sent back to France. The migration began on September 3, when baggage and furniture were taken in carts down the steep road that led to the river and loaded on two small rafts, which were poled downstream and landed on the south bank of the Missouri. Mother Audé, Sister Lamarre, and three of the pupils followed after a tearful good-bye from many of the children of St. Charles, who clung to the nuns and exhausted the patience of the waiting boatmen. At La Charbonnière they were met by Father Dunand, pastor of St. Ferdinand, and Father De La Croix. The former had brought carts that were loaned by the laborers working on the new convent; the latter, those belonging on the Bishop's farm. "They made seventeen trips from the river to the farmhouse," noted Mother Duchesne. "This does not mean that we have great possessions, however, for a one-horse cart can carry only three people, or baggage in proportion."

> This expedition [she continues] was followed by a second, when Mother Octavie left with two of the older girls in an open carriage sent by the father of one of them. I intended to bring up the rear that afternoon with the cows, the calves, the chickens, and

307

Sister Marguerite. But our cows revolted when they found themselves tied and obliged to walk in the sun, so we had to wait until early the next morning, when the rest of our belongings was packed into three carts, along with cabbages to appease the cows. These animals started off on the rampage, but soon they were mastered by their ropes and by fatigue, and they decided to follow with their calves. I perched on top of a cart, dividing my attention between the care of my relics and that of the chickens. After driving about ten miles, we crossed the Missouri just opposite Florissant on a raft. When we landed, Marguerite lined up the chickens with motherly tenderness and gave them food and water. I did the same for the cows with my cabbages. Then Father De La Croix appeared on horseback to show us the way. As we had let the cows loose, he had to gallop after them every time they tried to run into the woods. By evening we reached the little farmhouse.

Describing this new residence Mother Duchesne wrote:

It is composed of a single room, which will serve as the children's dormitory, refectory, parlor, and classroom. Above is a loft under a roof that is pierced by many holes. This will be our living quarters night and day. We shall stop up the holes as best we can and use the loft also as kitchen, refectory, and storeroom.

The farmhouse was a log cabin of American type, measuring about eighteen feet square and having two windows with solid wooden shutters and a single entrance fitted with a door of thick planks that was fastened with a wooden latch on a leather thong. A stone fireplace at one end accommodated enormous logs. Soon a great fire was roaring up the chimney, giving light and warmth to the room, for the erratic Missouri weather staged freak changes that September, with freezing temperature following close on the burning heat of the moving days. "We are in a situation that calls for continual self-renunciation," wrote Mother Duchesne, "at times pestered by visitors, without a corner to which we can withdraw for prayer; now overcome by heat in such crowded quarters, and now racked by the cold and wind that come in on all sides." [1]

Another circumstance that distressed her was the illness of Father De La Croix. In order to give the nuns and children a home, he had vacated the log cabin and taken shelter in a dilapidated corn crib, "as open as a bird cage," commented Mother Duchesne. Exposed to wind and cold, he contracted a fever and for several days was quite sick.

We could not even pass a chair into the place through the hole that serves as door and window. When the Bishop was informed of his condition, he ordered a two-room house to be built—one room for the priest and the other for a chapel. Some old timber was at hand, a few workmen were put on the job, and within a week Father De La Croix had a roof over his head, and the Blessed Sacrament reposed in the little chapel, and we were settled in the way we most desired, for "he who has Jesus has all."

To the surprise of the nuns, the school began to increase immediately. First came Mathilde Hamilton, at whose home near Ste Genevieve many of the young French and Italian priests who came as missionaries to Missouri spent several months in order to learn English "in a family that spoke it correctly and where they could not use any other language." [2] On October 19 three more pupils arrived—Virginie Labbadie, a cousin of the Prattes, and the Rolette sisters, Emilie and Betsie.[3] They were gentle, womanly girls, and like their companions they were drawn to Mother Duchesne because there was about her such a complete lack of affectation, such simplicity of speech and manner, such unobtrusive tact and sincere friendliness. On their coming to the cabin-convent, she commented: "People are so accustomed to poor lodgings in this country that even the wealthiest families do not mind sending us their daughters." She was happy to welcome these new pupils, but they increased her anxiety at a time when she had her hands full.

All the tenants on the farm contracted fever [she wrote in her *Journal*]; and as they could not help themselves, Sister Marguerite cooked their meals. Mother Eugenie had to milk six cows morning and night—two of ours and four belonging to the farm. This did not last long, but another trial followed, for Mother Octavie and two of the children caught the fever. As there is only one room for all the children and one for us, we feared everyone in the household would catch the disease; but Divine Providence was watching over us, and today, September 28, all are well.

The Bishop called on us yesterday. He named Father De La Croix as our chaplain. This priest was first his secretary and then his treasurer. The Bishop calls him his angel. He is a young Fleming who was in the seminary at Ghent when Bonaparte forced all the seminarians into his army. He rides horseback well and on his difficult missionary trips he easily crosses the most dangerous rivers by swimming his horse across. He is the first priest ever seen in many parts along the Missouri. He is going to live in a little house that stands on the same property as our convent in Florissant.

The defying challenge offered by the one-room cabin with a loft called forth the finest virtues in Mother Duchesne and stimulated like virtues in her religious. There was plenty of room for discouragement at times, but there was always at hand that dauntless combination of faith and hope and trust, all glowing with love. Although the community and school were lodged so inconveniently, Philippine noted appreciatively several advantages that compensated for their discomforts:

> We have an abundance of fruit and vegetables; we have salted down a little heifer; we get bread and corn meal from Florissant on credit for six months. The wood that was used in making the bricks [for the new convent] will furnish us with fuel for the early winter months. Many of our fifty chickens will lay eggs all winter. And there are the frequent visits of the Bishop and missionary priests, the assurance of the presence of Father De La Croix and of the pastor, who is using every cent he has to pay our workmen. All this makes us realize that it would be very ungrateful and very wrong for us ever to fail in trust toward Divine Providence in either spiritual or temporal affairs.

Besides her account of the transfer to Florissant and the first weeks in the log cabin, two letters written by Mother Duchesne in September, 1819, are extant. Six months had passed since her last letter to Father Barat, though she had received many marks of kindness from him during that time. Without apology for her silence she wrote by candlelight in a corner of the cabin loft while the household slept on the night of September 17:

> You certainly give us proof that we are still your daughters, for your solicitude for us does not diminish, but rather increases. Your letters to Mothers Octavie and Eugenie did them the greatest good and strengthened them in the path of perfection along which they are determined to walk. Far from being frightened by difficulties, they are never happier than when they have something to suffer. . . . The money shortage is being felt sharply in the United States also. A large number of banks have stopped payment and this means total loss for all who hold their notes—which is the kind of money in use in the country. It is very rare to find a few dollars or other coins among the paper notes we receive. I know that because of the money shortage Monseigneur wanted to stop the work on our house, but it is going on and we shall be in it within a month, even if they do not plaster it until the spring.

We had the pleasure of a visit from the Bishop yesterday. He still wants three more of our nuns, and he treats us as his daughters. We are lodged in a little house belonging to him, from which we can see Florissant, surrounded by orchards and farmlands where we may gather whatever we need. Monseigneur was delighted to learn that a little house of the Society has been founded at Bordeaux. He thinks very highly of the religious who have joined the Society there.[4]

I was really sorry the details of our straitened circumstances caused you and our Fathers and Mothers in France any anxiety about us. That was a temporary situation, and I assure you such experiences bring very real delight, and one must be on guard against taking pride in them. Divine Providence does not keep us waiting long, and in spite of the uneasiness caused by moving into our new house with a debt of perhaps 20,000 francs (they have not yet stated the exact sum), I have not the slightest doubt that we shall find a way to pay it in a short time, since we were able to live at St. Charles with so few pupils and still not incur the least debt. . . .

Among the many holy priests I have met, I do not find one who helps me. It seems as if my soul were quite alone—but I have too little feeling to be distressed about it. I do not know what condition my soul is in. I am unfaithful and I do not worry; I am haughty and impatient and I taste only the sweetness of Jesus. I rarely humble myself, yet the strongest conviction I experience is that of God's goodness to me. Father Richard did not handle me gently, and I am grateful to him for that. Yet with him, as with our Bishop, respect does not call forth that confidence which puts the soul at ease. My own is, as it were, passive, without movement except toward the soul of Jesus, toward Mary and St. Regis.

Please distribute the letters we are sending. . . . It is nighttime and I am nodding with sleep, but I must thank you on the part of Monseigneur for Sister Nativité's work, which he took even before he knew it was for him. We cannot hide anything from him. He sees through everything, exterior and interior, spiritual and temporal. . . .

Ten days later she opened her heart to Mother Barat, laying before her some of the problems that were weighing heavily on her. The spectre of debt was creeping up to haunt her for many a day and in circumstances that tried her severely. But the picture she sketched was never entirely dark, for her buoyant spirit and unfailing trust in God lifted her above the workaday worries that lay like snares in her path. Recommending her letter to St. Anthony, as was her custom, she wrote on September 27:

It grieved me to learn that you have been anxious about us, but it was very sweet to be told: "I should like to have a letter from you every month." I had not received that loving invitation when I omitted writing from April until July. . . . I received your April letter before that of March. The latter told me all the gifts you planned to send us; the former announced the shipment of these things. . . . What we need most of all just now is money. Monseigneur's purse is drained for his seminary at the Barrens and his college in St. Louis, not to mention the cathedral. Our building overwhelms him with embarrassment, so it is very urgent for us to pay our debt. . . .

I do not yet know the total cost of the building. At one moment Monseigneur was for stopping the work on it for lack of funds, but the pastor at Florissant took upon himself the business of urging on the work and even of adding another story, giving the brickmaker a piece of land in payment and spending his last cent on the house. He shows extraordinary eagerness to have us in his parish. . . .

I was the more deeply touched by your gift of the *piano* when I realized that you had purchased it with money you needed. Oh, my dear Mother, believe me, we suffer only when we learn that you are suffering. . . . Neither Eugenie nor I can understand English yet, and even Octavie, with all her facility and assurance and constant study, cannot understand some Americans nor make herself understood by them. A miracle is worked in favor of the priests, I think. . . .

Early in October Bishop Du Bourg paid the nuns a visit in company with Father Felix De Andreis, superior of the Lazarist Missions in Missouri.[5] The Bishop was pleasant and friendly, praised the children's singing, even asking for a repetition of the hymns sung at his Mass, and gave the community a deed to the plot of ground on which the convent was being constructed. "Then he required Mother Duchesne to write a letter to Mr. Mullanphy, asking the loan of $2000, as there is no money on hand for the completion of our building," Mother Duchesne recorded in her *Journal*. Next day she sat down to write to Mother Barat, yet strangely enough she made no mention of borrowing money from John Mullanphy. Instead she betrayed the emotional strain of the day before by giving free rein first to a reminiscent mood, then to a little daydreaming about St. Charles. Only after she had actually received and used the money did she write about it. That October 10 her quill touched on happy memories and shadowy hopes:

Our house will not be ready before December. That month is already dear to me and full of memories, for it brought me back almost miraculously [in 1801] to that happy solitude where you adopted me [in 1804], and where I saw you for the first time. There we often celebrated together the feast of St. Francis Xavier, whom we both love so much. And now this month becomes dearer by reason of the fact that it will see the opening of the first house owned by the Society in the New World. Monseigneur will add to our happiness by having a retreat given to us soon after our installation. That will reanimate our zeal for the work, which is going to increase, as several children will then come to us whom we cannot take now because of limited space.

Having learned already the ways of the mail between Europe and the frontier, she added:

Please accept the prayers we offer continually for you and which we renew in a special manner today as New Year's wishes in union with all our dear families. May we equal them in love and respect and not be far behind them in merit before God!

Early in November she sketched in a few lines the life of the nuns on the Bishop's farm:

Our days are filled with work for the children and our spiritual duties, along with chores to which we were formerly unaccustomed. As we have no servant, we have frequently to gather wood in the forest. In this country, people would look with scorn on the little fires we made in Paris. Here, when we have a visitor, we burn up our whole provision of fuel in a single day; then we have to bring in more wood. We gather corn, apples, vegetables in the garden. When the children go for a walk, they often bring back wild fruits and farm provisions, but we sometimes lack meat and often have only corn meal for making bread; and even this is expensive.[6]

Bishop Du Bourg was at Florissant again for the feast of the Presentation, November 21, presiding at the renovation of vows, preaching, and giving Benediction of the Blessed Sacrament. By this time Mother Duchesne was so well acquainted with him, she could interpret with fair accuracy the look in his expressive eyes—now puzzled and uncertain, now hardened into resolution, and again genial and laughing. She knew the set of his sensitive mouth, the lines of his fine forehead and weak chin. It was a handsome face in which obstinacy rather than strength seemed to dominate. The

Bishop's magnificent physical build gave him an imposing appearance, while his exquisite courtesy made him a charming guest.

All was pleasant enough that day until he again broached the subject of changes he wished to make in the Society's rule of life. "We would not consent to these," Mother Duchesne noted laconically in her *Journal;* and the Bishop must have admired her courageous loyalty. At least he took no offense, for he proceeded to arrange for the promised retreat to be given at the cabin-convent during a missionary trip Father De La Croix was planning. Up the Missouri River was the Indian country where white men were penetrating for fur trading, trapping, and hunting. No priest had as yet gone into those woods and prairies to carry the Gospel to the savages. There were settlers living in villages on the lower reaches of the river beyond St. Charles, and among them, too, the missionary hoped to sow the seeds of a rich harvest.

In a letter to Mother Barat written about this time Bishop Du Bourg expressed his admiration for "the rare virtues and remarkable gifts of the religious whom you have sent me. I cannot tell you how excellent an impression they have made in this part of the world. Mother Duchesne is a saint." [7] Meanwhile she herself touched indirectly on his visit in a letter to Mother Barat which is a sort of running comment on life at Florissant:

> The last letters we had from France were written in April. . . . We had hoped to be in our new home by the beginning of November, but we will be fortunate if we move in by January 1. In the meantime we live on the Bishop's farm. He has given us the legal title to the land on which our house is being built. . . . Recently we borrowed 10,000 francs from rich Mr. Mullanphy in order to get the building finished. His three daughters, about whom I wrote to you, are at Lyons instead of Poitiers. I hope you do not mind if our chaplain, Father De La Croix, has some material from Flanders addressed to you in Paris. Please have it shipped to Bordeaux for him and sent here. He is in great need of it.
>
> Our consolation in this wilderness is that our boarding pupils are much better off here than at St. Charles. Several show signs of vocation, but we must be very prudent in this matter because of their wealth and the opposition of their families. The daily regulations here are the same as at Grenoble. The uniform is magenta, trimmed in black velvet, without flowers or tulle or lace. One very irksome thing here is the scandal the Americans, especially the Protestants, take at the least game or outing on Sunday. I spoke to the Bishop about this and he said we must respect

the opinion of the people here. He experienced the same thing at the college in Baltimore. . . .

If any of our religious come to join us, I wish they would bring some pairs of sabots as models. These are greatly needed here, where one goes around daily through water rounding up the animals, with no servant to help, and where the kitchens are built at a distance from the house for fear of fire. Prairie fires and forest fires have done great damage this year. We have seen them at close range.

So much about material things, dear Reverend Mother, but my heart is with you and with the Societies of Jesus and of the Sacred Heart. When I meditate on the fact that I belong to our Society, my soul expands with joy, tears of gratitude flow, and I see only happiness in privations. Could God do more for me? Only one greater favor could He bestow—the privilege of martyrdom. But on my side, how much more I could do! What sorrow I feel at having corresponded so poorly with grace.[8]

Father De Andreis arrived for the retreat on December 5, and for a week held his audience of five nuns and a few of the older pupils under the spell of his fervent preaching and personal sanctity. The carriage that came to take him back to St. Louis brought Mother Duchesne a letter from Mother Barat dated July 9 and containing some reflections that Philippine noted in her *Journal:* "Our Mother General regrets that our first convent was not built either in New Orleans or in St. Louis. She insists that we establish a mother house and novitiate, from which small missions might be founded later on. But for the present she considers it very unwise for us to divide our group." Next day she made a very characteristic entry, writing in a completely impersonal tone of matters that were most dear to her heart and giving facts precious to those who would know her life-story in detail:

Today we commemorate the anniversary of Reverend Mother Barat's arrival at Grenoble [in 1804] to unite the convent of Ste Marie, where Mother Duchesne was living, with the Society. At eleven o'clock in the morning, which was the time at which she arrived, we all gathered in the chapel to sing the *Laudate,* the *Magnificat,* and the hymn in honor of St. Regis. Mother Duchesne also recalled her own return to Ste Marie, where she had been a pupil and later a religious novice for 4½ years before and during the great revolution in France. She had been obliged to leave in September, 1792, and she returned there in 1801. The building had been recovered from the government under Napoleon the very year of his concordat with Pope Pius VII.

The transfer from the Bishop's "chateau" in the woods to the new convent in the village has been described in detail by Mother Duchesne and Sister Lamarre in charming letters:

> We moved from the Bishop's farm in very cold weather [wrote Philippine], when the pastor of Florissant informed me [on December 20] that "the holy land was ready and could be entered before Christmas." I set off next day with a young American girl [Mary Ann Summers], who acts as our interpreter with the workmen. As we reached the village I heard the bell for Mass, so we went first to the church. The pastor announced that this was the feast of St. Thomas the Apostle. It gave me a thrill of joy to think that we were taking possession of our new home on such a day, and I begged this saint, along with St. Francis Xavier and St. Regis, to obtain for us the grace that all our labor might be for the glory of the Sacred Hearts of Jesus and Mary.[9]

The two-mile tramp through the snow and the two days of labor to clear the building of debris and prepare it for the community and children are in her estimation negligible details. Of importance, however, is the fact that

> on December 23 Mother Octavie with one of the Sisters and six of the older girls trudged through the snow to join me. They were wrapped up in blankets and had stockings over their shoes to prevent them from slipping on the ice.

The Sister in the party was Catherine Lamarre, who seems to have enjoyed this event of winter sport and wrote of it in her gayest manner:

> You cannot imagine any funnier sight than we were. It was bitter cold, and Mother Eugenie in the abundance of her charity had wrapt our bodies in blankets and our heads in shawls, leaving only our feet a little liberty. Enveloped in all this covering, we set out on our tramp. Never have we laughed so much in all our lives. We looked like a band of Indians, and by way of amusement we called ourselves a family—father, mother, and children. And I? Oh, I was grandma. We got safely to St. Ferdinand; and when Mother Duchesne saw us, she exclaimed, "What sights you are!" And laughing all the more, we began to strip off the wrappings that had kept us nice and warm, though the cold was intense.[10]

Taking up Mother Duchesne's account again, we read:

A wagon hauling our baggage and furniture followed them. I rode back to the farm in it to make up the last bundles and pack the chapel furnishings. That afternoon another wagon took the remaining children, escorted by Father De La Croix on horseback. On the 24th we sent Marguerite in a little wagon with our boxes and bundles. Later Mother Eugenie and I set out on foot, hoping to conduct our last cow across the fields in a friendly fashion. We had never been able to lead her with a rope, and she had no calf to attract her this time. I filled my apron with corn in order to coax her to follow me. But she preferred her liberty and ran headlong through the bushes and trees along our path. As we tried to keep up with her we floundered and fell several times in the snow, tore our veils and habits on the brambles, and at last gave up and let her go back to the farm, while we pursued our way to Florissant. The snow was falling more heavily now and we had only pig tracks to guide us. We were such a sight to behold, we actually frightened a herd of these half-wild animals. I was carrying our money and papers in my pockets, but the string broke and everything, including my watch, fell into the snow. We had a very hard time recovering our possessions and carrying them, for our hands were numb with cold and could not take hold of anything. So we were very late in reaching Florissant because we had lost our way. But we had to hurry with the work of preparing the chapel. Owing to the severe cold, the room intended for it had not been plastered. We removed the lumber that had been piled there and hung sheets as a curtain behind the altar which we set up. After supper we decorated it during the hour of *veillée*, then went to confession. At midnight Father De La Croix offered the Holy Sacrifice of the Mass.

In her *Journal* Mother Duchesne recorded other details: the nuns recited Matins promptly at eleven o'clock that Christmas Eve; the midnight Mass was followed by a second one, and both were attended by the "pious Irish workmen" who had built the house. There was a third Mass on Christmas morning, with joyous Christmas hymns, as at the other two, and in the afternoon Vespers followed by Benediction—both "solemn," though it is difficult to understand in what the "solemnity" consisted. The Bishop came next day to bless the new convent, and the children in their bright uniforms sang "some couplets expressing gratitude to him." Father Dunand was also present, so two verses were addressed also to him. General Pratte attended this little reception and next morning directed traffic in the village, for a stream of carriages brought visitors, some coming through curiosity, others, like the Pratte family, to attend the Bishop's Mass, at which Therese Pratte and Mary Ann Summers received their first Holy Communion. The year 1819 closed with the customary Benediction of reparation and gratitude, and the New Year opened with festive wishes expressed first to Mother Duchesne by both nuns and children, then to Father Dunand and Father De La Croix.

The boarding school increased with the arrival of the Leduc, Chenier, and Cabanné girls in January, and with them on this day of gifts came some handsome ones from the Bishop—oil paintings of the Sacred Heart, St. Francis of Assisi, St. Agatha, Benedict Joseph Labre, and one representing the death of St. Francis Regis. Now a little shrine could be set up temporarily in fulfilment of the promise made to honor him on the American frontier. A letter to Father Barat, begun on January 2 and continued at odd moments during at least ten days, shows Philippine grappling with problems less easily solved than that of the shrine:

> It is a long time since I wrote to you. I have made up for this in part by speaking often of you and recalling your advice. We must accept the fact that we shall never see you again, and you have often said to us: *God alone—we must give up seeking consolation.* It is true that in our relations with you there were fruits more valuable than consolation. But God has brought about this separation, this privation. That fact alone suffices to make us resigned to it. He has at the same time put into the hearts of the men of God whom we meet out here more zeal for us and interest in our work than we deserve, and they all assure us that we shall never be left without spiritual aid. I have every reason to believe them. . . .
>
> English is a very difficult language. I do not speak it, nor can I understand it yet. Mother Eugenie stammers out a little, and Mother Octavie speaks it badly and will never be able to teach it, so Monseigneur thinks, because of the extreme difficulty of the pronunciation and the very delicate ear needed for speaking it. But all the parents require the study of this language, and we have no nun to teach it. Mother Octavie is aided by an American pupil. Pray that God may destine her for our Society. Her innocence of soul and her natural disposition would make her an outstanding subject and just the kind we need for teaching English.
>
> We still have no novices, and the problem of their joining us is more difficult now. I wrote to our Mother General about it in my last letter. Monseigneur has again asked us to make changes in the Rule. We stated our opinion in our letter, and we shall hold to

whatever our Mother General may decide. But I do not believe these modifications would satisfy the pride that requires them. If such people do not complain about rank and costume, they will do so in regard to employments for which ability and education alone can fit a person. The more I think about it, the more I see the difficulty involved in acceding to all the Bishop asks. For how can we change the attitude of a whole nation, when that attitude is supported by the natural bent of human character? . . .

We moved into our house during a spell of severe cold weather, which has continued, making this the coldest winter they have had here in twenty years. We have kept well, but several of the pupils who were promised to us have not come, and it is another problem to know how to make ends meet. . . . All the state banks are failing and this is causing a panic throughout the country such as they have never experienced before. The only paper money that has any value is that of the Bank of Missouri. . . .

We persevere in the hope that we shall be well established some day. But just now the clouds are too thick to let us even glimpse that day. We know by experience that happiness can be combined with much suffering. We are satisfied with our lot; we have no regrets; and we are even disposed to abide in peace in the midst of failure. Poverty costs us little when it means merely privation for ourselves. It is the debts that stab the heart. But we embrace our poverty—abject, dependent, repugnant though it be—because it is like the poverty of our Lord and comes to us from the Heart of Jesus. And what I write is the unanimous sentiment of all your daughters here in Upper Louisiana, who call themselves your humble daughters *in Corde Jesu.*

On Friday, March 17, a heavily loaded wagon lumbered out from St. Louis, bearing the long-awaited cases that had been shipped from France the previous spring. Their contents delighted the nuns and children alike: silver-plated candlesticks and crucifix for the altar, material for vestments, clothing, an assortment of writing paper for letters and classroom use and of colored paper for the manufacture of the highly prized flowers, books, seeds, and last and largest, the piano—to delight, and at times nearly to madden, all who dwelt in the convent. On the following day another cart unloaded several cases of provisions sent from New Orleans by the charitable Ursulines.

These were busy days for Mother Duchesne, but not so busy as to prevent her from writing letters to France when an opportunity for sending them presented itself. On March 19, Bishop Du Bourg ordained two young Italian priests, and each expressed the desire to say his first Mass at the Convent of the Sacred Heart. That very afternoon Father Angelo Inglesi was welcomed cordially. This was the man styled by the Bishop "my most beloved son . . . whom Divine Providence has placed at my side . . . a new Timothy," than whom he thought "no one to be more acceptable" as his successor.[11] As the young Roman stood at the altar, no one suspected the truth about him; and when he announced his immediate departure for Europe as the Bishop's personal representative, Mother Duchesne hastened to write letters to France. That Inglesi delivered them is something in his favor. With joy and gratitude Philippine wrote to Mother Barat to tell of the arrival of the gifts, but she had to admit that they had cost 400 francs for shipment up the river, besides 900 francs in customs duty. "The thousand franc note you sent paid the duty," she added, "but the remaining money had been spent for us, so we are obligated to the father of one of our children for the freight charges. He is willing to wait for his money." [12]

Learning a week later that there was still time to send letters by what she considered an excellent opportunity, she wrote to the Jouve family:

> In a long-delayed shipment that was sent us I found two letters from you along with a superb present. Our humble chapel will equal the churches of France when we make up that beautiful vestment. It is the second I have received from you, and it will be very dear to me as a proof that you do not forget a sister who often thinks of you in the presence of God, begging Him to grant you happiness in answer to her feeble prayers.
>
> All the details you gave me about the family interest me very much, especially about your children. Euphrosine also keeps me informed. . . . I do not write here of my situation as I do not want to repeat myself too much. . . . You ask, my dear Sister, what would give me pleasure. I have few personal wants, trusting greatly in Divine Providence. Still, our debts force us to buy only the bare necessities. I cannot make up the beautiful vestment without some galloon—but choose the simplest pattern. That could not be found anywhere in the United States. A little thread and some green silk would also be needed. I would also like an abridgement of Ancient and Roman history, as our house follows the same plan of studies as those in France. Give my love to my brother and sisters.[13]

A few lines in a letter to Madame de Mauduit reflect her loving sympathy:

I have just received a letter from you well-calculated to rejoice a heart as sensitive to affection as mine is. But that heart suffers in knowing you are so isolated and lonely. . . . May you find peace for your heart and solace for your soul! These graces often make for happiness in the midst of suffering. I pray St. Regis, our mutual friend, to obtain for you all the consolation my heart desires for you. . . . Please have a Mass offered for my intention at his shrine.[14]

Meanwhile there had been much activity around the convent, for a real frontier house-raising was under way. Logs for the parish schoolhouse had been cut and trimmed under Father Dunand's direction, and on March 21 twenty-six men of the vicinity assembled to erect the building in a day and to enjoy a hearty dinner, prepared by the grateful nuns and served more bountifully by the addition of raisins, preserves, and other delicacies drawn from the provisions sent by the Ursulines. The feast of the Annunciation brought the second young Italian priest to Florissant to say his first Mass. Father Philip Borgna, C.M., whose sister became a Religious of the Sacred Heart in Italy, proved to be a steadfast friend of the order and a zealous helper both in Missouri and in Louisiana.[15]

In St. Louis and the settlements nearby there was excitement that twenty-fifth of March when a handbill went into circulation— a kind of frontier "EXTRA"—announcing the "happy intelligence" that the Missouri State bill had passed the Congress in Washington "without restrictions"; this meant that Missouri was now numbered among the nation's slave states. The news had been brought by a traveler who carried in his satchel a copy of the *National Intelligencer* of March 4. So the paper was three weeks old when it reached St. Louis, but its contents were news and called forth demonstrations in town and country. Mother Duchesne did not allude to it in her letters for several weeks, for she was preoccupied with matters more directly connected with the church and convent at Florissant.

Holy Week was at hand with its liturgical ceremonies and devotional exercises. Through the night of Holy Thursday, Philippine knelt in adoration at the repository. There was deep peace in her soul, but intense pleading in her prayer. On Good Friday *Tenebrae*, and the *Tre Ore*, and the solemn Way of the Cross, and on Holy Saturday the long morning liturgy—all were carried out in simple solemnity. One reads the record with astonishment. A retreat during Easter week prepared a group of children for Confirmation on April 6. The Bishop seemed preoccupied. He spent much time in conference with Father De La Croix. The Father Prior was invited at times to join them, and he was sad at heart as he confided to Mother Duchesne the subject under discussion.

On April 22 this was made public when Father De La Croix was named pastor of St. Ferdinand. Father Dunand, who had taken up his residence there in 1814 and had been the lone missionary in the entire area until the coming of Du Bourg, was now obliged to move from the rectory in which he had been living and build a little house for himself in the neighborhood. The situation that developed was very unpleasant. The trustees of the parish were devoted to the Father Prior and resented the Bishop's action as unfair to him. The parishioners sided with their old friend and the choir, "both men and women," refused to sing in the church when the new pastor made his solemn entrance.[16]

Mother Duchesne was now caught between the upper and the nether millstones. Gratitude to Father Dunand turned her sympathy to him, for he had certainly proved himself a generous and devoted friend. She still owed him at least one thousand francs, and now he was in poverty, without parish or fixed missions, after years of unselfish zeal for the salvation of Catholics on the Missouri frontier. On the other hand, loyalty to authority was a sacred duty. The Bishop was acting within his rights with regard to the pastorate of St. Ferdinand, though his action seemed untimely and inconsiderate. Mother Duchesne dreaded the consequences to all concerned and seems to have realized how far-reaching these consequences would be. In the minds of the parishioners who loved Father Dunand and the Catholics of St. Louis who already disliked Monseigneur Du Bourg, the Religious of the Sacred Heart were linked inseparably with the Bishop, whose unpopularity increased alarmingly through the coming years.[17]

As Mother Duchesne was under the impression that the Trappist was leaving soon for France, she wrote letters early in May which she expected him to carry back to the homeland. Her note to St. Madeleine Sophie was unusually brief, but a postscript practically doubled its length:

> We have received many invaluable services from Reverend Marie-Joseph Dunand, religious of La Trappe. He is the one who directed the building of our convent; he urged forward the work; he sweated for it and advanced money to help us. We still owe him one thousand francs, which he paid out to purchase many

useful things we needed. We promised payment in France to his Father Abbot de Lestrange or to himself, if he decided to return there. I beg you to draw on the money still owed us by the convent at Niort. . . . This is a sacred debt.

P. S. I thought this letter would be enclosed in Reverend Father Dunand's, but he sent it back to me along with his own, for me to send myself. I add just a few lines to repeat my affectionate and respectful sentiments and to beg you to send us two more nuns who are essential here, one to be superior, the other to take charge of the kitchen. . . . If the dear Lord should inspire you and enable you to send a larger group of nuns, it would fulfill all our hopes and be so very helpful.[18]

To Father Barat, Philippine expressed more fully her anxieties and her sentiments in regard to Father Dunand, to whom she and her community were so deeply endebted:

Sometime during this year you may see a priest from this section of the country. He is a religious of La Trappe, and it is chiefly on his account that I am writing this letter, for we owe him a thousand francs, for which he will accept payment in France. This is a great help to us as we are always short of money here. If by any chance you have a thousand francs to spend on us, I beg you to hold it in order to pay this sacred debt, in case there is not enough left in our fund to meet the payment. I hardly dare hope there will be any money left, so it might happen that this good priest would not be paid without your aid. All that comes to us through Mr. Du Bourg in New Orleans is used to pay Monseigneur what we owe him, and he still expects the 15,000 francs he asked our Mother General for. I have harbored no such an illusion.

The Father to whom we owe this money is the one who directed the building of our house. It was really watered by his sweat and it witnessed his care of us. We would not be living in it now if he had not procured a loan which he only could obtain. How much opposition there is to active zeal! After laboring fifteen years on this mission and a great part of that time alone, he must give way before the accusations and complaints that are made against him and see his place in this parish given to someone else, the pretext being his desire to return to his convent [in France]. We went through a difficult time on his account. We owe so much to this Father, and yet another type of spiritual director was more suitable to us. Each side was trying to gain our support, and we could not take sides either against gratitude or against the welfare of our house. We could only let those in authority act and on our side commend the whole affair to God.

It would have been very despicable of us to say a word that might influence the departure of a priest who had made every sacrifice to have us in his parish.

We now have 20 boarding pupils, the majority of them docile. We are trying to get our property enclosed, but have not succeeded yet, for in this part of the country the fences are made like ladders. [Here Mother Duchesne inserts a thumb-nail sketch of a rail fence which she labels *escalade*.] We are not rich enough to afford a board fence such as the Ursulines in New Orleans have. As for stone, there is none.

Repeat to our Mother our plea for religious. Three American postulants have just left, having neither vocation nor aptitudes. Vocations will be rare out here. For the welfare of us all we should have a good superior and a good cook. Among the nuns here no one has both the health and the ability for the latter employment. I think Monseigneur's good judgment will make him approve of a change of superior. There is no one in the community who is not suffering. I will never gain the confidence of either the community or outsiders, but everyone trusts my two companions, and they use this confidence to do good. . . . I am the least useful in the community, but I am happy to share the hard work. I wish I were put in just that kind of employment; then I would be content. It is heartbreaking, after such ardent desires, to see our success hindered or slowed up and to realize that I am the obstacle. Happy, too, would I be if, having no support from anyone on earth near me, I were deprived even of those consolations that really are too sweet for a life that is dying in Jesus Christ. That is what I desire, though I am not preparing myself for it by my fervor. . . .[19]

In the postcript to another letter written that same day Mother Duchesne shows Florissant in a brighter light:

I thought, dear Mother, that there was an immediate opportunity to send you this letter, but it failed me, so I am adding a few more lines, otherwise you might think me brief indeed, telling you nothing about our situation here. When we realize that we have been in this country less than two years, we cannot but marvel at the ways of Divine Providence. After some delays and some trifling privations God has put us in possession of a convent of our own, has kept us in good health, has established us in such a way that we may hope to pay the debt contracted in building, has provided spiritual help for us, and this often in abundance. Is this not really wonderful? And still more remarkable is the work accomplished by Monseigneur Du Bourg. In less than two years he has a cathedral built, a seminary founded and functioning, three or four schools in different sections of this immense diocese, all parts of which are visited at least from time to time by priests. The Catholic population is so sparse in places, it would not support a resident priest. We have twenty-one boarding pupils. Say then with us that God is good.

May brought a trio of new pupils, Maria and Adeline Boilvin and Elisa Bosseron, all of whom would in later years enter religious life. Maria would be obliged to withdraw on account of poor health. Elisa would die at an early age, and Adeline would become an outstanding religious of the Sacred Heart, one of those who came to know most intimately the mind and heart of Philippine Duchesne. Another pupil, Emilie St. Cyr, the aunt of the Boilvin girls and only a little older than they, had been at the Sacred Heart since the first year at St. Charles. From her pen comes a word picture that shows Mother Duchesne among the children as a religious educator:

In my childhood I always looked on Mother Duchesne as a perfect model of all virtues. It was my good fortune to have our holy Mother Duchesne as class mistress during more than two years. Never once did I see her lacking in poise and self-control; never did I notice in her the least movement of impatience in dealing with the group of children who were so difficult to handle. She showed the same gentle kindliness toward all. More than once I called the attention of my schoolmates to the heavenly radiance that shone on her countenance. One might have mistaken it for sunshine, but the light was softer than that. Then we would say, "Mother Duchesne has just come from the chapel. She has had an ecstasy," and we were sure she had had a vision of our Blessed Lord. We certainly had a saint for a teacher. Even the most troublesome girls venerated her. She never brought the class period to a close without some little word about God, but she never talked at length or let us lose a moment of time. During my religious life I have always considered Mother Duchesne as a perfect religious, a superior quite impartial and so mortified there is no one with whom I could compare her. She was completely dead to nature and self and faithful to the very least points of the Rule.

Father De Andreis was at Florissant for the feast of the Sacred Heart, June 9, which was celebrated with all the pomp and ceremony the convent could muster—solemn high Mass for the renovation of vows, sermon after Vespers, the Act of Reparation at Benediction, along with the singing of the Litany of the Sacred Heart by all present. Nothing filled Philippine's heart with greater joy than days like this, and she was careful to give St. Francis Regis his due on June 16, the first time the patronal feast was celebrated. There were other days recorded in the *Journal:* "July 4—*congé* for Independence, with a play based on our voyage to America." So successful was this first dramatic production on the convent stage in Missouri, it was repeated for the same audience on July 22, when there was a general holiday in honor of Mother Barat's patron, St. Mary Magdalen. The summer months brought short holidays, for the pupils' vacation began only on August 18, and classes were resumed on September 1.

An outstanding event occurred, however, during that short period when Mother Duchesne welcomed Mary Ann Layton, the first American postulant to persevere in religious life at the Sacred Heart. She was a nineteen-year-old girl from Perry County, Missouri, whose land-rich father, Bernard Layton, had donated more than fifty acres on which the county seat, Perryville, was laid out. In the southeastern part of the county, along the Brazeau Bottom and the Saline and St. Cosme streams, lay the open prairie called "The Barrens," where descendants of old Maryland-Kentucky families had settled—Mannings, Moores, Haydens, Fenwicks, Laytons. They were a Catholic group who treasured their religious heritage and handed on to their children the knowledge, love, and reverence with which their own lives were enriched and their worship guided.

Mary Layton had been born in Kentucky on July 2, 1802. Her mother died when she was a little girl, and Mary became the idol of her devoted father and brothers. The child was spoiled and not well educated. Yet she had more than book learning or domestic training, and from her earliest years her great desire was to love and serve God by belonging to Him alone. Her father had placed her in a special manner under the protection of the Blessed Virgin, and Mary entrusted to her spiritual Mother, under the title of "Mary Immaculate," her desire to belong to God. It was Father Henri Pratte who first told her of the arrival of the Religious of the Sacred Heart in Missouri, and the Lazarists at St. Mary's Seminary who guided her to Florissant. She came from the Barrens with Father Rosati, who was joined on the way by Fathers Borgna and Deys. From these visitors Mother Duchesne gathered much of the information she retailed to Mother Barat on August 29, the third birthday she celebrated in America:

I have picked up some interesting information that may call forth some prayers in return. An event that gave me the greatest amount of pleasure recently was the deputation that reached St. Louis from the Osage Indians, a savage tribe. The chief came to ask Bishop Du Bourg to pay a visit to his people.[20] The Bishop is going there next month with some Missouri River traders who have promised to help him in every way so that he may be treated with respect among these peoples, something like the way the Portuguese merchants helped St. Francis Xavier. . . . Monseigneur gave this Indian chief a crucifix, which he accepted very reverently. He then went into a store. The merchant who owns the place wanted to see whether or not he really valued the crucifix, so he offered him in exchange for it a very handsome saddle, then some liquor, then a big sum of money. The Indian refused all three, saying he would not part with the gift which he had received from the man who talked with the Author of Life. Father De Andreis, who is a saint, told me in a prophetic tone that someday I would go to the mission among the Osages just as surely as I would go to bed tonight. I will inform you of the outcome of the trip the Bishop is going to make. He is very eager to have the Jesuits from Georgetown make a foundation at Franklin. . . .

Yesterday evening we had as supper guests the two priests who are at the head of the Lazarist seminary at *Bois-Brulé*. They are also in charge of the parish there, which is like the primitive Church in fervor. On Sundays more than sixty persons receive Holy Communion, and there are not eight people in the parish who fail to go to Communion every month. There are no dances or cabarets in that place, though elsewhere these cannot be suppressed. . . .

To her beloved Cousin Josephine she sent a letter on that fifty-first birthday:

It is a long time since I wrote to you, but I know you often read the letters I write to other members of the family, so you always have the most recent news from me. That satisfies your loving heart that is so faithful to your old friend. Sometimes people say old hearts grow hard or lose their tender sentiments. But by experience I can declare that quite the contrary is true. The names of Josephine, Augustin, and Camille will always call forth the purest, tenderest sentiments of friendship and gratitude from my heart. Now that the dear ones whose faces these names recall are no longer the direct instruments of Divine Providence in my regard, God uses other means to show me His loving kindness.

We left St. Charles on the Missouri last Septetmber. In the midst of many comical incidents accompanying our transmigration, we were deeply touched by the tears of the children we were leaving with no further means of instruction. As the new convent at Florissant, or St. Ferdinand, was not ready, we camped in a farmhouse until Christmas Eve. Then at last we were at home—in a house built for us but on which we still owe a debt, as we had to borrow money in order to make it habitable. I have not the slightest doubt that Divine Providence, which has guided us here through so many dangers and difficulties, will complete the work by hidden means which seem to disguise God's way of furnishing help, but which only make them appear more wonderful in the eyes of those who follow Him along the paths of His goodness. Our pupils are distinguished for the fact that they come from the oldest families in this section of the country, and their influential position gives us more prestige than we deserve. . . .

This year Missouri has become one of the federated states of the Republic. St. Louis is to be the capital for six years.[21] The father of our very first pupils is the most influential man in the town and is very devoted to us. At present the laws of the state are being drawn up. The most disputed point and the one that has caused the greatest conflict concerns the admission of slavery. It seems that all those who now own slaves will be allowed to keep them and that the children of their slaves will belong to them, but there can be no more African slave trade. We do not want slaves and we have no money to buy them, yet we scarcely know how to get along without them, especially as we are cloistered and do not go about. No one wants to hire out as a domestic servant; all want to be on the same social level. Up to now we have given a home to some young girls who are orphans and who have been placed with us legally until they are twenty years old. . . . Believe in my undying affection.

The second scholastic year had scarcely begun when Mother Duchesne fell dangerously ill. Bishop Du Bourg came several times to see her, bringing Dr. Todsen with him from St. Louis, but Philippine preferred the village doctor, who handled the case skilfully and *gratis*. For two months she was confined to her room, for she had been obliged to accept a room during her illness, at least, though she clung to the little cubbyhole under the stairway that led from the rear of the lower hall to the second story. In her eyes that *petit trou* had several advantages—poverty, inconvenience, discomfort, but best of all, nearness to the chapel. She chafed under the regime of convalescence, especially since it rendered her incapable of helping care for Mother Octavie when she met with an accident. News of the death of Father De Andreis added grief to pain, but two weeks passed before she was able to write to Mother Barat. On October 30 she gave her an account of what had been happening at Florissant during the autumn and revealed the working of grace in her own soul:

> Never have I been in greater need of a letter from you and never have I had to wait so long for one. At last here is the packet entrusted to Monsieur de Menou, and we are consoled by your letters and those of dear Father Varin and our Sisters, and also by the hope that some religious are coming to join us. My preceding letters, which must have caused you anxiety about the health of Mothers Octavie and Eugenie, made you realize our need of recruits and this one will give you still further proofs of it. After these generous souls have been delivered from their bleedings and blisterings, I too had an illness that has lasted two months, including the convalescence. I received Holy Viaticum and was never so near to meeting my God. After having burned with desire to be with Him, at the moment when I could hope for it I felt only the emptiness of my life, the severity of God's judgments, and the hardness of my own heart.
>
> The disease was erysipelas. It covered my whole body and was accompanied by a fever that became malignant after the sores on my body disappeared. As I was delirious, Monseigneur brought his own doctor to treat me. He put me through three blisterings and gave me two mustard plasters. After that treatment I was no longer delirious, nor have I taken any more mercury, a drug widely used in American medicine. I felt many ill effects from it —sore mouth, salivation, continual weakness in my limbs, and my head so unbalanced that for a long time I labored under the illusion that I was two people; if one of them died, I said, there was always the other one left, and I tried to find her. Before I stop writing about myself, I want to show you once more how wonderful Divine Providence really is. A young American doctor treated me with the tenderness of a son for his mother, saying he saw in me a resemblance to his own mother. One morning he came as many as four times, and he charged nothing at all.
>
> Scarcely had I begun to regain some strength when Mother Octavie, shod in her beautiful new black velvet shoes that had just come from France and had very slick soles, slipped and fell and broke a bone in her leg; now she will be in bed thirty or forty days. This is just the seventh day, and yesterday she was delirious with fever. She is better today, but she is already tired of lying in bed.

Before I quit this topic of illness, I wish you would ask Monsieur Geenich's opinion about *mercury*. Here it is regarded as the very best remedy for fever, especially for yellow fever, but they use it for almost any disease. It made me so sick, I told Monseigneur the medicine was worse than the illness and that in future I was going to insist that our doctors use no more mercury in treating us. He thought this a wise idea. He and the whole diocese, and we in particular, have suffered a great loss in the death of Father De Andreis, provincial of the Lazarists and first vicar-general. He was a man of great holiness, remarkable gifts for the ministry, and prodigious learning. . . . Father Richard, our first chaplain, is replacing him as a saint and as vicar-general. Father Rosati is now superior of the Lazarists. He sent us a postulant and has suggested another, but how very difficult it is to explain religious life to people who speak a different language and know nothing at all about it and are accustomed to entirely different ways in food and clothing! . . .

You made us very happy by holding out to us the hope of three more companions. Send them at once. Our building for day pupils is ready and we could open the school if we had one more nun, for the children come from such distances, they can stay only a few hours a day. They never have sewing class as they have neither needles nor thread. So when the prayers have been said and the lessons heard and Catechism taught, it is really best to send them home. We need most of all the Irish nun you mentioned, but if she knows only the Irish language, that is not English. We have a great many Irish settlers here whom the English-speaking Americans cannot understand. . . .

Since Father De La Croix took charge of the parish, he says Mass in the church twice a week and we have it the other five days. We shall have it every day when the new church is built. It will stand on ground belonging to the Bishop and be contiguous to our house. Then our chapel will be a choir, as at Grenoble, opening on to the sanctuary, and we shall be able to assist at all the services. This arrangement is very necessary where there are few priests. I hope I shall not die before I have a chance to build a public oratory dedicated to the Sacred Heart in this country. I spoke to Monseigneur about this and he decided that the church at Florissant will be dedicated to the Sacred Heart, with St. Ferdinand as second patron, that the altar of the Blessed Virgin will be opposite our choir, and the shrine of St. Francis, which I also asked for, will be in a corner of our chapel. . . .

I know you will make an effort to help your poor mission that stretches out its arms, but cannot reach across the distance to you. As for me, do with me just as you wish. All desire but that of doing God's holy will is extinguished in me, and my illness has rooted me still deeper in indifference. Monseigneur has ordered me to take care of myself and I am doing so quite simply. Today I am writing my first letter. I have eaten four meals and I remained in bed until seven o'clock this morning.

Mary Layton had adjusted herself to convent life with surprising courage and proved so fervent in her quiet, friendly way that Mother Audé, to whom her training had been entrusted, was soon suggesting that she be clothed in the holy habit. Bishop Du Bourg gave his approval, but he was not present at this first reception of the religious habit by an American girl in the trans-Mississippi West. He was at the convent on November 18 to bid the nuns goodbye before leaving for New Orleans, where it was hoped he would be respectfully received. On November 22 Sister Mary Layton was clothed in the religious habit and began her long and fervent career of more than half a century in the Society of the Sacred Heart.

On February 19, 1821, Father De La Croix laid the cornerstone of the new church that was to stand beside the convent. The ceremony was very simple, but the joy it gave was very great, for a fervent hope had begun to be fulfilled—a church dedicated to the Sacred Heart of Jesus had begun to rise on the American frontier and its cornerstone had been presented by Philippine Duchesne herself.[22] In deference to her wishes, moreover, her beloved St. Francis Regis had also been chosen as a secondary patron of the church— strikingly prophetic choice, and a special shrine in his honor was to be arranged in the convent chapel. On the eve of the ceremony her mind was filled with joyous hopes and anxious fears as she wrote to Mother Barat:

I have been deprived of news from you for a long time, as the ice on the Mississippi detained the steamboats downstream during the winter. Owing to a thaw, however, a boat has arrived, bringing us several packets of letters, some thirteen months old, the most recent written last August. More than a month ago I had one from our dear protector, Father Barat, written in September and sent by way of New York. He enclosed the triplicate of the note for $571, which I hastened to turn over to the man to whom we owed 10,000 francs. People say he had his eye on our house, holding the mortgage as he does and knowing the extreme difficulty with which people like ourselves get any money. I prefer to reject such an idea as dishonorable to him and contrary to the goodness of

God, whose Providence toward us had been manifested in a thousand ways.

Tomorrow we shall have the laying of the cornerstone of the new church which the Bishop is having erected contiguous to our convent. It will be named in honor of the Sacred Heart and will bear on the facade this inscription in English: *My Heart will abide here.* . . . The schoolhouse for day pupils had been completed at our expense and paid for; but when all was ready, not a child appeared. The roads were too bad and the weather too cold. We shall open it in the spring, and by that time I hope to have two novices prepared to teach the American children. . . .

Mother Octavie is a great favorite with the children. They talk about her; they ask for her; everyone loves her; and she would be a good one to put in charge of the school if her great kindness did not make it almost impossible for her to act firmly. . . . Mother Eugenie has just finished a retreat that filled her heart with consolation and peace. . . . She is fundamentally humble, loves correction, and always seeks what is lowly and poor. I am the worst of all, the greatest obstacle to good. How I long to be given a lower place! I feel disposed to obey everyone in the world. I would have no difficulty in giving up my position, except the care of the business affairs, which are such a problem here. Our religious really guide themselves. As I cannot speak English, Mother Octavie talks without embarrassment to the doctors, workmen, and merchants, and Mother Eugenie manages to get along with the children. She is training our novice, who perseveres in all humility, complaining only that she is not corrected often enough. You can form no idea of all this novice suffers in tending the cows in the mud, snow, ice, often wet to the skin or numb with cold. One day we had to chop the milk in her pail with a knife and hammer, as one cuts loaf sugar. . . .

I was delighted with the letter from the Irish novice. Her command of English will make her very useful here, but she should be given a true picture of our position—inconvenience in everything, especially our lodging, having no place even to put a sewing basket or writing pad, not a table for one's own use, food that is often disgusting, and very little variety in it, severe cold, prostrating heat, and practically no spring weather. *God alone and the desire of His glory:* nothing else matters.

After a forty days' prayer for this intention, three vocations were decided in the boarding school—young girls of sixteen to eighteen years—two Americans and a French Creole. The last named [Emilie St. Cyr] has her parents' consent. . . . Another [Eulalie Hamilton] has not obtained this yet. The third [Mary Ann Summers] is an orphan whose guardian does not object. She is sixteen years old, manages the kitchen with astonishing ease, is skilful along all lines, and might do well at studies, were it not better for her spiritual formation to keep her a little in obscurity. . . . She speaks and writes both languages well and reads so intelligently as to need no correction whatsoever. . . .

Another letter, written that same day to Josephine de Savoye-Rollin, reveals the thoughts of her heart and the bond of affection between these middle-aged friends:

It is a very long time since I received a letter from you, but I know how much you have been concerned about me, and Mother Barat told me that you contributed 500 francs to a sum of money she was sending me. In this I recognize your loving heart and your zeal for good works. For even if ours is so insignificant and if we are unprofitable servants, still God, who sees the intention, will reward your purity of intention and return you a hundredfold. And He wills me to add once more an expression of my gratitude for so much kindness and generosity on your part. When I go over all that equips our little sacristy, I say with pleasure to my companions: This came from Madame de Rollin, and this, and this, and the list is long. All that you have given us is the more precious since I cannot ask anything from France, for fear of being unable to pay the freight charges. If, as I hope and expect, we can some day divide our community and have a second house in New Orleans, then the expense would be cut in two, at least.

We are the grain of wheat dying in the earth; can we repine at such a destiny? But we are full of confidence and wholly animated with courage to persevere, hoping that someday our work will bear fruit. It matters little whether we taste of it in this life, provided only that we serve God's cause. He let it happen that when we arrived in St. Louis money was plentiful and the price of land and houses was excessively high. It seemed better for us to build here at Florissant. That was not my opinion, but I had to follow the opinion of others and borrow money to complete the building. And now the failure of the banks has caused the disappearance of the paper money which was practically the only currency here. We could buy lands and a house in St. Louis for nothing today, yet we must pay back the loan at a time when the money is worth ten times as much as when we borrowed it. These are the unexpected occurrences against which human prudence can offer no protection. But Divine Providence is with us, and we can count so trustfully on God, we shall stand firm at our post. So sincerely are we persuaded that God Himself wants us here, not one of us regrets her position. . . .

The year 1821 was to be crowded with joys and sorrows, hopes and anxieties. March opened auspiciously with letters from France —always a great event for the community, and one from Bishop Du Bourg describing "the holy enthusiasm with which he had been received in Louisiana," and giving permission for the reception of the holy habit by the postulants. On March 7, Philippine sent one of her long, chatty letters to Father Barat. She wrote as she would have talked, with delightful vivacity, with sly humor in the midst of serious matters, with knowledge of the world around her and a spontaneous uplift of mind and heart that revealed the supernatural atmosphere of her life:

> It was a great pleasure to learn from your most recent letter that you are still in Bordeaux and so can act as father to our little colony. No one except our reverend Mother has given us as much help or shown as much sympathy and kindness as you have. I am often so embarrassed by all the trouble expended on us, by all we have cost the Society, that I might regret our persistent efforts to come here if I were not thoroughly convinced that it is the will of God for us to be here. I quiet my anxieties also by the thought that the Sacred Heart, for whom alone we intend to work, helps us in every way and is our greatest reward.
>
> Shall I lament or rejoice over the departure of the Jesuit Fathers from Russia? If some of those from Siberia are looking for a mission field with the same type of work and the same climate during a good part of the year, they might come to our section of the globe. It takes souls of that quality to persevere out here; and if they went to a mission among the savages, they could even hope for martyrdom, either at the hands of the Indians themselves or with still more certainty at the hands of the lawless men who trade with them. . . .
>
> Because of the scarcity of money here now, everything is worthless. People talk only of auctions for the payment of debts and the rigorous execution of justice, of poor settlers who see themselves stripped of all the fruit of their labors for the payment of a small debt. A pair of oxen sells for $3, which is about 15 francs in France; 18,000 arpents of land can be bought for $100, which is 500 francs. In such a situation one cannot rest easy if one has debts. We still owe 15,000 francs, part of that sum being held under a mortgage which the creditor boasts about. Divine Providence will not allow him to foreclose on us—God has been on our side too often for us to fear that, but the man may act with us as with his other debtors. As no purchaser for our house has been found, it might bring him at auction just the amount we owe him, though it has cost us nearly 40,000 francs. This situation is very

different from the one we faced at Grenoble, where we never had a feeling of debts piling up. But it is only right that I, having more sins to atone for, should do more penance and should purchase the joy of founding a convent of the Sacred Heart in America at the price of some anxieties. . . .

You ask news of Miss Emilie Chouteau. She has gone home for the third time, wishing to make her decision once and for all and to obtain the consent of her family. She will not get that for a long time; and between you and me I fear she will not hold out against the many offers of marriage that are being made to her and the many allurements to pleasure and affection. Miss Emilie Pratte gave in more easily. She is about to be married to an excellent Catholic. Her parents are delighted and she certainly merits high praise. Miss DeLassus, who also finished school with us, has refused three offers of marriage, but she will accept one some of these days.[23] There is also an American girl, a really superior person, who might have been the Aloysia of America had she not left school hastily to go home. She belongs to a very pious family, but it is the only one in that part of the country, where no priest is stationed and there are no regular religious helps. Father Richard predicts that she will come back to us. I hope so. In the meanwhile her sister, a very lovable girl, but less gifted, is asking admission as a novice, but she has not yet received permission.[24] Two postulants will receive the habit on the 19th of this month. . . .

I wrote that to our Mother last month by way of New York. She gave me news, and so did you, of the agony my dear Aloysia is enduring. But when one is out here on the other side of the ocean, one can only hope to see one's loved ones again in heaven. It is there I picture them all, though I myself become more and more earthbound. I am by nature most fitted to be a servant. Something quite different is needed in one who guides souls. But God does His own work. My two young religious sisters advance steadily toward perfection and relish all the poverty and abjection from which they suffer so much, for ours is not a life of convenience. That should be the disposition of all who come to join us. They must accept suffering and have *God alone* as their support. . . . Our Mothers and Sisters here are fairly well and I am more vigorous than ever, but I have few teeth left. . . .

While Mother Duchesne was writing in such depreciating terms of herself, it is well to note what others had to say about her in their letters to France. In April of this year, 1821, Mother Berthold told St. Madeleine Sophie:

Charity binds us closer and closer to our Mother Superior. I obey her, but my love for her is so great, it may deprive me of the merit of obedience, for it sometimes makes my motive too natural. We are so happy under her care. Her three years [of superiority] are up, but, Reverend Mother, do not listen to her request to be relieved of office. What would we do without her? There are seven of us in her little family now. We love each other very much and our hearts are all one with hers. . . . Furthermore, she knows the country and the character of the people. Anyone else would be an apprentice, as it were, at all this.[25]

The very next day Sister Catherine Lamarre was writing to Mother Prévost at Amiens: "Last fall we came very near losing our dear Mother Duchesne, but our Divine Master knows how necessary she is to us and so He restored her to health. What a terrible loss it would be if she were taken away! May the Sacred Heart be blessed a thousand times for having saved her for us."

In the reception ceremony on March 19, Emilie St. Cyr, "a Creole girl of 15 years," [26] received the habit of the choir religious, and Mary Ann Summers, aged sixteen, became a coadjutrix novice. To honor St. Joseph, Emilie took the name of Josephine, a practice Mother Duchesne had carried over from Visitation days and continued for a decade on the frontier. There was another pupil of the boarding school who watched this ceremony with deep soul-stirring. Eulalie Hamilton had heard the call of Christ and her generous heart had given a full, glad response, but as yet her mother had made no reply to the three letters she had written on the subject. The strain of waiting was beginning to tell on Eulalie, so Mother Duchesne took up her quill two days after the *prise d'habit* ceremony to request Father Rosati's mediation with the Hamiltons.

Miss Hamilton [she wrote] greatly desires to consecrate herself to God in our house. She fears she will be sent for before she receives an answer to the three letters in which she asked her mother's permission to become a religious. We know that letters are often lost between here and Fredonia; perhaps that is the reason for the silence on the part of Mrs. Hamilton. We hope that through your mediation this matter will reach them and we shall receive an answer. Your zeal for the salvation and perfection of souls has encouraged us to write this letter, which has the glory of God for its object. We are also eager to express our deep regard for you and tell you of the many prayers we say for your holy institution.[27]

Spring had come to Florissant Valley when a heavy cart made its jolting way out from the Market Street landing in St. Louis to the convent, laden with substantial gifts from Philippine's faithful friends in New Orleans, the Ursulines. "Barrels of sugar, rice, codfish, raisins, and preserves," she noted with astonished gratitude. There were still four weeks of Lent ahead, so the codfish was welcome, though it would appear more often at community meals than on the pupils' menu. An early April entry in her *Journal* reveals once more how precious was every item of news she received from France. Each detail was used by her to strengthen the bond between the parent stock and the frail cion she had planted on the American frontier. Lovingly she summarized the news and wrote the names of the Mothers she had known in what may have seemed now a rather remote past, though she had left them just three years before:

April 3. We learned that the General Council of the Society has come to a close. Its most important decision was the transfer of the Convent of the Sacred Heart from Rue des Postes to the Hotel Biron, Rue de Varennes, in the Faubourg of St. Germain, Paris. Mother de Charbonnel is the First Assistant General, Mother Bigeu, Second, and Mistress of Novices. The other Mothers of the Council are Mothers Grosier, de Gramont, Desmarquest, Geoffroy, Prévost, Deshayes, etc. The letters also described the reception given at the Sacred Heart for the Grand Almoner of France, ecclesiastical Superior General of our Society, the Cardinal-Archbishop of Paris, Monseigneur de Perigord, on the feast of the Sacred Heart.

As she wrote these lines, Philippine went back in spirit to the convent she had prepared so lovingly in the spring of 1816 as the Society's first home in the capital, to the Mothers and Sisters she had welcomed there, the many relatives and friends who had visited her, and their loving goodbyes when she set out for America. Now the Jesuit Fathers were installed in the house in Rue des Postes. That was a consolation. She talked of all this to the Florissant community, giving the novices that thrilling sense of belonging to a great family whose hearthfire, lighted from the Sacred Heart, burned in Paris and radiated its warmth to the most remote and insignificant member of the Society.

There had been news of a more personal nature in letters from Grenoble. While Aloysia Jouve was nearing the end of her short and holy career, her sister Amelie and cousin, Caroline Lebrument, became postulants at Ste Marie. At the Visitation in Romans her old aunt, Sister Françoise-Melanie, had died, and Sister Claire Euphrosine, who was not so old, had been elected superior, while her own loved sister Melanie had been given the office of directress of the school.[28] Of these dear relatives Philippine often spoke admiringly, praising their virtue and their work in contrast to her own.

Lent was always a time of intense fervor for Philippine. This year she encouraged her community to special efforts during the week preceding the feast of the Compassion of the Blessed Virgin for the intention of obtaining the consent of Mrs. George Hamilton for the entrance of not just one, but two, of her daughters into the novitiate. The affirmative answer came on the very day of the feast, and Philippine's soul was filled with joy and gratitude. That day she also learned with a sense of relief that John Mullanphy was leaving soon for France. This meant he would not dun her for at least some months, and it offered an opportunity to send letters safely and post-free, so she gave herself the pleasure of writing to her sisters and nieces, to Mother Thérèse Maillucheau and Mother Barat. These letters, remarkably varied in content, show us Philippine in turn as a loving sister, a devoted aunt, an intimate friend, and a true religious, bearing the responsibility that weighed so heavily on her and giving a faithful account of persons and things.[29] To her sisters she wrote:

A gentleman of our country is going to France to bring home several of his daughters who have been at school there. This gives me a fine opportunity to write to you and so strengthen the bond of tender friendship that unites us and that distance only draws tighter around my heart. True, it must be supernaturalized to last through all eternity, but it is already consecrated by nature and religion. Even though I am so far away from you in this life, I have the firm hope that we shall all be the closer in heaven and our reunion there will be all the happier. What I say of you I mean also for all my brothers-in-law and all your children, many of whom you entrusted to my care. It gives me great consolation to learn that the nieces whom I know are leading virtuous lives as worthy daughters of the Church, holding fast the purity of faith as well as the observance of the Commandments. . . .

I hope my sister Melanie does not fail to help me with her prayers, as did our venerated aunt. I learned of her death and the burden laid on Aunt Euphrosine. I earnestly beg her to recommend me to her holy community, in whose good works I want to have a share. . . . Adieu, my dear Sisters. Pray for me and have your children pray.

To her nieces at Sainte Marie she wrote, not knowing that Aloysia had died nearly three months before this:

Father Barat has written to tell me that you are together at Ste Marie, one bedridden, the other a postulant. How much patience the one must exercise and how bravely the other must struggle against the affection of her parents! But courage, both of you! When one has given all to God, what is there to fear in illness? And what could Amelie find in the world to compare with the Divine Spouse who has asked her to belong entirely to Him? I could have had no sweeter joy than that of hearing that Amelie and Caroline, whom I have always suspected of a vocation, desire to leave all for the Heart of Jesus. He will make up to them generously for all their sacrifices. They will find the hundredfold in this life, and God usually blesses the families that give Him the first fruits He claims as His own.

How sweet it is for me to think about that convent that is so dear to me and that was my spiritual cradle three times, to know that the dear Lord is calling my beloved nieces and children there one by one. . . . Here we have three novices, three postulants, twenty boarding pupils, ten day pupils. After class hours we find time to work in the garden, gather firewood, help with the washing, as we do the children's washing ourselves. . . .

This letter to her nieces was enclosed in one to Mother Thérèse Maillucheau, then superior at Sainte Marie, in which she wrote:

All the news I received recently from France was very interesting and stirred such a variety of sentiments in my soul, but they all come into unity in the will of God. We have a very limited apostolate, but the few people with whom we do come in contact would have no one to help them if we were not here, and they would never have learned their religion well nor have known the lovable Heart of Jesus. We ourselves are firm in perseverence. Not one of us is sorry she came here and we all desire to die here. Far from lamenting our poverty, we love it and would be uncomfortable in convenient surroundings. We laugh about our humble occupations as others do at their feasts, and we shall never be ill because of sadness. . . .

Through the letters of our Mothers and Sisters I realize the immense good that is being done in your school. This must fill you with consolation. . . . I cannot take time to tell each one in particular how grateful we are for their remembrance of us. Their letters reached us only yesterday. Mothers Octavie and Eugenie greet all their Sisters in their novitiate home and we offer you our loving respects in the Heart of Jesus.

The letter to Mother Barat is crowded with details, only a few of which are quoted here:

> In three years I have had only one letter from Father Perreau and one from Father Varin. Tell them that although this silence pains me, it reminds me of the silence of the soul that is closely united to the Heart of Jesus. In this intimate converse no word is spoken —and it is there I remember them and express my gratitude to them. . . . Father Barat made no mention in his letter of nuns coming to join us. This grieves me, for we must have some nuns. You know the doctor who examined Mother Octavie said she has a bad heart condition that might carry her off suddenly. . . . Mother Eugenie grows more and more capable of administration. She has keenness of judgment and prudence that saves her from rashness in action. She has firmness and zeal, is pleasing in appearance and conversation, and she knows enough English now to direct American subjects and give them religious instruction. . . . Marguerite is always very good, though weak in health. Catherine has many employments and teaches a small group of day pupils. . . .
>
> If Mr. Mullanphy brings you my letter in person, please welcome him in all simplicity, but keep the contents of my letter to yourself. You would never believe he is the richest man in this section of the country. He could buy up all St. Louis, and he is one of the shrewdest of bargainers. He is going to France to fetch his daughters and to see his son, who is in Paris. He is the man who loaned us the 10,000 francs at ten per cent, and he has in hand your remittance of 3000 francs which was somewhat reduced in the exchange.
>
> Yesterday I had a most agreeable piece of news: the best of our children, an American, has obtained her mother's consent to her taking the veil. She is already trained well enough to teach a class. Her older sister vacillates, but she has gifts that fit her remarkably for the Society. Father Rosati, superior of the Lazarists, will continue to urge her to follow her vocation.

The vacillation of Mathilde Hamilton called for action on the part of Father Dunand as well as Father Rosati. She was his godchild. He was sure of her vocation. He would fetch her himself from the home and family she loved so tenderly. Setting out for Fredonia in his caleche that was a familiar sight on the rough roads of Missouri, he returned in triumph ten days later with Mathilde beside him in the old buggy, just in time for the First Friday of May and the reception ceremony of Eulalie Hamilton, who took the devotional name of Regis. Father Dunand had been correct in his judgment of Mathilde Hamilton. Though she passed through stormy days as a novice, she became an excellent religious. The zealous Trappist had the satisfaction of seeing her clothed in the religious habit in June. Soon after this he left Florissant Valley to return to France and the silence of La Trappe, but the heart of Philippine Duchesne was not silent in his regard and her gratitude expressed itself in prayer and loyalty.

2. 1821 — 1823

> *Give heed, O Lord, to the unutterable love*
> *in the Heart of Thy dear Son.*
>
> Secret Prayer, Mass of the Sacred Heart

BISHOP DU BOURG WAS IN ST. LOUIS in June and called at the Florissant convent on the seventh of the month. He came on serious business which Mother Duchesne summarized in her *Journal* and would repeat in many a letter before the year was out:

> He proposed to us a foundation at Opelousas in Louisiana, where Mrs. Smith, a rich widow, offers us a house, lands, furniture, and money for traveling expenses. We have accepted, and Monseigneur, who had already arranged for his niece to keep at her home the two religious who are said to be coming from France, thinks one of us should go down to Opelousas to await their arrival, as they will go directly there on reaching America.

In falling in so readily with the Bishop's suggestions and advice, Mother Duchesne was acting within her delegated powers. Before writing of the matter to France, she discussed it many times with Mothers Berthold and Audé and prayed earnestly for light to know the will of God and the line of conduct that would bring the greatest glory to the Sacred Heart. Her counselors were in favor of accepting the offer, though they had no idea where Opelousas was, except the vague term "in Louisiana," and Mother Audé was particularly eager to share in the labors of the enterprise. The Bishop came again to celebrate the feast of St. Francis Regis, accompanied by Father Joseph Tichitoli, C.M. "He gave the veil and holy habit to Miss Mathilde Hamilton, who took the name of Xavier. That day we had five Masses [noted Mother Duchesne]. The reception ceremony preceded the Bishop's Mass at six-thirty. The last one was sung solemnly. After dinner there was a panegyric of the Saint."

During the day, the projected foundation was discussed again, and the religious were impressed more than ever by the many advantages stressed by the Bishop. Remoteness and isolation, difficulties of transportation and communication, insecurity as to a resident chaplain, sparsity of population in the vicinity, all were passed over in silence. The prospect of recruits coming soon from France and the fact that in their own convent at Florissant there were now five excellent novices in training and several postulants asking admission seemed to point up the advisability of sending a small group of nuns to Louisiana in the near future. But the plans were as yet only tentative, and Mother Duchesne was busy with her four French-speaking novices and happy to see that Sister Layton was beginning to understand when she spoke to her in French.

Meanwhile letters had come from France informing her of the death of her beloved Aloysia, along with a short sketch of her life and religious virtues. The knowledge that this favorite niece had fulfilled the Mother Foundress's dream of a perfect religious of the Society stirred in her new depths of joy and gratitude to the Sacred Heart. Later letters carried the news that the emaciated little body of Aloysia was intact, despite the frightful condition in which death had seized upon it, that the sight of her in her coffin after some months in the crypt at Sainte Marie had brought about the conversion of her dissipated, rationalist brother, François Henri, and a hardened old sinner-soldier, Claude, who worked for the nuns at Grenoble. For years Philippine had prayed for the godson to whom she had been allowed to give the name of her Jesuit favorite, François Regis, when she held him at the baptismal font. Now as she read that he was to enter the Company of Jesus, exultant gratitude surged up in her soul, and her joy found expression first in prostrate prayer. Then she shared her joy with the community, for that was her way with them.

As it was from Mother Thérèse that the first sketch of Aloysia's life came, Philippine thanked her for it at once and poured out the sentiments of her heart to a confidante who had long understood her:

I was deeply moved as I read the short summary of the life and virtues of our dear Aloysia, and I shed many tears as I thought over that career, so well filled in so short a time, while my own life, already rather long, shows no real virtues that could be of value in that eternity to which I am drawing near. How true that sentence is: We carry ourselves about with us always. One is as imperfect in a foreign land as one was at home. Martha bustles about with good intentions, but it is Mary—the soul that is humble, solitary, recollected—who is approved by Jesus. But it is very difficult to change one's character; and if God leaves me on earth for a while longer, I believe I could set out for South America, going either to Lima under the protection of my patron, St. Rose, or to Cartagena under that of Peter Claver. . . .

But let us go back to Aloysia. I often tell St. Regis he ought to consider his own reputation and not leave me so wicked when through the intercession of St. Aloysius Gonzaga our own Aloysia became so virtuous. God gave her to you for a short period to console you for having made nothing out of me. After God and her holy patron she owes all to you, for you were the one who taught her to curb the haughtiness of her character and turn her pride toward the lofty ambition of becoming a saint. . . .[30]

On June 30 Philippine put before the Superior General the proposal for the Louisiana foundation in a letter that seems to have been written with more care and deliberation than were usual with her. The projected establishment had been described to her in so rosy a light that she had set her heart on it and now endeavored to picture it to Mother Barat as she herself envisioned it. But there were other matters closer to her heart, and she began with them:

The loss of Aloysia does not pain me except in so far as it makes me reflect on myself: that life so short, so well filled, makes me realize the uselessness of my own life and my abuse of so many graces, which leaves me still so imperfect and immortified. The more I think about them, the more they astonish me and make me tremble. Among them I prize most of all that of belonging to our beloved Society, and I brought Aloysia to it, also. May her merits repair my faults and obtain for me from God an opportunity to repair the past.

The news of the choice made for us of three religious to help us overwhelmed us with joy. I conclude that Mother Lucille Mathevon is in charge of the group while traveling. A letter from Bishop Du Bourg tells us Father Dusaussoy is in New Orleans. Father Anduze praised him so highly that the Bishop decided to keep him there as that city is in such need of priests.[31] Monseigneur also has plans for our nuns which I am going to outline to you.

Mrs. Charles Smith, a rich widow who lives sixty leagues from New Orleans in a place called Grand Coteau, has established a parish there and built a church; now she wishes to procure an educational institution for that section of Louisiana. She has given Monseigneur 400 arpents of land, partly woods, partly farmland where corn and cotton are raised. A house is being built there, larger than the one we have here. This lady offers to pay the expenses of several religious for a year, to give them a Negro family as servants, to furnish the house and pay all the expenses of the voyage from Paris. Monseigneur dwelt at length on the advantages of such a foundation, which would procure for Lower Louisiana the good we have tried to do up here. The nuns would not be exposed to such cold winters nor to the epidemics that occur in New Orleans and oblige parents to withdraw their children from school every summer or keep them at home. That section of Louisiana is rich and would furnish more pupils than this area does.

Monseigneur proposed that I should go down to talk things over with Mrs. Smith, but considering first the expense of a long trip, and second that Mothers Octavie and Eugenie could not go together and leave me without an interpreter, I thought that Mother Eugenie could do the most good because of her appearance, her virtue, her genial manner, and the ease with which she now speaks both English and French. I suggested to the Bishop that she should take charge of the foundation, but be ready to return here if you should so order. . . .

We all agree on the need of a second foundation, first, because a house in Lower Louisiana is necessary to support the one in Upper Louisiana; second, because the milder climate agrees with some temperaments; third, because when the expenses of the trip are repaid, we in turn could pay off our most unpleasant debt. We shall never be able to do it without some outside help, as we still owe 13,000 francs. Fourth, because we now have five good novices, so there would be a sufficient number of us left here and we could accept the postulants who are asking to enter. It is not possible to do this if we receive the nuns from France, as several already sleep in the attic. That place is simply unbearable in winter, so every night they had to make up their beds in a classroom or in the refectory.

With two establishments we would not get involved in more debt, but rather liquidate the present obligations. Then too, we should be able to double the number of new religious, of pupils, and of poor children, and to spread devotion to the Sacred Heart of Jesus and set up new altars in His honor. These are very pressing motives. I realize that it is a very serious matter to change the destination of the religious you are sending us, but I believe this falls in with your intentions. So I have written to our nuns who are coming to follow the instructions left for them by Monseigneur. I have promised to send them Mother Eugenie, hoping she will send Mother Lucille to us. She will be very useful here because of her age, should anything happen to me. . . . Mother Eugenie will go courageously to her new destination when word comes that our nuns have arrived. God has fitted her for authority. . . .

July was a hot, busy time. There was work for all in the community, especially Mother Duchesne, whose active hours were devoted partly to the children and partly to the novices. They were her hope for the future, and from the very beginning she fostered strong virtues among them, that they might become humble, brave, self-sacrificing religious. She taught them to probe deep into the heart of the spiritual life, to free themselves from the subterfuges of self-love that blinds the soul to truth, to enter into the dispositions and sentiments of the Sacred Heart, and to find therein the model and motive for their entire religious life. Constraint had no place in her method, but self-renunciation was motivated so generously by love for the Sacred Heart that she had often to restrain the striving of these American girls who had determined to achieve independence by giving their wills to Christ and their lives to obedience.

She watched them prayerfully as they knelt at adoration, endeavoring "by the purity of their homage, the fervor of their love, and the fulness of their oblation to make reparation to Him for the outrages He everywhere receives." She listened with restrained happiness as they pleaded to remain awhile with her at night before the tabernacle. She was glad when she saw them follow Mother Octavie's humble reparation of the slightest faults, or Mother Eugenie's generous devotedness, when they were eager in their rivalry to help Sister Marguerite in the pantry or the parish school, and Sister Catherine in the linen room or the laundry. But there were times when she was overwhelmed by a sense of powerlessness in the face of the spiritual difficulties encountered by scrupulous little Emilie St. Cyr and passionate Mathilde Hamilton, whose natural temperament exposed her to temptations Philippine herself could scarcely understand. But the Holy Spirit was directing her work with these souls, and Divine Providence gave her prudent friends and advisers in Father De La Croix and the Vincentian priests on whom she relied for help.

The fairly even tenor of life at Florissant was interrupted slightly on the feast of St. Vincent de Paul, when the children of the parish school filed into the convent chapel, occupying the places of the boarding pupils and singing the Mass in honor of their patron. They returned for Vespers and a short sermon and enjoyed a little party prepared for them before they scattered for the vacation, which would last until the harvests had been gathered in.

A more serious interruption occurred on July 30 when Bishop Du Bourg arrived, not to celebrate the feast of St. Ignatius, but to insist that Mother Audé should go down to Louisiana before the arrival of the religious who were expected from France. It was an unwise step and Philippine opposed it, but there was no resisting the Bishop. When he announced, as he mounted his horse next day, that a steamboat was leaving St. Louis for New Orleans the following Sunday and he would reserve places on it for two religious, the reality of the venture was determined. There were four days in which to prepare for the departure. All that could be spared, and much that could not, was packed into boxes and satchels, and Mother Duchesne supplied one hundred dollars for the steamboat fare and the incidentals of the trip. Mother Audé and Sister Mary Layton left the convent early on the morning of August 5 and three hours later boarded the *Rapide* at the Market Street landing.

Within a week of their departure Mother Duchesne began to be troubled by anxious fears in their regard. These were aroused by news communicated to her by the Bishop. On the feast of the Assumption she opened her heart to Mother Barat on the subject, then added details about the boarding school at Florissant, which began its yearly vacation of two weeks that very day:

> From several different letters we understood that our dear Sisters had set out last March to join us. But a letter to Monseigneur from Bordeaux, dated May 1, does not mention any embarkation for this mission. This news causes us much anxiety and Monseigneur does not know what to think of it. He was all the more eager for their arrival as he was planning a second foundation at Opelousas, as I explained in detail in my letter of June 23. I fear that new house, for which I gave my approval, may cause you anxiety, but I shall repeat here the urgent reasons that influenced my decision.

After doing so at some length she continued:

Mother Eugenie felt strongly attracted to this work, and I thought she was better fitted for it than I am, for she understands English and can express herself in that language. She is quite able to direct both the community and the external works; she is very skilful and can meet any situation that may arise in a house. Her health has been declining noticeably and she needs a warmer climate because of her weak lungs. True, we have prostrating heat here in Missouri, but the weather changes suddenly to severe cold and it is difficult to take the necessary precautions. Last year we feared we might lose her, and her soul was more affected than her body. Her recovery was only temporary. A serious and persistent eye trouble developed, along with a cough and fever. All this made me fear a complete breakdown. God seemed to manifest His will in disposing her to undertake the direction of a house so willingly, though her humility must suffer under the burden.

It was arranged that she would not leave here until we had news of the arrival of our Sisters from France, but the very uncertainty of their arrival suggested to her the question: "Should we fail to accept the advantageous offers of Mrs. Smith on that account?" and "Would it not be better for her to go down to Louisiana in order to get all in readiness, so that on arriving, our Sisters might be able to live at once according to the rule?" I was astonished by these questions at first and acted as if I paid no attention to them. But I was impressed by them. They pleased Monseigneur very much, and on the eve of the feast of St. Ignatius it was decided that Mother Eugenie would leave here with our first novice, Sister Mary Layton, on the following Sunday. They would travel on the same steamboat that was carrying the grave and holy Lazarist who gave us a retreat in May [Father Andrew Ferrari] and several pupils of the Bishop's college who were under the care of a very good Negro woman whom the family had sent to St. Louis to accompany them home. She promised to take good care of our nuns also. I gave Mother Eugenie 500 francs for the trip, the necessary clothing, and furnishings for the chapel, thinking she would be supplied by what came from France.

As to books, she took all the duplicates we had, a copy of the Constitutions, and one of each of the books and note-books we use in the classes. She will have copies made, just as we have had the novices and pupils do here. Monseigneur added some books, vestments, candelabra, and four handsome pictures. No one has lost more than I by this departure: Mother Eugenie was my right arm. Monseigneur thinks very highly of her. He would have given her his whole house, had he been able to do so. He wrote to both the pastor of the place and the benefactress of the new house

letters that were very complimentary to the Society and to Mother
Eugenie. He told them he did not want them to meddle in any
way in the direction and administration of the convent and said
that such was our custom and that it was better that way. . . .

We have at present 22 boarding pupils. I learned today of the
failure of the Bank of Missouri, the only bank whose notes were
considered acceptable. I do not know how this will affect the
school. The four novices we have here are very good, especially
the Americans, and among them Sister Regis is an angel of candor,
sweetness, and devotedness. She is the one best fitted to take
Mother Eugenie's place in the work of the school and in the
pantry, but like Mother Eugenie she eats too little and takes no
care of herself. The novices are studying Rodriguez, the Catechism
of Perseverance, and Sacred History. As I could not get an
orthodox abridgement of Sacred History, I made one from a large
Catholic Bible, English translation, and the novices are copying
this and learning it by heart. I also translated or summarized from
English books the history of America and Roman history, and I
made an outline of Ancient history. All this has furnished material
for teaching the classes. As the novices have not had much formal
schooling and not one of them had a copy of *L'Hommand's Grammar*, I also made an outline of that which each one copies and
studies from. We have had to make copies of the arithmetic
and geography books in use in this country, printed in English. I
hope you approve of these methods—books are so scarce and the
children cannot buy them—no one has any money. . . . When I
first came to America I thought I had no further missionary ambition, but now I am devoured with interest in Peru. These desires,
however, are more tranquil than those that made me importune
you so impatiently in France. . . .

Classes reopened on September 1 with the reading of the School
Rule and distribution of charges the day before. The novices had
their share of classwork now, and Mother Octavie filled the post
of mistress general. The tuition had been lowered to $140 a year,
but there was little money coming in, though it was understood
that the school bills were "payable in advance." Mother Duchesne
made no reference to her straitened circumstances when she wrote
an affectionate little letter to her sister Euphrosine on September
17:

I received your letter and that of my brother-in-law, which the
customs officer must have taken from the box you were so good as
to send me, but which I have not yet received. I am so grateful for
these gifts you sent me. They will be so useful to us. I hope they

will reach us by the first opportunity. Your letters came by mail. I already knew the consoling details about dear Aloysia and her sister and my dear godson. I call you a very fortunate mother, for the heart-suffering you feel at the separation from your children can never equal the sweet consolation of giving saints to religion and heavenly protectors to all your family. I wrote to our Mother General in Paris, asking her to indicate to you the use to be made of the income, as I have no right to dispose of it myself. But you must be sure to keep the 150 francs due you from the religious in New Orleans. They sent the money to me.

I should like to write to you at greater length, but my eyes are giving me much trouble. As the ice cuts off the steamboat traffic at this time of the year, I am enclosing this little sheet in a letter going overland to New York. A thousand messages of love to my sisters. It is a great pleasure to have detailed news about them from you and Madame de Rollin. We have begun a second foundation in Lower Louisiana, where a lady donated a house and lands. It is 300 or 400 leagues from here, but that is like 30 leagues in France, for long trips are quite ordinary in this country. Regards to my brother-in-law. . . .

Philippine was right about travel habits in America, and she was often pleasantly surprised by visitors who found their way to Florissant. The Lazarist missionaries were particularly friendly toward the Religious of the Sacred Heart and often stopped for a visit and a meal, or at least some refreshment. Father De La Croix welcomed them cordially to his primitive quarters, and later on the sacristy of the new church was used as a lodging place by many an ill or weary priest.

I admit that this is something of an expense [wrote Mother Duchesne in defense of her own generosity], causes some loss of time, and interferes with regularity in the community, but I believe it is justified. These poor priests, worn out by their labors, find a little rest and a change of air at Florissant, and there is no one to care for them but us. And besides, this is part of my vocation, as I told you one day before I left France. I said, "Even if I could do nothing but cook for the missionaries, I should be perfectly satisfied." [32]

Bishop Du Bourg was at Florissant in September, 1821, with Father Rosati from St. Mary's Seminary. They chatted encouragingly with two new postulants who were finding religious life more difficult than they had expected, and Father Rosati expressed his desire to have the Religious of the Sacred Heart open a school at the Barrens. He even had some definite plans to submit. Father Acquaroni often stopped on his way to or from Portage des Sioux, where he was working among Indians, half-breeds, trappers, and traders—as motley a mixture of humanity as the frontier could breed. He was at the convent early in October, when the Bishop held a little conference with him and Fathers Niel, Deys, and Anduze.[33] He spent a long afternoon in conversation with Mother Duchesne, telling her about his work, his needs, his hopes and plans; and when he left, she was aglow with new zeal, thrilled with renewed ambitions. At once she took out her letter pad to propose to the Mother General her latest missionary projects, giving also homely details about debts and novices, hopes and anxieties, and beginning quite abruptly:

> The most important thing just now is to help Mother Eugenie at Opelousas, not by sending money, but nuns. When she left here, we thought our Sisters were already in New Orleans. This delay must be a great disappointment to dear Eugenie. . . . Our boarding school must inevitably diminish, as the Bank of Missouri has failed, and so have the banks of many other states. Money is so scarce, even the largest landowners have none. All trade is carried on by barter and we are getting absolutely nothing. There is some question of a new issue of bank notes backed by the value of one-thirty-sixth of the uncultivated land which Congress has turned over to this state. Until these notes appear, we shall receive little money from anyone. As creditors may even refuse to accept them, only by a stroke of Providence shall we be able to pay our debt that falls due in November, 1821. . . .
>   The novices are getting along very well. Sister Xavier has a good memory and translates both languages fluently. That is a great help in getting our French books into English. Sister Regis is more attractive in appearance. She has not the shrewd penetration of her sister, but she does everything so quietly and correctly. Grace finds no obstacle in her and so flows sweetly into her soul as pure water seeps into well-prepared soil. Her appearance is dignified and is made more attractive by the combination of evenness of manner, uprightness, and innocence. Sister Mary Ann Summers manages the kitchen and in this difficult employment always shows the greatest sweetness of manner. Sister Josephine St. Cyr is just fifteen years old. She is not very gifted, but she is very devoted. She milks the cows, bakes the bread, and teaches a class in the parish school. . . . We shall go on accepting postulants even if the enrollment of the boarding school does diminish, for we have already several tuitions to be paid in merchandise or

produce, so we shall have enough to live on. The money shortage has made the price of produce drop very low. Corn is down to 25¢ a bushel, meat to 2½ or 3¢ a pound; soap is only 8¢. . . .

Father Rosati is asking us to send a group of religious to his parish at the Barrens. The building would be erected by the parishioners—they have the material ready. They would contribute the flour needed by the community and would provide a chaplain and a doctor. But the foundation that would be most in accord with the original purpose of our mission is the one at Portage des Sioux, the most northern parish in the direction of the Great Lakes and Canada, which lies beyond them. And that parish stretches westward with no boundary this side of Asia. A zealous priest stationed there [Father John Acquaroni] ministers to three parishes. He teaches a school, trains a choir, and runs a farm, and he is a true father to the poor, living just as they do. The town is the *rendezvous* for all the Indian canoes that come down the Mississippi and for the boats of the traders who go into the wilderness in search of peltries. In their isolated posts, separated for whole years at a time from their wives, these traders often take to themselves for a time Indian women. They do not know how to provide for the children born of these illegitimate alliances. They leave them with their mothers, and so the children of Christian fathers are brought up like little animals. Many of these traders, however, are rich; and if they knew where to place the children, they would certainly have them educated. This is the good priest's project: he is going to build a house and provide a farm for the institution for orphans and half-breed children. He believes, and rightly, that since meat costs practically nothing in this section of the country, provisions of this kind could be salted down. The Indians in the neighborhood often kill deer now just to get the skins; and being completely improvident, they discard the meat or give it away for nothing.

This seems to me to be the most useful kind of establishment we could found, and the easiest. It also resembles the work done by Marie of the Incarnation in Canada and is most closely conformed to the purposes that drew us to this country. I have no other desire than that of consecrating my life to this work, if God so wills. If Divine Providence enables us to pay our debts, we could this very year help to found such an establishment. Sister Marguerite would also be well suited to this work . . . which would be to her liking and not beyond her strength. . . .

Several of our pupils are persevering in their desire for religious life. Miss Emilie Chouteau has the greatest difficulties to overcome. Girls are free in this country at the age of eighteen . . . and at eleven or twelve out here they are as well developed in body and soul as are those in France at fourteen years. Thinking over the obligation I have of helping my religious daughters in every way, I have sometimes judged myself blameworthy in not urging them more to use holy practices of penance. But when I see these children of fifteen and sixteen years baking bread, milking cows, cleaning the dormitory, doing the cooking, and having at most only one community recreation period a day because they help in the parish school, I am afraid of killing them if I add anything more. It seems to me the corporal penances can be introduced later on, when the work is divided among a larger number and when their physical strength is more robust.

This letter, begun on October 8, was written at odd moments over a period of three or four days. Philippine had sat down to finish it on the twelfth, but she was interrupted by the sound of voices, then a knock at the front door. She opened it to welcome Father Acquaroni and a priest of whom she had heard much—the celebrated Father Gabriel Richard of Detroit.[34] They stayed a long time talking of their great interests—mission work, the salvation of souls, and the means to achieve their high designs. Philippine enjoyed this visit thoroughly, so she continued her letter to tell the Mother General about it:

As I was finishing this letter, we received a visit from a French Sulpician from Canada. For twenty-three years he has been pastor of Detroit, the largest town in Michigan territory, having fifteen hundred inhabitants, French and American, Catholics and Protestants. About twelve years ago he formed a group of young women whom he had prepared for their first Communion and whom he has continued to direct ever since. The eldest, who is now thirty, has just been elected superior of the little congregation. The election was held in the presence of Bishop Flaget of Kentucky, who confirmed it. The good pastor of Detroit Father [Gabriel] Richard, had them read Rodriguez more than ten times, gave them a rule, and allowed them to make temporary vows. Monseigneur Flaget wants them to make their novitiate under a superior who knows religious life, before they bind themselves by perpetual vows. He wanted to send someone from one of the orders in Kentucky, either the Sisters of Charity, who have a modified rule, or the Penitents, who resemble the Trappists. They had not enough money to undertake this long journey, and besides, Father Richard and his nuns are Canadians, and they do not want to merge with Americans, so nothing has come of it at all. They want to be trained by a French religious, and Father Richard is asking us to send them a superior. I told him it is impossible just now, and besides, we should have to get permission from you. I promised to write to you all about this.

Detroit has a Canadian climate and one needs a fire there as early as September. The country is poor and we should have few boarding pupils able to pay even 450 francs, and few day pupils able to pay anything, but living is cheap and there are many souls in need of help. It takes at least a month to get to Detroit from here, going by way of the Illinois River, then three leagues overland to a river that flows into Lake Michigan, which you cross full length [south to north] in a sailing vessel. This brings you to Michilimackinac, where you undertake the navigation of Lake Huron [north to south] to the St. Claire River and down to Detroit. There is an overland route, known only to the savages [who act as guides]. This takes two weeks, and one must sleep in the woods at night, no matter what the weather. A third way is to go down the Mississippi as far as the Ohio, and up that river to Louisville, then overland to Detroit. They say there will be a Bishop there soon, perhaps Father Nerinx, a native of Flanders, or a Russian priest. There is already a new Bishop for Cincinnati in the state of Ohio. He is bringing Dominicans from Rome, but he is a Jesuit at heart, a zealous missionary in the full extent of the term.[35]

As Philippine's American geography was always a bit hazy, she certainly could not have mapped the wilderness routes she was describing, but her zeal for souls made her ready for the trip if obedience sanctioned it. Meanwhile she would struggle on at Florissant in her great but obscure task of training workers for the Society. The novices prepared for their patronal feast by a fervent novena, and on November 13 another white-veil was added to their group when Mary Mullanphy took the coadjutrix habit with the name of Frances. From the beginning Mother Duchesne had been careful to introduce among them all the customs she had seen in practice in the novitiates of the Sacred Heart at Ste Marie and Paris. Their special consecration to the Holy Heart of Mary was made for the first time at Florissant in December of that very year, and devotion to our Lady had a prominent place in their spiritual life. Communicating to them her own love for the Blessed Virgin, she taught them the prayer she had used since girlhood, when she first became acquainted with the spirituality of Mother Marie of the Incarnation:

O divine Spouse of my soul, what shall I render to You for the exceeding great love You have shown toward me? I give You thanks

through Your Blessed Mother. I offer You her Immaculate Heart
as I offer Your Heart to the Heavenly Father. Allow me to love
You through that holy Heart which has loved You so much, to
offer You that body which served You, that virginal sanctuary
which You deigned to inhabit. I offer it to You in thanksgiving for
all Your benefits to me. I offer it for the amendment of my life,
for the sanctification of my soul, and to obtain the grace of final
perseverance in Your service and in Your love. . . .

And now a great day was at hand. Father De La Croix had
chosen the date out of deference to the Religious of the Sacred
Heart, who celebrate the feast of the Presentation of the Blessed
Virgin with dual solemnity. From St. Louis on the eve came
Fathers Deys, Acquaroni, and Anduze, with two altar-boys. Let
Philippine's *Journal* tell the story:

November 21. First Mass in our chapel for Holy Communion and
renovation of vows at 5:30. At 6 o'clock, Mass of Thanksgiving.
At 7:30 a third Mass at which the Children of Mary received Holy
Communion. Then a fourth Mass offered by Father Acquaroni.
At 11 o'clock all the clergy went in procession from our parlor
to the new church, which Father De La Croix blessed without
chant. High Mass was then sung in the church by Father Niel,
pastor of St. Louis. Our children sang the Mass, accompanied on
the piano by Father Deys. Father Anduze preached on the
solemnity of the day, after reading the Bishop's decree abolishing
trustees and ordering them to remit to the pastor the money on
hand and the furnishings of the old church. . . .
November 29. The solemn erection of the shrine dedicated to St.
Francis Regis. It had been impossible to fulfill our vow sooner.
The altar stands in our choir at the left near the balustrade where
the religious receive Holy Communion.

Above the altar hung the picture of St. Francis Regis which the
Bishop had presented to Mother Duchesne. In company with the
holy missionary of Vivarais, she kept her night-vigils before the
tabernacle, sometimes allowing the novices to share this privilege,
but more often alone with the Divine Lover of souls, to whom she
yearned to draw all hearts.

Although the *Journal* makes no mention of special recreation
in the community in honor of these ceremonies, it does record on
December 14, "rejoicing in commemoration of the arrival of
Mother Barat at Grenoble in 1804, when she received Mother
Duchesne and her companions into the Society of the Sacred

Heart," and on December 21 "another *congé* in memory of our moving into the convent at St. Ferdinand." Between these two holidays Philippine described to the Mother General the blessing of the new church, adding quite casually: "The pastor says Mass in our cloister chapel whenever the severe cold threatens to freeze the wine in the chalice if he remained in the church itself." [36]

Christmas came, bringing midnight Mass in the convent chapel "just for us," with *Noëls* and exposition of the Blessed Sacrament immediately following and through the whole happy day, and the parish Masses at four and eleven a.m., and sermons in French and English, Vespers and Benediction. Philippine was in her element on days like this, and she strove to impress on her novices a true sense of worship. With her adoration was acknowledgement of her own nothingness in the face of God's All. It was reverence and awe in the face of His infinite holiness. It was tender filial love that was prepared to go all lengths in generosity to make return to the best of all Fathers, whose Providence never failed her. The inspired beauty of liturgical worship, with its exterior graces and its interior spirit, appealed to her quite as strongly as did the intimate communing of the soul with God in silent watches before the tabernacle, or the devotional closing of the Old Year with its *Te Deum* of gratitude and *Miserere* of reparation. Each year her soul expanded in strong, sweet praise of God's abundant gifts, then sank low in self-humiliation as she realized her radical incapacity as a creature to attain to the supernatural perfection to which she aspired or to accomplish the work entrusted to her. In this she was living the Society's Rule; with profound humility she "looked upon herself as the last of all," longed for the lowest employments, "never quit the thought of her own lowliness and nothingness." But faith in the grace of obedience was her support as she endeavored to develop in her novices an ever-deepening appreciation of, and fidelity to, their vocation as spouses and victims of the Heart of Jesus. One of them caused her much anxiety, and she wrote to Father Joseph Rosati about her:

> The elder of the Hamilton sisters is in a state of temptation that goes beyond my experience to handle and makes me fear for her vocation. Nevertheless she has remained firm and has not yielded to the invitations of her brother. There is no one here on whose decisions I can fully rely, and I realize more and more how much I lost in the death of Father De Andreis.[37]

On February 2 a new work was inaugurated at Florissant when

Mother Duchesne accepted as "orphans" two little motherless girls. The work was placed "under the spiritual protection of the Blessed Virgin with the hope of soon being able to give a home to a greater number of children." She mentions this in a letter to Father Barat a couple of weeks later and introduces him to another "charming child" in whom she was deeply interested. And again her anxiety about Mathilde Hamilton appears:

> There are a few vocations among our pupils and in time these will spread the work of education and religious worship. I believe the increase of our institution will be the surest means of spreading religion in this sterile country. What can you expect a priest to do out here when he can find neither lodging nor clothing nor food? Mediocre virtue will not stand up under such trials. . . . We have often had the pleasure of supplying linens for these poor ministers of Jesus Christ; nearly all the material sent from Amiens went to them, as well as all our handkerchiefs. I do not desire to be better off except in order to spread the good work. We have been asked to take several more children gratis, but we had to refuse. I promised, however, to take two motherless little Presbyterian girls, aged five and six. . . . Several of our Protestant boarding pupils have their parents' permission to be baptized. Do pray earnestly for a charming child with heavenly sweetness in her looks and character. She desires the same favor, but will scarcely obtain it. . . .
>
> One of the novices certainly needs your direction. I have tried to curb her pride, and I wonder whether she is subject to simple temptations or opposed to all dependence and self-control. It is hard to tell. Pray that she may overcome these difficulties quickly for the sake of her vocation, as the other lovable sister has done.[38]

The spiritual trials of Mathilde Hamilton continued to be a grave anxiety for Mother Duchesne. When Father Cellini, C.M., called at the convent early in March, she asked him to talk to the novice, who was "tempted to think ill of our Divine Saviour and of His ministers."[39] Mother Duchesne hoped that greater peace of soul would result from this visit, but there were severe storms ahead for Sister Xavier. Meanwhile, Father Henri Pratte had come from Ste Genevieve with another postulant, Judith Labruyère, and a letter from Bishop Du Bourg told of the arrival in New Orleans of Mothers Lucille Mathevon and Xavier Murphy. In her eagerness for news from France, Philippine was just a trifle hard on Lucille when she wrote to Father Barat on April 1:

The Bishop sent Mother Xavier to Opelousas and will bring

Mother Lucille here himself. She also wrote to me, but her letter told me all about her trip and not a word about our Fathers and our Mothers in France. From this I concluded that she is not accustomed to writing many letters, as she had not the intuition to choose what would be the most interesting news to put in a letter. No doubt she is bringing me some mail. She did not mention the fact, and this really annoyed me. The Decrees of the General Council, the Summary of the Constitutions, etc., etc., which we were awaiting with so much eagerness—all, she writes, are in Mother Xavier's trunk and have gone to Opelousas.

Madame Josephine Meneyrond also arrived in New Orleans on Christmas Eve. That news greatly astonished me—and also Mother Eugenie, with whom she is already lodged. We do not know the motive of her trip nor who sent her; and all her letters are so long-winded; I see rather clearly that she came against our Mother General's wishes, for the latter had written me that she was trying to dissuade her from this venture. She is asking to make her final vows at once and says you are the one who sent her and that you must have written to me about her. If you did, the letter got lost, for I have had no word from France about her coming. . . .

I have thanked you several times for your precious compilation, which I received just after it was published. It is read eagerly by all your children here.We must rejoice in the good that befalls others, but you will not forbid me to lament the fact that we have no Jesuits in this part of the world. They are greatly needed. The soul is utterly alone here.

The ceremonies of Holy Week, a retreat for first Communicants, the preparation of several children for baptism—all this absorbs our time. Miss Sarah Benton, the child of my heart, feeds her soul on hope.[40] She wants to become a Catholic and a religious, but her parents are opposed to this. Pray earnestly for her. She has so many fine qualities. I saw Miss Emilie Chouteau yesterday. She had nothing to say about herself. I realized that her soul was troubled, but she lacks strength of character. . . .

There were many times when Mother Duchesne found great consolation in the work that was being accomplished at Florissant. That Easter Monday nine children received baptism. A week later Mother Mathevon arrived under the escort of General Pratte, and Philippine could note with satisfaction: "She gave us all the news about our dear Society and informed us that through the kindness of our Mother General our debt to Mr. Mullanphy has been paid. He went to see her in Paris." [41] In the early hours of April 16 she was writing to thank for this help and to give details of the success with which God was blessing the apostolate on the frontier:

Yesterday, April 15, we had the joy of laying eyes at last on our beloved and long-awaited Mother Lucille. She had been welcomed, as we were, both in New Orleans and in St. Louis. . . . We had planned to have several of our pupils baptized on Holy Saturday, but we put it off until Easter Monday in order that the parents might be present at the ceremony.We decorated the baptismal font and the children wore white dresses. I stood as godmother for the step-daughter of General Clark, the Governor, a very prominent man in St. Louis.[42] . . . Mother Octavie and I also stood for two of the orphans to whom we give a home. They were the foundation stones of the little orphanage we have inaugurated and housed in the parish school. Besides these four children, there were five others, four of them pupils of the parish school, and a little boy who had not even a pair of stockings for the ceremony. We furnished clothing and a feast for these poor children in order to impress more deeply on their untrained minds this day of grace. My dear Sarah Benton and her friend, Caroline Hamilton, cried all day because they could not have the same happiness. . . . Tomorrow our chaplain leaves for the Osage mission. A Lazarist priest will replace him during his absence. That Congregation of the Mission is very friendly toward us. . . .

I cry for joy at times when I realize that in one way or another more than one hundred people are learning to love Jesus through our efforts here. I do not know how to thank God for this. Mother Eugenie will have greater success than ours, once her house is firmly established. She is very glad she undertook the work alone. God blesses quite visibly all she does, even at times seeming to work miracles for her. But I miss her so much. . . .

A tender, wistful little letter to Mother Thérèse, crowded with memories of Sainte Marie, reveals the heart of Philippine as in spirit she retraced the route Mother Mathevon had traveled from Grenoble to America:

I would rather write you a short letter than none at all. Mother Lucille arrived yesterday. I have had only the night hours to read the letters that are so dear to me and to answer some of them with the greatest haste. As the steamboat leaves at once for New Orleans, I must finish before daybreak. This silence of the night lends itself to the sentiments of the heart. Mine is always deeply moved when I think of my loved Mothere Thérèse, and of our sweet conversations as we sat on the rocky ledge at Ste Marie. Those walls, the very thought of which thrill me with gratitude, have become even dearer to me since they shelter the mortal remains of one who was not just a dear niece and beloved pupil, but a spouse of the Sacred

Heart whom our Lord united to Himself by suffering, and whose humble fidelity He is glorifying.[43] Thank you so much for having gathered all the details about her precious life and for seeing that the manuscript reached me. . . .

The departure of Father De La Croix on a missionary trip to the Osage Indians was always an occasion for holy envy in the soul of Philippine. She followed him in spirit as he made his way up the Missouri with the river traders, then plunged into the forests to meet the savages in their squalid encampments. There was as yet no possibility of establishing a regular mission among them, but the valiant priest did what he could at the risk of his life and was supported in his efforts by the prayers that were offered continually for him at Florissant. Meanwhile other plans were stirring in Philippine's mind and heart, other opportunities beckoned to her, and she put her thoughts on paper, begging Mother Barat to allow a few of the religious to reopen the school at St. Charles. After a lengthy defense of her proposal, she added:

> You were worried, Reverend Mother, by the suggestion of the new foundation at Grand Coteau. But just think, that is the only means by which we could support ourselves. By it we can now receive more postulants and be able to feed and lodge them. You will see that within a year Mother Eugenie will be as far advanced as we are after four years. It will be the same at St. Charles. All we need is the spirit of sacrifice. If a mission is established by priests among the Osage Indians, they will also want two nuns to teach the children, but *there* complete death to nature! It would be flying in the face of all prudence, but I would be very glad to devote myself to the work if you approve of it later on. . . .
>
> You must often have trouble reading what I write, but we do not have at hand what we need for writing well. . . . Monseigneur has sent us two more paintings. . . . What we really need is a banner of the Blessed Virgin. We carried her statue—already rather disfigured—in the procession of the Blessed Sacrament, which took place within our enclosure. All went off very well, even on the part of the Protestants who were present. Next year we would like to have banners that are not so shabby. . . .[44]

Back from Louisiana in company with Father Hercules Brassac early in July, Bishop Du Bourg paid a visit to Florissant at once and stirred the household to activity resembling that of the previous summer by the news he brought from Grand Coteau. The annual retreat of the pupils had been scheduled for the week preceding the feast of St. Vincent de Paul. Father Brassac gave the instructions to the majority of them in French, while Father De La Croix preached to the Americans. Mother Duchesne could give little time to these retreatants, for she was busy packing boxes and satchels and guiding little Emilie St. Cyr through the spiritual exercises in preparation for her first vows. What a day was that of July 19! Crowded with religious ceremonies, last minute instructions and advice to Mother Octavie, who was being left in charge of the convent as mother assistant, and at least one letter. This was posted by Mother Duchesne herself before boarding the steamboat in St. Louis on the afternoon of July 20 and told the reason for this hurried trip south:

> Monseigneur reached here a few days ago. He informed me that Madame Josephine Meneyrond has returned to France, that a coadjutrix novice from New Orleans has left Grand Coteau, that Sister Layton has made her first vows, Miss Carmelite Landry has received the habit, and Mother Xavier Murphy has made her final vows and is having some difficulty getting accustomed to things, and last of all, that Mother Eugenie is in urgent need of help. All this, along with complete silence on her part—which is most unusual for her and so causes me to suspect carelessness on the part of someone who was entrusted with her letters—all this has determined me to accompany the two young religious whom I was sending to her. One is a choir nun who made her first vows today in view of the long trip ahead of her and because of her courage in obtaining her parents' consent to the departure. The second is a coadjutrix novice who will take charge of the kitchen, which Mother Eugenie is still managing herself. As Mother Lucille is ready to handle any emergency, her presence here makes this trip possible. Monseigneur hastened my decision in order that we might travel on the same steamboat with four priests, and I can return on this boat before the winter freeze sets in. Monseigneur distributed the prizes at Opelousas and says the children are making astonishing progress there. Some people in St. Louis say the standard of our boarding school has gone down since Mother Eugenie left. That is not true.
>
> Today we had first Communion, besides the ceremony of first vows of Sister Josephine St. Cyr, which brought tears to many eyes. Monseigneur preached a beautiful sermon. He wants to allow the other second-year novices to make their vows in order to give them more control in the boarding school, where they help continually. All our Protestant children want to become Catholics. The interesting child, Sarah Benton, was withdrawn by her grand-

mother in fury. It was a sight to behold. The child will be severely persecuted and is in danger of losing the graces of baptism and first Communion. Miss Émilie Chouteau, who is now eighteen years old, sent me word secretly to let her know when I would pass through St. Louis. Perhaps she plans to follow us south. I am writing to her on the eve of leaving. Monseigneur will take us at daybreak in the carriage that brought him here. . . .

When Philippine set out on this mission of charity, she little dreamed of the adventuous journey that lay ahead. Nor could she realize how fascinating an account her letters would make. When she is her own biographer, the pages come alive with her vigorous personality, and the story glows with her own animation. She had already visited Grand Coteau and was on her way to New Orleans to board a northbound steamboat when she wrote to Mother Barat from a dingy inn at Plaquemine, Louisiana, on September 8:

Before I left St. Louis, I wrote to you by way of New York to tell you I was going to Opelousas, and on my trip down the river I repeated all this to the superior at Bordeaux, sending her at the same time a packet of letters we forgot to post in St. Louis. I wanted to make this trip when we first found out that Mother Eugenie had been ill. Then I put the idea out of my mind, once I knew our Sisters from France had arrived. . . . But when Monsiegneur returned from Louisiana, I realized again that I should make the trip and bring some help to that convent, for there was no priest in the neighborhood and the enemies of the pastor had forced him to leave. Monseigneur had withdrawn the convent chaplain in so imperative a fashion that the priest would lose his faculties for administering the sacraments if he remained a day beyond the time appointed for his departure. . . . Mother Xavier Murphy was ill at ease in her new home; Mother Girard was even more so; and help was needed. Two young novices with much good will can be of service with the work, and one of them can teach. The house will now be able to get along if they do not accept more than 30 pupils, and I believe they will never have more than that.

One can have no idea of what this section of the country is like unless one actually sees it. There are about 20,000 people in the whole area. The boarding school will draw its pupils from four small towns nearby, for access to the place is most difficult, there being only one route through swampy woods and a number of bayous and pools. Two of these bayous make a waterway which opens into a sort of basin, but one of them is navigable only in springtime, so I made the trip on the other.

We left St. Louis on July 20 by steamboat. A former pupil of ours [Therese Pratte], who is devoted to Mother Eugenie, had obtained permission from her parents to go with us at their expense. So there were four of us traveling together. There were also three priests on board [Fathers Brassac, Cellini, and Desmoulins], but they were no help whatsoever.[45] We counted on hearing Mass at Ste Genevieve on Sunday, July 21, but the captain wanted to take on a cargo of lead at Herculaneum,[46] so we stayed there until evening. Our Lord made up for this disappointment by allowing us to meet two little girls, who followed us step by step along the river bank with their dog. Soon their father came up to us and asked if we were Roman Catholics. We replied that we were and talked to him of his responsibility to have his children baptized. It turned out that the older one had received that sacrament, and the man was eager to have the other child baptized. She was too young to need instruction, so we called one of the priests and the baptism took place, to the great joy of the parents. Our pupil acted as godmother and the priest promised to visit this place on his mission rounds, though there are very few Catholics in the vicinity.

On July 22 we stopped at Ste Genevieve. There we had Mass and the joy of offering our Communion in union with all our Sisters for our very dear Mother General. From then until the 28th we could only offer to God the great discomfort of the intense heat of this season, the proximity of the boilers, and the other arrangements on the steamboat. We were all covered with prickly heat and mosquito bites. In the evening we had recreation on the deck and passed the time singing hymns, led by Father Desmoulins, one of the priests, who has so fine a voice it gave him quite a reputation at St. Sulpice. He left us at Baton Rouge on the left bank of the Mississippi, where he has been named pastor.

On Sunday, July 28, we hoped to reach Natchez in time for Mass, but the priest had already reached the elevation, and as he does not keep the Reserve in the tabernacle when he is absent, we were deprived of Holy Communion. We went to the home of the pastor, Father Mano[47] [Constantine Maenhaut], a young Flemish priest whose health is greatly undermined, more, I think, from heart-suffering than from physical toil. Very few Catholics live at Natchez; the little wooden church stands humbly among beautiful Protestant temples. There are five different sects in the place. Such a crowd was going into a Protestant church, we followed along; but were informed of our mistake, so we turned away with sad hearts and went to witness the solitude that surrounded the Catholic church.

Father Mano told us he sincerely regretted having allowed Mother Eugenie to leave Natchez. He thinks a foundation would have been better located in that fairly prosperous town on the great river where there is continual traffic, than in a little hole like Opelousas, where we can never reach more than a very restricted circle. But we were just badly informed and God allowed it to happen in order to recompense the faith of Mrs. Smith and to save the souls of the children in those parts who are so idolized by their parents that they would never have had the courage to send them to school at a distance. There will be few day pupils, and one could hardly place a novitiate there because it is so inaccessible at any season and so difficult to provide for. One must lay in supplies in the spring by means of rafts, which cannot reach there at any other season, and the carrying charges are so high: the transportation of one medium-size *armoire* from New Orleans to Opelousas cost 120 francs; each chair cost five francs.

On July 29 we left the river boat and waited at an inn at Plaquemine for a chance to board the bayou steamboat, which was undergoing repairs. We spent seven days there at 20 francs a day, besides 60 francs for transportation three leagues to where the steamboat was. Then we had to pay 35 francs apiece to travel for 24 hours on that boat. We had hoped to reach the landing in it, but the receding waters had left the place so miry, the oxen could not be driven into it. So the boatmen decided to transfer us and our baggage to a small boat that cost us 50 francs to travel four leagues on another little bayou which, they said, would bring us to dry land. As the captain considered this a good plan, I thought it best to do what these men who knew the country advised, so we got into the canoe. The men at the oars were soon pretty tired, and from the second little bayou we passed into a third.

You can form some idea of the place we were in if you recall the descriptions of the waters surrounding Tartarus. The water was black and evil-smelling. As far as the eye could see, it flowed through the most dismal forests which stand in water all but one or two months of the year. The trees have only a little dark foliage high up near their tops, and this is almost hidden under the long gray beards that hang from every branch of these old trees. (This hanging moss is a parasitic plant; when dried and beaten, it becomes a kind of fiber from which the countryfolk make mattresses.) The further we advanced, the denser the forest became; but there was no dry land in sight, not even a sign of it. The day wore on. We had only a little bread to feed the eight people in the boat. I said to the guide, "I think you have lost your way. Would it not be more prudent to turn back and find a place where there is dry land, no matter where?" He replied that that was impossible, and his embarrassed manner convinced me that we were lost in the swamp. Just then we heard shouting. "Listen," he said,

"they are calling from the bank to tell us they are waiting for us."
I answered, "But notice, the shouts are coming from a very different direction."

At that same moment we saw coming rapidly from behind us a canoe filled with Indians, Negroes, and whites, mostly naked except for loin cloths, the most frightful looking men, yelling and whistling as they are represented when rushing to an assured victory. Our boatmen grew pale and not one of them would have been able to put up any resistance. My three young companions were terrified, though they never dreamed of dangers as great as I was picturing to myself. I told them to pray earnestly to God and place themselves under the protection of the Blessed Virgin, and I immediately promised a novena of Masses in return for our safety. The canoe was already upon us. The savages stared at us as if petrified, then passed by, after having stopped some time close beside us. They eyed our water bottles, which they thought were filled with the liquor they are so crazy about. They seemed to have nothing to eat with them, yet they left us without asking for anything. I thought they had passed us by just to go ahead and wait for us at a place where they could attack us more easily, so I gave myself up to prayer, recommending my soul to God in preparation for death, but to my companions I only suggested prayer and patience. As the boatmen were exhausted with rowing, I feared my complaints might annoy them.

At last, just when I was positive we were lost in the swamp, dry land suddenly appeared, and we saw a cart drawn by four oxen waiting for us. It was like a resurrection—I really was not ready to die. I shall never forget the names of those animals: *Flambeau, Rousseau, Gaillard, Tout-Blanc*—the words rang through the woods every minute, for the driver had to urge them on continually over the muddy ground. We spent the night at an inn, where a few days before all this the travelers staying there had been robbed. But we were quite safe. At two o'clock in the morning we set out again in a cart and at nine o'clock [on August 7] reached the convent of the Sacred Heart.[48] Father Rossi, pastor of another parish in the Opelousas district, was just leaving. He continued to say Mass for us twice a week while I was there, as the priest whom Monseigneur has named to serve as chaplain had not arrived. I have had no news from either France or St. Louis. Letters ordinarily take six weeks to reach here from St. Louis. I asked Mother Octavie to hold at Florissant any that might come during my absence, as I thought they would not reach me at Opelousas. . . .

Mother Duchesne gives not the slightest hint of the good she accomplished at Grand Coteau by her fervor, her sympathetic love and interest, her self-forgetfulness, nor of the reaction of the community to her visit, but Mother Eugenie Audé described to Mother Barat the emotional welcome this surprise visit called forth from her, and Mother Xavier Murphy wrote to the Mother General on August 27:

> And now, my dear Mother, your prediction has come true. On the 7th of this month I had the sweet consolation of embracing our dear Mother Duchesne. You can easily understand my joy that day. Like the old man Simeon I might have said I have nothing else to desire, and I was willing to end my pilgrimage. I had made a novena to the Sacred Heart to obtain the grace of a visit from her. I had such need to pour out my heart to someone in whom I had confidence. Yet in that state of soul I knew that there was no sacrifice I would not make for the greater glory of God, no privation I would not endure in this dear land of my adoption. Still the fear of offending God, of breaking the solemn promises I had made before the altar alarmed me. But Mother Duchesne, to whom I revealed my thoughts, quieted all my fears. She understood my French, and I have never spoken confidentially to anyone with more ease and never experienced more peace and consolation than when she gave me her answers. She is a woman entirely according to my heart.

Mother Duchesne had, as Mother Eugenie expressed it, "time to examine the little house of Grand Coteau and judge for herself how it is being conducted." She met the seventeen pupils of the academy, among them Mary Ann Hardey, who, as Mother Aloysia, would become illustrious in the Society's annals. She discussed with Mother Audé the unhealthy physical condition of the nuns and the means that might be taken to relieve some of them of their too heavy load of work. She was puzzled by a certain aloofness in Mother Audé's manner, though she did not know that the young superior had during the past year made quite definite efforts to have her convent withdrawn entirely from the supervision of Mother Duchesne and placed directly under the Superior General in France. That very request had caused St. Madeleine Sophie to emphasize the fact that Mother Duchesne was, as it were, her Provincial—though that title was not in use in the Society. "I have given her full authority. . . . I have given her full powers. Have recourse to her in all ordinary cases." [49] There was, however, a strong bent toward independence in Mother Audé and this would show itself as the years went by.

Mother Duchesne spent her fifty-third birthday at Grand Coteau. There was no Mass in the convent chapel that August 29, but Mother Murphy noticed that she spent long hours that day before the tabernacle. Only at the evening recreation did she tell the little group that the day had special significance for her. On September 2 she told them goodbye. "Judge of our feelings!" wrote Mother Murphy, *"Dieu seul! Dieu Seul!"*

The trip to New Orleans took almost a week. There Mother Duchesne and Therese Pratte found hospitality for a few days at the Ursuline convent. Several friends came to call, among them Fathers Borgna and Ferrari,[50] but Philippine found time to write a sheaf of letters, one of them to Mother Marie de Brossec, whom she had met at Poitiers in 1818. In her friendly fashion she wrote:

I received your letter in New Orleans on the 9th of this month. I was obliged to come down here on my way to St. Louis from Opelousas, where I had brought two novices to Mother Eugenie to keep her from killing herself with work. There was no way to go back up the river except by coming here to take a boat bound for St. Louis.

Our new house in the Opelousas country is charming. It is as large as that of Florissant. The chapel is pretty and devotional, the sacristy well equipped with sacred vessels, thanks to the generosity of several priests. There are 17 children in the boarding school and five or six others are expected in a few days. God is quite visibly blessing that house, which is well established at the end of a single year and is out of debt. But an even more evident blessing is the astonishing progress of the children in piety and studies. . . . The parents are all well pleased, and this school has roused a desire for a similar one in this city. Several priests are urging it and two who are in the best position to help us spoke to me yesterday about a large estate located far out in one of the suburbs, which a rich man is willing to give for educational purposes. He will also allow us the free use of a house for two or three years. And last of all, he will procure the money without interest, or at a very low rate, with which we could build a convent and school. I am leaving here in a few hours and have already sealed my letter to our Mother. Having neither space nor time to add to it, I beg you to give her this letter, which will show her more than ever the goodness of God in our regard.

I beg you to recommend your Sisters of Louisiana to dear Mother Grosier and to all the community. We love to talk together about our Sisters in France, for the ocean that separates us seems to put no distance between us. Our hearts cross it rapidly to unite themselves to you and share in your merits. We do very little over here, but we hope we are preparing for a future that will bear much fruit.

My companions at St. Ferdinand will have more recent news from France than I have, for while I am running around the world, I cannot hope to receive letters. They would not catch up with me, even if they were sent to me. . . .

In another letter written that same day she commented: "I leave today by a steamboat that is going upstream. It is a long, expensive trip, but it was necessary; and Divine Providence is never wanting where necessity is concerned."[51] *Today* was September 11; the steamboat was the *Hecla;* the trip would last *80 days.* After the harrowing experiences of the first six weeks, Mother Duchesne wrote her classic letter of October 30, 1822, "On board the steamboat *Cincinnati*":

It may astonish you that, having written to you at the beginning of September from New Orleans, as I was about to leave that city, I have not yet reached St. Louis. But God has punished me for some of my faults by leaving me to wander about the world for so long a time with no spiritual help whatsoever.

They had assured me that there was no danger of yellow fever in New Orleans this year. So I went with all assurance to ask hospitality with the religious of St. Ursula. But the pupil who was traveling with me was not feeling very well, and I developed a little fever on the eve of our departure. I realized that the nuns were frightened lest we should contract that dreaded disease which, they say, only attacks people who are not used to the climate. The doctor and the superior both thought it wise for us to leave at once in order to escape the disease. I wanted to do this myself, though I knew I was in no condition to undertake a trip of 300 to 400 leagues through the wilderness to St. Louis. How I do wish we had a house of the Sacred Heart in New Orleans! The place they offer us is quite safe from the contagion of yellow fever, which is prevalent only in the central part of the city. But God seems only to hint at that foundation which I so desire as a link with you and with Opelousas.

They ordered a carriage for us and I went in horror to the steamboat. There my fever went up again, and on the second day of the trip, within 24 hours, we had three deaths on the boat: the captain, the first mate, and a passenger. A young man who had been sent from France by the hospital at Lyons was traveling with us. That same day he felt so ill, he got off the boat at a village where they tell me he died. Fortunately there was a priest in the place.[52] Serious cases of fever continued on the steamboat and I was suffering in every way, seeing men die like animals, with no help either human or divine, without that tender sympathy that alleviates suffering, and hearing people singing gay songs beside the very bodies of the dead.

I thought it prudent to get off the boat at Natchez, which is 100 leagues above New Orleans and is the last town or village on the way to St. Louis.[53] But on reaching there, we learned that we could not enter the town as we came from New Orleans and they feared we might bring yellow fever. So we got off the boat and remained on the sandy shore opposite the town while a passenger tried to find us lodging. We were refused at several houses, but finally a man took us in. He had lost his wife just three weeks before, and he gave us her bed, which still retained the odor of medicines and other marks of illness. The bedding had not been washed since her death. I was at the very crisis of the fever, but I held myself as straight as I could in order to hide the fact. I succeeded to some extent for four days, for they spoke only English and I remained hidden, as far as possible, treating myself. And God blessed my efforts, for since then the high fever has gradually worn off and for a week I have been quite well.

I wrote to the pastor [Father Maenhaut] in order that I might see him and find a lodging where there were some women. He was ill at the time, but on the fifth day he came to see us and had us received into a very fine home on the same side of the river, where we had every physical care that could relieve and rest the body. The lady, a Mrs. Davis, is a Catholic of Spanish origin, who speaks English, Spanish, and French perfectly. She offered us just everything, even carriage and horseback rides. The pastor had promised that he would return to hear my confession, but I waited another week, for he did not have money for the trip across the river. I tried to get into the town to go to Mass on Sunday. The doctors had a conference on the subject, along with several other people, and the reply was negative. This contributed to my having another attack of fever. Never have I felt a greater need for Mass and the sacraments. This came from having seen death at such close range.

My fever was a good excuse for not appearing at dinner when several officials from Natchez were present. They had been told that there was a nun in the house—a superior, what's more—and they wanted to see what kind of an animal that was. They kept on asking my traveling companion if I would not appear at least after dinner, and how I was dressed. One in particular, who spoke French, said it would give him much pleasure to talk with me. All this was repeated to me that evening by the mistress of the house. I told her I was delighted to have had an excuse to remain in my room.

Two days later the pastor came with charity to hear my confession, but that is the only spiritual help I had had since leaving New Orleans: neither Mass nor Communion nor any other confession, and that with a trip of 10 or 12 more days ahead of us if the navigation was smooth. In all it will be 60 days of the most rigorous fast I have ever made, perhaps in all my life, even including the time of the Revolution. Still in the midst of these hard privations I always see the Arm of Divine Providence stretched out to us. We came upon the steamboat *Hecla* which we had left at Natchez. It could no longer navigate; its boilers had burst: the steam had killed two men and burned several others badly, and thirteen men had died of the fever on board. One could not fancy a sadder situation than that of the three men left to guard the boat in a place where they could procure nothing. There is practically no doubt that we also would have been among the number of those who died, had we remained on board. During his illness I talked several times to one of those who died. I trust the dear Lord was lenient with him; he had no religion and was not baptized.

I learned at Natchez that there had been much sickness at St. Louis, that Monseigneur had been ill and had lost one of his best priests—the very one for whom I had told you Sister Catherine might have been able to conduct a school. I have had no news from St. Ferdinand. The length of my trip and the accidents I have experienced have made it impossible for letters to reach me. This makes me very eager to get home. I had written to Mother Octavie that I might have to return to Opelousas for the winter, but no steamboats went downstream while we were in Natchez, and as this one was going upstream, I thought the will of God was indicated by that circumstance. I am sorry, however, that I held out that hope to Mother Eugenie, who has had a severe illness. I do not know how a letter from her reached me at Natchez. It informed me that she had a fever, along with 3 or 4 of our Sisters. That grieves me the more because I am going far from her. But the fevers in that part of Louisiana are not dangerous and I trust them all to Divine Providence. Mother Xavier is expending all her charity on them.

Mother Eugenie is so attracted to New Orleans, she talked to me about it continually. I was obliged to warn her to make neither advances nor promises, for she is the one to whom they are writing on the subject. . . . Our confessor at Florissant wants us to open a mission among the Osage Indians. I do not know what to think about such an undertaking, so far away, with so few priests, and without government support. The Jesuits always had that help.

During my trip I have been reading about the voyage of the Count de Laperouse. While writing as a philosopher, he shows the good that was being accomplished in California.[54]

After summarizing Laperouse's descriptions of the Jesuit and Franciscan missions of the eighteenth century, she continued:

The more consolation I drew from all this, the more I realized the impossibility of doing a similar work unless the Congress of the United States would adopt the Catholic religion for missions among the Indians. . . . This has already been proposed in an effort to civilize the Indians living within the boundaries of the states.

P.S. [undated]

I intended to finish this letter when I reached St. Ferdinand, but the slowness of our trip makes me want to close it now, so that if by good luck I can find an opportunity of mailing it before my arrival there, it will be ready. I made my retreat on the steamboat. Everyone on board spoke English, and those who understood French did not speak it at all. So I took advantage of being alone with God, for after such a long absence I foresaw it would be difficult to get my retreat in after I reach Florissant. I had no books except a Bible I found on the steamboat and my little Office book. For the meditations I tried to recall those of St. Ignatius and Bourdaloue. The woman who shares the same cabin with me comes there only to go to bed. I received in New Orleans the letter in which you tell me about Mr. Inglesi, and also that final vows cannot be made before the age of 21. . . .

Part Two of this adventurous story appears in the letter she wrote the day after reaching home.[55] Exhausted though she was— for she had been obliged to rest in St. Louis for two days with the Pratte family before driving out to Florissant—she was eager to undertake new works of zeal. Her insatiable love for the Sacred Heart of Jesus and her desire to bring into His kingdom the neglected children of the frontier whom she had seen at close range in her travels urged her to plead with Mother Barat the cause of ventures for which she had no human means of accomplishment: [56]

My last letter to you was written on board the *Cincinnati*. I had already sealed it when the steamboat ran aground on a sandbank in midstream about 100 leagues below St. Louis near New Madrid. I wanted to finish the trip by the overland route, and that would have been quite possible. But in this land age must bow to youth. The young girl with whom I was traveling did not want to go that way. People sided with her and built up imaginary fears in her mind. They tried to deceive me; and as I would not in conscience leave her to travel alone nor make the difficult trip myself without a companion, I remained there doing nothing until Divine Providence inspired a French lady in New Madrid to invite us to her home.[57] We went there in a canoe and stayed five days until the water rose in the river and lifted the steamboat off the sand bank. Then we returned to the boat by canoe with two young ladies who were going to St. Louis to make their first Communion. One of them, twenty years old, knew very well how to curl her hair and dance and sing, but she could not make the Sign of the Cross nor say the Our Father or the Hail Mary, nor did she know the meaning of Mass and Communion. The other, aged fourteen, is going to attend our boarding school; she thought herself well instructed, but did not know what first Communion meant. Neither of them had ever been to confession. I tried to teach them their catechism, and after much explanation on my part I got from one of them the information that on the night before He died our Lord changed bread and wine into stone.

On this trip I have seen so much ignorance in the many little villages that have sprung up in the last four years along the neck of the river, that I am more than ever convinced of the great need there is for teachers who could be placed gradually in the larger towns where there are priests—towns like New Madrid, where there are sixty or eighty Catholic families. . . . I wish you would approve of our training some of the girls in the parish school for this work. Later on they could become members of non-cloistered Sisterhoods if they were not suited to our own order. I cannot tell you what Monseigneur thinks of this idea as he is absent just now. He has been in Baltimore for the past two months. I did not know this, as I received no news from my Sisters here during my trip. . . . That trip ended, fortunately, on the eve of St. Andrew's feast, during the novena to St. Francis Xavier.

I found everyone well when I reached here, but nearly all the community had been ill, several dangerously, also some of the children and three priests—these latter all at the same time in the sacristy [which was turned into an infirmary for them].[58] The chaplain came home from the Osage Indian mission in an almost dying condition. Florissant never had so much sickness before, and the same is true throughout the United States. . . .

Mother Octavie governed the house very well during my absence. They tell me Bishop Du Bourg has announced that he is going to live at the rectory in Florissant and take his meals in one of the sacristy rooms, so as not to bring distractions to our convent.[59] On my trip I missed 120 Masses, counting just one a day,

80 communions, about 20 confessions, and practically all the Benedictions of the Blessed Sacrament for four months. But I believe all these sacrifices are not without value; perhaps several foundations may come from them.

Kneeling in spirit at your feet, dear Reverend Mother, I offer my wishes for you to the Heart of Jesus. May He bless the year that is ahead of us, may He take care of you, help you bear the burden you carry, and never let me add to it by my faults.

eight

Stability in Suffering and Joy

I. 1823—1825

Receive, O Holy Trinity, this oblation . . .

Liturgy of the Mass

DURING THE WEEKS THAT FOLLOWED her return from Louisiana, Philippine learned much that distressed her. Mother Octavie's management of the household had been less satisfactory than appeared at first sight. Lacking firmness, she had let the children get out of hand. Mother Duchesne found it hard to reprove her, but that was her duty. She was troubled, too, by the worldly ways reported of former pupils of the Sacred Heart and made a subject of gossip in St. Louis. The town was just then agog with scandal over the conduct of a group of prominent Catholics who were taking advantage of the Bishop's absence to foment discontent and carry out a scheme that did them little credit, yet only a handful of the faithful were upholding the Bishop's cause. There was danger that the nuns at Florissant might be involved in the unhappy affair if they were asked to shelter the luckless prelate. Although this and much else was weighing on Philippine's heart as the New Year dawned, she began her letter to Mother Barat on January 4, 1823, with an outpouring of affectionate memories:

> This time of the year renews in my heart all its keenest and most grateful sentiments toward you and toward God, recalling that famous retreat during which you admitted me into the dear Society. So deeply attached to the Holy Mountain as I was then, I never dreamed that I should one day find myself so far away from

373

you who captivated me with such loving bonds. God, who willed that I should be here, gave me grace to break the chains I loved so dearly; and I have reason to marvel at the power of His grace, which makes me so happy and contented in the separation from all I loved most and without the least success that might make me forget my sacrifices. After that long trip [to Louisiana] during which I feared several times that I was going to die far away from a convent of the Sacred Heart, . . . it was a sweet joy to be with my Sisters once more and able to live again according to our holy rules. But there is pain in learning that most of the pupils who have left our school are giving themselves up to worldly pleasures and forgetting God.

There is no denying the fact that temptations are great in St. Louis, and it adds to our distress to realize what we have to fear for the girls who are still in our school. I consider St. Louis as bad as Malacca in the days of St. Xavier. After a short period of fervor, or rather effervescence, there has followed a time of great indifference as regards religion and of excess in the pursuit of pleasure. Our children are taken to balls, shows, speeches, have bad books in their hands, live in idleness. Already several vocations have been undermined in these surroundings, and I foresee that here, as in the time of Jesus Christ, the poor will be chosen to work for Him in preference to the rich. Since I came back from Louisiana I have admitted two postulants. . . . I hope they will take the training; we have such need of helpers. At New Madrid we saw girls twenty years old who did not even know how to make the Sign of the Cross.

I could not correct some abuses that crept in during my absence without reprimanding gently the one who through kindness had not held to *discipline*. But if this is lacking, everything is lost here where insubordination is considered a virtue. Even the orphans are complaining about their food and work, saying they are treated like slaves. Father Martial carries on his work with a firm hand, and in Kentucky Monseigneur David, who is Bishop Flaget's co-adjutor, conducts a large college with severe discipline, while in our vicinity [St. Louis], where they tried to be easy on the pupils and compromising, the institution is going downhill.[1]

Things are going badly for religion in St. Louis. As the debt on the church has not been paid, those who hold the mortgage [through loans made for its construction] want to sell the property of the presbytery, including the Bishop's house and garden, etc. Monseigneur [Du Bourg] is in Baltimore just now and the priest who holds the power of attorney for him dares not make a move to buy the church and shoulder the debt.[2] All this is a bitter blow for Monseigneur and his priests, toward whom these men are

acting with the greatest ingratitude, having given them no remuneration for their services. I was told that the Bishop might be
forced to come here to live—perhaps these people were just sound-
ing me out. Our own church still has a debt of 3000 francs. The
pastor has nothing left, and we are clothing him. I beg you to give
me an answer with regard to a foundation in New Orleans and
also with regard to Sisters for small [rural] schools. Mother
Eugenie says you never want us to make foundations for small
communities of three or four, but many villages cannot support
more than that. . . .

On the account sheet which I am closing . . . the amount spent
on food is in no way proportioned to the other expenses because
we receive so much help in this matter from our garden, which
yielded a hundred bushels of potatoes and many other things, and
from the milk of our eight fine cows and the eggs of our sixty
chickens. The repairs include the replastering of some rooms along
with some wainscotting, and the building of a long plank fence
instead of a wall. We do not owe Monseigneur any money now,
but we do owe 2500 francs to a gentleman who cleared us of debt.
Such is our financial standing at the close of five years, whereas
Mother Eugenie at the close of one year gave us more than 4000
francs. From this you may judge of the real necessity there is for
our having a convent in New Orleans to help support our work.
Here, far from receiving help from anyone, our first duty is to aid
the priests, and perhaps Monseigneur himself.

Mother Lucille is excellent, except that she is inclined to run
up bills too quickly. Mother Octavie is always amiable and everyone loves her. Sisters Catherine and Marguerite have grown stout,
but they are active and helpful. The five novices have good will
and are taking the training. I hold very much to study and I have
put Mother Lucille back to it; for if she is ever superior, she will
need it. . . . I have not yet received the sketch of Aloysia's life.
One must always recommend letters and parcels to St. Anthony of
Padua. He never fails. . . . My last letter went off on a steamboat
that got icebound on the river. This one will go by post to New
Orleans. I am addressing it to kind Father Richard. He was
stricken with yellow fever, but has recovered, as has also one of
the vicars-general [Father Philip Borgna], but another one [Father
Andrew Ferrari] died of it, and this is a great loss.

Dear Reverend Mother, please forgive me all the past and pray
that in the future I may do better. I am with profound respect in
the Sacred Hearts of Jesus and Mary, your unworthy and entirely
devoted

PHILIPPINE.

Some days later Philippine sat reading the *Missouri Republican* for January 9. Scanning the Post Office Notice inserted by Wilson P. Hunt, postmaster in St. Louis, she saw her own name listed among the 247 persons notified that letters were waiting to be called for.[3] Four letters on hand in St. Louis! At once the convent factotum, Martin Lepere, was dispatched for them. Though they required no immediate answer, Philippine had much on her mind and heart that could be expressed only to Mother Barat, and she was happy to have an excuse for a second letter within the month. Her reference to Monseigneur Du Bourg as "our Seer" (*notre Voyant*) seems slightly ironical, but it is impossible to know the exact connotation with which she used the term on January 16, 1823:

> I received two letters from you at the same time. There is universal joy when we hear from you, for then we feel nearer to our Mother and to the dear religious family, and that is a very pleasant feeling, even if it is an illusion. Your first letter went to Opelousas before coming here. Perhaps it was enclosed in a packet of mail. The people in New Orleans always prefer to send things to Eugenie rather than to me, so completely has she won the esteem and affection of all who have the good of the Society at heart. That is what happened to the box Mr. Jouve sent me, and I was so eager to get it, for it contained galloon for a pretty vestment I am making. He had already sent me the material, but there is no galloon to be had in this country. I wrote so often to Grand Coteau about it, I finally got my galloon, but not the other things that were in the box. I beg you, my very dear Mother, not to pack in the same box things that are for them and for us. It costs almost as much to send a box from New Orleans to Opelousas as to St. Louis because of the difficulty of transportation, and the return and forwarding charges are an enormous expense. Mother Eugenie is quite as well off as we are—if not better, and she has not our obligations and our debts. She receives many presents, and just recently a beautiful clock. There is great inconvenience in not having a house in New Orleans to receive the mail. Recently a letter for us was found in a table drawer at the Ursuline Convent, and it had been there quite a while. Another time our letters were put on a vessel sailing for Havre, though they were addressed to Bordeaux, and it would have been better to wait for the right vessel, for I had requested the superior in Bordeaux to forward by opportunity letters that I had sent her and that were not urgent. Then, too, the paper we get here is not so good nor so thin as the kind we get in France. I do not want to be importunate in asking for things, but in our country one must save if one is to live.

I do not know where we shall get the 6000 francs we owe in France.[4] We are in neither Peru nor Mexico nor in the rich islands, but rather close to Canada which, far from enriching France, cost her dearly and was the land in which her missionaries suffered most. Here we can hope to gain only souls—and a very small number of them. Only our desire to support our work and have more children in the school urges me to plead for New Orleans. I still hope the letter I wrote from Opelousas about New Orleans may change your decision, since we are not asking any help for the foundation, and it really is necessary to make a change at Opelousas. Those two heads do not fit into the same bonnet. There is no talk of this new foundation just now, for we have said we must first have your consent. Our *Seer* is away just now. I think he went to Baltimore to straighten out a misunderstanding with his colleagues or to ask the Jesuits to help with missions to the savages. I feel that nothing of this kind can be done without them. We are still nursing the priest [Father De La Croix] who made the last trip to the Indian country and came back in a most pitiable condition. What is needed for these poor people is many missionaries who will attract them and live amongst them. The trips to their part of the country are too long, too costly, and too dangerous to be undertaken often, and where shall we get the funds necessary for them? Oh, how hard it is to see a minister of the Gospel suffer so much in so magnificent a cause and to be unable to help him!

Your second letter (September, 1822) came by way of New York and, I know not how, was entrusted first to the Archbishop of Baltimore, who is a long way from here, and then to our Bishop, who was away from here at the time. Through the newspaper I learned that there were letters for me in the post office in St. Louis —they advertise letters so people will come for them. How eagerly I sent for them, hoping for news from you, and what a joy it was not to be disappointed. We had a reprimand from the *Seer*. Besides, my letter had been unsealed, as had also a large packet for him which had been sent to Baltimore; at Louisville it had been unwrapped, then sent back to St. Louis. They do this kind of thing in order to find money, and they think he has plenty. . . .

After some complicated explanations about money matters, she continues:

I am really chagrined and humiliated to think you lost that note for a thousand francs. It happened as a result of the naïveté of our Sisters.[5] They had not been in New Orleans fifteen minutes when they gave a scrupulous account of all the money they had to the person interested. That person wrote to me the same day, pointing out to me the *beauty* of our position, and saying that in conse-

quence he was going to dispose of the 1000 franc note on Bordeaux.
The same thing happened to the 1500 francs Mother Eugenie sent
me, in spite of my cleverness in hiding the money. We owed him
that, however, so it was a matter of justice to pay him.

In my last letter I sent you a copy of our accounts for the year,
and I told you I had found the children quite out of hand. I attribute this in part to the departure of some of the older pupils, to
the weakness of the surveillantes, and to the illness that tried the
convent: three priests to nurse at one time—one for 50 days, and
all the active members of the community ill, one after another.

The single entry in Mother Duchesne's *Journal* for February,
1823, is made up of jottings that paint a sad picture:

The withdrawal and complaints of two postulants who had no
vocation; the illness and death of Miss Leduc; [6] the worldliness of
our pupils who have left school and their forgetfulness of us; [7] the
indocility of the present pupils; calumnies circulated about us. All
this makes us feel the weight of the cross. And to it must be added
our poverty and an illness that has attacked nearly all the religious
and a number of the children. [8]

There is, however, a note of hope in the entry: "We have
learned that Father Rosati, superior of the Lazarists, has been
named Coadjutor to Monseigneur Du Bourg. He has asked us to
make a novena for his intention without telling us what it is."

The news regarding Father Rosati's nomination was not accurate. True, he had received apostolic letters from Rome in
November, 1822, informing him that the territories of Mississippi
and Alabama had been erected into a vicariate apostolic and that
he had been appointed Vicar Apostolic of the region with the title
of Bishop of Tenegra *in partibus infidelium*. These letters, bearing
the date of August 13, 1822, had been brought to America by
Archbishop Maréchal upon his return to Baltimore from Rome.
Believing that circumstances justified a petition on his part to be
spared the episcopal dignity, Father Rosati returned the apostolic
brief to Rome. He did not know at the time that Bishop Du Bourg,
on learning of the appointment in Baltimore, had written a strong
protest to Rome and had recommended Rosati as his coadjutor
with special jurisdiction in the upper portion of the vast diocese of
Louisiana and the Floridas. [9] The misinformation circulated in and
around St. Louis regarding Father Rosati's appointment reached
Florissant at about the same time as the letter he wrote to Mother

Duchesne begging prayers, and is reflected in her reply of February 17:

> I received your two letters, the first in answer to mine, and the second asking for prayers. I had these begun immediately and await a successful outcome from the goodness of God—perhaps not according to your own wish, but for the greater good of the mission to which you have consecrated yourself. I believe that what distressed you so much was the news that you are to be a bishop, as we have just heard. Although it is one of the laws of charity to mourn with those who mourn, it is impossible to obey in this instance. For a long time all eyes have turned to you when Monseigneur spoke of choosing a coadjutor, and I saw on my trip south how general this wish was. Our own interest adds to our contentment. We have experienced so much kindness and such unselfish zeal on the part of the members of your Society, that it is very dear to us, and all that tends to strengthen it in this country contributes to our happiness. . . .
>
> I am told that Father Cellini has not adjusted himself at Opelousas. If this is so, you know it. If the choice of his successor depends on you, we would like it to fall on Father Dahmen in the event that he is no longer contented at Ste Genevieve.[10] The Bishop seemed desirous of assigning him to Opelousas and has already told my Sisters how much they would profit by such a choice.

Three days later she wrote a pathetic little letter to the Mother General:

> I have already told you about the storm raised in St. Louis over the church debt. To collect on their loans, these men wanted to sell the property right up to the rectory. The lawyer for the Bishop's enemies has said very violent things against him. They went so far as to say that the King of France had made his gifts, not to Monseigneur, but to the city of St. Louis. Monseigneur was already disgusted with this sterile and ungrateful diocese; now his trip to Baltimore—the purpose of which is not known, the nomination of Monseigneur Rosati to the episcopacy (he was superior at the seminary), these recent events, about which the Bishop is informed, and several other happenings that preceded them, all make some people believe that he will accept the archbishopric of Baltimore and never come back to this part of the country. This is not certain, but it is possible; and if he does remain in Baltimore, a number of priests say they will not stay here. What will your poor daughters do then? But we are not discouraged. If we have

fewer spiritual helps, we shall try to profit better by what we have.

We received two postulants, each of whom brought her clothes tied up in a handkerchief. They left at the end of 19 days, complaining about the cold, the work, etc. That has been noised abroad unpleasantly. When a child has a chilblain, it causes a sensation—they say we let the children get their feet frozen. Chilblain or freezing—it's all the same thing here. You can understand how we come in for a share of the hatred felt for the priests. Can they love us when they expose to danger the young girls who leave our school? It is hard for these girls to struggle when their own parents thrust them into temptation. The most outstanding pupil we had last year gave herself up immediately to balls, comedies, expensive clothes, hence to loss of time and neglect of prayer. And these are the fruits of our labor.

Just now we are in a bad position: we shall be obliged to send home the oldest girl in the school, and what a furor that will cause! Her parents want her to be a nun! Pray for me, advise me, Reverend Mother. I would have more courage if I were close to you, for then I should have less fear of making a mistake.[11]

Father Philip Borgna, who had been stationed in New Orleans since his ordination and had suffered from an attack of yellow fever in September, 1822, passed through St. Louis on his way to Europe in March, 1823, and spent some days at Florissant. This gave Philippine a safe opportunity to send letters across the Atlantic. The handsome clock presented to Mother Eugenie had roused in her a desire for a similar one, recalling, as it did, the old timepiece she had known in her youth at Grâne. Now she would have one on the frontier if she could enlist the help of her family, so on March 21 she wrote to Madame Jouve:

I am eagerly waiting for news from you, and now I have a way of getting information directly through Father Borgna, a Lazarist missionary. He is a man of great merit, who does everything he can for us. He will be in Lyons for two weeks, and perhaps he will be able to see you.

Each year I have sent my life certificate to my brother and have never gotten a penny from the state. This time I have sent copies of these same certificates to our cousin, Augustin Perier, hoping he will push the matter with some zeal. If he does get any money for me, ask him to purchase for me a clock like the one at Grâne. It cost only 100 francs. Perhaps it would be even less now. Such things are very expensive out here. The route by Bordeaux is slower now than that by Havre. Vessels are sailing for New

Orleans from the latter port continually. Tell my cousin this, or
my brother, if they send me the clock. I hope that in a few years
we shall have a house in New Orleans. Property has been offered
to us, but it is very difficult to build a convent. . . . If you visit
Fourvière, do not fail to pray for us to Mary, Mother of us all.

To Mother Barat she gave news of the novices, who were a
grave responsibility for her, and of the hardships they faced so
courageously:

The priest who will deliver this letter is one of our most fervent
Lazarist missionaries. His superior is sending him to Rome on business connected with the mission to which he is completely devoted. For two years he has braved the danger of death during
epidemics in New Orleans. He expects to return there in a year. If
we make a foundation there, it would be very safe for two of our
religious to travel with him. He acts as our devoted commissioner
in that city and buys all provisions for Mother Eugenie.

I shall write no Jeremiad in this letter, for on Sunday during
the novena to St. Xavier [March 4-12] I had the consolation of
seeing the veil given to Sister Elizabeth Huber, a pupil of our
parish school. She is sixteen years old, an active worker, and seems
very firm in her vocation. A still greater joy was ours on the
feast of St. Joseph, when Sisters Xavier and Regis Hamilton and
Mary Ann Summers made their first vows. These are the *élite*
among our novices. Regis thought she would not live through the
day, so great was her joy; and she repeated this so often I began to
fear she might be right. That would have been a terrible loss for
us. There is in that soul no obstacle to grace. She does all the good
she can. Her capacity for study is mediocre, but she is not yet 18
years old, though she is quite tall, so she may develop further intellectually. Her sister has great talents along all lines except those
of household duties—these will be Regis' part. Xavier will have to
work harder for perfection, but she has real courage and devotedness. All three have the advantage of speaking and writing the two
languages. They are Americans and have learned French since
they came to us.[12] We would have postponed the ceremony until
after the Bishop's arrival, but the novices were already in retreat
when he wrote that he would be here only later on. They expect
him any day in St. Louis. . . .

I was hard pressed to clothe our novices in new habits for their
vows. An old soutane left by the Trappist Father made a choir
cloak for one. Sister Mary Ann's shawl and veil were made from
a black crepon dress left by a pupil, and Sister Xavier's habit was
entirely new except for an old cape which she wore in honor of

her Spouse, the Poor Man, by choice. There are advantages in the life of hardship and privation here. I must admit I fear for those who have had a life of ease and convenience. Here we must be ready for anything; one of us milks the cows, not in a stable but often in mud ankle deep, in rain, in snow; another makes the fire in the kitchen; another heats the bake-oven; at almost any time they have to cross the swampy yard that cannot be drained properly. Clothing and rooms suffer from these inconveniences—no sabots or galoshes, as these are unknown here. We are waiting impatiently for the life of Aloysia. . . .[13]

On the feast of the Finding of the Holy Cross, May 3, the community and the children of the boarding and day schools gathered in the meadow and went in procession to the little grove beyond to assist at the erection of a devotional cross that faced the convent and stood out against the background of trees. It was the first outdoor shrine Mother Duchesne planned for Florissant. Bishop Du Bourg saw and approved when he came on May 8 for first Communion and confirmation. He had just returned from the East by way of Kentucky and had much to tell, though little time for the telling. Mother Duchesne noted all briefly in her *Journal*, then wrote it all to the Mother General, along with comments on persons and things that reveal more about her than do the bits of information she delighted in recounting:

FLORISSANT, May 20, 1823

MY REVEREND AND BELOVED MOTHER,

It is a long time since I had any news from you, and this is a great privation for my heart. None of your last letters told me you had received those in which I told you about my trip to Lower Louisiana, during which I reminded you about the project of a foundation in New Orleans. Your replies to my former suggestions in regard to this indicate rather plainly that you are not in favor of it. Monseigneur Du Bourg, who was among the first to speak of this establishment, no longer shows any interest in it. Unquestionably he considers us too few in numbers to attempt such an enterprise without help from you, and he knows you have no one to send just now. . . .

Monseigneur himself told us this news when he returned from Baltimore. He spent hardly any time in St. Louis, came on the feast of the Ascension to give confirmation in our church and first Communion to 14 children, boarders and day pupils, left the next day, and that was the extent of his visit. He made far fewer inquiries than usual about what concerns the convent. People say he is no longer our Bishop, and as a matter of fact he signs himself Bishop of New Orleans now, and not Bishop of Louisiana, as formerly. It is rumored that our new Bishop is a Sulpician—others say Father Rosati, a Roman priest and a member of the Lazarist order. I believe that neither of them will be more than coadjutor to Monseigneur Du Bourg. His hurried departure for the South [on May 11] is causing the departure of several priests. One is going to join a religious order in Rome; others are to be parish priests in Lower Louisiana. Our own pastor is thinking of going south, for he says the Jesuits will serve us adequately.

If you do not yet know what took place at Georgetown between Monseigneur and the Jesuits, that last sentence may surprise you. Bishop Du Bourg did not give us all the details about that fine and inestimable acquisition for this part of the world, where the desire for the greater glory of God should be one's only riches and support. A priest told me that the Jesuit superiors were considering the closing of the novitiate [in Maryland] because there were too many foreigners in it.[14] Among them seven young Flemings, full of ardor, zeal, and devotedness, raised a great hue and cry, protesting that they had been brought to America, that they would not leave the house, unless they were placed in another novitiate of the Society of Jesus. Thereupon the superior decided to send them to Missouri, along with the Master of Novices and his assistant, some lay-brothers, and some Negro slaves. They are coming, I am told, in complete dependence on Divine Providence, but they are perfectly happy about it.

According to an agreement made between them and Monseigneur, the latter is giving them his Florissant farm, for which he paid 20,000 francs, and the horses and cattle on it. As the house is too small for the 12 or 15 people who are coming, he told us that some of them will live temporarily in the rectory. Unfortunately the roof and ceiling have not been finished, and we haven't a penny to help with this work. The pastor was having the house completed slowly, as he too is entirely dependent on Providence. There will be no furniture except what we try to give them, and we do not want to be outdone by these good Fathers in trust in Divine Providence. Monseigneur has assigned to them the Missouri country to visit, with St. Charles and two other villages. This is a great deal of work for two priests, as none of the novices have been ordained. . . .

I shall not beg you again to let us make little foundations. As he was passing through Kentucky, Monseigneur secured twelve of the Sisters whose order was established in that diocese by Father Nerinckx, a Flemish priest. These Sisters are called Lovers of Jesus at the Foot of the Cross, and for short Daughters of the Cross.[15] They are very austere. . . .

The convent at Opelousas is flourishing. Mother Eugenie is already thinking of putting up a new building. I am very much opposed to this because of the instability of institutions in this country—they change with the wind. One must go slowly and surely if one is not to get into trouble. It requires just one malicious tongue to empty a boarding school of its pupils. The Religious of the Visitation at Georgetown had 40 boarding pupils and now have only 19, without any hope of increasing that number, for the money shortage is felt in the cities of the East as well as out here.

As for us, we have only 18, and several of these are gratis; others are slow to pay; besides, we have six orphans and seven novices or aspirants who did not even furnish their own clothes. I should like to send home the pupils who do not pay, but several of them might lose their faith, and we should prefer to deprive ourselves of everything rather than have that happen. An establishment in New Orleans would have supported this house, but God does not will it, *Fiat;* for the money-shortage, *Fiat;* for the illnesses, *Fiat.* I have been afraid that Mother Octavie has contracted consumption. She has had several abscesses in her mouth; these have healed, but one of them came through on the outside of her neck. She suffers with the greatest sweetness; her perfect fidelity makes me fear that she is very near her eternal recompense, and her loss would be a severe blow to our convent just now when we are in such a depression. I scarcely think we shall ever get out of it. I even expect to lose other children soon—money is so scarce. . . . Our parish school is also small. You could not find more careless, inept, and unappreciative children. But God be praised in all. All our privations, all our humiliations would not have been too high a price to pay for the happiness of witnessing the success of our Fathers the Jesuits and their heroic virtue. This happiness is so great, I dare not count on it yet, and I dread lest once more someone has built for us a beautiful castle in Spain.

It was not, however, a "beautiful castle in Spain," but a great reality—the Jesuits were at that very moment nearing Shawneetown on the Ohio on a double "broadhorn" raft, and a new chapter was about to open in the life of Philippine Duchesne—a chapter in which joy and pain were strangely intermingled. For five years she had hoped and prayed, yearned and anticipated, pleaded and almost insisted in prayer. If only Divine Providence might send Jesuits to the American frontier! On June 2, 1823—it was a Monday afternoon—Father Charles Felix Van Quickenborne, S.J., arrived at Florissant with Brother Henry Reiselman and Brother Peter de

Meyer and three couples of Negro slaves. On Thursday, eve of the feast of the Sacred Heart, came Father Peter Joseph Timmermans and seven novices.[16] The liturgical feast was celebrated solemnly, but there is no least note of exaltation in the *Journal* entries, nor any allusion to the circumstances of their journey to Missouri.

Mother Duchesne soon learned, however, the story of their poverty in Maryland—so dire that it had threatened to dissolve the novitiate, and the hardships of their journey to Missouri.[17] They had traveled on foot from White Marsh, Maryland, to Wheeling on the Ohio along the old Cumberland Road, accompanying a light spring wagon that carried provisions, kitchen utensils, and the "altar trunk" containing vestments and other equipment for the celebration of Holy Mass. Two larger wagons had been hired to transport the baggage and other furnishings to Wheeling, which the entire party reached on May 7, after about four weeks on the pike. Two large flatboats of the "broadhorn" type were now purchased, as the most economical mode of travel, along with a copy of the *Riverman's Guide*, and the Jesuit community loaded on them their baggage and provisions, their slaves and themselves, to begin a remarkable voyage down the Ohio. The protection of Divine Providence was patent day and night, until the party landed safely at Shawneetown on May 22 and began the long tramp of 150 miles through southern Illinois to St. Louis. On May 31 they caught their first glimpse of the town rising on the western bank of the Mississippi. Ferrying the river they reached the wharf and made their way up the steep, dusty lane called Market Street to the Catholic rectory on Second Street, where they were welcomed by the cathedral priests, Fathers Niel, Saulnier, Michaud, and Deys.[18] They had still some fifteen miles to travel before reaching "the Bishop's farm," which they were to occupy.

Their arrival meant change, and on June 14 there was grief in many hearts as the nuns and children bade farewell to Father De La Croix, the friend and guide of the past four years. He was going south to join Bishop Du Bourg in Louisiana, hoping that the milder climate might restore his shattered health. Mother Duchesne's reverent affection and gratitude toward him came out in her letters to him through the years that followed. He had been so cordial and sympathetic, so ready to accommodate himself to the circumstances and needs of the convent, so eager to help and so grateful for help—all this she would miss, and she seemed already to sense the fact that Father Van Quickenborne, "an excellent religious . . . of too vehement a temper," [19] would be less cordial in his dealings with the nuns.

As Father De La Croix had urged her to send recruits to Opelousas with him aboard the *Dolphin,* the convent was again the scene of a hurried departure, this time for Sisters Marguerite Manteau and Mary Ann Summers. Another of her first companions to America was being sacrificed for the good of the Louisiana mission, another of her best young nuns—and the only one skilled in the preparation of meals. But they were going under very safe escort, and Mother Duchesne was happy on that score. As they left the convent on June 18, she gave them a letter for Father De La Croix, written that very morning:

> I received the little packet of mail which you sent from St. Louis, containing a few books and some unimportant letters. Following your advice, however, and in fear lest our Sisters at Opelousas should kill themselves with work, I decided to let Sister Marguerite [Manteau] and Mary Ann [Summers] go south with you. I might not find so favorable a time or opportunity to send them later on. Under your care they will feel less sharply the sacrifice of separation. Sister Mary Ann is past eighteen years of age and has made her first vows, so she is free to go and does so quite willingly. If, however, there is time, it would be very nice for her to see Mr. Hubert and Mrs. Pratte. The former was her guardian, and Mrs. Pratte has been most kind to her. . . .
>
> As to the expense of the trip, I am giving them $50, which will suffice, I hope, for the steamboat fare. If any unforeseen need for money should arise, Mother Eugenie will pay the rest of the expense. Our prayers will always follow you and all those who have expended so much care and kindness on us. The community sends you respectful greetings. Please accept mine also, along with the expression of my esteem and gratitude in the Heart of Jesus. . . .

By this time Mother Duchesne was acquainted with the entire Jesuit community, though it took her many a day to master the spelling and pronunciation of their names. They were Fathers Charles Felix Van Quickenborne, superior, master of novices, and pastor of St. Ferdinand, and Peter Joseph Timmermans, assistant master of novices, seven young Belgian novices—Felix Verreydt, Francis de Maillet, Judocus Van Assche, Peter John Verhaegen, John Baptist Smedts, John Anthony Elet, and Peter De Smet, and three coadjutor Brothers, Henry Reiselman, Charles Strathan, and Peter De Meyer. She came to know the three couples of Negro slaves, too—Tom and Polly, Moses and Nancy, Isaac and Succy. There was no language barrier to be broken down, for the Jesuits all spoke French and soon all mastered English. But from the outset there was a cool, deliberate aloofness on the part of the Reverend Father Superior and his religious sons that baffled Philippine. She was friendly, eager to help and be helped. She had expected a return of friendship like that to which she had been accustomed in France, where the Jesuits were *nos Pères* ("our Fathers") to the Religious of the Sacred Heart.

For five years she had yearned for spiritual direction of the Ignatian kind, and on June 26 she noted in her *Journal* that the community and novices had gone to confession and placed themselves under the direction of the Jesuit superior. But this was quite contrary to the taste and conscience of Father Van Quickenborne. There had been no mention of the spiritual care of the nuns at Florissant in the agreement drawn up between Bishop Du Bourg and Father Charles Neale, superior of the Maryland Jesuits. There is nothing to indicate that Father Van Quickenborne had even been informed of their presence in his new parish before he reached St. Louis. Had he known it, he would certainly have asked some directive in their regard before setting out for Missouri. As it was, soon after his arrival in Florissant he was writing to his superior in Maryland to know whether he, being a Jesuit, could take charge of the *Dames du Sacré Coeur*, hear their confessions, and attend to them as his immediate predecessor was accustomed to do. The answer was that the matter would be laid before the Father General in Rome and his answer relayed in time to Father Van Quickenborne, but *ad interim* he was authorized to attend to the "nuns *du Sacré Coeur*," provided Bishop Du Bourg gave him the requisite powers to do so.[20] It was autumn, however, before this answer reached Florissant.

In mid-July Mother Duchesne received news that caused her anxiety. *The Dolphin* had run aground on its downstream trip. The passengers had been transferred to another steamboat, with some additional expense, and Father De La Croix hoped that he and his party would reach their destination safely. They did so on July 1, but Mother Duchesne was unaware of this when she wrote on July 18 to Mother Barat in a very serious vein:

> My last letter of June 19 must have given you real consolation, for in it I told you of the arrival we had so longed for—the arrival of our Fathers [the Jesuits]. But you must not think things are the

same here as in France. Their interest in us is not the same at all, and already—four times within this present month—they have told me they would have nothing to do with us if the highest authority did not impose it on them. [several words illegible] This condition still exists, and I depend on Divine Providence not to leave us without spiritual food. This would be all the harder to bear since no one would sympathize with us, thinking that we preferred the Jesuits to all other priests, and that three of those who could have stayed here and helped us need not have gone to Lower Louisiana.

The plague of penury is felt down there as well as up here. Even before I was informed of this with certainty, I realized how few religious there are at Opelousas, how many more pupils they have to care for than we, and how delicate Mother Xavier Murphy's health is. So I considered it necessary to give them some help. Not being able to go myself, I sent Sister Marguerite, the oldest among us, with Sister Mary Ann Summers, an aspirant. They left with three priests on the best steamboat on the Mississippi, but through the recklessness of the pilot it ran aground 40 miles from here. They continued their journey on another steamboat which was passing downstream, but I have not yet had word of their safe arrival. The departure of these dear Sisters leaves a great hole in our ranks, and this is enlarged by the departure of Marguerite Tison, coadjutrix novice, who had been with us about ten months, but has given us continual doubts about her vocation. Her place has been filled by a French-speaking postulant of 21 years who is gifted for studies and seems very well disposed for religious life. Her name is Therese Detchemendy.[21]

In spite of our poverty I had to call a doctor from St. Louis to treat Mother Octavie, who had such a repulsive ulcer close to her mouth. It is much better now. . . . The other religious are fairly well. All find consolation in the direction of the Father who is both rector and master of novices. He is a Baltazar Alvarez, a real Rodriguez. He told me the Jesuits at Georgetown are very poor, for their best crop was tobacco, and this has dropped in value and no longer supports them. There were 70 in the community; now they are divided among eight or nine institutions, and they are refusing postulants. . . .

We have had the honor of being severely criticized, and in order to undermine our work still further, report has it that we are leaving here. There are people who wish we would. We must devote ourselves more and more to the poor and to our own perfection, happy to work among thorns and to be aided by living models, imitators of Him whom we propose to imitate. What joy I have had cutting out and making up clothes such as I had seen on our

Holy Protectors! Here they are wearing the regular Jesuit costume. . . .

When Father Van Quickenborne wrote to his Maryland superior a week later, "We *all* go in full Jesuitical dress at all times and in all places," [22] he might have added, "thanks to the industry, ingenuity, and self-sacrifice of the *Dames du Sacré Coeur*" who were such a thorn in his side. To no one did this "full Jesuitical dress" give greater satisfaction than to Mother Duchesne, and in her *Journal* she recorded on July 31: "Feast of St. Ignatius, celebrated solemnly in the church. On this day the Jesuits, all wearing their religious costume, sang both Mass and Vespers. Father Niel preached and the *Te Deum* was chanted after Benediction." Kneeling close to the shrine of her beloved Jesuit patron, Philippine listened to the deep tones of the men's voices, her tired eyes sightless with tears of joy, her whole being surrendered to God in an élan of praise and gratitude. What if her nuns no longer had their enveloping choir cloaks to wear at liturgical services, or decent habits and underskirts to don on Sundays and feast days! What if the Father Superior was stern and gruff, strict and even severe! What if he spurned the extras she tried to supply for the novices' meals! He had been grateful for the clothing that she and her community had tailored for them, and she had a Jesuit director for herself, her nuns, and her novices—a privilege and a security for which she would never cease to thank God.

A new school year opened on September 1, after ten days of vacation. There were just eleven girls enrolled in the boarding school. In a long letter to Mother Barat that month, Philippine touched on many topics but made only a passing mention of the school at Florissant. By reading thoughtfully both the lines and between the lines, one comes to realize more clearly what sort of person she was. Her character was of an extremely positive type— clearheaded, strong-willed, warmhearted. Part of the charm of her personality lay in the fact that it was colorful, vivacious, enterprising, and often varied with unexpected slants and changing moods. Faith, courage, self-forgetfulness, and humor undiminished by her austerity—these were ingredients that made her life beautiful against the drab background of the frontier. As her constancy would have done honor to the martyrs, so too would her acceptance of the obscure and ordinary sufferings that purified her soul. And no one understood her better than the friend in France to whom she wrote on September 25, 1823:

I do not know what delays your letters, or whether you have forgotten us. Never before have we been so long a time without news from you. The last letter from you was more than a year old when I received it, and that was six months ago. The most recent news we have had came from kind Father Barat. He must have had great consolation in learning that his Jesuit brethren are carrying on the missionary work he wanted to do in this sterile region. They alone could regenerate it, and to do so one must have a love of sacrifice, unwavering zeal, and sympathy to share the troubles of one's neighbors, all in the highest degree. We see all that in the angels on earth whom God has established here as our guardians. The more we see of the Father Rector, the more we appreciate his direction and recognize in him the spirit of his Father, St. Ignatius. I have found a Father Master. I no longer do as I please, but he is not yet satisfied with my efforts. He insists on deeper interior life, greater detail in the account one gives of one's soul—and you know I never have much to say! He gave a retreat of three days on the occasion of a prise d'habit [Therese Detchemendy's] and first Communion, which occurred on the 14th, feast of the Holy Name of Mary and of the Holy Cross. If it could only have been longer! He has the power to persuade and move hearts. Seeing your daughters in such good hands, I am now quite tranquil as to their spiritual direction.

This Father knows several of our religious in Paris. His name is Van Quickenborne. He also knows Mother de Peñeranda. He and all his religious brethren are Flemish. He would be quite capable of converting a kingdom, but up to this time he has accomplished very little. The whole country is going downhill. They [the Jesuits] are putting up a building on the Bishop's farm. I did my best to induce them to build nearer the church, but there was no getting them to do so. They do not want to be near us. I was deeply grieved at this, realizing fully that in spite of their courage we should often be without Mass in winter. They have their own chapel on the farm and our church is terribly deserted. The settlers in the neighborhood rarely come to it, and we have only eleven children. Of these just two are assured for the whole year, as their tuition was paid in advance. The others may be withdrawn any day.

So you see we are entirely in the care of Divine Providence, and it is very sweet to remain there in peace. We have never lacked what is absolutely necessary; we even have a little more money than formerly when we had more pupils. This gives me security for the future. Sometimes we have even been able to help the Fathers, who are much poorer than we. They are *suffering*, and how I wish some of the magnificence of France might be turned a little to their profit. Help will be slow in coming to them out here. One rich man has refused them a loan. They have cultivated some fields with great difficulty, and a freeze during this month of September has killed all their hopes of harvesting the most necessary crops.

Here again one must adore God's Providence, and abandon oneself entirely to it. One does not find friends and protectors easily out here. Each one thinks of himself, and no one will sacrifice his ease and pleasure for the sake of good works. There is not *faith* enough for that. Our greatest suffering does not come from being mocked and calumniated in social circles by our former pupils, but rather from seeing them rushing headlong on the road of pleasure and indolence. The one who was longest with us and who left school only three months ago [Pelagie Chouteau] died a holy death before being captivated by worldliness. One of her closest companions [Zoë Leduc] had preceded her into eternity in the same dispositions. . . .

Mother Eugenie's house will suffer as a result of the economic distress prevailing this year in Lower Louisiana. She has not paid me all she owed on the traveling expenses of the nuns I sent to help her. She has tried to build up her establishment too rapidly and has gotten many things she may not need. A wise economy is absolutely necessary here more than in any other country, for nothing under heaven is stable in the section of the world in which we live. Fortunes and institutions suddenly collapse. Many people who owe us money pay us with calumnies. The loss of pupils is not the thing that worries me most at Opelousas; it is Mother Xavier's health. She has been advised to go to Mrs. Smith's home to recuperate. Perhaps she is already there.

Monseigneur [Du Bourg], who sees everything through rose-colored glasses, has given the Fathers reason for concern. They were expecting more than they have received. And while I was talking to him about our loss of pupils, he told me he had an offer to make me of an establishment that would help us very much. It is at a place some 30 leagues above New Orleans on the river, which would make communication very easy. The people of the parish will build the convent. But he asks for *six choir nuns* from France, religious of tried *virtue* and *discretion*. . . . I replied that I did not think you would accept that foundation, that you had warned us not to expect any subjects or money in the near future, and that Mother Octavie's ill health has taken from me all idea of dividing this community.

I realize, however, how little chance there is of doing anything in St. Louis, where we are abhorred at present, along with Monseigneur. On the other hand, I have been pondering over the strange condition of Mother Xavier's health. I strongly suspect that it is the result of continual nerve irritation, for I do not believe she can ever see eye to eye with Mother Eugenie, and perhaps she would be even less sympathetic with conditions here. I believe she may be one of those persons who need activity of both mind and body in order to be in good health—a person like Mother Bigeu. I think Mother Xavier could govern the establishment Monseigneur now proposes. He admires her very much because of her virtue and her command of English. On her side she has great confidence in him and would be living near him, for it seems he is going to take up his residence at that distance from New Orleans on the other side of the river, perhaps in order to live in a healthier parish where he could keep his eye on the most populous part of his diocese. I do not desire him to live in St. Louis again. He would lack everything he needs and have only constant vexations. As for ourselves, the Jesuit Fathers attend to all our spiritual needs.

This establishment at *La Fourche*—the name of the place—would replace the one projected for New Orleans, where there would be little success for a long time, as commerce is in stagnation there and several epidemics have laid low that section of the country where God is so forgotten.[23] We certainly could give a few subjects to Mother Xavier. Her Bishop in Ireland considered her quite fitted to be a superior, and Mother Eugenie thinks she is capable of governing a house. Eugenie is the only one to whom I have expressed my thoughts. It would be time enough to speak of it to Monseigneur after we have your answer, which I beg you to hasten to send. I dread this remedy of leaving cloister for the sake of health. I should not give permission for it. It was suggested for Mother Octavie. I saw her growing weaker, but happily the Father Rector took my side instead of ordering the change as he was urged to do. He is going to give us a retreat in November, which I hope will strengthen the religious spirit of this poor house. . . .

Philippine was learning the doctrine of the cross from within her own heart. While suffering much from the criticism of people who should have appreciated her work, she felt more keenly the trials in which her sympathetic heart gave her a share. One of the severest was the frequent serious illness and the continual physical suffering of Mother Berthold. Another was anxiety with regard to the new project at La Fourche. The Bishop seemed to have set his heart on it and might persuade Mother Audé to undertake it without sufficient approval and help from France. There was also her interest in the Jesuits, whose poverty she longed to alleviate. As winter came on and cold winds whipped around the little brick convent, she knew that the suffering of those who were living in the Bishop's "chateau" was increasing and her own slender resources were diminishing. Her inability to help them was in itself a heavy cross.

Before the close of the year Philippine received a letter from her sister Amelie which roused her to the realization that many months had passed since she last wrote to members of her family. Money was scarce and postal rates were high, so she economized in ways that were particularly costly to her. She had made the perfect surrender of her dearest earthly ties, yet the love of this woman of strong and deep affections seemed to grow more tender and intimate with detachment. This is evident in the letter to Amelie de Mauduit on December 28, 1823. It was a brave letter in which she tried to depict favorably her drab frontier surroundings:

> I received your letter. In it your whole soul is portrayed—you are always so kind, so expansive, so zealous for good. You know full well the interest I take in all your dear ones. You have joys, you have sorrows—that is life. It seems to me that the joys, which are always so short-lived, are given just to enable us to rouse our courage to carry the cross. For it would overwhelm us if God did not strengthen us by some of His consolation.
>
> Remember me to your husband, your children, especially dear Amelie. I still love her, in spite of her silence in my regard. Remember me also to my Sisters. At such a great distance it is difficult to keep up a correspondence with those whom I love. Often I can only confide to the Heart of Jesus all I would like to write. I also put before Him the needs of all my family, and you are never forgotten. I form very special wishes for you at the opening of the New Year.
>
> Perhaps your heart longs to know just where we live in the New World. On a map you would find the place on the right bank of the Mississippi, between the mouth of the Missouri and that of the Arkansas River. Each of these streams is more than 500 leagues long. We are further upstream than where the Ohio flows into the Mississippi on the left side. If your map is detailed, New Madrid and Ste Genevieve may be marked; we are further north than these towns—they are really only villages, particularly New Madrid, which suffered greatly in an earthquake whose center was right there. I stopped there last year coming upstream on my way home from Opelousas. I had gone there accompanying two of our nuns to our new foundation, which already has more pupils than we have, as that part of the country is not so poor as this. Steamboats have been improved so much, they can now cover the

400 leagues from New Orleans to St. Louis in 15 days. But I spent three months on my return trip. That has taken away my taste for travel. Only the desire to work for God can make a religious endure the inconveniences of such a long trip.

My health is very good and would allow me to do much more work, but I must be satisfied with what God gives me to do. I would not choose rest just because I fear pain, but it would be very sweet to have it before I die, for the natural element often insinuates itself into the holiest enterprises and makes us lose the merit of them. If Father Feréol is still alive, remember me to him, and ask my old friends to pray for me, especially any who go on pilgrimage to La Louvesc.

The village in which we live is five leagues from St. Louis, the principal town in the new state of Missouri, and about the same distance from St. Charles, our first place of residence, which has been for some time the capital of the State. Ste Genevieve, where we had to go once, is thirty leagues away, and New Madrid is 100. Our convent is built of brick and joins the newly erected parish church, which is also of brick. Monseigneur gave the land for the church and made us a gift of the property we own, consisting of a big meadow, a small woodland along a creek, and a garden with a courtyard and a pasture for our animals. We have about 100 chickens, 7 cows, 1 horse. We do not have to buy feed for the animals—we just open the gate and let them out; in the evening they all return to exactly the same gate without shepherd or shepherdess. I forgot to mention our five lambs and sheep and some very handsome geese. In good weather all the livestock graze in the common fields and woods, and in winter these animals have no shelter except a shed covered with thatch.

Philippine's first letter of 1824 gave details that are as so many strokes of an artist's pencil sketching the cartoon for a picture of frontier life. Describing the retreat she had made under Father Van Quickenborne's direction, she mingled humor and realism:

Those eight days were really a time of spiritual abundance. The devil was jealous, however, so he arranged for the delivery of nine large hogs that we had bought. They arrived on the second day of the retreat. As somebody had to take up the disgusting work of caring for them for two days, I was the willing victim. I took the work as a punishment for my lack of recollection. The following days were peaceful, and that happy retreat closed on the feast of the Immaculate Conception. We had five exercises daily and a conference. All were full of the most solid doctrine and were very devotional.

Realizing that the number of our pupils is bound to diminish still further, we are trying to make for ourselves all we possibly can. We make our soap, candles for both the house and the church, altar-breads, our butter, woolen yarn, and cotton and linen thread. We sowed some cotton this year, but had no success with it, as the seeds were not suited to this climate. We hope to succeed better another year and to purchase a loom for weaving cotton and woolen cloth. We know how to dye in several colors—black, grey, and yellow. There is no expense in this as we obtain the dye from native wood or plants. We are going to plant some indigo to obtain a blue coloring matter which is easy to use. Salted pork, milk, vegetables from our garden make up our food supply. But I have written enough about the animal side of life. I beg you, pray to the Sacred Heart of Jesus for us, that He may assure us of one day possessing eternal life. There we hope to see you again someday.[24]

In her first decade in America, Mother Duchesne suffered practically every hardship the frontier had to offer, except the threat of Indian massacre—poor lodging, shortages of food, drinking water, fuel, and money, forest fires and blazing chimneys, the vagaries of the Missouri climate, cramped living quarters and the privation of all privacy, and the crude manners of children reared in rough surroundings and without the slightest training in courtesy. The thing that seems to have astonished her most about the parish school children was their apparent ingratitude toward the nuns who tried to teach them. But these same children came at times with the best gifts they could offer—wild berries, nuts, honey, fresh eggs, even a side of bacon or a block of homemade soap, and Mother Duchesne poured out on them all the treasures of her mind and heart, longing to draw them to knowledge and love of Christ.

Another frontier hardship was the loneliness of remote places and a foreign tongue. But she had friends in and about Florissant, and her letters to Father De La Croix are filled with little news items about the parish of St. Ferdinand and the people who had been so deeply attached to him during his pastorate there. The drudgery of farm and household work wore down her strength, but she did not complain of this. Only the slowness of mail from France seemed really to tax her patience.

This often kept her for months in ignorance of the sorrows that came to her family. The death of Josephine Perier's husband occurred on July 31, 1823, when the Baron de Savoye-Rollin was sixty-eight years old. Through more than twenty years he had been a loyal and generous friend of Philippine, and in his will he remembered her with a legacy. News of his death and of the legacy had come to her in a letter from Mother Barat,[25] which reached Florissant just a week before the one in which Josephine herself told Philippine of her widowhood. Answering immediately, Philippine wrote on February 16, 1824:

My dearest Cousin and Friend,

I have just received your letter of last summer, and I have shared all your sufferings. My tears have mingled with yours, and this sympathy is shared by all those who, like myself, have benefited by your generosity. How often I have spoken to my companions about your goodness to us! And it is always very sweet for me to tell them about my first and dearest friend, of all she has done for me—and this is very apparent at our religious ceremonies—and of the life-companion who made her days so happy and who, because he shared her loving interest in me, was the first to help in opening my way to happiness.[26]

My sentiments of gratitude have never diminished toward that happy couple who have been so blessed by God. You may judge, then, my beloved friend, how, as I spoke to my Sisters of the blow that has struck you, they shared your suffering and offered their most fervent prayers in union with you. But I have suffered most. And that last mark of kindness toward me on the part of your husband was certainly calculated to touch the tenderest chord in my heart. I offer for him in return the Masses, the Communions, the little we do in the line of good works, and I trust that God has already heard these many prayers offered for his intention to speed his entrance into a blessed eternity.

Our Mother General wrote to me about you and about the legacy you turned over to her for us. She realizes its value as much as we do. Among the religious here are two who knew you, Mothers Lucille and Octavie. They cherish great respect and affection for you. The latter has endured much severe pain this year: an abscess in her mouth had to be lanced by the surgeon and has now opened on the jaw, which makes us fear cancer. After causing intense pain, the wound has healed, but the continual indispositions which this dear sick Sister bears make me fear a return of the disease. She is a religious most precious to us because of her piety, her education, and her attractive character.

My dearest one, you have, no doubt, received the letter I wrote you at the time of the death of Tante Perier [Josephine's mother]. When I think of all the sorrows the dear Lord has sent you since we parted, I am deeply moved. There would be no understanding these mysteries of sorrow if faith did not tell us that they are but the reminders of the fact that true happiness is not to be found here below, and that we must look forward to that more blessed city on high, where loving husbands and wives are united again, where friends will meet once more, where those who have carried the cross after the example, and in the footsteps, of Jesus Christ will gather about Him who went ahead of them on the way of the cross.

The dear Lord has prepared much suffering for me, too, since the days when we opened our convent here with such a promise of success. The scarcity of money has caused the withdrawal of the majority of our boarding pupils—only 10 remain. This same circumstance, in conjunction with the persecution of the Bishop in this corrupt town [St. Louis], has forced him to withdraw 400 leagues from us [to New Orleans]. But the hardest of all has been the fact that practically all the pupils who have left us and who seemed so fervent and thoroughly good, have fallen back into their former neglect of religion, as a result of their natural levity and the influence of pleasure and bad example. I still hope that their faith is not dead and that age, reverses, and other trials from the hand of God will someday bring them to repentance—that is my only hope for them. But we have also the opportunity of offering to those whom God will call to His service a haven in which to practice virtue far from the contagion of the world. This will be our most enduring work here, and it has already drawn a shower of blessings on us and on those who have joined us. Up to now there have been twelve religious trained here and at Opelousas. We have had other foundations proposed to us, but prudence warns us not to undertake them until we receive more nuns and more money from France. These cannot be sent just now. . . .

You realize how consoling it was for me to learn that Aloysia, the first of my nieces to give herself to God, closed her earthly career in so holy a manner. I wept at her death—but the tears were for myself rather than for her, since I knew that in so short a time she had traded well with her talents, while I still have gained nothing with mine. Yet the time for rendering an account draws near, and I have already had several warnings to this effect. If I had any regret in giving up this life, it would be caused by the thought of leaving our work here in so unstable a condition and in the hands of religious, some of whom are too young and others too ill to carry it on. But God knows what will happen, and I trust I shall still have the pleasure of receiving many letters from you. I shall always answer them eagerly and with that tender affection which I bear you in the Heart of Jesus. Remember me to Augustin and his wife and to all the family.

The progress of the Church in Missouri was a matter of vital concern to Mother Duchesne and often formed the subject of whole pages in her letters. On February 19 she told Mother Barat:

> The coming of the Sisters of Loretto from Kentucky has taken away all idea of our forming small communities. They will do this work. They are under the direction of Monseigneur Rosati, co-adjutor of Bishop Du Bourg and a member of the Congregation of Lazarists. He is well chosen for this position and is quite friendly toward us. I understand Monseigneur Du Bourg is not re-turning to St. Louis. He has asked to have his vestments and books sent to him. It is in the parish where he is taking up his residence that Father De La Croix wants us to make a new foundation. . . . I really spoil everything. When you discharge me from office, you will do the greatest service to this house. I realized, when I was named to it, that I merited it not as a favor, but as a penance; still I wish always to be perfectly submissive to you.

The consecration of Bishop Rosati, which took place on March 25, 1824, at Donaldsonville, Louisiana, put an end to a peculiar situation that had arisen in the diocese. For more than a year he had been a bishop-elect, but only in December, 1823, had he received the papal brief appointing him coadjutor to Monseigneur Du Bourg. By a rescript obtained from the Prefect of Propaganda the new bishop was not compelled to sever his connection with the Congregation of the Mission, but continued to reside as superior at St. Mary's Seminary.

After an informal visitation in parts of Louisiana, Bishop Rosati boarded the *Dolphin* and arrived in St. Louis on May 19. Two days later he was at Florissant. Uppermost in his mind and heart was the problem of missions among the Indians. As it was not possible to send missionaries into the Indian Country before the Jesuit scholastics had completed their training, Father Van Quick-enborne had taken up Bishop Du Bourg's suggestion and opened, at Florissant, St. Regis Seminary for Indian boys. On May 11 two little Sauks, aged six and eight years, were received into the school. Three Iowa lads followed in June.

Mother Duchesne was keenly interested in the new school and eager to help with its support. That her generosity towards the Jesuits had been reported to the General is evident from a sentence or two in her next letter, but she did not dwell on the matter when she wrote to Mother Barat on June 10:

> . . . I admit frankly that I am as much concerned about the

Jesuit foundation as about our own convent, and even more. And I sincerely regret that I can do no more for them than the fly on the coach-wheel did to speed up the coach. They are severely tried, but they are not discouraged. The fine old spirit of zeal, courage, and poverty lives again fully in them.

Alas, the poor Rector has no priest of the Society of Jesus to help him now, and he has far more than he can do. His companion, Father Joseph Timmermans, died suddenly a week ago as a result of exhaustion following on missionary labors during the Eastertide. His trips took him through sections of the country now in flood condition, now in drought. He slept in wretched huts made worse by standing water and filth, and he often had only the bare ground to lie on. He is the first Jesuit to die in Missouri, for the early missionaries always lived in the vicinity of the Illinois [Indians]. He was buried in our church beside the altar. The Office for the Dead was chanted solemnly by his brethren. The Father Rector is in very poor health. Now he has four parishes on his hands, along with several remote missions, the direction of the studies [of the scholastics], the buildings, which will not be completed before September because of lack of funds, recurrent illness among the Brothers, Negroes, and Indians. The first two savages are dangerously ill just now with whooping cough, which has carried off more than a hundred children in St. Louis and causes severe suffering. I avow to you that when I see how calm he [Father Van Quickenborne] is in the midst of the many anxieties and occupations which pull him this way and that, I cannot but conclude that his soul is stabilized in those high regions of peace which are reached by way of complete self-renunciation and union with God. On Sundays he says two Masses, preaches three times, presides at the catechism lessons, and hears confessions at all intervals between services. To live in the neighborhood with saints has such an attraction for me that I delight in our poor countryplace more than I would in the most brilliant establishment in town.

Government aid for the civilization of the savages will be given only after the work has been undertaken. Then the missionaries must follow the plan outlined by the Secretary of War in what regards both the boys and the girls. As the Father Rector cannot take the latter group, we hope to do so, trusting in the help of Divine Providence. Food will cost very little; we have a place to house them; and we shall beg clothing for them. The chief agent of Congress for treating with the tribes in this part of the country [General William Clark] approves of this plan. He is going to Washington and will see whether the Secretary of War [John C. Calhoun] is willing to appropriate money for the traveling expenses of some more of our religious to help with this work. That would be an unprecedented favor for Indian girls, and the agent has little hope of obtaining it. But we must do everything in our power to further this important work which has been the object of so many prayers, which really brought us here, and which is in itself so interesting and offers us more hope of success than anything else does. The Father Rector speaks with great satisfaction of these two little lads, who are so docile and innocent. One of them has already been baptized, for they feared he was dying. . . . We often pray to St. Regis for the conversion of the Indians, and we are saying the forty-days' prayer to him to obtain more laborers at once.[27] But they must be really dead to self, for nature finds no satisfaction in this work. Faith alone and love for our suffering Jesus find their solid nourishment here.

The Religious of the Visitation at Georgetown, whose community had increased so rapidly as to number fifty-six, are in great distress and may be obliged to divide into two groups. After having had forty boarding pupils, they now have practically none, and they have gone into a good deal of debt for their chapel. All the institutions in the United States experience these sudden reversals, so one must be very prudent and advance quite gradually. . . . On the missions the treasure of poverty will never be lacking. . . . If my skin were worth any money, I should willingly sacrifice it to support our missions. . . . The Heart of Jesus is infinitely rich. Can we fear to be poor with Him?

Monseigneur Rosati paid us a short visit when he returned to this part of the diocese after his consecration. He showed great interest in us and in the Jesuits, whom he urges to open a college in St. Louis. He also urged us to go to Donaldsonville, a small town on the Mississippi thirty or forty leagues above New Orleans. In a letter which he brought me from Bishop Du Bourg the same suggestion was stressed. . . . I replied that you do not want any more establishments in small places, and I was not convinced by any of the arguments he used. These hopes of success are but flashes that amount to nothing in the end. It seems to me that if we are not wanted in or near New Orleans, we should do better, since we must be insignificant, to devote ourselves entirely to the savages and establish our convents in the vicinity of the apostolic men who should serve as our models, who keep well at a distance, and who never make us waste time. . . .

If a third convent is opened, I am convinced that Mother Eugenie is the best person to direct it. In one of your letters you suggested that Mother Lucille should replace her and that I should remain here, close to the Indian country, with Mother Octavie, who really could not guide a house alone. Ever since the wound on her face healed, she has had a sore throat; and she often suffers severely from it. . . .

The death of Father Joseph Timmermans brought about a condition of affairs that sorely tried the community at Florissant and caused Mother Duchesne to write to Bishop Rosati on June 24:

Since the death of Father Timmermans we are often deprived of Mass and Communion, for the Father Rector has others to care for as well as ourselves. We earnestly desire to make up for this deprivation by Exposition of the Blessed Sacrament, which is quite frequent in our convents. But the difficulty is to have It replaced in the evening after It has been exposed in our chapel in the morning. If, in place of exposition, you would allow the tabernacle to remain open during the day in our cloister chapel where we make our adoration, and let us close the tabernacle in the evening, we would have the same advantage without giving the Father Rector the trouble of an extra trip, which he often cannot make. Monseigneur Du Bourg would not allow exposition in the parish church because of the lack of adorers. But we beg you to allow it on feasts common to ourselves and the Jesuits, for the proper solemnity is possible only in the church, and real inconveniences result from public exposition in our private chapel. I assure you adorers will not be lacking on such days. . . .

The Bishop received this letter on July 7 and answered two days later:

In the great dearth of workers from which we suffer. . . . this misfortune distresses us greatly. . . . Nevertheless, we must resign ourselves to the will of Him who rules and disposes all for the advantage of His elect and for His own great glory. I am deeply moved by the privations which this accident brings you. But it is an arrangement of Divine Providence and undoubtedly for the best. The desire of your holy community to enjoy the privileges now granted less frequently will be a stimulus to redouble their fervor and to appreciate as far as our weakness can the enormous value of the graces God gives us in admitting us to Holy Communion. I heartily approve of your idea of supplying for this by adoration, for that is the very best way, especially if one joins to it spiritual communion. But I cannot approve of leaving the tabernacle open. First of all, the adoration would have to be kept up continuously, and second, it would be a great irregularity to allow religious women to do what the Church allows only to priests and deacons. So you must be content hereafter to adore our Lord enclosed in the tabernacle for love of us, and offer Him once more the sacrifice of the holy satisfaction that comes from the sight of either His sacramental presence under which He hides Himself in order to abide with us, or the ciborium in which He abides. Lively faith can make up for this sacrifice. . . . Let us try to submit whole-heartedly to God's will and to profit by the trials He sends us. Let us all pray for this and never cease begging Him to strengthen the good works He has begun in this country and to increase the number of workers in this almost abandoned section of His vineyard.

Philippine's reaction to the decisions of the Bishop was expressed in a few simple lines written on July 31:

Please do not think that these untoward occurrences discourage us. We accept as coming from God both the pleasant and the disagreeable. We shall always be happy if we retain your approval and protection. If God, who knows our desire to work for His glory, is satisfied with our good will, we too shall be content, even though we are unable to carry out our desires.

The letters Mother Duchesne sent to France can often be understood only with reference to the ones she received from the Superior General, and these were frequently more than a year old when they reached Florissant, whether they crossed the ocean by post or in the dispatch case of a French consul or the satchel of a missionary or the pocket of an American gentleman bringing his daughters home from school in France. In August, 1823, St. Madeleine Sophie wrote affectionately:

I still cherish the hope of seeing you before I die. Now keep that little overture to yourself; for if it is impracticable, there is no use rousing similar hopes in others. I also want to whisper something else in your ear, but it must be a secret. . . . We are thinking seriously of petitioning for the Holy Father's approbation of our order. Ask special prayers in your two convents, but keep the intention to yourself—or perhaps you could tell Eugenie, but bind her to secrecy. Pray and ask prayers for me, your Mother. Believe me, I often pray for you. Who, better than I, understands your many anxieties and privations? I have so many of my own to offer to God. What miseries there are in poor human nature! What patience and forbearance are required in those who direct souls! You will find these virtues in the Heart of Jesus, my dear Philippine. That Heart was opened for us; let us go to it and draw from it the strength and courage of which we stand in need. In that Heart, dear daughter, I remain very lovingly united to you.

Mother Duchesne responded affectionately, reassuringly, but with all honesty:

We have just celebrated the feast of St. Mary Magdalen, recalling such dear memories. We tried to rejoice in spirit with all our Sisters who are gathered around you, trusting to the Heart of Jesus our love and our good wishes. Mass, Holy Communion, and a little extra recreation was all circumstances permitted by way of celebration, but we do not want any community in the Society to surpass us in heartfelt affection and devotion to our loved Mother.

I am afraid that news about the Catholic institutions in the United States may make you uneasy about us. But I beg you not to worry. We wanted the cross and not honor, poverty and not ease, the will of God and not our own. So even if the work is hampered, we can always gather from this circumstance the precious advantage of being in a situation that can unite us closely to Jesus Christ, our Divine Spouse. All those among us who wear the black veil are in these dispositions—Mothers Octavie and Lucille, Sisters Xavier, Regis, Catherine, and Ignace [Judith Labruyère], who made her first vows on the feast of the Sacred Heart. As for the novices, two are firm in their vocation; the third, a young Spaniard, wavers a good deal.[28] If she leaves, that will make the third to do so in a year. Of all my trials that is the most painful, for I am to blame for this lack of perseverance, as it can be attributed to lack of care and good example on my part.

I am eagerly awaiting the happy day that will set the seal of papal approbation on our Constitutions. I wanted to have them translated into English by Sister Xavier Hamilton, but the thought that some changes or additions might be made caused me to wait. We should like a copy of the formula of the vows, both first and final, and tell me who should sign the documents besides the new bride of Christ. That is not indicated anywhere. I also want to know the exact number of Masses we are to have offered each month. . . . It may happen at times that we cannot afford to have them said, as the stipend is fifty cents.

Since the death of Father Timmermans we are often without Mass, though the Father Rector goes far beyond his strength in his efforts for us. If he succumbs—and his health is not good—we shall really feel the weight of the cross. He no longer speaks hopefully of other priests coming to help him. It would be very desirable if preparations for the missions to the savages could at least get under way. The five Indian boys the Fathers have give them a great deal of trouble now. They do not like to wear clothes; they want to sleep nude; they do not want to work; they are very greedy. One day when they felt they had not been given enough meat for dinner they charged up to the scholastics' quarters, demonstrating that the skin on their stomachs was not stretched tight.

I do not know when we shall be able to take the Indian girls. We are all eager to do so, but this has been a year of disasters. The Missouri has flooded to a great width and carried off the farm-houses and cattle of many settlers and ruined the crops. There will be almost no grain or vegetables, and we shall soon have only three or four pupils. The main thing just now is to support our little community. The Religious of the Visitation at Georgetown are obliged to divide their community. About twenty nuns will remain there and twelve or fourteen have asked a home in Quebec and the same number in New Orleans; and they say the Ursuline convent in New Orleans that was doing so much good, has gotten into a bad financial condition as a result of the large new building they erected. . . . I should be very sorry to begin a foundation in that city just now—it might look as if we were taking advantage of their misfortune.

In this section of the country there are so many reverses of fortune, so much instability in enterprises, so little support to rely on, one would almost need the visible finger of Divine Providence pointing the way before one would change one's residence. Here at Florissant we are no longer afraid of starving to death, and that is something. If God takes from us the means of doing good, we must accept His will. Sometimes I think God upset all our original plans and our first school in order to build up gradually the important work of training the savages. One really must merit a share in that work by humiliations and other sufferings. Do not worry about us. Not a single one of us is discouraged. I am the most dissatisfied because I have reason to think I have turned God's blessing from our labors. You are the only one who can remedy this, Reverend Mother.[29]

What Philippine wrote with regard to the Visitandine monastery of Georgetown was not a rumor picked up in a conversation, but firsthand information. When she came to America in 1818, one of the first letters she wrote was to the Sisters of the Visitation to introduce herself and her community and to ask the help of their prayers. Early in 1819 a French priest, known in the United States as Father Clorivière, became chaplain at Georgetown while the monastery's foundress, Mother Teresa Lalor, was still superior.[30] Father Clorivière took an active interest in the community and encouraged the expansion of the institution as well as the adoption of more exact uniformity in the way of life at Annecy. On July 26, 1820, the first stone of the new chapel was laid, the community depending on funds which Father Clorivière hoped to obtain from France. The money was slow in coming and by 1822 the community had gone so unwisely into debt that bankruptcy threatened. The idea of dispersing the Sisters had to be faced, and negotiations for a merging of groups of them with the Ursulines in Canada and Louisiana were actually under way when in 1824 the Sisters were spared this trial by providential help that came from both America and France.

Mother Duchesne had been in correspondence with Father Clorivière and the Visitation nuns during these years, as entries in her *Journal* show, and she quotes the chaplain on September 1, 1824, to her Superior General. This letter was written in answer to suggestions from Mother Barat that the convent at Florissant be closed, since it could scarcely be supported on the tuition of half a dozen pupils, and that Mother Duchesne and her companions go to Louisiana to staff the second establishment which both Bishop Du Bourg and his coadjutor had urged her to accept. In these paragraphs one feels the soul of Philippine Duchesne at grips with circumstances that threatened to destroy the frail cion she had nurtured for five years in the Valley of Florissant, which in her case had so belied its name:

> Ever since you told me your hopes for the approbation of our holy Constitutions, I have been waiting with keen impatience for the happy news. Following your recommendation, we are praying for the success of this project. . . . It seems to me I can want no greater consolation on earth than this—no further reason for life—I am ready to die—not that I haven't many fears for my last hour, but I realize that I am not capable of advancing the Society's work in this country. I am the more convinced of this because the Father Rector has so often told me to ask you to send us a new superior. I told him I had often begged you to do so, adding that you had not promised us anyone as you were pressed for religious to staff the new foundations in Europe; but I suggested that if my Sisters made the request, you might pay more attention to it, as the need would then be more evident. He did not like that suggestion at all, so I am left with the sorrow of thinking that I am not fulfilling my duties, that souls suffer in consequence, yet I have

no hope that in the near future I shall be put in my proper place. I beg you to weigh before God the interests and needs of this part of your religious family, which is all the dearer to you because it is so insignificant and so suffering.

Do not listen, I beg you, to Mother Eugenie's proposal to transfer me to Lower Louisiana in case of a new foundation there. I carry in my heart a great fear of spoiling things wherever I shall be, and this because of words I think I heard in the depths of my soul: "You are destined to please Me, not so much by success as by bearing failure." This may have been an illusion or a figment of a too lively imagination; still I cannot rid myself of this thought, and so I dread undertaking anything, lest I should hinder its success. If I had only to follow the dictates of obedience and carry out the work planned by others, I should not have all this interior distress, but the condition in which we are living at present strengthens me all the more in this conviction. Since the Bishop was obliged to withdraw from here, we have been completely forgotten; or if we are remembered at all, it is with contempt or a kind of pity that results from indifference. The children who have left our boarding school follow the broad road of pleasure, and we have almost no influence with those who attend the parish school.

The sufferings of the Jesuit Fathers are also ours. I hope they will succeed, but the difficulties, privations, ingratitude they are experiencing, all weigh heavily on my heart. It would be too great a joy for me to be able to contribute munificently to the important work they have begun. Divine Providence has arranged matters, however, by a secret means I cannot explain to myself, so that I have been able to lend or give them a little now and then. For although we have only seven boarding pupils, we still support three orphans, pay for the upkeep of the church, etc. And of our seven pupils, two pay nothing at all. The number may be further reduced, though I lowered the tuition to $100, or 500 francs, a year. There is simply no money in the country. All that is in circulation here comes from either France or Spain. And as pleasure comes before all else, there is not much left to pay for a good education. There may still be a few people who desire to assure this to their daughters, so we are keeping the large convent for that purpose, and we are going to try to organize in what was formerly the parish school building a boarding school more in conformity with the general poverty of the country, charging 180 or 190 French francs, but this is to be paid, not in money—that cannot be found in the country—but in corn, potatoes, lard, beef, and butter. This would furnish food for the girls, and they would take turns helping in the kitchen, milking the cows, doing the laundry, and cultivating the kitchen garden. They would also learn to spin and weave cloth for the convent and for the little Indian girls whom I hope we shall soon have—a very few at first, and we shall have to beg help to support them.[31] I have already asked Madame de Rollin in my last letter to form a little association among our relatives and friends who would be willing to contribute something each year for this good work, which may have more success than our efforts among the white children. The savages whom the Fathers are educating conduct themselves now in church better than do the children of the parishioners, and one of them is smarter than any of these children.

I wrote to you some time ago that the Religious of the Visitation at Georgetown were going to be obliged to divide their community and separate. Now their confessor, Father Clorivière, writes me that some unexpected help is enabling them to remain in their monastery, but he fears this will not continue for long.

We have just lost one of America's great missionaries, the Flemish priest, Father Nerinckx, founder of the Daughters of the Cross, for whom he opened at least ten convents. Only recently he paid us a short visit. He had taken up his residence in this diocese, where the Sisters are establishing schools, and he hoped to go with them to the missions among the Indians. Death overtook him just after he had returned from a visit here with the Reverend Jesuits, six of whom came from Europe with him on his last trip—for he had gone back several times to beg help for his missions.[32] Yesterday the Jesuits held a solemn service for him, at which there was a funeral discourse. It seems as if this holy man came here just to spread with his last breath his love of the poor. He remarked that the one means of planting religion firmly in this country is through the education of the poor, for the rich are very indifferent to this matter.

One of my anxieties is the fact that it is so inconvenient for the Jesuits to care for our spiritual needs. The distance of their farm from the church causes them much trouble. The Father says Mass on alternate weekdays here, the other days at the farm, but on Sundays he is obliged to come at an early hour to hear confessions, and all his community have to come also—in the heat of the summer, in the downpouring rain, in the most severe winter weather. The creeks in floodtime are difficult and dangerous to cross and frequently quite impassable. They really ought to own our house, which is contiguous to the church. But if we gave it to them, we should lose all the fruit of our struggle to get established, and we should have to begin all over again somewhere—and I am too lazy for such an effort. In St. Louis success would be uncertain and housing expensive. Here our cows cost us almost nothing, for they graze in the common meadows and return by themselves at milking time. Firewood is less expensive here than in St. Louis. I know of no one who would contribute enough to counterbalance such a sacrifice, and what would we do for spiritual help in St. Louis?

We are in complete obscurity here, but it is very sweet to lean for support on Divine Providence, awaiting each day what we need for soul and body. On the other hand, who knows but there may come a letter from the higher Jesuit Superiors forbidding the Fathers here to continue with our spiritual direction. I have had reason to fear this several times, but there is no way in which I can parry the blow, so I just live in complete abandonment. Even if there were several priests in the community, they would not want to reside near the convent, and given the farm as their residence, the inconvenience of the cross-country trip is serious. Our house stands between two creeks which are so swollen this year that our gardens and yard have been turned into a lake and the little bridges and our fences have been washed away several times. Coming to the church or returning home, the Father has had to let his horse swim across, and he has at times crossed on a floating log. One day we saw the horse come trotting up without saddle or rider. We looked at one another in terror, fearing the Father had been drowned. But after a while he arrived, wet from head to foot. His horse had thrown him. The young man who found the saddle said in an insolent tone, "What will you give me if I return it to you?" Such is the courtesy, the helpfulness, and the gratitude of his parishioners. . . .

While describing with simple accuracy the anxieties and external hardships that made up such a large part of life at Florissant, Mother Duchesne gives no hint of the extent to which she carried on personal mortification. Since, as time went on, things grew not easier but harder, she might have been expected to accept these God-sent circumstances as penance enough. But that was not Philippine's way with God. Possessed of great vitality of mind and body, she gave herself to the duty and privilege of serving Him with astonishing energy. She rose early to secure time for prayer before she gave the morning call to the community. Then she made her way to the sacristy to prepare for Holy Mass. The eve of a feast usually found her in the chapel or church late at night, decorating the altar and shrines. In her work as sacristan she experienced contact with the admirable qualities as well as the rough idiosyncrasies of Father Van Quickenborne. There were clashes between them at times; and when she held her ground, she knew she was likely to suffer for her courage. Where principle was involved, she would not compromise, and on occasions she felt it her duty to appeal to Bishop Rosati.[33]

Mother Duchesne's day was long and arduous. Often keeping the roughest manual work in the house for herself, she gave the novices a rare example of loving God "not in words, but in deeds." They reverenced her already as a saint, yet they were not shy or ill at ease with her. The lesson of self-sacrifice which made up the fabric of her day impressed itself indelibly on their souls. Her position as superior would certainly have entitled her to a room for her own use, but it also gave her the privilege of claiming for this purpose the cubbyhole under the stairway leading from the hall to the second story—a place of stifling heat in summer, of bitter cold in winter. In this as in so much else, she imposed on herself privations and austerities which she would not have tolerated for her Sisters. When she gathered up the fragments of food that remained after the children's meals, she kept them for her own use at table; but when the children brought in nuts and fruit after their rambles in the woods, she saw to it that the nuns had a share in these.

As Mother Duchesne was the first in the household to rise in the morning, she was the last to retire at night. After making the rounds of the visit to assure herself that lights and fires had been extinguished in the house and its dependencies, and windows and doors fastened securely, she often sat down in the little parlor to write letters—a relaxation from the tensions of the day and an outlet for a heart that needed comradeship, to bring her *Journal* up to date, or to balance the convent account book. This done, she would make her way noiselessly to the chapel for a last hour of prayer—an hour of soul-surrender to God. Before the tabernacle her awareness of the Divine Presence was almost tangible. Recollected in her union with the Sacred Heart of Jesus, she made Him more than ever the term of all her endeavor, the inspiration and reality of her life. In prayer she came to judge as He judges, to desire only what He willed, to hand herself over without reserve to the Providence of God. It was a complete and wholehearted surrender of self, yet there was frequent need of renewal when particular circumstances and renunciations called for a deeper plunge into the Sacred Heart.

Sometimes her absorption in prayer kept her kneeling upright for hours. Sometimes, wearied with work and anxiety, she fell asleep and woke only at dawn. "One night as she passed before the picture of St. Regis, she lifted her lantern to get a better view of her beloved patron and stopped to pray. Her eyes, heavy with sleep, closed, and she lost consciousness. Firm and erect she stood there until one of her religious, coming to look for her, found her asleep on her feet." [34] She laughed off the incident, but Mother Mathevon tried after that to keep a discreet surveillance on her superior's nocturnal devotions. Her own fatigue, however, made the task hopeless.

The strain of life at Florissant was often relaxed by Philippine's delightful stories of Sainte Marie, Paris, and St. Charles, or of her childhood and her family, by her sly humor within the community circle, by holidays and little "celebrations." [35] Sometimes she took the novices for a ramble across the meadow and through the woods for relaxation and nature study, in which she found real delight. They came to know just what to expect when Mother Duchesne drew out her watch and examined it attentively, suggested a little rest on logs or stumps or boulders or in the tempting swings dropped by wild grapevines, then took from her capacious pockets some *rafraichissement* in the form of apples or nuts or raisin cakes or a little chocolate.

Her gay spirit enlivened recreations and encouraged all to contribute to the conversation that added interest and amusement to community gatherings. She was constructive in her approach to character training, endeavoring to plant virtue rather than uproot faults; and she showed endless patience with difficult characters. Respecting the personality of each, she made no attempt to force souls into a common mould. She was too deeply imbued with the Society's spirit to adopt such a method.

She could give a severe reprimand when necessary, along with a suitable penance as a means of reparation, but she was never coldly unjust or partial. [36] She knew she could ask more of some than of others, but all were conscious of her maternal love for them—a love so supernatural that it was always counted on and always the same. Very sensitive herself, she had great sympathy with those who suffered from depression or discouragement, and she offered no mere conventional compassion. She knew what it meant to be self-willed and headstrong, to shudder under humiliation, to cringe under pain, to lose all sense of proportion in the very intensity of one's fervor. So she was prepared to deal with her nuns and her novices in a cheerful, practical way, ready to listen, resolute and self-possessed, ready to joke a little and let things drop.

Her greatest consolation in this work of training souls lay in the tremendous confidence she placed in Father Van Quickenborne. The change in his attitude toward the *Dames du Sacré-Coeur*, whose presence at Florissant he had at first resented, is described by Philippine, along with other things, in her letter to Mother Barat on November 24, 1824:

> I just received a letter from you that presupposes one written before it and seems to be a continuation of it. I am told there is a small packet of mail for me in St. Louis. I hope it contains that beloved letter; but I cannot put off writing to you until I get it, as the steamboat remains only a short time in St. Louis and the winter freeze makes river communication very rare. This letter will not reach you before New Year's, but my wishes and those of my Sisters here will always be welcomed by the most indulgent of mothers. She knows well that if this little portion of her family has no other good qualities, it is eager to be recognized by its appreciation of its Mother and its desire to please her by its fidelity, and to increase her happiness by the continual prayers it addresses to God for her.
>
> Your letter expresses the acute suffering of your heart over the sad condition of Mother Octavie last year at this time. But ever since we had the idea of asking you to write to Prince Hohenloe, her condition has improved and she is practically well now. I cannot call it a miracle, for medication was continued; but if it is one, I am inclined to attribute it to the Father Rector. He asked to see the troublesome sore and little by little he cured it. God made use of the medicine he used. It was mercury, used internally and externally over a long period of time. There remains only a scar at one side of the mouth, but the Father Rector uses it as a matter for humiliations; he asks her to let him see it, then he says "Oh, how ugly it is!" He has worked earnestly on that soul and with success, leading her in the way of renunciation, detachment, and humility.
>
> We are all very fortunate in having such direction. I much prefer poverty in the shadow of the Jesuits to the comforts of life under any other influence. For quite a while I feared this good fortune would not last, either because of their poverty or because of the rules of the Society of Jesus. But the Father Rector told me recently that the Father General has given the necessary permission. The Rector no longer keeps aloof from us and has gone so far as to say he might someday build us a little house at St. Charles, with a street between the Jesuit residence and ours. As soon as

there are two priests in this group, I think one of them will reside there, as there is no priest north of the Missouri yet, and crossing the river was so dangerous this year, the Father Rector realizes the necessity. He was highly pleased with the choice of Monseigneur Rosati as our coadjutor bishop. He will be titular bishop very soon. Between them [Van Quickenborne and Rosati] confidence and esteem are mutual. The good Bishop speaks earnestly of his love for the Society of Jesus. He solemnly baptized a little savage for whom Mr. Mullanphy and one of his daughters were sponsors. He gave minor orders to several of the young scholastics and has conferred the sacrament of confirmation.

Since the Bishop's departure for the Barrens, where he resides, the Father Rector gave a retreat to his sons, and then one to his *daughters,* as he has called our nuns several times. Last year we were only *Mesdames!* This change of title delighted our Sisters, who had a perfect retreat. He spoke six times a day, for the four meditations, the consideration, and an introduction. The points of meditation given in the evening were repeated in the morning. The good Father also gave his time generously to each one individually, though he and a companion were also making their retreat. I was in charge of the pupils, and Sister Catherine had the care of the orphans. She has had to walk a chalk line recently under Father Van Quickenborne's spiritual direction. . . . We have only five boarding pupils. One of them owes a year's tuition and board, and there is no hope of collecting a cent. Another is the youngest Miss Mullanphy [Octavie], who was placed here to prepare for her first Communion, after the Father Rector requested it.

Monseigneur Du Bourg does not write to us any more. You know, I am sure, that he does not want a convent of the Sacred Heart in New Orleans. He told Mother Eugenie, by way of excuse, that it was because of the frequent epidemics in the city and the detriment another institution might be to the Ursulines, who have moved into their new house. The old convent, which they gave to Monseigneur, furnishes him with a church. He lives at the college, which he has entrusted to a secular priest. It has only day students. Mother Eugenie, realizing your disappointment at not having a convent in New Orleans, is very eager to accept an offer of one on the river. I invited her to come here to discuss it, as I cannot leave Florissant. It would be good to see each other again and to let her choose the nuns who might best aid her. She says we really should have two houses in Lower Louisiana to support this one, if we take the Indian girls, and she can show me a letter from you giving permission, if we consider the conditions advantageous.

I cannot answer your other letters, my dear Mother, because I have not received them yet, but I did so want to write to you. I beg you not to forget to send Miss Mathevon's 600 francs for the Fathers. They are impatient to get the money. If you have not already sent it by a bill of exchange, Father Borgna would be the best one to bring it. But you must impress on him that he is to give it personally to the Fathers, or to us for them. They need so much more. The Father Rector told me he had not money enough to buy a single hog, and pork makes up half of life out here. He has no altar for the chapel at the farm. A few days ago I received a worn-out piece of heavy cotton material with this note pinned to it: *Please mend this for us. It is our antependium for the altar. Miserere nostri.* Something more suitable that had come to us from our dear France replaced that ragged thing at once.[37] Everything that has ever been sent to us has been useful and precious.

We appreciate Father Barat's interest in us. I have often wanted to write to him recently, but I do not want to be importunate. The Father Rector here has his spirit and his method. This paints the most perfect picture of him, according to our heart. I cannot conceive how Mother Eugenie could advise our abandoning this house. Though it is poorer, I find it much happier than hers. The *essential spirit* can be preserved here always under influence of this good spiritual direction. . . .

2. 1825—1826

May our offering be a gift acceptable to Thee . . .

Liturgy of the Mass

ON NEW YEAR'S EVE a letter from Mother Audé informed Mother Duchesne that with the sanction of the Mother General she had accepted the offer of a foundation at St. Michael's, Louisiana, on the Mississippi River. Father De La Croix, the pastor there, had been working zealously to bring this about and had collected $4000 to finance the building of a convent. The negotiations had been carried on by Mother Audé, and Philippine's reaction was generous and impersonal. As the school at Florissant was now practically empty, it seemed only reasonable to encourage a new beginning that offered every promise of success. But Mother Duchesne's heart was in Missouri, and she showed more enthusiasm for projects there than for those in the deep South when she wrote to Mother Barat on February 28, 1825:

There is disillusionment in store for anyone who comes to this country in search of success, honor, pleasure. But those who desire only the pleasure of God abide in peace even in the midst of failure, for God has not told us He requires us to be successful. All your daughters whom God has chosen for this mission are contented with their lot. None of them long for any other distinction, not even that which would place them at your side, and that would be the most tempting for them. The character of your American-born daughters may be rather unstable, and that is why it will always be well to have among them some European religious trained at the center of the Society and able to direct them according to the spirit.

On this point I have much with which to reproach myself, but every day I invoke the Holy Spirit to help me carry on the work, and also St. Regis, and more especially *Our Lady of Good Counsel.* . . .

In my last letter I wrote you about the establishment at St. Michael's. They have already raised 75,000 francs in voluntary contributions. Mother Eugenie, who has accepted the offer, will have given you all the details. I think that house at St. Michael's will do much good in Louisiana and will support the one here in Missouri, where there are only three boarding pupils now. I expect Mother Eugenie this very month. She is coming to get some of the religious in our community. She cannot take anyone from Opelousas, and her departure will leave an enormous place to be filled there. It seems to me that Mother Xavier Murphy, who was well trained in France and who has gained the confidence of the people, is the person best fitted to replace her.

Banking entirely on confidence in God, the Father Superior of the Jesuits has bought the house we formerly lived in at St. Charles. He wants to erect a church near it and has promised the people there that we will open a school. I am very much in favor of doing so, as we have so little to do here. St. Charles has a larger population, and the canal planned by the Government and already completed between New York and the Great Lakes is going to establish communications between the two oceans by way of the Missouri River. That will attract more settlers to its banks, and that is the region assigned to the Jesuits by Monseigneur Du Bourg. They have sent no one there permanently yet because they lack priests; but when one is stationed at St. Charles, it seems to me that we could not refuse to work in a section that is so destitute of educational helps. St. Louis is satisfied with its Protestant schools. Very few people want us there, and no one is willing to sponsor us. A boarding school for poor children is the only kind we could establish just now at St. Charles, but it could be run nicely by Mother Lucille. God blesses her work, but I do not think she would be physically able to go down to Louisiana or willing to sacrifice the spiritual direction of the Jesuit Fathers. The Father Superior admires her greatly because of her virtue, her peaceful manner, etc.

Although I have spoken of our abandonment to Divine Providence, I must admit that we are waiting impatiently for the arrival of Father Borgna, who will, I hope, console us with some recent news of you and some help for the Jesuits. . . . We are all in good health, but we are pining for news from France. On February 2 Miss Timon took the holy habit of a coadjutrix Sister, with the name Aloysia. Her brother, a man of great virtue and talent, is at the Lazarist seminary and soon he will become one of the most distinguished priests in the diocese.[38] We have no postulants at present. . . .

For nearly a year Mother Duchesne had been looking forward to the arrival of Father Borgna. Her anticipation had been whetted on learning that he was to be accompanied by Father Louis Dusaussoy, nephew of Mother Barat, who had "inherited some of his uncle's attachment for the Religious of the Sacred Heart," as the holy foundress put it. He had been chaplain for a while at the convent of La Ferrandière, Lyons, but missionary ideals had urged him to a venture in America. Mother Barat recommended him in an affectionate manner to her nuns, and they were happy to welcome him.[39] The arrangements for the foundation at St. Michael's were going forward swiftly—too swiftly for Mother Duchesne, who wrote in evident alarm to the Mother General on March 8, 1825:

I have just received a letter from Monseigneur Du Bourg telling me of the arrival of Fathers Borgna and Dusaussoy. He adds that they have brought many letters for us from you. They will send them to me when they come up to the Seminary [at the Barrens]. . . . Monseigneur writes that you told Father Borgna I should go to St. Michael's, and so he wrote that to Mother Eugenie. I do so wish he would go more slowly, for I think I should wait for a direct and positive letter from you before making so extraordinary and so unexpected a change. Quite a while ago you named Mother Eugenie for the foundation in New Orleans. Since that cannot be made because Monseigneur does not want it, St. Michael's takes its place. Mother Eugenie is well known in all that part of the diocese. She will build up a good reputation for the house and she is quite capable of sustaining it by her zeal, her prudence, and her talent for handling children. I have already written you all my thoughts on that score, especially in my last letter of February 28. Here, more than in France, the old and the ugly are held in low repute. I grow more unsightly every day. Gray hair, no teeth, horribly roughened hands, all make me in no way suitable to cut a figure in that fastidious section of the country. They are all right here in the village where, indeed, they call me quite affectionately *"poor devil."*

Philippine certainly quoted this good-humoredly. God had planted in her soul a personal contempt for the world and the things it esteems, yet she knew they could be used effectively for furthering the interests of the Sacred Heart. Eugenie Audé's talents and abilities were frequently the theme of her praise, and she was sincere in urging the Mother General to entrust to her the new enterprise at St. Michael's. There was a further reason, and Philippine continued:

If I should dwell on the spiritual side there would be still greater disadvantage in sending me. So I really think Eugenie is the only one suited to be superior at St. Michael's. Mother Xavier Murphy is the one for Opelousas, where she is known and loved. As to this community, I realize full well that I should be in the last place. But the Reverend Father, with whom I discussed the matter, said that, if such a change were made, this house would soon be closed. True, it is miserably poor, but for that very reason it is dear to me, and it was never before so favored, as far as spiritual help is concerned. The Reverend Father now takes a great interest in it, and in time we will develop the work for Indian girls, which we so desire. I have even been told by him that if Mother Octavie or another religious whom he named was at the head, neither he nor any of his brethren would take any more interest in the house.

I am simply telling you what I think I should. When one vegetates in this country, one must be satisfied with one's lot. Except for food, we are not in want of anything, not even clothing. We can get some help from the South. And if, as our Rule says, the poor should be preferred to the rich, we have no reason to envy Opelousas. We care for as many souls as they, and we shall always have more novices. You know Mother Eugenie has trained only one novice so far, and here ten have persevered. This number will increase when the new type of spiritual direction has overcome the old prejudices. I did not want to write to you before receiving your letters that are still in New Orleans, but I feared Monseigneur might press me for a decision. I beg you to make it, taking into consideration my age, which makes me expect death soon,[40] my defects, and my incapacities. We are all fairly well.

The Fathers have received $500 from the Government for the Indian boys. . . .

Mother Audé came up to St. Louis on the steamboat *General Brown* and arrived at Florissant on March 21. "She brought us $160 from various friends in France and America and a supply of provisions from the kind Ursulines," Philippine noted in her *Journal*. "She informed us of the prosperous condition of her convent [at Grand Coteau], where there were 27 boarding pupils, and also told us the collection for St. Michael's has amounted to $7000 in free gifts." There was no temporal prosperity at Florissant for her to boast of, but there were spiritual riches such as Eugenie had not enjoyed since her departure in 1821: Palm Sunday, with the blessing of the palms and the liturgical procession, the Passion chanted at Mass by the rich voices of the young Jesuits; *Tenebrae* chanted by Jesuits and nuns in church and choir alternately as dusk fell in the valley on Wednesday, Thursday, and Friday of Holy Week; adoration on Holy Thursday kept up by the Jesuits during the day and by the nuns at night. On Easter Sunday morning Matins and Lauds were recited at half past five, followed by meditation and an early Mass with a first Communion ceremony for children of the parish, who spent the day at the convent, regaled at both breakfast and dinner on the supplies received from the Ursulines.

But there was an unexpected and triumphant joy for Philippine when in the late afternoon of April 6 Father Van Quickenborne arrived at the convent and presented to her two little "savages" as the first pupils of the "Female Indian Seminary" she had dreamed of opening. Housed in a little building by themselves and cared for by Mother O'Connor, these little Indian girls became Philippine's delight and a shining jewel in the crown of Mother O'Connor.

On April 17 the little church at Florissant witnessed the first profession ceremony of a Religious of the Sacred Heart in America when Mathilde Hamilton made her final vows, receiving the gold ring of perpetual espousals and the silver cross of full membership in the Society. With her Mary Ann O'Connor pronounced her first vows as a strengthening preparation for the labor she would expend and the mortification she would practice in caring for the Indian children. Mother Duchesne wrote of all this in a happy vein to Mother Barat on April 23:

Mother Eugenie reached here on March 21 and will leave again about the first of May with young Mother Xavier Hamilton, who will be a great help to her in making the new foundation. As I have begged you for a long time to shorten her five years of aspirantship, and also as I received from you her profession cross, I thought I was sufficiently authorized to allow her to make her final vows on Good Shepherd Sunday. The Father Superior presided at the ceremony and preached a fine sermon. The other Hamilton sister, for whom you also sent a profession cross, is not yet twenty-one years of age, but she begs you to allow her, as soon as she reaches that age, the same happy privilege as her sister, who is our first American professed member and the first choir nun chosen to help in a foundation. With her will also go Sister Ignace [Labruyère], an excellent coadjutrix aspirant, and Sister Aloysia [Timon], an American coadjutrix novice. These are the three Mother Eugenie has chosen, and they are all we can possibly give, for we now have three groups of boarding pupils—those who pay 900 francs, those who pay 179 francs, and the Indian girls who have begun to come at last. We put them under the care of an Irish religious who made her first vows on Good Shepherd Sunday. She speaks English, is about 40 years of age, and is a person of solid virtue, so she is the best qualified among us for this work, which occupies part of her time during the day and keeps her separated from us at night in the Indian school house. The little savages call her *Mamma*, and they all dance around her wherever she takes them, whether to the cows or the chickens or the garden. We let them spend their time in these active occupations, for they cannot endure a sedentary life.

Mother Eugenie has shown us the plan for the convent at St. Michael's. It will be agreeably situated and very commodious. Everything seems to indicate that this foundation, which is better located than the other two, will succeed. I beg you, Reverend Mother, get prayers for us all and for our mission. There are always obstacles confronting us, but in the midst of these we see the finger of God who directs His work. We are very fortunate to see it carried on at all, and more fortunate if, leaving that consolation to others, we keep for ourselves only the cross and complete abandonment to God in all things.

The departure was set for May 12 on the steamboat *Magnet*. While preparations were under way, Mother Duchesne received from her sisters Amelie and Euphrosine letters she had been long expecting. In April of the previous year Mother Barat had written her news of the deaths of her sister Adelaide, and of her niece, Louise Lebrument, who had followed her mother so quickly into eternity. But it was only in May, 1825, that Philippine received direct details from the family, and she hastened to answer their letters on May 10, writing to Madame Jouve:

MY DEAREST SISTER,

I received your letter and that of Madame de Mauduit telling me of the death of our dear sister Adelaide, but they reached me a year and two months after that sad event occurred. My Superior General had already written to me about it, taking for granted that I had received the details from my family, so I awaited them with anxiety. In the midst of such deep heart-suffering, faith and piety find great consolation in the heroic virtues of one who was such a good mother, and in the resignation of her poor children and husband who loved her so tenderly.

Distance from you prevents my writing all that my heart suggests. I beg you to send on to that dear afflicted family this little note of sympathy, which is a very feeble expression of my sentiments and prayers for them. I am so grateful for the details you gave me about your own family and that of Madame de Mauduit. Please express to her my sentiments of sorrow, and also to Melanie at Romans and to my brother. How I regret not being able to write to them all just now! Four of our nuns are leaving for Louisiana sooner than I expected, and I shall probably never see them again. They are going to open the third house of the Society in America, so I must give them every moment of time before they leave us tomorrow.

In spite of all this, I cannot let the steamboat go without a letter to you, and through you to my sisters and your husband. I received some time ago the magnificent brocade material which was sent to me as a gift by M. Jouve. Monseigneur was so eager to have it, I just had to give it to him. It certainly will be more suitable on the Bishop in New Orleans than in our little village. And I really made use of it in the way that gave me most pleasure, for I enjoyed being able to present a gift to this good Bishop who has taken such an interest in us. I am all yours in the Heart of Jesus. . . .

During the weeks immediately following the departure of Mother Audé and her companions, Mother Duchesne was particularly concerned about the Indian school. She was eager to do her share of begging and more eager to see aid given to the Jesuits. When friction arose between Father Van Quickenborne and Bishop Du Bourg, she was caught in a conflict of loyalties that was unpleasant for her; but when she found herself involved in a misunderstanding with Father Van Quickenborne himself, she paid bitterly for her zeal. On June 8 she wrote to Mother Barat:

> If Father Niel, pastor in St. Louis, comes to you to beg financial help, will you please state the purpose of what you give him— whether for the Jesuits or for ourselves, since we are carrying on work for the Indians.[41] They now have ten boys, and we have six girls. The government has appropriated a sum of money for the civilization of the Indians. As the Secretary of War is in charge of this, I am writing to him to ask support for four teachers and money to help erect a school building which will cost at least three thousand francs. The policy of the government is to give aid and encouragement only to associations which have means to found institutions. So even if he gives us something, it will be but a fraction of our expense. But we must rely on Divine Providence and not do less for God than the Protestants, who have schools for the Indians in many sections of the states. . . . I beg you to get much prayer for our work. We shall call again and again to you: *Money, money,* but you will not mind since it is for the savages, the objects of all our prayers, for it was through love for them that you sent us to this country.
>
> Monseigneur Du Bourg had promised the Jesuit Fathers the alms he might obtain from France for mission works, but they have received nothing, and I believe Monseigneur himself is the poorest priest in the diocese. There is, as a result, a little friction between them. In order not to increase it, you might send directly to them [alms intended for the missions]. This will always be the best way; and since there is no privacy about our financial affairs in New Orleans, it would be better to send all by way of New York, even at the risk of losing in the exchange. . . .
>
> We must rely on God alone—and it seems almost miraculous when you think that we have been able to live according to our Rule in this country for so long a time. . . . The Father Superior told me to write and ask you to recall Mother Eugenie here, but I consider her more necessary in Louisiana, for with the spiritual direction we have here a mediocre superior can avoid mistakes; down there the danger lies on all sides and the very climate goes to one's head. . . .

Philippine's letter to the Secretary of War drew upon her head the wrath of the Jesuit superior. Of course the letter was never put into the mail, as she later recounted, but in early June of 1825 they were both sick; both were weary and overworked; both were strong-willed and hotheaded; and both were zealous and holy religious. His changing judgments on her as a superior must have been particularly hard to bear, perhaps even baffling, for she relied on his spiritual discernment. Had she been less frank and confiding, she certainly would have escaped some hard blows. Perhaps the severest humiliation she ever received occurred as a consequence of a lively argument they carried on in the sacristy one summer day. There was question of some minor change in the arrangement of the sanctuary. Tradition says it was all about a little piece of carpet on which she wished him to stand.

> Both held to their views on the subject with that tenacity which is sometimes to be observed in the saints when there is question of what is for the greater glory of God. Father Van Quickenborne went so far as to threaten to have the altar removed, as he said he had given it to the church. "In that case," replied Mother Duchesne, "I shall take the tabernacle, which belongs to me." An altar without a tabernacle, or a tabernacle without an altar—either condition would have been embarrassing—so very embarrassing that the matter rested there. But the feast of the Sacred Heart was at hand. On the eve Mother Duchesne presented herself for confession, but instead of absolution which she had come seeking, she heard this terrifying sentence: "Tomorrow you will not renew your vows," and the shutter closed, putting an end to her pleading. Next day the poor superior, in order to avoid comments, could only feign illness and remain in bed instead of leading the community to the altar rail for the renovation of vows. When she was sure they were all in the chapel and no one would see her, she crept noiselessly across the hall and prostrated herself behind the chapel door, weeping silently. When Mass was ended, she went back to her cubbyhole, to spend a day of agony and shame. And only after a week of suffering was she accorded the absolution she had sought.[42]

This is the story that must be kept in mind as one reads Philippine's letter of July 3, 1825. The original is not extant; the existing copy is mutilated, but the missing portion may be supplied from the authentic source quoted above. The *Journal* entries for this period make no allusion to personal suffering on the part of Mother Duchesne, though they do mention Father Van Quickenborne's illness on, and immediately after, the feast of the Sacred Heart, and Mother Duchesne's recovery on the feast of St. Francis Regis. The letter cited below is stamped with the affectionate interest, earnest sympathy, and ardent zeal that always marked her attitude toward the Jesuits:

Tomorrow we celebrate the feast of *Independence* in this country. There will be rejoicing among all social classes and in all regions, for the Catholics do not forget that this day gave them freedom of worship. Up to that date [1776], at least so I am told, anyone could kill a Catholic with impunity in Virginia. As for myself, I shall anticipate July 22 and celebrate in my heart now and always the treasured and inspiring *dependence* that binds me to you. Yes, I shall bless God for it to my dying day, and we shall be united in spirit to all the good wishes addressed to you on the feast of St. Magdalen.

In my recent letters I told you my health was failing. I did not know myself, I was so changed. On the eve of the feast of St. Regis I was very weak, but I did not ask for anything or pray for a cure. Then on the day of the feast I found myself in my former state of good health.[43] And in order that I might recognize with certainty the hand that had touched me, everything just then should have contributed to sap my strength: very great heart-suffering, troubled future, disturbed conscience, ill success, difficulties as superior, long and anxious waiting for news from our Sisters who left on the feast of the Ascension, prostrating heat. It only remains for me to make better use of the time ahead. Still, as this is uncertain, I beg you to let me know your wishes with regard to the government of this convent in the future. The work for the Indians is at last under way; since it is so dear to your heart, I trust you will decide to send here a person with a good *head* and one young enough to learn English.

I presume that the feast of the Sacred Heart was celebrated with pomp in the Paris convent this year. It was a very different matter here. I could not even have Communion on this, our most solemn feast, and in consequence I could not renew my vows in public. I could do so only in the depths of my heart. . . . Low Mass, no sermon; none the following Sunday when the feast was celebrated in the church, which is dedicated to the Sacred Heart. When the choir was still singing the Kyrie they saw that the priest had finished reading the Epistle. He felt indisposed, so the rest of the Mass was in silence. . . . One priest cannot serve four parishes, two communities, and the sick people living at great distances from here. His life is in continual danger. Lately, while crossing a river on horseback, he was thrown from his horse, but he held on to the reins until his feet touched the river bank. On his way back the water was even higher, and though he was on horseback he was drenched from the shoulders down from the splashing of the horse as it galloped so eagerly to get home.

The strictness of this holy priest displeases many people, especially the French, who say that he does not like them and that they will go to another priest. There is no other. He is the only one we have. . . . I realize from conditions close at hand and at a distance that a second priest would bring comfort to many hearts. One could not find a priest of greater merit, but sometimes the weaknesses of human nature need to be humored a bit. . . . And since an abundance of spiritual goods is very helpful, listen to my request, I beg you, and urge the Father General to allow some of the scholastics here to be ordained. It is argument enough to speak only of the vast apostolate which the Indians and the white people offer. In their widely scattered villages they are exactly *like sheep without a shepherd.*

I intended writing to the Secretary of War to obtain help for the Indian girls. But the Father Superior, who is acquainted with the government's intention of putting the boys and girls together here as in other *seminaries* of this kind, told me that I should be cutting his throat if I did so. That was enough to stop me. He wrote instead and stressed the advantage of separate education for the two sexes. I have small hope of success. The Presbyterians watch keenly for any advantage, and they will make an outcry against the novelty of the plan.

Through the weeks that followed the writing of this letter Mother Duchesne had frequently to record in her *Journal* "No Mass," for illness prevented Father Van Quickenborne from making the trip from the Jesuit farm to the church. When Bishop Rosati became aware of this condition of affairs, he sent Father Leo De Neckere to officiate at St. Ferdinand and give the Rector an opportunity to recuperate. But this arrangement displeased the irascible Rector. Yet Mother Duchesne judged him leniently. No one knew him better than she did. For two years now she had stood almost daily at the sacristy window in the early morning and watched for his figure to appear. At times dust-covered, perspiring, and weary almost before the day had begun, at other times drenched with rain or chilled to the bone with snow and sleet, the priest would be seen tramping across the fields, his black cassock flapping as he walked. Or he might come on horseback, his voluminous cloak held tight under his knees and billowing out around him like a balloon. She learned to interpret his moods— gruff and taciturn, or cordial and interested. She had suffered keenly under his sharp criticism, his brutal frankness, his unexpected rebuffs, and she had grasped hopefully at the judgments he expressed as to her incompetence, repeating them to her Superior General in the belief that they might bring about her

release from the office of superior. In every letter addressed to
her from the Mother House in France she looked for that news,
but instead, there came in September letters written many months
before in which St. Madeleine Sophie spoke her mind and heart
as only the saint could do. In the letter of January 10, Philippine
read:

> Now a word regarding your request to be relieved of the office of
> superior. If you will just reflect a little, you will realize that this
> is impossible, for I have no one to put in your place, and if you
> make a third foundation, how can you hope to be relieved of
> superiority? Besides, my dear daughter, would someone else do
> better than you? I think not. She might, perhaps, have more vir-
> tue, but certainly less experience and less self-diffidence. In a spirit
> of zeal for the work confided to you and for the salvation of souls,
> can you not make greater efforts to acquire the virtues you lack?
> When you have such powerful motives for advancing in perfec-
> tion, what can hold you back? Alas, I have little right to preach to
> you. I need this lesson far more than you do, my dear Philippine.
> How much reason I have to reproach myself! Still I must con-
> tinue to carry the burden, and it grows heavier every day. Then
> let us both put our trust in the Heart of Jesus. He will uphold our
> weakness, repair our foolish mistakes, and bring good out of them.
> If He has always acted in this way toward your Mother, who is
> so unfaithful, so blameworthy, what will He not do for you?

And in a letter written three months later the saint told her
self-diffident daughter:

> I approve of all you have suggested regarding the new foundation
> at St. Michael's. . . . You may also admit to final vows those
> whose names you proposed, only be very certain of the stability of
> their vocations. I have given up all thought of an establishment in
> New Orleans, so you see I am in perfect accord with you in all
> that you have done. . . .
> Now, my dear daughter, you are going to have three convents
> in America. You realize that two of these are entrusted to young
> superiors who will need guidance. The enormous distance that
> separates them from us makes it impossible for me to assume their
> guidance without serious ill-consequences. You have experienced
> the fact that long delays in correspondence bring about many
> abuses. So it is only fitting that the eldest of those to whom I have
> confided the American mission should be in charge of the whole
> of it. Now to you, my dear Philippine, I entrust the direction of
> these three establishments. Though we have not adopted the term

provincial in the Society, you must function as a provincial in Louisiana. You will begin to groan again at that new responsibility, but God will help you bear it. And, moreover, since you are living close to our Fathers, they will give you advice, and indeed it is from that source that there flows the fresh stream that waters our poor labors.

You see, my daughter, that I have entered into your views and I applaud the desire you expressed to remain at Florissant. You know from previous letters that I hold as strongly as you do to conserving that house because of the presence of the Jesuit Fathers in the neighborhood. If they do open a church and residence at St. Charles, I shall approve of putting some of our nuns there again . . . provided God gives us the recruits for the work. You may make the arrangements you indicated . . . but follow the advice of our friends. I realize that your position in no way resembles ours and that you must have a certain amount of liberty for your work, but hold to cloister as far as possible. Let no one leave the convent property without real necessity. You know the reasons for this injunction.

There followed the welcome information that the loan of 6000 francs, borrowed in 1822 to satisfy Mr. John Mullanphy, had been paid off by Madame de Granville. Gifts from her brother, from Josephine, and from other benefactors in France had been a substantial aid to Philippine in the past year. Mother Barat added another piece of information that was of vital interest to her American families:

Our affairs in Rome have met with delay. The main work is done, but several articles in our Constitutions present difficulties, especially the matter of cloister. We insist, however, that we shall not have *grilles*. Now I ask you, where would you be in Louisiana if you were fettered by that impediment? Keep on praying, for the matter is so important. When you write, mention Father Varin, for we pass your letters on to him, and it is only right that our Father should find his name among those you mention. . . . As for you, my dear Mother, receive the assurance of the tender and inviolable attachment with which I am

Your Mother,
BARAT

On September 14 Philippine answered, first revealing anxieties that were disturbing her peace of mind, then with greater emotional intensity accepting the Mother General's decision that was so repugnant to her. Years before she had offered herself wholly to God, and He had taken her at her word. Perhaps this accounts for that sense of disgust with self that appears so frequently in her letters.

This feast of the Cross [she wrote] recalls a day when our little girls at Grenoble acted out a little play for you on the love of the cross. You yourself had asked them to, and we enjoyed it as a recreation. Experience teaches that always and everywhere the drama of crosses may be renewed. Personal crosses are light in comparison with those that are a drawback to our work. And I see so many of this kind, they actually hinder me from desiring death. That desire is a delightful sentiment when one is prepared and when work will not suffer by our loss. While I do not love life, I do love the houses we have founded, and I realize that the least important person—if she is sincerely devoted to a house—is a support necessary to uphold it. . . . The religious most essential to the good of this house is Sister Regis Hamilton. She has to take on all the heaviest and most unpleasant employments, one after another, because she is so solidly virtuous and courageous. But she is greatly needed for the classes, being the only one having a good English pronunciation—a thing so highly prized here that nothing else is considered comparable to it. What I tell you is true of the other houses and may prove to you, notwithstanding Monseigneur Du Bourg's opinion, that good coadjutrix Sisters, well trained and courageous, humble and ready to supervise the kitchen, would be quite as useful to us as choir nuns and would give the latter a chance to devote their time to the classes. . . . The school here is rising from its ruins. For a while we had only four pupils; now we have eleven, and several others have applied. I do hope all will run so smoothly, there will be no cause for complaint. . . . The Father Superior wants you to send us religious capable of governing a house, as here he finds no one to his liking on that point. I am the least fitted for the position, but the other two [Mothers Lucille and Octavie] lack the gift of organization and firmness, though they are very virtuous. My hope for the future of this house rests on Sister Regis, but she is not yet 21 years old. She is so good, I asked you to let her make her final vows when she reaches that age. . . .

I am far from capable of holding the office you impose on me. I bow my head in submission, but I realize my incapacity. If I were at the source of light, near a Father Varin, or a Father Perreau, or a Father Barat—but here all thought is but confusion when I want to do good—poor blockhead that I am—old, without talents, without lovable qualities, without virtue. Beg from these dear Fathers

I have named an intention in their holy prayers for their Brothers and Sisters, for our white children and our Indians. God alone can see the outcome of our work, but there are terrible obstacles in the way of success. I desire to live only in order to sacrifice my life to the hardest labor. I realize that repose is not for this life. One must put one's body on the rack and one's heart in the wine press. If I can be useful in the least little work for the glory of the Sacred Heart, I am willing to spend a long old age here, without success, without friends, as my only means of imitiating the Sacred Heart.

On October 27 Philippine recorded in her *Journal* the arrival of Father John Theodore de Theux and Brother John O'Connor, who had at last come to the aid of Father Van Quickenborne. This assured daily Mass again for the religious and the liturgical ceremonies that were so dear to Mother Duchesne's heart. There were other joys to record: in November the opening of the convent at St. Michael's by Mother Audé, with Mother Mathilde Hamilton as her assistant, Sisters Mullanphy, Labruyère, and Timon, and the choir novices, Sophie McGowan, Philippine Jourdain, and Aloysia Hardey; [44] the installation of Mother Xavier Murphy as superior at Grand Coteau, with Mother Carmelite Landry as assistant and treasurer; and in December the entrance into the Florissant novitiate of Anna Shannon and Suzanne McKay, "both former pupils of this house and both Irish." Of importance, too, was the addition of a small cabbage patch adjoining the convent property which Bishop Rosati gladly turned over to the nuns on her request. His letter of December 19, 1825, granting this favor, introduced Philippine to another young Irish girl who would one day become a prominent member of the Society of the Sacred Heart. The Bishop wrote:

There is a young girl of seventeen, Eleanore Gray, among the boarding pupils of our religious here. She was born in Ireland and came to this country with her parents four years ago. She has been at the Loretto convent about a year and has been well behaved. There she decided to become a religious, but she is not attracted to this community, so she has not entered it. She wants to go to your house and is willing to be a lay-sister if you do not think her sufficiently educated for the work of the choir religious. She can read and write well and seems to have very good intentions. In the event that you can receive her, please let me know. She could enter the convent next spring. In this way you will make an exchange with the Sisters here, for on the day after this coming

Christmas one of your boarders, the Spanish girl Maria [Canale] will receive the habit here. After a fervent postulantship of three months she appears undaunted by the austerity and poverty of her future religious life. . . .

Mother Duchesne answered the Bishop's letter without delay on December 29:

We shall be happy to receive, especially from you, the young Irish girl who offers herself for the Society. The points in our way of life that present the greatest difficulties are entire obedience and indifference to house and employments. It is on these articles that she must examine her strength and devotion.

I am delighted to learn of the course taken by Miss Maria Canale, who was not only a boarding pupil with us, but also a novice. Even then she preferred the [Sisters of Loretto]. . . .

Our Mother General, in answer to my petition, has given permission to Sister Regis Hamilton to make her final vows when she comes of age, without waiting for the completion of the five years required by our Rules. I also ask you to grant her this grace and so reward her virtues. She will be twenty-one during this coming Lent. . . .

Like a Christmas gift from Divine Providence came a packet of mail from France to Mother Duchesne, including a letter from Mother Barat answering her own letter of June 8. This exchange of correspondence within little more than six months was a vast improvement over the long delays they had experienced in the past, though it was by no means permanent. To Philippine's satisfaction the Mother General renewed her sanction of the projected reopening of a convent at St. Charles, but she made it clear that no help could be sent to America within a year or even eighteen months. The news that a general council of the Society would meet in 1826 inspired the unselfish missionary letter Philippine addressed to the holy foundress on December 27, 1825:

We are all kneeling in spirit at your feet to share the happiness of our Sisters as they offer you their good wishes for the New Year. May we add to your consolation by living up to your training and by working generously for Him to whose glory all your efforts are directed. Nothing helps us more in our work than the letters we receive from our Mother, who shows us the will of our Divine Spouse and who is animated by His spirit. I received your letter of August 4 containing so many interesting details, along with the sheet of decisions and permissions. I find only too great

latitude in your permissions, and I am so unfaithful, I fear the
spiritual blindness that results from this and the mistakes it may
cause me to commit.

I am delighted to know about the council that will meet in the
spring.[45] Next to getting us the three more religious we so desire,
the most helpful suggestion for us would be to propose that a little
annual fund might be assured us by a donation from each house,
taken from the alms for the poor given by the children. This could
be used to support one or two priests in the Missouri missions. A
vast field is opening up here for their zeal, and many are eager to
work in it. But a superior cannot send out his missionaries to face
almost certain death from starvation or the diseases that result
from it. The Father Rector suggested that I ask you for an annual
fund drawn from our boarding schools or those of the Jesuits.
Assured of this, he will take measures to extend the missions. All
the missionaries who worked in Paraguay received 1000 francs
each, yearly, from the King of Spain, and this supported the men
themselves, their churches, and the poor. Dear Mother, please take
this matter to heart. So much good would come of it.

The policy of the United States government is to drive all the
Indians out of the settled states. Agents buy their lands and push
them into uninhabited regions. The chiefs say: You are stronger;
we must give way to you—and they withdraw, but not without
great suffering, for they have not enough room for hunting. The
Sac tribe has made a treaty with the government and reserved a
large area of land where the French and half-breed people of their
nation will form a settlement at the junction of the Des Moines and
the Mississippi Rivers, about a four days' journey from St. Louis,
going north on the river. This is outside the present territory of
the United States. The head man there would be glad to have a
priest in residence, but the people are so poor, they could not
assure him a living. If this could be assured by a fund from Europe,
then this settlement of half-breeds, along with the Sac tribe and
the Foxes, among whom they say Jesuits were once martyred,
would very soon be evangelized. The Osage are farther away and
much more savage, for they have not been brought into contact
with ideas of the true religion as have the tribes near Canada. Take
this matter to heart, Reverend Mother, and may all turn out well.
Many people pretend that the Jesuits are rich; quite the contrary
is true out here, and no one thinks of helping them. So long as
there is no priest stationed at St. Charles I know it is impossible
for us to return there. Probably there will be one in the course of
the year. I am so glad you approve of that foundation when we
are able to make it.

I hear nothing from or about Grenoble. Sometimes I think God wants me to give up all correspondence except with you—but I am not sure—I see for and against it. We now have sixteen pupils, enough to support us. I beg only for our neighbors—that ought to be something to my credit! For myself I ask only prayers, especially for a holy death. In this matter I count on the prayers of Fathers Perreau, Varin, Barat, Ronsin, Roger,[46] to whom I offer my humble respects. Mother Xavier Murphy thinks M[onseigneur] D[u Bourg] is planning to return to France. It is astonishing how this country discourages people. This only goes to show that an association of some kind is needed to support the missions.[47] Poor America! When one thinks that between here and Canada and to the west as far as the Pacific Ocean there is not a single church, not one priest, it is just heartbreaking.

The New Year opened with the usual distribution of prizes for scholastic achievement, or good conduct, or encouragement, as the case might be, in each of the three little schools—Indian, parish, and boarding school. Then came the thrilling days when the first two Jesuit scholastics were ordained at the Barrens and returned for Mass at Florissant—John Baptist Smedts on January 29 and Peter John Verhaegen on March 11. It was like a personal triumph for Philippine. On the First Friday of March, moreover, Anna Shannon received the habit and white veil, and one month later Suzanne McKay's reception took place. Now Sisters Stanislaus and Aloysia, as they were called, began their formal novitiate training. They were earnest, fervent, and mature beyond their years, and their progress was a consolation to Mother Duchesne.

Father Van Quickenborne's project of a church at St. Charles seemed to be taking definite shape, so Philippine consulted Bishop Rosati on the matter of a convent there. His gracious reply giving "all the permissions necessary on my part"[48] had not reached her when she wrote to Mother Barat on February 18, 1826:

> I have twice acknowledged the receipt of the list of permissions you sent. You have divined all that could put us at our ease and make less of a trial the enormous distance that separates us from you. Only two points trouble me greatly. The first regards myself and is the responsibility to watch over three houses when I manage just one so wretchedly. My heart yearns more than ever for solitude, and I have neither silence nor solitude. I am growing old; my health is declining. I should weep in reparation for many years of my life, especially those of my religious life. I accept the work as penance, but it robs me of the spirit of prayer. If you only

give heed to my request, I shall gladly obey anyone whom you may give us as superior.

The foundation at St. Charles will not take place immediately, for the Reverend Father says he will not send a priest there until the stone church is built, and the stone is still in the quarry. I believe that if we follow the desire of the Pastor of St. Louis [49] and open a school in that town, it will be the only means of supporting ourselves with security in this part of the country. The plan of going to St. Louis pleases me all the more since the suggestion came from you. I wish we could keep just a parish boarding school here, at 180 francs a year. The first-rate boarding school at 500 francs a year will need a suitable building in St. Louis, and its location will depend on what we can find.

Monseigneur Rosati is planning to bring the Jesuits to St. Louis. The Father Rector has not told me all, but he has suddenly decided to allow two of his young deacons to be ordained. One of them preaches well. I have no doubt but that the project will go through—another reason for desiring to found a house of our own in St. Louis. . . .

Projects were moving ahead rapidly and getting somewhat complicated. Father Francis Niel was using his influence with Mother Barat for the founding of a convent and school in St. Louis. Bishop Rosati was urging the Jesuits to begin work in St. Louis. Father Van Quickenborne had his heart set on a new church and a convent at St. Charles. Mother Duchesne had the Bishop's permission to cooperate in the work at St. Charles, and also the Mother General's, and was being urged by her to consider the St. Louis foundation as of prime importance. But she had neither money nor nuns for a foundation anywhere. On March 1 she made this entry in her *Journal:* "The Father Superior has purchased from Madame Duquette the house and property where we lived in 1818. He is going to make all arrangements to build a stone church there."

This matter is not referred to again until after Monseigneur Du Bourg's last visit to Missouri. On April 26 he was given a little reception by the children of the boarding school at Florissant. On the thirteenth of the month he baptized six Indian children and confirmed sixty persons of the parish or neighboring missions. Then he made a trip to St. Charles with Father Van Quickenborne, returned to St. Louis, and set out for Europe, "after making over to the Jesuit Fathers the Church of St. Ferdinand, reserving for us in perpetuity," noted Mother Duchesne, "half of the tribune, the first sacristy, and the opening of our chapel on to the church." The Bishop carried with him letters for Mother Barat and Josephine de Savoye-Rollin which Philippine had written hastily on May 2. One paragraph to the Superior General told of the plans that had taken shape:

> The church at St. Charles is at last under way and our original house there is being repaired to receive us a second time. You have already named Mother Lucille superior. For that little convent she will need only nuns who understand English, as that language is generally spoken there now. It is agreed that she could not carry a heavier burden, especially not that of the novitiate. I believe Sister Regis can be trained for that after her final vows, for which you have given permission, but her youth has kept her from making them until today. She is one of our best religious, and she wears the last silver profession cross we had on hand. There are none left for our two oldest aspirants and for our good Irish nun [Mother O'Connor], who is really faultless. She is about forty years old and can help Mother Lucille at St. Charles, and even replace her in an emergency. . . . I shall write by post after Monseigneur's departure. I left him alone in order to write to you. . . .

During the summer of 1826 it was becoming apparent that the schools for Indian children at Florissant were doomed to be short-lived. This was a poignant sorrow for Philippine, for the goal of her venture to America had seemed in sight. There was compensation, however, in the increased enrollment in the boarding school. Twenty-four pupils filled the little dormitory and crowded the two or three classrooms. Among them was Ellen Mullanphy Chambers, a grandchild of John Mullanphy. "*La petite Chambert*," as Mother Duchesne called her, has preserved some interesting details in her reminiscences about Mother Duchesne and the convent school.

> I was impressed by the strength and kindness of Mother Duchesne's character [she wrote in later years]. In appearance she was not prepossessing. She was rather florid looking, though a blonde. This was probably due to her exertions in the garden and laundry, for no work was too hard for her. She had pale blue eyes and high cheek bones, but her face was strong and tender in spite of its lack of beauty. She had a great love for little children, gathering them around her whenever possible, though at this time she spoke very little, and very broken, English. The girls all loved to be with her. Though times were hard and provisions often very

scarce, the children had the best that could be procured, and every Sunday, as a special treat she took us to the pantry, where each could choose for goûter what she liked best in the scanty larder. The favorite delicacy on these occasions was usually huge sour cucumber pickles. She was interested in all our games, too, and personally arranged little dramas to be acted in the school room. These plays were all adapted from familiar Bible stories. What they lacked in proper costuming and scenery was made up for by the earnestness and interest of the little actors, inspired by Mother Duchesne. She was often very original in the methods she used with us; for example, in winter when she feared the children might catch cold from kicking off the bedcovers, she had them sewed up, like a bag.

She was an excellent needlewoman and taught the children sewing; her darning was especially beautiful. She also taught them to make the soft shoes worn by the religious. Her days were spent in unending labor. The rising sun found her in the garden, digging, planting, or gathering the ripened fruit and vegetables. On wash-days she hung out the clothes, took them in, and sprinkled them so they would be ready for those who were to do the ironing. Besides her manual labor, she taught the higher classes several hours each day and found time to read aloud for half an hour or so each day from some spiritual book to her little community. Holidays found her in the convent parlor making vestments for the altar, and canopies and banners for the many processions that used to take place in the little church and village. No work was too hard for her, and no matter how much there was to do, nothing however small was neglected. No matter how crowded the day with busy tasks, she found time for many little visits to the chapel. . . .

I was with her a great deal. Being the youngest in the school, my hours of class were short. Nothing made me happier than to plod along beside her in the garden, picking up the potatoes as she dug them and listening to her quaintly told stories of France and the convents there, of the children in that land which seemed so far away. Then often her stories would be about people in the Old and New Testaments. She was a noble and brilliant woman, but withal as simple as the child who followed her along the potato row.[50]

With the larger school came increased anxieties. A season of high water had set in, and once more the convent was isolated by the flooding streams that encircled it. There was illness among nuns and children, but worst of all was the condition of Mother Octavie. She had been stricken with fever early in April, and for nearly three months she was in a most pitiable condition, which Mother

Duchesne's efficient nursing could not relieve. Another sorrow came from Grand Coteau with the shocking news of the death of Sister Mary Ann Summers, first Religious of the Sacred Heart to die in America, and hardly out of her teens. But from St. Michael's there were glowing accounts of progress and prosperity. Mother Duchesne's letter to Mother Barat on July 15 touched briefly on the topics that were closest to her heart:

> God seems to raise great obstacles to the work of teaching the savages. The government is buying their land and pushing them out of the states of the Union, forcing them to live within the narrow limits of restricted territory that has not nearly enough space for hunting, and that is their only mode of subsistence. The various tribes thus herded together make war on each other and so destroy themselves, or at least the weaker nations are wiped out. Beginning this year the Indians are no longer allowed to hunt in the state of Missouri, so the parents of several of our Indian children have come to take their boys from the Jesuits and their girls from us, and we had no means of keeping the children here. Their parents simply said they could no longer come to see them, and as they are pagans they could not bring themselves to make this sacrifice. . . .
>
> The church building at St. Charles is rising. The walls are now up to the level for the window frames, and the masonry will probably be completed within a month. They have planned an opening on to the sanctuary for us, as was arranged here. They are very eager to have us there, but, Reverend Mother, unless we receive some re-enforcements from France it will be impossible for us to furnish the four nuns who will be needed. . . . Mother Octavie is not improving. It seems as if her body is made just for pain. . . . She can barely teach her class now, but even that is a great help, for most of our pupils are new (there are now twenty-four) and at different levels, and I cannot suffice for all. Mother Regis Hamilton made her final vows on the feast of the Sacred Heart. I hope she will become one of the finest religious in this country.
>
> Poor Mother Xavier Murphy is making a rough novitiate of superiority. She has lost quite suddenly Sister Mary Ann Summers, a religious who was such a great help to her. This death is a severe blow, especially as two other members of her community are ill, and Sister Marguerite is aging considerably and gets around so slowly.
>
> A week ago the flooding of our two creeks carried away our fences and bridges and destroyed our garden. Never have we seen the water so high. The lower part of the parish school was submerged, and this gave us great anxiety as the wooden building

is not solidly constructed and is supported on only four wooden posts. Mother Lucille was terrified and came back on a horse to the big house, which was perfectly dry, though the water surrounded it and the church completely. For a while we could not make a fire as we had no wood for fuel. . . .

There were times when the loneliness of life at Florissant weighed heavily on Philippine, when the way of the spirit was particularly rough, and she knew she must travel so much of that way alone. The sense of God's love was often lacking to her, and seldom did she find true and congenial companionship in America. There was no softness or sentimentality in her make-up, but a depth of affection that expressed itself lovingly, tenderly, in letters that were to travel thousands of miles to loved ones of her own family or of the religious family to which she belonged. Her yearning for news from home betrayed itself in a little note she sent to Josephine in August of this year, after she had learned of the fire that had destroyed a huge section of the chateau of Vizille, where Augustin Perier and his family had their country home.[51]

My dearest Cousin,

Have I been remiss in the duty I owe you? Since your letter telling me the sad news of your widowhood I have had no news from you. Indirectly I learned of your moving from Paris to Grenoble, taking with you the remains of your beloved husband, and of the unfortunate accident that caused a considerable loss to two of your brothers. I have shared deeply all these happenings, and not being able to express my sentiments to anyone but our Lord, I have talked to Him very frequently about you all. I trust He has sent these trials only to raise your souls higher. We may not understand His will for us in time, but in eternity the veil will be withdrawn and we shall see that He acted only for our happiness.

Our three American houses are carrying on their works. The faith is making progress; the erection of new dioceses and of Catholic boarding schools will serve, I hope, to spread it more and more. We have more non-Catholics than Catholics in our little school, and the same is true in several convent schools recently established.

Remember me to all our loved ones—they are all dear to me—and be assured of my deep affection for you. . . .

In the autumn of 1826, Mother Duchesne received from St. Madeleine Sophie a somewhat disconcerting letter, urging her to take steps at once to open a convent and school in St. Louis. Father Francis Niel had called several times at the Mother House in Paris and had painted so rosy a picture of prospects and advantages in the town to which he had no intention of returning that the Mother General wrote with enthusiasm:

> Yesterday [June 15, 1826], my dear Daughter, I saw Father Niel, the excellent pastor of St. Louis. He has returned from Rome, and I think we shall keep him for some months in France. He is considering seriously the establishment of a convent in St. Louis, and after all the details he has given me of conditions there, I have not the slightest doubt that such a foundation is necessary. The motives and reasons I need not recount to you. You are on the spot and so you ought to know and understand them far better than I. If, then, my dear Daughter, after weighing the matter before God, you are inclined to make this foundation, here is what Father Niel proposes to me: buy a piece of land in St. Louis for ten or twelve thousand francs; on this you can build. The good pastor will find means, he says, to aid you. You will have as a fund about 6000 francs which Mother Audé has drawn on me in New Orleans as a loan. I give you that for St. Louis, with about the same amount which our parting missionaries will bring you. I do not want this business undertaken before Father Niel's return. The property, however, must be secured as soon as possible, lest the desirable site be sold to others, or the price raised. There are two places available, I understand—the one rather small, the other large. I prefer the latter, but before concluding the purchase you must inspect the property. . . .

Philippine was baffled by these instructions. She had not been looking for property in St. Louis. She seems to have had no idea on what land Father Niel was building the new institution as he talked to the Superior General. His begging tour in Europe had not been very successful, and where else would he find means to aid her? The academy at St. Michael's had been opened but six months, and Mother Audé was not yet able to refund the 6000 francs. The arrival of religious from France, "the parting missionaries" referred to, was problematic; as a matter of fact, they reached St. Louis twelve months after this letter. From Louisiana Mother Duchesne was receiving news that weighed on her. The illness at St. Michael's was God's own gift of the cross, but the prospect of no chaplain at Grand Coteau called for a representation to Bishop Rosati, administrator of the diocese. There was much else she wished to tell him, so she wrote on October 3:

I have received two letters from our superior in Opelousas telling me of the departure of Father Rosti.[52] With her and the people of that district, from whom you must have received a letter, I too would have begged you to leave him in the position he holds, to the satisfaction of all, . . . if I had not thought that our reasons are not as weighty as yours and could not make you change your decision. If there is still time, let me join my petition to theirs, asking you to leave with my Sisters this priest who has their confidence and the approval of the entire parish. . . .

There is much sickness at our house of St. Michael's. The nuns have been so disabled that the children had to be given a vacation. Such a beginning would be unfortunate if we were not convinced that God has willed it so.

Father Niel, who was in Paris in June, has convinced our Mother General that a convent of the Sacred Heart in St. Louis would be very successful, and she writes me that she believes it necessary for us, telling me to foresee the means to make it succeed. Bishop Du Bourg had often spoken to us of a school for this city, and at his last visit he gave us the land. This has since been sold, and Father Van Quickenborne, to whom I spoke about writing to you, does not approve of the project. Our Mother General insists, however, and I foresee that our house here may not be large enough to accommodate the children who are applying. We can take only thirty, and this number may possibly be reached in a few months. Many Americans are desirous of placing their daughters with us to learn French. I should like to know your wishes in this matter. In any event, there are many children in St. Louis who are not able to pay for board and who could be day pupils. . . . We hope to see you with Bishop Portier and to receive your blessing. . . .

Bishop Rosati acceded to Mother Duchesne's petition regarding Grand Coteau and answered that Father Rosti would remain there *"provisionally,* that is to say, until the time when I can replace him by another priest who speaks both languages." He also added: "An establishment of your Society in St. Louis will do much good here in every way. So I must second the views of your Superior General. This is the first I have heard about the sale of land that the Bishop gave you for this purpose. Bishop Portier plans to visit you at Florissant, and I shall have the pleasure of accompanying him." [53]

Meanwhile Philippine had written to Mother Barat:

I have been awaiting a letter from you with great impatience. You had announced the holding of the General Council in June or July, and I had calculated when I might get the results, with other

news about the dear Society. Your letter written on the feast of
St. Regis reached me in about three months and told me the Council had been postponed. As to the religious you propose to send us,
I want only your choice. You will certainly pick those who will
fit in best. I only add with regard to Sister Boisson: if God gives
her the health, she would be most useful here, as we do all the
sewing for the Jesuit community. She would also teach our children to sew. But she should be the fourth or fifth member in the
party, as each convent needs a choir religious. . . .

The little house at St. Charles cost the Reverend Father 3,500
francs, for which I told him we would reimburse him if we reopen the convent there. But work on the church has stopped, and
there may be a lawsuit with the contractor. And how can we go
there without a priest? Father Van Quickenborne could easily
station one there now. I do not know why he will not do so. Far
from rejecting St. Louis, however, I am eager to go there because
of the many children who can never attend boarding school and
who would be day pupils. A Paris newspaper announcing the
resignation of Monseigneur Du Bourg has reached us. That means
a great loss for this ungrateful diocese that made him suffer so
severely. . . .

Perhaps the most significant event ever recorded in Philippine's
Journal was the approbation of the Society of the Sacred Heart
by Pope Leo XII on the feast of the Sacred Heart in 1826. The
news, announced in a circular letter in July, reached Florissant on
November 9, and Mother Duchesne gathered her community in
solemn conference to read to them the message which the Foundress clothed in words well calculated to renew loving fidelity to
the rules which now had become doubly sacred to them:

> The solid fruit which the Heart of Jesus expects from us in re-
> turn for such a favor is, without doubt, more punctuality, more
> generosity in the observance of our Holy Rules. Let each one
> now make them her special study; and to encourage herself in
> practicing them, let her say often to herself: "I am sure of obeying
> the Church and of doing the will of God." The more we fathom
> their spirit, the more we shall banish from our midst feminine
> pettiness and the softness inherent in our age, which is quite
> capable of stifling the seeds of virtue that at all times have made
> great souls and saints.[54]

Mother Duchesne wrote the glad tidings immediately to Bishop
Rosati and received an answer that was gracious and encouraging:
"I am deeply grateful for the happiness that Providence has sent

you, and for your kindness in letting me share your joy. A house of your Society in St. Louis will be completely in accord with my desires." [55] Meanwhile she poured out her heart to Mother Barat at great length and in the buoyant style that always revealed an upsurge of joyous enthusiasm in her soul:

> Your letter of September 2, 1826, brought me the purest joy I can have here on earth, next to that which the soul experiences in its union with Jesus Christ in Holy Communion. We had the fore-shadowing of the happy day of our approbation when Pope Pius VII favored us with his special blessing, and later when our present Holy Father so kindly sent us his blessing through one of our missionary priests.[56] But what a joyous thing it is to have secured that approbation we had almost despaired of! How it obliges us to tend to perfection! And how ashamed it makes me, to realize what I am, after the many favors with which we have been over-whelmed! They have not even made me a worthy member of the blessed Society to which I have the happiness of belonging. . . .
>
> All my Sisters here have shared in the joy of the whole Society, but the Father Superior, more than anyone else, showed special interest. He repeated several times that no news could have given him more pleasure. He wanted to announce it himself to the community and then to the children. As the next day was Sunday, he had a solemn Mass of thanksgiving offered, with deacon and sub-deacon, and he had each of his priests offer three Masses for the same intention and each of the brothers say the beads three times. He would have granted as many Communions as anyone might ask. So it is that in great events enthusiasm for the glory of God shines out in the saints. Since what I wrote you happened, there have been no more reproaches on his part, but he is not in favor of the establishment in St. Louis. I told him that, confined in so small a village, we were practically unknown and that far from finding subjects capable of becoming superiors (he argues that we should train superiors here before going to St. Louis), we should receive only a few mediocre recruits from time to time.
>
> Strengthened by your authority and that of Bishop Rosati, administrator of the diocese, I shall prepare the way. I am so eager for the arrival of the religious from France. Before going to work, they will need rest and time to get accustomed to the ways of the country. I think there is no reason to wait for Father Niel, if we can find a house. . . . I fear we shall get no help from the people of St. Louis, nor from Father Niel, for he will have trouble enough rowing his own boat. In your precious letter I found the letter from Madame de Rollin promising the gift of a thousand francs. I

shall use it as you desire, trusting confidently that God will give success to the new foundation. . . .

Mother Octavie's health seems to be improving; all the others are about as usual, especially myself, but I am no better spiritually. I recommend myself to the prayers of Fathers Perreau, Varin, and Barat, who all observe a very rigorous silence, and I have no longer any reason to induce them to break it. Please ask Mother Bigeu to write me a long letter.

Another laborious year was drawing to a close, and characteristically. On Christmas Day a scene in the convent parlor brought bitter grief to Philippine and must have made her regret the imprudent haste with which she and Father De La Croix had accepted the immature and sentimental piety of young girls newly in contact with religious teaching and devotional practice for genuine faith and doctrinal understanding. The *Journal* describes the shocking scene:

On this great feast day we had the sorrow of seeing and hearing one of our former pupils—one who had received baptism and first Communion in this house—blaspheme against our holy religion, and that right here in our own convent. Another of our pupils has denounced to their parents those of her companions who are inclined toward the Catholic faith, and the parents, being Protestants, have withdrawn their children. At the close of this year we have 23 boarding pupils, 10 Indian girls, and 12 day pupils in the parish school.

No hint of these unhappy incidents finds its way into her New Year's letter to Bishop Rosati. She writes, however, of a personal anxiety of conscience that would recur more than once in the years ahead, and that she would always submit to him with the utmost simplicity and confidence.

All your religious family at St. Ferdinand [she wrote on December 30, 1826] offer you their wishes for a holy New Year. She who has the privilege of writing in their name feels more than anyone else that esteem for her first Pastor which is always in her heart, making her thank God for His gifts and begging Him to keep this Father with us always. . . .

I have already taken some steps toward the foundation in St. Louis. It is going to be extremely difficult in view of the lack of interest in the city toward such works and our own lack of funds, for we are never able to put aside any savings. I have no doubt, however, that someday it will succeed. What troubles me greatly

—and on this I need your advice—is my vow of poverty, by which I no longer retain the right either to receive, or own, or dispose of anything. I did not advert to this when, without warning, Bishop Du Bourg gave me the land where our house now stands and told me to make my will in favor of two of our religious. Later, when I explained the matter to him, he gave me the necessary dispensations. Now I shall have to do the same thing for the new foundation. Our Mother General, not wishing to remove my burden, wills rather that I should be charged in a way with all the houses of our Society established in this country. I beg you, Monseigneur, tell me what I can do in conscience in order to secure the ownership of the property for our houses. I ask you to excuse my bad handwriting and the lack of order in my letter. You are a Father to me, and this gives me confidence.

With the Bishop's reassurance and further explanations, the ghost of a scruple was laid for the present, and Philippine committed herself and her work once more entirely to the Sacred Heart.[57] She might know fear, hesitation, anxiety, yet her supernatural conviction of faith in the reality of God's Providence never seems to have wavered. Lacking all natural security, she went forward all the more courageously, just because there appeared no human help on which to rely. If He willed her to work in St. Louis, He would furnish both the means and the grace for the enterprise.

A City House in St. Louis

I. 1827—1828

*Giving thanks always and everywhere through Blessed Joseph,
prudent and faithful servant of God.*

Preface of St. Joseph

FLORISSANT VALLEY LAY BURIED IN SNOW as the New Year began. In the coldest hours before the dawn Mother Duchesne made her way through the icy chapel to find even the altar in the church covered with snow.[1] Great drifts, as of fine white powder, were banked up in the sanctuary. The sacristy, too, was white with the snow that had sifted in around the doors and windows and through the long cracks in the poorly ceiled walls. There was work to be done even before meditation this morning; and after a prolonged adoration, offering, and acceptance, Philippine began to sweep out the dry snow, to wipe off the altar, communion railing, and sanctuary furniture, to sweep again, and then prepare for Mass. The best vases and candelabra were already on the altar—all reminders of her dear ones in France. What were they all doing this New Year's Day? Turning her thoughts from them, she wondered whether the pastor would be able to make his way across the two-mile stretch of snow-covered countryside.

Coming back into the church, she found Sister Shannon at work cleaning the floor and benches. The task was self-imposed—that was how novitiate training showed itself. Sister McKay was laying a fire in the nuns' chapel, and Mother Mathevon was wiping snowdrifts from the window sills. Then all were kneeling silently in prayer, offering to God the New Year with whatever it might

442

hold for them. At six-thirty there was a stir in the room above, where the children were rising in the bitter cold and huddling before the fires Sister Catherine had kindled on the hearths at either end of the dormitory. Quickly and quietly they dressed under the eyes of Mother Hamilton, donning woolen stockings, soft shoes or moccasins, and pantalettes, knitted petticoats, hug-me-tights, flannel underskirts, and Sunday uniforms of heavy black serge. Even the slimmest among them grew rotund as successive layers of clothing were applied. The ice in their mugs and pitchers was left quite undisturbed. The strokes of the community bell gave the signal for the nuns to recite the morning Office. The children knelt for prayers, while downstairs the sound of shuffling feet and whispers told that the Indian girls had come in from their log house with Mother O'Connor. Then heavy stamping outside the sacristy announced that Father Van Quickenborne was there.

The church that morning was completely deserted of worshipers. The day was too cold for visitors, so Philippine had time to write to Josephine:

It is quite a while, my very dear and much loved Cousin, since I received your letter of August 30, telling me of a new gift of 1000 francs. I am so filled with gratitude, I do not know how to express myself. I can only beg the ever kind and generous Heart of Jesus to pay the debt I owe you and to give you a hundredfold in return for all you do for us. Everything around us speaks of your generosity. Our chapel decorations and vestments are from you; and whenever we go there, we are reminded of you, of your husband, of Tante Perier, and of all your family. I had learned from my brother of the dreadful accident that occurred at Vizille. I beg you to tell Augustin and his wife how I sympathize with them in this, but still more in the loss of their beloved daughter.[2] Madame Teisseire and her husband also have many claims on my gratitude, and their loss of Marie has touched me deeply. One of our nuns who knew her at Sainte Marie speaks of her as a model of perfection.

When you see Father Rambaud, present my respectful greetings,[3] and tell him I shall never forget all the hardships he endured for me, and say that what he continues to do at Ste Marie with so much kindness inspires still more gratitude in my heart. If death has not taken away Fathers Joué, Luc, Bernard, and Delagré, I beg you to ask them to pray for us and for our converts, who are so exposed to apostasy in this country, where a change of religion is made quite as easily as a change of clothing. The work for the Indians is of very doubtful value. To carry it on successfully, the miracle of miracles is needed—that is, to change their very nature, which is corrupted from their earliest years. One would need to live in their midst. So far no women have risked this; and priests who have done so were not only unable to obtain support from them, but had to give them material assistance. Every year many Indians die in wretched poverty or as a result of drunkenness.

The American government has followed the policy of buying up the Indian lands within the boundaries of the states in order to secure public peace. The Indians have been required to move into more distant territory. This is the last year the savages will be allowed to hunt in, or even to travel across, the state of Missouri. Having been herded together in restricted areas, they no longer have sufficient land for the hunt, and this makes them more and more miserable. Some efforts have been made to get the Indian children into schools, but the parents only allow them to remain for a short time, then come and reclaim them. The children are worse off then than before, because when they take up the old licentious life, they act with more knowledge of right and wrong. Some Presbyterian missionaries, supported by a society in New York, took up residence near the Osage Indians, but they complained loudly about the conditions in which they had to live. They could not hold the Indian children in the school and had only half-breeds. It is rumored that they will give up the mission. Some Lazarist Fathers [4] who journeyed along the Arkansas River, which is more than 500 leagues long and flows beyond the borders of Missouri, were begged by the pioneers in that region, which is being opened to settlement, to reside among them, . . . but there was no means of subsistence for the Catholic missionaries, while those of the Methodist sect . . . are supported either by the government or by different organizations. All this is a reason for greater zeal on our part.

I beg you to excuse my illegible writing, but we are having such severe cold just now, the ink freezes on the point of the quill, even here beside the fire.

As you always take an interest in our Society, I shall give you some details: our two houses in Louisiana, one a day's journey from New Orleans, the other four or five days', are doing very well. The former in particular, though begun just a year ago, has more novices and pupils than we have. Many of the novices are excellent subjects, coming from the best Creole families. We have less success with the Americans on account of the quarter method of education in vogue here: three months to learn French, three months for music, three months for art, and then the education should be completed. Just recently four children left us, each having been here three months. Then, too, the Protestant parents fear their children may become Catholics. They all desire to do so, and the parents say they are free, but they always find some reason against the step.

Adieu, dear friend. Let us remain close friends in time, hoping that our union will be even closer in eternity in the Heart of Jesus.

PHILIPPINE

There is no hint in this letter of the principal problem that was absorbing so much of Philippine's thought and prayer and activity at this time. She had been trying to enlist the cooperation of her acquaintances in St. Louis in the foundation of an academy in the town. The need was patent, but the means were lacking; and no one seemed willing to help her. She took the long, cold drive from Florissant more than once. She talked of the advantages a convent in town, *une Maison de Ville*—a City House—would have over the existing *Maison de Campagne*—the Country House—so far out in the country. It was all to no avail; no one was interested. In desperation she wrote to John Mullanphy. He knew about the efforts she had been making, but he had offered no help so far. She had discussed with Father Van Quickenborne the advisability of approaching the town's richest Catholic. The Jesuit Superior was not very encouraging; but since he had not forbidden it, she wrote.

On February 10 she went to St. Louis again, this time to talk matters over with Mr. Mullanphy himself. He had an offer to make, and she listened thoughtfully as he outlined the plan. Then she drove with him to see the property offered—twenty-four acres of high, rolling land and a two-story, twelve-room brick house just seven years old. That was a generous offer, but the conditions made her hesitate. If only Bishop Rosati were near; he had been away for many weeks on a winter trip to Kentucky. She could not give the immediate answer that Mr. Mullanphy desired; she must consult Father Van Quickenborne. He was vehement in his opposition, then modified his views. Father De Theux was in favor of accepting.

Philippine knelt before the tabernacle and reread the letter of February 7, 1818, in which St. Madeleine Sophie had given her authority to sell or acquire property in the name of the Society. She had acted before on that authority, and she had delegated that authority to Mother Audé in Louisiana. Now, after long hours of prayer, she acted again. On March 1 she wrote to tell the Mother General what she had done, and was doing, to carry out the wish the foundress had so often expressed for a City House in St. Louis.

I have not written to you since December 25, 1826, when I sent you the accounts for the past six months and in spirit crossed the wide ocean to find myself close to you with my dear Sisters, offering you all my good wishes for the New Year. It would be difficult to wish you a happier year than the one just past which gave us what is most precious in all the world [the papal approbation]. I received Mother Bigeu's interesting account, and I am enclosing in this letter a note of thanks to her. The little word you added at the bottom of her letter leaves us in doubt about the date of departure of our Sisters. They are expected daily in New Orleans. With that hope in mind I have pushed the matter of a foundation in St. Louis, feeling it a loss of both time and opportunity to wait for Father Niel's return, and many people say he is not coming back since he did not succeed in getting the financial aid he sought.

After making many inquiries, I realized that we should need at least 30,000 francs on hand in order to procure a house in St. Louis as good as this one, that we could not count on Father Niel for help, and that Mother Eugenie will not be able to pay us the money advanced to her for several years. I knew, moreover, that I could not count on the 6000 francs you spoke of in a preceding letter, since in the last one you mentioned only 1000 from Madame de Rollin. So I wrote to Mr. Mullanphy, asking him if he would not give us a house, as he owns a great many, and that on favorable conditions in view of our intention of opening a free school for the children of the poor. He answered by asking in turn how many orphans we would house on the following conditions: 1. that he would give us a brick house built about seven years ago, situated at a distance of a fifteen-minute walk from the Catholic church, with 24 arpents of land around it, not cultivated except for a vegetable garden, the house having 12 fairly large rooms, but not being as large as our convent here; 2. that he or his heirs would give each orphan at her entrance the sum of 50 francs for her bed, etc., and 25 francs yearly for clothing; and 3. that he would give 5000 francs cash for the initial expenses of the foundation. I replied that we would accept 15 or 20 orphans; he wanted 20, and they were to be presented by himself or his oldest daughters.

I went to inspect the house and found the site somewhat similar to that of Ste Marie, though less attractive. It is high, solitary, and in a healthful location overlooking the Mississippi and the city, from which it is well removed. It seemed to me we should be going against our own best interests to refuse this offer. True, we are taking on a burden for which we shall be responsible, but think of a debt of 20 or 30 thousand francs, or the necessity of being confined to a village where we are shut in by six feet of water up to our door five or six times a year, and that quite suddenly and with such force as to wash away the bridge leading to our house, to flatten all our fences, to destroy our entire garden, which has produced nothing these last two years, as the vegetables have rotted in the water. Besides that, there is the probability that if we do not take the lead [in opening a school], someone else may do so, and we shall be without any means of supporting ourselves. Are not these facts worth taking into consideration?

You counseled me to ask advice, and I did so. At first the Father Rector was opposed to the plan, then he thought better of it, though he was not enthusiastic. Perhaps he would have preferred St. Charles, but construction work on the church has been discontinued, and he does not want to station a priest there; and no secular priest will accept the parish as it lies within the area assigned to the Jesuit mission. I told him that you considered an establishment in St. Louis necessary, that you had told me to make plans for it, and that this should come before any other undertaking. The other Jesuit Father [De Theux] is wholly in favor of the St. Louis foundation. So I accepted, and things are getting under way, though the first contract that was drawn up has not been signed. Mr. Mullanphy is much interested in the repairs and is having them made at his expense, that is, with the money he promised to give. It was necessary to add a kitchen and a room above it for a hired man, also to repair the floors, etc. All will be ready by Easter, and we could open the institution then if the desired help comes from France. It was impossible for me to wait for an answer from you in this matter, as several parties were interested in the property—and how could I say when your answer would reach us, with the dangers and delays of sea travel? I am sorry you are not sending a good superior. . . . The people of St. Louis would certainly appreciate a religious who is American in both language and character. No other nation in the world admires itself as this one does. If for the moment I am disappointed in my hope, I cling to the thought that the religious who are coming are younger than I and may be able to learn the language and customs of the country.

I think it best for me to go to St. Louis for the foundation. The position might offer some dangers for others, as it is unwise to be too friendly at first with people, lest one make undesirable intimacies. Then, too, there are many well-educated people in St. Louis, and some of our religious might not make a good impression. Relying on the protection of St. Joseph and St. Regis, I have the utmost confidence that our work both here and in St. Louis will succeed. Each convent will help the other, one in temporal, the other in spiritual matters. The nuns can go from one house to the other for their retreats or for a change of air, etc. One can make the trip back and forth in a day. It would have been very satisfying for me to know I was carrying out your intentions in all this, and I should then have acted with more assurance. But in a country so destitute of opportunities for the education of youth, should I have held back because of the orphans? We have the responsibility of training them, but we also have the good will of the most influential family in this part of the country.

Mr. Mullanphy also reserved for himself the right to build two rooms for his grandchildren, whether still boarding pupils or out of school. If we keep a boarding school here at Florissant, the academy in St. Louis will develop slowly. The building in St. Louis will need to be enlarged, so we shall welcome the money promised for this foundation. We shall have a good number of day pupils, and if you agree to this, we shall use their tuition fees to support the orphans and their teachers. This work will be rather light in the beginning.

Bishop Rosati returned to Missouri at the end of February, but not to St. Louis, and left for New Orleans without having learned of the contract between Mother Duchesne and Mr. Mullanphy. Hearing that he was at the Barrens, Philippine wrote on March 8 to inform him of the steps she had taken, to request a formal letter of episcopal approval, and to say that the opening of the new school was set for May 1. She closed her letter with a little heart-cry: "I have learned with sorrow that Mother Xavier Hamilton is very ill. I begged her to come back here if she could stand the trip. This climate agrees with her, for she was perfectly well when she was here. I wish at any cost to save her. . . ."

It was too late to save young Mathilde Hamilton. Her death had occurred at St. Michael's on March 1, at the age of twenty-five. The Bishop learned this as he stepped from the steamboat in New Orleans, and he hastened to send the news to Mother Duchesne, his letter of March 11 crossing hers of March 8 somewhere on the river. He was still unaware of the activities that were afoot in St. Louis, but he had talked to Father De La Croix, who had come from St. Michael's to meet him, and he had been imbued with "Southern sympathies" when he wrote:

On my arrival here I learned of the loss your community has sustained in the death of Mother Xavier Hamilton. We must resign ourselves to the dispositions of Providence. She was ripe for heaven. Her death was that of a saint. Nonetheless, I understand how much a sacrifice like this costs you. According to what I have learned from Father De La Croix, Mother Eugenie has felt this death acutely, and so much the more since the number of religious is far below the needs of the boarding school at St. Michael's, which increases daily. At present there are ninety young ladies there.

I believe that the welfare of your Society in America, and that of religion in general, demands that you maintain this house, which will infallibly sustain all the others. I am of the opinion that it would never do for you to withdraw any of the religious from it, particularly those who teach. Otherwise you would destroy what has been accomplished. In a country like this, where there are so many prejudices against religious vocations and so many obstacles placed in the way of young ladies who wish to consecrate them-selves to God, it seems to me also that we ought to treat with great respect the affection of parents. If they see their daughters sent four hundred leagues from home, they will persist in refusing their consent. And although for the religious it would be better to be always at a distance from their families, nevertheless the good of religion demands that we have regard for the weakness of parents, who do not know the way of perfection. . . .

I understand the situation in which you find yourself just now; but if the establishment of a convent in St. Louis cannot be made without withdrawing religious from St. Michael's, then I would advise you to wait a little longer. It would be very unfortunate to ruin a house which is more promising than others and which at the moment, though still new, counts twice the number of boarders that are in the other houses. You must have regard to the health of the religious who, if overburdened with work, cannot long continue their apostolate. . . .

When Philippine's letter of March 8 reached the Bishop in New Orleans, he hastened to reassure her, fearing the misconstruc-tion she might put on his last letter and the soul-suffering she would experience as a result. The consideration shown by the young prelate must have been a balm to Philippine's troubled soul, and the postscript a subject of laughter in the community. The days of blotting-paper were still in the distant future when the Bishop wrote from New Orleans on March 23:

I have always believed and I still believe that an establishment of your Society at St. Louis would do much good. That is why I have so often made known to you my desire to see it begun. What I wrote you on that subject in my last letter of the eleventh of this month may possibly have made you fear that I had changed my mind. No, I am more than ever convinced that one must be made. I only wanted to tell you that if it could not be done without taking a religious from St. Michael's, it seemed to me better to defer it for a little longer than to ruin this house, which promises more than the others and will infallibly be the support of all your other establishments in America.

I bless Providence for having given you the means to do what we have so earnestly desired. I believe, however, that $5 a year and $10 at entrance is too little for the maintenance of an orphan. But I hope that Providence will do the rest. You must carry out the contract you made with Mr. Mullanphy. You cannot even think of withdrawing from the obligations you have assumed. You have my full consent, and to give proof of it in accepted forms I send you the enclosed letter. Recommend me to the prayers of your holy community, whom I bless in Our Lord. . . .
P.S. I have poured ink instead of sand, and I have not time to write another letter.

While awaiting the Bishop's reply, Mother Duchesne pushed her preparations ahead. On Easter Monday, April 6, Anna Shannon and Suzanne McKay made their first vows after a year in the novitiate. These were religious on whom the Society would rely for splendid, loyal service, Suzanne giving more than thirty years of active devotedness and Anna more than twice that long. Mother Shannon was, without a doubt, Mother Duchesne's most "illustrious" recruit for the Society. She lived with Mother Duchesne for many years and became one of the outstanding figures in the history of the order.[5] From her comes precious information about the convent at Florissant and its Mother Superior when the foundation in St. Louis was about to be made:

The main building [wrote Mother Shannon], which was occupied by the community and boarding pupils, was equipped with all the furniture and appurtenances necessary for regularity and for carrying on the works of the house. There were, besides, three other buildings detached from the principal one. Of these, one [formerly used for the second-rate boarding school] was set apart for the use of the priests; another was occupied by the free school; and the third was the Indian girls' seminary. . . . These girls slept on the floor—some on pallets, others on buffalo skins they had brought with them. During the day the pallets and buffalo skins were rolled up and put away, for the same large room answered also for class purposes. The girls were intelligent and learned quickly; they were soon handy with the needle. . . . One of them became very ill and was the object of Mother Duchesne's care and solicitude for two months. . . . She suffered greatly, but was a very privileged soul . . . and her short but holy life was crowned by a happy death in the arms of Mother Duchesne.

The children of the boarding school were good and pious, and in manners and deportment compared favorably with any I have met since. . . . The majority of them understood French, and all had to study it. Mother Duchesne understood English and could write it quite well, but she never trusted herself to speak it. She used to give the General Instruction herself,[6] and her exhortations, supplemented by her holy example, sank deep into their hearts. . . . The families of these children were very generous; whenever they came to visit them, they delighted to bring gifts of produce from their farms, or groceries received from New Orleans. If they received a quantity of French wines, for instance, a box or two was sure to arrive on their next visit to the convent. Such articles were carefully put aside to be served to the Bishop and priests when they dined at the house.

We had several good cows on the place and plenty of milk. . . . The religious all helped with the cooking, Mother Duchesne being always first at the hardest work, though meals were not always improved by her share in getting them up, for her gifts did not lie in that direction. In the management of the farm work, however, she excelled.[7]

The kitchen and dining room were housed in a separate log building behind the convent. The children had their meals first, then the religious. The diet was seldom "balanced," but it was wholesome and abundant, though Mother Shannon recalled being hungry almost all the time. Whatever was left from the service of the children was used, with additions, for the religious. Of course, reheated dishes are familiar items on convent menus, but hardly ever to the extent that occurred at Florissant in those days. No food was wasted, not even crusts of bread left by the children. These the Mother Superior gathered up for herself.

Mother Duchesne made the recreations very pleasant [continues Mother Shannon]. The dignity of her manner did not detract from her amiability, while her extensive and varied information, her ready command of French, and above all the love of God which seemed the very breath of her life, made her conversation not only entertaining and instructive, but also calculated to keep alive the fervor of us all. There was a singular earnestness and unction in everything she said that gave her a kind of power for drawing souls to God. The recreation after dinner was followed by the Office, which was always said with the greatest punctuality and exactness. . . .

Mother Duchesne slept very little, for besides her prolonged vigils before the Blessed Sacrament, she used also to sit up with the sick whenever this was necessary; and when dressing in the morning, the religious often found their shoes and clothing mended and knew whose charitable hands had done the work. . . . She also reserved for herself the night visit of the house and the morning call. . . .

Father Van Quickenborne was the superior of the Jesuits of the mission. He greatly appreciated Mother Duchesne and lost no opportunity of trying her by the sharpest mortifications. On one occasion, when she presented herself to receive Holy Communion, he gruffly refused her. Mother Duchesne stood up and returned to her place with unaltered countenance. The community and the people in the church had noticed the incident, otherwise it would probably never have been known, for she did not mention it. Nor did she ever speak of the frequent rebuffs she met with from the same quarter.

Mother Shannon was impressed by two seemingly contradictory facts—the occasional harshness of Father Van Quickenborne's treatment of Mother Duchesne and his otherwise amicable relations with her and her community. "He was a real father to us," she wrote, "and we could always count on his help when we needed it. He and Mother Duchesne were on the best of terms. She and her daughters were used to his oddities and did not mind them."

The influence of the Jesuit Rector on the training given the novices of the Sacred Heart was evident in the introduction of corporal penances after 1823. Mother Duchesne had been loath to impose them, but by 1825 the novices were familiar with many devices for self-inflicted penance, the common ones being the discipline and the chain. They also kept the Church's fasts with penitential severity. "After Mass on fast days those of the religious who wished to do so took a cup of sweet-herb tea, sweetened with a little molasses. Nothing else appeared on the table."

The clergy and laity, in fact everyone who knew her, esteemed Mother Duchesne as a saint. She was gifted with an admirable spirit of prayer [Mother Shannon continues] and often spent whole nights on her knees before the Blessed Sacrament without any support whatever; and when our Lord was exposed on the altar, she spent long hours in His Presence in the same attitude. One Holy Thursday night she kept me as the companion of her night-long vigil, and she never changed her position, kneeling upright without any support, except to rise to go up to the Repository to trim or replace the lighted candles. At the end of five hours I was overcome by sleep and began to nod . . . She noticed it and said to me: "Go to bed now. At four o'clock others will come, and I can remain alone until then." She was as alert and wide awake as if it were twelve o'clock in the day.

Mother Duchesne's soul seemed to be steeped in the fervent spirit of prayer and almost superhuman austerity of religious life in the early ages of the Church. . . . And from the very beginning she accustomed her daughters to make prayer the constant companion of their labors. While digging, hoeing, etc., we used to lighten our toil by frequent ejaculations and vocal prayers.

When I lived with Mother Duchesne, she was still strong and vigorous. She was rather tall and well proportioned, with a noble countenance and bearing and fine manners. She had blue eyes, and though slightly pitted by the small pox, her complexion was fair and clear.

So an artist might picture her in the late afternoon of an April day in 1827, sitting in the community room at Florissant and speaking in her singularly earnest way to her little religious family, telling them the arrangements she had worked out with Mothers Octavie and Lucille. There would be more work for them all, as she was taking with her Mother O'Connor, Mary Knapp, an orphan, and Julie Coutremanche, a half-breed girl. The other orphans would follow later on. The trimester prizes would be distributed to the three schools on Sunday, April 29; a *congé* would follow on Monday, and Mother Duchesne and her companions would leave on May 1, in accordance with her promise to Mr. Mullanphy.

The last announcement called forth a subdued protest. May 1 was the feast of St. Philip the Apostle, and Mother Duchesne's feast, too. They would not hear of her leaving them on that day. As she knew they were sincere in this affectionate outburst, she yielded to their pleading. She would leave on May 2—and she would come out to see them as often as possible.

So they feasted her in the simple Sacred Heart fashion. They gathered, too, for a last evening recreation. She gave them her blessing when the bell rang and went for a last adoration in the chapel that looked into the church which at her suggestion had been dedicated to the Sacred Heart of Jesus. It was her last night under the roof with the Blessed Sacrament for many a week; but she could say now, as she had said so often before in the cause of Christ: "I am ready for anything."

May 2, 1827, fell on a Wednesday. The Mullanphy carriage was at the convent door. The Misses Mullanphy were calling for Mother Duchesne and her companions, whom they were honored to take to St. Louis. Baggage and some furniture had gone ahead in a cart. The good-byes were joyous in spite of tears, and the vehicle moved off. It was springtime in the valley, with a shimmer of green on the trees, a sunny warmth in the air, and the smell of newly-turned earth. Bobwhites whistled in the meadows and thrushes sang in the hedgerows. The drive was long, but pleasant enough. Once they reached the city they headed east, then south, taking the road to Carondelet and branching from it, once they crossed the Mill Creek, into the traces of wagon wheels that led as a road to the brick house which became that day the Convent of the Sacred Heart, St. Louis.

Nine years had passed since Philippine Duchesne had set sail from France with St. Louis as her intended destination—nine years since she had made her first acquaintance with the frontier trading post and its friendly, hospitable people. She had known them in less amiable moods at times since then. She had seen the village spread from a place of three streets paralleling the river to more than twice that number and double its population. Americans had been moving in steadily through these years, and English was now the language of the town, though one had best be bilingual to be really at home. Philippine had been in the town many times during the past nine years and was familiar with its dusty, or muddy, lanes, its noisy traffic, its dingy shops, its more pretentious stores, its abounding life. She was personally acquainted with its handsome, red-haired, young mayor, Dr. William Carr Lane, and had also known Missouri's first governor, Mr. Alexander McNair, whose untimely death had brought grief to many a heart.

The Indians on the streets were no curiosity to her now, but always objects of compassion and prayer. She had learned that they often encamped on Chouteau's Pond, a pretty body of water that lay to the west of the property Mr. Mullanphy had given her and that was drained by the Mill Creek, "*le ruisseau de Monsieur Chouteau,*" she called it. That creek was something of a problem to her just now, for she knew she would have to build bridges over it. That, in turn, meant that she had very real need of the services of

Martin Lepere. She had known him for four years and had great confidence in him. Father Van Quickenborne had objected when she offered Martin the job in town, but she had held to the arrangement and the man was moving to St. Louis.

"The work will be rather light in the beginning," Philippine had written optimistically to Mother Barat, but it was drudgery from the start, for the house had stood vacant for some years and the workmen hired by Mr. Mullanphy had left a litter of debris in every room, besides the mud tracked in from the garden, where great mounds of loose earth were piled up from the excavating of the cellar. She and her companions were hard at work that first afternoon when Father Saulnier, the Cathedral pastor, arrived to offer his services and to promise that he and his assistant, Father Lutz,[8] would do their best to see that the convent had Mass, at least on Sundays. It was a cheering promise, but one the good priest would find difficult to keep. In material matters, however, he was more helpful, for he sent the nuns a cow, to Mother Duchesne's satisfaction, and a quantity of useful furniture—the tables, school benches, and other equipment from the defunct St. Louis College, and bade them help themselves from his garden and orchard, though at the moment there was not much to be gathered.

On Sunday two other visitors called—Mr. Mullanphy and Mrs. Bernard Pratte. The latter had two more daughters to place under Mother Duchesne's care as soon as the school was inaugurated. On Tuesday, Father Van Quickenborne appeared on the scene. "He was quite pleased with the house and its location," noted Mother Duchesne in her *Journal*. He returned next day for Mass—and on that Wednesday, May 9, St. Joseph was solemnly chosen as patron of the new institution. On the following Sunday he arrived at noon, but she was fasting hopefully. The chapel had been prepared as well as possible, but there was no ciborium and so the Blessed Sacrament was not reserved. There could be no severer trial than this, Philippine thought, but there were worse days ahead.

She had the satisfaction, however, of showing the Father Rector the letter written by Bishop Rosati on March 23, along with the enclosures. This formal approbation gave her a tangible sense of security, but it left the problem of the chaplaincy unsolved, so she laid the difficulty before the Bishop at once, along with a solution that had presented itself quite unexpectedly.

I had hoped [she wrote on May 10] that one of the two priests in St. Louis would offer Mass here for us on Sundays, but Father

Saulnier says he is already offering two Masses and Father Lutz goes to a mission station. . . . Meanwhile Father Richard is asking to be our chaplain, having heard that a convent was to be opened in St. Louis. He asks only lodging and meals, which is very convenient for a new house that still has so many expenses to meet. Father Richard, moreover, is a member of a religious community and very well suited to our needs.[9] There only remains your consent to be secured and some way of arranging so as not to inconvenience the Ursulines; they, however, have never liked Father Richard as much as we do. While awaiting your decision, I shall speak to no one about the matter. . . .

Many visitors came to call on the nuns the following Sunday— a Sunday without Mass at the convent. "Old friends, former pupils, parents offering us their children," noted Mother Duchesne, "but we could not accept them at once. We are not ready." That evening she gave Mother Barat an account of her first ten days in St. Louis:

The heading of this letter shows you that we are at last in the place you have long considered most suitable for a convent of the Sacred Heart. . . . I wrote you that the Father Superior did not like the contract with Mr. Mullanphy; and even after signing it with us, he urged us to get the approval of the Bishop before having the contract notarized. Fortunately the Bishop boarded the very steamboat that was carrying my letter to him, and it brought back his answer quickly. Along with his personal letter he enclosed a formal act of approval. . . .

That enthusiastic approbation under the seal of the Bishop and your frequently repeated wish give me the consolation of thinking that I am where God wills me to be, and that St. Joseph has greatly aided in this matter. So he is the special patron and protector of this house. The five thousand francs given by Mr. Mullanphy have already been used to pay for excavating a cellar and constructing a brick kitchen and a room above it that could serve as a convenient lodging for a priest, as it is well floored and ceiled and has outside shutters, etc.

I promised to take possession on May 1. The approach of my feast and the distribution of prizes gave an opportunity to reorganize the classes and install a new teacher without delaying my departure from Florissant later than May 2. Not a room in this house was ready, so we did not have Mass until Sunday. To my surprise and joy the priest said the Mass of St. Joseph, as this was permitted in the *ordo* of the diocese.

After touching on the problem of securing a chaplain, she continued:

> We shall not accept pupils until our Sisters from France arrive. Remember, very reverend Mother, you promised two extra religious if we made a foundation in St. Louis. Meanwhile I have had requests from the most prominent families in the city of classes for their children. But how shall we manage? The Father Superior says we shall destroy the boarding school at Florissant if we open one here, and I fear he is right. . . . I hope you will allow us to accept both paying day pupils—they would be the main source of income—and poor children. I think the hope of drawing Catholic children from Protestant schools in which boys and girls are grouped together is a consideration that will have great weight with you. An even greater good we can do is to offer a center where converts will find the means of strengthening their faith and of living their religion. . . .
>
> From all sides people are sending us gifts of food, so at present we are in want of nothing. I do so wish you would write to Mr. Mullanphy to thank him. He may help us build a chapel. He could do so and never miss the money, but he wants to do things on his own initiative. He cannot be pushed. He is a power because of his wealth and ability; he could rule a kingdom. His married daughters are very kindly disposed toward us. Miss Octavie, whom he placed for a while in our school at Florissant, has just left for France to be with her mother, who recently lost her eldest daughter, a very fine person.[10] If Octavie pays you a visit, please be very cordial toward her; she needs your friendship for many reasons. She is deeply attached to us and very virtuous.

Mother Duchesne had not received an answer from the Bishop with regard to Father Richard and the chaplaincy when she wrote to him again about another difficulty raised by Father Van Quickenborne, who seems to have been set at times on giving her trouble. Had he been officially named ecclesiastical superior of the Religious of the Sacred Heart in Missouri, he could scarcely have exercised—or attempted to exercise—more authority. This time the Reverend Father was objecting to Martin Lepere's moving to St. Louis to work for the nuns. "I am in real need of this man to attend to our affairs," she wrote on July 1. "He understands our rules and regulations and can direct the work for which a knowledge of the two languages is necessary." After some further defense of Lepere, whom Van Quickenborne considered lazy, she added: "As I could not get in touch with you quickly enough and as Mr. Martin was willing to make the change, I have not retreated from my position in spite of the Father's protest, and I shall carry the arrangement through, unless you counsel me to do otherwise."

By this time the bridges had been built, a well dug, the feast of the Sacred Heart celebrated with Mass and an outdoor procession of the Blessed Sacrament, a novice "with absolutely no training" added to the community, and the academy opened with a mere handful of pupils. Early in July, Father Van Quickenborne announced that he would come no more for Mass, nor would he send a substitute, as his priests were going to make their tertianship. "I have shed bitter tears over this decision," Philippine confessed to her Superior General. "There is a slender hope that the Father Provincial [Francis Dzierozynski] may decide otherwise; they expect him from Maryland this month." But he did not.

> Meanwhile we must live on privations. We have had no Exposition of the Blessed Sacrament either in the Octave of Corpus Christi or in that of the Sacred Heart; often we lose four Communions a week. These are my fast days, for I just cannot take any breakfast while I am hoping that some stroke of Divine Providence may bring a priest to give us Communion. . . .
>
> We still need to build a fence of planks or upright posts. This will be expensive, and we need a stable and a servant's house. The latter is necessary because of our isolation from all other dwellings. This isolation, however, has its advantages—no one can ever look in on us. We are going to leave part of our twenty-four arpents in woodland, where we can gather wild grapes, which are often quite delicious, hazel nuts, strawberries, and blackberries in abundance. But we shall still have plenty of land enclosed for a garden, an apple orchard, a little woods for walks or playgrounds, where there is a very good spring that never goes dry, and fields for corn and potatoes, but these fields have never been cleared for tillage.
>
> I have been greatly aided by several ladies of the town. One of them put at my disposal both her vehicles and her servants for all the trips I might need to make to Florissant. . . . If our religious from France had got here and we could have made the most of the general interest our coming aroused, our two institutions would have been filled with pupils. But I begin to feel like a fabricator of tales when I speak of their arrival in the near future. I am particularly embarrassed in the presence of Mr. Mullanphy.[11]

The strain of the first months in St. Louis was telling on Philippine; her nerves were on edge. When a letter from Bishop Rosati seemed to imply that the idea of Father Richard's coming to St. Louis had originated with her, she wrote in self-defense that she had had no intention whatsoever of attempting to withdraw the Ursulines' chaplain from them, but that he himself had written to tell her that

> he had given notice to the Ursulines that he was going to leave them and that he would offer to be our chaplain without remuneration, asking only lodging and food. Propitious as this offer was, I did not answer immediately, thinking that perhaps the St. Louis priests or the Jesuits, who are planning to open a college here, might supply our needs. However, when they both explained to me their difficulties, then I answered Father Richard, saying that if his transfer were agreeable to you, we should be delighted to have him. I also wrote to you about it, Monseigneur, sending the letter with Father Dahmen.

After repeating to the Bishop the substance of her interviews with both Father Saulnier and the Jesuits, she continued:

> I told the Father Superior that there have been saints who became holy without Mass and that I was ready to make the sacrifice in view of future good, but I already perceive the discouragement of my companions. . . . The Father Superior was annoyed that I took Mr. Martin for the St. Louis convent. When I told him my plan, he said nothing against it; but he showed his displeasure to others. Since then he has calmed down . . . and I believe the difficulty has been removed with the change in superiors.[12] I can never sufficiently express our joy over this. It is a great grace from God for which we shall never cease thanking Him. . . .[13]

The Bishop's reply was gentle and reassuring, and came to Philippine within a week:

> I am entirely convinced that you have not tried to take Father Richard away from the Ursulines. I also know that this holy man has for a long time wanted to leave Louisiana, where the heat is very hard on him. I should have had no problem in allowing him to go elsewhere, and certainly much less in seeing him go to your house, but it is absolutely impossible to replace him just now. Father Richard, as you have also seen by his letter, realizes this fact. That is why he did not venture to speak to me of it. Nevertheless, I shall write to France to have a priest sent who will be agreeable to the Ursulines. We must be patient while we wait for him and be reconciled to whatever is best. The loss of Father

Boccardo has upset me and has ruined part of my plans, for he was an ecclesiastic of merit. God be praised! In the sum of $2000 lost there was none for you. . . .

[P.S.] You know the Holy Father has decided my lot according to our own desires. Still I must retain the administration of the diocese of New Orleans for the present.[14]

The mention of Father Angelo Boccardo's loss gave Philippine a shock. She had hoped the religious from France were traveling under his escort. She knew the Bishop counted much on his coming, and that he was expected to arrive in New Orleans in July. Inquiries revealed further details of the unfortunate accident and its regrettable consequences. Father Boccardo had sailed from Europe as expected, the bearer of important letters, documents, and some funds for Bishop Rosati. All these he put for safety in one satchel, which he allowed no one else to carry. The vessel from France had docked at New Orleans and Father Boccardo, satchel in hand, was making his way down the gangplank when he stumbled and dropped his precious burden into the river. The tawny stream flowed over it and on, carrying the satchel away in its swift undertow. Fishing, dredging, diving were of no avail—the treasure was gone. So great was the impact of this accident on the distraught priest that he took ship back to Europe at once, and the Bishop was deprived of a helper he had counted on at a very critical time. Before Philippine had recovered from this disappointment, another unhappy difficulty arose, and she told the Bishop about it in confidence:

I have just received a letter from Father Van Quickenborne, who is displeased because of a little article Mother Octavie wrote for the Charlestown newspaper and with which I had nothing to do. The priest who copied the article about the Indian girls is hurt because in the eyes of the government they are part of his school. I find the article badly constructed and I beg you to suppress it if there is time. I strongly dislike seeing ourselves in the newspapers, and if you really want some little word about us, I should like it to be as short as possible. . . .[15]

The Bishop suppressed Mother Berthold's little report on Florissant because he had already sent to Bishop England an article containing what he wanted published on the state of the dioceses west of the Mississippi, but he let Mother Duchesne know what he thought of moderate newspaper publicity when he wrote:

I believe that without failing in Christian humility we can make known the condition of the churches in the United States. This is done for public edification and to close the mouths of sectarians who try to depreciate the Catholic Church because of the pretended small number of her members. That is what Catholics do in Rome, in Canada, in Ireland, in France. They have printed annually the status of the clergy and religious establishments. I read one of them which contained all the religious communities of women, and they mentioned your house in Paris.

You must abandon yourself to Providence. God will not fail to give you the consolation of Sunday Mass. Father Caretta is going to spend a few weeks in St. Louis and has promised me he will procure you this happiness during his sojourn in the city.[16] Before the month of November there will be a third priest in St. Louis. So take courage. I hope that I myself can soon spend the greater part of the year in that city. In the meanwhile, let us follow the lead of Providence. In the event that you have no Mass some Sunday, I am of the opinion that the children should remain at home [as well as the religious]. Let them hear Mass in spirit. . . .[17]

Philippine had now waited many months for the recruits she had expected from France to help her with the St. Louis foundation. The summer had been a long, hot succession of trials and disappointments, drudgery and privation. Her reaction to all this is evident from the tone of her next letter to Mother Barat. There is anguish in every line, but most keenly sensed in the closing paragraph. The Mother General did not approve wholeheartedly of the contract made with John Mullanphy. Two points of it were deemed unwise—first, the property was not donated outright, but merely leased to the Religious of the Sacred Heart, though the time-span was for 999 years; and second, the care of twenty orphans in perpetuity on so meager a support as five dollars a year for each was an almost preposterous condition. "That is a heavy burden," wrote the Mother General, "but God will aid you, I am sure." So Philippine wrote to her on August 18:

You have never subjected me to so severe a trial as this one of postponing the coming of our new religious. Father Boccardo, who was bringing us letters, let them fall into the Mississippi. As a result, I am in complete ignorance regarding the plans of their voyage. Every letter I receive from our Louisiana houses makes me tremble, and I am in dread lest Mother Audé, who does the most to keep them going, should succumb under her burden and the work should perish.

Sometimes I glimpse a little hope in the thought that you may double the help you are sending, since you know that the convent in St. Louis has been opened. You promised me this. . . . In the first group of nuns I include the American lady.[18] She is known and esteemed by the Jesuit Fathers, who agree in thinking that she will do much good here. . . . I really ought to be replaced by a person who knows how to attract people and make converts. Under my guidance everything will stagnate. . . .

It grieves me very much to know that you do not approve of the contract with Mr. Mullanphy. At least your desires are partly accomplished. Bishop Rosati, who has been appointed definitely to St. Louis, told me he intends to reside here part of each year. That will assure us of more spiritual help. I have no hope that the Jesuits will come to St. Louis in the very near future. The Provincial was impervious to all my pleading for a chaplain. We had only a glimpse of him. . . .

On Sunday, September 9, the long-awaited religious from France arrived—Mothers Helene Dutour, a Savoyard, and Xavier Van Damme, a Fleming, with a postulant, Miss Marguerite Short, a recent convert of Bishop Fenwick of Cincinnati. They had traveled down the Ohio with Mothers Dorival and Piveteau, the former on her way to Grand Coteau, the latter to St. Michael's. "The American lady," Mrs. Baker, had quit the party somewhere in the East, "too ill to travel to St. Louis." This was a blow to Philippine, for she had built great hopes on her, but the lady was not heard from again, though she had traveled to America at the Society's expense.

That very afternoon Mother Duchesne took the newcomers to Florissant, returning next day with only Mother Dutour, as Mother Van Damme had insisted on remaining at the country house to make a little "spiritual review" under Jesuit direction. This was a bit disconcerting to Philippine, but she mentioned it only casually in a letter to the Mother General which she began on September 11:

On receiving new gifts from you, must I not feel my gratitude increasing? I want to express it as far as in me lies, and especially since our dear Sisters have arrived. The Blessed Virgin brought them safely to us. I had felt a bit discouraged when all our novenas to the Sacred Heart, to St. Regis, to St. Ignatius brought no results, and even those made for the feast of the Assumption and the Immaculate Heart were unavailing. Then on the morning of the feast of the Holy Name of Mary, when I was pouring out my heart to her, I heard these consoling words: My protection will never fail you. I put aside the thought as illusory, but after Mass I seemed to hear the same words again, and an hour later the beadle of the parish came in all haste to tell me that our religious had arrived at the rectory, and being there they would attend the Mass that would be offered at ten-thirty. So they got here just in time for dinner.

After Vespers I drove with them to Florissant, where the joy of seeing them was very great. On Monday the prizes were distributed by Father De Theux, who was accompanied by another priest. Father Van Quickenborne was away on a mission trip to the Osage Indians. Kind Father De Theux had taken part in our novenas and had offered Holy Mass that very day for the safe arrival of our religious. Mother Dutour and I returned to St. Louis that afternoon. Mother Van Damme wanted to remain a few days at St. Ferdinand in order to make a review. I made her promise to come back here, telling her that both her youth and her facility in speaking English would enable her to procure the glory of God here. . . .

Interrupted while writing, Philippine could find no opportunity to finish this letter in the days that followed. News of the approaching visit of Bishop Rosati stirred the little convent to full activity, for there was much to be done before all was in readiness for the blessing of the house. When nearly two weeks had passed and Mother Van Damme still remained at Florissant, Mother Duchesne wrote to Mother Berthold to come for a visit and bring with her the reluctant member of the St. Louis community. They drove in on September 24 and Mother Duchesne gave them a cordial welcome. She had understood from the beginning what was going on in the soul of Xavier Van Damme and she wrote sympathetically about her: "The very narrow quarters in which we live, the small number of religious forming the community, and our great poverty, all combined to astonish and discourage her a little, but her virtue seems to have conquered this trial. As to Mother Dutour, she was at home immediately." [19]

On September 29 Bishop Rosati paid his first visit to the St. Louis convent. Mother Duchesne was happy to introduce to him the religious from France, to show him the copies of the brief of approbation and the new edition of the *Constitutions* which they had brought, and to tell him of financial help received from Josephine de Savoye-Rollin, Father Perreau, and the convent at Amiens. He returned three days later to offer the Holy Sacrifice of the Mass and bless the house, and on the following day he gave solemn baptism to Elizabeth Dodge in the convent chapel.[20] He had arranged as best he could about the chaplaincy, appointing Father Lutz to the post temporarily. And now he had a new enterprise to suggest. Mother Duchesne must have been astonished at the proposal, but she listened attentively. The Bishop was presenting them with a new opportunity for spreading the knowledge and love of the Sacred Heart, and Philippine could not turn a deaf ear to it, though wisdom lay in refusal. When he had driven away that afternoon, she took up her unfinished letter and wrote:

> Bishop Rosati called on us today and seemed quite satisfied with our location here, as he finds the place very pleasant. He laid before me a proposal that requires a prompt answer from you, for you have expressed the wish that we content ourselves with our four houses for the present, so I cannot accept a fifth without your approval. The Daughters of the Cross [Sisters of Loretto], who have a good number of convents in Kentucky, opened a school at La Fourche, near St. Michael's in Louisiana. Father Bigeschi, a holy priest who has since returned to France and whom you may have met, built them a convent and gave them land, furniture, etc.[21] But they are all English-speaking Americans, so they cannot go on with their work at La Fourche, where the language and customs are French. They find that they are unable to train their novices or teach the children, since only one among them can speak and teach a little French. Because of this situation they want to unite with us. Monseigneur Rosati and the priests in Louisiana are also in favor of this union. The Bishop has explained to the Sisters our organization and mode of life. They agree to all, so only your approval is lacking. Will you refuse to help this well-populated area, when all the convent needs is a religious superior?
>
> I think Mother Carmelite Landry would do well there. She has been Mother Xavier Murphy's assistant; but since Mother Dorival arrived, she has not been so necessary at Grand Coteau. She seems just made for that convent at La Fourche. She is well known to the people there and is one of them. We would send these good Daughters of the Cross to our other houses where there is need for religious who can speak English, and in their place we could put some French-speaking nuns. In this way and without asking for more help from France, we could form a very desirable institution. Mother Eugenie could send there the children she cannot take at St. Michael's because of lack of room; she could also keep an eye on that convent and help it in many ways. Please, dear Mother, give me an immediate answer. I have asked Monseigneur Rosati for

a delay of four months, hoping to receive your reply in that time, and I trust it will be favorable. I am asking it from our Lord through the intercession of Our Lady of Sorrows, the title under which the Blessed Virgin is especially honored at La Fourche. She has let me know that I shall always have her protection. . . .

The religious from France had brought with them supplies of many kinds for the American convents, but their baggage had gone astray en route from New York to St. Louis. Mother Duchesne considered this no reason for a delay in thanking for the articles she hoped soon to receive, so on the following Sunday she gave herself the pleasure of writing a letter to the Paris community. She knew that some unfavorable comments about the St. Louis house had already been sent to France, and she may have hoped to counteract the impression created by these criticisms. But she was too honest to do more than make light of the difficulties and inconveniences of which others complained. So she wrote as she would have loved to talk to the whole Society:

Our dear Mothers Dutour and Xavier Van Damme reached St. Louis on the feast of the Holy Name of Mary and have given us the news of you which we were awaiting very eagerly. They told us that nearly all our houses in France had contributed either to the cost of the trip or to the gifts sent to us. These, however, were shipped by another route and have not reached us yet. But whatever they are and to whatever convent they go, they call forth my sincere gratitude, and they are much appreciated on every score. We have never received anything from France that we could not make use of, and gifts coming from our own houses have a value all their own, being proofs of the holy and lasting bond that unites us in Jesus Christ. When we receive letters from you, or when anything comes from France, we no longer think of the vast ocean that separates us from you, and we fancy ourselves in France, witnessing your labors and your joys and learning at the school of your virtues. We even forget our own present situation—the crowded little buildings, the poverty of foundation days, the small number of religious in the community, the difficulties arising from different religions, different languages, different customs in the country, and the obstacles we encounter in trying to establish order in the community and the schools, that order which is so necessary, but to which we can at present only tend with all our hearts.

After reviewing the steps that had led to the foundation of the convent in St. Louis, she added some details that were not entered in her *Journal:*

> I was acting without the least promise of success. Mother Octavie was ill; Mother Eugenie refused to send anyone to help me; I had one leg so crippled with rheumatism, it threatened to incapacitate me. . . . I had to come to St. Louis with just one Irish aspirant. The house was not ready; there were no teachers for the classes; and we could have had a crowd of children at the moment, but now that we can take them they are going elsewhere. Our greatest trial is the uncertainty with regard to spiritual help. Beg our Lord to remove this privation by one of those strokes of His Providence that cost Him nothing at all.
>
> Our chapel is most unworthy of the Divine Majesty. It is located in what was formerly the kitchen, partly underground—what they call here a *cellar*. You can touch the ceiling with your hand. The fireplace serves as an altar.[22] I have killed several toads down there and some other horrible creatures, and huge spiders that chirp a little like birds.[23] They kept up their music at night when I was there alone in the chapel. There was also a fierce big cat that had gone wild and made a home under the roof. These were the only ghosts we discovered in the house. I must admit that I was less afraid of them when we first came here than I was of living human beings, for the place is so isolated. . . .

As the La Fourche project had been the absorbing topic of conversation during the Bishop's last visit, several matters on which Philippine wished to consult him had escaped her mind, so she wrote about the most urgent of them:

> If you are willing, Monseigneur, when you next send an extra priest to St. Louis, would you please assign him to be our confessor, if he is not too young and if you judge him capable of directing religious women. Father Lutz does not speak English, and Father Saulnier knows so little of either French or English, our nuns have a hard time getting used to him.[24] I myself have two things against him: first, that he rarely gives me absolution, and second, that he is very much opposed to giving Communion outside of Mass. This means that some religious must lose their Communions when they cannot be present at Mass, and it is sometimes necessary for them to remain with sick children.[25]

Some days later she had another problem to present to the Bishop:

I do need enlightenment on a difficulty I am having with the Father Rector. He is giving me qualms about using novices in small employments here, saying that if they do not persevere, I shall be in part responsible. I am still using the only novice we have here, and a postulant, though our Rule says that they shall be employed during the time of novitiate only in their own religious formation and in manual work. My reasons are: first, I still consider this house as a foundation in the Society and have no older religious to relieve the young ones of their work; secondly, this was done in all the foundations in France. . . . I avoid going to confession to the Father, for if he should say the same things to me in the confessional, I should be in much greater difficulty. . . .[26]

The Bishop set her conscience at ease, assuring her that since "necessity allows no choice in the matter and is above every rule," she might safely continue to employ the novice and postulant, adding: "The example of your houses in France will show you the justice of this principle." [27]

The gaiety that characterized New Year's Day in St. Louis seems to have found no echo in the woods beyond Chouteau's Creek. The motley bands of maskers roaming the streets on the eve and singing the *Guignolée* from house to house came nowhere near the convent property. Croquignoles and pralines find no mention in Philippine's *Journal*, and the New Year began the hard way, without Mass at the convent and with illness in the community. There had been no news from France since September, and the letters from Louisiana had added to her anxieties. On January 4, 1828, she wrote to the Bishop, who was then in the South on a visitation tour:

. . . I have as yet received no answer from our Mother General regarding our reunion with the Sisters of the Cross. It seems that this was proposed to Mother Eugenie at St. Michael's even before you spoke of it to me, and it was discussed openly at Opelousas when she was there [in September].[28] Mother Eugenie is afraid that a foundation of ours so close to St. Michael's might hinder its progress. Mother Xavier, the superior at Opelousas, thinks that Mother Carmelite [Landry] is absolutely indispensable to her, while at the same time she admits that she would make an excellent superior for the proposed house. All these difficulties will disappear if our Mother General gives her approval, and I have urged her to do so.

I am faced with fresh difficulties here. The Father Superior of the Jesuits, to whom we proposed a foundation at St. Charles,

came to ask me if we were going to fulfill our obligations. I replied that we could not do so without a new permission from our
Superior General; for after we made the foundation here, she
told me that this was enough and that we should strengthen our
four houses. He insisted on having *yes* or *no,* saying he must have
an answer. I was unable to say *yes,* and I thought *no* would
satisfy him, since he was asking something quite impossible at the
the moment. So I gave him *no* as an answer. He seemed satisfied;
this made me feel sure he had other plans and wanted to get out of
the situation if possible. But now, contrary to my expectations, he
has become irate, saying he announced at St. Charles that there
would be a convent and so the townspeople were ready for his
plans. Our refusal, he said, was doing him a great deal of harm.
My excuses did not mitigate his indignation. He is extremely put
out with me and added that my highhandedness was causing great
trouble in our convents. If you know anything about this, Monseigneur, please be good enough to tell me, believing in my utter
submission to your least word and that I am forced to retain the
position that I hold. I have always cherished the last place and
longed with all my soul for peace and solitude. I have again asked
our Mother General to let us divide forces so we can make the
foundation at St. Charles. But answers are so long delayed in
reaching us that many things happen before we can receive them.
. . . Our nuns who arrived most recently find the going very
hard, and the one who seemed the more robust is nearly always
sick. . . .[29]

On January 24 she wrote again to the Bishop:

. . . Mother Eugenie is against us in this matter [of the La
Fourche convent] and has perhaps written to our Mother against
it with greater eloquence than to me. She says 1. that this foundation will harm St. Michael's; 2. that she herself wants Mother Carmelite there; 3. that our Mother said to make no more foundations
in Louisiana. Without contradicting her opinion . . . I should
like to answer: 1. that since an orphanage is desired, it would be
better situated at La Fourche in a building already constructed
than at St. Michael's where there is an already overwhelming
amount of work and where we should need to build and so be in
debt again; 2. that Mother Xavier, superior at Opelousas, can give
up Mother Carmelite only in the extreme need of finding a
superior. . . . 3. Finally, our Mother did indeed advise us not to
make any more foundations for a time. She was afraid we would
ask her for money and subjects which she wanted to save for the
foundation in the East, but which she is now postponing. I am surprised at Mother Eugenie's displeasure—of which she says I am

partly the cause. Our Mother General, in spite of my representations, has given me charge of all the houses in this country. Mother Eugenie refused to give any religious for this foundation and she has kept a Sister from here whom I need—but I left her there. Now her community numbers seventeen, and she wants to take a very necessary member from the Opelousas community, which numbers only five. Do you think this is fair? Because I told Mother Eugenie she was going beyond her power, she has taken offense. I cannot say that something wrong is right. And I have been telling her for a long while that, instead of getting herself into even greater debt by expansion, it would be wiser to limit her enrollment to the number of children that can be actually cared for.

Not only did I write our Mother General about a foundation at La Fourche, but also for one at St. Charles, and I need both these answers. . . . The Father Superior was very bitter and said he would never come here again, etc. . . . He accuses me of being the sole cause of the refusal. I represented this case to our Mother, saying I should much prefer to go alone to St. Charles than to have this rift. If I should receive her answer by spring, and if you still desire our union at La Fourche, I plan to accompany one of our nuns to Opelousas, where I feel I am much needed. The return trip would present some difficulty. All this, however, is quite indefinite. . . .

But in Louisiana matters had taken very definite shape, and in ways of which Mother Duchesne was unaware as she wrestled at a distance with the problems that lay within her jurisdiction, yet not within her control. Both Bishop Rosati and Mother Audé had gone ahead on the La Fourche project without informing her of the steps they were taking. A letter from Mother Audé to the Bishop reveals the astonishing fact that they had taken for granted the Superior General's approval, at least two months before it arrived. On December 27, 1827, Mother Audé wrote:

I have just received your Lordship's letter and I hasten to answer. If you think it wise for me to receive in this house the novices of the Sisters of the Cross who have an attraction for our kind of life and who desire to embrace it, they may come whenever they wish. We shall be happy to receive them and also disposed to love them sincerely in the Heart of Jesus. I fear, however, that they will miss the edifying example and holy direction of their good Mothers Xavier and Regina, which they will be far from finding in your humble servant. Have the goodness to warn them of this, Monseigneur, that they may be less surprised and disedified. . . .[30]

As Mother Duchesne learned of the transfer of the novices only in mid-March, she must have wondered then what conclusions the Bishop had drawn when he received her January letters. His reply was, perhaps, more puzzling to her than Mother Audé's displeasure. After writing enthusiastically of his visit to Grand Coteau, he added a noncommittal paragraph:

> Regarding the matters on which you ask my advice, I think that with time and a little patience all can be straightened out to the satisfaction of everyone. I have always been of the opinion that the convent at Assumption [La Fourche] should be united to your Society, so I have not allowed it to be closed. That would be to act contrary to the desires of those who have borne the expenses of it and to betray the hopes of the public. Besides, it will never become a rival of the house of St. Michael's because it will have a different objective. I do not believe, however, that Mother Carmelite is suited to be its superior. Her virtue and prudence are well known, but we also know she has not sufficient education to inspire the confidence of the parents. A stranger would be better. I am of the opinion that you cannot take her from Grand Coteau without harming that house. That is what I have observed. As to the establishment at St. Charles, be patient. Time will furnish you the means for it; your postulants and novices will be formed; all will work out eventually.[31]

Meanwhile things had been working out in St. Louis. A free school had been opened in March and installed in the room above the kitchen, which Martin Lepere had vacated. As the number of pupils increased, Sister Catherine Lamarre was transferred from Florissant to take charge of this important work. Mother Duchesne's confidence in St. Joseph was strengthened by the arrival of mail from France. In a letter written on November 29 of the preceding year, Mother Barat consented to the union of the La Fourche convent with the Society of the Sacred Heart and advised Mother Duchesne to make a trip to Louisiana, decide with Mother Audé on the details of admission, and let her carry them out. The Superior General insisted, however, that the Sisters must be received individually, placed in their proper rank, and given the regular novitiate training.

> Leave the house at La Fourche [she wrote] on the same footing as those we have established in France as orphanages. Mother Eugenie will send there the orphans she has received at St. Michael's and discontinue that work in her house. There can also

be a boarding school at La Fourche for daughters of the less wealthy planters of that area. The instruction need not be carried as far as that planned for boarding schools in France and the pupils could be allowed to pay part of their tuition in farm produce, as is now the custom in the school.

In another letter Mother Barat reviewed some complaints she had received about conditions in the convent in St. Louis and made suggestions for their improvement, adding encouraging words of praise for measures Mother Duchesne had taken and again advising her to go to Louisiana on a little visitation tour. "Your presence really is needed both at St. Michael's and at Opelousas," she wrote on December 13. Mother Duchesne was reluctant to make the trip south. She sensed, moreover, the imprudence of trying to regulate the work to be done at La Fourche on the model of schools for the bourgeoisie in France. Her experience at Florissant had shown her that this arrangement would not work, yet she expressed herself with reserve when she wrote to Mother Barat on March 23, 1828:

> I learned through a letter from Mother Eugenie that Bishop Rosati has already sent her five novices of the Sisters of the Cross, two of whom she has sent home.[32] The Sisters who have already made their vows must decide for themselves whether they desire to unite with us or return to their former community. . . . Mother Eugenie also told me she had your permission to accept orphans at St. Michael's. As she seems opposed to the union, I suggested that rather than overburden herself with orphans, it would be better to place them at the new establishment. She could help support them there. . . . That section is as yet rather poor, and the people cannot send their children to school at a distance. The necessity of crossing the Mississippi to get to St. Michael's is a very real obstacle to this and to visiting them, and it would be a great benefit for the country to have another of our institutions there. But it is repugnant to the American spirit to have two different class regimes in the same institution. . . . I do not agree with Bishop Rosati's opinion of Mother Carmelite. The fact that she is from La Fourche and a member of a highly respected family there would give her the chance to do much good. She has quite as much education as is needed for the position. . . .
>
> In my last letter I spoke to you of the necessity of building here in St. Louis and asked for the loan of 19,000 francs. With that we could build what we really need. But dreading debts quite as much as you do, we have cut down our plan rather than postpone the

work. A brick building that will give us a dormitory with thirty beds, a chapel, and a sacristy with rooms for a priest will cost only 6000 francs. I can borrow that much at 10 per cent, which is equivalent to 6 per cent in France plus the exchange. So if you have not borrowed the money for us already, it could be postponed for a year or two. . . . We now have 12 boarders, 10 orphans, 10 day pupils who pay tuition, and 30 in the free school, besides a Sunday school for mulatto girls whom we instruct after the parish Mass. That makes 60 children to whom we have the happiness of making the Sacred Heart known. If the work far surpasses the material income, is it not all the greater gain in heaven? I am very happy about it.

The Father Superior, who has been appeased by the hope that we shall go back to St. Charles, offered the Mass and preached here on the feast of St. Joseph, and today when he was leaving for a month's trip to the Osages, he gave me the deed to the house at St. Charles. . . .

The suggestions Mother Dutour made to you are really impossible: 1. for the building project we could manage to pay back 6000 francs, but never a larger sum; 2. stone walls around property are in use here only around soldiers barracks. Congress can afford them, but we cannot. 3. If we tried to fence in all our land, no one could get to our house, either in a vehicle or on foot, for the house is built in the center of the property, and on one side you can neither see nor hear visitors who might want to come in. With two groups of day pupils, how could we have gates locked at a distance from the house? Such a thought is just silly. 4. As to cleanliness inside the house, it really is very difficult to keep it as it should be because of the quantity of mud brought in both by ourselves in our various occupations, and by the day pupils, and we have only the orphans to help us with the cleaning. 5. I must add, with regard to the enclosure, that hedges are unknown here, and that we could not even obtain posts for an ordinary fence. The Ursulines in New Orleans have plank fences, and we have the same kind around a fairly large portion of the property which is used for walks and playgrounds.

As to making a trip to Louisiana, 1. it is quite unnecessary. Mother Eugenie has the esteem and confidence of all the clergy in that section. 2. There is the expense. It would certainly cost 1000 francs for two of us. I need the money for our building. 3. Mother Octavie is sick again. If she grows worse, I shall be obliged to go out there for a while. People used to prefer her to me; but since I moved in here, they say I handled the children better than she does. In order to keep that boarding school going, I left Mother Regis Hamilton there, for she is the best-trained religious we have for that work, and she could carry it on by herself if she were not so young and if there were not so many calls to the parlor.

Spring rains turned the walks and playgrounds into streams and pools of thick mud and washed down earth into the poorly ceiled basement chapel. Mother Duchesne and the orphan girls labored hard to clean parlors, halls, and classrooms, as well as the chapel, especially on Thursdays, which was the day pupils' weekly holiday. Rough manual work was never repugnant to Philippine, though she often felt the fatigue far more than she was willing to admit. At her work she was frequently absorbed in prayer and thought, planning, calculating, wondering how to grope her way out of the thicket of difficulties that seemed to encircle her. She always went about her tasks in forthright fashion, but her mood was very grave these days.

Sometimes, when the work was done, she sat for a while in the little sacristy, making or mending vestments. Taking refuge from anxieties in happy memories, she would let the past unroll before her inward gaze. The scenes she had so loved in childhood, the hopes that had come apparently to such paltry fruition, the affections that had played such a happy rôle in her life—these were precious and holy things to recall, fragrant with grace and love, consecrated by wholehearted sacrifice, inspiring an ever increasing spirit of gratitude toward God and rooting deeply in her soul the conviction of her utter insufficiency.

Such was her mood on a Thursday afternoon in April when she realized that Josephine's birthday was at hand. When had she last written to Josephine? She would write this very evening, April 10, 1828, and she did, beginning affectionately:

It is a long time, dearest Cousin, since I had news of you, and it is very pleasant for me to renew contacts with those to whom the bonds of kinship, friendship, and gratitude unite me. And I may add with more justice, the bond of religion. Your zeal for our holy faith has made you shower me with gifts and aid me in founding this convent in St. Louis. Though we lack sufficient space and the number of nuns needed for the work, we are now instructing more than seventy children as day pupils or as boarders. . . . The health of the religious who came to America with me has suffered a great deal. Mine has improved during the last year.

I am anxious about you, having had no recent news. When I recall how many in our family have been claimed by death since 1818, the year of our separation, I dread the fresh blows that each letter may bring. My dear one, we shall meet again. God did not unite us in friendship merely for the short period in this life. After this separation—you in one hemisphere, I in the other—we shall soon be reunited in an eternal union. How very beautiful and consoling our faith is! For the little work we do here on earth, it promises us in return all the joys of assured happiness. . . . How blessed we shall be if at the price of even great sacrifices we shall have made God known and loved by one more soul!

Visitors were not rare at the convent, though it was remote and somewhat inaccessible, but Mother Duchesne was sometimes surprised by those who came. That was certainly the case one April morning when she was called to the parlor to meet a stranger who presented her with a letter of introduction from Bishop Rosati. Opening it she read:

Sister Johanna Xavier Miles, former superior of the Convent of Assumption [La Fourche], will give you this letter. She wants, and has wanted for some time past, to be admitted into your Society. . . . I beg you to receive her with that kindness which is characteristic of your Society. She has no brilliant talents; her health is poor; but I think she will not be useless. I spoke to you in another letter about the Convent of Assumption; the plan that Mother Eugenie proposes for the superior to be placed there will, I hope, meet with no opposition on your part. I beg you to agree to it.[33]

For the last two sentences of this letter Philippine was even less prepared than for the first. Yet she greeted the unexpected postulant with cordial charity. It was in moments like this that constant interior mortification gave control over feelings and exterior movements. Within a few hours Mother Xavier, as the postulant wished to be called, was on her way to Florissant in a carriage borrowed from either "kind Mrs. Pratte" or "dear Mrs. Chouteau." Next day Mother Duchesne wrote to the Bishop, telling him of the postulant's arrival and entrance at Florissant, and adding:

Mother Eugenie has said nothing to me about who is to be superior at La Fourche, and she cannot supply one. Mother Carmelite was recommended to our Mother General on the condition that you should approve of this choice. She is well able to manage a house, which ought not to be as large as St. Michael's. Otherwise it might be detrimental to the latter. . . . Here we are beginning to build our chapel.[34]

For the moment things were running fairly smoothly inside the St. Louis convent. But outside it was springtime again, and down by the bridge that led from Fourth Street to the convent property there was a sheltered stretch of water in "Monsieur Chouteau's Creek" that had for many years been the favorite swimming hole south of the town. The swimmers could not be seen from the convent enclosure, but day pupils soon reported their presence to the nuns, not perhaps so much through maidenly modesty as through indignation at the taunts and teasing hurled at them by the boys who were splashing in the water near the bridge, or called from the bushes where their clothes were hanging. Such a nuisance could not be tolerated, of course. So Mother Duchesne addressed herself to no less a person than the city's mayor, the honorable William Carr Lane, sending him one of the very few letters she ever wrote in English:

SIR,

I have recourse to your authority for the redress of an abuse which I look upon as very much against the welfare of our establishment. You know, Sir, that our young ladies, day schollars [sic], in order to reach our house have to pass the creek that runs all around our house. The warm weather invites a number of men and boys to swimming in the creek, and every day our young ladies meet with that disagreeable sight, both coming [to] and leaving the house; and as I understand that some regulation of court forbids swimming in public places, I suppose that it is merely by some negligence of the sheriffs in discharge of their duty that it takes place.

As you are, Sir, the father of an amiable family I need not say how much that rudeness is against the delicacy of sentiments we strive to endow our young ladies with, and I am convinced that you will be so good as to use your power to remove that obstacle. I offer you beforehand my thanks and beg you to believe me with deep respect,

Sir,

Your most obed. servt.
PHILIPPINE DUCHESNE
Supr.[35]

The response of Mayor Lane to this appeal is not extant. One can only hope that the sheriffs were called to order for their negligence and that the sensibilities of the young ladies were no longer confronted with "that disagreeable sight." As for Mother Duchesne, she had other matters confronting her. When she learned from Bishop Rosati that Mother Audé had proposed no less a person than Mother Regis Hamilton as superior at La Fourche, she wrote to him: "It is impossible to accede to Mother Eugenie's desire to put Mother Regis there as superior. It would ruin her health and possibly upset her spiritually. The sudden death of her sister was a great shock and she has been seriously ill several times since then." [36]

Mother Duchesne had a deep maternal love for Regis Hamilton. The strong bond uniting them was intimate and supernatural, a friendship of the most beautiful type. There was in the soul of Philippine Duchesne a natural need for affection and a tremendous power of love. She was conscious of this inward urge and knew there was no imperfection in it. And for that very reason the stream of her affection flowed warm and rich from her great loving heart, lifting, ennobling, sanctifying. She realized that God in creating friendship had made it very good, and she clung tenaciously to the family and friends she loved. It was particularly when loneliness and isolation pressed in upon her that she called across the ocean to loved ones in France in letters that gave little hint of the suffering from which they sprang. Such was a letter to her sisters on June 3, 1828:

It is a long time since I heard from you, . . . a long time, too, since I wrote to you, but that is a consequence of my vocation and the distance that separates us. I have learned of so many deaths in our family since I came to America, and deaths of members younger than we are, I do not know whether I can count among the living many of the friends of our childhood. You and I understood, when we said *adieu*, that it was for life. We have only to keep intact by our good works the sweet hope of being reunited forever in the next world. . . .

Does your love ask for news about a sister who always loves to get news? I have been in the episcopal city of St. Louis for a year. Our house here is still in its infancy, but it gives greater promise than the others because it is in a town that is becoming the central meeting place for all who are going into the Indian country and to the posts on the Mississippi and the Missouri for fur trade and the exploitation of the rich lead mines. I have not yet lost any of the companions who came with me from France, but we are living in four different convents. . . .

Our holy religion is making great progress in this country through the zeal of missionaries; and in spite of the return of Bishop Du Bourg and many priests to France, God has not left His vineyard without workers. The seminary established here has trained many good priests and promises many more. Pray often for this mission, but above all pray for me. I am growing old and I am not becoming holy. If you could arrange for a Mass for me at Notre Dame de Fourvière and one at La Louvesc, I should be very grateful. Please give my regards to your husbands, to your children, to the Lebrument family, to our relatives at the Visitation of Romans. I heard that Melanie is now at Valence.[37]

The new chapel was used for the first time on the feast of the Sacred Heart, though it was not yet plastered. A few days later the Bishop was in St. Louis, a very busy man. Mother Duchesne recounted some of his activities and some of her own to Mother Barat on July 3:

The Reverend Father Superior was highly pleased with your decision regarding St. Charles and asked me to thank you for it. Bishop Rosati is also delighted with your answer about La Fourche. I am very sorry Mother Carmelite cannot be named superior there. Having met Mother Dutour, Monseigneur asked for her to fill the post. I refused at first, but that evening she told me she could not put out of her mind the thought that she would go to La Fourche, and I realized that she would be happy to do so. Everyone is pleased with this choice, and as a phrase in Mother de Charbonnel's letter proves to me that you leave me completely free with regard to Mother Dutour, I decided I had the authority to make this appointment. I am obliged to take Mother Regis from St. Ferdinand, though she is such a help to Mother Octavie. But I simply must have her here in order to make the children love this convent. Many of them have found things repugnant for reasons which you know. . . .

The superior of the Daughters of the Cross at La Fourche came presumably to make her novitiate at Florissant, but she did not persevere. Bishop Rosati was quite displeased at this inconstancy. He arrived in St. Louis on the eve of the feast of St. Aloysius Gonzaga. On the feast of St. John the Baptist I went with him to St. Ferdinand and next day to St. Charles to see the church and our future convent. . . . On July 1 he gave confirmation to some of our pupils and left us on July 2. . . .

This month of July always recalls your feast and the happy days when I used to offer you my good wishes in person. While I long to see you, Reverend Mother, I have never wavered in my missionary vocation, neither have the four companions who came with me. Our attraction for the missions is inseparably bound up with an incomparable love for the whole Society and its Mother General, whose lowliest daughter I am.

As the Bishop had not yet assigned a chaplain for the convent in St. Louis, Mother Duchesne made another effort in that direction. To the joy of all concerned the choice fell on newly ordained Father Regis Loisel, first St. Louisan to enter the priesthood.[38] His very name was music in the ears of Mother Duchesne. The appointment had not gone into effect, however, when she wrote to Mother Barat on July 24:

> We spent your feast at the foot of the cross, without Mass, as there was only one priest in St. Louis, and he could not leave the parish without Mass just because it was your feast day. He came, however, to give us Holy Communion and Benediction. As we had all the day pupils of both schools here that day and as Mother Dutour was leaving the next day, we put off the extra recreation until today, Thursday. I considered seriously going with Mother Dutour, as Mother Xavier Murphy has been urging me to do. The people of Opelousas are pleading with her to transfer her establishment to their town. I consulted Monseigneur on the matter when it was first suggested, and he was against it. Being unable to ask his advice about taking the trip, I sent a letter to the Reverend Father Superior by a messenger who rode out to Florissant during the night. He replied that the trip seemed unnecessary. That set my mind at rest. . . . As Mother Dutour's departure leaves a great hole in our ranks, it would have been very difficult for me to go away.

The projected transfer of the convent at Grand Coteau to the town of Opelousas did not take place, but the merger at La Fourche was carried out. Mother Dutour's appointment as superior was confirmed in time by Mother Barat, but the Bishop took this for granted at once and announced her coming to Sisters Regina Cloney and Rose Elder, promising that they would soon be sent to the novitiate at St. Michael's. This would have been in accord with the Superior General's instructions. As a matter of fact, these two religious donned the habit and white veil of the choir novices of the Sacred Heart, but remained at La Fourche, carrying on the work they had inaugurated in 1825 and becoming excellent Religious of the Sacred Heart. Mother Duchesne, however, was left in ignorance of what was being done in Louisiana.

Mother Dutour took up her mission at La Fourche with more zeal than prudence, though she had held positions of trust in the Society before coming to the United States. St. Madeleine Sophie had expressed high regard for her and thought she would be very efficient on the American mission. She was a Savoyard, like Mother Audé, and Mother Duchesne may have expected this fact to create mutual understanding between them, but that was lacking. With only four in her community, Mother Dutour attempted to put the La Fourche school on a curricular footing with St. Michael's. Mother Audé, who, in spite of her ready acceptance of the Lorettine novices, was opposed to the merger, at once took a determined stand against it. She had had ample time to express opposition during the twelve months preceding Mother Dutour's arrival in Louisiana, yet only on August 25, 1828, when the latter had been less than one month at La Fourche, did she write to Mother Barat:

> Mother Duchesne writes that we should send to La Fourche the orphans we are housing here. But how can we do this to the poor children? They wait on themselves, are poorly clothed, have plain food, are trained to do all kinds of work and prepared to support themselves by manual work. How can they be placed with the boarding pupils at La Fourche, who are as fine ladies as our own pupils (*aussi grandes demoiselles que les nôtres*)? Would that not make a contrast harmful to some and humiliating to others? I await directives from you, Reverend Mother, to regulate my actions. Whatever you tell me to do, that I shall do. But I cannot resist the urge to tell you that you were poorly informed about that house at La Fourche. It seems to me that if you had known all, you would never have accepted it.
>
> You want to know, Reverend Mother, whether I ask advice of Mother Duchesne. I consult her, as I consult you, on all that concerns religious virtue, which she possesses after the manner of the saints. But in all other matters I prefer to have recourse to you. Your answers come as quickly as hers but with this difference— yours give me the assurance of acting in the Society's way and hers do not offer the same assurance. I am no further from you than from Mother Duchesne. . . . Then, dear Reverend Mother, let me have direct recourse to you. Do not refuse this favor to your Eugenie. . . .

It is patent that by this time Mother Audé had practically withdrawn her convent from Mother Duchesne's authority, and the Mother "Provincial" was aware of the fact. Moreover, while St. Michael's continued to prosper, enrolling eighty pupils, besides the group of orphans referred to, Mother Audé seems to have been obsessed with the groundless fear that *her institution*—and the personal element is only too evident—would be endangered by the activities carried on at the little convent located across the mighty Mississippi and some thirty miles or more down Bayou La Fourche. Answering this letter Mother Barat wrote:

> I send you a letter for Mother Dutour; read it and send it to her. Mother Ducis received your August letter. . . . Write me the full details about La Fourche and tell me whether my last letter on the subject made sense. At such a distance I do not know what to say, nor whether what I say is wise. . . . Your own house seems to be making great strides. Your prosperity would frighten me, my daughter, if you did not refer all this success to the Heart of Jesus and ground yourself in deep humility. . . .[39]

Through the autumn of 1828 Mother Duchesne was aware of the friction and rivalry developing in Louisiana. In September she welcomed two choir novices from St. Michael's, Maria L'Eveque and Eulalie Guillot, the former being one of six sisters who entered the Society,[40] the latter one of the three La Fourche novices. They were scarcely the exchange Mother Duchesne had expected as replacing Mother Dutour, for they were both delicate young women for whom, it was hoped, the Missouri climate would be beneficial. Maria made her first vows in October; Eulalie continued her novitiate at Florissant. Mother Audé refused to send any further help to St. Louis.

One of Philippine's rare joys this autumn was the entrance into the novitiate of another of her Florissant pupils, Adeline Boilvin, a niece of Mother Emilie St. Cyr. Mother Duchesne had taken a special interest in this delicate and gifted motherless child, who had been raised by her Grandmother St. Cyr and had lost her father in a river accident in 1824.[41] Adeline had proved worthy of the care and affection given her and had returned it with a personal devotion that grew stronger through the years, making her treasure the notes and letters written to her by her spiritual mother. She was preparing to receive the habit and white veil when she wrote to consult Mother Duchesne about a patronal name and received this reply:

> It will give me great pleasure to have you bear the name of a saint whose virtues, I hope, you will imitate. Choose among these: *Louise, Louisia,* or *Gonzague,* for Aloysia has already been taken.

I hope Mother Octavie's illness does not interfere with the novitiate, but rather draws down many graces upon it. Your loving hearts will be happy to procure for her the sweetest satisfaction she could enjoy in the midst of her sufferings—that of seeing you work courageously to merit the title of spouse of the most perfect and most loving Heart of Jesus.

You, more than anyone else there, can contribute to the fervor of the group. The yoke of the Lord which you have borne joyously since childhood has prepared you to practice the virtues of religious life and to walk manfully under the banner of the Sacred Heart of Jesus. On that banner one sees no other words but these: *patience, simplicity, recollection, obedience, regularity, silence, sacrifice.* May you deserve to have said of you what was said of the patron you have chosen, of Berchmans, and of many religious whom I have known—that you never, through your own fault, neglected the practice of the least point of observance. This is the happiness I wish for you. . . . Give a special message of affection to each of your companions.

Early in October Mother Duchesne was notified that the dedication of the new church at St. Charles was fixed for the twelfth of the month and that it was hoped that the reopening of the convent there would coincide with this event. She had understood the previous June that the old Duquette house would be repaired and made habitable before the nuns took up their residence again in it. She had chosen two religious on whose abnegation and fidelity she knew she could rely, no matter what the difficulties to be faced. She had worked with them at Florissant, knew the bright disposition, keen sense of humor, and quick intuition for the things of God that made them such congenial companions. Mother Mary Ann O'Connor was about ten years older than her superior, Mother Lucille Mathevon, whose merry laugh and sweet, clear voice made her a delightful community person.

Mother Duchesne reached St. Charles with them and Mother Berthold after an early morning drive from Florissant on October 10. The provisions they brought along were meager, and the conditions they encountered were appalling, even to women long accustomed to frontier life. It called for courage even to enter the old wooden house, and for stamina sustained by supernatural love to clean it and make it habitable.

Inner doors, as well as window frames and glass, were gone. In places the floor had rotted and fallen into the low basement, where pigs and sheep of the neighborhood had found shelter for the past years. The atmosphere was foul with musty dampness and decay. With the aid of an Indian woman who had come with the nuns from Florissant, they soon had the rooms in a presentable condition. Village carpenters closed the gaping holes in the floor and roof and laid in place the stones of the foundation which had been rooted out by animal intruders. The work accomplished was phenomenal, for by the afternoon of the second day the central room had been transformed into a temporary chapel. An altar was set up, and roughly constructed benches ran the length of the room on two sides. At six o'clock in the evening a small bell tinkled. Bishop Rosati and twelve priests filed in processionally, took their places, and chanted the Office for the Dedication of the Church "with all the dignity and piety that befit the liturgical service."

At dawn the following morning a series of nine Masses began in the little chapel on the altar stone prepared for the new church. The priests, long accustomed to pioneer life, accepted good-humoredly the breakfast served them in turn on top of an empty barrel. There was food in plenty, for the village folk had supplied roasted meats, corn bread, and many other provisions. Their generosity won the heart of Mother Mathevon before she had been a day in their midst. At ten o'clock the dedication ceremony began. . . . The Religious of the Sacred Heart assisted at it and shared the enthusiasm of the people, who flocked to the church the following day when the Bishop confirmed sixty-six persons and preached in his simple and captivating style. Mothers Duchesne and Berthold remained another day, then returned to St. Louis.[42]

Those strenuous days at St. Charles were followed by weeks of anxiety that lengthened into months of distress as Mother Duchesne became aware that trouble was brewing in Louisiana. An indignant protest from Mother Audé reached her at an unpropitious moment, adding to the worries that were pressing upon her. The convent purse was empty. Florissant was in need of financial help. Mr. Mullanphy had asked her to give hospitality to the Sisters of Charity from Emmitsburg, Maryland, and Philippine had only the sacristy rooms in which to house them. That in itself was embarrassing, for the superior, Mother Xavier Love, was quite ill when they arrived. Keen distress, born of sympathy, had also been weighing on Philippine for ten days since Bishop Rosati had called on her for just a friendly visit and told her how troubled he was about the heavy debts left on his shoulders by Monseigneur Du Bourg and the priests who had returned to France,[43] and she had

had absolutely nothing to offer him, except, perhaps, a taste of good French wine from the "groceries" in which Mr. Reilly paid his daughter Isabelle's tuition.

And why had Eugenie sent her protest to Mother Duchesne? Its tone and contents may be judged from some lines from Philippine's letter to the Bishop on November 17:

> My reason for writing to you is a letter I received from Mother Eugenie, enclosing a copy of a newspaper clipping, which gives the prospectus of Mother Dutour's school. . . . Mother Eugenie complains that all the subjects we teach are offered there at a lower tuition, which will, she thinks, take pupils away from her house and perhaps prevent her from paying her debts. She adds that a group of people at La Fourche have sworn to make St. Michael's close in favor of La Fourche. I find, too, that Mother Dutour has completely disregarded the conditions laid down for her foundation. She has done things that only the Mother General may do. . . . I warned her about all this, but my warning had no effect. I beg you, Monseigneur, insist that the conditions be held to and inform these good gentlemen of these conditions. . . . Forgive me, Monseigneur, for taking up your time with this business, but I feel that I am speaking to a father who encourages my fullest confidence.

Philippine's prayers were weighted with other intentions, too, that autumn. Through letters from France and through the local newspapers she had learned of the political disturbances rife again in the homeland and of the religious persecution that accompanied them. Mother Barat had written of "dreadful days" and "sad times" and of the expulsion of the Jesuits as a part of the radical plan to rob youth of Christian education. From Josephine de Savoye-Rollin had come information about the active part the Perier men were taking in the political life of France. Four of them were in the Chamber of Deputies now, and they were all men who knew their own minds: Casimir, always conservative, sat on the right; Augustin, center left; Camille, left; and Alexandre, extreme left.[44] But this difference in political opinion made no rupture in the close bond among the Periers. There had been family sorrows that drew them closer than ever, and Josephine had given the full details in a letter that was more than five months old when it reached St. Louis. Hastening to answer, Philippine wrote on November 25:

> In your letter you gave me such a concise and interesting picture

of the present state and circumstances of our large family. You forgot nothing of all that is dear to me and all I am bound to by ties of gratitude. Your heart guided your pen. Sensing the desires of my heart, you have written about all that touches me most poignantly. So I appeal to your heart to express my loving sympathy to Madame Augustin Perier and Madame Camille Teisseire in the sorrows that have come to them. Having known the children to whom they were so tenderly attached, I can appreciate their grief at losing them so soon.[45] In such trials there is nothing to do but bow the head and adore the ways of Divine Providence, which are not our ways. But I am firmly convinced that God has cut short these splendid young lives only to reward the sooner those virtues which worldliness might have tarnished. . . .

Then she gave free rein to her pen, describing with evident satisfaction the ceremonies she had witnessed at St. Charles in October and the progress of the other convent schools in Louisiana and Missouri. "Here in St. Louis," she concluded, "we teach at least one hundred children, but most of them are in the free school. The money shortage has left us few pupils in the boarding school."

The seal on this letter was scarcely dry when word came that Mother Berthold was desperately ill again. Mother Duchesne felt she must again make the sacrifice of Regis Hamilton, who exchanged places with Mother Therese Detchemendy on November 29. The sorrow of the one was the joy of the other, and Therese appreciated the privilege of living once more with Mother Duchesne, for she lost no time in telling Mother Barat: "I am now in St. Louis with my dear Mother Duchesne. I cannot tell you how hard she works or how she deprives herself in order that we may have more. One can truly say she is like a victim continually immolating herself in the interest of our dear Society." [46]

2. 1829—1830

Blessed is the one who comes in the name of the Lord.

Liturgy of the Mass

IN HER NEW YEAR'S LETTER Philippine offered Bishop Rosati the greetings and prayers of the community of the Sacred Heart "who thanked the Lord for the progress they have made under your guidance." After giving him news of the convents in Missouri, she again stressed the Mother General's wish that La

Fourche be kept on a level lower than that of St. Michael's, and begged him to use his influence with Mother Dutour, "who is extremely self-willed in her plans, and does not answer my letters at all, hoping to obtain all she desires directly from France." Two weeks later she told the Bishop, "No news from La Fourche." [47] And at this juncture the death of Père Antoine Sedella obliged Bishop Rosati to go to New Orleans, so he was absent from Missouri when Mother Duchesne received another letter from St. Madeleine Sophie advising her to go to Louisiana to see things for herself and to confer with Mothers Audé, Murphy, and Dutour as to the best means of securing uniformity in the American convents and an understanding among the superiors themselves. Mother Duchesne was still reluctant to undertake the mission and pleaded with the Mother General "to consent to whatever they will regulate among themselves." [48]

There were, indeed, several obstacles to her leaving St. Louis just then—Mother Berthold's serious illness, her own rheumatic condition, aggravated by a fall, the expense of the trip, and the lack of a mature religious to fill her place during an absence of two or three months. She went to St. Charles, however, to discuss the matter with Mother Mathevon, accompanied by Sister Mary Layton, who became the third member of that community. Mother Mathevon's reaction to the visit was expressed in a letter to Mother Barat a week later:

> I had been here at St. Charles four months before I had the happiness of receiving your letter. What joy it brought to my heart! And I had another very delightful pleasure recently in the thirty-six hours that Mother Duchesne spent with us. That visit lifted our spirits and renewed our courage to endure the many hardships facing us. . . . We live in great peace and union here and in an entire dependence on our dear Mother Duchesne, to whom we write frequently. She was well pleased with the conduct of our thirty-six children. Not a word was spoken in the studyroom that day during the time we were obliged to leave them to do their work alone.[49]

In Mother Duchesne's relations with Bishop Rosati there are many heart-warming incidents that show the prelate's understanding and sympathy. He had accepted a generous gesture with which she had refused a share, even a mere thousand francs, of the money provided for the missions of the diocese in 1828 by the Society for the Propagation of the Faith. "After all he had told me of his own needs," she explained to Mother Barat, "I had not the courage to accept the money. I prefer to suffer." But before his hurried departure for New Orleans in January, 1829, he instructed Mr. Mullanphy to give her a thousand francs as soon as the letter of exchange for the money was paid to him. Being now in actual want, Philippine applied to Mullanphy as soon as she was informed of the Bishop's kindness and obtained "$30 in advance," although the agent had not yet received the money from Europe.

Responsibility for the Louisiana convents was weighing heavily on her when she wrote to Bishop Rosati on April 5 to express her gratitude and to ask him to grant Mothers Audé and Murphy permission to come to St. Louis to confer with her. She had to admit that physical suffering was now her constant companion, but there was pain of another kind much harder to bear:

> Father Saulnier has been saying for some time that he wanted to talk to you about me, but he decided to tell me himself what he had to say. It concerns my manner of acting with my Sisters, which is too severe. Evidently they have been complaining to him about me, and this does not surprise me, but it is a fact that makes a meeting of the superiors all the more necessary, for Mother Octavie is very weak and she is suffering from several ailments.[50] St. Charles is getting along very well, having thirty-six day pupils now. I sent Sister Layton there and they are very happy to have her. . . . But be assured, Monseigneur, that I shall be submissive to all that you may decide in regard to me and that I am well aware of my faults.

This letter crossed one from the Bishop which must have pleased Mother Duchesne and at the same time increased her uncertainty as to what steps she should take, for the picture he drew of the La Fourche convent was, on the whole, quite favorable, and he urged the continuance of the work then being accomplished by Mother Dutour. After praising the simplicity, unworldliness, and economy he had noted at the convent on the bayou, he argued strongly in its favor and concluded with a paragraph of appreciation which contained a hint, at least, at one of the chief causes of disunion in the Society in Louisiana:

> I am of the opinion that you should see things for yourself, for it is just possible that seculars may perceive a kind of jealousy in the fears for the welfare of St. Michael's which are utterly unfounded, fears that these people should never have been allowed to hear

expressed. It is the interest I take, first of all in the good of religion in general, and then in your own institute, which is so useful in our dioceses, that makes me speak this way. I have no prejudice and no preference. All your convents are equally dear to me, and it is a real joy for me to see them prosper and increase.

In spite of this assurance, Mother Duchesne retained many misgivings with regard to conditions at La Fourche. One thing, however, was clear—she must send help to Mother Dutour. The question was whom to send. She scanned her list of the Missouri communities. There were just three nuns at St. Charles; and no one could be spared from Florissant, where the superior was ill and where regularity was necessary on account of the novitiate. As she pondered in prayer, a great act of confidence in Divine Providence welled up in her soul and she made her decision. She would make the sacrifice of young Therese Detchemendy, who was proving quite capable in the classroom, and send her south with Mother Van Damme, who might find more happiness in Louisiana than she had in Missouri.

Nearly six months had passed since Philippine's last letter to the Mother General. Her letters to the Bishop were always carried downstream by passengers on the steamboats and delivered for her without expense. Letters to her family had gone with travelers bound for Europe. There was reason for her silence toward the Mother and friend she loved so ardently: she simply had not enough money to pay the mailing cost on a letter to France, but she wrote on May 18:

We have had the cross of poverty this year to such an extent as to prohibit us from writing to you, as we had not the money to spare for the postage and were not able to get some mail out of the post office for the same reason. The convents at St. Ferdinand and St. Louis have often been several days without a penny, and we have had to pretend that things were otherwise, so as not to lose credit at the stores. At last, however, Mother Eugenie wrote me to draw on her for the money which you were so good as to instruct her to give us. Then Monseigneur gave me 1000 francs from what was sent him by the Society for the Propagation of the Faith. So we were able to repay the 3500 francs we borrowed last year, along with the interest. That is a sharp thorn drawn from my foot, for we have such scanty resources—eight boarding pupils, twenty-seven people to feed, nineteen of them to support entirely, and 1250 francs to be paid to the hired man. The eighteen day pupils who pay tuition have kept us alive this winter. Day pupils also support St. Charles, where there is only one boarding pupil, along with several orphans who are cared for gratis. . . .

We have sixty children in the free school, and within a year that school will have given us four postulants. So you see what the convent in St. Louis is accomplishing. We shall have many vocations from that group, which is so characteristically American, and very few from the boarding school. This, of course, will keep us in poverty, as we must provide everything for them, but several of them will be gifted for studies.

The convent at St. Ferdinand is better suited than this one for the novices. Though always suffering, Mother Octavie trains them well. There they do not have the distractions we have here. A continual movement goes on, with nearly a hundred children in a small house. They bring in all the news, and there is so much business, etc. Mother Octavie came here for six days to help me prepare for Mother Xavier Van Damme's departure for St. Michael's. She was never happy here; the children did not like her, neither did their parents. Several times she refused to speak to people, especially Father Dusaussoy, after asking to do so. She made many acts of humility before leaving, protesting her attachment to the Society and hoping to please Mother Eugenie. I sent her there for two reasons: she will be in surroundings like those of France, and Mother Eugenie will be the one to guide her. That house has all the characteristics that will please her, as it is better equipped and better regulated than ours, more on a French footing.

Monseigneur Rosati is delighted with the house at La Fourche and does not want us to limit the number of pupils. The other two convents are complaining a good deal that it is doing them harm. I think Mother Dutour could be satisfied with thirty pupils. She is a person who will push her requests until she gets her convent on an equal footing with the others. I cannot possibly leave here to go on a visit to Louisiana. I have five classes, all the religious instruction, spiritual reading, Office, the prayers in common to say, and what is more, the surveillance, which is very difficult.

I beg you, please give Mother Van Damme time. A fresh period of trial for her will not hurt the Society and will be very useful to her soul. Also please consent to whatever regulations our three superiors in Louisiana may decide upon. I am nothing but a worn-out stick, fit to be cast aside right now. But I beg you not to agree to the suppression of one of the houses in Missouri. St. Charles will be an educational opportunity for the children of the vast spaces of the western country. This convent is in the episcopal city, the most important place in the state. St. Ferdinand is the novitiate and has a boarding school with a lower tuition than we charge here. Mother Octavie agrees with me in all this. . . .

This letter reached Mother Barat about the same time as one from Mother Audé containing the following crisp sentences:

Mother Duchesne wrote to me that she could not come down here. She wanted me to go up there instead, but I cannot leave here now. As she foresaw this might be the case, she invited Mothers Xavier, Dutour, and me to meet and discuss the following points: 1. whether the houses of St. Louis and St. Ferdinand should be merged into one; 2. whether the number of establishments in Louisiana and Missouri should be limited to six; 3. what dispensations in matters of rule are needed in this country. She gave as her opinion, and that of Mothers Octavie and Lucille, a *No* for the first two points. I have allowed myself only too often the liberty of expressing my opinion on these same points in the several letters I have written you recently. The third point can be handled quickly enough right here. No dispensations are necessary, or if one or two have to be requested, they are of small importance and not absolutely necessary. . . .

It was a far cry from Paris and Lyons and Grenoble and Rome to the frontiers of the United States in 1829. Although St. Michael's and Grand Coteau were in a prosperous section of the country and in the midst of a Catholic Creole population, there had often arisen need for latitude in the application of the Society's rules and regulations. In Missouri circumstances had made that need more frequent. With only three religious at St. Charles and five at La Fourche it was impossible to expect exact observance in all details. For more than a decade of years Mother Duchesne had striven with all the energy of her loyal will to keep intact the spirit of the Society among the religious whom she had brought with her to America and to plant that spirit deep in the souls of the novices whom she accepted as members of the order, and she had succeeded magnificently, though the letter of the rule had sometimes to give way before the exigencies of circumstance. Love for the Society and its holy foundress were, with her, second only to love for the Sacred Heart, the Catholic faith, and the Church, and she transmitted that love to all her religious daughters with such steadfast conviction and ardor of spirit that the strength of the bond she created has never weakened nor the flame of love burned low.

The summer of 1829 was marked by few "events" to record in the *Journal* which Mother Duchesne kept so faithfully. The feast of the Sacred Heart was celebrated with not one, but two high Masses, and the inauguration of the Confraternity of the Sacred Heart in the school. Five postulants came to talk with her on their way to Florissant, and in August Bishop Rosati called with Father Anthony Blanc, pastor of Baton Rouge.[51] Later in the month he came a second time with Fathers Evremond Harrissart, and Fouché, who confided to Mother Duchesne a secret—they were going to enter the Society of Jesus. She learned, too, that the Bishop was planning a trip east in September. A little letter to Madame Jouve, written the day he was leaving with Father Jean-jean for the Council of Baltimore,[52] may have traveled as far as the seaport in an episcopal pocket. The beautiful supernatural sentiments and tender sympathy of the first paragraph contrast pathetically with the weary note struck in the second, but it is a very characteristic bit of writing:

My dear Friend and much loved Sister,

God, who takes care of our family, sends us from time to time some consolations. I have enjoyed none more than the knowledge of the deeply religious sentiments in your soul and the graces you receive from the goodness of God and through the trials He sends you. I understand how great a sacrifice it is for you to give up Constance, how alone you are after raising so many children. But remember, they belong to God more than to you. You have offered them to Him more than a thousand times in your heart, never dreaming that, when the moment of giving came, your heart would experience such suffering. But help yourself by the thought that even in this life your children enjoy more happiness in the service of God than they would in the most brilliant marriages. I have heard only recently of Constance's response to her vocation and of Henri's departure for Rome. I hope perseverance will crown their generous sacrifices.

You want news of me. I consider myself still young because I do what I did in my younger days, but I often hear this comment, "My, but you are old!" I trust I shall not survive you, as I have already survived two sisters who were younger than I, Adelaide and Melanie. Do not fail to remember me to my brother, to Madame de Mauduit, to your husband, to all your children who know me, and obtain for me all the prayers you possibly can. Adieu, my loved Sister. All yours in the Heart of Jesus.

For several months Mother Duchesne had been hoping and praying for recruits from France for the American houses. It was plain that Mother Berthold could no longer carry on the work at Florissant, and Mother Duchesne was finding it almost beyond her strength to fill the offices of superior, mistress general, treasurer, class mistress, and surveillante at the City House. The children were unruly, the parents exacting in their demands, the gossips were at their old tricks, and through it all she had before her the Superior General's instructions to go to Louisiana. Then came the long-expected travelers, Mothers Catherine Thiéfry, Félicité Lavy-Brun, and Julie Bazire, and Philippine's happiness poured out in a short letter to Mother Barat on September 13:

> My dear Mother, my very consoling Mother,
>
> My last two letters were Jeremiads, and I was preparing another one just as sad. The parents of our children have been acting in a most unreasonable manner, demanding two months of vacation, two outings a week, etc. Then they held a meeting at the home of one family and gave out the report that I was leaving the city because the institution was going to pieces. I ignored all this, however, and was counting on leaving for the South when the Reverend Father Superior held me here almost by force because of the danger of yellow fever and the perils of the river at this season. I yielded at last, fearing I should otherwise be guilty of disobedience toward this good Father, who is vicar-general of the diocese. That very day I received your letter announcing the coming of our Sisters, and the very next day I had the joy of welcoming them. They are so humble, so good, so regular in observance, I can never thank you enough for sending them, and especially the one who can be superior. That will facilitate my trip, for now I can make it under the escort of Father De La Croix. . . .

This letter was enclosed in a much longer one which Mother Bazire sent to the Mother General the day after her arrival in St. Louis and in which she wrote:

> At last our desires are fulfilled. Yesterday at three o'clock in the afternoon we set foot in this holy house. I can never tell you, dear Mother, all that I experienced on seeing this convent, and above all when I found myself kneeling before Mother Duchesne. As she was not expecting us so soon, she was taken by surprise and had all the greater joy on seeing us. We went at once with her to the chapel to adore our Divine Master in the tabernacle—a consolation

we had been deprived of for such a long time. Dear Mother, how much one appreciates the happiness of the cloister after being out of it awhile. . . . By the grace of God I am more determined than ever to strive for solid virtues, and to purify my heart, for one must do that if one is to save souls. Yes, dear Mother, I shall try never to betray the ideal they have here of novices trained under your direction, and I shall also endeavor to lighten the burden of our Mothers who are so exhausted, especially Mother Duchesne. She is distressingly thin and has aged a great deal. . . .

The presence of the reinforcements from France made possible a reorganization of classes and a reallotment of employments. Moreover, Mother Duchesne could plan her trip to Louisiana with a sense of security, for Mother Thiéfry was quite capable of directing the convent during her absence, though her English was as yet halting and uncertain. She was a fine looking woman, cordial in manner, attractive in conversation. She had been educated by Benedictine nuns and had entered the Society twelve years before coming to America. Much of her early religious life had been spent at Amiens, where in 1818 she had seen Sister Catherine Lamarre set out for Paris to join Mother Duchesne's first band of missionaries. Desiring to make to God what she considered the fullest sacrifice of herself, she asked to follow them, but only in 1829 was her request granted by St. Madeleine Sophie.

The scholastic year opened on September 30 with just seven boarding pupils, though day pupils were numerous in the academy, and the free school was crowded. The regulation was working smoothly when Mother Duchesne found time on October 11 to write to the novices in France, among whom she hoped to strengthen budding missionary desires:

A month has passed since we welcomed with great joy the dear Sisters who brought us your precious letter. As we received one at the same time from your dear Mother Desmarquest,[53] it was only right that we should answer hers first. I did so and sent it by opportunity, along with letters for Father Varin and our Mother General, fastening my letters and those of our religious to a little Indian basket filled with raw sugar extracted from trees in our woods.

I learned with great joy that my niece Amelie has made her final vows and also that Constance, whom I saw at Grenoble in her first enthusiasm for religious life, has entered the novitiate. But what gave me still greater joy was the knowledge that many among you are attracted to our poor mission. If you had already experienced many trials in religious life, such an attraction might be very natural, the result of a desire for change, but to be willing to give up the happiness of a well-directed novitiate, the pomp and majesty of religious ceremonies, the abundance of spiritual helps that are presented to you under the most devotional form, in order to embrace a life of want, crude living conditions, inconstancy, ingratitude, poverty—certainly that shows true love of the cross of Jesus, who was lonely, humble, despised, and who went before us on the narrow path along which He beckons us to follow.

I can assure you there is great happiness in all this, and the ties that bind one to the life grow so strong that among the five of us who first crossed the ocean, not one has ever cast the briefest glance of regret on what she left behind. Instead, we have always said—yes, *always:* I have carried the cross and I will carry it. But it is really our Lord who carries it, for He knows how to make the soul content with little or no consolation. One can always find strength in the *Ita, Pater,* and in *God alone.* Yes, a vast field for your desires is opening up before you, I hope, but you must expect to find thorns in it. The Heart of Jesus gives us these sufferings, and it is in this Heart, my dear Sisters, that I am all yours. . . .

The *Missouri* was listed to sail for New Orleans on Thursday, November 5, but it was only on Saturday that the cables were loosed and the big steamboat nosed away from the levee and out into the murky stream. Seven years had passed since Mother Duchesne had traveled on the river, but the experience of that terrible trip in the autumn of 1822 was fresh in her memory. Now, however, the chill of the oncoming winter removed the danger of yellow fever, and progress in steamboat construction had made travel safer and more pleasant. Moreover, the presence of Father De La Croix on board the boat relieved her of many little worries. He found her changed in appearance—thinner, older, with a slight halt in her walk that would increase to a limp as the dampness penetrated her stiffened joints. The expression in her fine blue eyes was often troubled and suffering, yet they could grow luminous again when a genial and friendly smile broke over her features.

She had aged considerably in the past three years, but this fact was less noticeable because of the more close-fitting frilled cap she wore now and the black bandeau that hid her pale gray hair. These modifications in the religious habit, adopted at the most recent General Council, were a great improvement, but the dampness of the river soon threatened the starch of her cap frill. So she and her companion, Mother Maria L'Eveque, for whom the doctors had advised a return to her native climate, sat in a sheltered corner on the deck or in the "ladies' parlor," talking, reading, knitting, praying. Sometimes Mother Duchesne drew from her pocket the letter from St. Madeleine Sophie that had sent her down the river at last on the mission she faced with such strong misgivings. Again and again she read the well-worn sheet which she had brought with her as a credential, though she realized that it gave her no increased authority:

> I see with anxiety [the Mother General had written in June] that union is somewhat compromised. The house at La Fourche is the cause of this—or the pretext. Believe me, dear Mother, it would be best for you to take a little trip to Louisiana; assemble Mothers Eugenie, Dutour, and Xavier at St. Michael's, and regulate affairs. I name you to preside at this little council. You can come to some definite agreements, as for example: 1. to make no more foundations for three or four years; 2. to decide on three first-class academies and fix the other three on a lower level [about grammar school level]; 3. make regulations regarding uniformity in the matter of closing exercises, invitations to Prizes, etc. Then examine the decrees of the General Councils; decide which are not practicable in America and write this to me. At least let all the American houses do the same thing and let the dispensations or modifications be uniform in all our convents there. This little meeting should heal all breaches of charity and encourage each one to put the general interests of all before the particular interests of her own house.

At other times, as she sat writing, her quill raced across the paper and fixed there the thoughts that filled her mind and expressed themselves in the chatty style she had not used in many a month.[54] But she did not write on Sundays. To her great astonishment Father De La Croix had asked her not to do so. She had made a note of that, and on returning home she put the matter before the Bishop in connection with another narrow view that puzzled her: "I always forget to ask you, Monseigneur, whether it is permissible to play the piano on Sundays and feast days. In France there was no objection, but it seems that it causes scandal here. Father De La Croix did not even want me to write on Sunday on the steamboat, which greatly astonished me." [55]

As the *Missouri* dropped downstream, fatigue and weariness

abated and Mother Duchesne was better able, physically, to cope with the situation she so dreaded. Her loyal will was one with the Mother General, whose instructions she desired to carry out. There was no flagging in her spirit of obedience, but she soon found herself unable to cope with the circumstances or fully to execute the orders she had received. Her authority was practically paralyzed by conditions too complicated by personalities to be easily resolved. Mother Audé was smooth and inflexible, determined to do as she thought best for her institution, regardless of general interests. Mother Dutour was unreasonable, changeable, yet set on her own will and judgment. Mother Murphy was generous and sympathetic, sincerely attached to Mother Duchesne, but she refused to yield where there was a question of what she considered her "rights." No one has analyzed the situation better than Msgr. Louis Baunard, first biographer of Philippine Duchesne:

> At this time [he writes] and until 1839, all the convents of the Sacred Heart, in the New World as well as in the Old, were directly under the Superior General, who still found it possible to fulfill this task of government. *De facto* and *de jure* local superiors had recourse to her as the one supreme authority, and a feeling of filial affection and veneration made all her daughters naturally desire to treat directly with so wise and holy a Mother. This was especially the case with Mother Audé, whose attachment to Mother Barat inclined her to repel anyone or anything that was an obstacle to her relations with this loved Mother.
>
> "I consult dear Mother Duchesne on spiritual matters," she wrote, "for in these she excels." And she limited her consultations to just this. Mother Duchesne had no support for her authority when she advised or decided anything, save a vague mandate emanating from the personal desire of the Superior General, but having no foundation in the statutes of the Society, and no precedent in its history. Hence the repugnance she experienced toward the position of presidency at a local council arose as much from her wisdom as from her humility. As head of a conference where all was to be decided by plurality of votes, her authority rested mainly on her experience, enlightened but scarcely to be considered successful. . . . And she had good reason to fear that her manner of acting might be considered severe in comparison with that of Mother Audé, who obtained such attractive results at St. Michael's.[56]

After a brief stay at the convent on the Mississippi, Mother Duchesne went to La Fourche for a friendly visit, then returned to St. Michael's, accompanied by Mother Dutour. This little trip gave her a clearer knowledge of the geography of the river and bayou parishes, involving, as it did, a short navigation west-north-west across the Mississippi by steamboat to Donaldsonville, and a change to a bayou boat or a wheeled vehicle to go some thirty miles south among the bayou plantations and settlements to Assumption de La Fourche, today called Plattenville. Moss-hung trees, thick reeds, and trailing vines lined the water's edge on either side, with clumps of palmettoes here and there. Small farmhouses of French type, built of cypress timber, with front galleries for shade and homey hospitality, stood back from the stream in groves of stately live-oaks. Here and there a mansion could be seen, like that of Colonel Pugh, whose broad acres, lush with fertility, spread along the upper reaches of the bayou. It was not, on the whole, a rich district, nor was it as poor a place as Mother Duchesne had been led to believe. It was a section of French-speaking, home-loving people, still without affluence or aristocracy, still looking askance at the Americans who were making their way into the quiet bayou country where Acadians had pioneered as early as 1755. There were many Catholic girls here in need of education.

When Mother Xavier Murphy reached St. Michael's, the work of the council began. There were private conferences of the individual superiors with Mother Duchesne and some general discussions of problems facing the several houses, of abuses calling for correction, of dispensations or modifications to be granted uniformly to the American convents of the Sacred Heart, but only a few minor regulations were agreed upon for all and submitted to the Mother General. Although she represented the three Missouri houses, Mother Duchesne seems to have had but one vote in the council, and this placed her in a difficult, and at times a heart-breaking, position, for she was obliged to struggle for the very existence of her poor little institutions. In a letter to St. Madeleine Sophie, written while the council was in session, she touched on a variety of subjects and described conditions in the bayou convent, but made no mention of decisions arrived at in the conferences.

S.C.J.M.   St. Michael's, December 11, 1829
                                    Recommended to St. Anthony

My very reverend Mother,

This month of December always recalls the happy day of your arrival at Grenoble, December 13, 1804. Twenty-five years have passed since that day when I was admitted into the dear Society. In it my happiness has increased steadily with the progress made by the order, for what do we desire but the glory of Jesus! He has brought the Society through many trials, but those were to be expected when we contracted our noble alliance with Christ. Once when we were reading the chapter of the *Imitation* on the Royal Road of the Cross, I drew from it this aspiration: *Portavi et portabo* [I have carried it and I shall go on carrying it]. Now that Mother Piveteau has given me a copy of Mother Cahier's beautiful hymn, I too shall say to my divine Spouse: *A Vous les coeurs, à moi les douleurs* [Souls for You, suffering for me]. I have nothing but my whole heart to offer you with my wishes for a Happy New Year. The year will have begun before my letter reaches you; still I shall be closely united with all my Sisters in France at the very moment when they offer you their greetings for the New Year, for hearts can be united across the greatest distances.

I have written to you several times since the arrival of our last three religious in St. Louis. They told me that you have approved of a foundation in New York. I believe there is not a better place in America, both for prosperity and for usefulness, for a convent there would be a link between our convents and you, and in a very few years it would draw American postulants who would greatly aid us. Our biggest difficulty is the language. In talking about this foundation, Father De La Croix said the person best fitted to take charge of it is Mother Xavier Murphy. You yourself said she would be assured of the protection of Bishop Dubois.[57] As a well-born, well-bred, well-educated Irish woman, she would gain the esteem and the good will of the Catholic population, which is in great part Irish. Nearly all the clergy of Louisiana have great respect for her, and in this country the wealthy Irish are closely united with their compatriots. They are also the most generous Catholics in the country; and although nationality may form a line of demarcation among the clergy, anyone who is prudent will be aided and supported by both groups. A number of our former pupils, now married, are living in or near New York. They would be delighted to have a convent of the Sacred Heart there. When Mother Dutour and her party were detained in New York on their way out to Missouri, a wealthy citizen there wanted to entrust to them his eight daughters as day pupils. In a city as well-built-up as New York, things cannot be done shabbily—but where can we find donations large enough to help us begin there?

As Mother Xavier no longer had a religious teaching music at Grand Coteau, I thought she could get along without Mother Félicité Lavy-Brun. The latter was so at home with us in St. Louis and so eager to remain there, I asked you to allow her to do so. But that was a false hope on my part. The music master has already left Grand Coteau, and the children are very impatient to continue their music lessons. This will hasten my return to St. Louis, where Mother Félicité is teaching my classes, as well as music. Mother Xavier has sent you 3000 francs. She gave 1000 to Father De La Croix to repay the money he advanced for the last ocean voyage of our nuns. She also told me that she had sent 500 francs to St. Louis to pay the expense of Mother Félicité's trip down the Mississippi. To my great regret there is no one here who could take her place. I was fortunate to have saved 500 francs from what remained of the money for the last ocean trip—otherwise I could not have met the expenses of this steamboat trip down and back up the river. There is no money anywhere in the Missouri convents. I left on November 6, I think, with a religious who had come up to St. Louis on account of her health and who was returning to Louisiana. She dreaded being sent back to her former superior, so since her health is really much better, Mother Xavier asks to have her at Grand Coteau. The three of us will set out for that house in a few days.

I hope to bring back with me Mother Carmelite Landry, whom you first named as superior at La Fourche and who does not always get along well with lively Mother Dorival. Her health will improve in her native air, which is, of course, La Fourche. I do hope she will be a help to Mother Dutour, if only she will let herself be helped by a professed religious. She seems determined to have a novitiate at La Fourche, in order to train her own teachers and to continue to teach as high as the third class inclusive, which she has organized according to the Society's methods, saying you gave her permission to do this. That house of La Fourche—what an obstacle it is to our complete agreement, and how tenaciously Monseigneur Rosati holds to it! I am going to tell you, point by point, exactly what I see. Mother Eugenie has praised that house to me, and I have seen no sign of jealousy in her; but she does insist that it should be organized on a footing lower than St. Michael's, as the two institutions are so close together. She and Mother Xavier agree in saying that very few children go further than the third class in their academies, and that if La Fourche goes that far also and has a lower tuition fee, it will cut down their enrollments. St. Michael's, moreover, still has debts and needs to enlarge the building, as the community is too crowded for health and regularity.

Mother Dutour has named as portress the choir aspirant whom I sent down to help her—a religious who has fulfilled all the ordinary school duties at St. Ferdinand. The portry in a country house is no occupation at all, so the young nun is drooping around without real employment, while Mother Regina Cloney, who teaches the upper class, never appears in the refectory and has not enough time for her spiritual duties, prayer, etc., and she is only a novice. The second religious, Mother Rose Elder, complains that she cannot be at Office and is overwhelmed with work. The coadjutrix Sister whom Mother Eugenie sent to La Fourche had been trained well for the kitchen at St. Michael's, but she teaches singing, is surveillante of the 43 boarding pupils, many of whom are girls well on in their teens or somewhat younger. She also has their linen room and their refectory. A postulant has the little girls for class and does some of the housework. The class she teaches was taken away from the aspirant, but Mother Regina tells me that the aspirant taught it nicely and that the children loved her. She was removed from her classwork because of some fault of character—but such humiliating treatment can only increase the fault. I do not think it would be wise for me to change the aspirant's place of residence, 1. because she is better at La Fourche than in a house of novitiate; 2. because her voice supports the chant at Office, which they have begun to recite in choir, but they cannot always do so; 3. because the house is so poorly organized just now, and I know from several sources what is going on. The aspirant was told that she need not give me an account of the affairs of the house. Mother Eugenie and I got an account from Mother Dutour in conference together at St. Michael's. We could not budge her on these three points: 1. to continue teaching the third class; 2. to enlarge the building; 3. to train her novices at La Fourche. She wanted me to move the aspirant and allow Mother Carmelite to go there.

Fearing what might result from this lack of union and spirit of division, I told her that it was not for her to staff her own house, as superiors were not free to choose and train the members they wanted. At one moment she seemed to agree with us . . . but we had to admit the inadvisability of organizing schools on different social levels. Monseigneur stands by her firmly and so do some of the priests; the children and their parents are pleased with the school. But I dread the consequences of that spirit of isolation that refuses to be held in check. When she has obtained one point, she wants another. She said it would take 2000 francs to build a priest's house—now she needs 5500. . . . A chapel must be built out of respect for the Blessed Sacrament, for our Lord is very poorly housed. I suggested something simple like ours, but now she wants a building made entirely of brick.

Father Richard thinks it is unwise to displease the Bishop and the priests and the people of La Fourche, one of whom gave the property for the education of children in that section. He also says we really cannot refuse the parents' request for a school there, as it is often very difficult for them to cross the Mississippi to go to see their children at St. Michael's. I believe Mother Dutour is acting contrary to her own best interests. Still, in spite of the many problems connected with that house, we want to carry out your wishes and keep it going. . . . I shall return here from Grand Coteau, but that is a very difficult trip, so I shall post this letter now, anxious as I am for you to give the final decisions. I have been obliged to tell the superiors that I have no real authority, that I come as a Sister, an equal, that you wished us to consult together but reserved to yourself and your advisory council the decisions to be made.

During the conferences Mother Duchesne was ill at ease. "What influence can I have," she wrote, "in a house where all is admiration from within and from without, while in St. Louis I am in just the opposite position? I gave my opinion on every point discussed, but I was convinced that I should step aside without pressing my point in any way except in friendly fashion as a sister would act among her sisters." [58]

The conferences seem to have lasted about two weeks. Mother Duchesne had intended to leave at their close with Mother Murphy for Grand Coteau, but death visited St. Michael's again, and they remained for the funeral of Sister Borgia Boudreau. Mothers Duchesne and Murphy had barely boarded the steamboat for Plaquemine when Mother Audé, who was dissatisfied with decisions that had been made relative to her convent, wrote in harsh and critical tones to Mother Barat on December 21:

Our little meeting is over, Reverend Mother. Regarding this house it was decided, 1. that parents of the pupils will not be invited to the distribution of prizes at the close of the year; 2. that we shall not continue to send reports about the children's progress; 3. that we shall no longer display in the visitors' parlor the list of competition places.[59] I agree quite happily to the first point, as I had decided ahead of time to follow our Constitutions hereafter in that matter. The second, and still more the third, points distressed me to some extent, for I know the parents will not be pleased. They hold very much to the reports. When they see that several changes have been made at the same time—no more public examinations, no more lists in the parlor, no more reports—they will think the institution is going downhill, and that will be harmful to it. As a matter of fact, curtailment in these last two points will certainly not establish uniformity between our convents in Louisiana and those of Missouri. If you would only have the goodness to send as visitatrix one of our Mothers who is thoroughly imbued with your spirit, she could judge of the truth of what I am bold enough to state, and her visit would do the greatest amount of good in our little American mission. Without this step on your part it will gradually lose all resemblance with the Society in France. With your permission, Reverend Mother, I shall continue to send the report cards just as is done in France. . . . Will you have the goodness to answer me at once on this matter? . . .

When one recalls that Mother Audé had known the Society just four years in France, whereas Mother Duchesne had been a member thirteen years before coming to America, one cannot but wonder at the tone of superiority in which she writes, at the naïveté of her haughty self-assurance, at the scorn implied in her severe criticism. Yet Mother Duchesne had judged Eugenie with magnanimity, had praised her for her ability and achievements, and had justified her to the Superior General the day before this scathing comment was written. She had admitted, however, that she felt more at ease with the young Irish superior of Grand Coteau when she wrote: "Mother Murphy is the one to whom I feel most personally attracted. We really could not help expressing our desire to live together in St. Louis. But who could fill that Mother's place at Opelousas?" [60]

The trip to Grand Coteau with Mothers Xavier and L'Eveque was a tiring expedition that kept them traveling on Christmas Day, but Mother Duchesne enjoyed the affectionate solicitude of her companions and the warm welcome that greeted her. She was happy to gather the community around her in that friendly, maternal way that made her loved so loyally by those who appreciated her high supernatural spirit and her lowly opinion of herself. Of the ten nuns in the group she knew all but three— Mother Dorival, Sister Cecile Boudreau, whose holy mother had just died, and Adele Aguiard, a young Creole novice who would exchange her white veil for a black one while Mother Duchesne was at Grand Coteau.

How lovingly she greeted her old companion of the *Rebecca*, Sister Marguerite Manteau, and her first choir novice, Emilie St. Cyr! And there was Mother Carmelite, whom she had known since 1822, and Eleanor Gray and Mary Frances Mullanphy, aspirants now. They all welcomed Mother Maria L'Eveque with cordial love, and for three weeks enjoyed a happiness that was enhanced by the very evident joy of their own superior. There was a bond of union between Mother Murphy and Mother Duchesne that sprang not only from supernatural charity but also from congeniality of temperament. They were cultured, vivacious women, marked characters who understood each other, seeing usually eye to eye and looking always from the vantage ground of faith. There was no pettiness in their make-up, no self-seeking in their apostolic work, and the younger nun was eager to draw with joy from the fountain of the older woman's spiritual depths. One day they walked together to the little cemetery where there was just one grave, and Mother Duchesne told the story of Mary Ann Summers and her vocation.

On January 16, 1830, Mother Duchesne left Grand Coteau. Somewhere on the way to St. Michael's, at an inn or on a bayou steamboat, she wrote to her Cousin Josephine on January 18:

> I can think of no better way to relieve the tedium of a long trip than by offering you my New Year's wishes and chatting with my dearest friend. My wishes are late in reaching you—this trip is the reason for the delay. It was occasioned by the need we had of taking counsel together regarding our six convents. They are located in such very different climates, and I may say, among such very different classes of people, that adaptations are required to safeguard each group of houses. I have the poorer portion, and I came down to visit the more prosperous ones. But this year they are not so well off by reason of the poor sugar crop and by the fact that many planters have had to give up growing cotton, as there is small profit in it in Louisiana because it is now grown in such abundance in other states.
>
> I left Missouri on November 7. Winter had already set in. Reaching here I found in December and January what can almost be called summer weather. People in good health here have no fires in their houses; the gardens are flowering as in May in our section of the country, and the parlors, and still more the chapels, are richly decorated with many kinds of blossoms. It has given me much satisfaction to visit our three Louisiana houses. I had known only one before this. Now I am on my way home, and I trust this trip will be more pleasant than the last one I made up the river. This season of the year is more favorable for travel than summertime, being free from the disastrous epidemics, which were more widespread last year than ever before. This fact has made people fear that there may be annual scourges both in the new towns and in New Orleans.

Thank you so much for the news you gave me about all my old friends. I asked Madame Teisseire to give my regards to a great many of them, but you know you are always the one to whom I trust my messages for our dear governess, Madame Luc, and for Father Dumolard. I am at present without news from France or from the convents in Missouri, for they did not know where to address letters to reach me. Perhaps I shall find one from you awaiting me in St. Louis. If all goes well on the trip, I shall reach there sometime in the first half of February.

In spite of the year's poor harvest, Louisiana is growing rapidly in population and beautiful homes. One sees an amount of luxury unknown even in France. This tends to breed laziness and love of pleasure among the children. Religion, however, is greatly on the increase. Several new churches have been built and the Catholic congregations are growing apace. Monseigneur Portier, a native of Lyons and recently named Bishop of the Floridas, has just returned from Europe, where he has been on the hunt for missionaries to help him in his apostolic work. They say he was very successful. . . .

Adieu, dear Cousin. I tell you again that I am growing old, but my affection for you has all the depth and tenderness of our youth. . . .

Back at St. Michael's on January 20, Philippine was writing to Mother Barat about her visit to Grand Coteau. The one thing that worried her there was the presence of so many non-Catholic children in the school. She felt that religion had no part in the lives of many of these girls and she stressed this fact to the Mother General: "I am ashamed to say it, but one does not dare to speak to them of God. The study of the catechism is not insisted upon through fear of losing pupils. . . . To tell you the truth, the mixture of religions produces an indifference that is deplorable." [61] She had not lost her sense of humor, however, and she regaled the Mother General with a description of her departure from Grand Coteau in the torrential rain of a subtropical storm. Father John Rosti, C.M., who was accompanying her in a vehicle of some kind, seemed to her unduly nervous, and the Negro boy who rode horseback ahead of them as a guide on the muddy road was too frightened to do more than cling desperately to his mount and utter low moans. At frequent intervals the priest turned to Mother Duchesne and said in awesome tones: "Look there, Madame, that is a sinkhole," or "Here is where I saw a wagon stuck in the mud for six hours recently," or again, "That is where I was attacked one night by a Negro."[62]

Philippine was eager to begin the homeward river trip, but steamboats going upstream were scarce on the river at that season and she was obliged to wait for two weeks at St. Michael's. This gave her time for prayer and reading and resting. Among the twenty-two members of the community, eighteen had been strangers to her when she arrived in November. With seventy pupils in the academy the young religious and novices were kept busy. Only Sister Judith Labruyère came frequently to talk to her. She was preparing for her final vows and turned with love and confidence to the Mother who had initiated her into religious life. Judith was pale and noticeably thinner; a hacking cough interrupted her at times as she talked, but she made no complaint. There was joy in her soul and her desires soared to an ideal of loving service that would make her worthy to wear the cross and ring of a professed Religious of the Sacred Heart.

Mother Duchesne had leisure for letters, too, and her thoughts turned to Mother Barat, to whom she longed to give an ever clearer picture of conditions in the convents she had visited.

I do not know [she wrote on February 1] whether God has been pleased with my trip or not. Your will alone made it pleasant for me. My heart leans always to the side of the less fortunate, and that is Missouri. I am not made for a life of leisure, and I have not succeeded in bringing about the union which you desired to have re-established. Bishop Rosati's letter has made you decide to leave La Fourche as it is. Father Richard also told me to tell you that he believes that convent is really needed in that section of the country; he thinks it would give great offense to people if it were reduced to a lower scholastic level. There is a kind of rivalry between the parishes on the two sides of the Mississippi, and Mother Dutour has already found more sources of outside help than the other houses have, for that section is religious-minded and offers many influential backers among the rich planters. She is, moreover, under a great trial right now: the one priest stationed there is ill; she herself has had a hemorrhage and has had fever for a month; and her nuns, so few in number, are nearly all ill. Mother Xavier Murphy had seemed willing to let Mother Carmelite Landry go to help her; now she refuses to give up either her or Mother Dorival. I urged Mother Eugenie to send her at least one nun—I think she could have done so—but she does not want to. . . . Will you please send directly to me a copy of the instructions you send

Mother Dutour, so I may not suggest anything to the contrary, and if possible word the articles so definitely that we shall have done with objections. . . .

I shall try to combine the two boarding schools in St. Louis, as you desire, and so bring together the religious who are teaching. I shall not repeat myself, as I have already written you the details of this plan, but I beg you to consider it well before it is carried out. . . . Please accept, dear Mother, my apologies for the mistakes you will notice in my letters. Old age, which weighs on me, is my excuse.

While Mother Duchesne was in Louisiana, Mother Barat received reports from St. Louis that praised Philippine herself, but represented her convent in a very unfavorable light. The young religious were represented as "nearly all without much training yet, but this is not surprising when one considers Mother Duchesne's many occupations and the fact that she has been working almost singlehanded here. She spends the greater part of her nights praying or writing, and the whole day in the boarding school." [63] And again: "One must be satisfied with loving God and praying for the conversion of this wicked town of St. Louis. . . . This dear convent is worthy of Mother Duchesne, for it is poor, persecuted, and the happy dwelling-place of the Cross." [64]

On February 2 Mother Duchesne had the joy of assisting at the religious profession of Sister Judith Labruyère, and on the seventh of the month she boarded the *Oregon* for St. Louis. Again she was to experience the uncertainties of river transportation, but this time she considered the circumstance a happy arrangement of Divine Providence. At the mouth of the Ohio the *Oregon* ran aground and the passengers were obliged to disembark and continue the trip by oxcart. This gave Mother Duchesne an opportunity to ask hospitality of the Sisters of Loretto at the Barrens and talk over with them the delicate matter of La Fourche. As it was from this community that Sister Joanna Miles and her companions had gone to Louisiana at Bishop Du Bourg's request, these religious felt keenly the unusual steps taken by Bishop Rosati to bring the Sisters at La Fourche into the Society of the Sacred Heart. But their charity and religious spirit lifted them above personal resentment and made a deep impression on Mother Duchesne.

From the Loretto convent she went to St. Mary's Seminary to see Monseigneur Rosati, who had returned in January from his long trip to Canada after the Council of Baltimore. On reaching home he had found there the papal letters appointing Father Leo De Neckere, Bishop of New Orleans. The Bishop-elect was also there to greet him and would remain until May, when his consecration was scheduled to take place in his see city. Mother Duchesne was delighted with the good fortune that enabled her to discuss with these prelates the changes decided in the council for Missouri and the problems confronting the convent at La Fourche. The Bishop-elect seemed to understand all that she put before him and promised to do all in his power to sustain the institution on the bayou and "to take on himself the office of ecclesiastical superior of the three convents of the Sacred Heart in Louisiana." [65]

On leaving the seminary, Mother Duchesne put into Bishop Rosati's hand a folded paper. She had driven away in the rough, two-wheeled cart when he opened it and found enclosed a note for $100. It is easy to imagine the prelate's emotion as he read the few lines she had written that February 22, 1830:

> Monseigneur, I realize that the $100 I have been able to save on my trip for the convent in St. Louis is more needed at the seminary, at least until you receive payment in March for your pupils from Louisiana. If it can be of use to your treasurer to pay the tradesmen, I shall be only too happy to relieve him of an anxiety with which I am only too well acquainted. . . .[66]

The report sent by Mother Duchesne to the Superior General regarding the American convents contained many heartening facts. The statistics she compiled showed that the Religious of the Sacred Heart, after twelve years in the Mississippi Valley, had six institutions, in which more than 350 children were being educated. Of the sixty-four nuns carrying on the work, fourteen had come from France, fifty were Americans. There had been only three deaths in these twelve years, one at Grand Coteau and two at St. Michael's. The account of the meeting of the superiors was less satisfactory, as Philippine learned from a letter written by Mother Barat in the spring of 1830. The Superior General felt that through it "much good had been accomplished," and that "the essential affairs" had been regulated, but that there was much more to be done. She approved of a new building at Grand Coteau and the remodeling and enlarging of the convent at La Fourche. She was also inclined to allow Mother Dutour to develop the scholastic level of her school as she thought best, but she added: "Without your consent, however, I shall not give this permission, for if you see any real objection I shall come back on the matter and write to the Bishop, but I know he will make further representations and not be very well pleased." [67]

In St. Louis Mother Duchesne was faced with the task of carrying out the changes decided on by plurality of vote at St. Michael's, and she set to work immediately, though she doubted the wisdom of her own action. The Florissant convent was to transfer its boarding pupils to St. Louis, retaining there only the free school and the novitiate, and depending for support on Divine Providence. This meant changes in personnel. Mothers Berthold and Hamilton accompanied the pupils to St. Louis, while Mother Thiéfry took charge of the Florissant convent as superior and mistress of novices, having Mother Shannon as her chief helper. While these arrangements were being carried out, another group of nuns prepared to go south. Mother Julie Bazire and Sister Tesserot were destined for La Fourche, Mother Lavy-Brun and Sister Lucille Roche for Grand Coteau.

Jottings in her *Journal* show Philippine faithfully recording all these moves, along with some encouraging events and circumstances that occurred that spring:

> *March 19*—Feast of St. Joseph, our beloved patron, whose assistance we experienced during these days of suffering and sacrifice. Bishop Rosati said the Mass, preached, and gave the veil to Misses Shannon and Missé. The classes have been reorganized, day pupils separate from boarders. . . .
>
> *March 31*—A visit from the Bishop, accompanied by Monseigneur De Neckere. He has received funds from the Society for the Propagation of the Faith. We shall receive $453 as our share. The Bishop has given permission for the liturgical ceremonies in our chapel during Holy Week, a privilege that was refused us in former years [by Father Saulnier].

There is an overtone of joy in the *Journal* as Philippine notes the early Mass offered on Holy Thursday by Monseigneur De Neckere, who hurried off to assist the Bishop at the Cathedral; the celebration of Easter with Father Peter Walsh, S.J., at the altar; the presence of both the Bishop and the Bishop-elect on April 12, when Eulalie Guillot, Marguerite Short, and Josephine Miller made their first vows. Both the Reverend Father Superior, whose name she had not mentioned for quite a while, and the Bishop-elect were at the convent on April 13, when five of the pupils of the academy received their first Holy Communion, "among them Miss Anne Stegar, a convert from Protestantism, about twenty years of age, who wishes to become a religious."

ten

Years Surcharged
with Suffering

I. 1830—1832

> *Mindful of the blessed Passion of Christ,*
> *most blessed Passion.*

Liturgy of the Mass

GENERAL WILLIAM HENRY ASHLEY, fur trader, explorer, politician, and officer of militia, paced the front gallery of his mansion on Third Street. The air was pleasant that Sunday afternoon in the spring of 1830, but the General gave little heed to its warmth or to the fresh beauty of the leafing trees and bushes in the garden. He was anxious about many things, especially his sick wife. It was not five years since he married Eliza Christy, and she was fading like a flower under his very eyes. She had the best of care and all that wealth could provide, but she was feverish and restless, and also quite upset about Anne. Why had he kept Anne in St. Louis?

She was his sister Nancy's daughter and had come from Virginia for a visit. Her father was dead, and the General had thought to show his love by giving the girl some further education. The McNair children, who lived across the street, went to the convent school. They were younger than Anne, but she had joined them as a day scholar and had been greatly attracted to the nuns, especially to Mother Duchesne. When she began to talk of changing her religion, the General had gone to discuss the matter with this nun. He had found her broadminded and understanding, so he had not made objections; he only insisted that the girl be well

509

instructed and not allowed to go impetuously into Catholicism. Many of his best friends and some of his keenest competitors were of that faith, and the Catholic Bishop was the most highly respected man in St. Louis. Bishop Rosati had examined Anne and found her not only pious but also sincerely convinced in her faith, so the General had gone again to the convent for the Communion ceremony on April 13. But when his niece had declared her intention of joining the nunnery, he had refused his consent. Now he had let her go alone to visit the nuns, and he wondered what the outcome would be.

At the convent there was subdued excitement that Sunday afternoon, and Mother Duchesne had need of wise guidance. Instinctively she turned to the Jesuits, who counseled the utmost circumspection in the affair. But she could not drive Anne Stegar from the convent. She had decided to let the girl remain when quite suddenly the problem solved itself, and she could write on May 6:

> When Mother Thiéfry came from France, she brought us a white statue of the Blessed Virgin which is charming in our chapel. That room is so small we could not erect there an altar on which to put the statue, so we had a metal niche made for it, painted to resemble dark gray stone, and this makes the statue stand out clearly. It was before this shrine that one of our pupils, a recent convert, came to pray when she left her uncle's home. He had consented to her change of religion, but the women of the household, zealous Presbyterians, gave the girl no peace. Last Sunday [May 2] she asked to visit us. She jumped the fence to get in and took refuge in the chapel near the shrine of Our Lady, praying with all her heart to be allowed to remain at the convent and become a religious. That evening the General, her uncle, sent his carriage for her. She told the Negro driver that it was useless for her uncle to send for her as she was not going to leave the convent. Her age allowed her to speak in this manner, but we were in a difficult position with regard to the family. The Jesuit Fathers whom we consulted said we should send her home at once, as they feared the consequences of allowing her to remain. We composed a letter to the family but were hesitating about sending it when, without any warning, her uncle sent to the convent all his niece's belongings—bed, clothing, etc. She hopes this means that he approves of her action. For the time being we are in suspense about her and are praying to Our Lady to take this dear girl under her protection. She was born in Virginia, where she never even heard of the Catholic religion, and now she has reason to fear that she may be forced to return there.

In this letter to Mother Prévost, superior at La Ferrandière, near Lyons, Mother Duchesne tells of her trip to Louisiana and the convents she visited, with their prosperous boarding schools, then adds:

> In Missouri, where there is little wealth, nearly all the children are day pupils or orphans whom we teach gratis. I had hoped to bring some boarding pupils back with me from Louisiana, but the distance is too great and the trip too dangerous. These facts will show you that we are in straitened circumstances here and always will be, and we have many other problems because of the independent and restless spirit of the people. Our brothers, the Jesuits, do a much more important work than we, but they also have a large share in the chalice. Out of their 110 pupils, 100 are day scholars who pay nothing. But the Fathers have to live and pay for their new building. Happily we got a share of the funds sent by the Association for the Propagation of the Faith, and this paid our personal debts. Thank Our Lady for this. . . .
>
> Mother Thiéfry has gone to the convent at Florissant to train the novices, who are suffering because of the change of Mistresses, while on her side Mother Octavie, who came here with a few boarding pupils, was in better health out there than she is here. But she could not carry on the training of the novices; her voice is gone and her infirmities are increasing. . . .

Mother Duchesne had certainly been guided by the Holy Spirit in dealing with Anne Stegar. Even the death of her Aunt Eliza Ashley on June 1 did not shake her resolution, though she sympathized lovingly in the sorrow that had come to her uncle. Her novitiate was tempestuous, but both Mother Duchesne and Bishop Rosati understood her and trusted her, and they were justified in this confidence.

Not all the pupils in the academy were as satisfactory as Anne Stegar. Many of them chafed under the restraint, and their parents encouraged them in this, coming frequently to the convent to ask for them privileges which Mother Duchesne considered quite unnecessary. "We are continually bothered by the demands of the parents," she noted, "to visit their children on school days and to take them out for holidays." Excitement mounted high in the school when two of the boarding pupils ran away to attend the social event of the season, the marriage of Julie Cabanné to Lt. James W. Kingsbury, U. S. Army, "and spent two whole nights dancing and feasting." Julie had attended the convent school in 1827 and 1828 and was kin to at least half the pupils enrolled in 1830, so the wedding must have been a strong temptation to more than two of the *demoiselles*, as Mother Duchesne always called them.

A new type of anxiety appeared at the convent when fire broke out in the sanctuary twice within a month and Father Saulnier forbade Exposition of the Blessed Sacrament. To Philippine this was a suffering harder to bear than physical privation, and she turned for help to a newly made friend. Through the good offices of Father Doutreluingne, C.M., the ban was lifted, at least on feast days when he was able to spend some hours at the convent.[1] It was in circumstances like this that Philippine came to realize more fully that the whole burnt offering she had longed to make to God was not consumed in one great fire of love, but was sacrificed over a slow fire that was refueled daily by unstinted giving.

Through the summer of 1830 she was kept informed about the progress of the Louisiana houses. When Mr. Landry of La Fourche visited St. Louis, "he blamed Mother Dutour severely for undertaking to erect a $12,000 building without funds."[2] This worried Mother Duchesne, for she knew the conditions laid down by the Mother General regarding expansion on the bayou. At Grand Coteau a new building had been begun "with full permission and $7500 on hand." When Mother Xavier Murphy pleaded again for religious to help in the academy, Mother Duchesne sent Margaret Short and Mary Shannon south. Large enrollments were reported by the three Louisiana convents, with St. Michael's well in the lead. These flourishing boarding schools contrasted sharply with the one in St. Louis. If Mother Duchesne could count one hundred children present at Mass on the feast of St. Vincent de Paul, she knew that at least seventy of them belonged to the free schools, and even among the boarding pupils some were enrolled gratis. Then, too, not many of the convent's debtors were as honest as Antoine Dubreuil, who gave the convent his Negro Joseph in payment of the tuition of his daughters Adelaide and Emilie.[3]

On August 19 Bishop Rosati confirmed Anne Stegar and remained for a visit with the community after the ceremony. Speaking privately afterwards to Mother Duchesne, he told her that he had information about a revolution in France. Just when it had occurred and what had happened he did not know. Philippine turned to prayer, trusting all to the Immaculate Heart of Mary and to St. Louis of France, whose feast coincided that year with our Lady's. Then she began a letter to Josephine:

> I wonder if you received my letter of thanks for the last help you were so kind as to send me. It was announced to me by the treasurer of the Paris convent about the same time as you wrote to me yourself. Let me thank you again, and at the same time renew the expression of my deep gratitude to you and to all the members of your family who in the past have helped me so much. . . . Your friendship has followed me to these distant regions where one sees very few examples of attachment as generous and as lasting as yours.
>
> Now I am going to ask a new proof of it: please write me the facts about the events that took place in France toward the end of July. An extraordinary newspaper dispatch from New York has already informed us of some things. The news was brought by water on a vessel from Liverpool, which had it from France by way of London. Although the American nation gained its independence with the help of France, the American people do not love the French very much. I fear the news is not reported truthfully, and you understand how earnestly I desire to be correctly informed. If my letter and your answer travel as speedily as some others I have seen, I should hear from you in January. That is a long time to control my impatience. I know you will satisfy me as soon as possible. No one else has your gift for putting so much into a single letter. I might learn far less from many letters other people would write.
>
> I am concerned about Madame Teisseire's health, and the fate of our beloved Mountain grips my heart.[4] Do not put any enclosure in your letter; there is no economy in doing so. The least extra paper added inside a letter doubles the postage.
>
> There is no news to give you beyond what was in my last letter, except that my health is better. I had a very sore leg, which was considered serious enough to be taken care of. It got well in spite of my neglect of it, and I am better. My greatest anxiety at present, and the one which I trust entirely to Divine Providence, is the matter of the donation of this house to us as an orphanage. . . . Now that the town is growing so fast, this property has gained much in value, and I have already been faced with very disagreeable accusations on the part of the donor, who can raise the most unpleasant difficulties for us if he so desires. Being really helpless in the matter, I can only trust in patience, hoping the more tractable heirs will find consolation in our establishment. We treat these poor children as well as we can in order to fulfill our duty and give no cause for calumny. They took their places at the

Prizes, dressed just like the pupils of the boarding school, recited poetry, and received rewards, just as the other children did. Our pupils of Opelousas send me each year for my feast quite a quantity of very nice clothes for the orphans. . . .

The *Missouri Republican* brought information more quickly than Josephine could send it. Under the heading "Revolution in France," the issue of September 21, 1830, carried news of the dethronement of Charles X and the establishment of a provisional government under the Lieutenant-General of the Kingdom, the Duke of Orleans. The name of Casimir Perier seemed to dance up and down the printed column: Minister of the Interior—one of the wealthiest bankers in Paris—head of large industrial plants— "although an ardent advocate for rational freedom, he has not the reputation of being a mere revolutionist"—"his talent for government appears to have been generally acknowledged, except by the late monarch and the party opposed to doctrines which Monsieur Perier entertains along with the Liberal Deputies."

Three times Casimir's name appeared in the list of Deputies to meet in Paris to remedy the serious dangers which threatened the security of persons and property. Philippine, reading this, did not know that the thirty deputies had met at Casimir's own home in Paris. A dispatch from a London paper stated that "Casimir Perier had issued a proclamation stating that obedience was no longer due to the Government which was to be considered at an end." And further that "Casimir Perier was one of the four Deputies who went amidst the fire of the musketry to the Marshal Duke of Ragusa, representing the deplorable state of the capital—blood flowing in all directions—and made him responsible for the fatal consequences of so melancholy an event."

News of the succession of Louis Philippe was brought to Philippine by Bishop Rosati some days later, and early in October she learned of the pillage and destruction that had occurred in the palace of Archbishop de Quelen in Paris and at the Jesuit college of St. Acheul. The *Missouri Republican* of October 13 devoted much space to the events that had taken place in the French Chamber of Deputies on August 6 and 7, and Philippine read attentively the speeches made by Monsieur Gerard and General Lafayette, who was courageous enough to declare himself openly "a disciple of the American school" of government. But it was the ceremonies of August 9 that interested her most deeply, when the Duke of Orleans, in the presence of the Chambers and an immense crowd of spectators, took the oath to the Charter and was admitted to the sovereignty of France. . . . The fleur-de-lys had been removed from the throne and four large tri-colored flags were disposed to the right of the throne. . . . Warlike music announced the arrival of the Duke of Orleans without military guard. . . . The Lieutenant-General [Louis Philippe], seated and covered, invited the Peers and Deputies to be seated. Then addressing Monsieur Casimir Perier, President of the Chamber of Deputies, placed in front of the throne, he said: "Mr. President of the Chamber of Deputies, please to read the declaration of the Chamber." M. Casimir Perier rose and in a firm and clear voice read the declaration . . . then continued: "In consideration of the acceptance of these articles and propositions, the Chamber of Deputies declares that the universal and urgent interests of the French people call to the Throne His Royal Highness, Philip of Orleans, Duke of Orleans . . . The Lieutenant-General—Louis Philippe. . . .

There followed the King's declaration of acceptance "without restriction or reserve" and the solemn oath he had taken to observe the Constitutional Charter and "to act in all things with a sole view to the interests, happiness, and glory of the French people," for Louis Philippe was "King of the French." As Philippine read the printed words, her heart echoed the cries of *Vive le Roi*, and with all her soul she prayed for the homeland that was so dear to her, for her family, and for the Society in France.

Through the autumn of 1830 her heart was heavy with anxiety about La Fourche. Unhappiness in that community worried her far more than temporal distress. On November 23 she wrote to Bishop Rosati:

I received a letter from Father Tichitoli, enclosing one from Mothers Bazire and Detchemendy, who are both in anguish over their present situation. The letter seems to imply that the spiritual needs of the convent are as great as the temporal ones. I wrote to Bishop De Neckere, while awaiting our Superior General's decision, to authorize the giving of the temporal jurisdiction to Mother Eugenie and the spiritual responsibility to Mother Aloysia [Hardey] or to Mother Regina [Cloney]. I told Mother Dutour herself that I thought it would be wise for her to ask to be replaced as superior.

Since then I have received a letter from our Mother General; while at Chambery, she saw Father Caretta. He is quite worried about La Fourche, for he fears we will offend you if we in any way antagonize Mother Dutour. However, he knows nothing at all about the building, the debts, and the discontent. Please be good enough to tell me what to do. Would you be willing to tell her you approve of a change for her? May I venture to ask you to answer this? . . .

The Bishop's reply is not extant, but on December 29 Mother Duchesne wrote to him:

I have the honor of sending you a letter from the Bishop of New Orleans concerning La Fourche. I beg you not to let anyone know the contents, but to be good enough to suggest some way of supporting this work. I have already written to our Superior General, asking her to send someone to La Fourche, since the two oldest religious can no longer endure to live there. I received two letters yesterday from Mother Bazire asking for a change of house. If the money you promised us on the part of the Society for the Propagation of the Faith is still in France, I shall use it for the traveling expenses [of a religious to replace Mother Dutour]. . . .

On that same December 29 Bishop Rosati replied:

In regard to the house at Assumption, I believe that you must for the moment follow the counsels of Bishop De Neckere: let Mother Therese [Detchemendy] remain at St. Michael's, Mother Dutour at Assumption, and persuade Mother Bazire to be patient. It is in circumstances such as these that we must practice the Christian and religious virtues. *It is necessary;* we are obliged to do so. Thus Mother Bazire must make this sacrifice. While waiting for your Superior General to send you a good subject from France, write to name her [Mother Bazire] superior. Her merit will not fail to win confidence. . . .

In suggesting Mother Julie Bazire for the office of superior at La Fourche, Bishop Rosati was making as serious a mistake as when he first chose Mother Dutour, but only time and experience would reveal this fact, and the Bishop himself would, perhaps, never know it.

The winter of 1830–1831 brought much physical suffering to the people of Missouri. There was deep snow from December until the close of February. So severe was the cold that cattle died in large numbers from exposure, and a shortage of wood for fuel increased the suffering and brought on much illness. In the convent infirmaries Mother Duchesne nursed the sick day and night.

Orphans, pupils, religious—all were the object of her efficient and motherly care.

At Florissant there was suffering, too, combined with penury, for the convent had no income whatsoever since the transfer of the boarding school to St. Louis. Mother Duchesne did all she could to relieve the privations there, but her resources were very meager. She was especially concerned about Anne Stegar, who had received the habit in the autumn and been sent to the novitiate for her training. Anne was showing much good will, but the severity of the winter and the consequent privations had tried her physically, while her difficulty in understanding Mother Thiéfry's newly acquired English put a strain on her spiritually. Mother Duchesne often spoke to Bishop Rosati about her, knowing his interest in the girl. In January she suggested that Anne might profit by the mild Louisiana climate and the training given in English by Mother Murphy at Grand Coteau,[5] but the Bishop was not in favor of the move and advised that Anne be brought back to St. Louis and trained by Mother Duchesne herself. This advice was followed and Anne's happiness and perseverance were assured.

Bishop Rosati spent the day at the convent on March 19, his name day and the patronal feast of the house. After Vespers he told Mother Duchesne that he wanted to give Mother Regis Hamilton the pleasure of seeing her brother George advance a step nearer to the priesthood and planned to confer the tonsure on him and Hilary Tucker in the convent chapel. These two young Americans were leaving soon for Rome, where places had been provided for them at the seminary of Propaganda Fidei. The tonsure ceremony was set for March 28, Monday in Holy Week. So preoccupied was Philippine with the event itself that for once she forgot to record in her *Journal* the names of the "several priests" who assisted the Bishop that day. A letter from Monseigneur Rosati on the following day, however, shows the generous offering she had given him as he left the convent and reveals the simplicity with which he felt he could call on her for service:

I shall do as you tell me in your letter with the $50. I have already given $10 to Brother George [Hamilton]. If you had time to make for both him and his companion two pairs of cotton drawers, I should be most grateful to you for this service. In this case ask Martin Lepère to buy the cotton material you need; I will repay him. . . .[6]

Philippine's talent for handling both needle and scissors was equal to the Bishop's confidence in her, and two days later Martin Lepère carried to the cathedral rectory on Second Street a parcel containing the finished underwear, with a note asking what more the nuns could do for the seminarians.[7]

Although Bishop Rosati had done all in his power to provide spiritual help for the Convent of the Sacred Heart in St. Louis, Mother Duchesne clung to the hope of having Jesuit guidance and direction for the community. When she noted in her *Journal* on February 28 that Father De Theux had replaced Father Van Quickenborne as superior of the Jesuits in Missouri, she was optimistic enough to think that the new superior might take an interest in the spiritual welfare of her community. She even went so far as to ask Bishop Rosati's permission for this. He responded, "I gladly grant permission to Reverend Father De Theux and his confreres to hear confessions and give instructions at your convent."[8] But he prefaced this permission with a remark that may have puzzled Philippine in its context: "Human miseries!" he wrote. "We shall always be surrounded by them; we shall feel them; and in our turn we shall many times make others feel their effects."

Father De Theux came to offer the Holy Sacrifice of the Mass at the convent on April 10. While he was at breakfast, Mother Duchesne told him that Father Lutz, the chaplain, was about to start on a mission trip among the Indians of the Upper Mississippi Valley, and asked if he would allow one of the Jesuits to replace him for a few weeks. The fact that she produced the Bishop's letter of approval may have annoyed good Father De Theux and stiffened his attitude toward the nuns, for he was adamant in his refusal, and had the unanimous support of his council in the matter. Happily there were other priests more willing to help at the Sacred Heart, and Mother Duchesne wrote next day to Bishop Rosati about entirely different matters.

The "paying day school" on which she had relied so hopefully when opening the convent in St. Louis had been discontinued in the spring of 1830. A juvenile feud between day pupils and boarders had wrought havoc with discipline and school spirit, and with the transfer of the boarding pupils from Florissant to St. Louis, Mother Duchesne had decided to eliminate the day pupils and concentrate the efforts of the community on the boarding school. While the enrollment had not been large enough to support the institution, she was more concerned about the fact that the day pupils were attending private non-Catholic schools and receiving no religious instruction. Love for souls, taking ever deeper hold in her own soul, increased her zeal, and she longed to try even the impossible for Christ. A second project that had taken shape in her mind shows this longing even more patently. She could confide in Bishop Rosati, knowing he would always understand.

> I have been thinking a great deal [she wrote on April 11] about the advice you were kind enough to give me during your last visit with regard to our paying day school. It seems to me that, since Divine Providence has given us a chaplain, we could take up this good work again without upsetting the household and disrupting the boarding school. It was the boarding pupils who scarcely tolerated the day scholars and even abused them. If we make the regulation that no children will be accepted for less than a year or six months and that payment must be made in advance, we shall be able to avoid continual withdrawals and the sorrow of seeing pupils leave us without having made any progress. . . . If you approve of this plan, would you be good enough to speak of the project to those who might be interested? We need all the money we can get in order to prepare the house. In this way we shall again have the consolation of making another trial at a day school without contracting any debts.
>
> We had a visit recently from one of our mulattoes from St. Ferdinand. She longs with her whole heart to enter with us, but we may not accept her as a religious. This has suggested to me the idea of offering our house out there for the use of colored girls, either like the Sisters of St. Martha or like the St. Michael nuns in Paris, who were founded for girls whose parents complained of them. Many of these girls, being strongly urged by grace, wanted to become nuns. A very edifying community was established for them, having its own rule, but occupying a separate building within the same enclosure. Could not we, too, gather together colored girls who want to leave this world and set aside for them one or two of our own nuns until they would be able to continue on their own as a community or congregation according to their special calling? Of course, we could do nothing for such a good work without the approval of our Mother General, so I hasten to propose the matter to you. If you approve of the plan, I can tell her so and in that way avoid the long delay that is necessary since the Revolution. . . .[9]

On April 20 Mother Duchesne learned that the Superior General had followed her suggestion regarding La Fourche, reliev-

ing Mother Dutour of her duties there and sending her to Opelousas. She had put the financial affairs of the convent in Mother
Audé's hands and named Mother Bazire superior *pro tem*. Some
days later Philippine told the Bishop:

> Mother Dutour has written to me in a very religious manner.
> Mother Eugenie says that she showed great virtue in leaving La
> Fourche and that the departure did not cause a big stir. The debts
> are heavier than we had thought. Bishop De Neckere, however, is
> eager to keep the school open, and Mother Eugenie, who has
> already negotiated with several of the creditors, will do her ut-
> most to carry out the Bishop's desire. . . .[10]

Life continued to present a succession of trials for Philippine
that spring and summer. Early in May Mother Regis Hamilton was
taken very ill. "Small pox," the doctors said, and for three weeks
Mother Duchesne nursed her day and night, convinced that the
diagnosis was incorrect and that it was not necessary to close the
school. It was a risk, but no ill effects followed, and the nuns were
not deprived of the meager tuition fees that were their only means
of support. News from La Fourche was not encouraging. Mother
Duchesne told Bishop Rosati on May 14:

> Today I received letters from Louisiana, one of which was from
> Bishop De Neckere about the business at La Fourche, which is by
> no means finished. When Mother Eugenie realized that the con-
> tractors would come to no agreement with her and that they are
> planning to sue Mother Dutour, she advised her to go further
> away, and I do not know what tells me that she may be on her
> way to St. Louis on the *North America*. Though I resolutely dis-
> approved of her actions, I do hope she will not be afraid of her
> Sisters. Will you be kind enough to assure her of my feelings for
> her?
> And will you allow me, Monseigneur, to enclose my answer to
> Bishop De Neckere in yours in order to lessen the expense and in-
> sure its safety? There is also a note from Mother Regis for her
> brother George. She has received four or five letters from him
> which she has not answered, and this must worry him. He seems to
> be in good health and is waiting for your answer before setting
> out for Italy.

"What next?" Philippine may have wondered. The answer was
not long in coming, for the *Journal* contains the following entry
for June 3:

There was a frightful storm during the night. Lightning struck a chimney and knocked it down. It fell through the roof and the ceiling of the room in which all the orphans were sleeping. Several of them were hurt, but not dangerously. We were obliged to get the roof repaired at once, even though the work had to be continued on Sunday, for the rain was pouring into the house. It took several days to complete the repairs, and we have put up a lightning rod.

As usual it was to Bishop Rosati she turned for help on the morning after the accident. After describing the damage done by the storm, she added: "May I impose on you by asking you to loan us your workmen tomorrow and to speak to them yourself, for we know nothing about such work." [11] Two days later she was asking him to arrange for a triduum of recollection for the nuns in preparation for the feast of the Sacred Heart, and she added: "Mother Eugenie confirms in part what you were good enough to tell us: that the business at La Fourche has been arranged satisfactorily. On her side she paid $2700, and with the help of friends $3,666 in all. An equal amount remains to be paid on the known debts." [12]

The Bishop spent the feast of the Sacred Heart at the convent, pontificating at the High Mass and presiding at the singing of the Vespers. He had news from France which he knew would interest her and call for her most fervent prayers. Since the accession of Louis Philippe, Casimir Perier had not only been President of the Chamber of Deputies, but had also sat in the Cabinet without portfolio. On the fall of the Lafitte ministry he had been summoned to power as Prime Minister, taking the folio of the Interior on March 13, 1831. A very independent character, Perier held the Cabinet meetings at his own home, and not at the Tuileries. The French government was now in energetic and capable hands, and within a year civic order would be restored and national credit re-established. This strong, clear-sighted man could hold Paris in check by the force of his personality and quell revolts in the cities in which he had spent his boyhood—Lyons and Grenoble. His cousin Philippine was helping him with her prayers, while members of the family in France were enjoying a little reflected glory. "So Casimir Perier has become King of France," wrote Henri Bergasse. "I hope the whole family is going to feel the happiest results from this event." [13]

Through the long, hot summer the religious were at work in their classrooms, when they were not ill in the infirmary. "We have had continual illness in the convent since May," Mother Duchesne told the Bishop in mid-August, "and so our Sisters have not been able to work on the albs. This work had to be turned over to the orphans . . . and I see with regret that they have not been as successful as I had hoped. All could be finished, however, for the feast of St. Louis if we had the other albs to which trimmings are to be added. We should like to have everything soon in order to finish on time." [14]

While Philippine strained to complete the work for the Bishop, Mother Thiéfry was deeply concerned about her, knowing the long hours she also spent nursing the sick, so she wrote to Mother Barat on August 21:

> Do ask prayers, dear Mother, for our dear Mother Duchesne. We must beg God to take care of her for us; she certainly does not take care of herself. Just think of it—she has spent eleven successive nights at the bedside of one religious who was very ill, and she does not allow herself any respite from work. I cannot understand how she does it at her age. I think it is miraculous.

In the midst of the summer's trials came a letter from Mother Barat containing some cheering news. From Chambery, where she had found refuge during the revolution in Paris, she wrote:

> Thanks to your splendid cousin, Madame de Rollin, we are able to keep the convent of Sainte Marie for nine more years. At the end of that time I trust God will help us find a means of remaining there still longer. I am sending you some recruits. Mother de Coppens will go to Mother Audé's house; her health calls for a warm climate. . . . Mother Toysonnier goes to La Fourche; Mother de Kersaint is for your house; and the fourth will be for St. Charles.[15]

On August 24 Mothers de Coppens and de Kersaint reached St. Louis. Though destined for St. Michael's, Mother de Coppens had stopped at St. Louis instead of going south with Mothers Toysonnier and Prud'hom, who were on their way to La Fourche with Father Caretta. From the newly arrived religious Philippine learned much that had taken place in France in the past months. In fact, so avid was she for news that evening had come before she wrote to inform the Bishop of the day's surprise:

> This is the first moment I have had today to write to you. I should have liked to do so as soon as Father Brasseur, a Flemish priest,

came to tell us that two of our religious had arrived by steamboat last night. Mother de Kersaint, a Breton related to the Rochejaque-lin family, will remain here. Mother de Coppens, a Fleming, was to have gone directly to St. Michael's under Father Caretta's escort, but she felt unable to continue the trip. There were four in the party from France. . . . I think our nuns paid the passage of Father Brasseur, who greatly desired to come here as a missionary to the Indians. He knows nothing about this country and told me he did not even know where to find a lodging. I offered him our little sacristy room for the priests; and if you do not object, he may stay there whenever he likes. Our religious speak very highly of him. Mother de Coppens is the bearer of the letter to you from Father Niel, who was on a begging tour in Flanders. She wants you to know that what he is spending is for missionaries, but he is going into debt in Paris to such an extent, he will never be able to meet his obligations. She wants to see Father Rondot, whom she knows. . . .

Through the year 1830–1831 Mother Duchesne had never shaken off the impression made on her by the contrast between the flourishing institutions in Louisiana and the cramped and poverty-ridden convents in Missouri. More than ever a distressing sense of failure oppressed her, for she knew Mother Barat had been disappointed not only with the outcome of the conferences at St. Michael's, but also with the small success achieved by the City House in St. Louis, on which she had built great hopes. With the coming of Mother de Kersaint, Philippine thought she saw a way out of the office of superior and on August 28 wrote to Mother Barat:

Do name Mother de Kersaint superior. I shall keep so quiet in my corner as never to be in her way. I should add that I am ready to go anywhere you may send me, though I realize that wherever I go I may be in the way because of my age and my years as a professed religious. And, too, I can never deal easily with the parents of our children. The Americans do not understand me. The Creoles want good looks and attractive manners. The best thing for me to do is to disappear, either teaching a class or caring for the sick. I tell you this in all sincerity, and I shall act accordingly.

Such sincere insistence, repeated many times, could not fail to influence Mother Barat. She was inclined also to believe the letters written to her by a few of the religious who had come to Missouri within the past five years. They said that in her humility and unworldliness Mother Duchesne had let the convent in St. Louis stagnate, had refused to furnish it in a suitable manner, had neglected to make it attractive enough to draw pupils. The critics felt, too, that she had alienated the best families by holding too rigidly to strict discipline in the matter of outings and holidays, that she insisted unswervingly on things being done as she had known them in the early years of the Society's existence and in the first schools it had conducted in France. She was not progressive enough, they thought, for the St. Louis that was emerging from frontier conditions and developing a sophisticated urban life. She was, moreover, too generous in her charity, especially toward the Bishop and the priests who served the convent. The time had come, they urged, to yield to her own appeals and give the institution in St. Louis a chance to expand and develop along normal lines.

Mother Barat hesitated to take the step that was being represented as necessary. She knew the heart and soul of Philippine Duchesne, knew her love and loyalty toward the Society and toward herself, knew the motives that had impelled her to cling to old ways and rules and discipline. The principle of union, underlying all Philippine did in regulating the communities and schools under her direction, had maintained intact the bond between the Society in France and the little offshoot in the Mississippi Valley. That had been vital, and in that she had succeeded far better than anyone then living would ever realize. But the foundress came to a decision after mature thought and intense prayer, and wrote quite simply to her old friend and companion on November 30, 1831:

> I sent you a letter quite recently, dear Philippine, answering one from you, but I had not then read all the mail that has since come from you, from your companions, and from the newly arrived religious. From the ensemble of details given me I cannot help being worried about the present condition of your house. For a long time I have been saddened by the small success attained in St. Louis and by the anguish this has caused you. I have tried to send you recruits for the community, such as Mother Thiéfry, and I hoped that you would be able to keep at least one of them to help you in St. Louis, and that the convent there might be established on a footing with St. Michael's or Opelousas. Friends had given me reason to hope for this. But after all I have read, it seems to me we shall never obtain this result unless we follow a course of action different from yours, dear Mother.
>
> I must then, for the sake of the general good, submit a plan to you. You will, of course, consult Bishop Rosati, to whose judg-

ment I refer it for final decision, and I beg you to follow his advice. This is what I suggest: let Mother Thiéfry take your place in St. Louis and give her, as Assistant, Mother de Kersaint, and perhaps Mother Regis as Mistress General. Do your utmost to build a separate orphanage first of all, then little by little on a well constructed plan erect the other buildings necessary as the academy grows and additions can be undertaken prudently. You, dear Mother, may go either to Florissant or to St. Charles, whichever you think the better.

I realize, my dear daughter, that at your age and after all you have suffered, the foundation of an American academy, which calls for so much care and perfection along all lines, quite surpasses your strength. For several years all those who have been at the St. Louis convent have complained of the lack of order, the shabbiness, even the uncultivated condition of the property. Alas! God forbid that I should blame you, dear Mother. I know only too well all that you have done and suffered. But times change and we must change, too, and modify our views. I realize from experience that it is unwise to leave superiors for long years in the same house. Good government requires a change of superiors once in a while. . . .

That letter was still on the high seas when Mother Duchesne learned of the death of her beloved Judith Labruyère at St. Michael's. "She was an excellent religious and rendered valuable service to the Society," was the comment inscribed in the *Journal*. Another letter told her that Mother Bazire was doing well at La Fourche and that Bishop De Neckere and Father Ladavière were making efforts to finance that convent, but this was uphill work.

New Year's Day, 1832, was a holiday for the pupils, but some of them returned next day with their parents, who complained indignantly because their daughters' hands were sore with chilblains. The winter had been so severe that Mother Duchesne had actually begged the Bishop not to expose himself to the rigorous cold by making his usual visits.[16] The complaints had subsided when Philippine wrote briefly to Josephine on January 14, 1832:

MY DEAREST COUSIN,

The latest news I have had of you came to me through Mother Barat, who had the pleasure of seeing you at Sainte Marie. Again you have come to the aid of that house and put me also under fresh obligations to you. I have already expressed my gratitude to you, but the mail is not always reliable, so I am repeating my thanks both for the protection you have given to that haven of my happiness and for the 500 francs I received in September. I beg you also to thank Cousin Augustin for his kind response to my request. His letter was dated from Paris and contained so many interesting details about his family.

Our houses in Louisiana are flourishing and those in Missouri remain small and poor—they are my portion and I love it. We have had to see to locking up more securely, as a thief got in and robbed us recently. This leads me to appeal to your charity, as in one of your last letters you asked if I had need of anything. Could you help us a little this year? I trust I shall not need to make this request again, and remember, you must never mind refusing me. Adieu, dear friend, with messages of affection to all our relatives.

The packet of mail which Mother Duchesne received on January 31 contained the letter Mother Barat had written the previous November. After reading it and praying about its contents, she sent a note to the cathedral rectory asking the Bishop to come to the convent as soon as possible and providing a carriage, as usual, for his convenience. There is no record of their conversation during the interview, but the letters they both wrote on February 1 indicate the decision Bishop Rosati imposed on Mother Duchesne. Following the interview, Philippine wrote to her Superior General:

I have received your letter of November 30 in which you tell me your new plan for the convent in St. Louis. My natural tendency toward lowliness will make me find happiness in my position, provided I am not left with nothing to do. And even if you thought that necessary, I believe God would give me the grace to endure it. I am fully convinced that I do not possess the qualifications a superior should have. And for a long time one of my most fervent prayers has been to obtain what I felt should happen and what I hoped would raise the standard of religious observance and schoolwork in this house and draw to it all hearts.

But she goes on to relate that when she consulted Bishop Rosati, as she had been instructed to do, he told her quite positively to remain at her post in St. Louis and make no change until she had heard again from the Mother General. Meanwhile he would write to her himself. His letter to St. Madeleine Sophie testifies to the deep veneration as well as the personal esteem and affection the Bishop felt for Philippine Duchesne:

Madame [he wrote in the formal fashion of the day], Mother Duchesne has informed me, according to your instructions, of your latest letter to her and of the changes you believe it proper and even necessary to make in regard to the government of your institutions in Missouri. After mature reflection on the plan you submitted to me, I have begged Mother Duchesne to suspend its execution until she heard from you again. I want you to think over what I am going to tell you.

In the first place, I believe there is no one among your religious who can gain as much confidence as Mother Duchesne justly receives here. All who know her respect and venerate her because of her virtues, which, joined to age and the experience she has acquired during her long sojourn in this country, make her esteemed by all. There are few persons whom I venerate more than this holy religious. She has the true spirit of her vocation and on many occasions, known only to me, has given most striking proofs of this. In the next place, I see by the complaints that have moved you to decide on the proposed changes that things have been misrepresented to you. I am well aware that no one wished to deceive you, but rather spoke from a lack of insight into the matter. If the boarding school is not larger, this is not the result of lack of space. The house can accommodate twenty-eight and has only eleven boarding pupils. The house is not elegant, as are your European convents, but it is suitable for this country. That is not the reason why parents do not send their children there. You have been told the property has not been properly cultivated; one of your religious newly arrived from France told me the same thing. I replied that after she had been here a while and had made attempts like mine, she would realize that in America, where land is cheap and labor expensive, a religious community cannot obtain profits from its farm produce, for this must be sold at a very low price.

You have been told that she has not cultivated the friendship of the Founder [Mr. Mullanphy] sufficiently, but I can assure you that I do not know anything more Mother Duchesne or anyone else could have done in this respect. Besides, I know the Founder. Once he has done what he planned to do, he will do no more. So I do not think Mother Duchesne should be blamed on this point.

With regard to the religious sent from France, whom Mother Duchesne has not kept here—this action was not prompted by the fact that she did not need them, but rather by her desire to work for the general good of all your convents. This generosity, which I admire and at the same time regret, led her to make sacrifices in order to satisfy the demands of the superiors of the Louisiana houses. These demands were such that had they always been heeded, the houses here would be empty. I speak from firsthand knowledge on this point. More than once she has had to make a change of house or climate to satisfy some of the religious or to prevent complaints. You yourself know that this is not rare in communities, where we feel the effects of human weakness unless we are well advanced on the way of perfection. Religious are also children of Adam, so this is not to be wondered at. On this point in particular Mother Duchesne has suffered very much. Instead of blaming her, we should pity her.

I am speaking very frankly, Madame, because I have at heart the happiness and prosperity of your houses in my diocese. I believe that the contemplated change will in no way contribute to this end. No religious whom you may designate to fill the position now held by Mother Duchesne could really replace her. I greatly fear this excessive desire to enlarge the house, to make it appear more like the French houses, and to put the houses here on the same footing with them. You have had an example of that policy at La Fourche. Very well, here it would be even worse. In this country we have not the resources nor many wealthy Catholics. At present the Protestants have their own schools and they fear to send their daughters to a convent lest they be converted to Catholicism. That is the real reason for the small boarding school. Is it prudent to go into debt and pay a high rate of interest to build new additions? As things are now, much good is being done with the orphans and in the crowded free school, and there are others who could pay if you received them as day pupils.

In all the convents good is being done and more is hoped for in the future. With the growth of population and wealth will come increased opportunities for good. The Ursulines of New Orleans and Canada have at times been in conditions much harder than those of your houses here, but now they are as well off as their Sisters in Europe, perhaps even better off. Let us follow, then, the guidance of Divine Providence; it will not fail to uphold us. That is what those newly come from Europe do not know and do not want to know. But we know it after years of experience. Their views must not be placed before those of experienced persons. I pray you to pardon me if I speak so frankly. I sincerely desire the prosperity of your convents. . . .

So Philippine renewed her courage in prayer and purified her motive of love for the Sacred Heart, and continued to carry her burden in St. Louis. Its weight was increased just at this time by anxiety regarding the health of both Mother Regis Hamilton and Mother Octavie Berthold, whose suffering seemed to grow more intense with every hour and who could no longer appear in public. Jottings from the *Journal* give information about the things that weighed on Philippine's heart during this period:

February. Father Cellini, a Roman priest and excellent physician, came from St. Michel des Mines [17] to St. Louis at our request to examine Mother Hamilton and suggest a treatment for paralysis of the nose. The remedies he tried were unsuccessful. An operation may be necessary.

February 26. Departure of our Sisters Anne Stegar, novice, and Helen Mayette, aspirant, for Grand Coteau, on the steamboat with Fathers Van de Velde and Paquin, who were accompanying some of their students home to Louisiana.[18]

March 7. Father Rondot said his last Mass at our convent. His mind is quite confused, so he is returning to France.

March 15. News from Mother Eugenie Audé, who informs us that she has been authorized by our Mother General to close the convent at La Fourche, with the approval, of course, of the Bishop of New Orleans. He gave his consent very reluctantly. The two superiors of St. Michael's and Opelousas carried out the instructions. On March 26 the five religious who remained at La Fourche will go to Opelousas; the others went to St. Michael's. The house has been closed and given back to the Bishop, to whom the property belongs. The religious of this convent, the pupils, and their parents were greatly grieved by this action.

The objective tone of this entry in the *Journal* contrasts sharply with the emotion expressed by Mother Duchesne in her letter of March 17 to Monseigneur Rosati. Socks and sugar and dinner on a fast day were but the fringes of her thoughts. A sudden terror had gripped her heart, and she bared it to the Bishop in all its stark reality, writing:

> Mother Octavie sent you only one pair of socks as a feastday gift; we want to add those which the orphans had the pleasure of making for you with the silk floss sent us by Mother Lucille's sister. She begs in return the help of your prayers that she may remain steadfast in faith under persecution. Our two postulants have come in from Florissant and are eager to take the veil on Monday [March 19]. My one anxiety is that you may want to return home fasting. We do hope that you will partake of our meager dinner in company with the priests whom you may choose to bring with you for the ceremony.[19]
>
> Letters from Louisiana give me very different versions of the closing of the convent at La Fourche. According to Mother Eugenie, she was about to have another lawsuit on her hands. According to those who were obliged to forsake that convent: 1. she would have had, on the contrary, a house that would have cost her nothing; 2. Monseigneur De Neckere was misinformed; they told

him the house at Opelousas would be closed unless it received the help of the religious from La Fourche. 3. The parents were distressed and offered to increase the tuition of their children, only five of whom went to St. Michael's. 4. They say Mother Thiéfry will soon be in charge here in St. Louis. . . .

These reports urge me, Monseigneur, to beg this favor of you: if they try to precipitate matters here in the same manner, please oppose them firmly, requiring that the article of the Constitutions which forbids the closing of a house of the Society without the approval of the Cardinal Protector be held to rigidly. It took just three days to destroy a convent that had cost so much painful effort. . . .

[P.S.] Permit us to share with you this bit of sugar, while waiting for more to come.

At his visit on March 19, Bishop Rosati quieted Mother Duchesne's fears with regard to the fate of the Missouri convents. He shared her anxiety about Mother Hamilton, and when Doctors Samuel Merry and Bernard Farrar were consulted,[20] as well as a physician at St. Charles, Mother Duchesne wrote on March 28 to tell him they agreed that an operation was necessary. His answer was a personal visit on the following day, when he brought with him,

a skillful doctor from Baltimore whom Divine Providence had sent to perform the operation on Mother Hamilton. We had feared there was no doctor in St. Louis who could do it and had been advised to take her to one of the Eastern cities for it. The matter was entrusted to St. Regis, and we recognized in the arrival of this good doctor an answer from our saint.[21]

Anxiety about Mother Hamilton was relieved temporarily, but heart-suffering of another kind was renewed. On April 6 Mother Duchesne received a letter from the Superior General which dealt with the matter of the supervision of the convents in the Mississippi Valley. Writing from Lyons on February 3, 1832, Mother Barat said:

The time set for the meeting of the General Council is approaching. I feel, dear Mother, that since your houses are so far away from the center of the Society, it is becoming more difficult to govern them from such a distance, at least as to details. So I have decided to have you all name an Assistant General for Louisiana and Missouri. She would have the necessary powers, and all would be bound to obey her.[22] In order to be enlightened on this matter, I want you to carry out this plan for me: in each of the five houses let the superior have the professed religious vote by secret but signed ballots. These will be sent under seal to you, and you will send them sealed to me—but recommend the use of thin paper. Do not make any of the changes I suggested until after the nomination of your Assistant General. God will give her the light to put all in order.

Mother Duchesne communicated this news to Bishop Rosati on April 7:

> Yesterday I received a letter from our Mother General. She is still of the same opinion about me. If you approve of her plan, she wants to have an Assistant General named for America, as she finds it more and more difficult to attend to all the matters of government at such a distance.
>
> I am quite sure that the little progress made by this house is attributed to me. . . . There is no denying the fact that in the academy we are weak for English. It seems to me that Divine Providence is offering us a means to overcome this: if Mr. Taylor would give English lessons several times a week, we would receive his two children as boarding pupils in payment. They are so young, it would be almost impossible for them to come as day pupils. Will you sound him out on this matter? [23]

Mother Duchesne's move to interest Mr. Francis H. Taylor in the work of the school was wise and successful. He was a convert to Catholicism who had formerly edited the *Catholic Press* in New Haven, Connecticut. Coming to St. Louis in the spring of 1832, he proposed to Bishop Rosati the idea of publishing a Catholic newspaper which would have as its objectives to inform and instruct Catholics in the Mississippi Valley and to combat the vicious, even scurrilous, attacks by which the non-Catholic press strove to "save the valley" from Romanism. The Bishop approved of the plan and assisted Mr. Taylor financially, giving the publication his backing to such an extent that it became known as "the Bishop's paper" and proved a powerful factor in Catholic development during the four years of its existence.

Bishop Rosati also approved of Mother Duchesne's suggestion of adding Mr. Taylor to the teaching staff of the convent school, but again he firmly opposed her change of residence. Philippine submitted once more. At the summit of her soul there was total adherence to the divine will, and this gave sovereign peace. But at a lower level she shrank from the suffering that was inherent in her position. She felt that instinctive dread that every human heart feels when faced with pain, humiliation, failure. For years she had realized how untenable was her position as "provincial," when such an office did not yet exist in the Society. But she had clung to the supernatural conviction that she had grace for any circumstance that might arise, and her love was ready to give its full co-operation. She had always the Bishop's friendship and support, and her confidence in his judgment was complete. He understood that her shrinking from positions of authority was not a weak evasion of responsibility, not cowardice or dread of failure and criticism. He knew that she was profoundly convinced of her own incapacity, but he also knew that grace was achieving a mastery in her soul that called for an ever fuller gift of self, an acceptance of the whole will of God sincerely, courageously, and without reserve.

In the midst of her own personal struggle she was in constant anxiety about Mother Hamilton. On April 30 she noted: "The doctor from Baltimore performed a second operation to remove the growth from Mother Hamilton's nose. She suffers intensely and the result is doubtful. It appears now that there is a second polyp in the other side of her nose." The children had been given a short spring holiday, and on May 2 classes were resumed. The enrollment in the academy was poor, but in the free school there were 93 pupils. This was a great consolation for Philippine, but it did not pay the bills. She could, however, put aside all personal anxieties and write to Josephine, whose charity was being directed constantly to the convent of Sainte-Marie-d'en-Haut:

> Your generosity toward the home of my delights—generosity that has cemented our tender friendship—urges me to break silence in order to express my gratitude. I trust that God will reward you and your dear family not only with honors and earthly goods, but also with the greatest eternal blessings.
>
> The details which in your kindness you so often ask me to give you are in my letter to Mother Paranque, who will share it with you.[24] And in order not to increase the weight of my letter I only beg you to tell Madame Teisseire how deeply concerned I am about her health. Tell Augustin how I treasure the memory of all he has done for me and how I enjoy every detail I hear about him. Tell Father Dumolard how touched I am by the affair that has occupied so much of his time and strength. I do not know whether you will see my brother and sisters in the near future—but I beg you to remember me to them all. Tell them I never forget them,

that I am growing old, but am in good health. I have lost none of the companions with whom I came from France. This section of the country is very healthful and fertile and is being settled by Swiss, German, and Irish immigrants, and by Americans coming from the Eastern states where the soil is very poor. . . .[25]

Quite unexpectedly, one day early in May, Mother Anne de Coppens arrived from St. Michael's. She had been unhappy in Louisiana, and thinking she was not needed in a community of thirty-five religious, who seemed quite sufficient to care for the one hundred and fifty boarders in the academy, she had presumed permission to travel north. Mother Duchesne gave her a kind welcome, but could not sanction the step she had taken. As a matter of fact "Madame Anne" became something of a thorn in her superior's side.

But there was more personal heart-suffering in store for Mother Duchesne. She soon began to note in her *Journal* the distressing news coming from France, where, it was reported, cholera had carried off thousands of victims. When the Bishop came to pontificate on the feast of the Sacred Heart and Father Verhaegen preached *"un beau sermon en Anglais,"* the several priests present discussed the news at dinner. During June the *Missouri Republican* had been printing the "latest from France," always about six weeks old. An item in the issue of June 19 reported that Monsieur Montalivet was performing the duties of the Minister of the Interior in consequence of the illness of M. Perier. That of June 26 contained the rumor that Casimir Perier was dead, but added that the report lacked confirmation. The Bishop and clergy were deeply sympathetic with Mother Duchesne in this personal sorrow, and she was grateful for the prayers she knew this sympathy would call forth.

Another interest they discussed was the new Catholic newspaper, *The Shepherd of the Valley,* the first issue being due to appear on Saturday, July 7. The convent had subscribed to it; and when it came, Philippine scanned the pages for news from France. The plague was reported to have been subsiding in mid-May. The issue of July 14 stated that Casimir Perier was better, but the *Missouri Republican* of July 17 told the sad truth—Casimir Perier was dead. Philippine's heart was heavy with grief for the handsome lad who had taught her arithmetic, the Deputy of the Opposition whom she had seen in Paris just before leaving for America, and with sympathy for Augustin and Josephine, "her first and dearest friends." *The Shepherd of the Valley* gave details of Casimir's last illness and death, but only later on did Philippine learn of the courage, even heroism, with which, after a slight attack of the plague, he had visited the Hotel-Dieu in Paris in company with the King while many cholera patients in the hospital were in their death-agony. Three days later he was stricken a second time, and after struggling valiantly, as his friend Guizot wrote, "with all his physical and mental vigor," he died on May 16, 1832. A great demonstration of national grief and gratitude testified to French sentiment in his regard and gave him the title of "Defender of Liberty and Father of the Poor." [26]

The dreaded plague was devastating Canada in July, and *The Shepherd of the Valley* was warning St. Louis to look to the condition of its streets and alleys.[27] In early August the danger of another revolution in France was not so vital a news item as the fact that the cholera was gaining headway in the United States. It was in Boston, Philadelphia, Baltimore, Detroit; and a letter from Chicago told that the dreadful epidemic was in that village.[28] It was a time for earnest prayer and sensible precautions. The health situation in St. Louis, however, was still normal, so the schoolwork was continued.

During the first week of August both Bishop Rosati and Mother Duchesne received letters from Mother Barat written from Aix on May 8 in answer to those sent from St. Louis six months before. To the Bishop the Superior General stated frankly her own views and gave willing acquiescence in his:

> I am very grateful, Monseigneur, for the frankness with which you wrote to me of all that concerns our convents in Upper Louisiana, especially the house in St. Louis, about which I have had much anxiety. Ever since it was opened I have regretted its failure to prosper, as have the other houses [at St. Michael's and Grand Coteau]. Many reliable people, as well as several of our Sisters, have told me emphatically that Mother Duchesne's manner of governing was to a great extent responsible for the failure. I love and revere that dear Mother with all my heart, Monseigneur, but I know that even here in France, where she rendered us such valuable services by her zeal and devotedness, she did not agree entirely with our way of arranging things. As a matter of fact, we never put her in complete charge of a boarding school just for this reason. The representations which have been made to me along these lines did not surprise me. They were in line with my own thoughts and the knowledge I have had for many years of this holy Mother's manner of governing a convent. But, Monseigneur,

I agree with you that she has gained experience through her long years in America and still more, a personal knowledge of the ways of the people, who are so different from ourselves.

Now that you assure me that the abuses which are said to exist there and the slow development of the school are either exaggerations or difficulties inherent in the location of the house, I gladly confirm Mother Duchesne in the position she holds and direct her to make no change for the present. It cost me much to decide to take her from this family which she has established with so much difficulty, but she herself has insistently urged me to do so, and that on the advice of spiritual directors. I yielded only to petitions reiterated through many years. I beg Your Lordship to add to the kindness you have already shown in warning me of the disadvantages which would accrue from the change, the favor of confirming Reverend Mother Duchesne in the position she now occupies. I have done so, but a word from you will relieve her of all anxiety and encourage her to continue her self-sacrificing mission with perseverance and confidence.

If Your Lordship thinks it advisable, I shall direct her to draw up a single entire plan for the convent and to add one wing or section now, so as not to go into debt. We shall aid as far as we can, for I believe the building necessary in order to attain the regularity befitting a Convent of the Sacred Heart. But in this matter Your Lordship must be the judge. I leave it entirely to your wisdom to decide what part of the building Mother Duchesne can, and should, undertake at present. . . .

To Philippine, St. Madeleine Sophie wrote:

Your letter of last February reached me on the 4th of this month, my dear daughter . . . and I want to send you an answer at the same time that I answer the letter of Bishop [Rosati], which reached me a few days before yours. I yield to His Lordship all the more readily since it cost me much to make the former decision. I had acceded to your wishes, so perseveringly and energetically expressed. And then, too, so many other seemingly well-informed people agreed with you. I am delighted to know, my dear Philippine, that they are mistaken, and that on your side it is humility alone that urged you to make the request. I trust that God will aid you, as He has done thus far, in the exercise of your difficult charge. Continue, then, to fill it as well as you can. This is the wish of your Bishop; it is also mine. I love to find myself in complete accord with him. After his decision we shall change nothing. Do what you think best for the three [Missouri] houses. . . . Consider whether you can build in St. Louis without acting imprudently. I made some suggestions about this in my last letter to you. If you accept these, we shall try to put 10,000 francs at your disposal within a year. You can pay us back later on.

The cholera is emptying our schools wherever it breaks out. Paris has been ravaged, also Beauvais, Amiens, Metz. They expect it in other cities. May the Sacred Heart protect us. . . . Oh, what calamities! Your cousin, Casimir Perier, our one and only hope in France, for he had a fine mind, will not recover; Scipion, Casimir's brother, died of this same disease, and so many others. Pray for us that we may profit by these afflictions and be truly converted. . . . Adieu, dear daughter. I could write you volumes of news about the Society, if only I had the time. Pray for your Mother and receive, for yourself and for all your religious, the assurance of the tender love I bear you. . . .

Philippine made a laconic entry in her *Journal:* "News from France. Our Mother General wishes us to build here in St. Louis and offers a loan of 10,000 francs." When and how could she ever pay back a loan of 10,000 francs? Bills for food and fuel and clothing kept her constantly pressed for funds. There was no one to whom she could turn. The mention of Scipion's death reopened an old wound in her heart—Scipion, the lad who used to trail her through the big double home on Grande Rue with a book in his hands, asking her to read to him when he dared not use his own eyes on the printed page. He had died in Casimir's arms more than a decade before this, but death had not taken him from her affectionate memory.[29] Her heart still gripped tenaciously every member of the family she had loved and sacrificed for Christ.

The scholastic year closed on September 6 with a brave little effort at entertainment:

> The dormitory was transformed into a reception hall and decorated by Mother de Kersaint to represent a woodland bower. Bishop Rosati, Fathers Verhaegen and Elet, S.J., and Fathers Condamine, Lutz, Roux, and Paquin attended first the distribution of premiums, then a little pastoral play composed for the occasion by Mother Berthold and addressed to the Bishop under the title of *The Shepherd of the Valley,* the name of his ecclesiastical journal.[30]

As a member of the teaching staff, Mr. Taylor was invited to attend these exercises. His interest was reflected in the paragraphs he inserted in the newspaper the following week and in the editorial comment: "What we saw did not surprise us, for we have long known the merit and skill of these teachers." [31] Two days after school closed Mother Duchesne went to St. Ferdinand to make her retreat. During her absence "the kind doctor from Baltimore, assisted by Dr. Walker, removed the growth in Mother Hamilton's nose. Afterwards he said, 'Just thank God and me,' and he very generously refused any other remuneration for this difficult operation." [32]

Classes were resumed on October 1 with fifteen pupils in the boarding school, but within ten days all but six had gone home, for the dreaded cholera had appeared in St. Louis. Mother Duchesne wrote to Mother Barat on the eleventh of the month:

> After ravaging Canada more frightfully than Paris, it is doing the same in St. Louis in proportion to the population. Our pupils went home at the first appearance of the scourge, and the fear it inspires will last for months, if one can judge by appearances. But God be praised in all! He is always a Father, always good. In the midst of these difficulties He has shown a special providence in our regard, for with death all around us it has not taken a single person in the three convents in Missouri since we came here.

During this enforced vacation, Mr. Taylor determined to keep the boarding school before the Catholics of St. Louis, at least in print. Under the heading *Education* in the issue of October 13 he wrote:

> The Female Academy under the direction of the Ladies of the Sacred Heart (St. Louis) is already well known by the accomplished young ladies who have received a finished education in it and who have brought from it to the bosom of their families, and to the world, a greatful [*sic*] affection for their teachers who, with tender and maternal care, guided them in their advance to virtue and useful knowledge. [33]

So the City House, St. Louis, had formally adopted the title of "academy" and was offering as comprehensive a study program as could be found in any girls' school west of the Alleghenies, along with all the arts and skills required in feminine education of that day. In her planning, at least, Mother Duchesne was not behind the times, but for the moment there was but a handful of children in the school, and these were for the most part the orphan girls. In mid-October the people of St. Louis were advised by the *Missouri Republican* to "Keep cool, remain at home, do not worry, and trust in Divine Providence for exemption from the pestilence," but it was admitted that out of ninety-three cases that week, thirty-three had resulted in death.[34] At the close of the month Mother Duchesne wrote:

> During these terrible weeks Monseigneur Rosati and Fathers Lutz, Roux, Bonniot, Lefevre, and Borgna have all shown the utmost devotedness and have brought about the conversion of many non-Catholics who were abandoned by their own pastors. The Jesuits transferred their boarding pupils to St. Ferdinand, but Father De Smet remained at the college and devoted himself to the service of the sick, converting many great sinners.[35]

St. Louis was in a frightful condition that autumn, for the cholera raged "with very alarming malignity," and there was hardly a person in the town who did not "weep the loss of relative or friend." [36] Early in November, however, the civil authorities felt that the disease was under control. It seemed noteworthy to Father De Theux that the two Jesuit communities, with their pupils, and the Convent of the Sacred Heart "did not present within their enclosures a single one of those lugubrious scenes which . . . spread desolation and alarm up to their very doors." [37]

If the convent in St. Louis had been spared, that of St. Michael's had had a frightening experience, had lost Mother Amelie L'Eveque, had seen Mother Audé desperately ill and the boarding school of one hundred and fifty girls dispersed. Grand Coteau had been spared, though they still mourned the loss of Mother Dorival, who had died the previous summer. Reports from New Orleans told of cholera, smallpox, and yellow fever, all three, ravaging the city, with hundreds of deaths recorded.[38]

On November 21 Bishop Rosati paid a visit to the convent, bringing with him a prelate whom Mother Duchesne had desired to meet for nearly fifteen years—Bishop Benedict Joseph Flaget of Bardstown, Kentucky. She had heard so much about this great missionary that she felt as if she was already acquainted with him, yet she was meeting him at perhaps the most difficult period of his long career. During the previous year Bishop Flaget, weighed down by responsibilities and suffering from spiritual depression and a conviction of inability to administer his vast diocese properly, had written to Rome, tendering his resignation and asking that the burden he had carried for twenty years be shifted to younger shoulders. During his visit to St. Louis in November, 1832, he learned that his resignation had been accepted and that Bishop John David, his coadjutor and two years older than he, had been named second Bishop of Bardstown. Along with this news came the information that the Catholics of Kentucky were loud in their protests against his retirement and the proposed changes.

Mother Duchesne could sympathize with Bishop Flaget in this painful situation when he came to offer the Holy Sacrifice of the Mass at the convent on the first of December. She was happy to be of service to him when Bishop Rosati, coming from the convent infirmary where he had visited Mother Octavie, proposed that she make the ex-Bishop of Bardstown a new cassock from the piece of purple silk she had on hand in the sacristy. At once she set to work, taking measurements while the two great missionary prelates discussed the situation in Kentucky and the heavy losses sustained by the Church during the cholera epidemic. Detroit had lost its hero-priest, Father Gabriel Richard, whom she remembered so well, and Cincinnati had lost its first Bishop, Edward Dominic Fenwick, a relative of Mother Regis Hamilton.

Mother Duchesne had been uneasy about the presence of Mother de Coppens in St. Louis since May and had discussed the matter with Bishop Rosati, even written to him, asking him to persuade her to return to Louisiana, as that had been her assignment from the Mother General. When she learned that he was accompanying Bishop Flaget back to Kentucky, she begged him to use his influence and authority. Mother de Coppens agreed to give the Louisiana climate another trial, and Mother Duchesne helped her pack her satchel and boxes. The *Journal* tells how "Bishop Rosati and Bishop Flaget started together for Kentucky, Mother de Coppens traveling on the same steamboat to return to St. Michael's. At Ste Genevieve, where the prelates transferred to an Ohio River boat, Bishop Rosati was obliged to send her back to St. Louis, as she was ill again."

2. 1833—1834

> *To these and to all who rest in Christ,*
> *grant a place of refreshment, light and peace.*
>
> Liturgy of the Mass

DURING THE BISHOP'S ABSENCE, Father Borgna, who was acting as chaplain at the convent, took on the duty of confessor also. At Christmas he said his three Masses at midnight and Father Lefevre came for two the next morning.[39] Sometimes Father John

Timon, C.M., came instead of Father Borgna. Then Philippine was more at ease, for in spite of her long friendship with Father Borgna she did not wholly trust him, and she had reason to believe that his influence on some members of the community was not strictly in line with religious spirit and supernatural obedience. The Bishop knew the circumstances on which she based her fears and understood what was implied in a little note she sent to welcome him home on January 27, 1833, when he returned from Kentucky:

> During your absence we have been tried by the illness of our Sisters. But their joy in your return has brought them back to good health and today all are really better. We were glad to hear that you had a pleasant trip. I am very anxious to know whether we may hope to see you this week [for confession]—or is it indiscreet even to expect this? Shall we go on accepting Father Borgna's services? I shall be submissive, but not indifferent, in this matter.

At the convent on February 1 the Bishop entertained the community with an account of his trip, dwelling particularly on his stay in Cincinnati. Mother Duchesne was happy to be able to tell him in turn of a letter recently received from Mother Barat approving the plans sent from St. Louis and urging her to begin building as soon as she received the money that was being sent to her from Paris. She had not the satisfaction, however, of a confidential talk with him, so she wrote on February 4:

> It was not the moment, at your first visit, to renew our demands on your kindness to us. It seemed selfish when I realized how overburdened you are with pressing affairs. But your silence worried me. I know well that your time is precious and that it must be difficult for you to give us part of it each week. I am greatly torn between the dread that you may decide against coming and the fear of being importunate. I can only abandon myself to your paternal goodness, which calls for our complete submission.
> I have a very great repugnance to undertaking the new building, for I dread getting into debt. Our sick religious, however, are so uncomfortably housed and our classrooms are so inconveniently situated, we would like to get the work under way as soon as possible, trusting all to God, who sees our good intention. I did not want to take up the matter with Mr. O'Neil [40] while you were away, Monseigneur, as I needed your explicit permission. I have been assured that the necessary funds will be loaned to us in the course of this year. But we have not got the money on hand, and

if any unforeseen event should prevent us from receiving it, we might be in a very embarrassing position. I beg you to decide this matter for us. If we delay too long, materials will be more expensive and nothing will be ready before the winter sets in. . . .

The boarding school had been reorganized after the cholera had completely disappeared from the town, but the enrollment was small. Some fragments of a letter to a religious in France penned in February, 1833, give a few realistic details about life at the City House in those days, but their importance lies in their tone rather than in their contents. Philippine was weary, even discouraged, but not without hope when she wrote:

Just fancy how cordially we would welcome you here, but accustomed as you are to large convents, you might find it difficult to accept our penitential life, for it calls for great self-renunciation. One has little room in which to move about; there are very few to chant the Office; one must take on many employments and expect them to be upset frequently. A class of five or six children, and frequently less, offers little interest, and success seldom corresponds to the effort one expends in teaching. And after spending oneself on them, one sees little gratitude or piety in them. They go away and there is little to show for all one's solicitude about them. They must be coaxed pleasantly to do the will of God, and long afterwards perhaps a soul may be saved eternally. . . .

Mother Duchesne was still disturbed about Father Borgna's presence at the convent. Matters had not improved when she wrote to the Bishop on March 8:

My joy was very great when I learned that you had not gone away. It would have caused me real pain if you had gone away without my having had an opportunity to tell you my great distress on learning that you had confided us entirely to Father Borgna's care. I realize what a burden it is for you to hear confessions outside your own church, especially when you have so many important episcopal duties. But please remember that my anxiety is based principally on that unfortunate occurrence which you know about and which has roused in me fears which only your kindness can calm, at least in the near future. I should prefer death to a life of anxiety, alarms, suspicions—even though they be involuntary—and to misunderstandings because of differences of tastes and opinions. Have the charity, Monseigneur, to change your decision, if it is such as I have been given to understand. Make the change later on, when some circumstance arises that forces you to do so.

Bishop Rosati yielded to her entreaties and continued to come to the convent for confessions as regularly as his other duties would allow. Only when stricken with illness in the following July did he give up this service which Mother Duchesne appreciated so highly.

There was cholera in St. Louis during May, but by the end of the month it was thought that the mild epidemic had spent itself. Several serious cases appeared in June, but the convent was again spared this trial. Then came the crushing news that at St. Michael's the plague had carried off five religious in four days, among them Mothers Xavier Van Damme and Therese Detchemendy. Mother Duchesne recorded this news in her *Journal* without comment, but added later:

> A letter from Mother Maria L'Eveque gives details of the ravages of the cholera at St. Michael's. After five of our religious had died, five others were dangerously ill, but they recovered. Three of the pupils died after going home. Mother L'Eveque praised in highest terms the courage and devotedness of Mother Audé in these terrible circumstances. . . . The epidemic has raged with terrific virulence in the river and bayou towns of Louisiana. The Ursulines have been attacked by it, and we have learned of the death of holy Father Richard, the constant friend and protector of our convents and our first chaplain at St. Charles.

The feast of the Sacred Heart was celebrated solemnly, with Father Le Clerc preaching "a very touching sermon" on devotion to the Sacred Heart. Within a month he was dead, Bishop Rosati lay dangerously ill, as did Mother Hamilton also, and Mother Octavie Berthold received the Last Sacraments. But on June 23, when Mother Duchesne learned of an opportunity to send mail to France by a dependable traveler, she could write far into the night, sending to Josephine a long, interesting letter in which her personal anxieties find expression only in the closing paragraphs:

> You simply overwhelm me, dearest Cousin, with your friendship and your gifts. I received your interesting letter along with the gift you announced in it. Nothing could have been more acceptable. We have undertaken the construction of an addition to our building, which was so small the school could not grow. We had no infirmary, no assembly room, no private rooms, and this was very hard on the sick—and these make up most of the community.

As for myself, I keep my strength and any place is good enough for me. I spend my most restful nights in the most crowded corners, and for several years I have not minded carrying my mattress from one room to another according to circumstances. I would roll it up in the morning and put it somewhere else the following night. I have understood by experience St. Augustine's saying: "It is better not to need much than to have much." So that good thousand francs—for which I thank you a thousand times—will be better employed for the general needs of the convent than for my own personal needs, and that will give me the greatest amount of satisfaction.

I hope you do not mind if I decline your invitation to return to Sainte Marie and rest. I prefer to die at work and, as they say, "in the fight." If the pagan Greeks praised that woman who reproached her son for having survived a defeat, you will not blame me if I cling to my desire to make God known to those who do not know Him. It has always been my ambition to die among the Indians, and in my youthful enthusiasm I thought this an easy thing to attain. But at close range one sees that one cannot hope for that, and where there seemed to be reality, one finds only a beautiful dream. The Indian missionary must have the sanctity that works miracles and the gift of tongues to be understood and to make an impression on a people given over entirely to things of the senses. There were such saints once upon a time; that is why some tribes in Canada and that vicinity have well-organized Indian missions, where the Divine Office is chanted by the Indians themselves, who assemble at the church every day. But it is only at the price of great suffering and unmeasured work that this change was brought about, and I am not holy enough to gather about me a school for Indian girls. We find closer at hand a kind of white savage, who lives without faith or in deadly indifference to religion. Of course, one can always win a few children, but how difficult it is to raise them to the level of generous virtue.

I am most grateful for all the details you give me of things so dear to my heart. You ask me many questions, and I fear to write more repetitions of what you already know, for the Catholic gazettes published in many cities are sent to France. They are cheap and abound in information. We have one published in St. Louis under the title of *The Shepherd of the Valley*. According to the statistics given, there are now 10 bishoprics and one archbishopric in the United States, 3 Jesuit colleges—one of them under the very eyes of Congress, which has just appropriated 125,000 francs for an observatory. This institution has already installed the best possible equipment and has, as far as I can recall, 180 pupils. The college in St. Louis has 100 and that in Kentucky about the same number. There are several other Catholic colleges, and numbers of Protestants prefer them to institutions conducted by members of their own faith, so these colleges enroll a large number of non-Catholic students. The one in Baltimore under Sulpician management is on the highest footing. There are now 3 convents of the Visitation, 5 of the Sacred Heart, 1 Dominican, 1 Carmelite, 2 Ursuline, more than 20 institutions conducted by the Sisters of Charity, and as many more under the Sisters of the Cross. Among the candidates for the office of chaplain of Congress there was one Catholic priest. They voted several times, and every time he got first place, so he took up his duties in spite of the opposition of several ministers, who in condemning Congress merely hurt themselves.

During the last cholera epidemic New Orleans was forced to recognize the fact that religion alone gives the courage to risk death in order to assist the unfortunate victims. A committee, visiting one hospital when the contagion was dying out, found there sick people completely abandoned for days, dying victims lying with those already dead, animals rooting among the bodies that no one had buried. The town council appealed to the Sisters of Charity to take charge of that hospital. These Sisters are spread widely in the East and here. A few days ago 12 passed through here, going down the Mississippi. They already had an orphanage in New Orleans, founded to care for 100 children. Cholera has reappeared in that city with fresh fury, and this fact has hindered the progress of our house at St. Michael's, which is our largest academy. This year the enrollment has diminished, and so that convent could not aid us with the expense of building, as Mother Barat had expected. . . .

I have never been so completely without a moment's peace. My heart is never free from suffering—and this is what attaches me most of all to this house, for how could I leave these poor, suffering nuns? There are 13 in the community, and today 7 are under medical treatment. That has been the condition for a long time. I have been waiting a month for time to answer several letters. Forgive me if I stop abruptly, but very affectionately, in the Heart of Jesus. . . .

A shorter letter written that night was addressed to her sister, Madame de Mauduit:

We do not write often to each other, but we love each other always. The Hearts of Jesus, Mary, and dear Regis, our favorite saint, keep us forever united. I often think of you and your family, and I come today to ask you to remember me to them all, especially to our relatives at Romans, with whom you are certainly in touch. Do not fail to give an affectionate message to Monsieur de Mauduit. Does he still love hunting and his old sister-in-law? Does he ever think of imitating his pious mother? That is my most urgent petition for him, the object of my prayers, for he is growing old, as are also our brothers-in-law Jouve and Lebrument. . . .

Give my love to your daughters. I am growing old, but I am always very busy, as some of our Sisters are in poor health. So much activity is often harmful to the soul. Pray, and ask others to pray, for me. Give news of me to my sister. I cannot afford to write many letters. . . .

Since early May Philippine had been putting off her letter of thanks to the religious and children of Grand Coteau for the gifts sent for her feast. Every year since Mother Xavier Murphy became superior, a large shipment of clothing for the Indian girls at Florissant or the orphans in St. Louis had arrived for the feast of St. Philip. One of the children who donated most generously to the 1833 gift was Célina Chrétin, to whom Mother Duchesne wrote on June 30:

When Mother Xavier, your dear Mother, sent me the clothing for our dear orphans, she told me that you had given the greater part of the generous presents which these poor children received. They would be happy to know the names of all their benefactresses, but they are especially glad to know yours, Mademoiselle, since you are the principal one. Please let me be the interpreter of their gratitude, for this gives me the very agreeable opportunity of contact with a family that has been so good to the convent at Grand Coteau—an institution that is very dear to our Society because of the excellent work it is doing. If your Father and Mother will accept this expression of my gratitude, I shall be very happy.

I hear a great deal about the expansion of your academy, and I rejoice with all my heart at Mother Xavier's success. Her pupils give her much consolation by their good conduct both while at school and after they return home, and I understand that you are one of those of whom she is justly proud. They tell me the pupils of Grand Coteau have contributed greatly to the progress of religion and to the erection of a new church building. The conduct of the young gentlemen from Louisiana who are attending the Jesuit college here gives their professors reason to praise them highly, and I take great pleasure in hearing them spoken well of on every score. St. Louis College will soon have 100 pupils. That number is practically complete now, and the institution is to be enlarged by a new building.

We, too, are erecting an addition, but the work is held up just now by a scarcity of bricks. A very severe storm a few days ago destroyed many dwellings, lifted the roof from several other houses, but cost us only part of one chimney, though we were in the storm center. . . . The cholera spared us, also, though it is raging all around and has reappeared in St. Louis. We must thank Divine Providence for the protection given and pray that it may be extended to Grand Coteau, also. . . . Please remember me to all your dear companions whom I had the pleasure of meeting, and especially to the Louaillier girls.[41]

The storm that this time spared the convent proved something of an advantage to it, as the notes written by Mary Ann Rourke, who enrolled in the school shortly after this, show:

The Sacred Heart Convent in St. Louis had been in existence about six years when I was placed there as a boarder at the age of thirteen. Mother Duchesne was superior at the time. Some French girls, the Misses Paul, who were themselves boarders, advised my Mother to place me at the Sacred Heart. Imagine my delight upon reaching the convent to find all my companions of the day school I had previously attended there before me.

Perhaps I should tell you first about that day school, "Mrs. Windship's School." This lady had come from Boston and opened a select school, which was soon filled with rich girls. The city was built along the river and Mrs. W's school was on the "hill," as Third Street was then called. One night a violent storm swept over the city and great damage was done—trees lying in the street, roofs blown off—such was the sight that met our eyes next morning when walking to school. The roof of Mrs. Windship's school was hanging off, so I turned back and never heard anything more of the lady, and this circumstance led to my being placed at the convent. A family connection of mine, Eleanor Gray, had entered the Sacred Heart as a religious when I was seven or eight, but I had never seen her.[42]

My recollections of Mother Duchesne are not very numerous. As she spoke English very imperfectly, the Mistress General, Mother Regis Hamilton, was the business woman for the English-speaking girls. Mother Duchesne and Mother Regis were closely united. They used to go through the school together, and I can see them standing at the door of the study room in close conversation. We knew they were occupied with us, and the girls used to say they were "two heads in one bonnet." Mother Duchesne was strict for order; and when the girls heard her footsteps, they straightened up. She used to take us for Latin class and we recited the Office with the nuns. In those days all the hemming of the frills for the nuns' caps had to be done by the pupils, and it was Mother Duchesne who had us for sewing. She was advanced in years, quick in her movements, with a sharp, clear eye.

We all knew she was holy, but I might add, we thought all the nuns in the convent were holy. I recall one morning we were conducted to the chapel and led to the altar railing to receive Communion before Mass. Mother Duchesne was present and read aloud the prayers. We were taught to pray to St. Joseph to find out our vocation in life. With great simplicity the girls would ask him for a good husband, if they felt that was their vocation. . . .

The school was on a solid basis and had a fine reputation. We were under the "French regime." We were taught to make a courtesy as we entered the parlor. A piano was in the pupils' parlor, and the pupils took their music with them and played for their parents. We had a musical contest, some taking from professors, others from the nuns. Mother de Kersaint's style was soft, the professors' brilliant. . . . The nuns were all distinguished in manner. Besides Mother Duchesne, who was Superior, and Mother Regis, the Mistress General, I recall Mothers Thiéfry, de Kersaint, de Coppens. Mother [Margaret] Murphy was an Irish nun who was greatly loved by the girls.

The strongest point of the education was religious instruction. Those nuns spoke like priests. I can still remember an instruction in which the Mistress was trying to make us understand the pain of loss felt by the reprobate soul. She told us the story of the Babylonian Captivity—how the Jews hung up their harps by the rivers of Babylon and wept in thinking of their homes lost forever. The picture of homesickness was brought out in all its details as "worse than death," then applied to the homesickness of the soul for God when it is freed from the body. The instructions were given in French; and if the Mistress told an incident or story, this was translated by my friend, Amelie Paul, at the end of class. The sermons in the church were in French; our textbooks were French. Those who did not know the language on entering the school were able to follow the classes in six months.

We had prizes every quarter, at which the ribbons and medals were distributed. We went home on Washington's birthday, even though it was Lent. . . . I was never intimate with Mother Duchesne, and I did not see her after she left us. But I have always kept a precious remembrance of my school days at the Sacred Heart, and I attribute blessings bestowed upon me to the solid religious training received at the convent.[43]

The grave illness from which Monseigneur Rosati rallied in late July and slowly recovered put an end temporarily to the devotedness he had shown toward Mother Duchesne and her community as their confessor. Her reaction to this decision shows how deeply she felt it personally, for she wrote to the Bishop on August 16:

> I have already told you of my sorrow at the news that we are no longer under your personal direction. You have tried to reassure me, but I am not at peace. I realize only too well that a Bishop's time is precious and that frequently he is no longer master of it. Moreover, I have pondered how grievous it would be and how culpable we would feel if we sought our own welfare rather than the general good of this large diocese, especially in your weakened state of health. Your prospective absence, which is being announced for next month, weighs me down still more, as well as the fact that we must address ourselves now to a priest who is more suited to persons of the world than to those who should have a piety that is both interior and serene.
>
> I must tell you, however, that several members of the community are not of my opinion, and are happy enough with the new arrangement, but their reasons seem to me to carry no weight. I am ready to sacrifice my taste and my peace of soul in yielding to the general good, but I shall not be satisfied until I have placed before you what I think would be for the greatest benefit of this convent, and it is to appoint for us, or at least for those who feel the need, a confessor who has the same rules as our own. . . .

Soul-suffering such as this was for Philippine "the secret of the King," and never did she betray to her family the anguish she endured. Bright, interesting letters crossed the ocean whenever she knew of a traveler going to Europe. Two days after her heart-cry to Bishop Rosati, she was writing to Madame Jouve:

My dear One,

I received your letter from Lyons in April after your return from Grâne. I am delighted to know that my letter reached dear Amelie, but believe me, this is not the only one I have written. I recall quite distinctly writing to her several times recently. In one of my letters I spoke at length about her daughter, Madame Bergasse. It is not surprising that letters from such a distance get lost. I have not received the one you tell me she wrote, but I sent her another, hearing that she complained about my silence, and my letter must have crossed hers, for I have not received the one you tell me my dear Amelie wrote at the same time you did.

Perhaps this letter I am writing will go to Lyons with Father Odin, a priest and missionary of this diocese. He is going to make a tour of his homeland on business. He is president of a college in

our state and is very successful. The college of St. Louis has been
erected into a university by the legislature of Missouri; it is conducted by the Jesuits. As they have nearly one hundred resident
students, they will need some of their confreres to help them. I
should love for Henri to be chosen for this work. He would find
in the state of Missouri and in the Territory beyond, which is
much bigger than the state, plenty of scope for his zeal. Religion
is spreading, and not a year passes without the erection of several
churches. The Cathedral in St. Louis will not be finished until
next year. It will be beautiful, and so will the church at the
seminary, thirty leagues from here, but it was planned on too
grand a scale for the country and so cannot be completed for lack
of funds.

Father Paillasson, who also came from Lyons, has exercised his
ministry in the midst of great suffering and distress. He is now at
New Madrid, a village founded by the Spanish and at one time the
chief town in this section of the country. Father Condamine, a
former vicar-general in Lyons, has left Kaskaskia, the oldest town
in Illinois, and at one time a Jesuit mission where they built a
church.[44] A community of the Visitation has been formed there
by nuns who came from Georgetown, near Washington. They are
a bit discouraged in surroundings so different from what they
were accustomed to.[45]

I thank God for having disposed all things by His adorable
Providence so that you and your husband can spend your days in
peace and happiness, and also Monsieur Lebrument. God will also
be favorable, I trust, to Madame Bergasse, who draws blessings on
her family, as did our dear Adelaide. Adieu, dearest one; my love
to all your dear ones, and especially to your husband. The love of
my heart for you will never grow old. . . .

On Philippine's sixty-fourth birthday Mr. John Mullanphy
died at his St. Louis residence on North Main Street. On the following day the girls of the orphanage walked in the funeral
cortege, dressed in black and white. Early in September it became
evident that Mother Octavie Berthold's suffering life was drawing
to a close. More tenderly than ever Mother Duchesne nursed her,
and more constantly. There was distressing news from Louisiana,
where cholera was raging again. Bishop De Neckere had been for
some weeks at St. Michael's, recuperating from illness and over-
work. All who knew and loved him prayed that he would remain
in comparative safety, but he could not be persuaded to do so, and
on September 4 his career was cut short by the plague in New
Orleans.

The distribution of prizes was set for September 16, but the Sacred Heart had other designs for that day. Mother Duchesne noted in her *Journal:*

> Our dear Mother Octavie Berthold took a sudden turn for the worse and at ten o'clock in the morning gave back her beautiful soul to God. She was assisted by Father Borgna, the Vicar-General. Her agony lasted but a moment, and she had received Holy Communion early in the morning. Her body was laid out in our chapel, where there were people praying continually. The altar was draped in black and the Office for the Dead was recited that evening. Next morning Fathers Borgna, De Smet, and Doutreluingne offered low Masses for her. At eight o'clock the High Mass was sung by Father Verhaegen with deacon and subdeacon. . . .

At the far southwestern corner of the convent property they buried Octavie Berthold in the little cemetery staked off the previous May. The first grave had been opened for Father Le Clerc, a cholera victim after just six weeks in St. Louis. Another victim, a Sister of Charity, had been laid to rest on September 9. Mother Octavie's burial was the last before the city began to cut streets through the Mullanphy grant and the cemetery was condemned.

Writing to inform the Superior General of this death, Philippine expressed her personal sorrow with great restraint, while paying a heartfelt tribute to her close friend and co-worker:

> Keenest grief fills my soul, dear Reverend Mother, as I come to add to the sorrow that already fills your maternal heart over the loss of five of our Sisters whom cholera carried off at St. Michael's. The terrible scourge spared us, but death, which had so far respected our convents in Missouri, has come in another form. Mother Octavie Berthold has at last succumbed to her long illness. She died on September 16. In her I lost the one on whom I relied most securely and her Sisters lost their most perfect model.
> Born in Geneva of Calvinist parents, Octavie went to Grenoble to devote her talents to education. At the age of twenty-four she had the happiness of receiving the light of faith and of becoming a Catholic. She was so faithful to the grace given to her that two years later she merited the further gift of a vocation and entered the Society, taking the holy habit at Grenoble and making her first vows in Paris on February 5, 1817. She made her final vows there in 1818 when about to leave for America. Her amiability, her sweetness of character made her loved by all who knew her outside the convent and by all within the community and school, and she exercised an influence which virtue alone can give. Never

did we see her falter, though for long years she suffered from a
painful malady, parts of her body being covered with open
wounds. Her zeal gave her strength far beyond what was natural
to her state of health, and in spite of the many employments she
accumulated because of the small number in the community,
never did she make a complaint. I found her always obedient and
docile, never omitting a spiritual exercise, and finding in her in-
genious charity the means of obliging her sisters. So all deeply regret her loss; all weep for her; and all feel a greater urge to imitate
her virtues. She died almost without agony and in full consciousness. She had received Holy Viaticum and Extreme Unction some
weeks before, and had received Communion many times after
that. So weak was her condition that Holy Communion was
brought to her at midnight on the eve of her death. In the morning the grace of absolution was renewed and the last indulgence,
and while we were reciting the prayers for the dying beside her,
she gave up her beautiful soul to our Lord in the sweetest peace
and entire confidence. She was 46 years and 18 days old. We
prayed beside her continually, either in her room or in the chapel
until the funeral, which took place the day after her death. The
Pastor and the Vicar-General asked the Jesuit Rector to preside at
the funeral and give the sermon which is customary here in the
case of anyone who is well known. Four times Mass was offered
while she lay in the chapel, the last one sung solemnly with deacon
and subdeacon. We followed this dear Mother to her last resting
place in our little cloister cemetery. The orphans led the procession in their blue dresses and white veils, the boarding school
followed in black, then the day pupils, our religious, and the
clergy. The Sisters of Charity helped carry the coffin, as our older
nuns were not strong enough to do this alone. I shall not enlarge,
dear Reverend Mother, on what this loss means to me—you
understand only too well; and while I am perfectly sure of the
happiness now enjoyed by that faithful soul, I beg you, however,
to ask for her the suffrages of the Society.[46]

It called for faith and courage and high supernatural resolve to
carry out the plans that had been made for the closing exercises,
but Mother Duchesne faced the duty, erect and self-controlled, and
gave a cordial greeting to Fathers Verhaegen and Lutz, and to the
parents of the children, who had been invited to the little gathering.
"They were well pleased with the new building," she recorded.
"The children's dining room is on the first floor, which is slightly
lower than the ground level; the study hall is above this, and the
dormitories are on the second and third floors." Mr. Taylor, who
again attended the performance, described it as the "Literary

Exhibition held annually at the Female Academy of the Ladies of the Sacred Heart," and reported that "one room in the spacious new brick building recently erected" was "elegantly decorated with specimens of embroidery, needlework, and several other branches of a female education." He was impressed by the "melody of voices," the "soft sounds of the piano," recitations of prose and poetry in both French and English, and the awarding of prize books and crowns for success in studies and deportment. In conclusion he remarked: "This establishment, we are happy to state, is daily growing in public confidence and is undoubtedly entitled to the most extensive patronage." [47]

Two days after the departure of the pupils Mother Duchesne sent half of her community to Florissant to rest and recuperate. This left her with only four or five companions and the orphans to do the heavy work of housecleaning and small repairs throughout the building. For two years she had relied on the help of the Negro man, Joseph, whom Antoine Dubreuil had given to the convent. Joseph had died quite suddenly in the sanctuary during Benediction in August, 1831, and Mother Duchesne had not been able to replace him, though she was still trying to do so. The news that Fathers De Smet and Odin were leaving soon for Europe turned her to letter writing. As there was no time for this by day, she used the night hours.[48] To Josephine she expressed her gratitude for a gift recently received.

> Dearest Cousin [she wrote], I received on the same day letters from you and Madame de Mauduit. That gave me a real feast and a cause for more gratitude, for here was another thousand francs from you before I thought my thanks for the last thousand could have reached you. Yes, you certainly will provide a room for me, and the most desirable one I could have, for while giving me a very convenient place as far as the works of the house are concerned, it will keep me always close to the Blessed Sacrament in health or in sickness, and that is a priceless advantage.
>
> I have done my best to find something that might give you pleasure, and I have only a pair of moccasins, but they will show you the skill of the Indian women. I am sending the parcel to Mother Ducis by two missionaries, one of whom—Father Odin—will visit both Lyons and Grenoble.[49]

The school year began in October with a fairly good enrollment, though the nuns must have been disappointed when there were a few empty beds in the dormitory. Mother Duchesne made no allusion to this, however, in a letter to Mother Desmarquest written on October 19. She seems preoccupied with the sorrows and losses of the past year, but in the last paragraph one feels that she is pleased with the new building, though it is not yet paid for.

The consolation that came to us from the news of our Mother General's cure and the letters from Rome has been counterbalanced by the sad losses sustained by the Church in the United States this year—two excellent Bishops and seventeen priests. The Bishop of Cincinnati [Edward Dominic Fenwick, O.P.] was a man of wonderful apostolic simplicity, a son of St. Dominic, who like his founder accomplished wonders through the Rosary. The prelate named to replace him is Monseigneur Purcell, former president of the college at Emmitsburg, near Baltimore. He crossed the ocean on the vessel Mother Dutour was traveling on.[50]

The Bishop of New Orleans died of yellow fever, a man of great virtue and learning, whose modesty often sought to hide his remarkable talent for preaching. All these gifts had made him loved and respected by his flock and by all the clergy, even the eldest among them, in spite of his youth. He was a very firm friend of our Society, and his death is felt keenly by Mother Eugenie, who has such need just now of comfort and support. The majority of the priests who have died this year were victims of their zeal for souls or victims of cholera.

Our own Bishop was so ill, they feared he would die. He is growing stout and his visits to us are less frequent than formerly. But he offered the Holy Sacrifice of the Mass for us on the feast of St. Joseph, patron of this convent, and also on the feast of the Sacred Heart, when he gave Confirmation here.

The distribution of prizes took place only on the 18th of September. For this occasion we used the studyhall of the new building, which is fifty feet long by thirty feet wide. On the floor that is partly underground the new building has a large refectory and a room in which we shall put a coal stove that will give heat from under the house. Above this is a large studyhall, along the full length of which runs a pretty covered gallery where one can enjoy fresh air in bad weather. This leads into a vestibule giving entrance to the chapel. Above all this is the dormitory and a small washroom. The attic is well plastered and will provide another dormitory. It adjoins the old one, which is now used as the children's linen room. . . .

During the autumn of 1833 Mother Duchesne's thoughts and prayers were turned constantly toward Paris, where she knew the fifth General Council of the Society was being held. That assembly would be concerned in a special manner with the welfare of the American houses. While the council was in session, she learned of the death of two more religious at St. Michael's. Along with other news items she noted in her *Journal* the providential help which came from several sources, enabling her to pay off almost the entire debt on the new building:

> Bishop Blanc writes that he has on hand the $200 left us by Father Benedict Richard. We also received $450 from Grand Coteau as a gift for the new building and $200 from Madame de Rollin. We have agreed to receive the two Grolet girls, orphans from Grand Coteau, for six years for $1500 in three payments, the first in advance. We marvel at the ways of Divine Providence. With this money we are able to pay almost all we owe on the new building, which cost $4000.

While rejoicing in this good fortune, Mother Duchesne also shared the happiness of Mother Mathevon, who was busy drawing up plans for a brick convent at St. Charles to replace the old Duquette house that was falling in ruins. Father Van Quickenborne, who was pastor there, was taking up a subscription to finance the project and had already collected $1500 when Mother Duchesne went to St. Charles for a short visit in November. The plans laid before her were almost identical with those of the Florissant convent, but there was to be a well-finished basement a half-story underground. The convent would stand on the first bluff, facing the river and closer to the new church than the Duquette house was. In the near future, it was hoped, it could be extended to the north so as to meet the wall of the sanctuary of the church and this addition would give the religious a cloister chapel like the one at Florissant. Mother Mathevon was proving a competent and much loved superior, and Father Van Quickenborne was mellowing considerably.

Joy and sorrow came together on January 12 when "the Bishop gave the veil to Miss Teresa Wise, preached two beautiful sermons, and spent the whole day at the convent." He also gave Mother Duchesne her heart's desire by promising to replace Father Jeanjean as confessor while the latter went south on business. Philippine felt once more the strength and sincerity of his friendship when that very day she received news of the death of another religious at St. Michael's. He sympathized with her, too, in her sorrow over the closing of the old monastery of Sainte-Marie-d'en-Haut. This

was a blow she had endeavored to avert by penance and prayer. Six
months earlier St. Madeleine Sophie had written to her: "A piece
of news that will pain you, dear Philippine, is the perspective
before us of having soon to evacuate your beloved convent of
Sainte Marie." [51] And in a letter of October 10 she announced the
fait accompli: "What a heartbreak it is to be forced to give up your
cradle, that house so dear to you. We were obliged to do so. The
city took it from us. Pray much for us." This letter had reached
St. Louis during Christmastide, and Philippine had answered on
December 28, 1833: "It must have been hard for you to decide to
abandon that house. It is still the place to which I am most deeply
attached and the greatest sacrifice I could offer at the crib of the
Divine Infant. If God strikes the green wood thus, what will He do
to the dry, worm-eaten wood we build with here?"

Father Jeanjean's trip to Louisiana gave Mother Duchesne an
opportunity to send mail free of charge as far as New Orleans, so
early in January she wrote a newsletter to Mother de Gramont,
knowing it would be circularized in many of the French convents:

> I am taking advantage of an opportunity to send by a traveler as
> far as the seacoast the accounts of the house of St. Ferdinand for
> the last six months, but I am much more eager to offer our affec-
> tionate good wishes to our Mothers and Sisters in Europe, whose
> virtue we should like to imitate, but we are still far from that per-
> fection. We have learned with real joy that France is now fairly
> peaceful and that in the shelter of this peace many fervent souls
> are exerting their zealous efforts in the cause of religion. That is
> what the Bishop of Charleston told his flock when he returned
> from Europe.[52]
>
> The United States has lost two holy bishops this year and more
> than a dozen excellent priests, the greater number through illness.
> Some new workers have come, but the number is too small, and in
> the Lord's vineyard many sections are left uncultivated. Happily in
> this free country nearly all the Catholic institutions prosper, and
> in time they will provide priests for the country. The Jesuit Col-
> lege in St. Louis has been recognized by the State of Missouri as a
> university and has nearly 100 boarding students; there are 150 at
> the Barrens in this same diocese. We also have in the diocese 60
> religious women: 22 of our Society, 12 Sisters of Charity, 10
> Visitandines, and the rest are Sisters of the Cross.
>
> Out of these 60, the cholera carried off only one—a Sister of
> Charity; but the same was not true of Mother Eugenie's commu-
> nity at St. Michael's. We have just learned of the twelfth death
> there this year, the greater number from cholera and its after-

effects and from consumption.[53] Mother Octavie is the only one of our nuns who has died in Missouri since 1818, and no children have died as pupils. In taking care of us with such goodness, God has counterbalanced with the crosses of penury, small success, etc. It looks as if He is going to change these now, for we are improving exteriorly. At St. Charles, our cradle in America, they will move this year from the rotten old wooden house to a new brick building. St. Ferdinand has 16 boarding pupils, and we have from 28 to 30, but there are always some at home because of illness.

St. Michael's, though struck so severely, still has 28 religious, 4 excellent postulants, more than 100 boarding pupils, and a good number of orphans, for whose support the state of Louisiana has just contributed 10,000 francs. And the parents of the pupils will soon have collected 15,000 francs to help with the erection of a larger brick convent and school building. That house has suffered an irreparable loss in the death of Bishop De Neckere. He had spent several months there during the past year, gave the retreats, and even went so far as to give lessons in advanced sciences to the young religious teaching there.

As for ourselves, we experience the most paternal kindness from our Bishop. He has again become confessor of the community. Illness and his visitations had interrupted this work. Yesterday he gave the habit to Miss Teresa Wise, a former pupil at St. Ferdinand, who came here for the ceremony. He preached in the morning at the ceremony, remained for dinner in the parlor in order to chant Vespers with us, gave a second sermon and Benediction. He always officiates here on the feast of the Sacred Heart and that of St. Joseph, his patron and ours.

Please let me express here our loving and heartfelt gratitude to those of our religious who have the kindness to copy for us the letters of our Mother General and the account of her visit to Rome. When we receive such delightful sheets, we joyously pretend that we are—and we really seem to be—in the midst of those who give us such pleasure by so many interesting details. . . .

I am enclosing in this letter the plan of our grounds and the new house. Our neighbors have proposed an exchange of our land for property further from the city. Our property is going to be divided into blocks, with corners on the streets that are to be opened according to the plan of the city. This will cut up our land in all directions and will be extremely disagreeable. We are told that if we try to make the exchange, we shall be hindered by the executors and heirs of Mr. Mullanphy. I greatly desire to have our Mother General's advice in this matter, and as she is perhaps absent from Paris, I humbly beg Mother de Gramont to transmit her message to me. She will learn with pleasure that Mother de

Coppens' health is quite restored. She is braving the cold, which
has been severe for some days; she teaches the highest class, has
the children's linen room, teaches sewing, and helps in the pantry
and the parlor. She is a very useful person and is devoting herself
to all this work courageously. Mother de Kersaint coughs a great
deal and is hardly able to sing. . . .

Her letter to Josephine, bearing the same date, is much more
personal. At the time she did not know that Josephine and all the
family were in grief again, this time for her beloved Augustin
Perier. He had stood close by Casimir's side with advice and the
support of his strong character, and Louis Philippe, recovering
from the shock of their common loss, had raised Augustin to the
peerage. The reception tendered him in the Chamber of Peers had
been an ovation.[54] He had enjoyed that honor just one year when
he died suddenly at his estate in Fremigny, near Paris. Baron de
Gérando, a friend since childhood, described the Augustin whom
Philippine so loved as "lively, sensitive, often impetuous, yet of
great moderation and wisdom in judgment; he was a man of Truth
who lived a noble and useful career, a man of hard work, high
standards, and kindly generosity." [55] This was the brother Josephine mourned, while Philippine wrote, all unaware of her grief:

DEAREST COUSIN,

I have received all your generous gifts—the two thousand francs
which you had the goodness to send me in two payments came in
quick succession. It is a joy to owe you so great a debt of gratitude, though you know my friendship for you has no personal
selfishness in it. I love you tenderly and value you highly just because of what you are in yourself.

I wonder why the greatest favor you and your dear husband
and your splendid brothers all took so much trouble about for us
now must come to naught. They write me that there is no way to
save Sainte Marie to the Society, that the convent must be closed,
and that the daughters of Sion can only weep because the holy
songs of praise are silenced. I never thought I might see that beloved place again, but it was a joy for me to think of it as a home
of God-fearing virtue, zeal, and innocence. It is very bitter for me
to think that perhaps I am responsible for the closing of that
house, because I did not merit the graces needed for its support. I
have no desire for new endeavors. It seems to me that what we
build here is but a house of cards compared with the massive pile
of that noble monastery, its vast proportions, its charming situation, its silent church remote from all distractions.

But while I say that there is nothing left for me to do but die, I feel my earthbound soul holding tenaciously to the body, and I often dream of possessing here in St. Louis some parts of the altars from our dismantled chapel of Sainte Marie. And that is not entirely impossible. Vessels come continually to American ports laden with enormous cargoes of Italian marble. In the national capital in Washington, the President's house is built almost entirely of this. The only difficulty is to get the marble to Marseille, for the sea trip is nothing—they even put huge blocks of marble in the hold of vessels just to steady them on the high seas. From Marseille to New Orleans and from there up the Mississippi to St. Louis is an easy matter. But the difficulty is not confined to transportation only—it might be hard to get these altars; I fear they may be claimed or sold very quickly.

Our new building to which you so generously contributed is now complete, except for the plastering. It presents such an attractive appearance, the number of boarding pupils has already doubled. I should not have believed this possible.

You will be glad to know that all the Catholic institutions in the United States are prospering at present. Congress has as its *chaplain*—that is to say, its *preacher*—a Catholic priest. The President [Andrew Jackson] is quite favorable to Catholic priests, and many Protestants prefer to entrust their children to celibate priests rather than to professors whose duties are divided between interest in studies and care of a family. New Orleans has at last decided to entrust its hospital to the Sisters of Charity. They have won the admiration of people of all creeds in St. Louis by their work in our hospital.

Remember me, I beg you, to Madame Teisseire, whom I never forget—she has been so kind to me—and to the other members of our family whom you see. You can rely on my constant remembrance of you, also of Father Rambaud. Beg him to pray for me and to give me a continued share in his works of charity. I have great confidence in his prayers.

In almost everything she wrote Philippine revealed herself. At times, however, a character trait is emphasized in an unexpected way. She was accused of being too severe a disciplinarian, too rigid and unyielding toward the parents who consulted her, yet she writes to Bishop Rosati on January 15, 1834:

I refrained from speaking to you this morning about our doctor, as he said he was going to talk to you himself about his only daughter. Since the death of their son, his wife cannot bring herself to part with the child. She came herself to ask if she might place her with us as a day pupil, and on Mother Regis' refusal she was greatly disappointed. I spoke to her afterwards and told her we would think it over and give the doctor an answer. Mother de Kersaint is quite opposed to receiving this little girl as a day pupil, 1. because others will want the same privilege or complain of preferences being made; 2. because it is against our regulations.

I answered her that I would not be afraid to say that we are making this one exception for our doctor who has taken care of us so generously, and that it would be difficult ever to repay him for his many visits. I should not have to give the same consideration to our other children whose fathers are doctors. There are exceptions to every rule and I shall do what you advise. I beg you to make the decision. I have avoided seeing the doctor so I would not feel obliged to give him the answer his wife desires.

In a matter of this kind Mother Duchesne might have made the decision without consulting members of the community. But she did not act independently. The burden of her responsibility seemed to grow heavier every day, and early in the New Year this was borne in on her in a way that made her heart cry out to Mother Barat:

I am entirely behind the times. Here one must now talk of advanced sciences, astronomy, chemistry, philosophy. But I am drawn to know nothing but Jesus as the subject matter of the one science necessary, and to seek Him in solitude. My patron for this year is St. Andrew and his cross. That cross, that good cross, I long for in one of two things: either the end of my life or the end of my position as superior.[56]

She was striving hard at this very time to restore union and charity in the community, which had been disrupted by Father Borgna's unwise direction and Mother de Coppens' critical spirit. This condition of affairs distressed her, for it seemed beyond her power to check and eradicate it. The matter was still preying on her mind and gnawing at her heart when she wrote to Mother Barat on March 2:

I have been deprived of news from you for a long time, and even from all in France. If it were possible to forget you, you would bring yourself to our minds by the very force of your great kindness. Mr. King, the New York banker, wrote me that he had been notified to send us 3000 francs, which in the exchange amounted to 545½ dollars or *gourdes*.[57] Since then we have received this money through merchants here who needed money on hand in

New York. I am sure that Mother Ducis has written to me about this money, but I have received no letter either from her or from any of our French convents. I do not even know what has happened to our dear house in Grenoble, which we all regret so keenly.

Our new building is being used in part, and at Easter, when the plastering is finished, we shall have the use of all of it. It has already brought us double the number of boarding pupils we had had—there are now thirty-four—and if more come, as seems certain to happen, we shall be no better off for the community than we were before. We still have no infirmary, no community room. . . .

I spend very little time in the boarding school now, for I really feel that I am not liked. I am not offended by this, for I realize that my age [she was in her sixty-fifth year] does not appeal to young people, and it is quite apparent. But I have plenty to occupy my time from four o'clock in the morning till eleven o'clock at night: treasury, pantry, sacristy, nuns' linen room, a class with the children of the free school, two hours a day with the orphans, surveillance of the workmen, visits, letters, etc.[58] You may think I want to do everything myself, but I may also have to take charge of the children's linen room, for the three choir religious who speak English have all they can do—not a quarter of an hour free—and so they cannot take this employment. The same holds for Mother de Kersaint, because of the music. Mother de Coppens, who was in charge, did the work so poorly, I am told, there were continual complaints. . . . Our infirmarian has been threatened with consumption, and she would be an irreparable loss.[59] Mother Hamilton is very busy, but she continues to act as Mistress of Health for the children. . . . I beg you earnestly to give us a surveillante for her and also three other religious of tried virtue. . . .

I have no doubt that you have received written complaints against me, for the spiritual director about whom I wrote to you, urged some of the nuns to do this, I am told, and he himself sent off the two letters. Things will turn out as God wills. I hold to nothing and I know they can make complaints about me that are very true. I long to see an end to my embarrassing situation. If I can believe Anne [de Coppens], the four younger choir nuns have formed a clique against me, but these four (more truthful than she) accuse her of falsehood in the matter, and Mother de Kersaint in particular says she would not dare repeat what she heard her say, and declares she never agreed with her when, on their arrival here, she said she could not get accustomed to life in America. One would need the power to read hearts in order to get at the truth in all this and form a fair judgment. I cannot write you everything about this religious [Mother de Coppens], but she does disturb the union in our community.

Please tell me whether we have permission to build a larger chapel, or whether you think it imprudent to do so, and whether we may hope for some more religious from France. We cannot expect help from the South. St. Michael's has more than a hundred children and Opelousas has eighty, a good number of these being Protestants and Americans. Our St. Louis children are a hundred leagues from any thought of religious life. The religious best suited to teach here are Mothers Hamilton, de Kersaint, and Boilvin. The last named can teach both music and English as well as French. She is a Creole. . . .

That letter had scarcely left the country when Mother Duchesne wrote in her *Journal:* "We have learned the results of the General Council that closed in November, 1833. The Assistants General are Reverend Mothers Desmarquest, de Charbonnel, de Gramont, and Eugenie Audé for America. She has received instructions from our Mother General to make a visitation of the American houses and then return to France to give her report." So preparations for the visitation began. Mother Duchesne was glad the new building would be plastered, finished, and in use by April, glad too that there were thirty-four pupils enrolled in the academy and twenty-two in the orphanage, but she realized that the convent in St. Louis would make a poor showing in comparison with those of Louisiana and that discontented members in the community might have a sympathetic listener in the Mother Visitatrix. But all was in God's hands, in God's will. She could repeat unwaveringly, *"Portavi et portabo,"* as she had in 1829.

Reverend Mother Audé arrived on April 13, having put Mother Bazire in charge at St. Michael's, with Mother Hardey as assistant and mistress general and Mother Louisa L'Eveque as mistress of novices. After three days with Mother Duchesne's community she visited first St. Ferdinand, then St. Charles. On her way the Reverend Mother Visitatrix drove by the handsome Jesuit college and the cathedral Bishop Rosati was building. The Bishop came to pay his respects to the new Assistant General. Mothers Mathevon and Thiéfry came to St. Louis to confer with her once more, then Reverend Mother Audé left for France. "She had edified us all and been lavish with gifts," Mother Duchesne recorded after her departure. She had, of course, taken advantage of this opportunity to write to the Mother General—a plain, matter-of-fact letter, with here and there a dash of the real Philippine:

I should have answered your last letter sooner, had I not been daily expecting Mother Eugenie, who can carry our letters to you without postage and in great security. She is here now and awaiting the first steamboat that will take her [up the Ohio] most directly toward her goal. She has visited all the houses and is in a position to give you an account of them better than anyone else could. She will tell you the steps she has taken with regard to the spiritual direction of this house and the success obtained in the matter. In this respect no houses are better situated than Florissant and St. Charles. These parishes are directed by the Jesuits and always will be, according to the contract with the Bishop. This is a strong motive for supporting these convents. They in no way hinder the progress of the house in St. Louis; and if they were closed one evening, they would be reopened next morning by the Sisters of Charity, who are highly esteemed by the clergy and the people, as they conduct hospitals, boarding schools, and orphanages for boys and girls—all equally well. More than that, they act as nurses for the colleges, even for the Jesuits and their pupils. All this makes them justly popular and provides them with means for success. If we do not maintain our schools well, they will put us in the shade.

I was struck by this sentence in your last letter: "When Mother Eugenie returns to America, she will bring precise orders; and I hope they will not meet with opposition." From whom do you expect opposition? Or what gave you cause to fear it? Mother Ann [de Coppens], who so often complained of being stationed here, is expressing no desire to return to France, but she may ask to do so later on, though Mother Eugenie's departure is offering her the best opportunity possible.

I have no least detail about the closing of the house at Grenoble. When you told me about it, you were kind enough to promise me 4,000 francs to help pay for our building, with the understanding that I would in turn help Mother Lucille that much with the building at St. Charles, and I told her this.

After repeating much that she had written in March about dollars and francs and the payment of debts, she concluded: "If I must go on handling the money, I must avow to you that it is very hard to be obliged to refuse to help the many good works that are needed here, and it is quite difficult to be restricted to giving only 50 francs [$10]. That is next to nothing out here."

When Mother Audé sailed from America, Mother Duchesne was ignorant of some of the facts about her departure. The Mother Visitatrix seemed the very embodiment of success that stemmed from natural ability, religious zeal, and supernatural courage. She had done fine work in Louisiana, endured frightful trials in the past two years, suffered physical collapse and long illness, and most of the time she had kept her troubles so entirely to herself that Mother Barat had had to demand news before she received it. Then Eugenie's courage faltered; emotion had overwhelmed her; and on December 21, 1833, she had poured out a dramatic account of the past seven terrible months. As she brought it to a close she wrote:

> My heart is broken; each religious who died took from me a part of my life. . . . A little while close to you would strengthen me, revive my poor soul, prepare me for further suffering. Oh, Mother, my dear Mother, will you not grant my request? But—forgive me; such a request is contrary to complete abandonment. Do what you will with your Eugenie.[60]

This appeal to the Mother General—not the first Eugenie had made for a return to France [61]—had crossed a letter written by Mother Barat on November 2, 1833:

> I hasten, dear daughter, to tell you that our General Council closed yesterday. The elections had taken place the day before that. . . . You have been chosen Assistant General for America. Our Mothers in the Council made their decision in accord with the plurality of votes of the professed religious in that part of the world. . . . We enjoin on you the duty of accepting this burden, which Jesus will help you to carry. As soon as you receive this letter, begin the visitation of the other four houses, if your health permits, then sail for France to give an account of your mission.[62]

So Mother Audé had assumed the office of Assistant General for America, but she would never see America again, not even when Mother Barat, whom she loved so dearly, expressed the need she had of her services. The American houses were now less unified than before, though in Missouri there was security in the presence of Mother Duchesne. She had lost all delegated powers when Reverend Mother Audé superseded her, but the power of her sanctity remained, as well as the influence she exerted on the religious who knew and loved her, and there were very few who did not recognize in her the true religious superior.

The "sickly season" was upon St. Louis early in June. A light form of cholera prevailed through July. Mothers Hamilton, de Kersaint, Boilvin, and Judith Shannon were so ill that the Bishop advised advancing the summer holidays. Reviews and prizes were postponed until the reopening of school, and most of the community went to Florissant to recuperate. Mother Duchesne and Sister Lamarre remained in St. Louis with the orphans. Reduced to penury, they were obliged to borrow money from the bank for living expenses.

Prayer and toil filled the long, hot days, and all was offered in a spirit of reparation. The terrible plague with which God had repeatedly scourged so many parts of the world, and particularly the Mississippi Valley, seemed to Philippine and to many holy priests with whom she talked a punishment for sin, for infidelity, for blindness born of worldliness, ambition, avarice. A lively sense of responsibility before God, a pressing sense of guilt that nothing seemed to relieve, kept her prostrate in spirit, pleading in prayer that there might be an end to this terrible condition, that souls might turn to God in sincere repentance. Saints are certainly more sensitive to the malice of sin than are the rest of people, and Philippine Duchesne was very close to God.

Realizing the presence of evil and being powerless to prevent it was terrible suffering for her. So she strove to make reparation for at least some fraction of it by her own penance and prayer and by strengthening the religious convictions of the children under her care—a mere handful of orphan girls. But fervent love could increase a hundredfold the value of their reparative efforts. So she tried to share with them the burning thirst of her incessant desire to bring souls back to Christ and to give Christ to souls. The dominant thought in her soul was always the thought of extending the reign of the Sacred Heart. In these August days of 1834 that thought obsessed her.

On the feast of the Assumption, adoration of the Blessed Sacrament was kept up all day, the orphans taking the places of the absent religious. The octave was a week of intense fervor.

> On the eve of the feast of the Holy Heart of Mary [Mother Duchesne recorded], nine of the orphans fasted on bread and water to obtain the cessation of our trials, if such be the will of God. These young penitents made a procession in honor of our Lady, walking barefoot and with ropes around their necks. A few days later our religious returned from Florissant quite recuperated, and several of the pupils came back.

The next entry in the *Journal*, under date of August 28, shows the breadth of her sympathies, for it relates the story of "the disaster that occurred in Boston when an infuriated Protestant mob set fire to the Ursuline convent. Everything was burned, nothing

saved, and the religious and their pupils escaped by a rear door."
The Shepherd of the Valley carried the details in its issues of September 5 and 12, but both the Bishop and Mr. Taylor reported the news dispatches to Mother Duchesne as soon as they received them. The horror of this incident, the hatred it displayed, the suffering it entailed, all seemed to impress her vividly, for she referred to it several times in letters to France.

The school year began with the postponed reviews and examinations, and the Bishop came to distribute the prizes on September 25. Mother Duchesne gave the event small space in her *Journal*, for a large packet of mail arrived from France next day bringing news and information about the convents in Paris, Avignon, and Parma, which seemed to her more important. A letter from her sister Euphrosine told of the death of her husband, Jean-Joseph Jouve, and Philippine wrote at once, "We have prayed for him and for you, my beloved Sister, who are so sad and so lonely."

Her letter to Mother Barat on October 5 contained a statement of the financial condition of her convent: the contractor had been paid; a Negro couple had been purchased for the service of the house; a promissory note for 3,000 francs had been signed in favor of Mother Lucille Mathevon, who was hard pressed for money to continue the work on the new convent at St. Charles; and another thousand francs was owed at the Bank of St. Louis. In the closing paragraphs she touched on difficulties:

> Mrs. Mullanphy has turned over to me the 750 francs she received for us in France, 500 coming from Madame de Rollin. She also brought us, among other things, the new plan of studies, the rule for the Children of Mary who have left school, the method of compiling accounts, and the biographies of our religious who have died. These touch me very deeply. One difficult point for me is the emphasis on that method of prayer and examen. I never could follow it in the past, and I am much less able to do so now, when my imagination wanders worse than ever. You told me once that you had the same difficulty, and that consoled me. As to the changes indicated in the *Règlement* for the boarding schools, I think we had better wait until Mother Eugenie returns before introducing them. She is desired as eagerly in Missouri as in Louisiana.
>
> The change in my health and physical strength makes me realize more plainly than ever my incapacity as superior, and I long for a discharge from the office. The message to be given to the Bishop with regard to Father B[orgna] is most difficult to transmit. The

more I think of it, the more I fear its consequences. The Father Superior [Verhaegen] is coming tomorrow at my request. His prudence and spiritual direction alone can guide me in such a difficult circumstance. The sad departure of Father Rondot and this last matter have drained me of all courage to persevere in my position.[63]

The consecration of the cathedral is set for the 26th of this month. Monseigneur wishes quite positively to have some of our nuns assist at the ceremony in a private tribune. We hope Mother Eugenie is already en route to America. . . . I enclose Mother Henriette's letter answering one she received from Mother Eugenie. It caused her to shed many tears, but I could not find out what it was about. Perhaps it had to do with the affair of Father B[orgna], for whom they retain a high esteem.

I am, in C.J., Your wholly wretched but very devoted daughter. . . .

The consecration of the St. Louis Cathedral had been announced and Mother Duchesne and her community were looking forward, not to attending the ceremony, but to the clerical visitors whom they expected and for whom the pupils would give a little reception, of which uniforms, gloves, curtsies, music, and an address were the traditional ingredients. The reception would take place as planned, but Mother Duchesne would not be at the City House to greet the guests. Unknowingly she had given the Mother General a last account of her stewardship in St. Louis.

As Mother Barat had stated that no changes were to be made in Missouri until Reverend Mother Audé returned to America, Philippine was unprepared for the letter that reached her on October 7, enclosed in a copy of a circular letter from the Superior General to the convents in Louisiana and Missouri. Mother Barat wrote after hearing Mother Audé's account of conditions prevailing in the American houses. The letter was dated July 29, 1834:

As I send off the circular letter to our American houses, my dear Philippine, I want to write a few lines to you to explain a sentence in one of my letters which you quoted in the last one I had from you. It was about the opposition that I encountered in regard to your change of residence. You recall that I was obliged to give up that plan—at least I was persuaded to do so. It was not you, my dear Mother, that I had in mind when I wrote that I hoped Mother Eugenie would help me overcome that opposition. As a matter of fact, one of ourselves on the spot can judge so much better than I can at such a distance. That is why, up to now, I have been so hesitant with regard to the direction of our American convents. Now I feel that I know the conditions better, and so I have not hesitated in deciding on a change of residence for you. Besides, it is in our recent decrees that we should not leave superiors more than six years in the same house unless it is impossible to do otherwise.

Moreover, dear Philippine, you need a rest and an easier field of administration. So you will call Mother Thiéfry to St. Louis to take your place, and you will take hers at Florissant. Mother Eugenie will write by this same post to your Reverend Bishop to inform him, or I shall do it myself, if I can—that would be better. I have also indicated some other changes, but I leave you free to modify these if you think it necessary. Confer with Mother Thiéfry about the matter. I want her to have charge of the novices. If she has a Mistress General and an Assistant, she should be able to direct them. . . . I shall be so happy to have your answer to this letter; give me details about your new place of residence. I recommend myself to your prayers, dear Philippine. Be assured that I pray for you with all my heart. You know how dear you are to me. . . .

Philippine began at once the preparations necessary for her departure, but she took time to write to Josephine on October 8:

I have not had direct news from you in a long time, but you speak constantly to me by your benefactions. A letter from Lyons informs me that 500 francs which I received through some ladies of our city who had been in Paris came from you. Really you are too generous, and I simply do not know how to thank you enough. That money came at a time when we were in such great need, I have thanked Divine Providence and my beloved provider-friend a thousand times. Severe fever and dysentery among the nuns had forced us to send home the boarding pupils. As a result, our funds were exhausted, yet I had thirty-eight people to feed and care for, counting religious and orphans. With this fresh proof that God is ever mindful of our needs, health was restored. I held up better than the others, then I had my turn—but not very seriously. Madame Teisseire's poor health is an anxiety for my heart. It is a consolation to know that you two are living together and are able to take care of each other.

So Sainte Marie has been given up! Surely it is not wrong for me to grieve over this. I do so even more legitimately than Jeremias once lamented over the ruins of Sion. This home of our childhood was the cradle of our faith and of the friendship that has united us and is so dear to me.[64]

I am going to move from the convent in St. Louis to that of St. Ferdinand, which I left six years ago to come here. It is just about five leagues from here. This change gives me additional work, so I must be brief. I learned from Madame Jouve of the death of her husband. Not knowing her exact address, I am enclosing my letter to her in this. A thousand loving messages to Mesdames Teisseire, [Augustin] Perier, [Hippolyte] Duchesne, and de Mauduit. The last named should not complain, for I have written to her several times recently. Moreover, she knows my love for her, and that love can never change.

Bishop Rosati came for confessions on Saturday morning, October 11. When she greeted him in the parlor as he came from the chapel, she gave him the letter Mother Barat had written to him, asking his approval of the changes. There was no "opposition" on his part, though he was reluctant to have her leave that very afternoon. But she was ready to make her sacrifice, and less than an hour later she was bidding *au revoir*, first to the children, then to her community—some of them her very dearest daughters, Regis Hamilton, Suzanne McKay, Gonzague Boilvin, Judith Shannon, and Catherine Lamarre—all of them so dear to her great, generous heart. Into the hired carriage they put her meager luggage, and she drove off alone, yet not alone, for those mid-day hours spent traversing the autumn-tinted Valley of Florissant were also spent in intimate converse with the Sacred Heart.

eleven

Sharing the Lot
of the Saints

1. 1834—1836

And to us sinners, Thy servants,
grant some fellowship with all Thy saints.

Liturgy of the Mass

THE CHILL OF AUTUMN was in the air. Sere and brittle leaves scurried and swirled around the Florissant convent as the sharp wind blew from the northwest. The atmosphere inside was damp and cold and penetrating, but Philippine gave little heed to it as she knelt in the cloister chapel, her eyes fixed on the tabernacle. She still seemed deep in retreat, though she had already completed the eighth day. It had been a time of spiritual aridity and trial in spite of the fact that she had used as her guide through the Ignatian Exercises the notes of a retreat given in Paris by Father Varin himself. Struggle as she would, she found it beyond her power to relinquish the hope she had had of being freed from her position of authority. And there were the recommendations made by the last General Council, stressing the use of certain methods of meditation and examen, which troubled her, though she realized their general usefulness.

The silence of the night was broken at times by whispered pleadings and offerings. Spontaneously the words she had loved and used since girlhood formed her colloquies. The prayers of Mother Marie of the Incarnation had inspired her in her youth, and by them she had inspired the children she had taught, whether in France or America, with devotion to the Sacred Heart. They often formed the substance of her holy hours or holy nights of adoration, and she never tired of dwelling with contemplative desire on the simple, all-embracing sentiments of love and reparation they expressed:

> O Eternal Father, I come to You through the Heart of my Jesus, who is the Way, the Truth, and the Life. Through this divine Heart I adore You for those who do not adore You; I love You for those who do not love You; I gratefully acknowledge You to be my God for all who in wilful blindness and contempt refuse this recognition of Your goodness. By this Divine Heart I desire to make satisfaction for the neglect of all mankind. In spirit I go through the whole world in search of every soul redeemed by the Precious Blood of my Divine Spouse, in order to make reparation for all through His Sacred Heart. . . .

The retreat left her spiritually disturbed. As she sat writing to Mother Barat on November 9, the lines in her strong, mobile face were deep-set; her friendly eyes were troubled. In all the world there was only one person to whom she could freely unburden her soul, and to her she poured out all the pent-up personal sufferings of the past month:

> I have just finished my retreat, which I made by myself shortly after coming here. I wish I could assure you that I shall lead a better life here in solitude and far from the occasions that so often caused me to fail. But it always seems to me that for my own security and for the good of others I should be in a position of lower rank, and I await this second favor from your charity. Besides the experience of my whole past life, these new regulations and directives frighten me. They are so detailed, and my memory is so faulty in regard to new things, much more so than for things of the past. My heart is so dry, I can scarcely think through all these rules and methods, so it will be far worse for me to try to carry them out. There are just three of us together in the evening before night prayers. If I can say three sentences in three minutes on the subject of the morning's meditation, that will be all, and I am sure the others will say nothing. . . . I have never been able to reflect on a subject. I see it as a whole, and what I have once seen I shall see for ten years without change or addition. I never see things in detail or in parts. I see a thing, there is the whole thing; I do not see its divisions. When I hear a sermon or listen to a long instruction, in spite of myself I reduce it all to a few words, and I cannot understand how anyone can develop a topic. In that

state of soul all methods and considerations become mere distractions for me, and I am so dry and brief in my words, they only cause aridity and disgust to other people.

I feel that I am a worn-out instrument, a useless walking stick that is fit only to be hidden in a dark corner. God allows everything to deepen this impression in my soul. I have never at any time attracted people's confidence, and the same thing is true here. The religious quite naturally think they should prefer the superior who preceded me, and not one of them has so far given me a word—I do not say of confidence, but of cordial politeness. Under the eyes of their class mistress two of the pupils wrote me a note asking me not to come to my French class, and they brought it to me with an air of triumph. I just told them to show the note to their mother. I went to the school to replace one of the nuns—the children asked me how soon the other teacher was coming back. A little later they suggested that if I knew how to do multiplication I might show them. Many other disrespectful actions strengthen in me the conviction that I am no longer fit to work with other people.

I came here in great peace of soul as to my assigned post, but the devil did not leave me long in peace. In the letters I received from St. Louis several persons told me the remark was made by some that they *never* wanted to see me again. From that I concluded that they wanted me to be sent further away, and I have not the courage to accept that. Here I have more spiritual help than anywhere else in the United States. This is all I ask for the rest of my life. I know Mother Xavier Murphy once said she thought I would spend the last years of my life near her, but I dread being sent [to Grand Coteau]. For three months they have had no Mass, not even on Sundays and feast days. My conscience is not tranquil enough to allow me to live in peace without the possibility of receiving the last Sacraments. I dread the river, the traveling, the heat especially, because of an illness from which I have not fully recovered.[1] I beg you, Reverend Mother, let me die here in Missouri. I shall obey anyone you place over me.

I shall have no peace of soul unless I tell you . . . that I have on several occasions given more than fifty francs in charity without asking the advice of my council or your permission, urged as I was by the desire to help a good work. This is just ten dollars here and is considered the least contribution one can make to churches, missions, etc. . . .

Here is a picture of spiritual suffering which was deepened by a feeling of incapacity, a sense of utter failure. She was a spent force; she was puzzled and bruised, and her sensitive nature cringed under the thoughtless blows that rained on her. All natural supports seemed to have crumbled, and she knew not where to turn. To accept the bitterness inside herself and not to add to it by external resentment or by cynicism called for high courage. If she seemed to falter inwardly, she only leaned the more reliantly on God for support, and the trials she suffered served to strengthen her faith immeasurably, while self was being slowly, painfully, ground out of her. So splendid was her self-control in this time of heart-suffering, she could write to Mother de Gramont the same day without betraying by the least hint the tumult in her soul:

> At the beginning of October I received letters from our Mother General and our Assistant General informing me of my change of residence. I spent some days putting many things in order and waited until Saturday, the day on which our Bishop usually comes to hear confessions. Then I gave him the letter informing him of my departure and expressed my desire to go that very day. He wanted me to pass by his residence, so he could show me his beautiful new Cathedral. I found some excuse not to do so, and the carriage that took him home returned to take me to St. Ferdinand. There I found Mother Thiéfry ready to leave, and I witnessed the sorrow of her community on losing her next day when she went to St. Louis, where she enjoyed the visits of all the bishops who came for the consecration of the Cathedral. The Bishops of Cincinnati, Ohio, Bardstown, Kentucky, Post Vincennes, Indiana, along with our own Bishop, all took part in the ceremony and all are churchmen of distinction.
>
> The consecration took place on October 26. Besides the four bishops there were twenty-eight priests and many clerics from the seminary present. Everything combined to make that ceremony very impressive. . . . At the elevation of the Mass the great bells brought from Normandy, the salvos of cannon, and the salute of the military guard that was present—all offered homage to God to whom that temple was being dedicated. And the large congregation present declared they had never seen anything so beautiful. Monseigneur Rosati had told me that the visiting prelates would come to St. Ferdinand, but on arriving here I found only five francs [$1] in the house, so I warded off the visit, or rather Divine Providence did so for me. I should have been so happy to meet Bishop Bruté, who is compared to Father Barat in learning and spiritual direction.

By the messenger who carried these letters to the St. Louis post office, Philippine also returned to Mother Thiéfry the retreat notes she had borrowed, adding to her note of thanks a few lines to Mother Gonzague Boilvin, who had written to her soon after her transfer to Florissant:

> You should have had no doubt, my dear Sister, as to the pleasure your letter would give me or the joy I shall have from those you intend writing when you have time—I do not say when you have strength, for I am persuaded that will not be wanting to you, especially what you need to carry with good grace all the crosses it may please God to send you. This is quite possible when one meditates on the mystery of the Cross, the crimson livery of our Spouse, and on the necessity of doing penance in order to enter heaven.
>
> Your cross has not yet been heavy enough nor in proportion to your debts to God. Make up your mind, then, to work without seeking rest, to pray without consolation, to suffer illness without the alleviations of tender care. In this way you will be a true spouse of the Sacred Heart. Ask Mother Thiéfry to allow you to read the verses by Father Varin which close his retreat. I am just now returning the copy. Tell Mother Regis I agree with her.[2]

Ten days later she was writing to Mother Barat on an important matter:

> Mother Thiéfry has written to ask my opinion about the fitness of Mother Stanislaus Shannon for final profession. She has placed the greatest confidence in her. I refused to pass judgment, for I was under the impression that this young religious was not sufficiently dependent on authority. But I did say that she loves her vocation sincerely, that she has just reached her twenty-fifth year, and that she has been very generous and devoted in the hardest kinds of employments. It is unfortunate that while she was so young she was placed second in authority in the convent, and she has had full charge of all business and financial affairs because of her knowledge of English. She has charge of the studies, and in this matter she has followed faithfully the instructions given her. But the Constitutions require that she be sent to the house designated for probation, and I do not see how she can be replaced here.[3]

During the weeks that followed, Philippine was troubled by the thought that in her impetuous outburst to Mother Barat she had shown a lack of abandonment and religious spirit. After submitting this scruple to her Jesuit director, peace of soul returned and she followed his advice, as her letter at the close of December shows. She was also ready to express the very favorable opinion she had now formed regarding Mother Shannon and to request from Mother Barat permission for her final vows:

> At this season of the year I always feel obliged to ask pardon for the pain I have caused you for so many years. I hope your charity grants it to me, along with the favor I have already solicited—of being freed from all official positions. Both God and men alike say that I am less fit than ever for them. I pray that in this coming year God will pour out upon you His best blessings, and also on the Society and on our kind Fathers. On the advice of one of them I wish to retract, though very regretfully, the request I made you not to send me away from here. I am ready to obey, no matter what it may cost me, in any change you may be pleased to make and no matter how I may dread that change.
>
> The aspirant who was Mother Thiéfry's right hand here is now in her twenty-fifth year of age and has completed the five years since her first vows. I did not want to express my opinion about her the first time it was asked, until I had tried her out a little. Since then I have formed a very good opinion of her. The difficulty is that this convent could not get along without her, and there is no one to take her place. I am like a stranger here to the Americans, as I cannot talk to them. This religious has charge of the temporal administration of the house and carries on the contacts with the parents of the English-speaking children. I want to ask you to let her remain here for the six months of her last probation. If you think it advisable, you could add the condition that she ask the help of the Father Superior and Master of Novices. She would have better direction here than in St. Louis and according to the spirit of our institute. . . .[4]

Her friendly and informal New Year's greeting to Bishop Rosati contains some pathetic lines:

> Although I have been deprived of the pleasure of seeing you for such a long time, I have not ceased recalling all your kindness to me, and indeed I can never forget it. I pray continually for your happiness and for the success of all your holy and important enterprises. Through fear of disturbing you I put off writing to you immediately after I left St. Louis. Later, however, I did write to you, but after reading the letter I tore it up. Now I should be humiliated if you thought me negligent of a duty which gratitude urged me to fulfil. It is this gratitude which makes my wishes for the New Year all the more ardent as I offer them in prayer to our Sovereign Master, so I beg you to accept them.

I say nothing to you about my position here. It is such as you can imagine. I love the solitude, and I would love it even more had I more of it. I am begging God to grant me this, without much hope of obtaining my request, for our religious are needed everywhere and charity makes it a duty to sacrifice one's personal inclinations. . . .[5]

Of her position at Florissant she had written some weeks before this: "My life here is about the same as in St. Louis. I wake the religious in the morning, make the last rounds at night, clean the outhouses, scrub, sweep—these are my ordinary occupations." [6] And of her solitude she would write six weeks later: "There is no news to give you from this house. The front door is not opened all day long, the parlor, opened once a week, stays closed from Sunday to Sunday. This solitude is entirely to my liking." [7]

A little note written in January to Mother Boilvin shows the strong bond that united them in a friendship that was rooted and grounded in love for the Sacred Heart. To the young aspirant, frail in constitution, sensitive in temperament, talented and gifted spiritually, the older religious—more than twice her age—gave strength, courage, and training that would make her an excellent religious. Never afraid to show her affection when she knew it would be understood, Philippine wrote on New Year's Day:

I received your two letters, my beloved Sister, and though you did not tell me you had made what you sent me, I had no trouble in recognizing you in all of it. Thank you so much for all, but especially for that which is the symbol of our union, the object of our dear devotion, the mirror in which we should both perceive our own faults and find the model of the virtues we lack. My great wish for you at the beginning of this year is that you may obtain these virtues, which can be drawn from the study of the Sacred Heart.

I do not need all His charity in order to pardon all your faults toward me, for I cannot recall a single one. As to the faults that have been displeasing to God, they are forgiven seventy times seven times if you detest them. As I have the same hope for myself, I trust that the Heart of Jesus will unite us once more in the same community. In Him I am all yours. . . .

Sympathy with sickness and suffering was a natural quality in Mother Duchesne's character. Her *Journal* at this period shows her concern for both the religious whom she had left in St. Louis and those whom she found at Florissant. At the City House there had been illness all winter, but in January it became alarming. The climate was, of course, partly to blame, for in Missouri, where the first snows, coming in November, melted quickly and were followed by "spells" of bright, mild weather, the real winter usually set in after Christmas. But this year, Mother Duchesne recorded in February, "the cold was something extraordinary, the worst in twenty years, and that throughout both the United States and Canada. . . . Actually our lips froze together, and at night our breath froze on the pillows and sheets."

At Florissant the one who suffered most was Sister Elizabeth Missé, a promising young coadjutrix aspirant. She had been in bed for two months when on January 6 Mother Duchesne gathered the community around the invalid's bed and began a fervent novena through the intercession of St. Philomena for her cure. On the ninth day Sister Missé was well enough to assist at Mass and lend a helping hand about the house. The cure was not permanent, but it was a consoling answer to prayer and lasted several months.

At the City House the greatest sufferer that winter was Mother Boilvin. Mother Duchesne had written to her before Lent began:

> Your letter gave me great consolation, for I read there the expression of your desires, the love you have for our holy vocation, and your eagerness to contract the alliance which will unite you more completely to the Heart of Jesus. Your perseverance will make up to Him and to us for the defection of several of His spouses. But to satisfy fully the love and longing of this adorable Heart, the heart you desire to give Him must be prepared for this divine union by marks of resemblance to His Heart. What special resemblance? He Himself indicated it when He said: "Learn of Me *meekness and humility*."
>
> Humility is the virtue that requires the greatest effort on your part. And since you want to know yourself, and to prune the vine before inviting the Divine Spouse to eat of its fruit, I should warn you to trim off the useless branches continually. By this I mean that good opinion you have of yourself, that too self-assured air, the surprise you show when found in fault, your coldness when a request for service causes a slight upset in your plans. There is also some negligence in training the children, a lack of order in your class and of neatness in the appearance of the children.
>
> As to penances, you are not able to perform them. The only one I ask of you is to speak English with everyone who understands it. That is a very good mortification and worth more for the glory of

God and the good of the convent than a fast on bread and water. So here are your penances: 1. speak English; 2. give some time to studying it every day; 3. study the English hymns; 4. examine the childen's clothes every day; if you cannot do it while they are dressing in the morning, then do it after breakfast; 5. everyday make two acts of humility, either checking an answer or an excuse, or something else of the kind.[8]

Anxiety about Mother Boilvin's health led Philippine to ask Mother Thiéfry to send her to Florissant where she herself might nurse the young nun back to health. On receiving a refusal, she decided to put the matter before the Bishop, who had always taken a fatherly interest in the Boilvin girls. So she sent him a pleading little note,[9] and early in March, Mother Boilvin came to Florissant to recuperate. It was a joy for Mother Duchesne to be able to care for her, a relaxation for her to talk with her in the little room adjoining her own, where the aspirant was lodged. French was a bond between them, and Gonzague was off her penitential English regime for the present. There were so many things to talk about. *The Shepherd of the Valley* was carrying alarming rumors of war with France over certain unpaid indemnities guaranteed in a treaty made during Casimir Perier's ministry.[10] And Father Jeanjean had refused the see of New Orleans—he was determined never to be a bishop.[11] There was good news from Louisiana, where St. Michael's had one hundred and fifty pupils and fifty orphans, and Grand Coteau had eighty girls in the academy. New convents had been opened in France, and Mother Duchesne could point out their location on an old map she had treasured through the years and dwell with loving insistence on the motivating force within the Society—the glory of the Sacred Heart and the love that urged its members on to works of apostolic zeal that would draw souls into the Kingdom of Christ.

Then word came from St. Louis of the fire that had burned a livery stable and the old wooden church that was being used as a warehouse, and endangered the cathedral. The intense heat had broken some of the stained glass windows and caused other serious damage. But these were the least effects of the fire in Philippine's estimation. "Monseigneur Rosati nearly died that night," she recorded in her *Journal* some days later, "and has been ill ever since." Out of her poverty she made him an offering, after consulting Mother Shannon as to how much they could possibly spare.

The brief note that accompanied it must have touched the Bishop's heart:

> I learned with sorrow that you are not recovering quickly, and I readily understand this after the terrible shock of that fatal night of the fire, which I cannot get out of my mind. To think that I was asleep while you were suffering such intense anxiety! I have been haunted by the thought of the great danger to which you were exposed. We have assembled together to pray for your recovery and for the cessation of the trials which are enough to overwhelm you. I wish it were in my power to repair all the damage done to the cathedral. I am sending you all I can spare just now, and I hope to double this small amount as soon as possible. I dare not take more of your time, but I beg your blessing for us all.[12]

After Easter Mother Duchesne sent Mother Gonzague Boilvin some lines of encouragement that show the strength and brevity of the spiritual direction she gave to those who confided in her:

> I received your letter, my dearest Sister—I do not recall its date—and I was not able to answer immediately. Profit by the little trials that come to you—that is the time to make progress. I shall always recall these words quoted to me by a man of God when I was in a situation similar to yours: *Unless the grain of wheat falling into the earth decay and die, it will not bear fruit; but if it decays and dies, it will bring forth much fruit.* It is often laziness that makes us wish for death, and then there is nothing to do but repeat the words of the hymn, "After death there will be suffering still." And what suffering there will be in purgatory! Remember that last farthing of which we must render an account. That stirs one's fear. Let us bear up under our suffering and leave to God how long and how much we must endure.[13]

Mother Duchesne was unprepared for a visit in May from Colonel Pierre Menard of Kaskaskia. Nearly ten years before, he had loaned her $500 to pay Bishop Du Bourg what she still owed him on the convent building at Florissant. He had charged no interest and the understanding had been that the money would be paid back in the tuitions of pupils whom he would send to the boarding school. He had sent only one child, and a debt of about $300 remained. Now Colonel Menard wanted a cash payment. As Mother Duchesne was accustomed to transact such business through Bishop Rosati, she promised the Colonel that the debt would be paid within thirty days, counting entirely on Divine Providence. The Bishop was at Florissant on May 31 for the patronal feast of St. Ferdinand, so Mother Duchesne had an opportunity to explain the matter to him. Acknowledging the receipt he sent her some weeks later she wrote:

> I am most grateful for the picture of St. Philomena which you sent me and which I treasure as a precious remembrance of our first pastor. I had previously received your letter enclosing the receipt from Mr. Menard. Your absence from St. Louis and the illness of our hired man prevented me from acknowledging it sooner. I could not but bless Divine Providence which, contrary to all likelihood, furnished me with the means of canceling the debt (always a sharp thorn to me) which the convent had contracted. One of the parents paid me the tuition for his children a year in advance, and so I had enough in one of our cash-boxes to pay in gold what was owed. . . . They tell me your health is better, and I thank the Lord a thousand times for such a great favor for the whole diocese.[14]

One day shortly after the Bishop's visit Mother Duchesne had the joy of presenting to Mother Shannon the Superior General's permission for the young nun's final vows, which was transmitted by Mother Audé. Arrangements for her probationary training had already been discussed with Father De Theux, S.J., superior and master of novices, when Philippine wrote to Mother Barat:

> I received a letter from Mother Audé which testified to your kindness in my regard. As to my health, it is good now. All desire is extinct in me except that of enjoying God and of preparing myself for that by withdrawing from all occasions of faults—but I shall always have these. It grieves me to be an obstacle to the advancement of those who are under my care, and I shall be until I am relieved of superiority. This is the request I again dare to present to you.
>
> The young religious who is writing to you along with me is very eager to make her first vows, and I beg you to grant her this privilege. Mother Stanislaus Shannon was delighted with the permission to prepare for her final vows. As she cannot be replaced, so necessary is her very name in this house, the Father Superior of our neighbors has consented, with zeal and interest, to direct her himself during the six months, which cannot begin before vacation. Could you not shorten the probation in view of her ten years of assiduous service to the Society?[15] That would give me as much

joy as it would give her. My eyesight is very poor today, so I cannot write more. . . .[16]

The temporary extinction of all lesser desires in view of the highest good was a spiritual experience that seems to have come frequently to Philippine Duchesne. It was a grace that led to more intimate union with God in the sanctuary of her own soul and to more generous imitation of Christ in the daily contacts of community life. She had no false or complicated notions of perfection. To her perfection lay in giving oneself wholly to God and in going the whole length of opportunity in the service of others. It was the reflex of this charity that made her enter so heartily into the joys and sorrows of her companions.

August was drawing to a close when one hot, humid day Mother Duchesne met Mother Shannon on the stairway—there was only one stairway in the little convent—and made her a sign to follow her. When they reached the doorway of her room, the superior said to her young treasurer, "Where do you expect to procure a profession cross for yourself?"

"From your cupboard, Mother," came the quick reply, and they both laughed heartily.

"Yes," said Mother Duchesne, "it is there, and you shall have it soon, for this very day you are going to begin your probation. Are you pleased with that news?" The answer was an explosion of joy, for that was Mother Shannon's way.[17]

She used to tell how her probation was directed by Mother Duchesne, who provided her with plenty of trials and humiliations along with enlightening explanations of the Rule and spirit of the Society, and by Father De Theux, who came for confession every two weeks and gave her very vigorous spiritual guidance. At the outset he presented her with a French copy of *The Ladder of Perfection*, printed in seventeenth-century type which she could not decipher with any degree of certainty. According to her own testimony she had reached only the second rung of the ladder at the end of six months. Her active duties were not interrupted by the contemplative additions to her daily life, for Mother Shannon had now become Mother Duchesne's right hand.

During these months of probation the young nun's love and admiration for her superior increased continually, and throughout her long life Mother Shannon always spoke of her as "my holy Mother." Years afterwards she used to say:

My holy Mother thought that a religious of the Sacred Heart was not worthy of her name unless she offered herself with ardent love to the work of reparation and expiation, and therefore led as penitential a life as her strength would allow. Perhaps we had strong constitutions or received special graces in answer to her prayers, but we certainly practiced great austerities and were none the worse for it. We lived as long as other people, and many of us have reached an advanced age.[18]

Another passage from the biography of Mother Shannon gives a deeply moving picture of the superior at Florissant at this time. The young nun was walking in the garden one day, saying her rosary. Ornamental plants and shrubs were not cultivated there in those days; only potatoes, onions, and other common vegetables grew in neat patches. Going noiselessly down a pathway hedged by berry bushes, she came quite unexpectedly on Mother Duchesne, who had been trimming off the rank outer leaves from the cabbages, but was now resting a little, seated on a boulder by the path. The commonplace, prosaic background of the picture was symbolic of the rough ways of humility and self-sacrifice along which Mother Duchesne followed her Divine Master, and Mother Shannon realized, as she stood watching her, that some deep sorrow was crushing her heart. The holy old religious was holding her rosary in one hand and with the other was trying to brush away the tears that were pouring down her cheeks. As she sat there, weeping silently, her whole posture and expression revealed unspeakable suffering patiently borne. The young nun could not hold back her own tears at the sight and longed to console her loved superior, but this sorrow was too personal, too sacred to intrude upon, and she withdrew as noiselessly as she had come, leaving her "holy Mother" alone with God.[19]

Perhaps it was just at this period that Mother Duchesne sent these undated lines to Mother Boilvin:

It has been hard for me not to write to you individually, dearest Sister. You know that you have always been very close to my heart. Still we must prefer to be very close to the Heart of Jesus, and how shall we be close to Him if we fail to do His will? It has been so unmistakable for me in this circumstance that it would give me great joy, if it did not also show me my innumerable defects. The will of God is plain for you also. Do it by accomplishing strictly all the duties laid on you by your Rule. The difficult step once taken, I have confidence, and almost assurance, that you will be at peace. I have found peace in this difficult situation. All I desire is retirement, silence, the forgetfulness of creatures, and to remain until death near the altar of St. Regis. . . .

Although the convent at Florissant was remote and solitary, it was a place to which many visitors were now drawn by the presence of Mother Duchesne. Old friends brought new ones, and she noted their names faithfully in the *Journal*. Father Brassac came with Father Lutz; Father Timon came with Father Badin, "first missionary in Kentucky"; Bryan Mullanphy brought Monsieur Nicollet, the noted French scientist and explorer; Father Van de Velde came with Father Carrell, a new recruit for the Jesuit novitiate,[20] and returned some days later with another interesting personage, a Mr. Pierce Connelly, "newly converted Protestant minister, who is going to Rome and will carry our letters and commissions." [21]

But Mother Duchesne had no letters to send, for soon she was desperately ill. August floods had brought the water so high that access to both church and convent was cut off for some time. As the waters receded, sickness began to take its toll in the community —first Sister Missé, then Mother Shannon, then Mother Duchesne herself. Her illness was so alarming that Mother Shannon sent for Mother Thiéfry in September, but Philippine would not allow her to remain. She felt that she could manage without her, and she knew the St. Louis community needed its superior. From her sickbed, however, she wrote on October 8 to tell the Bishop what she had done, for that always brought her peace of soul:

I have been ill since the end of August, and several times when I thought death was at hand I asked myself, "Shall I never see my venerated Bishop again?" I desire death for myself, but I was sorry to leave this house without a superior. I asked Mother Lucille to come to see me, as much to assure her of the property at St. Charles as to propose that in case of my death she might come to spend some time here until our Superior General would designate my successor. When I first fell ill I wrote to ask about this. Mother Lucille disagreed with me quite positively, and seeing her strong opposition I did not insist.

Now our young religious, who love Mother Thiéfry very much, suggest that I ask her to spend some weeks here as she offered to do so. I want you to make her understand that this is not the moment to do so. I think my illness is just a matter of old age, so I shall never be completely cured of it and this condition may last a long time. It would be better for her to reserve her kind services for a time when I shall be completely incapacitated or when I die. Between now and then an answer will come from France. At present her absence would be harmful to the convent in St. Louis, and she is not needed here. It is a great consolation and a source of peace for me to know that she is willing to come and stay here, but I repeat, it is not necessary yet. This illness is not the kind that gives sudden alarm; it just makes me linger on. I beg you to excuse the mistakes in my letter, as I have great difficulty in writing.

When Bishop Rosati was leaving for New Orleans early in November for the consecration of Bishop Anthony Blanc, Mother Duchesne took advantage of the chance to send letters to the seaport without postage,[22] and wrote to Mother Barat:

I think I wrote to you at the beginning of September and begged you to provide for the needs of this convent, fearing and hoping that God would bring my life to a close with the illness from which I recovered only at the beginning of November. Again I have lost most of my strength, but I now believe that if Mother Eugenie returns to us in the spring, as you hold out the hope that she will, I shall have the pleasure of seeing her.

After repeating what she had written to the Bishop, she continues:

As I did not lose consciousness during my illness nor the power to read letters, I could keep an eye on things, though confined to bed. I was not ready to die; I still have need and reason to do penance. . . . Our little boarding school is attended by Americans who speak English all the time. However, I give an hour and a half of French class daily to some of them, and I take an hour of surveillance in the studyroom.

To Mother Boilvin, who was anxious about her, Philippine wrote on November 15:

I have always answered your letters, my dearest Sister, and I have never been put out with you, except when you worry about my health, which really should not give you so much concern. I have reached that period of life when, as David said, one has nothing but miseries. For some it happens suddenly; for others it is a long-drawn-out affair. I suspect I shall have the latter experience, and I anticipate being ill a good deal this winter. But that will be a means of expiating the past and should be looked upon as an advantage and not as a humiliation, since nothing defiled can enter heaven.

As to what you are suffering, believe me, I am having the same trial. But let us take up the cross without cowardice. Let us fix our eyes on Jesus, reduced to the last extremity of suffering and desolation, and then ask ourselves if we wish to leave Him all alone. Would we have the courage to refuse Him anything? . . .

Early in November, Father John Odin returned from Europe, bringing parcels and a packet of mail for Florissant. There were letters from Philippine's family and from the nuns in France, little gifts and remembrances, some books—all carried in the satchel of this kind Vincentian friend. One letter called for immediate action and an answer by the first opportunity. In it Mother Barat had written:

> Mother Eugenie has answered your last letters, but I want to write to you myself. Though I refused your request, I understand, nonetheless, your need of rest, but I still have no one to take your place. . . . Be patient, dear Mother, and pray that the Heart of Jesus may send us capable postulants. . . .
>
> I often think that your convent at Florissant really ought to be closed. The works are so small. Then St. Louis and St. Charles would get aid and it seems to me these two establishments would be sufficient. Tell me what you think on this subject; consult your neighbors [the Jesuits]. If they advise this, then I shall write to Monseigneur and you will receive your obediences. I think it is high time we opened convents in sections of the country that would furnish us with vocations. . . . Mother Eugenie cannot leave France yet. Her health is very poor, and the doctors advise against her taking this trip. . . . Adieu, dear Mother; I have written enough for this time. Our friends send you affectionate greetings, especially Father Varin and my brother. They, too, are growing old. Soon we shall all disappear. Fortunately we have already left all things. . . . Oh, how I should love to follow your example and make the same request that you address to me. . . .[23]

After consulting Father De Theux, Mother Duchesne answered on December 20:

> We have heard of your grave illness, but only after you had recovered. We have thanked God for sparing us the terrible sorrow of losing you, and we continue to pray for the conservation of health that is so precious to us all and for the preservation of the

large religious family confided to your care. These are the New Year's wishes I would love to offer you personally, if that were possible.

Now I come to the chief topic of your letter—the merging of the Florissant convent with that of St. Louis. I wrote at once to the superior of the Jesuits to ask his advice. Here are the exact words of his reply: "It would grieve me to have your house at Florissant closed. I hope this will never happen. If Mother Barat has made up her mind about it, could you not suggest to her that this convent be used as a central novitiate for all your American houses, with only a free school attached to it? I think this would be an excellent way of forming your novices, and in this way your Society would continue its good work among us. But for goodness' sake, do not let them close your house! Offer my humble respects to Mother Barat, please. As to yourself, after having done all in your power to save this very useful convent, do not be discouraged. This is the way God treats His servants."

As for myself—if I may express my opinion—I think, 1. that this house with its little boarding school will give more recruits to the Society than the other two in Missouri.[24] The academy in St. Louis is not increasing in numbers and the pupils give the religious much cause for anxiety on account of the impiety and ingratitude of some of the non-Catholic girls, and the inconstancy of the parents who withdraw their children just when the religious are hopeful of good results. At St. Charles there is also a mixture of religions. 2. Here at Florissant we shall always be assured of the finest spiritual direction because of the Jesuit establishment near by. Many fervent apostles are being trained there. 3. None of the children of this academy would transfer to the other boarding schools, and the nuns from here would be a burden to other communities, while here we can live on the produce of our garden. . . . 4. We built this house at a time when prices were very high, so it cost about 40,000 francs. We could not get 10,000 for it now, and I am sure that if it were put up for sale, it would be bought by subscription to make a country house for the Sisters of Charity. . . .

I wrote to Mother Thiéfry to tell her what you suggested in regard to our convent. Though I am better, I am in no condition to drive to St. Louis. The least exposure to cold or dampness brings on fever and a bad cough. She will write directly to you, my beloved Mother. I hasten to finish this so I can send it by a traveler. If you follow the advice of the Jesuit Father, this house could be placed under Mother Thiéfry's guidance again. She has not built up the academy in St. Louis to any great extent. Mother Hamilton would be more pleasing to everyone there. Mother

Shannon would help Mother Thiéfry quite effectively where English is needed. . . .

Philippine sent other letters by that opportunity. In one to Josephine we read:

It is too near the beginning of the New Year, my dearest Cousin, for my greetings to reach you on time, but you know you receive them at every season, for you, my most intimate friend and best benefactress, are constantly in my thoughts and prayers, as are also your family, from whom I have received so many kind services and proofs of affection. Your letter of March 4, entrusted to Father Odin, arrived a few days before a second one, undated, which came by post.

I fear one of your letters to me was lost, for I never heard from you directly about the departure of our religious from our dear Sainte Marie, nor about the inauguration of the orphanage there. In those long fifteen months during which I had no word from you, I was afraid that God had taken you to Himself, and I spoke of this to Mother Lucille Mathevon, who came from Grenoble and esteems you almost as highly as I do. She is now superior of the convent at St. Charles, where we made our first halt in America. . . . Now we have a pretty brick convent there, larger than the one here at St. Ferdinand. . . .

Thank you so much for your generosity in offering me another gift. Keep it, please. If it reached me before my death, I would not use it either to enlarge this house or to improve it. The closing of Sainte Marie, on which I spent so much money, robs me of all initiative, and a three months' illness has weakened my constitution and made me hope that I shall not be much longer in this land of sorrow and tears. If, however, your gift were intended for poor priests, that would be a great charity; but with my vow of poverty I could dispose of the money only as you would indicate.

I share your grief at the loss of Father Delagré, and I beg you to offer my sympathy to Fathers Rambaud and Dumolard, to whom I owe so much. Remember me to Augustin's wife and family. Thank you for telling me about them. I can never forget Augustin, her splendid husband, nor you, my dearest friend. . . . I send you the love of a heart entirely devoted to you.[25]

The letter enclosed to Marine Teisseire was no mere repetition of what she had written to Josephine, but a sheet of jottings that reveal the interests of her mind and heart:

I was deeply touched by your remembrance of me, my dearest Cousin, and how I sympathize with your suffering during your long illness and the loneliness you feel because of the absence of your children—a circumstance well-calculated to pain a heart as loving as yours. I was so glad to know that your last daughter [Louise-Philippine] was not leaving you after her wedding, and that her marriage, far from withdrawing her from you, was bringing to you the support of a gentleman of fine, upright character.[26] The only one of your children whom I knew well is Madame Bergasse. Do not fail to give my greetings to her and her nice husband. I am not giving you any messages for my brother. A letter from Paris, more recent than yours, tells me he has been elected a deputy and has paid a visit to our Paris convent. I am sure his wife was with him.[27]

We have the consolation of seeing the Catholic religion spreading in the United States. Our priests fraternize often with ministers of other religions and ordinarily speak of them as "our separated brethren." Besides the Archbishop of Baltimore, there are twelve Catholic bishops. Many Protestants are enrolled in Catholic colleges, and this is the case in our houses in Louisiana, where there are 150 boarding pupils and 30 orphans in one convent and 100 pupils in the other. In Missouri we have not had the same success, and there are many non-Catholics who are hostile to us. In their newspapers they speak of convents as devil-houses that should be burned. One day I received word that our house in St. Louis had been burned. It was a false report, but there is no doubt that the stable near the cathedral was set on fire with the intention of burning that very church. The plan failed because of the metal roof. Only two windows were ruined, and the cathedral had but recently been consecrated. That magnificent ceremony roused the fury of the hostile sects. The burning of the Ursuline convent in Boston went unpunished, though it was premeditated and carried out by more than 80 people; and on the anniversary of that outrage, this year, they wanted to tear down the ruins that were still standing. The magistrates forbade such an action, and the Irish Catholics would certainly have raised a riot, had it been done. The Ursuline nuns were obliged to go to Canada, and they received no compensation from the city of Boston. That convent, a handsome building, had been erected later than ours, and so it is an example of the instability of works which are apparently quite useful.

I am really good for nothing any more, but even if I had ability and strength, I would have no desire to undertake anything new. I am thinking only of building my eternity, and I still have a great deal to do on that. . . .

New Year's holidays for the pupils had by this time become the custom in the boarding schools in and near St. Louis. This gave the nuns an opportunity to spend the last day of December in recollection and to take a little relaxation on New Year's Day. Philippine used a few free moments to compose a letter to her Mothers and Sisters in France, writing on January 1, 1836:

> The lowliness to which the Infant Jesus stooped is recalled to our minds at this season which is consecrated to His deep humiliations. Such thoughts will make you welcome the greetings and good wishes that come to you from the smallest and lowliest of all the Convents of the Sacred Heart. Our claim to this title was until recently disputed by the house at St. Charles. But Divine Providence, through the instrumentality of one of our friends, has procured for that community a brick house larger than ours, so we are secure in the last place. But we live in the convent dedicated to St. Regis. Here we have the shrine we promised by a vow in France to erect in his honor in return for his protection over our American missions. . . . The Jesuit church is contiguous to our convent, so we profit by their help. Their novitiate, at present composed of twenty excellent young men, gives great promise of stability. Their superior visits us at the Ember seasons and during retreats with incomparable kindness. . . . We have learned recently of the opening of a school for boys at St. Charles by one of the Jesuit Brothers, and success is already assured.[28] St. Louis University is having far greater success, for it has 200 pupils enrolled, fifty of them boarding pupils. . . .

A few days later she was thanking Mother Boilvin for a Christmas gift:

> I recognize the goodness of your heart, my dearest Sister, in the charity you have shown me by making these gifts that remind us of the love of the Heart of Jesus and of His cross. The last emblem you made seems to me more perfect than former ones. I do not know whether or not that was due to the finer material you used to paint on. You would make your two pupils here very happy if you gave them two small pieces of that same material, so they might copy yours, for they think it is very pretty. They both have real talent for that art, and it is well worth cultivating and quite useful in making religious articles. They are sending you back some of your models; they want to keep the others a little longer, though they have very little time for art work.
>
> Your letter gave me joy, for I read in it the unction that the Divine Infant poured into your heart as you knelt at His crib. The crib and Calvary are the two dwelling places dearest to those who

love Jesus. Pray to Him for me, that I may never leave those dwelling places.

On March 7, 1836, Mother Shannon made her final vows. The Bishop's absence was a disappointment to the community, but Father Philip Borgna, as vicar-general, presided at the ceremony and preached with unction and eloquence. Perhaps it was by visitors who came for the day that Mother Duchesne sent the following undated note to Mother Boilvin, for it belongs quite evidently to this period:

Be assured, my dear Sister, that you have not caused me any pain, but rather consolation, because I see in you a person who can render valuable services to the Society of the Sacred Heart. I fear in a way that you realize this and so may lose the merit which could be gained from your work. That is why I felt I should deal a blow to your self-love in order to make way in your soul for divine love and fraternal charity. The worst evil in the world would be to consider yourself free from faults. Being too greatly saddened by one's faults can come from having one's pride humiliated. Try to be like that Hospitaler Sister who got a chapter of fifty-two faults and just plunged with undiminished confidence into the merciful Heart of Jesus Christ.

I am rather put out with you because you did not admit sooner that you were suffering. You should not fast on Wednesdays. Whenever you feel the need of medicines, you must say so. Those in charge cannot always discover our ills simply by looking at us. It would be a real pleasure for me to take care of you. . . .

Boxes from France always caused a stir in the convent, and Philippine was quick to thank for all that reached the mission. On March 20 she sent a letter to her sister, Madame Jouve:

Just recently, my dearest Sister, I received your letter of April 3, 1835, dated from Conflans, and put in a case that was coming to us from Paris. In it was also the beautiful present you sent me. It is what I would have desired more than anything else, for the first vestment you sent me in 1819 is worn out and needed to be replaced. I knew from a letter that came more rapidly by mail that you had been to see your daughter [Mother Amelie Jouve], and I shared in the pleasure of that visit. As to the income of which you write, I do not recall the conditions, and it is not in my power to change them now because of my vow of poverty. But in any case it is most natural that it should go to Amelie, who is nearer to you and younger than I. In this way we would avoid bank fees and the risk of death, which, I trust, will come to me before it comes to your daughter. She can do much for the cause of religion, but my days are numbered. I am growing quite weak. In this country where I still do not understand the language well, I shall soon be useless. I almost forget that I am French; that language is studied only as a foreign tongue by the Americans, who are growing more numerous and now occupy all the prominent positions here.

I beg God to enlighten both you and your daughter Josephine as to the vocation God wills for her. I should grieve to see you alone, yet it would be a consolation to see her sheltered safe from the many dangers that threaten one's faith. Even the most enlightened maternal care has not been able to safeguard several of your children. By the generosity of your sacrifices for them you will increase your own merits and make their true happiness more secure. The world was saved by the Cross. Those who spread the Gospel preached only the Cross. And solid virtue flourishes only in its shadow. This necessity of carrying the cross and of living as a follower of Jesus Christ in toil and tears prevents the return of so many brothers who have wandered from the truth.[29] We do not want a religion that is sad, they say, or one that requires suffering; we want pleasures. They want Paradise without paying the price of suffering, but can they give the lie to the Gospel?

Let me close this, loved Sister, and add a note to Amelie. I do not know her address, and the least paper over and above the single sheet doubles the postal fee.

The packet of mail that reached her at this time contained a letter from Mother Barat that renewed in her soul an anxious dread that was to last for several years. The Superior General wrote:

I have been waiting for news of you, dear Philippine, before answering your last letter, which caused me such sorrow, as I read in it your expression of farewell. I hope these were not your last *adieux*. You have indeed suffered much, but God endowed you with a strong constitution, so I trust that you will recover your strength, and that we shall have the consolation of keeping you for a long time, to perfect your own sanctification and consolidate the mission you founded. I do not hesitate to tell you, dear Mother, that one means of doing this would be to build up St. Louis and St. Charles at the expense of Florissant. Since I am unable to supply these houses with enough religious to carry on the work properly, all three will remain poor and weak, while on the other hand they could do more good and do it more effectively if they had the religious from your community. You could go to

St. Charles for some rest and encourage, by your advice and example, that interesting foundation which is destined to do a great
amount of good, if we but merit that grace from the Heart of
Jesus.

This, however, is not an order; it is just a suggestion. I wrote in
the same vein to Mother Thiéfry, but I told her to act only with
the approval of the Bishop, to whom I refer the decision. At such
a distance from you and unable to judge *pro* and *con*, I bow to the
advice of those who are on the spot. You might ask the advice of
the superior of the Jesuits. If you close Florissant, I leave you free
to make whatever disposition of the property you may think best.
If you dispose of it for some other good work and get a few
thousand *livres* for it, that money could be used for the new
buildings at St. Charles and St. Louis, and that would be a great
help. But do what you think best. I leave it to you and Mother
Thiéfry. Confer with her. . . .[30]

Philippine discussed the matter again with Father De Theux,
then wrote to Bishop Rosati and Mother Thiéfry. Father De Theux
took the matter to heart so seriously that he also wrote to the
Bishop. His letter reached its destination, but Philippine's did not.

Permit me, Monseigneur [wrote the Jesuit superior on March 15,
1836], to commend to your consideration an affair of very deep
concern to the parish of St. Ferdinand. Madame Barat, so it appears, wishes to suppress the house of her Ladies at St. Ferdinand;
but, according to what I have been told, she would first know
your sentiments on the subject. I believe it accordingly to be my
duty, seeing that the village is committed to the care of our
Society, to observe to you that the suppression of that house
would work very serious harm to the village of St. Ferdinand, unfortunately perverse enough already, and yet destined by its
situation to develop shortly into a place of importance. We should
lose, besides the prayers and good example of these Ladies, the
day school, which they have decided to keep up regularly for
the future and which, together with the boys' school that I opened
last September, ought to give the Father Missioner a great ascendancy over the parish. In fine, who will keep up the church as
neatly as they do? And what will their house be used for if they
leave? A tavern? I will not insist further. *Fiat voluntas Dei et
superiorum.*[31]

Two weeks later Mother Duchesne wrote again to the Bishop:

I am overjoyed at the news of your return. I was awaiting it with impatience and some time ago sent Mother Thiéfry a letter to give to you at your first visit. She forgot to do so and returned it to me. It was good for nothing except to be burned.

The superior of our St. Louis convent [Mother Thiéfry] was told to ask your advice about closing this house of ours. There is nothing for me to do but accept what is decided. It will touch me personally, but me least of all. The idea of closing the house, however, has distressed me for a long time. I hope that no matter what happens, you will take a stand and protect this establishment in which such good can still be done, and that good does not need to be showy. . . .

The Bishop's answer is not extant, but the plan to close the Florissant convent was dropped temporarily. Early in April Mother Hamilton came for a brief visit, bringing Mother Boilvin to recuperate again and taking back to St. Louis Mother Mary Ann Roche, one of the few fairly healthy members of the community. Once more Philippine nursed the delicate little aspirant back to health, but this time she decided to ask the Mother General's permission to keep Mother Gonzague at Florissant.

Although Mother Duchesne does not mention the fact to the Superior General, illness had laid its hand on her, too, during the last weeks of Lent, but under Mother Shannon's care she rallied and was able to be with the community at Easter. Before the close of April, Florissant had quite an unexpected invalid in its infirmary. From Louisiana came Mothers Antonia Potier and Louise Penel, both unannounced and both tubercular, the former from St. Michael's, the latter from Grand Coteau. On their arrival in St. Louis, Mother Thiéfry decided to share with Mother Duchesne the problem of caring for them and so sent Mother Penel to Florissant. This new member of the community found it difficult to accept the conditions and the climate in Missouri, and very soon Mother Duchesne realized that she had not only an invalid but also a mental case to deal with. In a building as small and crowded as the convent at Florissant, this was a severe trial. No hint of this appeared, however, in Philippine's letters to her family that spring, but she showed another anxiety in writing to Josephine on May 10: "Our solitude is quite disturbed by rumors of war with France. I trust, my loving and incomparable friend, that this will not take place. If there is sea-fighting, what might happen to the mail? I think this letter can still reach you and an answer come back to me, if sent through a neutral country."

These rumors of war with France had been troubling Philippine for many months. Newspaper reports were now alarming, now reassuring. A diplomatic impasse had resulted from President Jackson's abrupt and undiplomatic pressure on France for payment of the indemnities guaranteed in 1831. For a time the American public expected war; then England offered her services in negotiations and the war clouds disappeared. But Philippine could not foresee this happy outcome of events when she expressed her fears to Josephine.

In May a very affectionate letter reached her from Mother Barat:

> This very moment, dear Mother and beloved daughter, I received your letter of November 1. It was balm to my afflicted heart. . . . I was dreading what might come of your long illness, and I thanked God when I saw your handwriting. Now we can hope once more to keep you on earth. May Jesus be blessed for this! I am greatly preoccupied about the convents in your country. How I wish I could send you recruits, especially a Mistress of Novices to carry out the plan suggested! . . . Dear Mother, beg the Heart of Jesus to send us subjects according to His Heart. Pray for me, too, and be assured of our loving union.[32]

Philippine's answer, written on Pentecost Sunday, May 22, 1836, reveals the workings of her mind and heart in the midst of very trying circumstances:

> I am so relieved and consoled to know that this convent will remain devoted to the Sacred Heart and forever consecrated by the vow you allowed me to make in honor of our patron, St. Regis. He is no longer honored at Grenoble. I feared this trial would go even further. As to myself, I am growing very old. I have never wanted to be in a position of authority; still less do I want it now, for I realize more and more clearly how unfit I am for the office of superior. To soul-suffering there is added bodily suffering that shows me even more plainly my incapacity. At one time I begged you not to change my place of residence because none of our other convents equals this one in drawing souls to the love and practice of solitude, and here we always have the best spiritual help. This convent is well suited to receive young novices, but the closing of the boarding school would take away the hope of vocations. We now have just fifteen pupils, but I believe this small group will give us more stable vocations than will any one of the other four boarding schools. . . . One must be in this country to appreciate the shades of difference in various localities. . . .

I sent you a letter, dear Reverend Mother, by Mother de Coppens, containing information about the few nuns here. She left us in poor health, but she traveled with our kind doctor and his wife and daughter, who were very attentive to her needs. This departure removes a sharp thorn from Mother Thiéfry's side, but she has plenty of others to suffer from. She wrote me that she is now carrying the heavy end of the cross I used to carry. I certainly would not want to carry it again, but I believe her excessive activity makes her suffer. She wants everything to run smoothly all the time, and she wears people out by continually changing employments and rooms. . . .

If you want my opinion about this house, it is to keep a small boarding school here always. We would always need a Mistress of Studies for second-year novices, and she could direct the work of a small group of docile pupils. We have now in the school two of Mr. Mullanphy's grandchildren,[33] and they have been joined by several other children of this parish. When their mothers come to Mass, they can visit with them. These girls would not go either to St. Louis or to St. Charles. . . . Monseigneur came here to give Confirmation, but as arrangements had been made with him in St. Louis, I said nothing to him about changes. In the confessional, however, he exhorted me earnestly to carry the cross.

In June Mother Duchesne and her assistant, Mother Shannon, who also retained the office of treasurer, were busy making up the expense accounts of the past six months, which were to be forwarded to the Mother House in July. Had Florissant ever sent in so good a record before? The house was not only out of debt, but also had on hand an almost incredible surplus, after having loaned one hundred and fifty dollars to St. Charles for the digging of a new well and the purchase of furniture. This improvement in financial conditions was due in part to the increase and stability of the enrollment in the boarding school, which Mother Duchesne attributed to Mother Shannon's influence, and Mother Shannon attributed to Mother Duchesne's prayers. The fate of the convent was still in the balance when Philippine sent the accounts to the Mother General with a brief letter on July 1:

The changes suggested for this house would come at a time when it is prospering better than ever before. We have more pupils in both schools than they had while Mother Thiéfry was here, and many others have applied. None of them will go elsewhere. I owe you this information . . . but *fiat*. Mother Penel is a very sick person. I am trying to nurse her, as well as our other two invalids, but I have reason to dread the coming winter. Who will care for them? . . . If only I could be completely hidden in a corner, so as not to be tempted to think about things that are really not my business! My recovery at Easter makes me fear I shall again have to face troubles and trials. I really am in no condition to nurse the sick and watch by them, to work in the garden, to give the morning call and make the night visit. But there is no one else to do these things. All are either too delicate or too busy.

In August death claimed an aspirant in St. Louis, Eliza Bosseron, who had been a child at Florissant. After the funeral Mothers Thiéfry and de Kersaint came for a short visit with Mother Duchesne, who had the joy of sending back with them another of her pupils, Mary Egan, who began her novitiate under the protection of the Immaculate Heart of Mary. New pupils were coming in at the end of the month—Louise and Adele Destrahan from Louisiana, sad children who had just recently lost their mother,[34] and *Mesdemoiselles* Keating, Lopez, Pitcher, Huff, Jane Pettigrew, and Ezelda Musick. Three of these were non-Catholics whom Mother Duchesne would have the happiness of seeing baptized in St. Ferdinand's Church. The pupils' vacation began on September 10, but the girls who had enrolled in August did not spend those three weeks in idleness. Had not the *Prospectus* stated that even this time of relaxation could be usefully employed? There were little outings planned for them, however, and they drove in groups to St. Charles with the nuns who had not yet seen the new brick convent there.

During the holidays Mother Duchesne found time to write to Josephine:

I received the letter you wrote me on my feast day [May 1], dearest Cousin. If it had reached me that day, it would have been my most precious *bouquet de fête*, as you have always been my most steadfast and beloved friend. Yes, when I commit faults that make me fear the divine justice, I can say what must touch the Heart of God: "What did I not sacrifice for you, my God?" Then the name of Josephine rises to my lips, as it is always in my heart. . . . Details about Sainte Marie always interest me. I thank God for keeping it a haven where He is glorified. . . . You know, my dear friend, that if we suffer from physical separation, our hearts and souls can find happiness in the assurance of one day being united again in a better world. What a joy it is to go back in thought over one's friendship with a person as rich in merits and good works as you are! . . .

During August I had the symptoms of an illness like the one last year, but now I am better, and I think I shall be able to care for our sick Sisters and help those who are teaching. As the number of our pupils has increased, I think that Divine Providence will give us the means to carry on the work. Really, I do not cling to life, for I am good for nothing in the service of either God or my neighbor. The heavenly country attracts my thoughts and draws my heart, but I am ever your grateful and faithful friend.[35]

The October enrollment was astonishing—twenty-four pupils in the boarding school! But the happiness of the community was overshadowed by a letter from the Mother General telling them not to count any longer on Mother Audé's return to America because of her broken health, and by the news of the death of Mother Xavier Murphy at Grand Coteau. "She was just forty-three years of age," Mother Duchesne wrote in her *Journal*, "and a violent fever carried her off in a few days." Within a week it had also claimed as a second victim Mother Rose Elder, who had nursed her with such loving care.

Winter came early to Florissant Valley, and the extreme cold brought Mother Penel so close to death that Extreme Unction was administered. The melancholy she had suffered from for several months now resulted in complete mental unbalance, a condition very depressing in so small a community. Under the pressure of circumstances the nuns were finding it more and more difficult to carry on their classes and housework and the duties of their religious life. The hired man, moreover, had given notice that he was leaving them. After prayer and consultation Mother Duchesne decided to try to purchase a Negro slave. Previous efforts she had made through the Fenwicks at Ste Genevieve had failed, so in December she turned to Father John Timon at the Vincentian seminary. He advised her to hire a reliable Negro woman rather than go into debt for a slave, and soon Mathilde was installed in the convent kitchen.

In a letter to Bishop Rosati at Christmas, Mother Duchesne expressed deep concern about Mother Penel's condition, and the year closed in depressing sadness. The *Miserere* was chanted on the Office tone after Mass. Benediction followed, at which a few voices tried to sing the *Magnificat*, for there were not enough nuns to attempt the *Te Deum*. A token kiss of peace was given in the evening without a conference, for so many in the household were ill. Short holidays gave a respite from classwork, and the children had just returned, when Philippine experienced once more the strengthening sympathy of Bishop Rosati's friendship. Through the snow and ice of a bitterly cold day he drove to Florissant to offer spiritual help. He visited Mother Penel, praying with her and for her, and consoled Mother Duchesne by his assurance that the devil had no part in the invalid's condition. "God heard the Bishop's prayers," wrote Philippine gratefully in her *Journal*. On January 15 lucidity returned and Mother Penel was able to receive absolution and Holy Communion. Just an hour later she expired. On the seventeenth, five Jesuit Fathers assisted at her funeral.

In February Mother Duchesne learned with satisfaction that Mother Aloysia Hardey had been named superior at St. Michael's and Mother Julie Bazire had gone to fill that office at Grand Coteau. On March 10 came news of the death of a very fervent and active religious, Sister Helen Mayette. That was the sixth of her Missouri religious to die in Louisiana and the realization of this fact was depressing, for Philippine had sent of her best religious to the Southern houses. However, a letter from St. Madeleine Sophie reached Florissant just at this time and afforded her consolation by the hope it held out of recruits from France and by the tenderness of its closing lines:

> What memories the months of November and December bring to my mind! Those happy days of long ago, gone forever! Now there is only the cross and naked detachment. It must be that way. . . . Adieu, dear Mother and beloved daughter. I am losing my hope of ever seeing you again, Philippine. . . . Adieu once more.[36]

2. 1837—1840

Through Him and with Him and in Him . . .
all honor and glory.

Liturgy of the Mass

IN THE BOARDING SCHOOL Philippine had the consolation of seeing the girls respond to Mother Boilvin's training. Although April began with "extraordinary cold and a fall of snow," the convent was aglow with joyous fervor when Jane Pettigrew was baptized and she and Ezelda Musick, another convert, received their first Holy Communion. These were American girls to whom Mother Duchesne could give little more than a smile, a few halting words of encouragement in English, and a festal goûter of pancakes and syrup, but her joy in them was great, for they had learned to know and love the Sacred Heart. Her regret at being unable to help actively in the apostolate with the children is reflected, along with her joy, in a letter of intimate self-revelation written to Josephine the day after the Communion ceremony:

Not long ago I received your December letter, my dearest Cousin. I am always so grateful for the proofs of your constant friendship, to which I make a glad and eager return. One thing displeases me in your expressions—they flatter me so much, and I am far from meriting them. Self is always with me, and in a double vocation which should lead me to sanctity, I cling to faults which many people of the world and in the world would have corrected in themselves. God sees to it that I expiate these faults. To be praised from afar and often blamed near at hand is a safeguard against vanity. This recalls to my mind St. Augustine's word about Plato: "What benefit is it to you, Plato, to be praised where you are not, if you burn where you are?"

It seems to me I have outlived myself. I see the time coming when I shall be good for almost nothing. As my health has taken on new vigor, that uselessness will be harder to bear after I have had so much to do. The children here all speak English; very few know French, and I cannot even teach religion to the two Negro women who work for us, nor to the little children in the free school, for although I can read English, as I know the meaning of the printed words, it is quite a different thing to understand it when it is spoken, or to speak it myself, because of the extreme difficulty of the pronunciation, which one can never master at my age.

Recently three more of our religious arrived in Louisiana from France, but none of them is coming to Missouri. They can scarcely replace the losses sustained by the house to which they were sent, where several excellent religious have died recently. Our part of the country is much more healthful. We have had very few deaths since 1819, when we first took possession of this convent of St. Ferdinand. The very first death here was in this year 1837, and the nun who died had come here from Louisiana in a critical condition. So I dread becoming a doting old lady in second childhood before death catches up with me.

In the meantime I shall have time to plant and tend our truck garden. They say we shall have small success this year, for the ground has been covered with snow three times since the beginning of this month, and nearly all the seed had been sown before that. I find in this quiet work one very great advantage—it brings such peace of soul, and this arises, no doubt, from contact with the beauty of nature, which lifts one up to the Creator.

The parish church here is contiguous to our convent. There was a ceremony of first Communion yesterday; two of our children who had been Protestants were among those who received their Saviour for the first time. The other two convents also have the consolation of making converts, and American converts make excellent Catholics. The people of the United States are quite remarkable for their care about external forms, their keenness of intellect, and their genius for science and art. It may be that from the Christian point of view they go much too far in their passion for knowledge, their personal ambition, and their desire for worldly success. Being so old-fashioned, I love simplicity all the more in contrast to the affectation of wealth and knowledge that I see at times. They tell me I could not recognize France today. Well, I can find real pleasure in the happy memories of our childhood.

If Father Rambaud, "the man of my peace," is still alive, tell him he will live forever in my grateful memory. That is a tribute I owe also to the Teisseires, though along quite different lines. They have always been so good to me and so generous. And what could I not say about Augustin, were he still alive! I share your loneliness in regard to him and trust that God was merciful to him in proportion to his charity.

I have not had answers to the last letters I wrote to my sisters, Mesdames de Mauduit and Jouve. I understand the latter is all alone. Look at the three of us—Amelie, Euphrosine, and me—each in different circumstances of detachment. There is not a single religious from France in the community here. But we meet at the same center—the Heart of God, whose Providence watches over us, whose arms uphold us. May He bless us! I am always your friend.[37]

By this time Philippine had learned that her niece, Josephine Jouve, had entered the Convent of Perpetual Adoration in Lyons. She waited, however, for her sister to tell her of this last great sacrifice—the fifth child she had given to the service of God. Then she wrote in loving sympathy and abounding joy to Madame Jouve. Tender and virile, the letter is a counterpart of its author:

I have just received your letter of March 16, my dearest Sister. The generous sentiments you express in it are very consoling to this sister of yours who loves you in a special way in God. But your loneliness and your sacrifices add to the tender affection which I have always felt for you and which can only increase as your trials are prolonged. If Abraham's oblation has been so highly praised, if God Himself rewarded it and praised it so nobly, what will He not do for you, who have offered five beloved children as victims to His grateful Heart? They were not undesirables in the family, led to the altar as good riddance for the household, in order the better to provide for children that were loved more tenderly. They were the loveliest ones, four of them your first fruits, like the offerings of Abel and Solomon. They were truly the chosen ones, the pride of the family, and they would have had a brilliant place in society, shed luster on their parents, married well. In every respect you gave the best to God in sacrifice.

If you are already receiving some part of the hundredfold in this world from the high esteem that people have for these children you gave to God, think what your joy in heaven will be when you see them all crowned in glory, blessing the hand that guided them and paying honor to their mother through the many souls who will accompany them and who shared in her guidance, as it were, and so walked in the way of salvation.

Do not fear that I love your daughter Josephine less than the others. God has created all the religious orders; He has privileged souls in all of them. Their paths may be different, but they lead to the same goal, where I trust we shall all meet. It is a joy for me to know that you can visit Josephine often and that you enjoyed Father Henri's stay in Lyons. When you see him again, tell him to pray for his godmother. His brethren in religion are increasing in the United States. They have three novitiates—one for Americans near the City of Congress [Washington, D. C.], a French one in Kentucky, and one made up chiefly of Flemings near St. Louis. The teaching, however, is done principally in English. In some districts of this country French, German, and more especially Spanish, are necessary, and it is not unusual to meet people who speak four languages. But that is not my case. All I have learned of the English language is to read it in print, to understand it in the simplest conversation, and to speak a very little bit.

You gave me consolation by telling me that Sainte Marie has been put once more to a good, useful, and religious work. After I heard it had been closed, I made a sketch of that dear house and wrote beneath the picture, "Sion weeps because no one attends the solemnities." Now I shall add the words, *"Tribus, tribus Domini . . ."* ("The people, the people of the Lord"). It is a joy for me to think that Madame de Rollin is also the originator of that good work. Thank her for me, for all that touches the glory of God is personal to me, and I rejoice in it as a personal gain. Do not forget to give my love to Madame de Mauduit. We are three old sisters. Our lifelong friendship will last forever, for God is the strongest tie that binds us to one another. . . .[38]

This letter had not reached France when Amelie Duchesne de Mauduit was stricken at Grâne and died of, a cerebral congestion. Many letters came to tell Philippine the news. Of her answers only the one to Josephine is extant:

I received your letter, dearest Cousin, telling me of the death of my dear sister Amelie. My brother was the first to send me the news, then Madame Jouve and her daughter Amelie. I sent answers to these letters and hope they have received them. I want to thank you very particularly for all the dear and edifying details you gave me about the death of this sister whom I esteemed so highly. I am sure her piety and good works have already gained for her the life of eternal happiness. I weep rather for us who remain "under the tents of Cedar," exposed in a thousand ways to losing the crown that is merited only by perseverance. Since death took our beloved Augustin and Scipion, Camille and Casimir, no loss has pained me so much as this one.[39] So many ties, natural and supernatural, united me to this dear sister, I cannot help thinking her death is a warning for me to prepare, and there is so much for me to do in order to assure a favorable judgment.

The author of the *Imitation* says that those who travel rarely sanctify themselves, and elsewhere, that change of residence deceives many. I had hoped to do out here something for the glory of God and the salvation of His children, and now I find myself with hands as empty—and perhaps not as clean—as when I was in my little cell on our Mountain of Love, Sainte Marie. . . . How glad I am that you, to whom I owed the first resurrection of our holy haven, have brought about a second, and not less glorious, one for strengthening the faith! What a joy for me, in this distant land of separation from my best friend, to learn that the voice of her charity—a voice unfailingly heard by God—rises continually from that happy refuge of childhood, to beg our common Father to shower His blessings upon her. I beg you to share the merit of these prayers with me and with Monsieur de Mauduit, whose condition is very sad.[40] I learned from Madame Jouve herself that she is living all alone, but she has the consolation of faith to sustain her, and our brother-in-law has not.

In the pleasant circle of our acquaintances around which you always take me in your letters, I did not see Casimir Perier's wife.[41] Some one wrote me that she bought an estate in the diocese of Meaux and had gone to live there. I am sure her virtues have increased with the years. Remember me to Madame Teisseire, whose messages touch me deeply; also to Augustin's wife and to my brother and his wife.

Your heart is asking, perhaps, about my health. I am well

enough, but Madame de Mauduit's death does not reassure me about living much longer. Madame Jouve thinks she had a cerebral fever. That illness often comes quite suddenly, so it warns me to be ready. If my kind Father Rambaud is still alive, offer him my humble respects.

Our little establishment supports itself and we have all the spiritual helps we need. Our Bishop is a man of outstanding worth. His seminary, two well-attended colleges, five or six convents for the education of girls, all combine to give great hope for the maintenance of the true religion. Several sects show animosity, but they cannot by threats and calumnies prevent the Catholic boarding schools from being filled with non-Catholic children. When I left St. Louis, it was the Protestant children who gave me the greatest proofs of affection. . . .

The severe judgments Philippine often passed on herself were in no way shared by those who lived with her at Florissant. It was during these years that they came to call her "the Francis of Assisi of the Society," as years before she had been called its "Xavier." In one way she considered herself less poor than in former days, for she could no longer claim the closet under the stairway as her living quarters. Mother Thiéfry had used the small room on the second floor which Philippine had been forced to occupy after several attacks of illness, and now she was obliged to accept this again. The community commented jokingly that she only camped there, for at first she scorned the little bedstead and put her mattress on the floor. Renewed illness, however, brought her to accept the service of the bed.

Her poverty was beautiful in the excess of its love, but her worn-out clothing was at times a sight to behold, and she would never have allowed her religious daughters to appear in the patched habit and veil that were her joy. Both naturally and supernaturally she was a lover of poverty, claiming that it was a matter of personal taste as well as a means of imitating the Poor Man of Nazareth. Perhaps the greatest suffering she endured in virtue of poverty was the bitter winter weather. Her letters and her *Journal* bear witness to the fact that in middle age and later life she was exceedingly sensitive to cold, yet she refused the luxury of a fire in her room, except when illness forced it upon her.

There were times when members of the community remonstrated with her for the severity of her mortification in the refectory. Stale bread and weak coffee for breakfast seemed to make fasting a year-round habit with her. But she had a ready answer: "Now what is that compared with the heroic acts of St. John of the Cross, St. Bruno, St. John Berchmans?" Sanctity was her goal; heroism, her model; and she would reach the heights, no matter what price she had to pay. Yet in her own eyes she was always walking the lower levels of the spiritual way.

Mother Margaret Cornelis described the remarkable activity of Mother Duchesne in this second Florissant period when she was approaching seventy years. She was always at work, and mending was a favorite occupation. When the household was asleep, she went noiselessly through the dormitories of both religious and children, examining shoes, stockings, clothing, carrying off what needed mending, making repairs at once or replacing articles with fresh ones—and all of this in the silence of the night. Only when her needle refused to thread easily would she seek out someone with good eyes who was still awake. The children, who slept soundly, could never understand by what mysterious providence the clothing they had left ripped or torn on their chairs at night was always intact when they put it on next morning.

She had a remarkable gift for nursing the sick, not just by caring intelligently for their physical ailments or disease, but by strengthening their souls through charity. She often brought her sewing and sat by the bedside, enlivening the long hours by her interesting and inspiring stories. Where the illness was grave, she refused to yield her place to anyone; and her services were bestowed not only on the religious and the children of the boarding school, but on Theotiste, the old Creole woman who acted as the convent commissionaire, on Mathilde, the Negro cook, and her frail little girl, on the wife of the hired man and on his children.

There is danger of underestimating the supernatural motive and value in all this charity, of taking it for granted that Philippine's character lent itself easily to this inexhaustible devotedness. As an actual fact her soul was frequently a battleground where human forces contended for the upper hand and grace triumphed only after a hard fight. She was a woman of positive tastes, strong likes and dislikes, intense affections, yet she embraced with her charity every soul that came within the ambit of her influence in her effort to be all things to them all and so lead them all nearer to the Sacred Heart of Christ. She loved Florissant with a kind of vehemence, loved its material poverty and inconvenience and solitude, its spiritual wealth under Jesuit direction. But she was often so weary that she could scarcely drag herself to the chapel for prayer or to the sacristy for work, so weak that she seemed more in need of nursing than those to whom she carried a cup of tea or a bowl of porridge. Only the strength of an indomitable will and the charity of Christ Himself urged her, upheld her, in the round of daily work and prayer.

The Country House (*Maison de Campagne*) at Florissant had, among other advantages in Philippine's eyes, that of offering hospitality to the religious from the City House in St. Louis. August and September brought Mothers and Sisters in small groups each year, some for their retreat, others for relaxation and a change of air, though there was really very little change. In August, 1837, Mother Duchesne made the acquaintance of some of the novices whom Mother Thiéfry brought for holidays at Florissant. Old friends came too, Mothers Hamilton, de Kersaint, Roche from St. Louis, Mothers Mathevon, O'Connor, McKay, and Guillot from St. Charles, and young Mother Mary Knapp, who was to join Mother Duchesne's community.

In the midst of these happy comings and goings the mail brought a letter from Mother Barat, who wrote from Rome on May 25:

> Your last letter reached me here in Rome, dear Philippine, and in spite of all my occupations I want to answer it at once. I see the cross is accompanying you to the very end of your life. Certainly you cannot do the amount of work you used to accomplish, but I know you do not give in to fatigue and your house gives glory to the Heart of Jesus. Why do you want to relinquish your cross voluntarily? Wait until we tell you to, and until then, do the best you can. I have given up the idea of transferring the novitiate to Florissant. Money would be needed to support that convent, and we have none. The postulants do not bring any with them—nor even the clothes they need.
>
> While awaiting the time when I can send an Assistant General to visit your section of America, this is what I have decided on: leave the novices in St. Louis under Mother de Kersaint. I think she will succeed with them. . . . You, dear Mother, remain at Florissant and sanctify yourself there. . . . We have lost our father and benefactor, Abbé Perreau. This will sadden you. He was deeply attached to you. Have a Requiem service for him. . . .
>
> Affectionate greetings to all, and you, dear Mother and old daughter of mine, be assured of my unalterable attachment in C.J. . . .

Philippine made an entry in her *Journal* like a litany of gratitude:

> Father Perreau was one of those who helped to decide our coming to America. He aided us from his own pocketbook and with funds he obtained for us from the Society for the Propagation of the Faith. He always remained an outstanding benefactor. . . . It was he who procured for us through Cardinals Litta and Fontana the approval and blessing of Pope Pius VII on our American Mission. He wrote us many very paternal letters. His gentle, humble manner, his whole life, which was so marked by simplicity, made him a living image of the Sacred Heart on earth.

The solemn Requiem service was held for Father Perreau on August 25. On the last day of the month the service was repeated for Father Charles Felix Van Quickenborne. He had returned from his Kickapoo mission in very poor health some months before this and had taken up the new duties assigned to him at Portage-des-Sioux, where he died on August 17, 1837, in his fiftieth year of age and his fourteenth year on the frontier. In his death Missouri lost one of its greatest pioneer missionaries, and Philippine lost a sterling friend in whose missionary ventures she had had a vital share through constant prayer.

New names, along with familiar ones, were being entered in the *Journal* now, as new pastors came to the Church of St. Ferdinand and new missionaries took up their residence at the Florissant novitiate. Fathers Paillasson and Van Assche were old friends, but Fathers Gleizal, Helias, and De Vos were new.[42] More interesting, however, were the visits of Father Christian Hoecken, after whose name Philippine wrote words that thrilled her soul: Indian missionary.[43] An even greater thrill came the day she said *au revoir* to Father Aelen and his companions as they set out for the Potawatomi encampment.[44] And it was more truly *au revoir* than anyone could foresee. But Philippine enjoyed most of all the little visits paid by Father Peter Verhaegen, now superior of the Missouri Mission, who took up residence at the Florissant novitiate in the autumn of 1837, and Father De Smet, who had returned recently from a begging trip in Flanders.

The crowning visit of that year, however, was an unexpected pleasure, when Bishop Rosati brought to Florissant the prelate whom Philippine had so longed to meet in 1834—Bishop Simon Bruté of Vincennes. At last she met the churchman of whom she had heard so much, and particularly that he greatly resembled

Father Louis Barat "in learning and spirituality." In her *Journal* she made no comment about him, because she was so concerned about other things, especially the servant problem.

Father Timon had advised against the purchase of a Negro slave, for prices were just then exorbitant. He had, instead, directed her to hire a trusty servant from a Catholic slave-owner in the vicinity of Florissant. That arrangement had worked well for a time, but at the beginning of winter the owner had withdrawn the woman and there was no one to tend the cows and cook the meals but Mother Shannon, who had as a helper "the Lynch girl, an orphan to whom we have given a home." Happily Mathilde, the reliable and efficient Negro woman, returned to work at the convent soon, bringing along her little eight-year-old girl.

A letter from Mother Barat, intended as an encouragement to Philippine, seems also to have added to her anxiety. The Superior General had written on July 20, 1837:

> I received your last letters, my good, my very dear Mother and daughter, and they grieved me. You have your troubles and I share them with you. My intimate affection for you has never diminished; neither time nor distance can lessen it. On the contrary, it has gone on increasing. Your zeal, your long years of labor for the Society in America have doubled it, for I am always mindful of all you have done and endured. I wish I were able to accede to your wishes and procure for you the rest you have so much right to expect from our affection and also from our gratitude. But please realize the position I am in. I cannot find superiors for the houses in France and other countries. Mother Audé cannot return to America. Who, then, can I find to take your place? You know well that I wanted to close Florissant and so help the other houses, but you yourself gave me good reasons for preserving that establishment whose solitude makes it so suitable for a novitiate. Just as soon as I can send a Mistress of Novices and provide a regular income for that house, you will be free from the office of superior, and what would hinder you from coming back to finish out your life in France? At least we could see each other once more. We shall provide for all that in our next General Council. Meanwhile pray for us. Cholera is at the gates of Rome and we cannot leave here. We trust our Lady to protect the city. Adieu, dear Philippine. Be assured of the unchanging love with which I am all yours in C.J.M. . . .

Mother Duchesne had wanted to talk confidentially with Bishop Rosati when he paid his visit in November, but that had been impossible, so on December 14, 1837, she wrote to him, exposing the matters of conscience that were disturbing her:

> I am lacking in the zeal that would help me carry my little burden generously, and God allows it to weigh more heavily as I grow older, and draw nearer to judgment. All the scruples I have ever had with regard to obedience and poverty seemed to pile up in my mind one night when I realized that I may soon have to render an account of my stewardship. The things that worry me most are contributions I have made without the permission of our Superior General. When at times I have tried to explain these things to her, either she paid no attention to what I wrote or her answers were so vague I could not decide whether I was acting in agreement with or contrary to her intentions. I said to myself: "Charity is the first, the highest law," yet in the depths of my soul I heard the words: "Obedience is better than sacrifice."

The Bishop's reply was calming, reassuring, and Mother Duchesne thanked him in her usual gracious manner, then added a paragraph that showed new anxieties of quite a different kind:

> Yes, Mrs. Pitcher, who died in a steamboat disaster, left her orphan daughter in poverty. We are happy to give her a home. And we fear the same fate has overtaken Mr. James Brown of Galena, whose daughter is also in our boarding school. We have had no news of him since he set out on a dangerous trip. Mr. Walsh, with whom he told us to communicate, has not been able to learn anything about him. If you get any news about him through newspapers or other sources, I hope that in your fatherly kindness you will let us know.[45]

The plight of these orphaned children, along with letters from France, brought memories crowding in on her and calling for some outlet, so she wrote to Josephine: [46]

> It seems like a very long time since I had a letter from you, my dearest Cousin. Perhaps I feel it so much because I never longed so eagerly for one. The reason for this is easy to understand. A letter telling me of trials in the Lebrument family speaks also of your sorrow at similar trials that have come to your nephews. How could I know that you and those dear to you are suffering, and not feel this myself, and not long to know from you yourself the true condition of things, and whether the Divine Goodness has not poured healing balm on your wounds to lessen the pain or heal them completely. Do not put off writing to me of your anxie-

ties, dear Cousin. You know, of course, that I cannot remove them, but I can share them. I can unite my prayers to yours in order to obtain the grace that better and more desirable gifts may replace those that the fickleness of fortune so easily snatches away.

A French book I am reading just now strengthens that hope in my soul. It proves that our country [France] is in a better condition now than before that terrible revolution you and I saw enacted. The author claims that finer buildings have risen from the ruins of the old ones; that zeal has doubled the number of religious, as well as generally useful, institutions; that piety and generosity respond immediately to the mere proposal of good works. One of our bishops, on a begging tour recently for his diocese, corroborated these statements when visiting us—he spoke with great admiration.

When you give me the pleasure of hearing from you again, do not fail to tell me about Mesdames Augustin and Casimir Perier, Teisseire, Jouve, and about Duchesne and his wife. Since Madame Barat and the other religious whom I knew in France no longer reside regularly in Paris, I hear very little from them. As the Society spreads and the older members die, we in America must seem like people who lived in ancient history. I am something of an antique myself. I am really ashamed of it, and I have no desire to be considered an Egyptian mummy.

In this country, where everything is new and where luxury and soft living are indulged in to a disgusting excess, I find delight in recalling the simple pleasures of our childhood: our modesty in dress, the good times we had at the convent, eating salad with our fingers, the two of us with a single plate between us and sitting on the same seat beside the fire—all of which moved dear Sister Colombe to tears. She used to say: "How those two children love each other!" I always think of Augustin reading the lives of the saints with me, and Scipion dogging my footsteps one Eve of All Saints to get out of eating his breakfast, and Casimir and Camille trying to teach me arithmetic. Those happy evenings in Grandmother's house; the simple but charming dinners on Sunday— and those on Monday; the presents given out gradually to each of the younger children. All this comes to my mind. Those happy days in the big family were surely preferable to the proud disdain, the indifference, the affected languor, by which people think they make themselves important and attractive. I continue to live in the same convent—a peaceful retreat suited to my age and tastes. My thoughts are often with you and about you, for you are so dear to my heart.

There was joy in the Florissant community at Easter when Mother Boilvin received permission for probation and final vows. There was sorrow at the end of May when Mathilde's little girl fell ill and died. The child had been baptized and was being prepared for her first Communion in view, one would suspect, of her delicate health. She was buried from St. Ferdinand's Church, and four of the pupils carried the little coffin to the cemetery.

A sentence in a letter from Mother Barat just recently received had set Philippine to wondering, hoping, praying hopefully, but with resignation: "I have a plan in mind, and I shall share it with you when I have matured it in prayer." [47] But she referred to it only indirectly when she wrote to the Superior General on July 2, 1838:

> As for myself, I am ready for whatever you may decide. I long for retirement and rest, and I have no hope of finding them in this life. I should not, however, want an inactivity that would expose me to the danger of napping all day long. But everything seems to point to the fact that there is no sweet retreat ahead of me. Wherever I have been, external and distracting work has been my lot and still is, though I am about to begin my seventieth year. There is no one else here to give the morning call, make the last visit at night, care for the garden, watch by the sick, or take care of the pantry, the linen room, etc. I cannot teach an English class or survey the study periods of English-speaking children, so the material employments fall to me. The other religious are really exhausted by their work, for the enrollment changes continually and makes it very difficult to teach the pupils in class groups. . . .

Then "thinking it might give you pleasure to know the present condition of our diocese," she launches into a lengthy paragraph of statistics worthy of, and perhaps drawn directly from, the *Catholic Almanac*. It was the kind of information she reveled in, but she checked her pen suddenly with the words: "I must bring this letter to a close regretfully, dearly revered Mother. An opportunity to send it to St. Louis is at hand. My regards to kind Fathers Louis and Joseph, to Mothers Desmarquest, de Gramont, and finally, to everybody." So hurriedly did she finish that letter, she had no time to call herself "wretched" or "unworthy" or anything else but "Yours in C.J., Ph. Duchesne, r.S.C."

The feast of the Assumption was celebrated with more than usual pomp that year, for the College Choir from St. Louis University came to sing the solemn High Mass and to furnish the music for the procession planned for the late afternoon. All went well enough at the Mass, and the twenty choir members were having breakfast at the convent when Bishop Rosati and Father Elet arrived unexpectedly. Provisions had by this time run low and the dinner served to the Bishop and his companion "suffered sadly, to our great confusion," according to the *Journal*. Fortunately the choir was invited to the novitiate for dinner, so the nuns were spared further embarrassment. Perhaps it was the strain of this unusual hospitality that discouraged Mathilde, the Negro cook. At any rate she left for a second time and "there is no one to take her place," noted Mother Duchesne pathetically.

While taking extra work upon herself, she was determined to give Mother Boilvin a lighter schedule during the weeks that immediately preceded final profession. On the outer, unused page of a letter addressed to herself, Philippine wrote her a little undated note to this effect:

> DEAREST SISTER,
>
> Would that I had the zeal and unction of your good Father to express to you my desires and sentiments at the approach of the holy ceremony at which you will contract your sweet, and I trust your eternal, alliance. Just one month, and the happy day will be here. We shall try to give you more time to yourself, more time for prayer and acts of humility and recollection. It is in the calm of solitude that your Beloved wishes to speak to you of His love, of the conditions of this alliance, of the graces it will draw down upon you, of the ornaments in which you should present yourself to Him. We are meditating today on these ornaments: the cross, the thorns, the binding cords—these are the jewels of Calvary and of the altar that will witness your vows.[48] Have courage! Others have worn them before us and have seen them changed into treasures immortal and incomprehensible in their grandeur. In C.J.,
>
>   PHIL.

It was time to arrange with the Bishop about the profession ceremony. He had been absent from the city for some days, so when Mother Duchesne heard of his return she wrote:

> May I beg you to tell me whether you can come to receive Mother Boilvin's vows, or shall we postpone the ceremony, or will you send someone else to take your place? I hope the carriage will not be too uncomfortable. Please order one of the nicest—one with

two horses. I am happy to be able to pay the expense. I hope Father Lutz will accompany you. I am in a great hurry. . . .

The Bishop's answer brought disappointment, but not delay. He wrote on September 7:

> I cannot be present at Mother Gonzague's profession, for I must leave tomorrow to assist at the consecration of Monseigneur Miles, Bishop-elect of Nashville, which will take place at Bardstown, Kentucky, on the ninth of this month.[49] I shall return in two or three weeks. . . .

The Bishop delegated Father Van Assche to represent him at the ceremony, which took place on September 30, six days after Adeline Gonzague Boilvin completed her twenty-fifth year. Mother Duchesne noted lovingly some of the details:

> At half-past seven the ceremony began, the solemn High Mass being sung by the Jesuit novices. Father Van Assche asked the questions in the ceremonial and blessed the cross and ring, wearing the cope; then he offered the Mass with deacon and subdeacon and before Communion received the vows of our dear Sister. After the Gospel Father Gleizal gave an appropriate little discourse. He offered a low Mass of thanksgiving, after which the Jesuit novices sang the *Te Deum* and the Blessed Sacrament was exposed until after Vespers.

A short note to her sister Euphrosine shows Philippine as she felt and described herself a few days after the ceremony:

> . . . I have not had a letter from you since the one you wrote after Amelie's death, but my brother has given me news of you since then, and so has Madame de Rollin. If you want some news about me I shall tell you that going into my 70th year I feel the infirmities of that age: I cough and totter and fall, and the thought of death is always with me. So many of our family who were younger and stronger than I have died. Join your prayers to mine; ask your dear daughters to pray for me; ask prayers at the shrine of Our Lady of Fourvière. On my side I promise you frequent remembrance before God. Love, family ties, religion, all inspire my prayer. . . .[50]

The tone of depression so evident in this paragraph runs through some entries in the *Journal* as winter came on—a hard winter indeed. Even the children were at times so intractable under the hand of their mistress general, Mother Boilvin, that there were no ribbons merited at the distribution of prizes before they took their New Year's holiday. Perhaps the most moving entry in the whole *Journal* is the one that opens the account of 1839:

> We have no servants at all, so we could scarcely find time to gather in the community for New Year's greetings. The one who could help us refuses to do so. We hired a young Negro girl, but she is just added trouble. She is not honest and has to be watched continually. So we are obliged to have our night recreation in the kitchen in order that she will not be alone with the orphan to whom we give a home. So side by side with them, in the midst of the noise of dishwashing and kitchen arrangements, with the wind sweeping in on all sides, we renewed our sacrifice as we remembered the evenings in France.

In the little group of nuns there was only one who "remembered the evenings in France," but she gave no hint of depression when she wrote to her sister in February. On the contrary, she seems to have been reacting deliberately against such feelings in the hope of cheering her lonely sister, whom she addresses not only as "My dear Sister," but also as "my loving Friend," clinging to the old form she had used with Euphrosine for more than thirty years:

> It seems to me that since we have lost so many members of our beloved family who have been taken from us by death, you are becoming doubly dear to me. But another idea comes still more forcibly to my mind. It is this: we are united by the same principles, and this makes us one in joy and sorrow. I share with the liveliest interest the consolations you have had in the children whom you have so generously offered to God. I have had the opportunity of hearing high praise given to the two who are in our Society, and the one who went to heaven is our protectress. Your son Henri, my godson, will enrich both his own crown and yours by drawing souls to God, and perhaps he is destined to bring back to his way of thinking the members of his family who have strayed from the right path. Remember me to him, and also to your daughter Josephine, who is your neighbor and your joy.
>
> I received the letter in which you remarked on how long mine was delayed. That always happens when we give them to people who are traveling, so I shall use the mail more frequently, as that is the safest and speediest way. Thank you a thousand times for the very useful gift you are sending me. I have not received it yet, but you put it in very good hands. We hope to receive one

or two more religious from France soon. I think they will take charge of everything that is being sent to us.

You are the last member of the family who has given me any news. Madame de Rollin writes from time to time, but in her last letter she complained of ill health, which caused me sorrow, for she is supporting so many good works. What astonishing changes have taken place in her family and ours! What a scattering of dear ones, and how many have died!

Religion is making progress in the United States, either through the labor of missionaries or through the immigration of large numbers of German and Irish Catholics, who keep their zeal for the faith. Twenty churches are being built this year in this diocese alone, and last year there were eight new ones. Some priests came recently from Lyons and Besançon, and two American priests returned from the college of the *Propaganda* in Rome, where they had obtained places to make their studies.[51] The Lazarists have also received some more priests. Pray for all our missions, and especially for me. I do not do much in this world, and I do still less that is of value for the next. Embrace your dear daughter for me and think of Philippine as your most steadfast friend.

The bitter winter weather continued into March, with biting wind and heavy snowfalls. The convent seemed more remote and solitary than ever, but there was plenty of activity within its walls and Mother Duchesne took a generous share in the labor. There were times, however, when she found time to write long letters, as one to Josephine on March 17 shows:

I was finding the time very long since your last letter, my dearest Cousin, when, among several that came in the mail, I recognized your handwriting. What joy that gave me! I am always so grateful to you for telling me about that dear childhood home of ours, where the shower of heavenly favors first began to fall upon us. All was sunshine for us then; but stormy days followed—the Revolution, the loss of so much we loved. Old age and infirmities have changed the outward aspect of our life, but not the Heart of Him whom we took as our model and whom we have followed. He warned us that this would mean carrying His cross, and He promised unending happiness in return for our struggles and sufferings. So we can always live in His friendship if only we accept His conditions. Yet I beg this good Master to soften for you all the pain and hardship that old age brings. May these words of Scripture be fulfilled: "God will deliver from evil days those who have been responsive to the needs of the poor and miserable." Your whole life has been spent in caring for the poor; your activity and your wealth have relieved their wants. How many priests you sought and obtained freedom for! Continuing the same passage, or at least its sense: "The Lord has promised to soften the bed on which you will lie in the day of suffering." It is very sweet to have friends near you in illness or sorrow. But what more lovable or more powerful friend could we have than the One who has all power over the soul and its frail wrapping, which is the body?

As for myself, I am really healthier than I like. During recent years I have often thought I should die soon. Now I fear I shall live to be a hundred—as there is no prospect of death in the near future. I am troubled at the prospect of the infirmities and uselessness of old age. However, I am not there yet. The lack of hired servants leaves me plenty to do. In this land of liberty it is very difficult, especially for us, to get help. Often an almost worthless Negro slave costs three or four thousand francs; and he must be supported. Frequently they are more difficult to manage than white servants in France. Besides that, they are subject to so many vices, we can scarcely take the responsibility for them. Just now we have a good German workman with whom we are well pleased. As he knows very little English, he will not be so quickly spoiled. As to the orphans to whom we have given a home, they are not so easy to manage as yours, and they require continual surveillance.

You gave me much pleasure in telling me about my old friends. Express my sincere gratitude very specially to Father Rambaud. How I wish I had turned his good advice to better account. I often recall his helpful words, and I unite my prayers to his, whether he is still on earth or is already enjoying his eternal reward.

At present we have in St. Louis the Bishop of Dubuque, a new city in Wisconsin Territory, fairly close to the Great Lakes and north of our state. This worthy prelate is from Lyons.[52] He was unable to take up residence in Dubuque during the winter because of the severe cold, so he remained as a missionary in St. Louis. Our own Bishop, who is as active in good works as his father and founder, St. Vincent de Paul, is going to hold a synod for the good of the diocese after Easter. With the exception of the diocese of Baltimore, our diocese has more priests than any other in the United States. With the cooperation of the Lazarists and the Jesuits the Bishop will, undoubtedly, form some new parishes soon, as he expects to build twenty new churches in the diocese this year. The church in Jefferson [City], the capital of the state, will be very beautiful, owing to the generosity of the Irish who have settled there.

During the summer of 1839, Mother Duchesne decided to improve the Florissant convent by the addition of a brick refectory and kitchen. The experiences of the past winter had proved that the old wooden building was no longer fit for use. Going to St. Louis in July to consult Mr. Hugh O'Neil about the work, she had an opportunity to inspect the new building erected by Mother Thiéfry for the boarding school. The increased enrollment and the desire for adequate accommodations for the novices had made this addition a necessity. Work on the Florissant project began on September 1. "It will give us a brick refectory and larger living quarters for the hired man," Mother Duchesne noted in the *Journal*. It had called for a good deal of courage on her part to undertake the work, for it meant borrowing some money, a thing she always dreaded, but she had Mother Shannon to rely on and that was a comfort to her. Satisfaction at the outcome of the undertaking is evident in the *Journal* entry three months later: "We are delighted with our new brick refectory, but [she adds ruefully] we have had to build a wooden house for the hired man, who has brought his family from Germany. One room was not enough for them, and we had the children on top of us."

While the Religious of the Sacred Heart in America were carrying on their laborious apostolate, some in prosperity, some in poverty, all in the joy of a life wholly dedicated to God, there was a struggle facing the Society in Europe that had no counterpart in the remote missions of the Mississippi Valley, yet its repercussions were to be felt throughout the entire order. In a circular letter from Paris in December, 1838, the Superior General announced that a general council would be convoked in the following year. The French capital was disturbed and revolution threatened, so Mother Barat chose Rome for the meeting place. Reaching there in April, 1839, she convoked the council to meet on June 1. Nine out of the twelve members composing the deliberative body were able to be present, among them Reverend Mothers Desmarquest, de Charbonnel, and Audé, the Assistants General, and Mothers de Limminghe, d'Olivier, and Maillucheau, old friends of Mother Duchesne. Mother Elizabeth Galitzin's office of secretary allowed her to take part in the deliberations. These religious were truly *one heart*, but they were not *one mind*, for some of them were too deeply imbued with the idea that there was need for sweeping changes in the organization of the order. Admiration for the Society of Jesus had engendered in them a desire to imitate its manner of life, while the Mother Foundress wished her daughters to be themselves, "to lead their own characteristic life, without the artificiality and constraint of trying to be something which was not their very self." [53] Two subjects were proposed as the principal matter for discussion: the modification of the fourth section of the *Constitutions*, which deals with the mode of government, and the choice of a fixed place of residence for the Superior General. The first motion was to relieve the Superior General of a portion of her burden by dividing the Society into provinces to be governed by Mothers Provincial, whose duty it would be to visit and direct the convents under their authority, but subject to the control of the Superior General. Together with the Assistants General the Provincials were to form the council that would aid the Mother General by advice and cooperation. Corresponding as it did to similar statutes in the Jesuit rule, this arrangement was unanimously approved. Twenty years before this Mother Barat had delegated the powers of a Provincial to Philippine Duchesne.

This was but the beginning of changes, however. Within a month the "reformers," led by Mothers de Limminghe and Galitzin, had brought about forty-six other changes in the *Constitutions*, all directed toward a closer resemblance to the Ignatian ideal. Most important of all was the decision which removed the seat of government in the Society from Paris to Rome, and it was this point that later on excited the most opposition. In the elections which closed the council Mothers de Charbonnel, Desmarquest, de Limminghe, and Galitzin were chosen Assistants General, the last named retaining the post of secretary general. Mother Thérèse Maillucheau was named visitatrix of the American convents and prepared at once to set out on the voyage, but for some undisclosed reason this nomination was canceled and she returned to France.

Late in November Mother Duchesne received a letter from her dear Mother Thérèse, telling of the appointment and of her keen sorrow at having to sacrifice the chance to see her loved friend again. The *Journal* entry is terse: "Mother Thérèse was all ready to set out for America, coming to visit the Convents of the Sacred Heart, but her destination was changed. She is returning to Nantes to inaugurate there the novitiate for the Province of the west of France. Our Society has been divided into provinces since the council." This seems to have been the first news Mother Duchesne received about the Sixth General Council's activities. Mother Barat informed the Society in November, 1839, of the changes initiated in the meetings and of the three-year trial to which they would be submitted. Her letter showed apprehension with regard to the wisdom and utility of the changes, but also the sincere humility with which she had bowed to her councilors.

In the American houses the new decrees were accepted, in as far as they were understood, and the good will to put them into execution abounded everywhere. The adoption of the Jesuit rule does not seem to have entered into the consideration of the religious in the Mississippi Valley as seriously as was intended by the councilors who drew up the decrees. Strangely enough there is not the least mention of them in Mother Duchesne's *Journal*. She records, however, the transfer of Mother Shannon to the City House in St. Louis early in 1840 and the arrival of Mother Anne Josephine Egan and Sister Catherine Campbell at Florissant. Then came the news that Bishop Rosati was leaving for Rome after the Fourth Provincial Council of Baltimore, which was to convene on May 17. Father Peter Verhaegen, S.J., was appointed Vicar-General of the diocese, and Father James Fontbonne, secretary, to replace Father Joseph Lutz, who was accompanying the Bishop to Baltimore and to Europe.

There is no estimating the sacrifice which the Bishop's departure exacted of Mother Duchesne. For nearly fifteen years he had been, quite literally, her best friend in America, a friend in the highest, finest sense of that beautiful word. She had been at ease with him; she had relied on him; she had turned to him in any need; and he had never failed her trust. He had understood her when so many others had not. Now he was going out of her life, though she did not know how true her premonition of this fact was. He came to pay a farewell visit and she gave him a letter for Mother Barat—of all her American letters the one written in the most careful and beautiful penmanship:

> I envy the good fortune of our venerable Bishop, Monseigneur Rosati, who hopes to see you in Rome. We are very much afraid his health may oblige him to remain in his native land. In that case our diocese would sustain a great loss. It is simply marvelous to see the remarkable changes brought about through his indefatigable zeal. God has visibly blessed his apostolic labors, and more especially his great piety and the charity that makes him a worthy follower of St. Vincent de Paul.
>
> We are eagerly awaiting the arrival of our Provincial, but if you are very hard pressed to give her some recruits for us, we can get along as we are. Mother Thiéfry was quite upset by your

reprimand and sent us an excellent Sister. With her help all can run smoothly in our little convent, even if God should call me from it. I would not leave a vacancy. Mother Gonzague Boilvin, though quite young, has natural talents like Mother Bigeu's for governing a house. She resembles her in other ways, and also Mother Eugenie, her former teacher. She would have as helpers two young choir religious, former pupils of ours, who speak both languages, and so does the religious in charge of the free school. That school can never be very numerous here. Even the free school in St. Louis has diminished. Mother Thiéfry is suggesting changes that would take Sister Catherine Lamarre away from here. That dear old Sister is now quite infirm. She has confided to me that she longs to finish her days here, where she can still find some scope for her zeal by teaching the free school children who speak French. As there is only one professed in this community besides myself, I have neither assistant nor admonitrix.

The City House in St. Louis seems to have a greater financial burden than it can meet. The enrollment in the academy has diminished; many postulants bring nothing with them when they enter—not even enough clothing; and more than fifty orphans have been accepted. When Mother Thiéfry asked my opinion with regard to postulants, I replied that it was imprudent to accept more than she can conveniently support. . . . The young women who have been our pupils will always make the best teachers and will be the most constant in their vocation. . . .

Before his departure Monseigneur blessed the little cemetery we had marked off. It will serve for the convents of both St. Louis and St. Ferdinand. Mother Thiéfry will have the bodies of our religious who are buried in St. Louis transferred here, as a street is to be cut through the convent cemetery in town. As for ourselves, no one in the community has died except Mother Penel, who was sent here from Louisiana. She was really on her way back to her family in France; but when she reached here, she was too ill to continue the journey. She is buried in the parish cemetery.

My dear Mother, my venerated Mother, accept the grateful expressions of a heart that realizes all its owes to you. The thought of death is ever before me, but it will not be as easy a passage as it would be if I had always occupied the lowest place in this holy house.[54]

The thought of death that so frequently finds expression in Philippine's letters was no obsession in her mind, nor did it make any practical difference in her activity. She was as laborious and industrious as her increasing physical infirmities would allow. She still reduced food and rest to the minimum for herself, still tried to do the hardest work, to give the most hidden devotedness. She seems never to have been disappointed with herself in a sensitive and personal way. She gauged her incapacity as she saw it and was not surprised at small success, but she had a constant dread lest God had been known, loved, and served less well because of her. Perhaps the gulf between the ideal and the actual depressed her sorely. Cut off, for the most part, from the apostolate she had envisioned, by the insurmountable language difficulty on the American frontier, she might have grown impatient with the vicissitudes that plagued her missionary career.

Yet the evidence all tends the other way. God had been working so secretly, so subtly in her soul that she had no perception of what His grace was accomplishing. Union with Him in prayer and love had developed in her a humility so great that it seemed to hamper her external work. In order that she might reflect in her life the passion of the Sacred Heart of Christ, her achievement had to be as secret, as obscure as His on Calvary. The apostle can never accomplish real good without suffering, and that in proportion to the good he does, to his share in the redemptive work of Christ. So it was with Philippine Duchesne.

Sometimes she steadied her will by rereading letters she had received from France and copied into her thick, heavily bound notebooks. One from Father Varin in the early weeks of 1840 was like a handclasp across the sea. He, too, was thinking of death, and like her he was in his seventy-first year when he wrote:

MY DEAR MOTHER AND ALWAYS MY DEAR DAUGHTER IN OUR LORD:

It shall not be said of me that I left this world without sending you a reassurance of the sentiments which I feel toward you. Long years ago, almost from your very entrance into the Society, I foresaw that the Divine Master would call you to labor in distant lands beyond the sea, to spread the knowledge and love of His Sacred Heart. Happily His will in your regard has been accomplished, and you have been an instrument of His mercy in those remote lands. *Courage* and *Confidence* to the very end! What a consolation it will be for you, when the Divine Master calls you to Himself, to leave behind you a large community which will continue with loving ardor the work for which you sacrificed your liberty, your rest, your life! [55]

As he wrote these lines, Father Varin knew of circumstances that would soon put to the test all the courage and confidence Philippine had stored up through the years. In the spring of 1840 the Superior General announced her choice of Reverend Mother Elizabeth Galitzin to act as Provincial and Visitatrix of the convents of the Sacred Heart in the Mississippi Valley, and to explain the new decrees and insure their proper application. She knew her secretary well, knew her ardor for foreign missions and her remarkable physical energy. She also knew her autocratic nature, her dogmatic vehemence, her close approach to despotic intransigence which Monsignor Baunard has described as *gouvernement à la Russe*.[56] In a letter to the American convents St. Madeleine Sophie prepared her religious for the arrival of her delegate, and on September 1 the Mother Visitatrix and her companions reached New York after a transatlantic passage of forty-five days. Traveling west over the Cumberland Road by stagecoach and down the Ohio River by steamboat, Mother Galitzin reached St. Louis about three weeks later.

She was a conscientious and thorough visitor, whose vigilance nothing escaped. Wherever she went, she noted the needs of sacristy and infirmary, parlor and pantry, school and community. Efficiency characterized her work, but sympathy was often lacking. Externals were carefully regulated, while sensitive souls quivered under the scrutiny of the Provincial. Perhaps the keenest sufferer was Philippine Duchesne, but the visitation began for her with joy. Going to St. Louis to greet the Mother Provincial on September 24, she knelt to kiss the hand of the representative of highest authority in the Society and to beg with all the old fire and impetuosity for release from her position as superior. Mother Galitzin was prepared for this request and granted it immediately in the name of Mother Barat. But when approached on the subject of an Indian mission, she gave an evasive answer which Philippine knew how to interpret, for on September 30 she wrote to the Superior General:

My reverend and beloved Mother,

We are rejoicing at last in the happiness of seeing your representative in the New World. We owe you a deep debt of gratitude for the sacrifice you have made in our favor of a religious who was so helpful to you. I beg God to bless this sacrifice and pour consolation into your heart by reason of the good a person of such great talent can accomplish in our houses for the glory of the Divine Heart of Jesus.

On my side I thank you most sincerely for having at last lifted the burden I have carried so inefficiently, a burden that would have been such a trial in my last hours. I desire death and I fear it. But God, who is so good, will give me the means of expiating my faults, for I realize quite clearly that crosses will follow me, though of quite another kind—if only that of changing from a very busy life to one of almost complete inactivity.

There is no hope of our going to the savages just now. Nothing has been prepared for such a mission. But besides that, I have perceived that whenever I have expressed my desires and my regrets on that subject, I have been judged unfit for the work. And even if there were only my age against me, that would be reason enough for a negative answer. I pray earnestly to God for interior spirit, and I have much to do to acquire it. . . .

Before returning to Florissant to gather together her precious notebooks and old letters, a few books, and some other personal belongings, as well as her scant supply of worn and mended clothing, Philippine wrote to Mother Louise de Vidaud, from whom she had received a letter when Mother Galitzin reached St. Louis. Thoughts of Sainte Marie came crowding in upon her as she began to write on October 1:

Your six years' silence has not kept me from thinking of you, my dearest Mother. Memories of France, and above all of Grenoble, are too much with me ever to let me forget you. However, it is less to the land of my birth and of my family that I cling than to memories of God's mercies in my regard, the marked protection of St. Regis, and the excellent religious who were trained on that holy mountain and who now work in all parts of France and in Italy for the glory of the Sacred Heart. I recognize the same love for our holy sanctuary of Ste Marie in all the religious who lived there and from whom I sometimes receive news.

Our house of St. Ferdinand has also received special favors from its patron, just as Grenoble did. Before sailing for America, we consecrated our new mission to him and he has been our refuge in all our needs. A beautiful picture of this charitable saint was given to us and so we were able to erect a shrine in our chapel, which opens onto the parish church of St. Ferdinand, who is also its secondary patron. That church was served for two years by a Jesuit who had resided in the house at *La Louvesc*, and he is still inspired by that holy place and always speaks of the saint in the most enthusiastic tones.[57]

I was greatly consoled by the details you gave me of all the good works carried on at Avignon. We are far from seeing so much fervor here; it will take many years to develop it. . . . I never forget your dreams of our going to martyrdom together or your delight in the procession of virgins *"who follow the Lamb wheresoever He goes."*

At present I cannot tell you to what community I belong. A week ago I came here from St. Ferdinand to see Mother Galitzin and her seven companions. They are all well. The foundation in New York will not be made until next spring. Reverend Mother will spend the winter in Louisiana and so avoid the severe cold of Missouri. The Jesuits have opened several Indian missions in this part of the world and are already having some success. . . . I beg the prayers of all my Sisters for my old age.

A few days later Mother Duchesne drove from Florissant to the City House and took her place, without distinction except that of seniority in profession, in the ranks of the community among the Mothers and Sisters who had for so many years looked to her as the representative of the foundress herself in the American convents of the Society. With the entry of this little trip Philippine ended the *Journal* she had kept so faithfully for twenty-two years.

twelve

Among the Potawatomi

1840—1842

Thy Kingdom come, Thy Will be done . . .
Liturgy of the Mass

IN THE INFIRMARY AT THE CITY HOUSE Mother Duchesne lay critically ill. The malady had been difficult to diagnose. Beginning with anguish of mind and heart and nervous depression which her strong will could not control, it had developed into a high fever accompanied by pain throughout her entire body. Her limbs were swollen; her breathing was labored; her pulse, uneven. The doctors ordered remedies of many kinds, chiefly mustard plasters. They dared not bleed the patient again, lest life itself be drained from her body.

Mother Shannon kept watch in the sickroom, yielding her place at times to her sister Judith or to Mother Regis Hamilton. They had not much faith in the efficacy of plasters to relieve the patient. They knew no amount of medication could draw the pain from her heart. Nor were they able to do so by their loving care and deep compassion. It would take time and the healing balm of grace from the Sacred Heart to supply the resignation, abandonment, and blind acceptance of the ruthless act that had so nearly broken the tenuous thread of health that kept body and soul together.

Sometimes in sleep she murmured, "A vow . . . a promise made in France . . . to God and to St. Regis." At other times her

623

tears flowed silently. No least sob escaped her, just great tears coursing down her sunken cheeks. Those who nursed her wiped them away, scarcely seeing through the mist in their own eyes, but they could not relieve the pain that caused those tears. Never would it be relieved, she had declared, for the shrine of St. Francis Regis had been taken from the chapel at Florissant. The picture she loved had been relegated to the attic, and that in spite of her protests to the Mother Provincial, who had ordered what Philippine considered a desecration. True, she had replaced it by a painting of the Sacred Heart, and that was the Society's dearest devotion, but the shrine had fulfilled the promise made in France to gain the saint's protection over the American mission. Argument and reasoning did not calm the old nun's distress, and the illness consequent on moral anguish and an already broken physical condition lasted many weeks.

But time and prayer and the continued loving care of those who nursed her brought a slow improvement, and by mid-December she was able to make her way, with some help, to the chapel. Once that was possible, she seemed to gain new strength; and by Christmas she was asking to move from the infirmary back to the room she had chosen when she was transferred from Florissant in October.

> You should see her room [wrote Mother Mathevon to the Superior General when she came from St. Charles for a visit]. Her bed is in a cubbyhole under a stairway. She says it is quieter there than anywhere else in the house, and to tell you the truth, there are few places available. She is an Alexis, a wonderful example for the St. Louis convent. . . . Though she is obliged to have mustard plasters on her swollen limbs, she drags herself to her superior's room to ask permissions. . . . Few canonized saints have practiced as much virtue as she does.[1]

Often she spent her hours of convalescence rereading the old letters she treasured or paging through her *Journal*. Work with the Indians was still her goal, and in these old manuscripts she found joy and a stimulation of her desires. She had never given up her hope of someday keeping the vow that she and her four companions had made on leaving France in 1818 to devote themselves to the salvation of the Indians. Thinking of her four companions, she realized that she alone could hope to carry out the vow. Mother Audé was ill in Rome; Mother Berthold had gone to her reward; Sisters Catherine and Marguerite, the one at Florissant, the other at Grand Coteau, were old and broken in health, while she had only her strong will, braced by faith and love, to rely on now. Circumstances, she knew, had indicated unmistakably the will of God and hindered the fulfilment of the promise, but through toil, privation, sickness, lack of success, and now a chronic state of ill health, the ardor of her desire had not slackened, the term of her ambition had not changed.

She recalled the arrival of the Flathead delegation in St. Louis and the enthusiasm with which she had written about it to Mother Barat in January, 1832. The answer had been only slightly encouraging: "For such a mission you would need religious of tried virtue and mature age who speak English. Where will you find them? . . . Write to me again about this project, if it is really feasible. Tell me the name of the bishop in charge of these tribes and what means of support and spiritual care you would have." [2]

Nothing had come of the project, for the difficulties inherent in it staggered both Bishop Rosati and Father Van Quickenborne, but Philippine had not given up hope. By her prayers and by small gifts of money, altar linens, and clothing, she had aided the Jesuits who had gone into the Indian country closer to St. Louis. How often their names were on her lips as she prayed: "Eternal Father, through the adorable Heart of Jesus I offer You all the priests who are working to spread the Gospel throughout the world. By His merits I beg You to fill them with Your Holy Spirit. On this Sacred Heart, as on a divine altar, I offer You in a very special manner . . ." [3] and their names came slowly, as she implored God's blessing on Fathers Van Quickenborne, Hoecken, De Smet, Verhaegen, and so many other splendid missionaries who were her friends.

One day in the late summer of 1837, just before she learned of Father Van Quickenborne's death, she had received a letter from Father Verhaegen that revived all her missionary zeal. He had been making a visitation of the Kickapoo mission which Van Quickenborne had established so laboriously in the summer of 1836. It lay beyond the western border of Missouri, where the frontier marked the fringe of white settlement and presumably gave the Indians a region all their own forever. So far the harvest garnered by the missionaries had been distressingly meager, but Father Verhaegen gave no hint of that when he wrote:

On June 20 I reached the Kickapoo encampment and was taken that morning to see the Indian lodges. When the chief of the tribe learned of my arrival, he came to visit me and showed me much affection. He is a savage in the full extent of that term. He paints his face black, with a little red around the eyes, and he glories in the fact that he has adopted no single article of the white man's dress. The savages come each week for the religious instruction which Father Christian Hoecken gives in their own language. He speaks it so well, the savages call him Father Kickapoo. Eight or ten adults have been baptized, and more than one hundred children. . . . They call God the Great Spirit and every morning pray for His blessing. If they feel sad or guilty, they blacken their faces and fast for an entire day, taking no food at all. When a brave dies, they bury his horse beside him, so that his soul may ride to the palace of the Great Spirit, which they think is far away from their village beyond the western prairie. . . . Pray, Mother, that God may send workers into this vineyard and may bless their labors for His greater glory.[4]

Mother Duchesne knew that, although the Kickapoo mission had received some aid from the Government and the Jesuits had endeavored earnestly to Christianize the tribe, these Indians had not responded to the efforts expended on them. Father Verhaegen soon considered the mission "utterly sterile," and in the autumn of 1840 he decided to close it in favor of a more promising field of endeavor for Christ. Mother Duchesne could trace in her *Journal* the beginnings of the Mission at Sugar Creek.

The Potawatomi were of Algonquin stock, closely allied with the Ottawa and the Chippewa. Their name, signifying "fire-makers," or "people of the fireplace," originated from the fact that they separated from the nation to which they had belonged and built for themselves a new fire, thus becoming an independent tribe. From their homes along Lakes Huron and Michigan they drifted southward into Illinois and Indiana. They were a warrior race and lovers of the hunt, little given to tilling the soil, even for a scant harvest of maize. Jesuit missionaries had toiled amongst them during the seventeenth and early eighteenth centuries, but without great results. The priests who came amongst them later on realized what the encroachments of white settlers would mean to these forest folk. The Government was pursuing its policy of dispossessing the Indians of their lands by forced treaties and assigning them other homes and hunting grounds beyond the Mississippi. Mother Duchesne had alluded to this policy again and again in her letters.

In 1835 a delegation of Potawatomi selected territory on the

Osage River in the present state of Kansas and began moving there at once. Some of them were Catholics. When their chief, Nesfwawke, learned that there were Black Robes in the Kickapoo settlement, he begged them to visit his people and instruct them. Father Hoecken made the trip in January, 1838, and found the Indians in heart-rending poverty and suffering. Though he had nearly lost his life in a blizzard and had done little to alleviate their physical miseries, he considered the journey well worthwhile, for he had given spiritual help and encouragement to a few faithful braves and squaws and had left them with the promise that missionaries would come to live in their encampment. Father Verhaegen went with him in the following May when he visited the Potawatomi and was so favorably impressed that he consented to the establishment of a permanent mission station among these Indians.

Their number had been increasing by the arrival of groups designated as Wabash and St. Joseph Potawatomi, and with them had come Father Benjamin-Marie Petit, a young missionary from France whom Bishop Bruté had ordained in 1837. His first and only assignment was with these Indians. He had witnessed the harshness and cruelty with which the trek of the Potawatomi had been conducted by government officials and soldiers, and he had shared the privations of his flock on the journey westward to Sugar Creek. Within a year he fell dangerously ill. Father Hoecken cared for him until he recovered enough strength to start for St. Louis, where he was received with great kindness by the Jesuits and visited by Bishops Rosati and Loras. On February 10, 1839, Father Petit died.

Mother Duchesne had noted these facts in her *Journal* under date of February 15, 1839, and would refer to them later on when pleading the cause of the Indian mission. She was deeply moved by the heroism of Father Petit; and after the Jesuits took charge of the Potawatomi Christians, she begged in letters to St. Madeleine Sophie and in talks with Bishop Rosati to be given a share in the work. She was seconded in this by Mother Lucille Mathevon, whose missionary vocation, like her own, had first been directed toward the Indians. When Bishop Rosati called on Mother Barat in Paris in the summer of 1840, the conversation turned quite naturally to this subject, and the Superior General surprised the Bishop by telling him that Mother Duchesne was pleading the cause of the Indians with such loving insistence that it seemed impossible to refuse her the permission. Knowing the precarious state of her health, the Bishop had some doubts as to the wisdom of her attempting such a mission, but he was delighted at the prospect of the religious at work among the Potawatomi and at once wrote to Mother Duchesne, sending the letter by Mother Galitzin, who was just setting out for America. The Bishop journeyed on to Rome, and in an audience with Pope Gregory XVI spoke of the missionary desires of Mother Duchesne and the prospect now opening up for her. By the end of November a letter from Bishop Rosati informed Mother Barat that the Holy Father had expressed a desire to see the Religious of the Sacred Heart at work among the Indians. Had Philippine but known it, the cause was won.

Meanwhile in St. Louis Father De Smet was using his influence to bring about the same result. In an interview with Mother Galitzin during her first visit there, he told her bluntly that the blessing of God on the Society of the Sacred Heart in America depended directly on the foundation of a mission school among the Indians. The Mother Provincial assured him that Mother Barat desired such a foundation with all her heart, but that both recruits and money were lacking just now. She spoke with her usual finality, but she did not know the missionary to whom she was speaking, and she left for Louisiana before winter set in.

On January 6, 1841, Father De Smet called at the convent in St. Louis. During a visit with Mother Duchesne he urged her to make another appeal for permission to open a school among the Potawatomi, promising on his side to raise the funds necessary for beginning the work. Suddenly she drew from her pocket Bishop Rosati's letter from Paris the previous July. Together they read:

> The example you have given in leaving Europe to make the first foundation of the Sacred Heart in America is still very powerful in influencing others to follow you. God be praised for this! But I am really surprised to learn that you are now pleading to leave Missouri in order to go among the savages. However, when one loves God, one never says "Enough." If I did not know you well, I might say it is too much for you. But knowing you as I do, I say: "Go! Follow your attraction, or rather the voice of God. He will be with you." I beg Him to bless you.[5]

Together the vigorous priest just entering his fortieth year and the broken old nun now past seventy discussed the possibilities of a school for Indian girls at Sugar Creek. The urgency of love and zeal smoothed away obstacles to their plans, and the vision of souls gained for Christ made every sacrifice seem paltry in comparison. It was agreed that she would write to Mother Galitzin at once and he would begin a begging tour for funds, not in St. Louis, for the Catholics of that city were neither mission-minded nor generously inclined to such appeals, but in New Orleans, where there was more wealth and more Catholicity.

On January 7 Mother Duchesne composed her letter to the Mother Provincial, beginning with a little summary of her missionary aspirations and the several times she had tried to carry out the promise made in France to work among the Indians.

> So far [she continued] we have been disappointed in our hopes—at least I have, for all my inclinations and desires urge me to work among these tribes. . . . Yesterday, the feast of the Kings, a visit from Father De Smet, who has come back from the Rocky Mountains, roused my ardor once more, and that to such an extent that I experienced a sort of physical resurrection as a result of the hope I feel that I may be among those chosen for a mission that is now offered to us under very favorable auspices.
>
> Beyond the western boundary of Missouri, this Father tells me, there is a very good tribe that comes from Canada, already partly converted to Christianity. They are called the Potawatomi. A holy Breton priest, Father Petit, consecrated his life and labors to them, and before his death he turned over his beloved flock to a Jesuit, who has since come to see us. . . . He now lives the same hard life as his new charges and finds great consolation in working among them. . . . The Government has contributed to the expense of building a log church and may also help build us a house. The missionary whom I saw yesterday considers it a duty for us to seize this opportunity before others of non-Catholic faith do so. I showed him the letter you brought me from Bishop Rosati, in which he wrote to me so positively: *Follow your attraction.* At the time I received it, I did not pay much attention to it; for my soul was crushed and all my offers were rejected. Now I think it really is the voice of God. Our Mother General has often expressed this desire, and our Lord will so arrange matters that you will lend a hand in this enterprise.

After suggesting the names of the religious whom she considered best suited for the work of the Indian mission, she added: "God is going to cure me. I shall be just an extra member of the group, helping with the housework and other labors."

Father De Smet's trip south gave Philippine an opportunity to send by way of New Orleans a brief note to her sister. It had been months since she had written, and what she had to say now shows how far from well she was:

> I do not want to leave you any longer without news of me. At our age and in the illness from which I am now suffering, it is natural to think that an opportunity to write to you might not occur again. I admit to you that it would be very bitter for me to survive you and realize that I was destined to see all my sisters—all younger than I—go before me into eternity. I am not jealous of the fact that three already enjoy the reward of their virtues, but I attribute the length of my earthly exile to the fact that so much is wanting to me in that respect. The last news I had of you came through [Mother] Amelie [Jouve].
>
> My present illness is a bloated condition, almost general, which they are treating with mustard plasters. God alone knows how much good they will do. As for myself, I live only for His will. Pray for me, tender friend and beloved sister. . . .[6]

At St. Michael's Mother Galitzin was astonished, when called to the parlor one day by "a priest from St. Louis," to find herself face to face again with Father De Smet. Her surprise increased when he presented her with a second letter from Mother Duchesne and five hundred dollars in gold, the fruit of his begging tour in New Orleans and among the planters of the Gold Coast of the Mississippi.

> The priest who brings you this letter [she read] is, as you know, the one who is carrying on the great mission work in the direction of the mountains. I hope he will be able to give more weight to the pleas I have already made. . . . Dear Reverend Mother, do hasten your return to St. Louis in order to take care of this important affair. Religious are not lacking for it, and I trust that God will let me be among those who are chosen. I know this work is one of our Mother General's most earnest desires. . . . When I consider how little piety our pupils show after they leave school, I realize how much more glory for God and consolation for ourselves there will be in instructing these fresh souls who are still in their innocence, far from the dangers of the world! What a joy it is to serve God freely, generously, without asking recompense! If we had just four hundred dollars to start with, we could go this coming spring. Our large houses in Louisiana can certainly regard this little gift as a mite in comparison with the huge sums spent on their buildings. It would give God glory if they curtailed

some ornamentations in order to furnish the indispensable for our poor Indians.[7]

Father De Smet left on record an account of what happened at St. Michael's:

> I was the bearer of Mother Duchesne's request. . . . At first the petition met with no success and was rather firmly rejected—"It could not be thought of." I humbly begged Mother Galitzin not to come to so hasty a conclusion on a matter of so great importance, to ponder it quietly and lay it before the Lord at the foot of the tabernacle. A few days after that the approval of Mother Duchesne's request was granted. I have as yet in my possession the letter of Mother Galitzin in which religious were named to commence the Potawatomi Mission. . . .[8]

Mother Galitzin was not to be hurried from Louisiana in midwinter, but from her answer Father De Smet concluded that his mission was accomplished. A month later she received from the Superior General the letter that was decisive in the matter:

> I am sending you a note from Monseigneur Rosati on the subject of a foundation which he desires us to make among the savage tribes. This matter should not be neglected. Remember, dear Mother, that our good Mother Duchesne in leaving us for America had only this work in view. It was for the sake of the Indians that she felt inspired to establish the Society in America. I believe it enters into the designs of God that we should profit, if possible, by the opportunity offered us by Bishop Rosati.[9]

The wish of the Sovereign Pontiff, Gregory XVI, was law for the Society of the Sacred Heart; and when Mother Galitzin reached St. Louis in March, she announced the decision that had been reached: two new foundations were to be made that year, one in the East, in New York City, and one in the West, at Sugar Creek. There were volunteers for the mission to the Potawatomi in the three Missouri houses, most vocal among them being Mother Lucille Mathevon and her close associate at St. Charles, Mother Mary Ann O'Connor. Mother Mathevon wrote enthusiastically to the Superior General:

> There are already more than a thousand Catholic Indians in the tribe. The Jesuit Fathers are obliged to teach even the girls. . . . These are *civilized savages*. They resemble the first Christians in fervor and have been begging for three years to have religious

come and teach their children. . . . Oh, how much good we could do, how many souls we could save! One must know this country as I do in order to realize how much real good our convents accomplish. St. Charles was just a little village where people lived according to their own ideas of right and wrong. We began by teaching the children to make the sign of the cross and say their prayers. Now it is a town in which religion is practiced with fervor. On all first-class feasts a hundred and fifty men and women go to Holy Communion. The confraternities [of the Sacred Heart, the Immaculate Heart, and the Rosary] have been established, and more than four hundred people have received the scapular.[10]

Mother Mathevon's nomination as superior of the Indian mission band was no surprise, for her ardent desire for this work was well known. Mother Regis Hamilton was named to take her place as superior at St. Charles and went there in April. Mother O'Connor accompanied Mother Mathevon to St. Louis, for she, too, had won a place on the mission band, along with Sister Louise Amyot. As yet there was no mention of other names. Mother Eleanor Gray, superior at the City House since February, tried to console her beloved Mother Duchesne, while Mother Galitzin gave her little encouragement because of her ill health and Mother Mathevon wrote to St. Madeleine Sophie on May 10: "Mother Duchesne is growing considerably weaker. I fear she would not be able to go far." "There is scarcely a breath of life in her," she had written two weeks before this, and Mother Duchesne admitted her condition honestly at the close of a letter to Mother Barat on May 18:

> I wrote to you not long ago. Sympathy urged me to do so. Pardon another letter so soon. It is written to reassure you with regard to the means of subsistence for the proposed Indian mission. There are farms under cultivation all around it. There are half-breeds who are saints, and so are some of the savages. In that mission one sees what is to be seen nowhere else in this country, so completely does the lively faith of these people recall the days of primitive Christianity. When the priest carries the Blessed Sacrament to the sick, two acolytes in surplice and carrying candles precede him; a third with a little bell accompanies him. They go on horseback, the priest wearing surplice and stole. The little bell warns the people that the dear Lord is being carried that way. At once they all leave their houses or cabins and kneel in adoration on the roadside. On Sunday the Mass is sung by the savages in an excellent manner.

I told Mother Bathilde [Sallion] that the Government has set aside a considerable amount of revenue appropriated for the education of the savages. There is no doubt that we shall receive a share of this, as other denominations have.

Father Timon, who will deliver this letter to you, has already refused to be a bishop, but they think he will accept the title for Texas, the country that separated from Mexico and is now developing into a republic like our own [United States]. Father Odin, who is also going to be a bishop, came here this morning and told me about his mission work in Texas, where he has traveled about 800 leagues. That country is as large as France. The chief city, San Antonio, is not yet settled in proportion to the size of the country. It can be reached from New Orleans in ten or fifteen days. Last year Father Odin asked Mother Hardey for religious from St. Michael's to work there. As she gave him an affirmative answer, he asked the President of Texas [Sam Houston] to give him an option on the most beautiful house in San Antonio, and he offers very easy terms (as long as we wish). Father Timon is going to renew the request to the Mother Provincial. Mother Bazire would do well on such a foundation. It could be made with 5000 francs for the first expenses, and pupils would be enrolled at once.

My writing and my scratching out show you the weakness of both my head and my hand. The miracle of my cure has not taken place. I await the will of God. Mother Lucille is to be the head of the mission band. I kneel for you blessing, Reverend Mother, with love in the Sacred Heart of Jesus. . . .

Mother Galitzin left St. Louis for the foundation in New York at the end of April, taking with her Mothers Catherine Thiéfry and Judith Shannon. They were joined in mid-May by Mothers Aloysia Hardey and Ellen Hogan from St. Michael's, and later by Mother Adeline Boilvin and Sisters Gallien and Pratt. It had been a satisfaction for Mother Duchesne to have the talents and virtues of her beloved "Gonzague" recognized, but they both knew that the parting was for life. It was not, however, a breaking of the ties that united them so affectionately, and Mother Boilvin treasured the letters she received from Mother Duchesne during a few short years. The first of these is dated June 4, 1841:

I have already sent a short note in answer to your letter from Pittsburgh, hoping to write at greater length when there would be an opportunity to send a letter by a traveler. Our music master will take this to you. His place is being filled by Mother Crawford from St. Michael's, a very lovable person.[11] She now has six pupils for either harp or piano. Mother [Evelina] L'Eveque is not very well. I suffer for her when I hear the long hours of music practice. Mother Aloysia [Hardey], to whom I send my regards, knew their delicate health and it was her prudence that inspired the recommendations necessary to save these two religious who are so useful.

The Chambers girls are away from school just now. The younger had the measles here. They have been together at home with their mother, and Miss Jane, who caught the disease from her sister, has a very serious case at home. Mr. Destrehan has come and gone. I did not even know it until after his departure, when I heard them speak of him at recreation. He refused to leave his piano for less than $300, and I fear Mother Prud'hom's method of teaching did not please him.[12]

They tell me you will not be installed in your new home before August. This time of waiting will be a very profitable period for you to grow in virtue and knowledge. I do not know what good learning has been to me; but when I recall how I enjoyed it, how I esteemed it, and how little use it has been to me, I rejoice in the thought that in heaven *all earthly knowledge will be lost in God.* There we shall say only the eternal *Amen* and "Holy, holy, holy Lord."

I have no hope now of finishing my embroidery. Adieu. A thousand messages to dear Sister Gallien. . . .

Philippine needed the grace to say that *Amen* even as she was writing this chatty news sheet, for all around her there was bustle and subdued excitement of preparations for the mission venture. No least share could she have in the work; and she found it difficult to understand why she was being spared fatigue that would have been a comfort to her, since there seemed to be no human hope of her going to Sugar Creek. She had almost resigned herself to the fact that, feeble and ill as she was, she could not bear the tiring trip nor the hardships of the life that awaited the missionary nuns. Yet she prayed the more earnestly, even for a miracle, were that the only means of securing the privilege. And miracle it would have been, judging from a description of her condition at this very time:

The doctor thinks she is in continual danger of death, yet she wanted to fast and abstain all during Lent. Since then the swelling has increased, and it extends from her feet up to her chest, so that she is liable to be smothered at any moment. She feels that she is very near to death, yet once our Mother General gives her the permission, she will consider it an order and no one will be able to hold her back.[13]

The date of departure had not been set when Father Verhaegen appeared at the convent one morning quite unexpectedly. He had decided to visit the Sugar Creek mission early in July and thought it advisable for the religious to travel in safety under his escort. As he talked with Mothers Gray and Mathevon, Mother Duchesne sat with them in the parlor, for Father Verhaegen never called at the City House without asking for her. They were discussing the business side of the trip—the steamboat, the baggage, the date and hour of departure, the reservations for the three religious. For three? Father Verhaegen had expected four. He turned to where Mother Duchesne sat praying silently, tears falling unheeded on the darkened, toil-worn hands that held her rosary. "But *she* must come, too," he said to Mother Gray, and his strong face lighted up with reverent affection. *She* was the person he wanted most of all at Sugar Creek. "Even if she can use only one leg, she will come. Why, if we have to carry her all the way on our shoulders, she is coming with us. She may not be able to do much work," he added, and his kind eyes narrowed to thin slits in a characteristic smile, "but she will assure success to the mission by praying for us. Her very presence will draw down all manner of heavenly favors on the work." [14]

How much of this vehement declaration Philippine understood is a matter of conjecture, but its outcome was immediately clear to her as Mother Gray put loving arms about her and said words so like those she had heard from St. Madeleine Sophie in Paris on a May day in 1817 when the holy foundress had consented to the American mission. Mother Mathevon, however, was reluctant to assume the responsibility for one so loved, so venerated, and so enfeebled, and Philippine was quick to sense this attitude without realizing its true cause. So there was heart-suffering in the midst of joy, but she could repeat the little prayer she had made her own: "Lord, I lean on You alone for strength. Give me Your arm to support me, Your shoulders to carry me, Your breast on which to lay my head, Your cross to uphold me, Your Eucharist to nourish me. In You, Lord, I shall sleep and rest in peace." [15]

The little mission band boarded the Missouri River packet on June 29, 1841. Besides the four nuns there were two Jesuits, Fathers Verhaegen and Smedts, and a diocesan priest, Father Francis J. Renaud. On the levee a crowd of friends had gathered to say

goodbye, and Bishop Jean-Marie Chanche of Natchez was there
to give them his blessing. The steamboat *Emilie* was booked to sail
at noon, but during a two-hour delay the Bishop remained with
the nuns, telling them of the problems that faced him in Natchez,
where there was but one priest for the whole newly created
diocese.

The river trip was pleasant; accommodations on the steamboat
were good, though not so luxurious as those on the smart packets
now plying the Mississippi. Mother Duchesne gathered fresh
strength as the boat ascended the muddy stream and was able to
walk the deck with a remarkably firm step. She was interested in
all she saw and heard and was a center of interest among the
passengers. By a spontaneous gesture these people took up a collection amounting to fifty dollars for the nuns, while traders on board
contributed provisions to the value of forty dollars. These were
confided to the care of Edmund, the young Negro from the convent in St. Louis, who had been brought along to help with the
heavy work of installation.

Mother Mathevon's account of the journey is a charming bit of
narrative:

> Our trip, as far as Westport, was very pleasant. We made it in
> four days. I should never have imagined that Missouri was so
> thickly populated. We passed fifteen towns, at least, containing
> several thousand inhabitants each. Some of them are really lovely,
> and there are delightful homes along the river. Yet this large
> population is entirely without churches or priests and has not a
> single school. . . . On July 4, the festival of Independence, Father
> Verhaegen preached to the passengers. When the sermon was
> over, great applause ensued, with clapping of hands and stamping
> of feet. Then everybody, ourselves included, drank iced sherry.
> We are all very well. As for Mother Duchesne, she walked up
> and down the deck as if she were young again. It took four days
> after leaving the boat to reach Sugar Creek, our destination. We
> could have made it in two, but the kind Fathers thought it best
> to travel by slow stages and so avoid greater fatigue. . . .
>   The Indians had been warned of our coming, so the entire vil-
> lage assembled and waited a day. We had stopped about eighteen
> miles away on the banks of the Osage River at the home of a
> French settler, where we were most kindly received. The Indians,
> impatient of our arrival, sent ahead two of their number to find
> us. These came and knelt before the Father Superior to receive his
> blessing. We gave them supper; then they started back to an-
> nounce to their tribesmen that we would be with them the follow-

ing day. As we advanced next morning, we met, every two miles along the way, two Indians mounted on fine horses. They had come to greet us and show us the safest and best road.[16]

About a mile from the mission house a band of five hundred braves appeared in gala dress—bright blankets, plumes and feathers, and moccasins embroidered with porcupine quills. Their faces were painted black, with red circles around the eyes that gave them a frighteningly grotesque appearance. As the mission wagon advanced, the Indians performed a series of equestrian evolutions, now in semicircles, now in circles, and always with such precision that never was a horse out of position.

We were given a reception that far exceeded anything we had expected [wrote Mother Mathevon]. A half-breed named Joseph Napoleon Bourassa made a fine speech in the name of the tribe and the 700 who were assembled to greet us. He told how glad they were that we had come to instruct their daughters in the true religion. I do not remember all Father Verhaegen said in reply, but he presented Mother Duchesne to the Indians, saying, "Here is a religious who has been asking the dear Lord for thirty years to let her come and teach you, and how happy she is that at last He has heard her prayer."

Then they all wanted to shake hands, and Mother Duchesne put her arms around all the women and girls; and they all shook hands with us. After that we had a fine dinner at the home of Mr. Joseph Bertrand, a very refined half-breed, whom we regard as a great benefactor. . . .

As Father Aelen had not been informed of our coming with Father Verhaegen, which was sooner than had been planned, there was no house ready to receive us. A good Indian named Manope let us have his cabin, as it was close to the church, and he went to live in a tent. His house was about fifteen by twelve feet in size. . . . We had two chairs, one of them reserved for our dear Mother Duchesne. She made a kind of desk out of the chair and kept her little belongings there—that was the full extent of her room—and from that chair she wrote to our Mother Foundress with the greatest joy in being able to practice holy poverty in this fashion.[17]

The first letter Mother Duchesne sent to St. Madeleine Sophie was headed: "From the Tribe and Village of the Potawatomi," and covered the sheet so completely, there was not even space at the end for a signature.

My dearly loved Mother [she began], At last we have reached the country of our desires. We left St. Louis with the Father Superior, who is replacing Monseigneur Rosati in everything that is not exclusively the duty of a bishop, and two other Jesuit Fathers. We traveled first by water, leaving St. Louis on the beautiful feast of St. Peter, after a visit with the Bishop of Natchez, who also gave us his blessing. He is going to have more difficulties than we are. There are no difficulties here except when people worry too much about *tomorrow*.

This tribe, which like many others was driven out of Michigan by the Americans, is now about half Catholic. These people have built their village at a distance from the pagans, who are being converted gradually. Once baptized, they never revert to drunkenness or stealing. Whatever is found is placed at the door of the church to be claimed by the owner. Not a single house has locks on the doors, yet nothing is ever missing. The Indians gather in groups [men and women separate] for morning prayers, Mass, and catechism. In the evening they assemble again for prayers. They eat seven times a day.

The pastor does not think it wise at present to teach the children another language. He fears this would lead them into evil ways, but that will be decided later on. He insists above all on manual work, for both the men and the women sleep part of every day. They also come crowding silently into our house, which belongs to one of the savages.

Mother Galitzin gave us 250 dollars, which she considered enough for the erection of a wooden house. I thought the money had already been sent to the pastor, and we were told in St. Louis that our house had been built. But it was the pastor's house, and also the church, for which he obtained money from the Government. On reaching here, we were greatly disappointed to find no house ready for us, and we showed our distress. But it was not the fault of the person who kept everything a secret from me and would not listen to any suggestion I made. I was not allowed to prepare a single package for the trip. They kept on telling me to the last day that the trip would make me sick. . . . When the steamboat passage was paid, we had scarcely twenty dollars left. But what pained me most of all was the fact that so many seculars were invited to come to see us before we left. They were a nuisance and ate up our time.

The pastor has given us two fine cows and put at our service a pair of oxen, a good horse, and a charette. It will be easy to plant a nice vegetable garden, so have we anything to complain about? We brought with us the Negro man from St. Louis. He is a carpenter and will help with the manual work. Our baggage has not arrived yet, so I was obliged to use this thick paper. I have been ill again, and I find it difficult to think. This is a weakness I never experienced before. It accounts for the condition of my letter, but the facts are correct. You may, however, receive some exaggerations.[18]

It was hard for Philippine to have to admit that she had been ill again, but it was much harder to realize that her feebleness cut her off from the activities of the other missionaries. The Indians, however, seemed to appreciate her from the moment she set foot in the Sugar Creek encampment. Even though she could not teach their children as Mother O'Connor was doing by mid-July, or cook for them as Sister Louise did, or read their language as Mother Mathevon could after three or four weeks amongst them, they loved her and respected her and brought her all manner of things—fresh corn, newly-laid eggs, chickens, wild plums, sweet, clean straw for her pallet. "Whatever they have, they bring to the *good old lady,* as they call Mother Duchesne," wrote Mother Mathevon in August. And later on:

> She stayed all morning in the church, so Sister Louise would take her a cup of coffee each day, and she drank it at the door of the church. After dinner she went again for three or four hours of prayer. The Indians had the greatest admiration for her, recommended themselves to her prayers, and called her Woman-who-prays-always. Everyone admitted that a great number of baptisms resulted from her prayers. Almost every Sunday afternoon three or four men or women and their families were baptized. Mother Duchesne inscribed all their names in the register.[19]

But in all this there was no sense of achievement, no reassurance. In her own heart, "last lurking place of self," she had to face the fact that to all appearances she had failed in the dearest hope of her life. She was completely unaware of the graces she was receiving or of those that were coming to others through her prayers, but the results were all the more powerful for this very reason. Her incapacity for active work brought her loneliness of heart which she admitted and accepted with love, but not without pain. The solitude at Sugar Creek was not merely a physical remoteness, but also a spiritual aloneness that grew out of the sensed fact that she was a burden on those who cared for her, an anxiety for them. Borne in close union with the mystery of Christ's loneliness, this suffering only drew her closer to His Sacred Heart, where she buried the pain by renewed and more loving surrender.

News of the venture into the Indian country had reached Philippine's family in France, and soon they were writing her letters and sending her gifts in the generous fashion that had characterized them through the past twenty years and more. One of the few extant letters she wrote from Sugar Creek was addressed to her brother and written from her armchair desk in Manope's hut on September 12:

Just a few days ago, my dearest Brother, I received the letter you wrote for kind Monsieur de Mauduit, at the end of which you assured me once more of your loving sentiments in my regard. As you said in your preceding letter that you would carry out your promise only after my arrival here, I did not fail to write you that I am here. But I was very agreeably surprised soon after reaching this mission to find enclosed in a letter from Madame de Rollin your note for 500 francs [$100] on the Bank of New Orleans. That was the best way to send the money, though bank failures are frequent, both in New Orleans and throughout the United States, even in the case of banks that have the best standing, and this sometimes makes it difficult to cash a letter of exchange. I sent the draft to St. Louis at once to the gentleman to whom we owe the most for the loan of money to pay our traveling expenses, and I am sure it will be readily accepted in partial payment of what he advanced.

There are four of us here in this new foundation, and we are all in better health than when we were in St. Louis. The biggest inconvenience we have experienced is that of having no house prepared for us to live in, as by some mistake they told us one was ready. It was described to us as much larger than the one now being built for us with the help of the people and the pastor of the mission at which we are so happy to find ourselves. The Indians cut down and transported tree trunks for the walls of our house. In two days twenty or twenty-five men put up these huge logs about a foot or more in diameter, after having squared them off, and so the shell of the house was raised. The roof was finished yesterday. It is made of small boards which in French are called *bardeaux* (shingles). While waiting for the house to be erected, we have used the rented hut of a poor Indian, who installed himself and his family temporarily in a tent. Our beds are built of wood against the wall, and we sleep well on them.

To remove from your mind all suspicion that there is folly in our enterprise, let me tell you that this little tribe is very good, professes our religion, and welcomed us cordially. Behind our house we have an excellent plot of ground large enough for a yard and a truck garden. And to add further details, the pastor has

put at our disposal a horse, oxen, and a charette for farm work
and transportation. He has sent us three fine cows, many chickens,
some geese, and a litter of little pigs. There are calves in a meadow,
and every day the cows give them a little nourishment. Then the
cowherds milk the cows, take what is needed for the priests and
others, and give us the rest. There is almost enough milk to suffice
for our whole nourishment, but we have vegetables and can get
meat at just five and a half cents a pound.

We cannot expect to do much with the Indians except
strengthen the character of the children and rouse them from their
laziness by interesting them in some kind of easy work. The
language is extremely difficult, and the alphabet, which has four
letters less than ours, is sounded just as in French. Our nuns have
learned quite readily to read the language and are teaching the
children as one teaches little children to read Latin, only here
things are reversed: the children—not one of them knowing how
to read before—understand the meaning of the words which we
do not understand at all. . . .

After giving Duchesne a language lesson in Potawatomi by
writing out the *Gloria Patri* and a dozen Indian words which she
had mastered at least on paper, such as God, man, woman, sun,
moon, salt, fire, finger, in true grammarian style, Philippine continues:

Let me add that some words in this barbaric tongue run to ten,
nine, eight syllables, and as yet there is no published dictionary,
no grammar, and just one book of prayers. I think I shall never
learn such a language.

Tell Madame de Rollin that I shall write to her just as soon as
I receive the letter she tells me is on its way to me. Say to that
dear cousin and to your wife all the most affectionate things you
can think of. After reading this letter, please send it to Madame
Jouve. I shall add here a few more lines to her and you both.
Adieu, my kind Brother. I pray to our Lord for you and hope to
see you once more in that life that knows no ending and is always
happy.

Your grateful sister,

PHILIPPINE

The few lines she added amounted to a second letter:

I am sure, my dear and beloved Sister, that my going the distance
of a six-days' journey farther from you has not caused you any
sorrow. Our trip was pleasant. We reached a village of Christian

Indians who had been partially civilized by some good missionaries in Michigan, one of whom spent 32,000 francs on them, and the last one accompanied them here, though his health was already shattered by his labors, and he has now finished his course.

This is the order of day established for the mission: morning prayers in the church when the bell rings, then Holy Mass, during which they sing hymns in the Indian language; this is followed by catechism for the children. The principal meal, at 10 or 11 o'clock, consists principally of corn and meat. Many of the Indians own cows and horses. In the evening there are prayers again in common in the church. On Saturdays the priest scarcely leaves the confessional, and on August 15 and also today there were more than one hundred Communions. In the church the men and women sit on opposite sides, and the boys have a proctor who holds a correction rod in his hand. I assure you there is need for this. The older Indians do not grow weary even during the longest ceremonies. Their good example continually draws other adults and these ask for baptism. Once they receive this sacrament they give up quarreling, drunkenness, stealing, and dancing. Nothing could be more peaceful than this village. One would think the very horses' hooves were cushioned like cats' paws. The animals are as tame as human beings.

Several neighboring nations (by nations they mean tribes of 1000, 2000, 3000, 20,000 people) are asking also for priests and churches. They do not like Protestant ministers because these men bring along their wives. I am hopeful of seeing missions established among these tribes. If Alexander wept for want of lands to conquer, I am tempted to weep because at my age I cannot rescue from barbarism so many poor people who are ruining their lives by their misconduct. Many tribes worship the evil spirit, and their improvidence makes them slaves of hunger. They search for bitter roots, insects, and other things for food, and so the death rate is high. In order to perpetuate the tribe, the girls are forced to marry. Now if, little by little, missionaries can eliminate these evils and establish the happy conditions that exist in our village, tell me, would they not be doing more good than if they were teaching the arts and sciences? Our Indians are decently clothed. They do not find a heavy blanket uncomfortable even in the month of August, and the clothes they wear under it are varied and bizarre. I have seen men coming out of church wearing red trousers with a white shirt over them, held by a blue sash. In the most elegant costume they can wear, they discard the shirt and put on a pretty jacket with a kind of short cape and two brightly colored neckerchiefs.

Now all I have written is enough to prove to you that there can be a real vocation to our present missionary work and that God can bless it and recompense it. All yours in the Heart of our good Master,

PHILIPPINE

In general Mother Mathevon agreed with what Mother Duchesne had written to her brother about the abundance of food and the improvement in the health of the missionary nuns. "On our Indian beds," she wrote, "we sleep better than we would in the palaces of kings. Dairy products, vegetables, rice, cornbread, and bread made of wheaten flour, lard—that is our diet. We have good appetites and our health is much better." [20] But her report to Mother Galitzin in the autumn contained a passage relating to Mother Duchesne that shows her physical condition:

> She is here just to suffer, for she has aged much in this short time and is sometimes like a little child. She no longer has the fine mind of other days. She is feeble; her limbs are swollen; her digestion is poor. I fear she will have a stroke. To tell you the truth, we cannot understand how the Father Superior could have insisted on bringing her here. But he said that she would pray for the missions and that she must be given the consolation of dying here. All she can do at present is pray, sometimes lying for a little while on her bed, and knit stockings. That is all. It is a great anxiety for us to have to care for her without being able to give her what she needs, for one has to send twenty leagues for things. We are doing all we can for her. She has done so much for the Society, it is only right that we give her all possible care in her old age. [21]

The religious took possession of their new log cabin on October 9. It was primitive and poorly built, but it was clean. There was not much privacy in it, for the Indians came and went as they pleased during the daytime, but the nuns had grown accustomed to this. A wood stove and some shelves occupied one side of the room. This was designated as the dining room and kitchen; but when winter came on and the icy wind swept in from the western prairies, the nuns and their Indian pupils huddled near the fire, even while meals were being prepared. Sensitive as she had become to cold, because of the fever that seldom left her now, Mother Duchesne suffered more than the others. Yet she made her way through the snow to the unheated mission church for Mass each morning. When Mother Mathevon forbade her to return to the icy building during the day, she accepted the prohibition in the spirit in which it was given. She knew Mother Lucille's love for her, though at times she felt that her superior misunderstood her or exaggerated her physical infirmity, which she herself would have liked to ignore.

The Potawatomi, like other Indians, were thoughtless and improvident by nature and had never learned to protect themselves against the bitter cold of winter. As a result there was much illness among them during this season. The nuns visited the sick, cared for them as far as they were able, aided and consoled them, and prayed with the dying. In this, at least, Mother Duchesne could have a share when she was able, and allowed, to drag herself from the cabin-convent to the native huts. The Indians were deeply touched by this kindness, especially when they saw her, feeble and worn by the rigors of the winter, bending over the rough pallet of a dying woman whose life she had failed to save, but whose soul had been won for Christ.

Mail came once a week to the mission when the weather was good, but it was often delayed when snow and ice or rain made the rough roads impassable. So it was mid-winter when Mother Duchesne received a letter written by Mother Barat on August 23, 1841:

> What a consolation it was, dear Mother and old daughter of mine, to receive your letter, undated, but addressed from the Potawatomi village! [22] So at last you have reached the Indian country you have so desired these long years! May Jesus protect you, my dear Philippine, and give you the means to do good there.
>
> By the most recent group of our nuns traveling to America we sent you some things, but unfortunately not much money, for our resources are exhausted. We shall try, however, to collect more another year. I hope we have provided at least for your most pressing needs by arranging with St. Michael's to send you each year what would have been sent to me. I shall be so happy, dear Mother, to have you profit at my expense. But you must pray for the donors. Some of the things we sent you were donated by a poor lace-maker and his sister, who is a seamstress. Each contributed a dollar out of their hard-earned funds. My little purse paid for the rest, with some help from the children. Have your little savages pray for us all.
>
> I was sorry to learn that you were installed in a cabin. I fear, my dear daughter, that you went too soon. Next year would have been time enough. But our dear Master allowed it all for the best. Have confidence! He will aid you. I keep on worrying about one thing: if you cannot teach your own language to the Indian children, how will you be able to instruct them? Certainly, at your age

it will be very difficult for you to learn the Indian tongue. Ask Mother Mathevon to write us all the interesting details about your mission—that is the way we shall get gifts for you, especially if you promise to have the little savages pray for those who help the missions.

Pray also for our General Council of 1842, dear Mother. It will be a very important meeting, and we have great need of God's help. Share this letter with Mother Lucille, and also my loving sentiments. Your friends, Fathers Barat, Varin, etc., and Mothers Desmarquest and de Gramont send you loving greetings. You know we just lost Mother Rivet at Chambery,[23] and you and I are drawing near the gates of eternity! I have been very ill this past year and have not fully recuperated.

The Holy Father blesses you and takes a very special interest in you. He was delighted with the courage you showed in undertaking your new mission. Dear Philippine, Jesus will ratify that blessing given by the Father of all the faithful. So have unshakable confidence and the utmost zeal in trying to save the souls that have been redeemed by the Blood of Jesus Christ. Pray, too, for your Mother, who longs to share your labors, but she is not worthy to do so. At least, my dear daughter, I console myself with the thought that you are taking my place with these savages who have always been so dear to my heart. . . . Be assured, dear Mother and old daughter of mine, of the loving and inviolable attachment with which it is always so sweet for me to sign myself

Votre Mère toute dévouée,
BARAT

The long winter wore on, with now and then a spell of moderate weather. In February, Mother Duchesne told her sister optimistically: "My health has improved very much in this part of the country. I have gained some strength; my eyesight is better; and I retain the use of all my faculties, though I am in my seventy-third year. Wherever I am, my heart goes out to you and I am glad to be able to assure you that I love you." [24] Mother Mathevon, however, wrote the following day: "Mother Duchesne is aging more and more. She is often in a very suffering condition. The life here is much too hard for a person her age." [25] But the valiant missionary was keenly interested in the work at Sugar Creek and alert to all that was going on.

Congress [she wrote to Madame Jouve] forced the Potawatomi to move into this region and will pay them an annual sum of money which, as long as the arrangement lasts, will save them from dire misery. This year we have seen them making good use of part of their money by buying shoes, shirts, and other articles of clothing such as the white people wear. But the blanket is always an important item in their dress. Christianity changes these unfortunate people so noticeably that a pagan among them can always be identified by his fierce and unkempt appearance. In our school some dear little girls are beginning to read in their own language and some in English also. More than twenty have learned to spin and knit; but even before we came here, many knew how to sew quite well. They are, on the whole, very interesting children, but they find it very difficult to stay at the same work for any length of time. The pastor guides this tribe as a shepherd leads his lambs. . . .[26]

Although Mother Duchesne was, in a sense, crushed by her own helplessness at Sugar Creek, frustration had no part in her reaction to circumstances, for these were for her the manifest will of God. At times her physical weakness may have left her powerless to think clearly, but she was very alert mentally when she wrote to Father De La Croix after seven months at the mission. Knowing his interest in all that concerned the Society of the Sacred Heart in America, she gave him news about people and places and left on record details about Sugar Creek that may not be found in other sources. With remarkable vigor and buoyancy she wrote:

SS.C.J.M.   CATHOLIC VILLAGE OF THE POTAWATOMI
                                                    February 20, 1842

DEAR FATHER AND KIND BENEFACTOR,

I have just received the letter you sent me by Father Lefevre, who is now Bishop of Detroit. He was consecrated in Philadelphia, along with Monseigneur Kenrick, coadjutor of Bishop Rosati, whom he preceded to St. Louis. We do not know when Monseigneur Rosati will return from his European trip. We understand that he has been commissioned by His Holiness, the Pope, to treat of religious affairs in Santo Domingo.

How can I ever express my joy on receiving your letter which is of such value to me? It is easy to see that like an affectionate father you never forget the children on whom you bestowed both temporal and spiritual goods. They will always miss you. I hope I can answer satisfactorily all your kind inquiries by giving you news of each of our religious families, even at the risk of telling you what you already know. I shall begin with the most recent foundation—that of New York, where the superior is a French religious [Mother Bathilde Sallion], but Mother Aloysia Hardey, the Mistress General, is the soul of the boarding school. The people of New York, and especially the clergy, have been very kind to our nuns.

Mother Louisa L'Eveque is superior at St. Michael's, and Mother Dutour is in charge of the orphans there. Mother Audé will never return to America. She is superior at the Trinita du Mont in Rome.[27] People thought the establishment at Opelousas would suffer severely after the death of Mother Xavier Murphy, but that condition did not last long, for the boarding school has already increased. The superior now is an English religious who came to Louisiana from France [Mother Maria Cutts]. Several of our religious have followed Mother Murphy to the grave. I mention Sister Marguerite Manteau in particular.[28] The Jesuits have built a fine college at Grand Coteau on the land given to the Church by Mrs. Smith, but they have encountered many difficulties. Louisiana and Missouri are joined in one province now. The college in St. Louis has expanded satisfactorily. Its new church is now roofed and will be more beautiful than the cathedral. The novitiate remains in that dear place where we first experienced your kindness and has a fine farm now.

I know St. Ferdinand interests you. The church building has been enlarged by a pretty chapel of the Blessed Virgin directly opposite ours, which has also been enlarged by the addition of the entire parlor. The novitiate for our Society in Missouri has been placed there. Father Van Assche is pastor and Mother de Kersaint is Superior and Mistress of Novices. They have no boarding school there now, just the parish school. Out there Mrs. Chambers and Mrs. St. Cyr are fine examples of holy women. The St. Louis convent has an Irish superior, Mother Gray. There are about fifty pupils in the academy and as many in the orphanage. A large addition to the building has got them into debt. St. Charles was also in debt because of the pretty brick convent they built, but they are almost free from debt now. Mother Regis Hamilton is superior there, and Sister Catherine Lamarre and Mother Thiéfry are in her community. We are expecting our Provincial, Mother Galitzin, to visit us on her way back from Louisiana. She went there again after the foundation was made in New York. It was she who forwarded your letter to me after reading it herself.

Now I come to my own story—the chapter since your departure. If I knew how to profit by suffering, I would be able to say, like you, that I am perfectly content. But I needed to be tried, and God has directed my steps along *vias duras*, even while guiding me to the mission for the savages, so long the goal of my desires. Here I suffer still because I can do nothing at all. First of all, I was transferred from St. Louis to St. Ferdinand, where there were continual threats that the convent would be closed. Then, in answer to prayers and representations, they placed the novitiate there. I was transferred to St. Louis, passing from a very active life to one of complete nullity, and I was ill for a long time. Father De Smet returned from the Flathead mission in the *Rokis*— a three months' journey—and his coming gave me new life. He led me to hope that we would make a foundation there within two years, and he vigorously urged our Mother Provincial to send us here to work among these Indians.

After narrating the story of the migration of the Potawatomi and the death of Father Petit, she continues:

Reverend Fathers Hoecken, a German, and Aelen, a Hollander, have continued the work with success. They have a residence here, and the superior is Father Verreydt, whom you know. There are just three of them here. They go on missionary visits to neighboring tribes and so bring many souls to Jesus Christ. We traveled here with Father Verhaegen, the Provincial, and Father Smedts, pastor of St. Charles. Mother Lucille is our superior; Mother O'Connor, an Irish nun whom you knew at St. Ferdinand, does most of the teaching; and Sister Amyot, a Canadian, is very skilful with all kinds of manual work. In this way they supply all the needs of these children, who can never be kept long at any work. They slip off at any moment and have not yet acquired a taste for learning.

There is not much hope of permanent missions among the neighboring tribes yet, not even among the Osages, who are fairly near and whose river we crossed on the way here. They are still pretty barbarous. They killed an American blacksmith and burned the home of the Protestant ministers. As there are, however, many half-breeds among them, Father Aelen visits them and is kindly received by the big chief. On one trip he baptized thirty people and received a gift of twenty-five francs for us from the chief, who said he hoped we would do something for the Osage children also. Several of the Osage Indians have come to visit our school. They enjoyed hearing the children read and seeing their work. We can take their children only as boarding pupils, but not yet. We thought we were going to find a convent ready for us when we arrived, but we had been misinformed. Our first shelter was the hut of an Indian in which we lived from July to October, when our house, nineteen feet square, was ready, but without a fireplace and without a stairway up to the loft, which was to be our dormitory. One climbs a ladder to reach it. The lower room is parlor, classroom, kitchen, refectory, etc. Neither the St. Louis

convent nor any of the others were able to give us much help.
Our Mother General sent us a gift that is to pay for an addition
that will double the house and give space for orphan children and
those of other tribes. We have not the means to feed them, however. The Government has done nothing for us, in spite of the
efforts of Father Verhaegen, who is himself in great need of
financial help to support the novitiate, to complete the college
church, and to carry on mission work. Could you not send us some
money to buy food for the little Indian girls? So many are ready
to come to the school, and there are the missions of the *Roki*
mountains, too. Give me only your prayers for a happy death and
your fullest blessing. . . .

P.S. Mother Lucille has decided to write to you herself, so I still
have room on this sheet to beg prayers more earnestly, especially
at the Holy Sacrifice of the Mass, for a happy death. That is a
moment to be feared when one has worked with so little fervor. I
want to add also a few more lines about our good Potawatomi.
The Catholic Indians live in a village quite separate from the
pagans, who honor the evil spirit in order to ward off harm.
Among the Catholics there is no drunkenness, no dancing, no
gambling. Every Sunday one sees at least a hundred at the Holy
Table; at Christmas four hundred received the sacraments. On the
feast of the Assumption fifty made their first Communion, the
greater number of these being newly baptized adults. Since last
July about seventy old people have been baptized, and they are
all persevering. In the church the men and women sit on opposite
sides and sing hymns in their own language. They do this also at
night and they say the family rosary, each one carrying a pair
of beads always. More than two hundred received the scapular
of our Lady on a single day. Charity is practiced among them as it
was among the early Christians.

The log church at Sugar Creek was a neat and spacious structure, situated on a bluff about a hundred feet above the level of
the bottom land and blessed on Christmas Day, 1840, under the
title of the Immaculate Conception of the Blessed Virgin. As the
entire mission was dedicated to our Lady, Philippine found herself
once more at *Sainte Marie*, but similarity to the Alpine monastery
ended with the name. The convent erected at Sugar Creek stood
close to the church on an eminence commanding a fine view of the
surrounding country, but the little stream, bordered by sugar
maples and called Sugar Creek, bore no resemblance to the swift
Isère of Dauphiny, nor could the Indian encampment evoke the
memory of Grenoble and the lovely Vale of Grésivaudan. Just half

of the convent had been built in the summer of 1841. Material for the second half was being prepared when Mother Duchesne and her companions learned news that distressed them. So she got out her writing materials again, feeling that there were many things she must tell Mother Barat, whether the news were correct or not. On February 28 she wrote:

We have just learned in our village that you have suddenly re-called our Mother Provincial to France; and she writes to us that, unless she receives a counterorder, she will not be able to visit us. We are all distressed at this news. There is not enough time for us to point out to you the need we have of seeing her and getting everything settled with the Fathers who are guiding our work. But our one consolation is to think of the pleasure you will have in seeing her again and of the great help she will be to you once more in your immense labors. We thank God for your restoration to health, and we continually beg Him to preserve it.

We are all in better health since we came to work among the Indians. We are never in want of anything, as far as food goes, having our good cows and just as good meals as those served in our larger convents of the United States. Only the lodging gives us some reason for sacrifice, for we still have only a log house nineteen feet square. The logs have been prepared with which to make it more than twice that size, but builders are lacking. The savages are not workmen. The men who built the church charged ten francs a day, and it cost fifty francs a week to feed them. The church was built at the expense of the Government, which spends a great deal of money for the civilization of these poor tribes, yet makes little headway. None of the schools opened so far have succeeded. This tribe is the farthest advanced, and all the progress has been made in the past year. Each member of the tribe received 175 francs this year, and the President promised their representatives 50,000 francs with which to pay for clearing the land. Then it will be divided among the Indians. A flour mill has been built for them, and they will be furnished with looms. These are already on hand, whenever the Indians want to use them.

The Father Superior has not been able to obtain anything for the support of his missionaries or our school, and we have been the mission's biggest expense because we needed a house. Would you believe it—and I saw this myself—eight oxen were unable to transport one of the logs used in our building. They had to get ten. And for four days, twelve were harnessed to the same wagon to haul the planks for the flooring of the two rooms, though they had already been brought halfway from the place where they had been sawed. I hope that, when the big logs are lifted one upon the other by the Indians, (that will cost only the food for twenty or thirty men during two days) the Brothers who directed the building of the church will be able at least to oversee what remains to be done on our house. Then the money you so kindly sent us will be sufficient to pay for the work. I do not believe there is enough to pay also for a little chapel.

Madame de Rollin wanted to send me something (500 francs), but the letter of exchange was not accepted. I have written to my brother about this. If Madame de Rollin has not died in the meantime, I think the money will reach us. Will you please let us use it for just one thing—a little wooden chapel opening into the large new stone church which is to be built soon? This would assure to us a private place. We have a place now beside the confessional, but we are always being chased out of it when anyone of importance comes—and that is usually on Sundays, when many members of this good tribe go to Communion.

They tell us that there are many saints buried in the little cemetery. When I walk alone out of doors, I always go there, and I kneel and beg of God the favor of being buried beside them. I feel, however, the same longing for the *Rocki* Mountain missions and any others like them, that I experienced in France when I first begged to come to America, the same longing I felt for the Indian missions, once I reached this country. They say that in the *Rocki* people live to be a hundred years old. As my health has improved and I am only seventy-three, I think I shall have at least ten more years to work.

I used to think it more perfect to wait for things to take their course and so decide my fate. But now, Reverend Mother, will you not authorize me to go farther west if they want me to do so? Of course, that is still rather doubtful, but here I am only a burden to others, as I have no real employment, and there is no doubt about it, they would be glad to have me recalled. I knew from the beginning that I was not wanted. One of the missionaries got permission to remain as long as he desired, even though he was wanted at the college. That makes me hope for a similar favor. . . .

The most experienced of the missionaries here says we really must overlook many things in the Indian girls and gain their affection by every means possible. Though he has tried to do this, he has not been able to hold twenty of the boys he fed—they all went home. He added that in dealing with the Indian children one must use methods entirely different from those used with white children. He says that the little savages never forget a refusal or a reprimand and that superiors at a distance cannot make regulations for them. He advises that we accept as boarders only the little girls who live at too great a distance to be day pupils. This priest is the one most skilled in the Indian language [Father Christian Hoecken]. He hopes soon to compile a dictionary, and he will let us use a grammar he has completed. He has sent the Father General what he wants to have printed in this language. With these helps he thinks a person can understand the language and make himself understood rather quickly. I can scarcely believe this, for other priests, after two years, have made little progress. In this very difficult tongue there is not a single word resembling a French word. There are some that resemble Hebrew and Greek, and the Father concludes from this fact that the savages are of Jewish descent.

I am ashamed of having taken up so much of your time, but I know you are a Mother, the most indulgent of mothers. Bless your daughter who kneels in spirit at your feet—the worst, but also the most devoted of your daughters.

The log convent was completed by mid-March. The crevices between the mural logs were packed with mud, while inside the cabins, set side by side about ten feet apart, heavy cotton cloth was stretched over the walls and whitewashed. On windy days this canvas often swelled out like the sails of a vessel, and when a fierce gale swept across the prairie it sometimes ripped the cloth from its fastenings. While the work was at its height, Philippine was begged to remain in safety in the church. Nothing could please her more than this, and there were such vital intentions to lay before her Eucharistic Lord: the mission and her dread of having to leave it, the coming General Council that was so important in Mother Barat's eyes, the novitiate at Florissant. As she knelt motionless before the tabernacle, lost in prayer, the Indians would steal into the church and watch her intently, then noiselessly approach her, kneel, and kiss the hem of her worn habit or the fringe of her old shawl. *Quah-kah-ka-num-ad*—Woman-who-prays-always!

The thought of Florissant had been in her mind persistently since she had received a wholly unexpected letter from Bishop Rosati, written from New York on January 13, 1842, as he was about to sail for the tropics on a papal mission.

On the eve of my departure for Haiti [he wrote], I believe it necessary to steal a few moments from my other occupations to write you a word on a subject of importance to your Society in America. I have learned that Mother Galitzin has decided to transfer the novitiate from St. Ferdinand to Conewago in Pennsylvania. I was greatly surprised at this, and I see no reason for it. It is certainly not the sterility of the novitiates located in Missouri and

Louisiana. You have now more than one hundred religious in your American houses, of whom only twenty have come from Europe. All the others have been formed in the novitiates of Missouri and Louisiana. The transfer of your novitiate to Conewago will close the door of your Society to the young ladies of the country that until the present has furnished you with such a great number of subjects. You cannot expect parents to consent to send their children a distance of some two thousand miles.

Even supposing they consent to it, who will accompany them? Who will furnish the money for the trip? If they do not persevere, how can they be sent home at such a distance? And how expensive it will be to distribute the subjects from Conewago to the different houses of the South and West! These expenses will be much greater than those needed for the support of the novitiate at St. Ferdinand. What difficulties the young religious will encounter!

You may argue that these difficulties are the same if postulants are sent from New York to St. Ferdinand and back again as religious. I admit this, but I do not think this is necessary. You can open a novitiate in New York, or, if you prefer, at Conewago for the houses of this section. This will remove the inconveniences, if you leave the novitiates of Louisiana and Missouri where they are. When you consider the immense extent of the United States, which is three or four times the size of France or Italy, you cannot think that three novitiates are unnecessary. You have two in Italy. The Jesuits have three in the United States. They are needed to prepare for the future of our country, which is now in its adolescence.

The growth of religion here during the past few years assures us of progress in the future. That is why we believe it necessary to erect bishoprics in sections that now have scarcely any Catholics. Your Society will stretch out to all the dioceses of the eastern part of the United States. So a novitiate in this section is necessary. To have it, however, does not require the destruction of what has already been founded in the West and South. At St. Ferdinand there was a nice little boarding school that was getting along very well. You suppressed it to place the novitiate there. The novitiate has been there scarcely a year, and you think of transferring it, thereby destroying all that has been accomplished.

Madame, it is in the interest of your Society that I write you this. You know how attached I am to this Society, which I regard as the most beautiful ornament of my diocese. I am rushed. Pray for me. . . .

Quite as unexpected as the Bishop's letter was Mother Galitzin's arrival at Sugar Creek on the eve of Palm Sunday for a two days' visit. She saw the mission in full activity, received a hearty welcome from the braves and squaws, complete with parade, equestrian demonstration, and hand-shaking, and examined the handiwork of the little girls. By some unexplained means the nuns procured a bed for her, and she was not permitted to climb the ladder-stairs to their dormitory loft. What she thought of the Bishop's wise letter is unrecorded; it certainly had no effect on the plans she had made and would carry out within a few weeks, to the later sorrow of the Society in the United States. One change, however, was decided on, though it was kept secret for the present from the one whom it most concerned: Mother Duchesne would have to go back to one of the Missouri convents within a few months.

There seems to have been no suspicion of the impending change in Philippine's mind when on Easter Sunday she stood as a witness with Brother Van der Borget, S.J., to the marriage of Pierre Drayard and Theresa Rose Kusto, Potawatomi Indians, nor even when she wrote to her sister two weeks later on April 24:

> I hope you will not object if I answer your letter and that of your beloved daughter Josephine together. I did not know her in France, but I love her dearly because of all I have heard about her and because of the joy she gives you. Tell her to pray much for me and for Mother Lucille, whom she loved so much at Sainte-Marie-d'en-Haut. She is here at the Indian mission with me. There are just four of us, but that is enough as we have only day pupils at present.
>
> One really could not find better people than these good savages. Two of them work for us, and as they do not like to stay at any one thing for long, they amuse themselves and laugh like children —always happy, yet looking as tall and straight as warriors. When we do our washing, they bring their soiled clothes, too, and their mending. The children who come to school are very skilful, but quite lazy. Of course we receive no remuneration from anyone and are obliged to furnish the materials for their sewing, etc. They have already exhausted our supply of needles for darning and sewing; thimbles, scissors, thread, all disappear quickly. They do nothing unless we furnish all the material. I saw one poor mother of a family whose husband was ill and whose children were in rags, but she could not borrow enough thread among the Indians to mend their clothes. Sometimes poor Indians come to us and show us their torn clothing, making us understand by signs that they have no needles and thread. And they go away very happy if we supply their need. So whenever you want to give me a present, I shall ask for some galloon—medium width, for a vest-

ment, some thread of different colors for cross-stitching, some needles, thimbles, scissors, and some small, light-weight knives. Since German-speaking people have opened stores in St. Louis, we can get everything else we need, but at a high price. But we cannot get church goods there.

You would be deeply moved by the piety of this good tribe, which had already been converted to the faith in large numbers before being moved into this region. . . . There are baptisms of adults almost every week, some even from neighboring tribes. The priest often calls on one of his catechists to give a little sermon for their benefit. The Indian rises quite readily. Wrapt in his blanket, with his eyes lowered, he begins to speak. As he becomes more animated, he stretches his arm from under the blanket, then finishes his discourse with the air of an experienced orator. The same thing happens at the daily catechism lesson. This is held in the Indian language, as are also the night prayers. The church erected with the help of 4000 francs donated by the Government is already too small. When they are able, the Fathers will build a larger church and use the old one as a hospital, for there are many sick people in the tribe who are not cared for properly as they have no homes, no relatives, no means of support. The death rate among the Indians is high, especially among the tribes where the evil spirit is worshiped, for part of their ceremonial consists of swallowing certain medicines that are really poison and that are given to their captives. The Osage tribe has diminished by half in the last few years. They are still fierce and unhappy, though they were the first with whom the white man traded in this section of the country. But their contact with those early whites only added drunkenness to their other vices. Recently I tasted some of the roots they eat when there is no game to hunt. The strongest woody old turnip would be delicious in comparison. Starvation kills off as many among them as does poison.

Do not think, my beloved Euphrosine, that distance from you dims my memory of you. In prayer I frequently beg God to bless you and yours. In return please have a Mass offered for me at Notre Dame de Fourvière. If you have an opportunity to speak to dear Mother Goeffroy and the community at La Ferrandière, tell them we are very much at home here. We are growing fat on the milk of our fine cows and we are all in good health. Adieu, my dearly loved Sister. . . .

That last extant letter from the Indian mission contains dramatic material for a mural: the Jesuit missionary and his neophytes in the log church, the baptismal ceremony, the young brave with lowered eyes standing among them, wrapt in his bright-hued blanket and speaking with dignified gestures to his fellow tribesmen of God, the Great Spirit now made known to them in the light of Christian truth, the intent, motionless figures in the background—men and women still groping in the darkness of paganism, and there in a corner by the confessional the old nun, clasping her rosary, the baptismal register on her knees and the rapture of heaven in her eyes. She had attained her goal. She had, all unconsciously, proved the constancy of her courage, the heroism of her faith, the unfathomable depth of her selfless love.

Yet a trial awaited her that would test, once and for all, the fine steel of her endurance. The bright vision of work among the Indians that had for more than thirty years steadied her faith and hope in the darkest hours at St. Charles, at Florissant, and in St. Louis, was to fade into the shadows of the past, like the momentary glory of a sunset, and she was to know a darker path and an even greater need for ardent faith and supreme confidence.

Springtime and early summer at Sugar Creek were crowded with activity. Mother Duchesne went about the mission with firmer step and more vigorous determination. Sometimes small groups of Indian girls gathered about her as she sat in a shady place, and she helped them with their knitting, or showed them the mysterious thing she still carried in her pocket—the watch she had brought from France so long ago, or let them handle reverently the big rosary she wore at her side.

She was looking forward to the visit of Monseigneur Kenrick, Coadjutor Bishop of St. Louis, who was coming in early June to administer confirmation at the mission.[29] She hoped he would be friendly and understanding like her good friend, Bishop Rosati, who was now back in Rome to report to the Holy Father the outcome of his trip to Haiti. She wondered about the new Bishop's French. That was always a problem for her. Bishop Kenrick was all that she had anticipated, except on one point—he disapproved of her remaining at Sugar Creek. The prelate who ten years later would call her "the holiest person he had ever known," was not content to let her "lay her bones to rest in the Indian cemetery," as she had so often expressed the wish. He counseled a return to St. Louis. It was not an order, but she knew there was more behind it than counsel. The weekly mail soon brought the dreaded letter from France—Mother Barat was asking of her "eldest daughter" the supreme sacrifice of the Indian mission.

As soon as Father Verhaegen was informed of the order, which was announced by another letter to Mother Gray, he planned a trip to Sugar Creek. He had escorted Mother Duchesne up the Missouri to the Indian Territory; he would bring her back safely, though it was a bitter disappointment for him to have to do so. On June 19 they left the mission, after a demonstration of affection on the part of the Indians that must have moved Philippine to tears. Traveling slowly in a rough, jolting wagon through dust and heat, they stopped to say goodbye to Napoleon Bourassa and his Potawatomi wife, Memetekosikwe, who had so often befriended the nuns during the past year. Four days later they boarded the river packet at Westport and reached St. Louis on June 29, 1842, exactly a year from the day they had set out for Sugar Creek. No sudden spurt of courage and generosity had carried Mother Duchesne through this hardest ordeal of her cross-strewn career, but the habits of a lifetime, above all the habit of simple acceptance of God's will through love.

After a short rest at the City House, Mother Duchesne drove to St. Charles with Mother Eleanor Gray. The cordial and loving welcome given her by Mother Regis Hamilton and her community helped to lessen the sorrow that weighed heavily upon her. In the hurried preparations for leaving Sugar Creek there had been some distraction from grief, but in the quiet routine of life at St. Charles, the realization of *failure* crept over her once more, bringing with it an agony of disappointment that summed itself up in the haunting thought, "All that effort of love in vain!" But she knew in her inmost heart that it had not been in vain, and peace came flooding into her soul as she knelt in the cloister chapel and renewed her complete surrender to God's will, a surrender involving what was most dear to her, the hardest submission God had asked of her. She must have found it bewilderingly hard to accept, yet not a trace of rebellion appears in the letters she wrote shortly after she took her place as the nineteenth member of the St. Charles community.[30] Interest in the welfare of others dictated them, but there was no artificial stifling of her own feelings as she wrote to Mother Boilvin on August 7:

> Two days ago, my dearest Sister, I sent Mother Bathilde two letters for France, and here are two more. I hope this is not ill-advised on my part. My correspondence with all in France will be more and more limited hereafter.
>
> I heard that you were miserable physically, and my loving interest in your health makes me fear you have tried to do more

than your strength allows. You have always needed to spare your voice in singing and to have a little more sleep than the rest of the community. So have the humility and the simplicity to admit your needs and accept the proper care.

From my last letter you learned of my departure from Indian Territory. I cannot forget the savages, even though I am surrounded by everything that can edify me and fill me with gratitude. The religious whom I had never met, as well as those whom I had known for a long time, are full of kind thoughtfulness for me.

I left our Sisters at Sugar Creek in good health. Just now there are at that mission Reverend Father Verreydt and the two Fathers Hoecken, who are both in poor health. Pray for their restoration, for the sake of the poor tribes whom they have gathered around them. A little five-room house had been built for us before I left. Many of the children had learned to read, knit, card wool, and spin. Some already knew how to sew when we went there, and they like this kind of work best of all. They are beginning to settle down; and as they are quite intelligent, we may hope that, with the help of the prayers offered to God and the perseverance of the nuns in caring for them, they will make progress in virtue and knowledge. The Father Provincial has recalled Father Aelen to St. Louis. A thousand messages of respect and love to our Mothers and Sisters in New York. . . .

One of the letters for France which Philippine mentioned to Mother Boilvin was written to Father De La Croix. In it she repeated her appeal for funds to help the mission at Sugar Creek, supporting her request with some information about economic conditions in the Mississippi Valley, where recovery from the financial crisis of 1837 had been very slow. She closed her letter with a touching little reference to herself:

I received a letter from you which you had given a long time ago to the Bishop of Detroit. It reached me only when I had gone to the Indian country. I answered from there, begging help from the Society for the Propagation of the Faith for our establishment, which has only one purpose, the instruction of the little savages. My Superior General considers me too old for that work, so she wrote me to return to St. Charles, our first American home. I thought I should write to you and ask you to address any funds you intend sending for the work among the savages to the Provincial of the Jesuits, who will be best acquainted with the needs and the situation of each mission. Already two have had to be abandoned, for drunkenness was introduced and nothing more could be done.

We have had no direct news recently from Father De Smet.[31] One traveler announced that he had reached the Flatheads beyond the *Rokis* safely. Another spoke of his success and said that one of the three priests in his mission band had descended the Arkansas River, going to beg in New Orleans. He will get little help there, as economic affairs are in a bad condition. Enrollments in our academies in Louisiana have diminished. . . . The same money shortage exists in St. Louis, so the academy there is reduced from sixty to thirty pupils. The novitiate has been transferred from St. Ferdinand to a place near Philadelphia, and there is only a day school left. At St. Charles, where I am living now, a good brick building was put up some years ago through the efforts of Father Van Quickenborne. As I live a very solitary life, I can employ all my time in making reparation for the past and in preparing for death. But I cannot put out of my mind the thought of the savages, and my ambition carries me even to the *Roki*. I can only adore the designs of God, who has taken from me the thing I had so long desired. . . .

thirteen

The Reality of God's Will

I. 1842—1847

Realizing the sweetness of Thy loving Heart,
may we learn to despise the things of earth
and to cherish those of heaven.

Postcommunion, Mass of the Sacred Heart

THE YEAR 1842 WAS CRITICAL in the history of the Society
of the Sacred Heart. The period of trial accorded the new decrees
formulated by the Sixth General Council was drawing to a close,
and the whole Society was in eager anticipation of the coming
council. "It will be a very important meeting," Mother Barat had
written to Philippine in August, 1841, "and we have great need of
God's help. Pray. . . ." During the autumn and winter of 1840–
1841 the Superior General had been very ill and therefore was
unable to carry out her plan of visiting all the convents in France
before the council took place. In June, 1841, however, she began
her visitation of the houses of northern France and Belgium. She
was well satisfied with these communities. Returning to Paris for a
few days, she set out again in September, visiting houses to the east
and south and arriving in Rome before Christmas.

In February, 1842, she received from Pope Gregory XVI the
unequivocal statement that she should return to France and make
that her ordinary place of residence. Consulting Cardinal Lam-
bruschini, Papal Secretary of State, as to where the coming council
should be held, she was told emphatically, "In France and not elsewhere, and this in order to accede to the wishes of the French
bishops," and the Cardinal named Lyons as the most suitable place.

660

Acting on this advice, Mother Barat issued a circular letter to the Society on February 21 to prepare the way for the Seventh General Council. At the same time she told Mother Galitzin of her intention of returning to France in July and holding the assembly there. Accordingly Mother Galitzin sailed for France in May with Mother Hardey, who was to represent the American province at the council. From Paris they went directly to Rome, only to find that Mother Barat was already at the convent of La Ferrandière in Lyons. They had the pleasure, however, of being presented to the Holy Father by Bishop Rosati and of experiencing his personal interest in all that concerned the Society's work in America and, above all, its great pioneer missionary, Philippine Duchesne.

The councilors who assembled at Lyons formed a numerous body—Assistants General, Provincials, several local superiors, and a professed delegate from each province. Of all who had been expected to take part in the deliberations only Mother Eugenie de Gramont was missing. In her stead came a letter from Monseigneur Affre, Archbishop of Paris. Arrogating to himself the title of ecclesiastical superior of the order, an office abolished in 1826, he forbade the Mother General to hold the council anywhere outside his episcopal city. Moreover, his letter carried an ominous threat: he had calculated all the consequences of this prohibition, and the Mothers would have reason to regret it if they disobeyed his orders. He had communicated his opposition to Lyons and his disapproval of the decrees of 1839 to the twenty-two French bishops having convents of the Sacred Heart in their dioceses, and they all joined him in his protest. Mother Barat could only appeal to Rome to enlighten the Archbishop on the matter of ecclesiastical superiority in the Society, but that meant weeks of delay while a commission of eight cardinals investigated the matter and answered the petition.

The Mothers who had assembled for the council went into retreat under the direction of Father Joseph Barelle, S.J. "The Lord gathered you together for important business," he said in his opening talk. "It seemed urgent . . . and lo! He says, 'Not yet, think of Me, and of your own soul. Fear not; your affairs are in My hands.' " [1] But when the exercises were completed, no answer had come from Rome, so there could be no council. As the Archbishop of Lyons had arbitrarily imposed silence on Mother Barat regarding the cause of the indefinite adjournment she was now obliged to give, the Superior General bore the full responsibility of it in the eyes of the astonished Society and the interested outside world.

At the end of August the Mothers Councilor dispersed, each to the house from which she had come, and Mother Barat set out for Besançon and Autun. The answer of the commission of cardinals, supported by a papal brief, proved clearly that Monseigneur Affre possessed no special jurisdiction over the Religious of the Sacred Heart, and in November Mother Barat submitted this answer to the Archbishop. The resulting complications necessitated Rome's re-examination of the *Constitutions* of the Society, which happily led to a decree confirming in their entirety the rules approved in 1826.[2]

In the meanwhile Mother Hardey had returned to America, bringing with her several recruits for the American foundations, among them Mothers Cauche and Cruice. They were on the high seas when, on October 24, Mother Duchesne wrote to Mother Bazire, now a member of the New York community:

> I want to thank you and Mother Boilvin for your interesting letters which gave joy to my solitude. I am very happy about the progress of your new establishment. The details about the foundations to be made in England and Ireland were very welcome, and also those about the convent of Notre Dame de Fourvière in Lyons, of which we had not heard before we got the list of our houses and their communities. . . .
>
> Louisiana prospered for a time; Missouri has always vegetated; now both seem destined to work under difficulties. Mothers Thiéfry and Gray certainly have their share of crosses, and this house could scarcely be poorer than it is. They say the upset condition of economic affairs throughout the country will continue for about two and a half years longer. I do not understand economics, but I do realize how bitter it is to be unable to contribute to the many good works that are in great need of aid. I believe they are better off at Sugar Creek than we are here, but what an immense amount of good could be accomplished if help could be sent to the missions beyond the Rocky Mountains. The farther the missionaries advance toward the ocean, the easier their work becomes. Father De Smet writes that they have baptized 1200 Indians and that there is work enough for twenty priests and twenty Brothers, if only they had them. How much it takes to support these missions! When one thinks of this, one is tempted to wish that one were rich. . . .
>
> Do they know in New York about the Confraternity of the

Holy Heart of Mary for the conversion of sinners? The Holy Father, Gregory XVI, by a brief has granted many indulgences to this association and it is bringing about extraordinary conversions. You would do well to help establish it in New York. The booklet about this association can be gotten at Notre Dame des Victoires in Paris. It was published in 1839 and is very interesting.

One of the two enclosures to Mother Bazire was written to Father De La Croix in the hope of obtaining financial help for the convent at St. Charles, where, she said,

> I find myself in a house even poorer than the one I left among the Potawatomi. It is very distressing for me to add a new burden here, being the object of so many charitable attentions on the part of my superior, Mother Regis Hamilton. This house has always been poor, but the poverty has increased since they put up the addition to the new brick convent.[3] The general stagnation of economic life has extended to this part of America, and they say it will last two more years. Everyone is hard up. All our boarding schools have lost pupils and those who remain pay very poorly. . . . I tell you quite frankly, Reverend Father, my purpose in writing to you is to beg some help to support St. Charles in these wretched times, if you have any funds of the Society for the Propagation of the Faith at your disposal.
>
> Recently I feared I was going to be the only one left of those of us who first came to America, for Sister Catherine Lamarre has been quite ill.[4] For thirty-eight years my great desire was to work among the savages. I even hoped to go to Father De Smet's mission in the *Rokis*. Then after one year of uselessness at the Indian mission I came back here by order of my Superior General, without having accomplished anything and without hope of ever accomplishing anything.

A letter to her sister, written the same day, has a more personal touch and a flash of the old fire. In it one feels how distressed she is at the poverty of the convent at St. Charles, but she does not beg financial help from her family:

> At the beginning of August, dearest Sister, I wrote to Madame de Rollin and asked her to share the letter with you. I took the liberty of accepting your offer and suggested that you send me some galloon for a chasuble. In my present life of solitude I have the very satisfying occupation of embroidering a cross for a chasuble with the remnants of the silks you sent me, and I use

them so economically, I shall even have a good deal left over. I am very fortunate to have saved them so long. You realize, of course, that my work is quite imperfect, but I enjoy it very much. I cannot finish the vestment, however, until I get the galloon. . . .

I hope soon to receive some of the income due me from the royal treasury, in which my father invested a trust fund in my name. I believe they think I have lived too long. At the time of the last payment they declared they would send me no more unless the judge who signed the attestation saying I was alive also stated that he had seen my baptismal record or birth certificate. I asked my brother to send me a copy. I should have received it by this time. Please ask him if he sent it. If he has not done so, tell him to have it copied on thin paper and sent by post from Havre. . . . Affectionate messages to this dear brother. I hope he does not regret his generosity to me at the Indian mission, where he predicted I should not remain two years. He was right, but I had no desire to leave there, and his money was used most beneficially. God will reward him for sending it. Madame de Rollin inquired the best way by which to send things to me. Tell her to send through the procuratrix, Mother de Lemps, at Rue de Varenne, Paris. I have just as much need now as when I was with the Indians. All our houses are in straitened circumstances as a result of the business depression which has been produced, no doubt, by the circulation of paper money that has met the same fate as our *assignats* in France long ago.

For an authentic picture of the home in which Philippine Duchesne spent the last decade of her life, one has only to read the description written by her niece, Mother Amelie Jouve, who visited her there in 1847:

The convent at St. Charles is very pleasantly situated on the bluffs overlooking the Missouri River. It is an unpretentious little building, enlarged on one side by a cloister chapel that looks into the sanctuary of the parish church. Here the religious can assist at all services and hear the instruction given by the Jesuit Fathers. At the [south] end of that chapel [beyond a partition wall] there is a small room, about eight feet wide by fifteen or sixteen feet long. These are the two places in which Mother Duchesne spent most of her time—now at prayer, now at manual labor. The furniture of her little room consisted of a low cot, a chair, a wooden box in which she kept her treasures—and what treasures they were! Some instruments of penance, some spiritual notebooks, some letters of our Mother General. There were two or three old pictures of pious subjects on the walls and some well worn prayerbooks on a little table.[5]

As Philippine sat by the window in her little room sewing or reading or looking out at the wide, turbulent river and the rolling country beyond, memories of her first year in America must have come crowding into her mind. She was by disposition reminiscent, and recreating the past was often a delightful distraction for her. From the back porch of the convent she could look up the hillside to the dilapidated old Duquette "mansion," now used as a wash-house. Often in warm weather she saw the children in their pink gingham uniforms and green sunbonnets playing on the gallery of the house or under the big trees on the playground. They were such a small group, it seemed at times a waste of effort and energy to run the boarding school for them, but Mother Hamilton clung to the hope that it would survive the depression years and be built up again. To this intention Philippine applied her most earnest prayers. At a short distance behind the church she could see the little cemetery that had been staked off before Mother Mathevon left St. Charles. One white cross was there when Philippine first visited it in 1842, and that marked the grave of Mother Eulalie Guillot, but soon there were other crosses driven into the little leveled plot at the base of the second bluff.

When winter came and the cold was severe, Mother Duchesne recalled the bitter weather of her first winter in Missouri and refused to have a charcoal brazier lighted in her room. What was the chill of the brick convent in comparison to the icy atmosphere of the log church at Sugar Creek or the unplastered room at Florissant? There were sick nuns in the infirmary who had more need of the little heater, she thought. Sometimes she made her way slowly up the steep stairway to visit them, to cheer them with thoughts of God and stories gathered from missionaries and Catholic chronicles and spiritual books. She often inserted stories in the letters she wrote to her family in France. A letter to her sister Euphrosine opens with a charming picture of Philippine in her little room on May 5, 1843, as happy as a child on Christmas morning:

> Surrounded by the wealth of gifts you have sent me, dearest Sister, I hasten to acknowledge the receipt of them. If I had prepared a list of all the things I wanted, you could not have succeeded better in satisfying all my desires. Accept my most heart-

felt thanks. I had sent you word by Madame de Rollin that I knew the package had arrived in America,[6] but it was delayed somewhere on our frozen rivers during the long, severe winter, and I received it only today. . . .

It seems to me that in leaving the Indians I left my real element, and now I can only yearn for that land from which there will be no departure. God knows why I was recalled, and that is enough. My greatest joy now is to hear about the hopes raised by the mission in the Rocky Mountains. The leader of these missionaries, Father De Smet, is obliged to go to Europe to beg help, for he must have money to undertake and carry on this enterprise. At the risk of telling you what you already know from Catholic publications, I am going to relate two incidents that show God's great mercy to this vast country . . .

And she was off on a storytelling expedition in company with Indian children, Black Robes, and the Blessed Virgin. Then she continues:

The mission where I was stationed, just beyond the Missouri border, is doing well. The savages are becoming more civilized; many are accepting Catholicism; and many are learning to farm. All this takes time, for they will be happy only when they can overcome their natural laziness. Our nuns write that they no longer have to urge the children to do their work; they love it. The Indian agent who visited that tribe was highly pleased and gave an order for all the school supplies they needed—pens, paper, books, cotton for spinning—and he promised to recommend the school to Congress. . . .

Louisiana, which was formerly so rich, is suffering very much economically, and so is Missouri, so there are very few people able to pay tuition fees, and as a result we, too, are in great want. But I am not in need of anything, and I am keeping for my work a good share of the fine supplies you sent. Adieu, dear Sister. I never forget you or your children. It is such a pleasure to be united with you in spirit. . . .

The work of the Society in New York and Pennsylvania was of particular interest to Mother Duchesne because it was being done in large part by religious whom she knew personally and whose names occur frequently in her letters. The foundation at Mc-Sherrystown near Conewago was made under Mother Galitzin's supervision in the spring of 1842, Mother de Kersaint becoming superior and mistress of novices and Mother Margaret Murphy from St. Louis, assistant.[7] Mother Mary Ann Roche soon joined the community, which included several novices from New York and Louisiana. The free school quickly enrolled fifty children, but the academy made little progress. Changes, accidents, and an alarming decline in the health of the community make the record of the years at McSherrystown sad history. When Mother de Kersaint was chosen for the foundation of the first Canadian convent of the Sacred Heart in the autumn of 1842, Mothers Caroline Cauche and Catherine Cruice, who had come from France with Mother Hardey, became superior and mistress of novices, respectively. In December Zoë Mignard, a novice from Louisiana, died of tuberculosis at McSherrystown—the first among many to succumb to the disease.

In March, 1843, while Mother Cauche was inspecting the work being done on the roof by laborers, about whose safety she was worried, a heavy plank fell from the scaffolding and struck her on the head. Her life was saved by prompt medical care, but the mental incapacity that followed called for a new superior at McSherrystown, and Mother Adeline Boilvin was chosen for the position, with the double work of guiding the community and school and directing the novices, as Mother Cruice was called back to New York, where Bishop Rosati's prediction was fulfilled and another novitiate was opened. Mother Boilvin had been but a few weeks at her new post when she wrote to Mother Duchesne, telling her of the changes and begging her prayers. On October 18 Philippine replied with sympathy, encouragement, and all the news she thought the community at McSherrystown might enjoy:

Yesterday, my dear Mother, I received your letter and began at once the novena you asked for; today I received Holy Communion for the same intention. I was completely ignorant of the fact that Mother Cauche was ill and that you had replaced her. I am not at all surprised that you were astonished at this change and distressed by it. But after all, God willed the blow that has struck you; His will is expressed by the orders of superiors and by the great need there was of replacing these dear Mothers. Your natural inclination is thwarted, and this shows that on your side there was nothing done even to suggest the promotion by which you—and such a little person you are—now find yourself a superior.

You must, then, bend your shoulders under the yoke of two heavy offices, those of Superior and Mistress of Novices. If humility is always desirable, generous humility is still more so now. Obedience has not destined you to be an Alexis or a Benedict Labre, but rather to imitate the courage of St. de Chantal and St. Teresa without the least human respect. . . . These women were great saints. I hope you will become one also by acting in your present position just as if you were engaged in the lowliest employments. I shall pray much for you and your large religious family. The family you gave up for God seems about as usual. Your Grandmother St. Cyr can still go to church and she seems physically stronger than Maria. I shall give them news of you, just in case you have not done so. They say Maria makes use of her infirmities to advance in perfection.

Mother Thiéfry is very happy at Sugar Creek, and they are delighted to have her there. She was quite ill when she first went there, and now Sister Louise is ill. Everyone is well in this community now and all are able to come to recreation. It is the first time this has happened since I came here. The upset condition in our convents and the opening of the free school by the Sisters of Charity, who also admit to it children who can pay, have reduced our boarding schools rather sadly. The Sisters have 200 children —almost all there are of school age. Our nuns in St. Louis have only twenty-eight boarding pupils, the same number of orphans, and fifty in the free school. Here there are fifty or sixty parish school children and nine boarding pupils, two of them paying nothing at all, one very little, and two paying just half the tuition. Imagine the penury and the cross! But Divine Providence has always been at hand in our need after trying our faith.

I have no news from Louisiana, except a great decrease in the number of pupils. The same is true of the college in St. Louis and, I suppose, of the one at Grand Coteau. Father De Vos has gone to the Rocky Mountains, Father Smedts is Master of Novices at St. Ferdinand, and Father Verhaegen, who was Provincial, is now pastor here at St. Charles, to the delight of the nuns and the parish. Father Van de Velde is now Provincial, Father Carrell is President of the College, Father Gleizal is pastor of the parish dedicated to St. Francis Xavier. They say the new church is very beautiful. One is also being built for the Irish Catholics under Father Hamilton's direction near the Biddle home, and another for the Germans.[8] The church near the Bishop's seminary is served by the Lazarists. . . . Our Mother Provincial has not arrived yet, but she is expected any day now.

Mother Galitzin had returned to America in the spring of 1843. Realizing the harm she had done in pressing too vehemently the acceptance of the Jesuit Rule and the decrees of 1839, she had begged to be allowed to revisit the convents in the United States and restore the original organization of the Society as established there by Mother Duchesne and her companions. She spent the summer in New York, Canada, and Pennsylvania, then turned westward over the route now familiar to her. When Mother Hamilton went to St. Louis to see her and report on conditions in the convent she was directing, the visitatrix made a swift decision and ordered the closing of the boarding school at St. Charles. It was Mother Hamilton's difficult duty to carry out this order in the midst of very trying circumstances. Within the space of a few days eight of the religious who had been teaching at St. Charles were transferred to either St. Louis or Florissant, where the boarding school had been reopened for the fourth time, and six of the nine pupils had joined their City House companions.[9]

Mother Galitzin was advised by the doctors in St. Louis to go south as soon as possible in order to avoid the rigor of the Missouri winter. On reaching St. Michael's, she found yellow fever raging. With the rashness that characterized her generosity she insisted on nursing the sick, and on December 1 she herself was stricken. God had accepted the sacrifice of her life, made the year before at La Ferrandière, when she thought the existence of the Society was threatened, and death came to her on the feast of the Immaculate Conception.[10]

Mother Duchesne's reaction to the upheaval at St. Charles and the death of the Visitatrix appears in a letter to Mother Boilvin, answering a New Year's greeting from McSherrystown:

> You took a very tiny piece of paper to write to me, and I am devoting the largest part of this big sheet to answer your letter, and still it seems small in comparison with all I have to tell you. First of all, let us talk about your Grandmother: Father Van Assche told me she is getting along as well as possible and goes to church almost every day. Maria is still very weak. She was in bed the last day the good Father was there. He is confessor of this convent on the Ember Days. You already know that Father Verhaegen fills the position of pastor here now. We are very much afraid this arrangement will not last long. . . .
>
> You have also learned of the great loss the Society has sustained in the death of Reverend Mother Galitzin. Mother L'Eveque, who cared for her during her painful illness, is inconsolable. With your sympathetic heart you can easily understand the sorrow felt in Missouri. Before she left St. Louis, she was ill with fever and so could not visit us at St. Charles. She sent for Mother Hamilton, and on hearing how few children we had and how much sickness there had been in the community, she struck us a severe blow—had

the children transferred to St. Louis, along with several of the nuns, and sent others to St. Ferdinand. There are just eight of us left in this big house. Only Mother Hamilton and Sister Couture speak French. In just a few days we found ourselves living in solitude, with the last—that is the parish school—having become the first. Our convent was offered to the Visitandine religious at Kaskaskia, who want to leave their present place of residence because of illness. They refused this one, however, wishing to establish their monastery nearer St. Louis. They may be there already.[11]

I still hold on to some hope that our Mother General will not sanction these measures, which are so heartbreaking, especially for me. I saw the work begin here, and perhaps I shall see it destroyed. I wrote to her with all the urgent entreaties I could employ, begging her to renew the life of this house and allow us once more to admit the children who would support it. At present we can take no measure by which to do so. They were counting, perhaps, on Louisiana, but money is as scarce there as here, and the enrollments are low. The Jesuits are suffering a great deal.

I have written enough to show you the state of my poor heart. Do not fail to get earnest prayers for our resurrection; and when you write to Mother Barat, plead our cause. You ought to tell her also that it would give great satisfaction generally, both outside the convents and inside, if we had a Mother Provincial who was American by birth and language. You know Mother Hardey well. You could tell our Mother General your opinion of her. She is the one I would choose, if my advice were asked. Try to bear up under your burden. God is very good to have eased it by the sincere and affable character that marks all your family. . . . Pray more earnestly than ever to St. Francis Regis for St. Charles and St. Ferdinand. I attribute all our troubles and anxieties to the destruction of his shrine. How I long to erect it again! The latest news from Sugar Creek was good. Adieu, my dear Mother. Pray for me that I may have a happy death.

Mother Duchesne wrote also to Mother Margaret Murphy that day, not knowing that she and several others in the McSherrystown community were very ill:

The more you enjoy your peaceful convent, the more you ought to compassionate ours, over which we can only weep. . . . Do not neglect any means of inclining God to be favorable to us. As Jesus has promised to refuse nothing to those who invoke Him through His adorable Name, put it always first in your prayers for us, then invoke Mary, saying the *Memorare* many times. If this trial lasts long, the convent will be closed. Pray that I may die before that happens. I do not believe I have the strength to bear such a sorrow. One must have experienced what I have experienced and seen what I have seen to understand its bitterness. But I have said enough about sorrows; resignation must have its place in our souls. Pray for that also for me.

In pleading with Mother Barat for the survival of the convent at St. Charles, Mother Duchesne had voiced not only her own sentiments but also those of many of the religious who loved that convent with special affection. Among them was Mother Regis Hamilton, who sent an earnest plea to the Superior General, representing how unsatisfactory the new arrangement was and how destitute it left the community. Six months passed before a letter from Mother Barat brought the desired answer: the academy was to be reopened the following school year and at least two members of the community would return from St. Louis at once. That the little group of nuns at St. Charles considered this letter as addressed to themselves is revealed in this entry in the *Journal* of the convent on May 2: "We have received a letter from our Mother General containing the joyful news that some of our dear absent Sisters are to return to us and that this house is not to be broken up." The letter was addressed to Mother Hamilton, the superior, and contained no separate answer for Philippine.

This was a great disappointment to her, a shock to her sensitive and affectionate heart, and she interpreted it as a reproof for having written as she did. On her recall from Sugar Creek she had written to Mother Boilvin, "My correspondence with all in France will be more and more limited hereafter." Now she seems to have renewed that determination, though it must have caused her keen suffering to carry it out.[12] But in this matter she was acting in accordance with a recommendation of the Sixth General Council which Mother Galitzin had emphasized and which would later on be written into a decree to the effect that, although all the religious were at full liberty to write to the Superior General, they should refrain from doing so except in a case of real importance and necessity, and this because of her numerous and important occupations. Mother Galitzin's orders and influence in the Missouri convents remained in force for several years after her death, as evidence will show later on.

The study of conditions facing the Mother General from 1843 to 1846 reveals a continuous need for visits to the many convents that had been opened in France, an increasingly heavy correspondence with superiors and other religious in posts of importance in these convents, and a proportionately lessened correspondence with the close friends to whom Mother Barat had been accustomed to write charming and deeply spiritual letters. No one felt this enforced silence of her beloved friend more than Mother Duchesne. But the knowledge that St. Charles was to continue its apostolate brightened her outlook, and her pen was often busy with letters to her family and to other religious and priests with whom she still exchanged letters.

Her needle, too, was very busy that summer and autumn on work for the sacristy of a church, presumably that of St. Ferdinand. Martin Lepere, whose name appeared frequently in her *Journal* and in letters to Bishop Rosati between 1828 and 1834, had prospered and was taking an active interest in parish affairs. A quantity of old vestments had come into his possession or been entrusted to him, all in need of renovating or remodeling. It was but natural that he should turn to the convent at St. Charles, where his daughter Agnes had been recently at school and where his good friend, Mother Duchesne, was residing. Philippine, in her seventy-fourth year, undertook the work and wrote to Lepere on July 30:

> I have been very eager to see you in order to decide with you what could be made use of for your church in the trunkful of vestments which you left at our convent. As I am the only one here who can give her time to this work, I decided to begin it at once, for my advanced age cannot let me count on tomorrow. First, I made a black chasuble out of the three pieces of material from New Orleans, but the velvet was so thick that the needle made many holes, some of which still show.
>
> Secondly, I have mended as well as I could the lace surplice and have also made a more substantial one for ordinary use. Thirdly, I left as it was what seemed to be the cover for a credence table, and I mended the altar cloth to the measure of our own, and on its width I was able to cut off material for some purificators. There remain on the material some spots caused by humidity which were impossible to remove. Fourthly, I trimmed the flowered cope with violet braid. . . . Fifthly, I cut off the long points of the banner, as the tassels could not be cleaned, and I mended the festoons.
>
> Now here is what I think about the rest. There are two canopy tops; one was white and lined, but now it is so discolored it could only serve as a funeral pall. Two vestments might be made out of

the second, one purple, the other white, by adding some material from the rose dalmatic. The two flowered dalmatics will never be used in your little sanctuary; you might sell them or exchange with Father Fischer of Our Lady of Victories, and if you wish, have them freshened up by dying the lining yellow. . . . but I really am not able to do this. There remains the border around the crimson canopy; but if two vestments are to be made of this, you will have to procure the galloon.[13]

News from McSherrystown that summer told that the cross of illness was weighing heavily on the community. Within the space of four months, three deaths occurred from tuberculosis, while a novice returned home to die of the same disease. Mother Margaret Murphy was the last victim at this time, but five other religious who had contracted the disease succumbed within five years. Bishop Kenrick visited the convent and sympathized paternally in these losses, but begged the nuns to continue their work. Partly out of compassion for the Bishop, who was experiencing the outrages of religious bigotry in Philadelphia, Mother Boilvin encouraged her community to perseverance, though it was evident that she herself was far from well.

When Mother Duchesne heard of all this, she wrote to Mother Boilvin:

Ever since I learned of the successive blows that have been test-ing your resignation to God's will, I have been continually occu-pied about you in prayer, begging God to be your strength and to let these great sacrifices work toward the good of your convent. Already the consolation you have drawn from the virtue shown by your daughters has strengthened your afflicted heart and proved to you that their eternal happiness far surpasses the pain you felt at losing them. I think, too, that the zeal and fervor of our dear Mother Murphy is going to be handed down to all those who saw and admired her virtue, and they in turn will imitate her. I trust that a sweet calm has followed the storms and that all that has happened will procure the greater glory of the Sacred Heart in your peaceful convent.

Every day we are expecting Mothers Cutts and Sallion.[14] The flooding of the Missouri River prevented them from going to Sugar Creek, so they went down to Louisiana to make their visitation before coming here. All I know is that we are going back to the former Rules and Constitutions of the Society and that our house and that of Florissant are again allowed to receive boarding pupils. But God sends successive trials that slow up everything.

We have had the worst flood ever known here, and it has ruined the entire countryside. It was followed by much sickness, and this continues. Families that had already lost their homes, furniture, cattle, crops, and harvest, are now reduced to the utmost misery, and no one here is rich enough to contribute large sums of money for charitable relief. They are doing a great deal in St. Louis, however, and some individuals, not particularly rich people, have taken in as many as seven sick families that came from the flooded districts of Illinois, and they are providing for all their needs over a period of six months. . . . Adieu, kind and dear Mother. No one takes a greater interest in all that concerns you than I do.[15]

The community at St. Charles was increased in August by the return of several religious to teach in the academy, which was reopened in September, 1844. The small enrollment might have been discouraging, had it not been for the joy in the hearts of the nuns at this new beginning. The presence of the children enlivened the convent, and Mother Duchesne took particular interest in the little Johnson girls and their cousins, all of whom were related to Mother Boilvin. At the end of October she went to St. Louis on business connected with the cutting of streets through the property still held by the Society under the contract and deed made to her by John Mullanphy in 1827. She told Mother Boilvin about this little trip and much else in a letter that traveled eastward in the pocket of Father Verhaegen. His departure for Maryland in December was a sacrifice keenly felt by all at St. Charles, but particularly by her.

I was greatly astonished one day when Mother Gray arrived out here to take me to the city to revise my will. She had had some difficulty about Mr. Mullanphy's grant to us. . . . The lawyer whom she consulted said I should make my will in legal form, giving approval of the improvements made since I left there. It took three weeks to complete this little bit of business; then Mother Aloysia Jacquet and Mother Prud'hom accompanied me back to St. Charles. We went by way of St. Ferdinand, which I had not seen since you and I parted there. Pray that that holy house may be reorganized successfully. Fathers Van Assche and Gleizal are eager for this. The latter says he can always recognize in the confessional young people who were our pupils there by the good method they use in approaching this sacrament. You deserve more praise than I for this, for you were the one who instructed them. See to it that your present pupils are as well trained. . . .

The Religious of the Visitation have two establishments in St. Louis now, as those who were left at Kaskaskia came to the city

at the time of the flood and are not going back. Their great benefactor, Mr. Menard, is dead. . . . The children of the Mullanphy
family go to the Visitation. Would you believe it—the Visitation
nuns were urged to buy our convent at St. Ferdinand, and Mother
Galitzin even offered them our convent here at St. Charles! But
those convents belong to St. Regis, and he saved them, I may say,
by a miracle. Comment on these matters is unnecessary.

In spite of myself I stumble upon St. Regis. I meant to begin my
letter with him, but I also wanted to tell you what God has been
doing in St. Louis. Have confidence in this great, this humble
protector. It is just when one is most depressed, most trampled on
by trials, that one experiences his uplifting help. How did I obtain from Napoleon the convent that was the joy of my youth?
Again, how did I, after prolonged pleading, finally obtain permission to come to America? St. Regis did it all. . . . So make a
promise—for that does bolster up one's prayers—and add to it
Masses at the tomb of St. Regis. That is where God is pleased to
glorify him by granting petitions. . . . Promise, for example, that
if within the next six months or a year not another person in your
community dies of lung trouble, you will have a novena of Masses
offered in your own chapel or at La Louvesc. I shall ask Father
Gleizal for the address to which you should write. The problem is
how to send the stipends. Our American paper money is worthless
over there. Within six months I shall tell you what Father Gleizal
says.

Less than two weeks later Philippine was writing again to
Mother Boilvin, about whom she was growing anxious, as she had
heard that her health had also been undermined and that there was
some question of closing the McSherrystown convent:

I wrote to you about two weeks ago, when Reverend Father Verhaegen came to ask what messages and commissions we wanted to
send to the East. He was leaving for Georgetown, as the Fathers
at that college had requested the Father General to send him there.
So he had to go, carrying the burden of both Provincial and
Visitor. The latter office will bring him to see you. . . . I have
written to Mother Geoffroy at Lyons, asking her to send you the
collection of the *Annals of the Faith*, from the establishment of
the Society that bears that name in 1822 to 1844. I think there are
in all fifteen or eighteen volumes. They are printed in seven
languages now. You ought to procure the English version and pay
the subscription fee of the associates, which will entitle you to the
six booklets published each year. Perhaps the association has been
established in Philadelphia or New York. You know the rates: one

sou a week. I have never in all my life read anything more interesting nor better calculated to enkindle zeal. . . . This reading is my delight. . . .

Put your trust in Divine Providence, dear Mother, and in the protection of St. Francis Regis, making him some promise, as I suggested in my last letter. But try to make one that you are sure you yourself can carry out. I fear the failure to keep the promises made to the saint for Grenoble and St. Ferdinand may have caused the closing of the house at Grenoble and the wretched condition now prevailing at St. Ferdinand. . . .

Among the treasures lovingly safeguarded at St. Charles for more than a century are the twelve bound volumes of the *Annales de la Propagation de la Foi* in which Mother Duchesne took such delight. Here and there on the printed page one finds corrections in her handwriting and even slips of paper inserted and pasted in, on which she wrote correct versions of stories she had heard or events she had witnessed or taken part in. For her truly apostolic soul it was a satisfaction to share in spirit at least in the sufferings, labors, and achievements of the missionaries who were leading souls out of darkness and error into the light of truth. Often she became so absorbed in these accounts, she would willingly have given her night hours to reading, as in the past she had given them to writing and to prayer, had not the community bell signaled to her that it was time to close the book.[16]

In May, 1845, there was sacrifice again at St. Charles, when Mother Regis Hamilton was relieved of her duties as superior and Mother Emilie St. Cyr was installed in her place. These two former pupils and novices of Mother Duchesne were very different in character and temperament, manner and outlook on life, yet they were both loyal and devoted to the one whom they considered the main channel through which devotion to the Sacred Heart had come into their lives. Where Regis was cordial and demonstrative, Emilie was timorous and reserved under the impact of responsibility. Mother Amelie Jouve attributed her overemphasis on strict observance to the fact that she was young and inexperienced. She was thirty-nine years old in 1845.[17] Never having been placed in authority before, she was inclined to interpret both her rights and her obligations in a somewhat narrow and rigid manner. She had been in Louisiana for twenty years and so had lost contact with the religious in Missouri. Mother Hamilton, on the contrary, had been mistress general at the City House for ten years before replacing Mother Mathevon at St. Charles.

The change of superiors would have been more costly for Mother Duchesne if Mother Hamilton had not remained another eighteen months at St. Charles as assistant to the new superior. A few days after Mother St. Cyr's arrival, Philippine wrote to Mother Boilvin:

> Reverend Mother Cutts came here last week, bringing with her your dear Aunt Josephine [Emilie] St. Cyr, whom she gave us as superior. Mother Hamilton remains here as her assistant. . . . At first I did nothing about the Masses at La Louvesc until I should hear again from you. I spoke to Father Gleizal, however, but he says he does not know anyone who is stationed at the saint's shrine now, and he would not take the responsibility of writing. So I have done it myself. I wrote to my sister who lives in Lyons. She can attend to it through one of my nieces who is in Mother Geoffroy's community, or through another who is at the Visitation in Romans. They can find frequent occasions through pilgrims who go each year to La Louvesc. But I did not know how many Masses you promised, so write the number in the place where I put "Number of Masses" between parentheses, then seal the letter, pay the postage and, if you think well of the suggestion, add a little note, but I think it can go as it is. Our kind Mother St. Cyr wants me to give you affectionate greetings. If, by distraction, she sealed the letter to my sister, just put a little note in with another seal.[18]

The letter had not been sealed, so Mother Boilvin followed instructions and sent off to Madame Jouve one of Philippine's loving, chatty letters:

> A few days ago, my dearest Sister, I received your letter of February 18. The mail has certainly been unreliable in delivery, for nowadays letters often come from France in six weeks. I have never failed to write to you over so long a period as you claim. It certainly would be long to delay a whole year in writing to one's only sister. There again the blame must be put on the mail. I read your letter quite easily, although you complain of poor eyesight. My own sight had weakened considerably, but I have recovered it to such an extent that I no longer need my spectacles; I can read fine print, and I thread my needles quite easily now. I am so grateful to God for this improvement, for needlework is a good occupation for old age.
> The past winter was very mild. I did not suffer from rheumatism in my limbs this year as I did the winter before, but I did have it in my hands, though I could keep on with ordinary work. Since

the 29th of last August I am in my 76th year, and I long for, yet fear, the hour of death, for I have amassed so little treasure for heaven, and old age is not the most fervent period of life. Today, the feast of Pentecost, is the anniversary of my first Communion. I was thinking somewhat sadly that it would have been a fortunate thing for me if I had died then, but God willed it otherwise. Certainly I never forget either you or your family in my daily prayers. I am so grateful to you for giving me news of them, especially of Constance, of whom I had heard nothing recently. Since the Society has grown so rapidly, we receive fewer letters than formerly. Nearly all the Mothers and Sisters I knew in France are dead or infirm. . . . The poverty of our convents keeps us from writing many letters, as postal rates are much higher here than in France. They talk of reducing them once the cheap paper money is withdrawn from circulation.

I want to ask a favor of you. It is, firstly, to have a Mass offered for me at Fourvière, and secondly, to have Masses said at La Louvesc in fulfillment of a promise which I counseled the superior of our convent near Philadelphia to make. She had great anxiety because of much illness in her community, and also had much to fear for a time when an anti-Catholic political party burned several churches with their rectories and schools and drove out the Sisters of Charity. Our convent in St. Louis was also threatened. Happily the mayor had a guard placed around the building,[19] and for several weeks eight or ten gentlemen who were friends of the institution slept at night in the parlors in order to be on hand in case of an attack. Now the danger has subsided. These facts show you how greatly we need St. Francis Regis as our protector. . . . I do not know the exact number of Masses promised, but I will have it written below. If you have no direct means of sending the stipends to La Louvesc, where St. Regis is buried, either Caroline [Lebrument], who is in Mother Geoffroy's community, or Eugenie [Lebrument] at the Visitation in Romans, can find a way.

Please give Madame de Rollin news of me, along with the most affectionate messages of love for her and her sister. Don't fail to remember me to my brother and his wife, my brothers-in-law and their families. All I can do for them is to pray for them, and that I do every day. Adieu, dear, kind Sister. . . . (Number of Masses: two this year and two next year.)[20]

With the coming of Mother St. Cyr, Philippine had more frequent opportunities to help Mother Hamilton in little ways. But this made her feel more keenly at times the restrictions placed on her zeal and activity. She was physically much better than when she returned from Sugar Creek. Her mind was clear and active, and she was as eager as ever to advance the Kingdom of Christ. Yet she was obliged to confine the urgency of her love to a little work with a few French-speaking children in the free school. She longed to lend a hand at household work, but she was unable to do this and so found herself alone most of the day. "But her solitude was brightened, sweetened, by the fact that she could always be close to Jesus in the Blessed Sacrament of His love, Jesus, the Friend who is faithful and near when all other friends disappear. He had not forsaken 'His poor servant,' as she called herself, and more than ever He let her experience the sweetness and joy of His presence." [21]

Besides the long hours she spent in adoration, she had the privilege of giving the Latin responses at all the Masses offered in the church or in the cloister chapel, for acolytes were few and unreliable. Even at the age of eighty years she continued to do this, kneeling upright without support, not only during one Mass, but during several offered in succession. She was also very punctual about the recitation of Office to the very last days of her life, as the private recitation decreed in 1839 continued to be the custom in the houses in Missouri for more than a decade, so slowly was the work of Mother Galitzin undone.

By a happy coincidence in the August of 1845, a letter from Josephine de Savoye-Rollin reached Philippine as she was celebrating in her own heart her seventy-sixth birthday. It contained a gift of money, as usual, and announced the shipment of a package that should reach St. Charles in the near future. But more precious to Philippine was the wealth of family news it contained. Answering on September 14, she commended her letter to St. Anthony of Padua, as had been her custom throughout the quarter-century she had spent in America, and wrote what is her last extant letter to Josephine Perier:

> I am always deeply touched, my dearest Cousin, by your generosity toward me and above all by the loving words that accompany your gifts. I do not know how to thank you, but our Heavenly Father hears, and will hear every day of my life, the voice of my prayers by which I try to pay my debt to you. My prayer has been heard long since, I trust. The interesting details you give me about your dear family, about the piety that reigns there, especially among the young married women who give so much consolation to their mother, all speak to my heart and make me realize that my daily prayers for Marine have been answered by the Sovereign Master, who has made gratitude a duty. [22] I draw

from His treasures to pay my own debt. The news that Masses have been offered for me at Fourvière and La Louvesc gave me great joy. The protection of heaven has been very evident and our house near Philadelphia that promised those Masses has been freed from illness and death, which had struck terror into the hearts of the young religious. . . . The founding of several new convent schools in the vicinity of St. Louis will draw many children away from our schools, but we desire only to serve God, and we must be content with the rather mediocre success we have. The generous sum you sent us will remove all fear about the coming winter, for it will buy the provisions we are most in need of.

Other members of her family were showing their love in the same generous way that had marked their attachment to her for nearly half a century in France and in America. From her brother came some precious volumes of the *Annals of the Propagation of the Faith*. From her sister came the sewing materials with which she was still able to make and mend vestments and altar linens. For her personal use she desired nothing. She was the poorest nun in the community and the most mortified. Never was she to be found idle. Even in the last years of her life she allowed herself no retrenchment of her ordinary way of living, no little comforts to ease the pain and weariness inherent in her physical condition. Her food was chiefly milk, vegetables, and fruit. On fast days she ate only one meal, taking a cup of black coffee in the morning and a cup of tea in the evening. She loved to read in the community refectory during meals, but her voice had become so faint that it was difficult for the religious to hear her. Still they did not let her know this, for it would have added to that sense of uselessness that frequently depressed her.[23]

A letter to her sister in March, 1846, shows her as interested and as interesting as ever, and as lovingly grateful for things that enabled her to compensate by a remarkable industry for the inactivity to which she felt "condemned":

Your heart, my beloved Sister and Friend, has found fullest expression in the promptitude and eagerness with which you are supplying my old age with holy and very happy occupations. I have never enjoyed reading and sewing more than I do now, when they fill my days, along with prayer. As soon as I receive the books, I shall let my brother know and shall express my gratitude to him. As for you, my loving Sister, I am always thinking of you; and even if I could forget you, the last two packages of sewing materials you sent me are certainly very dear reminders of you. They have enabled me to make six vestments. I thought at first that I should have scarcely enough for one. . . . This multiplication of material makes me admire more than ever the Providence of God, who takes such care of me. You may imagine what kind of embroidery I can do now and how incapable I am, but I am helping poor churches that are being built on all sides. Not a single Catholic paper I read but has an account of several new churches consecrated—and some of them are very beautiful. In general, all the churches have organs and good singing. . . .

The number of Germans coming to the United States has contributed greatly to the spread in this section of the country of the most useful of the fine arts. All our workmen and servants are German-speaking, as well as the majority of the children in the free school, and they are very easy to manage in the classroom. . . .

I often picture your home and the young family gathered about you,[24] and it gives me so much pleasure to know what great joy they bring you. Thank you so much for giving me news of the grandchildren and of other members of the family. Greetings to all who know me. Adieu, dear Sister. In the Heart of Jesus I am your faithful friend and sister. . . .

Through the spring months of 1846, Mother Duchesne was often to be seen kneeling in the cloister chapel, her gaze fixed on the tabernacle, tears flowing unheeded down her cheeks. She was wrestling in prayer for the existence of the convent at Florissant. For years she had hoped against hope that the Society would never give up what was to her its dearest home in America. She had saved it before when a like fate threatened—saved it by pleading with God and with the Superior General. It was nearly two years and a half since she had written to Mother Barat. The barrier formed in 1844 had remained, though St. Madeleine Sophie, overwhelmed by problems, anxieties, visitations, and successive illnesses of which Philippine had no conception, was quite unaware of the reason for her old friend's pen-silence.

Toward the close of May, Mother Cutts arrived at St. Charles. One reason for her visit was the decision that had been reached regarding Florissant. When it was announced, it took all the courage and fortitude Philippine could muster to accept the blow. And before she did so, she exerted every effort to parry it. From Mother Cutts she turned to Bishop Kenrick, but his answer to her letter brought her small comfort, though she recognized the supernatural truth he was suggesting when he wrote: "This is the cross that Jesus, your Divine Spouse, wishes you to carry for love of

Him." [25] Even before his letter reached her, she had decided to write just as she would have talked to Mother Barat, explaining her past silence and urging her present petition with all the earnestness of her glowing, if impractical, zeal:

SS.C.J.M.   ST. CHARLES, June 5, 1846

MY VERY DEAR AND VENERATED MOTHER,

It is quite a long time since I wrote to you, but that is because I wished to obey your recommendation not to write except in the case of real necessity. I thought it was such a case when I took the liberty to beg you to re-establish the boarding school here. I received no answer, but the Mother who was our superior at that time received one, which proved to me all the more clearly that I ought to be more reserved about writing.

When I expressed a desire to plead with you to save our first house, that dear solitude dedicated to St. Regis, the Louvesc of America, I was told that my efforts would be useless. My heart yearned so to return there, I would not be restrained by any consideration from using every means to obtain this favor. I implored Mother Cutts to allow me to keep that quiet little house open with just one Sister who could speak both languages, so we could continue the free school, take care of the church, and prepare the priest's meals. He is so poor, he cannot even have the leaking roof of the church repaired. That church has always been used by us as if it were our own. The Jesuit Fathers have never asked any remuneration as chaplains and have given us abundant spiritual help.

At first Mother Cutts said she thought my idea was good, especially as I assured her that I would not ask her for more religious or for money. To remove all hesitation that my advanced age might have caused, I told her that I come of a long-lived family, that I felt I had many more years of life ahead of me, and that I was enjoying much better health than I did some years ago. I said that such arrangement would tide us over until we had better times in this country, and that the convent of St. Ferdinand, being in a very beautiful locality, would be just the place for religious who were old, infirm, or convalescent. I also said that it was not surprising that there had been so few pupils lately, considering the influx of non-Catholic settlers and the number of new institutions opened in recent years. I told her we had often had as many as thirty boarding pupils and that number was almost never exceeded in the schools conducted by religious communities before the Revolution in France, with the exception of the royal school of St. Cyr.

The hope of obtaining what I pleaded for dried my tears, but they flow more bitterly today for, after I repeated to her [Mother Cutts] all I have written you in this letter, she told me before leaving this morning that you would grant me no part of what I asked, that you had made your decision. . . .

When I learned that the shrine of Saint Regis had been destroyed [in 1840], and that the beautiful relics brought from Rome by Monseigneur Du Bourg had been removed from the chapel, I expected a catastrophe to occur. When Mother Galitzin died, I knew it had happened. I could not help telling the Mother Visitatrix this. Even without such an occurrence, the suppression of that house causes a deep wound to my heart, for that house has furnished us with more vocations than any other. St. Charles may furnish some soon, also, but in St. Louis the academy is two-thirds non-Catholic, and the other third is composed of children reared in luxury. It has given no vocations so far, and perhaps never will. There will be some among the orphans, but they do not make teachers capable of gaining much confidence. Yet some of these girls and the coadjutrix novices compose the novitiate at present. To this you must add the withdrawal of several novices recently, one of whom got her name in the newspaper along with several criticisms of the convent. This shows that we must draw our recruits from the smaller convents where the pupils are well educated and the pride of the parents will not withdraw them from religious life.

Mother Cutts counts on selling the convent of St. Ferdinand to Bishop Kenrick, but he will never buy it. He is still burdened with debts left by Bishop Rosati and can barely support his seminary. The Jesuit Fathers have big debts on their churches. The Religious of the Visitation have left Kaskaskia insolvent. The Sisters of Charity make no foundation without an assured income, and they help themselves still more by fairs that bring in a great deal of money.

If there was less love of external show in our large houses, the small ones would have support. People think they will work wonders by external appearances, but those who are suffering and who see the uselessness of this are able to distinguish in this matter. This passion for external grandeur is accompanied here [in America] by a passion for knowledge. . . . People want to know all the motions of the planets and the stars, when they know nothing about Bible history or the cultivation of a garden.

Forgive this long letter. I count on your kindness. If you refuse my petition [in regard to Florissant], I shall submit, but I shall never be reconciled. The wound is too deep. I kneel at your feet awaiting the decision, and I retain always my deep respect for you and for the beloved Father who laid the foundation of our holy Society. I beg the Heart of Jesus to uphold you, and in that Heart I am, dear Reverend Mother,

Your very humble and unworthy servant,
PHILIPPINE DUCHESNE
r.S.C.

The decision regarding Florissant had long since been made and this letter remained unanswered. Months passed. When Philippine spoke with Mother Hamilton about this silence on the part of Mother Barat, they found no solution to the problem, such as there had been in 1844. If Philippine had grieved then, she was desolate now, for she feared that the friend whom she loved more than anyone else on earth was displeased with her. In her humility she attributed this to some serious fault on her part, yet the most searching self-examination failed to reveal any action that could have merited such punishment. There was no querulous resentment in her reaction to this unexpected silence, no least tinge of bitterness in her comments. When she spoke of it to Mother Hamilton, she was always hopeful: mail was slow; letters were often delayed, and many were lost. She had said these very things in her letters recently. Perhaps by New Year's she would receive an answer. Meanwhile the convent at Florissant stood vacant and the picture of St. Francis Regis had been left behind in the attic.

Then came another unexpected sacrifice—Mother Hamilton was transferred to Canada, leaving St. Charles on November 8, 1846. Philippine could not restrain her tears. She had found strong comfort in the sympathy and friendship of this beloved Mother. But now, a long, bleak road seemed to stretch before her, and she must walk its dark way alone, and yet not alone, for she could always put out her hand in the darkness and go forward unseeing, yet guided securely by luminous faith and unswerving trust. The desolation of these months was a dreariness that must be endured, and there seemed to be no way to deal with it except by a simple surrender of herself to the reality of God's will. Free from self-pity, she thought of herself as a creature of no importance, buried away unnoticed in the obscurity of the Society's poorest convent. Yet here was another seed growing silently and destined to bear fruit a hundredfold in her own soul and in the souls of countless members of the Mystical Body.

At New Year's she wrote in loneliness and gratitude to her sister:

It is a long time since I had any news from you, my dearest Sister. I wonder if you are dead. I would not want to survive you. It is too hard to see all those one loves pass ahead into eternity. I have the same fears with regard to Madame de Rollin, who has so many claims on my heart. Her last letter was so affectionate, it filled me with dread lest it was her last adieu. I had that same feeling the last time my Father visited me at Ste Marie. His parting words, *Adieu, Philippine,* left me in tears. I thought at once that he would not return to see me, and I was not mistaken. When you answer this letter, do not fail to give me news of my brother, of Madame de Rollin, her sister, and all that is dearest to us.

I never can thank you sufficiently for your gift of the *Annals of the Propagation of the Faith.* Those books are as enjoyable as they are edifying, and they are my delight. I have a great desire to be enrolled in that society, and such a thing is quite impossible here, as there is no branch established in this section of the country. Will you enroll me and pay the penny a week for me? If you cannot do so, please ask the superior of our convent on Rue Boissac to do me this service, presenting to her my respects and the needs of my old age by way of excuse. I do not know her personally, but I count on her charity. Recommend me to the prayers of your dear religious daughter who lives near Our Lady of Fourvière, so that she may pray to that good Mother for me and also ask the prayers of her Sisters in the community.

A few days ago I saw a missionary from the Rocky Mountains, which lie toward the Pacific Ocean. He made a voyage on that ocean, escorting a party of Belgian religious to Oregon Territory. These nuns have also one or two convents in the state of Ohio.[26] In a section of the Northwest settled by Canadians who have intermarried with Indian women they have already built a fine convent and have sixty boarding pupils, the children of these marriages. They also have schools for pure-blooded Indians. . . . The missionaries have made consoling progress among the tribes they have been able to reach. Among them one sees the fervor of the primitive Christians.[27]

Although her infirmities kept her most of the time in her own little room or in the chapel, Mother Duchesne went faithfully and gladly to the community recreations. She loved conversation and talked well, for her mind was stored with interesting information and lively stories of the past, of personal experiences, and of people whom she had known in France, in Louisiana, and in Missouri. As the years passed, however, her voice became a mere whisper and only those who sat close to her could hear and enjoy what she said.

It often happened that in good weather the community recreations were spent out of doors, where the religious walked for exercise and pleasure in the lanes and groves of elm and oak and maple on the convent grounds. Mother Duchesne spent these hours in the chapel, where she forgot her loneliness in prayer. "It was not," wrote Mother Amelie Jouve later on, "that the religious would not have been happy to spend this time with her, but the superior, young and inexperienced, disapproved of this, fearing that her own authority might suffer by such friendly contacts with this saintly old Mother. God permitted this little trial in order that Mother Duchesne might find her chief support in the cross." [28]

One of the pleasures she most enjoyed and was never asked to sacrifice was the visits of Father De Smet. He wrote about her and about his visits to her twenty years after her death:

I keep the memory of Mère Duchesne in the highest respect and veneration. Her praise has been and is on the lips, not only of her own Sisters in religion, but of all those who had the honor and the happiness of her acquaintance. On every return from my Indian missionary visits, I deemed it a most agreeable duty to pay my respects to good Mother Duchesne, and I never returned from one of these visits but with an increase of edification, with a higher opinion of her virtues and sanctified life, and always under the full conviction that I had conversed with a truly living saint. I always considered Mother Duchesne as the greatest protectress of our Indian missions. For years she offered two Communions a week and daily prayers for the conversion of the Indians. She loved these poor, benighted children dearly and nothing seemed to make her more happy than to hear of their conversions, of their fervor and zeal in the practice of their religious duties after having entered the true fold of our Divine Redeemer. I can entertain no doubt, many were brought over to the Holy Faith of Christ by the many acts of mortification she performed, and by the constant prayers she offered up for the salvation of these, her dearly beloved Indian children. . . .[29]

In 1847 Father De Smet, on a begging tour in Belgium, visited the Convent of the Sacred Heart at Jette-Saint-Pierre. One of those who listened to him made notes of what he said:

This holy missionary held us spellbound for an hour as he told us of his distant missions. He also spoke of Mother Duchesne, whom he had seen a short time before this. He said she had climbed all the rungs of the ladder of sanctity, and never had he seen a soul more ardent in love for our Lord. In his opinion she rivaled St. Teresa. Never had he known a person who was poorer in all that concerned her private life, and in this she imitated St. Francis of Assisi; nor a more apostolic soul, eager for the salvation of souls, and he thought St. Francis Xavier had shared with her his zeal for the conversion of the infidels. As he ended his talk, he said: Now she is on the sorrowful way to Calvary to which old age and infirmities have condemned her; but no matter how hard that road may seem to her, she is climbing it with all the fervor of youth. She has struck deep roots in American soil and they will one day bear an abundant harvest. I should not be surprised, the Father said, if someday she were raised to our altars.[30]

While there are no documents to prove the fact, it seems most probable that, from Canada, Mother Hamilton informed St. Madeleine Sophie of the distress which her silence was causing Mother Duchesne. When Mother Adele Cahier, then Secretary General, received a little letter from Philippine, she was surprised at the formal message in its closing lines: "I respect our Mother General's time too much to write to her. I beg you to offer her my regards and devoted affection, and the same to my very dear Father Joseph, the Assistants General, and Mother Thérèse." [31]

For several months the Superior General had been wondering why she had not heard from Philippine again. Puzzled by this silence and by the reports she had received, Mother Barat determined to set all at rights by the most acceptable means in her power. She had granted Mother Amelie Jouve's request for service on the American mission and had assigned her to the latest Canadian foundation. She was to sail from France late in July. Disregarding the geography of the route, Mother Barat directed her to make the journey from New York to Montreal by way of St. Charles, Missouri. Mother Jouve has left a brief, impersonal account of her meeting with Tante Philippine in September, 1847:

That fortunate niece was received by Mother Duchesne as an angel from heaven. After reading the letter sent to her by our Reverend Mother General, who was her dearest friend, she seemed transported with joy. Tears flowed down her cheeks, and she was speechless with emotion. After a little while she exclaimed, "So our Mother General still thinks of me, still loves me? She has been so good as to show me that love by sending you to visit me?" She was radiant with joy.[32]

More personal impressions occur in a letter written by Mother Jouve on September 14:

> I may say with Anthony that I have seen Paul in the desert. Yes, I have seen a great saint and one who is drawing near the end of her earthly pilgrimage. I found her very weak and her voice so feeble that it is hard to hear what she says. She received me like an angel come down from heaven. The cross has ever been her portion, and for sometime past she has suffered intensely, believing that she had incurred our Mother General's displeasure. An ecstatic happiness lighted up her face when she read our Very Reverend Mother's letter and heard that she had sent me to St. Charles just to see her. We had long talks about the past; the names of our Mothers and Sisters in France recurred over and over again, and the recollections of the early days of the Society.

And to St. Madeleine Sophie she wrote:

> You would be deeply touched, Reverend Mother, by the poverty of St. Charles. It could hardly be greater. Mother Duchesne's room is like a veritable sanctuary of this virtue. Certainly in the whole Society there is no one more poorly housed or clad or shod. Blessed Benedict Labre could claim her for his sister. And it is quite useless to argue with her in this matter—it is her *attrait*. I did, however, remove her Office book, which was in tatters, and substitute one that is somewhat less worn out.[33]

To Mother Barat, Philippine herself wrote on September 10, after reading the letter and examining the many presents brought to her by Mother Jouve:

> Your letter and your gifts, my dear Mother, chosen with such exquisite taste, have been a life-giving balm to my soul. Oh, how I thank you and the God of all goodness for them! I was sorrowfully convinced that I had lost my place in your heart; and because I thought it was through some fault of mine, my own heart was the more grief-stricken. . . .
>
> God has favored me here with a room that is next to the chapel. I go from one to the other. My greatest happiness is to pray for the missions, for the Society, for you, my loved and venerated Mother, who hold God's place in my regard. . . .

After commenting on conditions in the Missouri convents and regulations that had been established in 1840, she continued: "All our American houses accepted respectfully the changes inaugurated by Mother Galitzin because they considered them as coming from you. At a word from you now I am sure they would return gladly to the old order of things."

During her visit Mother Jouve did her best to discover what would give pleasure to her dear old aunt, or what had caused her pain. Neither pleasure nor pain seemed of interest to her then. She had the assurance of the unaltered love of her dearest friend, and that was enough. At length, however, she admitted that there were two desires in her heart: the rescue of the picture of St. Regis from the attic at Florissant and the return of Mother Hamilton from Canada. The first desire was not difficult to fulfil. Mother St. Cyr was able to arrange with the Sisters of Loretto, then living in the convent of St. Ferdinand, to return the picture, and it was given a place of honor in the cloister chapel. The second request took longer to accomplish, and four years elapsed before Mother Duchesne had the satisfaction of welcoming Mother Hamilton back to St. Charles.

On a third point Mother Jouve reassured Mother Duchesne: somewhere a letter from St. Madeleine Sophie had certainly gone astray. "Whether lost or intercepted" [to use Mother Jouve's own words], she could not say, nor did she lay the blame for its disappearance on any individual. Letters had been lost before, even so important a letter as the one from Mother Barat recalling Philippine to France twelve or fifteen years before this. "Thinking that America could do without her for at least a few months, Mother Barat wrote, 'Come, my dear Philippine.' That invitation would have been an order for Mother Duchesne, but it never reached her. Pressing affairs supervened and she was directed by Paris not to make the trip if she had not already set out." [34]

In her *Life* of St. Madeleine Sophie, Mother Adele Cahier writes: "It is impossible to say either how or why Mother Duchesne failed to receive Mother Barat's answers to her letters," but she blames no one.[35] Mother Marjory Erskine, in her beautiful volume on Mother Duchesne, brings out the fact that, after 1843, Philippine "relapsed into a silence which did not inspire Mother Barat to write," and, moreover, "the Superior General would naturally write seldom to one whom she loved when that one was no longer in authority." [36] This conclusion is borne out by the fact that in the years following Mother Jouve's visit in 1847 there were very few letters exchanged between them, and each complained that the other wrote so seldom.

One further point needs some elucidation in fairness to the religious who, after Mother Duchesne herself, suffered most keenly as a result of this whole unhappy affair. The blame for having intercepted Mother Barat's letter, or letters, to Mother Duchesne was laid rashly on Mother Emilie St. Cyr, superior at St. Charles during the years 1845–1851, and this not after her death, but during her lifetime, and the insinuation cast a shadow over the last years of her life. The accusation appeared in Monsignor Louis Baunard's *Histoire de Madame Duchesne*, veiled in so transparent a statement that Mother St. Cyr's name might just as well have been printed on page 513. The book, published in 1878, appeared while Mother St. Cyr was still alive. More than once she declared in private conversation that she had never been guilty of so deceitful, so unthinkable a deed. When toward the close of her life she was asked to speak out in self-defense, she replied, "No, no! That cross was the hardest and the heaviest of my religious life. It has been my sanctification. Let's leave it buried in the Heart of Jesus." [37] An answer worthy of a religious trained in the school of Philippine Duchesne!

Although Mother Jouve's visit to St. Charles lasted but two weeks,[38] one of its most satisfying outcomes was the correspondence it initiated between Mother Duchesne and her niece. The first of Philippine's letters to Mother Jouve was written shortly after their parting:

> I received the letter you wrote to me from St. Louis. It was hard to see you leave me forever, for we can never hope to see each other again this side of heaven. So we must strive to reach there, you and I, but by such different paths—I doing nothing and you accomplishing great things for God through the education of youth. God has given you the necessary talents, and you must use them to produce a hundredfold in His service. But never forget that the road to heaven is the way of the cross. Jesus has called us to follow Him, bearing the cross as He did. We have no choice about it—we must take it up and carry it if we are to be saved. You have made a big step forward in leaving France and all that you loved there. Now you must persevere courageously, in your sacrifice by renouncing legitimate satisfactions, accommodating yourself to the character of different nationalities, seeing God always in His creatures, and living with them as with the children of one common Father.
>
> I made my retreat shortly after your departure. In it God seemed to give me only the cross, so beg for me the grace to know

how to carry it well. I found it very difficult to read your letter. In future I hope you will use blacker ink. Letters coming from Paris are almost too pale to read. I shall try not to merit this same reproach. Here all is going about the same as when you left. Everyone looks back with pleasure to your visit. Give my love to Mothers de Kersaint, Roche, L'Eveque, Alphonsine [Shannon], Cornelis, Short, Hamilton. We hope to see the last named in our midst again soon—she was only loaned. . . . Beg all the religious to give me a share in their prayers.[39]

Mother Duchesne's joy in Amelie's visit would be difficult to describe, but it is reflected in her next letter to Madame Jouve, which contains quaint reassurances for the mother who had sacrificed this talented daughter to the cause of the American missions. Writing on December 12 she says:

Last month, my beloved Sister, I received your letter of September 26, in which you complain of having received no letters from me since last February. I am sure I have written to you since then; the last time was in September, when I also wrote to Madame de Rollin. It was your dear daughter who took those letters with her to mail them in New York, where she could send them directly by boat. It would be very difficult for me to put into words the pleasure her visit gave. More than thirty years had passed since I had seen her, and during that time she has acquired much virtue. She gave me all the details that delighted me about our big family, most of whom I do not know now, but I often recommend them to God, all together and individually. I marvel at the merit of your sacrifice in consenting to the departure of that Sister and friend whom I had here for a little while. The whole community of St. Charles was delighted to see her and wanted to keep her always. And it was the same in St. Louis, a much larger house than that of St. Charles.

Do not worry about her health. Canada is a very healthy place. All the Canadians I have ever met were quite robust, and our religious who bore the burden of the foundation there and several who were attacked by consumption and sent there are now in much better health than they were in either Missouri or Louisiana. And they have suffered less from the cold than we do in Missouri because the houses are built more solidly and are better heated. Except when they go out of doors, the boarding pupils wear the same kind of clothing in winter as in summer. Could they say that about Paris, which is at the same latitude? . . .[40]

Our first convent in Canada was situated too far from Montreal and so the boarding school did not prosper. . . . The second one, much larger, now has many pupils. It is called St. Vincent [on Ile Jésus]. That is where our dear Amelie is stationed. . . . A thousand affectionate messages to Madame de Rollin and my brother. Ask him to send me the rest of the *Annals,* from January, 1845, on. I did not know about your daughter's trip to America any sooner than you did.

In a long letter to Mother Amelie, Philippine gave small but telling space to herself when she wrote: "I have carried out your wishes and am well wrapped up day and night in the gifts our Mother General sent me. As to food, I am acting without scruple; and when I can eat my little piece of meat, I do so, making no secret of it. . . . Everyone loves you and prays for you." So Philippine thought she was making great concessions to nature by wearing a warm shawl by day and a woolen camisole by night, by eating a bit of meat prepared especially for her, and by taking a few other mild precautions during the rigorous winter season, but the religious who lived with her saw little change in the austere manner of life she prescribed for herself. She was obliged to go to St. Louis again on business in the late autumn of 1847 and enjoyed seeing many of the religious whom she had known in the past. Two months later one of them, Mother Thiéfry, gave news of her to Mother Barat when writing from St. Michael's on her way to Natchitoches: [41]

During my stay in St. Louis I had the pleasure of seeing our dear Mother Duchesne, who came there on some business. This meeting was a real satisfaction for us both. That venerated Mother is remarkable for her age. The improvements and changes at the City House in St. Louis pleased her very much, so Mother Gray did all in her power to keep her there, but her efforts were fruitless. It is evident that St. Charles suits perfectly her great desire for retirement. "There," she told me, "my room is right beside the chapel. I do not need to go up and down steps to get to it, and on Sundays we always have two Masses." Mother St. Cyr, who takes the greatest care of her, came herself to St. Louis to drive back with her to St. Charles. I say she takes the greatest care of her—she wants to, but what can she do? You may judge for yourself how seldom she succeeds. Mother Duchesne is so austere; as you know, she refuses all the care and attention offered her. Thus in the morning the Sister who sleeps in her room lights a little fire. As soon as she leaves the room, Mother Duchesne puts it out. Then the Mother Assistant, seeing no fire in her room, thinks

Sister is neglecting her—and so it goes all through the day, Mother Duchesne continually seeking means of mortification.[42]

2. 1848—1852

> *Lord Jesus, may we be found worthy to persevere*
> *and to grow in love of Thee until the end.*

Mass of the Eucharistic Heart of Jesus

THE YEAR 1848 brought Philippine fresh heart-suffering. News from France told of revolution in that country as well as others in Europe. It was, indeed, a year of revolutions, and the Religious of the Sacred Heart were among the victims of persecution in Italy, Piedmont, Switzerland, and France. As early as April 15, Philippine was asking her sister for news about her loved ones and about the homeland. Her note that day was short: "My eyesight has grown weaker this year," she wrote, "and varies from time to time. Today I can see very little." But her heart was full of the old affection, and she closed her letter with a touching phrase, *"Toute à toi, chère et tendre amie."*

She seems to have been gripped once more by the idea that it would be better for her to refrain from correspondence with friends, even members of her own family, in France. The revolution had cut off mail for a time; and when she heard from her sister in June, she immediately forwarded the letter to Mother Amelie, then confided to Madame Jouve:

> I have not written recently to my brother or to Cousin Josephine, not knowing where they were and fearing my letters might displease them. I have maintained the same reserve with regard to Madame Sophie, my highest Mother Superior, but you would give me pleasure if, being on the spot, you would find out where she is—they will know at Rue Boissac, Lyons—and write to her yourself. Tell her the convent at St. Ferdinand stood vacant a year and then was rented at a low price by the Sisters of Loretto, who are conducting a school there. As the house still belongs to us and a good deal of our furniture and chapel furnishings were left there, as if awaiting our return, we are eager to know whether we may take back that house for our religious who could come from France to live there. They could open an entirely French school. That language is well appreciated now, but it is difficult to learn it at the same time as English, for the children turn back to their

native language continually. But no education is complete without a knowledge of French, and people are very eager about it. Try to do as I ask in this matter and get an answer for me. . . .

This renewed effort on the part of Philippine to establish a community of the Sacred Heart once more at Florissant was in line with the movement throughout the Society to offer a refuge to its members whom persecution had driven from their convents. The American religious were stretching out welcoming hands across the sea to their Sisters in Europe, and in Mother Duchesne's eyes no refuge could have been more suitable than the little home she had built more than a quarter-century before this on the frontier. Once more her plans were impractical, her efforts abortive.

A very personal heartache for her that summer was the news that Mother Boilvin's health had broken under the pressure of work and anxiety, and she, too, had been declared tubercular. For a time she tried to carry on her work at Eden Hall, the beautiful convent she had opened near Philadelphia in 1847, but she was obliged to give up at the close of the first scholastic year. Hoping a change of climate might save her, Mother Hardey took her to Canada and entrusted her to the care of Mother Amelie Jouve, who had been named superior at St. Vincent, Ile Jésus, that summer. Learning of these events Mother Duchesne wrote to Mother Jouve on August 30:

> See, my dearest Mother, how God gives joy to some and sorrow to others! I come in between. I do not rejoice to see you in a position of trust, but I bless God, who lets you dread the position of superior so that you may bear this burden with self-diffidence and lean on Him for support. He is too good ever to leave you without support. Dear Mother Boilvin, who is with you now, went through the same trial, and the Jesuit Provincial, Father Elet, told me he had known few people more highly esteemed than she. . . . So say your *Fiat* generously.

In September Philippine learned that her nephew, Eugene Jouve, was planning to come to America. Her interest in him and his sister, Mother Amelie, as well as in the fortunes of the family in France, appears in a few lines she sent on the twelfth of the month in reply to her sister's letter:

> Could I have foreseen, my dearest Sister, the financial reverses

that you have encountered, I should have been more guarded in making my request for books. I have not received them yet, but I thank you sincerely for them. I am writing to you and your son under the same cover for the sake of economy, and I know you two are but one. I shall give you some news of your daughter in Canada, in case you have not heard it. She has been appointed superior of the convent, to her great distress, and that distress is so great that it has robbed her of both sleep and appetite. I trust she will recover both, once she gets over her surprise, for she has won all hearts. . . .

Someone who returned recently from Europe told me that in embarking at Antwerp (and the same must be true of Havre), one pays only 300 francs for passage to America, and the overland trip from the Atlantic coast to Louisiana or Missouri is less than 100 francs. I forgot to tell my nephew that French is spoken more generally in Louisiana than English.

Adieu, dear Sister. I sympathize intimately with you in all your cares. My heart is more in France than in America when I am so preoccupied about my beloved family. All yours with deepest affection. . . .

On October 22 Philippine received the news of Mother Boilvin's death. Her short career of thirty-six years closed in a manner that reflected the courage and holiness of her consecrated life. In the little cemetery on Ile Jésus they laid to rest this "child of Florissant and daughter of Mother Duchesne in pioneer days, Julie Adeline Boilvin, one of America's most distinguished religious of the Sacred Heart." [43] Then Mother Jouve sent a letter off to Tante Philippine, who replied immediately:

The sad news of Mother Gonzague's death was not a surprise, but just the same it was a great sorrow. For me she was a support and a consolation, for the Society a valuable and edifying member, for God a docile child and a faithful spouse of the Sacred Heart. I am firmly assured of her present happiness after so holy a death, but it is sweet and consoling to think about her and recall her virtues as I fulfill toward her the obligation we have to pray for our deceased members.

I received the letter in which you told me what a burden had been laid upon you, and I answered immediately, encouraging you to carry that burden with resignation. Happily God has smoothed your path by drawing to you the affection of all those with whom you live. That is what has been written to me from all sides. So take heart, since besides accomplishing the unmistakable will of God, you are able to contribute so easily to the prosperity and regularity of an institution that does so much good in a country where religion is still so highly honored and is so vital a force.

I had not heard about my brother's financial losses until I received letters from Madame de Rollin and my sister. The former, whose brothers are all in prominent positions, has the pleasure of being in their midst when they gather at their country homes. She told me everyone is hard up. . . . Your brother Eugene wrote to me, saying he wished to come to America and asking information about different states in this country. I advised him against settling in Texas, as it is an unhealthy place and is still in a disturbed condition. I know very little about Tennessee, but I praised our healthful climate and fertile soil. He is not a farmer, however, and has very slender means. . . . Your dear mother enclosed a letter to me in Eugene's. Constance is still at Chambery.[44] The people there were firm in opposing the destruction of the convent in the recent disturbances, and things seem to have calmed down a little, though Switzerland pursues its deplorable course of persecution. . . . I have had no letters from either my brother or Augustin Jordan since the revolution in France.[45]

I greet all your community in the Heart of Jesus, for I love you all in the Sacred Heart and in Him I am all yours. . . .

Through the winter of 1848–1849, Mother Duchesne worked steadily with her needle for poor churches and for the missions. In the spring she sent a large package of her handiwork to Father De Smet, whose note of thanks touched her so deeply that she at once packed up another bundle, writing at the same time:

It made me so happy to know that you had accepted the poor offerings of my making and had offered two Masses for my intentions. I trust you will also accept what I am now sending you for the savages—two quilts, one of them made of little stars, and the other a larger one, and some small altar linens. It is the gift of a poor person, offered to the poor, who are the true friends of Jesus Christ. Your charity will overlook all the defects.[46]

The courageous effort she must have expended on quilts and altar linens and knitted garments may be inferred from a letter to her sister at this time:

Each time I send you a letter I think it is the last I shall write in this life. Old age tells me this, and today an illness stresses it with more certainty. This illness is a swelling that goes from one side of my body to the other, and when it attacks some vital spot, they say, it will end my life. I have been in this condition, more or less suffering, since the end of November. I am far from trying to escape death; indeed I would long for it, had I not so much reason to fear the Judgment, since even the just man has no assurance of his lot, as *God must judge even the just.* That thought is terrifying, so pray and ask others to pray for me. I do the same for you and your family. I may, however, drag on for a long time. God alone knows when the end will come. . . . Adieu, dear Sister. Oh, the happy day when we shall be together once more! Then all sorrows will end and we shall have eternal happiness in the Heart of our Saviour, in whom I am your loving sister and friend. . . .[47]

If the misfortunes and disasters in France called forth Philippine's sympathy that spring, the terrible scourge of cholera that ravaged St. Louis and the great fire that wrought havoc on the waterfront filled her with sorrow and distress and urged her to more insistent, more persistent, prayer. Between January and August, 1849, the epidemic claimed more than six thousand victims out of the sixty thousand inhabitants of the city. In the vicinity of Chouteau's Pond and the newly settled district beyond the Mill Creek the plague was at its worst. The panic of fear that seized upon the people was increased as a flood of refugees streamed in from the South, for the plague had infested almost the entire Lower Mississippi Valley. The City House had escaped the epidemics of former years, but in 1849 six religious and three children died in less than three weeks, while many others were dangerously ill.

When Bishop Kenrick insisted on a change of air for all the household, the majority of the community went with the orphans to St. Charles, where there had been no cases of the disease. "It would be difficult," wrote the chronicler of those days, "to describe the charity lavished on us during our weeks there. Dear and venerable Mother Duchesne could not do enough for us." Charity, self-denial, and prayer were her way, along with an insatiable zeal for souls. In her letter of July 29 to Mother Jouve her spirit shines through the phrases of encouragement she uses and the descriptions she gives, and there is a zest and freshness in her style quite remarkable in an octogenarian:

In these times of epidemic and political upheaval, my dearest Mother, one really needs to draw consolation from one's friends. Our correspondence is carried on under great difficulties through the mail. It is easier to get an answer from France than from Canada. I expressed to Mother Hardey my anxiety about your discouragement under your difficult burden. She replied from

Halifax that she had received a letter from you in which you seemed more resigned. I sympathize sincerely with you in your situation, but I cannot change it. Every day I pray to Divine Providence for you and invoke the loving care of the Sacred Heart of Jesus and of His holy Mother. They are my best assurance that all will turn out well for you. If you suffer, you also acquire merit, and by your resignation you can draw down graces on our Holy Father, on the Church, and on France, which is resting on a volcano. Let us realize that we are sinners and so have much to expiate, and that others less culpable than we are suffer much more than we do.

St. Louis is the city that has suffered most cruelly from the ravages of the cholera. There were more than 100 deaths daily for a while, and some days 150 to 180. In a single week there were 900 deaths. Now the civil authorities are relieved when there are only about thirty deaths a week. But the epidemic has spread through the rural districts and is attacking people who have come recently from Europe. . . . We escaped the cholera, but it has ravaged the country around us. It is believed that the great fire, which destroyed 300 buildings on eight blocks and burned for several days afterwards, helped to increase the contagion. Try to form some idea of the poor who were left helpless and exposed to the weather and without food, etc. Of all the priests who worked day and night among the sick, not one died of the epidemic.

Having passed her eightieth birthday, Philippine wrote to her sister in a brisk and vigorous style, with a breadth of interest that ranged over Europe and America. It is easy to picture her rapt in prayer in the cloister chapel or bending intently over her needlework, but to fancy her sitting at her window scanning a newspaper might seem far-fetched, did not her own words put the authentic stamp upon this sketch of herself.

I must answer two letters I have received from you, dearest Sister. . . . The second, written in July, gives me details about the June revolution. I knew about it through our newspapers, which are so common in the United States that even the workmen and servants receive their own copies of the papers. They are printed in small towns as well as cities, and the telegraph, which is remarkably widespread in this country now, brings European news quite rapidly. It comes to the East from England and France in a week, and those two countries get it from all parts of Europe. Our city of St. Louis has three gazettes, two being daily papers, printed on large sheets, and the third a weekly, printed on sheets three feet long.

This city of St. Louis has just furnished us with a terrible example of the punishments God sends down on those who break His law by excessive luxury, drinking, disregard for the sacredness of Sunday by manual work and nonattendance at Mass. First there was a great fire that destroyed thirty-six steamboats in all and three hundred buildings on the streets near the river. The fire broke out on a steamboat and spread, burning for several days. Then it burst out again and burned five more steamboats. This disaster was followed by cholera and dysentery. These two diseases carried off nearly 10,000 inhabitants of the city.[48] . . . Next to St. Louis, the city most severely attacked by the plague was, I think, Cincinnati.

How earnestly I wish that the misfortunes of this deceitful world would bring my brother and my brother-in-law back to the service of God. Every day I bring them in prayer to the foot of the altar. Our dear Amelie wrote me from Montreal that she had had a visit from her youngest brother Eugene, who has settled in New York. She seems less burdened now by the office of superior, and she is greatly loved by her community. I hope she will be as good a superior as Constance is. . . . You will be interested to know that our Society now has ten institutions in this country, the Visitation has five or six, the Sisters of Charity, of St. Joseph, of the Cross, and of Mercy have many more than we have. The Jesuits have six or seven big colleges. There are Lazarists in many dioceses, also Redemptorists, Augustinians, Holy Cross Fathers, Trappists, etc.

During the cholera epidemic the President of the United States sent a message to every state in the Union, appointing the First Friday of August as a day of prayer, with all public works stopped, so that the people might humble themselves before God and obtain a cessation of the epidemic. This President, who was General Zachary Taylor, commanded the American Army during the war with Mexico. He often took his relaxation with a Jesuit Father who was chaplain of the Catholic troops, a very learned and perfect religious. He was killed by the savages whom he was trying to evangelize. . . . Find here, dearest Sister, the expression of my deep affection in the Hearts of Jesus and Mary.[49]

An unexpected joy came to Mother Duchesne as the year 1849 drew to a close. Among the religious who came from France that year was one to whom Mother Barat entrusted a letter—the first, it would seem, that she had written to Philippine since the one sent by Mother Jouve in 1847. It is not difficult to picture the old nun kneeling close to the sanctuary railing in the cloister chapel and reading:

I am so happy, my dear, good Mother, to think that Mother Guinand may have the consolation of seeing you and giving you our affectionate personal messages. She will tell you, dear Mother and old daughter of mine, that you are always in my prayers and that we often think of you and speak about you, especially to our young religious in order to rouse their zeal for the salvation of souls and their generosity and willingness to sacrifice all for the love of Jesus Christ. But alas, we get little response from them. Strong vocations are becoming rare, and parents raise so many obstacles. . . . The reason is that our life requires so much sacrifice, and health is much weaker now than formerly. Pray then with us, dear Mother, in order to obtain from the Sacred Heart of Jesus strong and generous souls like those our dear Master gave us at the beginning of the Society. . . .

What a long time has passed, dear Mother, without any news from you! My heart is eager to hear from you. When you have an opportunity, give us details about all that is of interest to us. If you are in need of anything, my loved friend, I shall be so happy to send it to you. Adieu, dear, good Mother. Be assured of my deep affection for you in C.J.M. . . .[50]

Philippine's answer was a cry of gratitude and joy, but she admitted that she was often lonely and depressed, for old age was, she thought, a sad time. Her weakening eyesight cut her off from the reading and sewing with which she loved to fill her days. "But God is good," she added to Mother Barat, "always so good. I have the consolation of spending my time in silence close to the chapel. By the grace of God I am still able to be up and around. Every day I assist at two or three Masses and almost every day our Lord admits me to His holy Table." [51]

Holy Communion often transfigured her. Those who saw her were struck by the glow that radiated from her countenance during her thanksgiving after Communion. As they left the chapel, the children often waited to curtsy to her in reverent silence; then they whispered to one another, "Mother Duchesne is still praying." Sometimes the radiance was noticed by people in the church who saw her kneeling at the altar railing to receive Holy Communion. "I never saw anything like it," said one old man to a member of the community. "Mother Duchesne is a saint," and he described the light he had seen shining from her.[52]

In February, 1850, she was again writing to Father De La Croix at the bidding of Father Van Assche: "He would like a bell for the church at St. Ferdinand, weighing about 1000 pounds, and in spite

of my repugnance to begging from you, he insisted that I be his
agent in this matter. Please let me know whether you can satisfy his
desire." At the close of this long, chatty letter giving news of the
Indian missions, the twelve convents of the Sacred Heart now existing in America, the fire and the cholera, and the failure of St. Louis
to reform its morals after such punishments, she adds a few lines
about herself:

> I have now reached my eighty-first year, and I have been in
> America thirty-one years. How little I have accomplished for our
> good Master! Pray to Him for me and please offer a Mass for me
> that I may have a happy death. I now have as superior, Mother
> St. Cyr, whom you knew at St. Ferdinand and at Opelousas. Give
> us both your blessing for the love of the Heart of Jesus.[53]

She had been busy that winter and spring preparing useful
articles of clothing and sacristy supplies for missionaries and wrote
to offer them to Father De Smet. His answer made her very happy,
for it contained the kind of news she loved to receive:

> I accept most gladly and most gratefully the gifts you are pre-
> paring for the missionaries. The time of their departure is not
> settled yet, but I sincerely hope some will be going soon, and in
> all probability I shall be of the number. The news I received re-
> cently from the savages is very consoling. Father Bax writes me
> from the Osages that he already counts more than five hundred
> Christians among them and that more than a hundred have had the
> happiness of being baptized on their deathbed. Father Hoecken
> writes that there are more than two thousand Christians among
> the Potawatomis. Father Nobili writes from New Caledonia, west
> of the Rocky Mountains, that he has baptized fifteen or sixteen
> hundred savages in that region. Father Joset informs me that the
> savages in our mountain missions persevere and continue to serve
> the good God.[54] He is asking us to send Fathers and Brothers who
> can go out and instruct the thousands of unfortunate people who
> beg to hear the word of God. So you must pray, Mother, to obtain
> help from Heaven for us.
>   I intend to visit St. Charles soon, and I shall accept with pleasure
> the two books by Father Surin which you offer me. . . . I write to
> you in French just to recall old times, and I recommend myself
> to your good prayers.

The month of May was drawing to a close when Father De
Smet paid his visit to St. Charles in company with Father Christian

Hoecken, another kind friend of Mother Duchesne and a great missionary. They were still at St. Charles when she wrote on May 30 to Mother Jouve:

> We have just been visited by Mother Cutts. She left us this morning and will leave St. Louis in a week. She begged us to pray for the health of our religious in the South . . . for workers are lacking for the harvest. St. Michael's has 140 pupils, Opelousas 110, Natchitoches 100, including the day pupils in the academy. I do not know the numbers in the other houses. . . . We are being urged to make foundations in San Antonio, Texas, in Milwaukee, Wisconsin, in Chicago in the Illinois Country, and in Detroit, Michigan. But it was difficult to find even two religious to help with the work among the Potawatomis. Mother Lucille has between fifty and sixty pupils, half-breeds and savages. Mother Bazire found her work there distasteful, as has been the case in St. Louis and at Opelousas. They fear no place will satisfy her but France.[55]
>
> I fear I am beginning to write nonsense—sometimes I use *vous* (you) and sometimes *toi* (thee). Forgive my old age, for I am eighty-one. . . . A long life is no reason for esteem, but rather for trepidation on the part of the one who must render an account of it.
>
> France is once more on a volcano. Your brother might succeed better in Mexico. It is a very Catholic country and those who fought there during the war praised the kindness of the Mexican people. St. Louis has become a Babylon since the influx of immigrants. That town, which had not 4000 inhabitants when we came in 1818, now has 63,000. Cincinnati, that scarcely existed then, has more than 100,000. . . .
>
> Here at St. Charles for the past two days visitors at the Jesuit residence have procured for us six Masses each day. One Mass was offered for my intention. I made the responses at another, kneeling between two altars [one in the church, the other in the chapel], where the Holy Sacrifice was being offered by our two greatest missionaries, Father De Smet, who has four times crossed the continent from here to the Pacific and has visited the native tribes in that area, and Father Hoecken, who is so skilled in the native languages he can speak twelve or fifteen, but he longs to undertake new conquests. Fancy my delight to find myself between these two saints whose charity toward me is so great that they often offer the Holy Sacrifice of the Mass for me. You would do well to procure from Paris the books on the missions by Father De Smet. They are printed in Lille, and also in Flanders, I think. He presented me with two volumes, each a separate work. I rarely

get any news from my family; you must certainly have heard more recently than I. . . . Share this letter with Mother Hamilton, if she is still at St. Jacques. . . .

In 1850 the Religious of the Sacred Heart were preparing to celebrate their fiftieth year of corporate existence. But that year of jubilee was marked by sorrow, for in April Father Joseph Varin died. Mother Barat announced this loss to the whole Society in a circular letter of April 19, and the European convents received the news promptly. But mail to America was still slow at times and often uncertain. Mother Barat's letter had been nearly two and a half months on the way and had not reached Missouri when Philippine wrote to her on June 30:

My beloved and venerated Mother,

I answered the letter you sent me by Mother Guinand. I have not had the pleasure of meeting her yet, but she has written to me. I did not know how to contain my joy on reading your letter, nor can I express my gratitude for your gifts. I tried to do so in my letter to you, but I could find no satisfactory words. So I must continually present to God the debt I owe you in order that He may pay it for me. I wrote to you a second time, but the last letter I received from you was that of September, 1849. I am certainly privileged to receive letters from you, as I have become perfectly useless. Charity alone can prompt you to write to me.

When I learned how the health of Reverend Father Varin was failing, I hoped we would receive letters keeping us informed about his condition. But it was in a Kentucky newspaper that I learned of his death. In that paper he was called the author of our *Constitutions*. How many memories his death has awakened! How much gratitude I owe him—a debt I could never repay! How deeply I sympathize with my venerated Mother, who had already been so sadly tried by the loss of a brother who was her support! [56] Only your great soul could bear the weight of so much sorrow, along with all the disasters caused by the revolutions. . . .

We are very eager to have Mother Hamilton back. She has a special talent for handling the parish sodalities. She was loaned only for a year, and she has been gone three years. The two Canadian convents are prospering after the initial trials, and in general so are those in the United States. Our convent now has as many religious and pupils as it can care for. There is some talk of an addition, and this is badly needed for the sake of health.

I was asked to give my opinion about allowing two mature aspirants to make their final vows. How I do hope they will not be kept back any longer! There are some others who completed their aspirantship some time ago. I think the lengthening of this period tends to disgust them, when they know that in other orders the time of waiting after first vows is only a year or two. That is why those orders have more vocations, for there is no risk of being dismissed after six or eight years in religion.[57]

It is evident that Mother St. Cyr and Mother Cutts considered Philippine's judgment unimpaired by age, or they would never have asked her opinion in so serious a matter as that of fitness for final profession. Evident, too, is the fact that she was wide awake to all that was happening at St. Charles and interested in all that concerned the growth of the Society in America. Because her character is so clearly revealed in her letters, nearly two-thirds of those extant have been cited in part, at least, in this story of her life. Her virtues were graphically sketched by Mother Jouve, who gathered information from the religious who were closest to Mother Duchesne during the years of her pioneering in the face of almost insuperable difficulties. Hence Mother Jouve's pen-portrait of her is of far greater value than any twentieth-century analysis or commentary.[58]

Among the many virtues which were so noticeable in Mother Duchesne, these, she thought, were most prominent: her devotion to the Sacred Heart in the Blessed Sacrament, her love of poverty, her deep humility, her self-denial and penance, her zeal for the salvation of souls, and her charity. This brief enumeration shows how "of a piece" was the development of her sanctity. The seeds of these virtues were planted in girlhood; they grew to strong and vigorous maturity under the action of divine grace during her active life in France and America; they yielded a hundredfold of harvest in the last decade of her life at St. Charles.

Describing that development, Mother Jouve stresses the fact that Tante Philippine was of a naturally serious disposition, yet she was always joyous and animated at the community recreations or when the religious came for little visits with her in her room. This attitude was the more meritorious because she was often at grips with spiritual trials, her soul submerged in dryness, bitterness, and an overwhelming sense of worthlessness. By reason of her natural disposition toward self-contempt and an exaggerated notion of personal responsibility for all that went amiss around her, "she was her own heaviest cross." In spite of her constant efforts to learn meekness and humility from the Heart of Christ, God left her with a certain brusqueness of manner that betrayed itself at times in the tone of her voice, the impetuosity of her actions, the roughness that frequently damaged the very things she was using or making. She misplaced the things she needed, forgot the things she had promised to do, spoke hastily at times. But never did she allow such faults to pass without reparation. Her apologies to her Sisters or to the community were but a shadow of the contrition which filled her soul and prostrated her in humblest self-annihilation before God. But long before her life drew to its close she had so conquered self that those who lived with her spoke only of her sweetness, her gentleness, her patience, her humble gratitude for the least service, and above all her spirit of prayer.

Into her sanctity there were welded depths of thought and sacrifice and union with God, self-renunciation and supernatural living of which the world can understand very little, depths, too, of calm and peace and joy which the world can never give. She judged herself severely. At times she was crushed with sorrow for sin, not only her own little faults of frailty that loomed so large in her eyes, but also the sins of the world, especially of that little world of hers on the Missouri frontier. The norms of ordinary life were never hers. Faith—living, active, informed by charity—led her to ever greater purity of intention and delicacy of conscience. In Father Peter Verhaegen she found a spiritual guide who understood and who was prepared to help her in the final stage of her ascent to God.

The ladder by which she continually made that ascent was prayer of adoration and love in the presence of the Blessed Sacrament. Prayer was her life, but she lived that prayer-life in a simple, yet heroic, way. At times she seemed to be struggling through a desert land, yet she had always the living water of grace to quench her thirst, and she drew that living water from its fountainhead, the Blessed Sacrament. In the years of her active life sun and shadow had fallen unpredictably across her days, but the long hours of her nightly vigils before the tabernacle had steadied her course. In the last obscure years, as she looked forward to the day that knows no declining, the privilege she stressed most frequently in her letters was that of living close to the Blessed Sacrament; the occupation she loved best was needlework for the sanctuary. Both her work and her prayer were worship, for that was the paramount purpose of both—not personal perfection or growth in holiness, but the worship and love of the Heart of Jesus tabernacled in the Blessed Sacrament.

> During the last years of her life [wrote Mother Jouve], when she was free to follow the attraction of her soul, she seldom left the chapel on days of Exposition of the Blessed Sacrament. One day a young religious, fearing that Mother Duchesne was exhausting her strength by her long hours of prayer, knelt beside her and asked in a low voice, "Mother, won't you come to your room to rest for just a little while?" The old nun looked at her with a smile and whispered, "Sister, could one grow tired when she is with our Lord?"

As it was from the tabernacle that she had drawn her strength and her inspiration in the years of heaviest labor, so in the years of utter weakness she found there both courage and the power to endure the physical exhaustion that was so great a trial. From the experienced reality of His Sacramental Presence she had learned to embrace the reality of God's will, expressed in every circumstance and event of life. And as she approached her eighty-first birthday, life was still very interesting to her. She was still writing lengthy letters to old friends like Father De La Croix, filling them with statistics, which she loved, in order to spread a numerical panorama of some sections of Catholic development in America. The pupils of her earliest mission days were remembered and mentioned lovingly—Emilie Chouteau, whose daughter, Philomena Smith, was then in the boarding school at St. Charles, and the five Pratte girls, all "good mothers of families"—and those earliest and kindest friends, General and Mrs. Pratte, and also Mr. and Mrs. St. Cyr. These friends were dead, and the thought of death was before her continually, urging her to beg for prayers and Masses.

In August Philippine learned of the death of her last surviving brother-in-law, Constans de Mauduit.[59] He had long been the object of her daily prayers, she told her sister, and she was consoled by the news of his return to God and reception of the sacraments. She was concerned about her nephew Eugene, who seemed to be roving the continent, and she wrote to his mother on August 4:

> He has gone to Mexico, whence I fear he will proceed to California, where the rage for gold is attracting crowds of people. But I believe what was stated in a letter from that part of the world recently—that for one person who makes a fortune, five hundreds are impoverished and have not even enough money to

pay their way home, for extravagance, dancing, and entertainments of all kinds are to be found side by side with suffering and extreme misery. . . .

Do not worry about my health; it is as good as could be expected when one is past eighty years old. You and I are closely united, being nearly the same age and having been bound to each other not only by family ties but by the closest friendship. I am all yours in the Sacred Heart.

News of the death of Josephine de Savoye-Rollin reached Philippine on November 8 in a letter from her brother.[60] "Mother of the poor and my closest friend," she called her, when writing next day to Mother Jouve, but there was no further comment, except a wistful sentence: "God, who saw that her soul was ready for heaven, took from her the consciousness of her approaching end, for she had always feared death." She apologized for scribbling so badly that day, and blamed this on her weakened eyesight, but undoubtedly the hot tears had welled up from her loving heart at the mention of her beloved Josephine.

The Society of the Sacred Heart celebrated its golden jubilee on November 21, 1850. Mother Barat was then in Rome on important business that concerned the whole order. It now counted two thousand and fifty-five religious, living in sixty-five convents scattered through France, Italy, Belgium, Austria, England, Ireland, Canada, and the United States. Such an organization could no longer be directed as a whole by the Superior General, even with the aid of Mothers holding the title of visitatrix and reporting on conditions in the houses they inspected. The necessity of dividing the houses into provinces which would be under provincial superiors was patent, but the refusal of the Holy See to allow this in 1842 made the reintroduction of the subject a very delicate matter. However, when a commission of cardinals examined the proposal in the spring of 1851, an affirmative answer was given. Pope Pius IX preferred the title *Mothers Vicar* to that of *Provincials* for the superiors who were to be placed in charge of the divisions of the Society, and these divisions were, therefore, called *vicariates*. Thus the "finishing touches" were given to the Constitutions of the Society during the lifetime of Philippine Duchesne.

Early in 1851 she began to experience sudden attacks of weakness which she feared might so incapacitate her as to make her a burden to the community. Telling Mother Jouve of this, she added: "I should like to write also to Mother Hamilton. Never before has she been silent with me for such a long time. But at the age of eighty-two I experience great fatigue from writing, and I console myself with the thought that she may be en route to join us here." [61] When Easter came and there was no indication of Mother Hamilton's return, Philippine wrote to Mother Barat:

> Last year I heard that you were going to Rome and that we should not write to you except in a case of real necessity. So I kept silence. But I can no longer force myself to keep silence, since I hear that our Reverend Visitatrix, Mother Cutts, has been ill for a long time at St. Michael's, and they think she cannot possibly come for her visit this year.
>
> We have reached the end of Mother St. Cyr's term of superiority. This being so, we had hoped to be governed once more by Mother Hamilton, who was loved by all because of her many virtues. Here, as in St. Louis, we need a superior who can speak English, for visitors always ask for the superior. True, Mother Hamilton dreads going to the parlor and still more being superior, for she is very scrupulous. But the big obstacle to her return seems to be the need they have of her at St. Jacques in Canada, where only a French person or one who speaks French can govern the house.

After pleading once more the cause of the young religious who had not yet been admitted to final profession, she continues:

> My beloved Mother, I am growing very old. Be so good as to help me to prepare for death by a little message of the sweet and touching kind you alone can give. I implore you to sustain this house of St. Charles. At present the one abandoned at St. Ferdinand has as many pupils as there are in our academy in St. Louis, and the Sisters of the Cross have put up an addition to the building. Dear and venerated Mother, I kneel for your blessing. [62]

In a little letter of June 12 she admitted to her niece that she was not able to write just then to Madame Jouve: "I beg you to explain to her why I do not write. . . . My mind is greatly confused and my body very weak." She suffered severely from the prostrating summer heat, but there was no evidence of mental confusion in the long letter she addressed to Mother Barat on August 18, 1851:

> I do not know where you are just now, my venerated Mother, but I think it safest to address this letter to Paris. Yesterday I had a long talk with Mother Bathilde Sallion about you and the Society,

and it was not without bitter grief on my part. She told me all about you and the great anxieties you have had. I had no idea they were so grave and so numerous. In turn I confided to her the fears and the many intimate afflictions that accompany my old age. Mother Cutts writes very seldom to us. She has not replaced our Mother Superior, whose five-year term of office expired last spring. I fear she intends to close this house, as she did St. Ferdinand, where those who replaced us now have seventy-nine pupils, and I do not know how low a price was accepted for that house.

As I want to ward off such a fatal blow from our little convent here, I begged the last two Jesuit Provincials to write to you and explain the advantages this house has to offer: 1. the spiritual direction of the Jesuits, three of whom serve this parish and a neighboring one; 2. the great salubrity of the air, which has enabled us to escape the epidemics that have ravaged St. Louis; 3. the beautifully situated property—Monseigneur Du Bourg admired the site very much. This little town offers us few pupils for the academy, but the great influx of settlers is peopling the rural districts, and ours is the only place for Catholic education in the territory north of the Missouri River, whereas non-Catholic schools are appearing on all sides.

I was completely disappointed in the hopes I set on those two Fathers. Having had occasion to see one of them, I inquired whether he had written to you. He answered *No*. That *no* re-echoed in my heart as I thought how, when they first came to Missouri, we had stinted ourselves in order to help them, and all I had asked was a letter that would give you correct information. I know very well that all the Fathers are not so hardhearted with regard to our insignificance, and many of them would gladly see us prosper. But with all the schools there are in St. Louis and in the vicinity, just a step outside of it, we have very little chance to prosper. To ferry across the Missouri costs the parents ten francs each time they visit their children; and sometimes, when the river is frozen in winter, there is no way to get across.

After telling you our problems, I beg you to sustain this house. Do not treat it as Florissant was treated. In spite of all the difficulties, we shall always have day pupils who pay a little, the poor children who have no other chance for education, and some boarding pupils from the vicinity and even from St. Louis, as we have at present, and they pay very well. All the American houses lament their lack of religious to carry on the work. The reason is that the time of aspirantship is too long, and as a result the candidates for religious life go to other orders.

If you could see the pretty place we have here, standing beside the church, as it does, you would not have the courage to take it from us, even if there were only four of us to carry on the work. . . . Mother Bathilde, who came for a visit with us and with whom I had long talks yesterday, told us confidentially that she is leaving us soon. She spoke to me of all the crosses you have carried. I sympathize with you sincerely, but I beseech you, take mine away by safeguarding the existence of this, our first dwelling place in America. . . . Pardon the condition of my letter; so much has been against me—pen, ink, etc.

Philippine's plea for St. Charles was heard, though she did not receive an answer immediately. She had news, however, that brought great joy to her affectionate heart—Mother Hamilton was returning to St. Charles. How soon she did not know, but she told her "dearest Amelie" in October:

I saw in a letter from Mother Regis that she had visited you at St. Vincent, but she has been delayed in New York on account of some business. I am writing to thank you for all your kindness to me. I have not written often recently—old age makes it impossible —and I have been hoping that Madame Jouve and my brother keep you posted with regard to our family. Madame Teisseire is very near death, if she is not already in eternity. She dreaded death, and it is a time in which we need many prayers. I beg you earnestly to procure them for her.[63]

I am growing very old, gradually losing my memory and my strength. Perhaps you will not receive another letter from me. I hope I shall always have your prayers and those of your dear community, to whom I recommend myself. . . .

Mother St. Cyr appended a little note to say:

I hope, dear Mother, that you will excuse me for not writing. Let me assure you that only a lack of time has prevented me from doing so. . . . The weakness of our holy Mother Duchesne keeps us in fear, but her fervor and regularity encourage us in the practice of virtue. Pray for her—pray for us all.

Mother Hamilton reached St. Charles in November and the convent journalist noted: "Our holy and venerated Mother Duchesne's declining days seem to have acquired renewed animation and vigor from the sight of her loved and devoted daughter, Mother Regis Hamilton." Soon Mother Hamilton was happy to be able to tell Mother Jouve:

You know that I am now back at St. Charles with my holy Mother

Duchesne, who, instead of saying her *Nunc Dimittis,* is almost rejuvenated. When I first saw her, the day I arrived, scarcely able to walk or to make herself heard, I was overcome with indescribable sadness. She asked me if I wanted to sleep in her room. Fancy my joy! I prepare her for bed at night; I help her dress in the morning; and I care for her as best I can, but not as I should like to; for she still has the idea that she must do penance, and she considers everything too good for her. The result is that we sometimes have little arguments. Now I win and now I lose.[64]

The improvement in Philippine's condition is evidenced by a letter she wrote on December 19, 1851, to Mother Alexandrine Brangier, who had replaced Mother Hamilton as superior at St. Jacques, Canada, and along with several members of that community had sent letters to her by Mother Hamilton:

We received your many letters—four of them were for me. The arrival of Mother Hamilton and her continual solicitude about me fills me with gratitude to God. I am now able to answer your letters; and before she came, I thought this impossible. Dear Mother, have the fullest confidence that you will succeed in your pious wish to maintain a very fervent community around you.

When I first desired to go to America, I thought only of Canada. That was the goal of all my hope, as I greatly admired Mother Marie of the Incarnation. Father Barat, the brother of our Mother General, told me that Canada was well supplied with missionaries and offered us to Monseigneur Du Bourg, Bishop of New Orleans, who placed us near St. Louis.

I thought no more about Canada, and I thank the Divine Goodness for having sent there Mothers more fervent than I, religious who greatly appreciate all that is being done in Canada. I beg you to offer my respects to your holy pastor. Tell him I am his daughter at least by my admiration for his work. Mother Hamilton often delights us with stories about the Bishop, the clergy, and the way of life in Canada. I cannot read my letter over, as my eyes are too weak. . . .

Through the winter and the spring of 1852 the community at St. Charles was in constant admiration at the change brought about in Mother Duchesne by the tender care given her by her devoted nurse. Those who had lived at the City House in the years when Mother Hamilton had so often been dangerously ill and Philippine had expended on her all the practical skill she had acquired through nursing the sick over more than thirty years, now saw the picture reversed and Regis sparing no effort to bring some strength back into the worn and wasted body that housed the ardent soul of her loved Mother in Christ. They often talked about the happenings in France that winter at La Ferrandière, where the Seventh General Council of the Society was being held. Its special purpose was to insure uniform observance of *Rule* and *Constitutions* as they were interpreted before 1839, to promulgate the modifications in government allowed by the Holy See in May, 1851, and to organize the Society's sixty-five convents into ten vicariates, two of them in America. Reverend Mothers Hardey and Cutts, who had represented the American houses at the council, were appointed to the office of vicar, the former to direct the nine convents in the eastern section of the United States and Canada, the latter the seven in the Mississippi Valley. To Mother Cutts, St. Madeleine Sophie entrusted her letter of February 18, 1852, for her loved "old daughter" Philippine.

> Our Mothers leave tomorrow, dear, good Mother [she wrote], to return to their dear Mission. I am sure Mother Cutts will hasten at once to visit you, to talk to you about the Society and your old friends who treasure such an affectionate memory of you. Above all, she will tell you how consoling our reunion was and, I hope, how profitable for the whole Society. I am sure this will be one of the consolations of your old age.
>
> My dear Philippine, confidence in the Society is increasing; the order is spreading in almost all parts of the world; and from all sides we receive requests which we must refuse. Ah, if we only had Mothers as zealous and selfless as those who first went into the land where you now live, we would not need so many religious for each house, and foundations could be made more easily. Pray, then, dear and loving Mother, pray earnestly that our sweet Master may have mercy on the souls who call for us and may send us apostles according to His own Heart. He will listen to you, I am sure, dear old daughter of mine, for you have always understood so clearly the value of souls and have never recoiled before an obstacle when Jesus summoned you to their aid. . . .

This letter reached St. Charles in mid-April, and Philippine set herself to the congenial, but now very difficult, task of answering it at great length. Her heart was full of joy, her mind alert to all that concerned the community and school, the Indian mission, and the whole Society. She was certainly very much herself as she wrote on April 22, 1852:

I was astonished and greatly consoled on receiving your letter. Since Easter of last year I have not been expecting to live through another twelve months; especially during last summer there were times when I could not even write my own name. When the weather got cool, that gave me back some strength, but my memory has been failing more and more, and also my eyesight. God gave me a great joy in the return of Mother Hamilton. For a long time hearts and arms had been reaching out to welcome her. The religious who knew her before had often been tempted to beg for her return, and those who had not known her rejoiced in the Lord, and all are very happy after many trials that had resulted from disappointed hopes. The Jesuit Fathers esteem her highly and are delighted; the boarding pupils are more attached to her than to her predecessors, and so are our friends outside the convent. All this is a subject for thanksgiving to God, who lifts us up after casting us down by trials.

The charity of our Mother Superior is a wonderful example for all. She sleeps in the same room with me, and this gives her an opportunity to exercise her charity. She has also had still more opportunities because of the illness and death of one of our Sisters and a pupil; they were buried at the same Requiem service.

We have enrolled a good number of new pupils, but we cannot take more than thirty-five without being greatly overcrowded and risking fresh cases of illness. There is real need for an addition to the building; and since I am so useless, I have begged God to take me to Himself, as that would give place for two more people. If the convent in St. Louis could help, the addition could be built quite easily.[65]

We are eagerly anticipating the visit of Mother Cutts which has been announced; she will explain to us the finishing touches that have been put to your splendid labors, which, I trust, will always be blessed by God, who is so rich in mercy and so generous in rewards. He has certainly been prodigal in blessing with success the council, of which we are so eager to know the full outcome. I suppose we shall have to await the arrival of the *Vicar* with Mother Cutts.[66] It was the latter who sent me your letter, for which I am very grateful, and also for the *Cross*, but that will never reach me if she is delayed long. I received the letter written by Mother d'Ainval for Mother Henriette.[67] I am very grateful to them both, but they could not read my scrawl; only the most maternal indulgence like yours can do that.

My love for the savages, however, urges me to describe to you the progress of the school we have in their midst. It is greatly retarded by a lack of teachers, but there are none to send. All the American houses are begging for religious. Mother Lucille

Mathevon wrote me that she has more than sixty pupils in her boarding school. There are four lay teachers (half-breeds) who help the nuns and who have religious vocations. The Government pays for the upkeep of all who are needed at the mission, both priests and religious, and of a certain number of pupils, both boys and girls. Funds for the support of the others come from the sale of surplus produce from the immense property given to the establishment, or from tuitions paid by the Indian parents. The lands are being cultivated, and this past year they had an abundance of corn to sell, more than sixty head of cattle, and plenty of vegetables.

It would be very easy to train, right there, both teachers and religious who would be assigned to that mission and later on to other missions where they are needed. Should such holy people be deprived of religious life just because they have Indian blood? For the most part they have as good minds as the white people, and they are capable of high sanctity. Recently there was a scourge of smallpox, which is very terrible when it attacks the savages. The vast majority of those who had it died like saints. Spiritual help is abundant there. The mission is now the residence of the Bishop of all that territory.[68] Five or six Jesuit priests reside there, and eight Brothers carry on the farming and other work, and they teach and aid the savages. They, too, receive support from the Government. . . .

Our own Archbishop in St. Louis has nothing like as beautiful ceremonies during Holy Week as the poor Bishop of the mission had. There he pontificated solemnly all three days. The Office of Tenebrae was chanted solemnly each day, the lessons being sung in three parts. One of the Jesuit Brothers, a fine musician, had trained ten young Indian boys to chant the Passion, taking the part of the populace, and they did it admirably. The Bishop himself gave the retreat for our nuns, and he also gives them an instruction every two weeks.

If you should wish to establish a novitiate at Kaw River [St. Mary's, Kansas], you must be careful not to interfere with the help given in the school by the lay teachers about whom Mother Lucille wrote to me. They would have to continue their duties with the children and not be withdrawn too much from the laborious work of which they are capable and which is so well suited to them.

I know very few people who have the happiness of seeing you now, but I am eager to recommend myself to Mothers Desmarquest, Thérèse, and Constance Jouve, whom I knew only as a child. My letter is very badly written, but I cannot see to rewrite it. I have strength, however, to kneel in spirit at your feet to receive

your blessing with all possible love and respect in the Heart of
Jesus. . . .

Summer came on gently that year and June was pleasant. Early
in July, Philippine received a letter from her sister which she
hastened to answer, not knowing that the Jouve family in Lyons
was in great sorrow over the death of Mother Constance Jouve at
Chambery on June 15 at the age of forty-five.

> Yesterday, my dearest Sister [wrote Philippine on July 7], I re-
> ceived a letter from you that was written in January. This sur-
> prised me very much, for letters reach us now without delay. No
> doubt God willed that I should feel not only the absence of my
> loved ones, but also that of news from them. One must be re-
> signed. For us there remain only the sufferings of old age, in
> addition to the events of life that are contrary to our desires. At
> our age we should like to enjoy peace, tranquility, and the sweet
> pleasures of friendship, and yet we must bear our burden of years
> along with the suffering that comes from unhappy events, whether
> in public affairs or in our personal lives.
> I am surprised that you are obliged to complain about silence on
> the part of your dear daughter Amelie, though everyone accuses
> her of laziness in the matter of letter-writing. But she is very active
> in her convent. They sing her praises loudly and all goes well. She
> rarely writes to me, while formerly I did not need to be urged to
> write, but I sometimes think it best to stop writing letters lest I
> appear ridiculous. This was especially true last summer, when I
> lost both memory and intelligence for a time. But instead of dying
> during the winter, which was very severe, I found myself stronger
> when spring came, and now I have stopped calculating when I
> shall meet death. It will be when God wills. Old age has many
> sacrifices to make, and it can be a period of great value as one's
> purgatory. It will certainly be a less rigorous one than that of the
> next life.

After telling Madame Jouve that the "mission for the savages is
doing very well," she gives a long paragraph about it, closing with
a sentence about the death of her good friend, Father Christian
Hoecken: "Last year the outstanding missionary, who could speak
fourteen or fifteen Indian dialects as well as several civilized
languages, died of cholera, which he contracted while attending
victims of the epidemic. Another is at the gates of death in the
Osage mission. These are great losses." [69] The last sentence of this
letter shows the union and charity that made community life so

happy under Mother Hamilton's guidance: "There is no one in this community who knows you, but charity makes us all pray for the loved ones of those whom we love in religious life, so you have a share in all our prayers."

With characteristic determination Philippine resolved to make the retreat with the community, though the weather had become very hot and humid and she was oppressed and very restless. "I thought it was my duty to begin my retreat," she told Mother Barat. "I spent most of each day in the chapel, and I grew wearier every day. Our confessor told me I did not need to apply my mind to the meditations, and I felt that myself." As forgetfulness and mental lapses became more frequent, Mother Hamilton grew alarmed and called the doctor.

> The doctor [wrote the patient herself a few days later] discovered that I had very high fever, but I did not mind that so much as having lost my head for awhile. In order to be able to face my present condition and the prospect of losing my mental balance, I really must hold firmly to the conviction that God does everything for our good. Everything possible is being done for me. Mother Hamilton sleeps in my room and attends lovingly to my every need. I meet with the utmost kindness from all my Sisters, and I ask you to include them all in the prayers I beg for myself, especially from our Mothers whose names I cannot recall, for all names escape me now. I humbly beg pardon for all the suffering I have caused you. I do not think I shall do so again. . . .[70]

On August 16 the dear old invalid was so weak that she asked for the last sacraments. Father Verhaegen came and anointed her. She thanked him with a radiant smile. Next day she was better and penned three little notes with a firm hand. That was a triple *adieu* to all she loved best in this world—the Society and its holy foundress, her family, and the Indian missions. To Mother Barat she wrote:

> According to all appearances this is the last time I shall be able to write to you. Yesterday I received the last sacraments, but God may still keep me waiting for the happiness of seeing Him. The mental wanderings I was suffering from were caused by a high fever that I was going about with all the time. At present I do not know when the end will be, but I come once more to kneel at your feet, beg your pardon, and assure you of my loving veneration.

To her sister her pen was again the interpreter of her heart:

I have just received a letter from you, my dear, loving Sister, which I must hasten to answer. Yesterday I received the last sacraments. I am leaving you with sorrow because you are so alone. But God has promised the hundredfold to those who leave father and mother for His sake, and you deserve the hundredfold, too, for your sacrifices have been far greater than those your children made. You share in the merit of all the good works they accomplish. Courage, then! One is always richer for having made sacrifices for God. Have your pious children pray for me. I carry into eternity with me the memory of them and of you. Adieu, loving and dear Sister.

PHILIPPINE

Father De Smet was in St. Louis when he received her little note of August 17:

Your kindness toward me in the past gives me the assurance that I shall see that kindness continue to the end of my life. Yesterday I received the last sacraments, and I hope you will not forget me in your prayers. If you do me the favor of asking prayers for me, that will be a great charity. Will you please write to Reverend Father De Coen for me? He will not forget me, either.[71] If God is merciful to me, you will have a large share in my prayers. I beg your blessing and I am your humble servant,

PHILIPPINE DUCHESNE

From St. Louis University the great missionary wrote to her on August 23:

I received your good letter of the 17th and I cannot tell you what consolation it brought me. Certainly I shall pray to the good God for you. I offered the Holy Sacrifice of the Mass on Saturday and Sunday for you, and every day I shall offer your good intentions to the Lord at the altar. I have also recommended you in a very special manner to the prayers of all our confreres in St. Louis. I expect Father De Coen to arrive here at any hour now, and as soon as he does, I shall deliver your message, and I know he will add his prayers to ours to obtain for you an abundance of graces from heaven. It is I, Madame, and our Indians, who are under great obligation to you for all the prayers you have offered to God for their conversion and welfare and for all your charity in their regard. I do not need to ask you to continue those prayers for us all. And after you have fulfilled the holy will of God here below and received the recompense of your labors, then in heaven more than ever you will pray for the conversion of the poor, unfortunate, and abandoned Indians. And I recommend myself to you in a very special manner. Do not forget me. I shall rely on the promise you made me in your letter.

When she had regained a little more strength, she wrote again to Father De Smet:

Your touching letter filled me with gratitude. God must be very good indeed to give me an intercessor like you. Thank you a thousand thousand times for the Masses offered to God for my poor soul, which I beg you to protect with your prayers, for if God sees fit to prolong my life in the midst of infirmities of both soul and body, I shall be exposed to many temptations. This is why I have recourse to your charity, that it may not abandon me in the midst of temptations to which a long old age exposes one. If God has mercy on me, I shall not fail in the duty of gratitude which I owe to you on so many counts.

I am with deep respect your humble servant,

PHILIPPINE DUCHESNE
who attained her 83rd year on
August 29.[72]

It was evident to Mother Hamilton and the community that Mother Duchesne was growing weaker every day. Neither the medical attentions of Dr. Behrens nor the mixtures he prescribed could check the gentle ebbing of her life. The convent stock of remedies was replenished: elder flowers, slippery elm bark, powdered Virginia snakeroot, orange peel and gentian, quinine, cordial, claret and honey, a pint of French brandy—all purchased for the sick.[73] But the invalid preferred a little milk.

Every morning at the hour for Mass she came into the chapel, almost carried by the religious who helped her, and took her seat close to the sanctuary railing. It was the Mass that mattered, and Holy Communion was her "Daily Bread." Feeble, tottering, bent, her gaunt frame clothed in patched garments, her once luminous eyes now dimmed, she might have evoked pity from a stranger who saw her seated there. But her Sisters in religion looked on her with awed love and veneration, knowing the truth of which she was unconscious, reverencing the sanctity of which she was unaware. Her message to them, though unspoken, was a message of lively faith. She had put God first in her life because she had realized with astonishing clarity that He *is* first, and also last—Alpha and Omega —and that between Him and all else in the universe there is, there can be, no comparison.

After the Holy Sacrifice she was taken back to her little room, to spend the day in quiet communing with God. She could no longer sew or read; she could only rest in the Heart of Christ and lose herself completely in God's will. Each afternoon she went to the chapel for adoration. Her prayer was a quiet looking and listening, the restless mind stilled, the eager will satisfied, petitions laid before the Master in faith and confidence and at once abandoned to His will. *"Je ne suis rien, je ne puis rien, je ne sais rien,"* was more than a quotation copied into her breviary. It was a conviction lived and loved. Her nothingness was a reality in her own mind, for she had given her all to God and fashioned the offering in a prayer she had written in a spiritual notebook years before, a prayer she had lived through nearly thirty-five years on the American frontier:

> O my God, I desire to live as a victim offered in a spirit of penance and love. Then let me prepare all that is needed for a sacrifice of love whose perfume will rise even to the Heart of Jesus. May my *whole being* be the *victim*, all that I am and all that I have. May my own *heart* be the *altar*, my *separation* from the world and all earthly pleasures the sacrificial *knife*. May my *love* be the consuming *fire*, and my yearning *desires* the *breeze* that fans it. Let me pour on it the *incense* and *perfume* of all virtues, and to this mystical sacrifice let me bring *all that I cling to*, that I may offer all, burn all, consume all, keeping back nothing for self. O Divine Love, my very God, accept this sacrifice which I desire to offer You at every instant of my life.[74]

Tuesday, November 16, was a dismal day of torrential rain, biting wind, and penetrating cold. Mother Duchesne wished to rise as usual to assist at Mass, but she was so weak that Mother Hamilton forbade her to do so, and she obeyed. During the course of the morning a carriage drove up to the house, there was an unaccustomed stir, and Mother Hamilton came to tell her that visitors had arrived just to see her—Mother Cutts and Mother Anna Du Rousier, who was representing the Superior General as Visitatrix in America. She had come to bring a last message to Philippine from Mother Barat. On learning this the dying nun gripped her visitor's hand and begged a blessing, which Mother Du Rousier gave in the name of St. Madeleine Sophie. In turn she asked a blessing from

Mother Duchesne, who raised her thin hand and traced a cross on the forehead of the Mother Visitatrix. "I still seem to feel that cross," Mother Du Rousier often said afterwards, "and I trust it to bring me happiness." When someone suggested that Mother Duchesne should offer her sufferings for the success of the Mother Visitatrix's work, Philippine answered quickly, "But I am not suffering." "Then offer your privations, Mother." "Yes, I will offer them," she said, and her feeble voice was steady and grave.

On the following day she was decidedly weaker, and a dry, persistent cough gave her no rest. Mother Hamilton was constantly at hand to give her a little soothing drink. Toward midnight when she presented the cup, Mother Duchesne refused, fearing to break her Eucharistic fast. "Take it," urged Mother Hamilton; "it is not yet midnight." "Are you very sure?" asked Philippine in a tone that brought tears to her nurse's eyes—for it was the Philippine of younger days checking on her religious daughter.

In the chill hour before the dawn, Father Verhaegen made his way from the rectory to the church and prepared to bring Holy Communion to the invalid. The community had already gathered in the cloister chapel for prayer. When Sister Couture kindled a little fire in the room, Mother Duchesne said reproachfully, "You think only of material things. It would be better to say a *Pater* and an *Ave* for the good of my soul." Mother Hamilton then told her the religious were all praying in the adjoining room. "Oh," she exclaimed, "how fortunate I am to die in a house where such charity reigns." The tinkle of a little bell announced the coming of the priest to hear her last confession and give her the Viaticum. Then he returned to the altar to offer the Holy Sacrifice. Later in the morning he came to anoint her again, for she was sinking rapidly. Yet when she heard the invocation, "Jesus, Mary, Joseph," she could answer audibly, "I give you my heart, my soul, and my life—oh, yes—my life, generously." As the noonday Angelus ceased ringing, that eighteenth day of November, 1852, the heroic life of Philippine Duchesne came to an end.

They laid her in a plain deal coffin, made by the village carpenter, and watched beside her in silent joy and grief. They chanted the Office for the Dead in the chapel and left her alone before the tabernacle for her last night of vigil. Father Verhaegen offered the funeral Mass in the Church of St. Charles Borromeo, with many priests in the sanctuary and an unexpected crowd of friends filling the pews. After the requiem service she was laid to rest in the cemetery on the hillside, and the pastor returned to the sacristy to record the burial. He had known the vigor of her early years at Florissant, the suffering and humiliation of the years in St. Louis, the pathos of her helplessness in the Indian encampment, the obscurity of her last years at St. Charles. He had known the inmost secrets of her soul and could say, "She was a perfect religious, and as far as I can judge, she never lost her baptismal innocence." Now that death had led her into eternal life, he wrote:

> On the 20th of November, 1852, I, the undersigned, buried the mortal remains of Madame Philippine Duchesne, professed religious of the Society of the Sacred Heart, aged 83 years.
>
> Madame Duchesne was a native of France, and came to the United States of America with a small number of religious of the Society of the Sacred Heart in 1818. She may be considered the foundress of all the houses of the Sacred Heart in the United States. Eminent in all virtues of religious life, but especially in humility, she sweetly and calmly departed this life in the odor of sanctity on the 18th day of November, 1852.
>
> [signed] P. J. VERHAEGEN, S.J.

In the convent *Journal* the story of Philippine's last days on earth is told in a simple, direct fashion that might have been modeled on her own style. But the love and veneration of the annalist, who wrote for the community, came to a focus in the concluding lines: "We had her daguerreotype taken in case she may one day be canonized."

EPILOGUE

Sanctity on the Frontier

CANONIZATION BY ACCLAMATION has long since disappeared from Catholic usage, but the witness of contemporaries forms a vital part of the evidence accepted by the Church in the process of determining the heroicity of the virtues of one whose cause is under consideration by the Sacred Congregation of Rites. A few days after Mother Duchesne's death, Mother Anna Du Rousier wrote from St. Louis:

> Mother Galwey has promised to give the details of the edifying death of our venerated Mother Duchesne. It is the general opinion here that we have lost a saint. The clergy, and the Archbishop in particular, speak of her with the greatest admiration. Monseigneur Kenrick declared she was the noblest and most virtuous soul he had ever known. Father De Smet says that while living she was worthy of canonization. Our American houses owe everything to her. She opened the way to us through many fatigues and privations. I feel that I am acting in accordance with the wishes of our Mother General in soliciting for her the suffrages prescribed in the Society for a deceased Superior Vicar. It is a homage of gratitude which we owe to the memory of this venerable Mother. I arrived just in time to receive her blessing and to recommend to her the needs of our missions, and she promised she would treat of them earnestly with our Lord. I count much upon her intercession, for I believe she is all-powerful with the Heart of Jesus.

PHILIPPINE DUCHESNE was beatified by Pope Pius XII, now gloriously reigning, on May 12, 1940. The Roman Martyrology for the seventeenth day of November reads as follows:

> Blessed Philippine Duchesne, Virgin, of the Society of the Religious of the Sacred Heart of Jesus, whose birthday is commemorated on the following day.

And for the eighteenth day of November:

> At St. Charles, in the State of Missouri, in (the United States of) North America, the birthday of Blessed Philippine Duchesne, Virgin, of the Society of the Religious of the Sacred Heart of Jesus, illustrious for the practice of severe mortification and for unflagging zeal in winning souls for Christ. Pope Pius the Twelfth

enrolled her among the Blessed. Her feast is celebrated on the preceding day.

PRAYER

O God, who lovest souls and hast in all ages chosen apostolic hearts and endowed them with Thy knowledge and Thy love, hear the prayers which we offer through the intercession of Thy servant, Blessed Philippine Duchesne. Kindle in us the zeal with which her life was consumed, and grant that after following her example in charity, self-denial, and prayer on earth, we may be admitted one day to the same glory in our heavenly country. Through Christ our Lord. Amen.

Appendix I | *Tables 1 and 2*

ANTOINE DUCHESNE, 1711-1783
m. (1737)
MARIE LOUISE ENFANTIN

Marie Louise 1738–1820 Visitandine Sr. Françoise-Melanie	Françoise 1739–1810 m. Jean L. Tranchand	X*	Marie–? 1742–1770 Visitandine Sr. Marie-Fortunée	Pierre-François 1743–1814 m. (1765) Rose-Euphrosine Perier	X 1748–1760 died as a novice Visitandine	Claire-Julie 1749–1830 Visitandine Sr. Claire-Euphrosine

Marie-Julie, b. 1768
Visitandine
Sr. Claire-Julie

Children of Pierre-François and Rose-Euphrosine Perier:

Marie-Adelaide 1767–1778	Marie-Amelie 1771–1837 m. (1786)	Charlotte-Euphrosine 1772–1857 m.	Agathe-Justine 1775–1776	Adelaide 1779–1824 m. (1798)	Hippolyte 1781–1854 m. (1814)	Augustine–Melanie 1786–1828 Visitandine
ROSE-PHILIPPINE 1769–1852 R.S.C.J.	Constans de Mauduit 1760–1850	Jean-Joseph Jouve		Henri Lebrument	Coralie Durand	Sr. Marie-Xavier

Children of Marie-Amelie and Constans de Mauduit:

1. Augustine 1787–1847 m. Augustin Jordan
2. Amédée 1790–1875 (Army officer, unmarried)
3. Amelie 1795–1869 m. (1818) Henri Bergasse
4. Adrien 1805–1817

Children of Charlotte-Euphrosine and Jean-Joseph Jouve:

1. Auguste
2. Euphrosine, 1796–1821 R.S.C.J., *Aloysia*
3. Amelie, 1797–1879 R.S.C.J.
4. Henri, 1800–18 ? S.J.
5. Hippolyte, 1802–1877 m. (1) Marie J. Neal (2) Amelie Bergasse
6. Alexandre, 1805–18 ?
7. Constance, 1807–1852 R.S.C.J.
8. Camille, 1809–1897
9. Josephine, 1811–18 ? Religious of Perpetual Adoration (Lyons)
10. Eugene, 1814–1887
(Five other children died in childhood.)

Children of Adelaide and Henri Lebrument:

1. Caroline, 1799–1854 R.S.C.J.
2. Henriette, 1800–1854 m. Dr. Tourret
3. Eugenie, 1802–1857 Visitandine
4. Marine, 1803–1861 m. M. Barras
5. Delphine, 1805–1833 Visitandine
6. Amelie, 1806–1828 m. M. Gauthier
7. Octavie, 1812–1893 m. M. Munaret
(Two other girls and a boy died in infancy.)

*X—according to Msgr. Baunard there was a son older than Pierre-François Duchesne.

JACQUES PERIER, 1702-1782
m. (1741)
MARIE-ELIZABETH DUPUY, d.1799

| Claude 1742-1801 m. (1766) Marie-Charlotte Pascal | Jean 1743 | Jean-Antoine 1744-1793 (?) | Hélène-Elizabeth 1745-1796 m. Pierre Jordan | Jacques-Augustin 1746-1793 m. Charlotte Carrier | Marie-Elizabeth 1745-1796 m. Alexandre Gueymar | Rose-Euphrosine 1748-1797 m. Pierre-François Duchesne |

See Table I:
The Duchesne Family

Hélène-Elizabeth / Pierre Jordan:

1. Camille, 1771-1821
2. Noel
3. Augustin

Jacques-Augustin / Charlotte Carrier:

Camille-Josephine, 1800-1826, m. François-Charles, Comte de Rémusat
Alexandrine, 1801-1824, unmarried
Adolph-Scipion, 1802-18 ?, m. Natalie Dumottier de Lafayette
Eugene-Fortunat-Paul, 1809-1849
Marie-Amelie, 1806-1827, unmarried

Claude / Marie-Charlotte Pascal:

1. Jacques-Prosper, 1768
2. Elizabeth-Josephine, 1770-1850 m. Jacques-Fortunat de Savoye-Rollin
3. Euphrosine-Marine, 1771
4. Augustin-Charles, 1773-1833 m. Louise de Berckheim ....
5. Alexandre-Jacques, 1774-18 ?
6. Antoine-Scipion, 1776-1821 m. Louise de Dietrick (3 children)
7. Casimir-Pierre, 1777-1832 m. Marie-Cecile Loyer (2 children)
8. Adelaide-Helene (*dite* Marine), 1779-1851 m. Hyacinthe Teisseire ....
9. Camille-Joseph, 1781-1844
10. Alphonse, 1782-1868
11. Amédée-Auguste, 1785-18 ?
12. André-Jean-Joseph, 1786-18 ?

Charles-Joseph, 1797-1858, m. Mathilde de Salcette
Amelie, 1800-18 ?, m. Louis Bergasse
Josephine, 1802-1803
Henriette-Marie, 1803-18 ?, m. Achille Chaper
Marie-Josephine, 1804-1822, unmarried
Camille-Alexandrine, 1803-1823
Emmanuel-Paul, 1809-18 ?
Louise-Philippine, 1814-18 ?, m. (1835) Charles-François Rolland

730

APPENDIX II | *Letters*

Letter 1.

NEW ORLEANS, June 3, 1818

Your names, which I carry both on my heart and in my heart, are constantly before my mind, and now I add to the pleasure of thinking about you that of writing to you. I do not know when this letter will reach you, but no matter how long it is delayed, it will in time tell you that I shall never forget you, and by it I shall bear witness to the fact that there is sweetness in sacrificing all for God, who has given Himself entirely to us. I have already seen the savages for love of whom we have undertaken this difficult journey. A great number of them come here to sell small baskets—you will see some samples of these—or the blackberries they gather in the woods. The skill with which they make these baskets and the shrewdness with which they do their trading prove that they are quite intelligent and so they are able some day to attain to a knowledge of God, if only they are brought to civilization and are thus enabled to become Christians.

But in this city, which is more corrupted by luxury and magnificence than any city in France, people are accustomed to treat the Indians like animals. They have only huts to live in, and they are much more wicked than those we shall deal with in Upper Louisiana. They are cruel, revengeful, and they repel whatever is said to them about religion. Those who come to the door of the Ursuline convent call the nuns the "women of the Great Spirit." The ones I saw were dressed exactly as our Lord is represented in the *Ecce Homo*, but the cloaks they wore were much more bizarre. One of them stuck his head in at the door of the church on Sunday. He had the air of a devil who wanted to put his head in at the gate of Paradise; then he made off like a thief.

That same day I went to the rooms where the Ursuline nuns were teaching catechism to more than a hundred people—poor Creoles, colored persons, Negro women. There are some among them who live like saints. One of these came up to me, her hands joined, to ask whether I would remain here. She devoured us with her eyes and was much saddened when we told her we were going farther on. But apart from some good ones, a great many of them are ignorant, wanting only fine apparel which they can procure from New York and Philadelphia, where there are no slaves. They often go barefoot during the week, then on Sundays appear in hats and dresses of pink or blue taffeta, which only brings out the black of their faces. Many of them wear dresses of net or shining white material. The slaves who have nothing with which to satisfy their vanity wait until their owners go away from home; then they go to balls dressed in their clothes. The washerwomen do the same with clothes that are left with them on Sunday. Oh, do pray for all these poor, ignorant, and sinful people. Workers are needed to instruct them. When a savage can make himself understood and asks pardon, he adds: Now no one teaches us any more.

They live in bands around a fire, and this is as acceptable to them in summer [as a "smudge" to drive off insects] as in winter. They sleep around it. The Negroes, too, never go to sleep without a fire, no matter what the season. The condition of these slaves is not entirely unhappy. They are given two or three hours each day which they may employ in cultivating a little land that is assigned to each family, commonly called the *desert*. They can work there and raise as much in this little time as people who toil all day in France. The Pope has given them a dispensation to work on Sunday. Each family has its own little house, the whole group of houses being called *quarters*. They all wear clothing. All along the Mississippi [on the way up to New Orleans] I saw plantations where there are as many as one hundred slaves. For that alone the master would have to be worth a million francs, since each Negro is worth more than ten thousand francs. In Cuba, which is called Great Cuba here, there are plantations with more than four hundred Negroes. In this country some planters make two hundred and fifty thousand francs' worth of sugar a year. Does that bring them happiness? I would much rather teach a little savage and eat the same kind of food she does than see myself in such great abundance and with the responsibility of so many persons, for whose salvation many masters are so indifferent, they leave them without instruction and without any practice of religion.

I shall try to enclose with this letter a plan of the vessel on which we sailed. After you have seen it, please send it to Mlles de Vidaud and de Jonquière in Grenoble, to whom I promised to write. The Seine, which you see in Paris, the Rhone, which is so beautiful and swift, the Loire, so beautiful at Tours, and lastly the Garonne—none of these can compare with the Mississippi. The width of one of the five channels at its mouth equals that of the Loire; all put together would equal the Gironde. The entrance to the river is frightening. From the Gulf of Mexico the boat passes into what they call the *white water* (which is really green), and there the sailors begin to sound for the floor of the ocean. At some leagues from the actual mouth of the stream its waters are carried out into the sea without mingling with the sea water to the right or left, and the vessel, sailing through this water, leaves in its wake a furrow of the sea water it has plowed into below the surface. The struggle between the sea and the river is very noticeable at the mouth of the stream, where the sea, repelling the river, has piled up sand and mud, which is held fast by the shores and rocks whose ledges stick up, and the whole mass forms a bank or delta. The river is not very deep here and leaves only a channel with sufficient water to carry the vessel, which moves in a very narrow lane choked by sand banks and enormous trunks of trees floating on the surface or caught in the mud.

As the vessel enters the river, the captain is all activity. The best pilot is at the wheel; another, with sounding-line in hand, casts it continually and sings out the number of fathoms he measures. The coast pilot goes ahead of the vessel with a spy-glass to observe the exact middle between two objects he has noticed and which mark an important spot. The other sailors and all the passengers are in tense silence and no one speaks until the captain says, "Now we are in the stream." There is no tide here, as in the Gironde, to help the vessel; it must be driven by a favorable wind, which often dies down. So thirty-two leagues may take a very long time. We were neither much favored nor much hindered. After the dangers at the entrance to the river we enjoyed the beauties spread before us: groves of the most beautiful green trees formed a lovely long curtain, which is nowhere broken by openings. The stream is so peaceful that it is held in check by its banks without any dykes. There are small cabins and big plantations where one sees orange groves, pomegranate trees, myrtles, pink and white oleanders growing in the gardens. There are fields of tobacco, maize, cotton, sugar cane, and between them herds of cows or other animals grazing. The milk here is always sweetened. When we bought it on the boat from farmers on the river bank, they always added a little sugar cane with it.

About half-way up to New Orleans from the Gulf the copsewoods give way to tall forest trees—live oak, sycamore, pecan, tall poplars, and willows. At the water's edge there are enormous palms with very large leaves which, caught together at the stem, form a huge fan. These palms are used for brooms; when bleached, they make very pretty straw hats; and the savages use them in making their baskets. They color them with herb dyes to form the patterns you will see. The Mexican Indians are naturally artistic and make very pretty things in shell work.

To finish what I wanted to tell you about the banks of the Mississippi, the part nearest to New Orleans has been stripped of its trees, and no good planting has been done to replace them. The land is swampy and not very good for vegetation. Grape vines dry up and die; neither cherries nor gooseberries will grow there;

the best plums are like our worst; peach trees degenerate; vegetables are very costly; figs and oranges grow well, but a winter extremely cold for this climate killed many of the orange trees, and even in the best years they never produce fruit as good as that grown in Cuba. On the voyage they gave us some oranges that were far superior to those of France, along with pineapples and bananas. Cuba exports these, along with tobacco and sugar cane, but the cane is not let ripen enough to attain its full sweetness. We eat raw sugar here; the refined sugar actually comes from France and is quite expensive.

The ocean is gray during storms, slate-color in better weather, and a beautiful blue mingled with violet rays when the sun shines full on it. But the sun is often no brighter than the moon, and it seems to sink at evening right down into the water. On other days the sunsets were like a burning furnace. Sunrise and sunset are, I think, much more beautiful on land, where the horizon is so much more varied. On the ocean one can see only about three leagues away, and this appears just about the distance from our convent [at Grenoble] to Val de Grâce because of the uniform flatness. I did not see any whales or even sharks or dog-fish, though some of them gnawed at the bait. But we did see several schools of dolphins, which are quite large, and the sailors caught two good sized porpoises, or sea hogs, and some doradoes, which are colored like the rainbow, a cod fish, a huge turtle that had four strong fins instead of feet such as land turtles have, and some flying fish.

In the Mississippi there were gray-colored crocodiles shaped like huge lizards, many snakes, water polyps, and shell fish by the millions, and there were thousands of them on the trunk of a cedar tree we saw in the ocean—it had drifted from the coast of Virginia or Carolina. The mosquitoes that attacked us at the mouth of the river are felt rather than seen. They bear a close resemblance to their venomous cousins in France. The only bird in this section of the country that sings is called the *mocker*. There are also *popes, cardinals*, and *bishops*. The pope is easier to raise than the cardinal. We also saw many pelicans and herons on the Mississippi.

In the convent of the Ursuline nuns who are so kind as to give us hospitality, there are about sixty boarding pupils, twenty orphans, and some day pupils. They receive only white children, except in the catechism classes on Sundays; we, on the contrary, shall have more colored children. I commend our mission to your prayers, and I have already felt the effects of your prayers. The main thing is to do good. Population increases daily in the territory to which we are going, and much produce is exported from there to this city, which had loaded more than five hundred sailing vessels this year and needs three hundred more to carry all the cotton, sugar, tobacco, and grain that is still to be shipped. Now I must finish this quickly by telling you that I have you all in my heart, and I try to put my heart in the Heart of Jesus.

PHILIPPINE

Letter 2.

TO THE RELIGIOUS AND CHILDREN OF THE SACRED HEART IN FRANCE:

ST. CHARLES, November 20, 1818

Though our New Year's greetings will be late in reaching you, the Heart of Jesus, to whom neither time nor distance makes any difference, will let you find pleasure in them, especially when we tell Him that we desire to be all His in union with you. We do not yet know whether you have received any of our letters, but we have had the joy of receiving several from you. . . . Father Barat has given us many proofs of his kindly interest. He has written to us five times, but his last letter was far from consoling, as we had hoped he might be coming out here. The Bishop is also disappointed, but he does not dare urge missionaries to come out here because of the hardships they must endure from the change of climate, manner of life, and the privation of many things. But God, who looks with mercy on this country, has inspired the superior of Georgetown to buy land in Upper Missouri, where it is very desirable. Every day there are American families, mostly from Kentucky, passing through here on their way to settle at Boonslick, where there are good salt mines. Many are also taking up land near Franklin, where the Jesuits will open their college, and small missions will spread for 2000 leagues farther, in regions where the faith is unknown. Only a religious order could undertake such an enterprise. The Jesuits will be the third order of men to labor in this vast diocese. The Lazarists have founded their seminary at The Barrens (or Bois Brulé), the most fervent Christian community in the region; some young priests of Father Liautard's group are opening a college in St. Louis.

People still believe that this section of the country is going to be very important and that this very winter Missouri will become a state of the Union. St. Louis will be its capital, just as New Orleans is the capital of Louisiana, Natchez [meaning Nashville] the capital of Tennessee, Bardstown the capital of Kentucky, and Kaskaskia that of Illinois. Kaskaskia was formerly an important town. It has a stone church—a rare thing out here, and a rectory that belonged to the Jesuits before their expulsion. When the Indians of the vicinity learned of the departure of the last Jesuit there, they leaped into their canoes, pursued and overtook him,

and brought him back by force, saying they wanted their father
and would keep him in their midst. After that there was no safety
for anyone traveling through their country unless he wore the
"black robe," and many seculars were obliged to wear this disguise
in order to travel in security in the vicinity of Kaskaskia. That
town was almost swept away once by the flooding Mississippi.
The high water was checked only when a holy priest led a procession of the people toward the rising tide, planted a cross in the
ground, and said: "Thou shalt not advance beyond this spot."

The love of the savages for the "black robes" is general throughout this country, even among the Sioux, a very fierce tribe. The
priest who lives nearest them frequently comes here [Father John
Acquaroni]. He told me that the Indians would gladly furnish him
with all the meat he needs, if he would accept it, but he does not
want to be obligated to them in any way, lest they ask whisky
from him in return. That is a kind of liquor made from corn. It
puts the Indians into such a condition that a drunken savage, here
at St. Charles, held his child in one hand and his knife in the other,
ready to cut the little one in two. Someone pounced on him suddenly and saved the child—and that child has been baptized. These
wretched people bargain anything they possess for this liquor.
Sometimes they go in a group to the priest's house, even at midnight, to demand liquor, but he is very careful never to have a
drop to give them. Owing to this condition of affairs, we are
obliged to guard against making friends with them. But Divine
Providence has Its own hours.

Here is the story of a remarkable conversion. An Indian who
was very ill was heard talking to himself and saying, "Once upon
a time I was in the presence of the Author of Life (he had had a
very severe illness sometime before this) and He said to me,
'Return home; it is not time for you to come to Me.' But now I
am going to the Author of Life." A Christian Iroquois named
Francis who was present said, 'The Author of Life sent you back,
no doubt, to get the water poured on your head.' The sick Sioux
answered, 'I really believe it was for that.' Then Francis asked, 'Do
you want me to go and find the black robe who will pour the
water?' The Sioux answered, 'Go quickly; there is not much time
left.' The good priest came at once, was satisfied with the answers
the Indian gave, and baptized him. The Indian died shortly after
that. He was given a solemn funeral, and the priest also baptized
his son who was very ill. This all happened quite near here, and
the priest is Father Acquaroni, a Roman Lazarist, who is one of
our zealous friends.

Another priest [Father Joseph-Marie Dunand], who is a
Trappist, has told us many stories that prove the love of the

Indians for him. He is always making missionary trips and frequently meets Indians, but they never have molested him in any way. Once when he went to Prairie du Chien, so called because the nomad Indians there have only cabins made out of deer skins which can be rolled up and packed on poles drawn by dogs, all the women came out of their huts, bringing their babies that he might bless them; men and women came in crowds to his Mass, but he could not teach them because of the difference in language. . . . The Indian women are really slaves: when the tribe moves, a woman may have to carry three children on her back, while the man goes off freely, carrying only his weapons. If he kills a bear or a deer, he leaves it where it falls, though he may cut a very heavy animal into sections. Then he goes to get his wife, tells her where the beast is, and she has no rest until she has brought it all in, carrying all on foot, even until ten o'clock at night.

We have no full-blooded Indian girls in our school, only some half-breeds, of Indian and white blood. We have one such girl as a domestic servant. Someday she may be a religious. When she was twelve years of age, her father sold her or gave her in marriage, but she would never go with her husband, kept herself aloof, and talked very little. She is a gentle, pious girl and speaks of giving herself to God. I am sending you a portfolio and a pair of Indian moccasins that will show you how well the Indians work in leather. They give animal names to those who go among them. They call Father Pratte, the pastor of Ste. Genevieve, "Son-of-a-white-fish." One day when they greeted him, they saw Bishop Du Bourg behind him. "Who is that?" they asked. "This," said the pastor, "is the Father of the Black Robes." Immediately the whole group came up to salute the Bishop, even those who were a bit drunk.

A very lucrative traffic has been established up the Missouri with the Sioux and other tribes. The merchants from St. Louis who go up the river in boats suffer quite as much as the missionaries, often being without food and spending as much as eleven months on one trip. The Catholics in Canada are aided by the English government, which is interested in holding the settlers in that country. They have beautiful churches with gilded domes, and there are five communities of religious women, nearly 300 priests, while in this enormous diocese there are just about twenty or twenty-four priests all told.

A Canadian Iroquois who had been for a time at Florissant died later on in his own country at a time when travel was impossible. His father scooped out a log, put the body in it, closed it, and put it up in a tree. When spring came, he was told that the boy's spirit cried out, "Let us go to Florissant." The father carried the body 600 leagues to obtain Catholic burial for his son and gave the priest an offering of 200 francs. In a church at Portage des Sioux the altar was ornamented through ignorance with two pictures—heads of Bacchus and Venus; now a picture of the Sacred Heart is to be seen on the door of the tabernacle.

Letter 3.

To the Novices at Grenoble:

> St. Ferdinand or Florissant
> In Louisiana [sic]
> March 1, 1820

I have just received, my very dear Sisters, a little packet of letters, some dated February, 1819, others April and May of the same year, among them two letters each from Sisters Aloysia Jouve and Louise de Vidaud. They came on a steamboat that was delayed a long time because of ice in the Mississippi. The steamboat remains at St. Louis only a few days and I want to take advantage of its trip downstream, so it is impossible for me to write many letters just now. And what is there to hinder me from using the same sheet to thank my dear Aloysia for her interesting accounts of happenings at Ste. Marie, and of congratulating Julie Dussausoy and Louise de Vidaud on their generous resolutions and their happiness, which is also mine, since I am so glad to be bound to them by new ties. Besides, I owe you all the fulfillment of a promise to write to you. Do you remember how sometimes when we were talking together, we would read interesting missionary accounts and I would tell you of my longing to work in the land of the savages? Then you would make me promise that, if ever I should go to foreign lands, I would send you back accounts of my doings? It is time I kept that promise, but I cannot tell you anything very interesting. This country has come but recently out of barbarism, I think, and so it offers nothing very remarkable for us to accomplish and nothing in the line of curiosities such as one finds in distant but civilized lands.

The State of Lower-Louisiana has no large city except New Orleans, its capital. Much of the country is fertile but uncultivated; however, it is being settled on all sides by Spaniards, French, and Americans—this last name is given to the subjects of the United States, naturalized citizens or descendants of the English. The climate of New Orleans and its environs is less healthful than that of the country farther north. St. Louis is the largest town in Upper Louisiana [Missouri] which is still only a territory, that is, a section of the country dependent on the United States, but having no part in the general government. This region is quite healthful, except in low-lying districts where there is stagnant water. However, there are frequently, and notably this year, epidemics whose contagion seems to originate from long ocean trips in southern waters. The travelers contract the diseases from one another and spread them rapidly. The passion for traveling is remarkable and does much harm among the young people. Some traders go as far as Philadelphia on business and bring back all kinds of luxuries, so that the poor people here often seem to have more than have our pupils in France, even those in easiest circumstances. The ordinary settler's wife, after eating her salted meat and corn bread, washing her linen and doing her kitchen work, puts on a hat bedecked with ribbons and flowers, colored shoes, embroidered dress, takes a parasol, and goes for a stroll. The men who go up the Missouri and the Mississippi for five or six hundred leagues to trade for furs and skins with the Indians bring back loose morals, a passion for gain, and savage ways. . . .

I have been told that there is in this country a kind of soil which has all the properties of soap and is used by the Indians to wash and soften the skins of animals which they trade for shot and powder, beads, blankets, and liquor. Drunkenness is a wide-spread vice here among both the savages and the civilized people. And dancing is another form of pleasure that develops into a violent passion.

Every householder here makes his own soap from ashes which have been steeped in water for some days and filtered slowly. The residue is then mixed with old corn or oats and boiled, and at the end of the process they have a strong, reddish-brown soap. Candles, too, are homemade, and this kind is used in church. They melt less readily than those made of yellow wax, which is easily procured, but is never refined.

The woods between St. Charles and Florissant are full of trees which they tap for sugar, this kind being used as much as that obtained from cane. Most of these sugar trees are maples. There is also much honey in the wild nut trees; the nuts cannot be eaten as the shell is too hard. There are wild grape vines, the fruit of which would make fairly good wine could it be picked, but the vines wind about tall trees to an inaccessible height. . . . You have seen the pecan, a nut native to this country, which is very much liked, but never used to make oil. The only oil in use here is that of the cod, very thick and hard to procure. Vinegar is made from rain water mixed with a strong liquor called whisky, corn, and sugar, and exposed to the sunlight.

There are very fine horses, more numerous than are the men who never go the least distance except on horseback. On Sunday the church is surrounded, having the appearance of a horse fair. The women ride to church seated on their horses and carrying their young children in their arms. Cows wander about everywhere, but come home night and morning to their calves, which are kept tied up. And what an uproar when the calves are taken from them entirely! The oxen and horses also come home regularly, enticed thither by salt and Indian corn. When they stray, men ride through the woods in search of them. It is often difficult to yoke oxen that are accustomed to freedom, so, to save time and trouble, they are left yoked together day and night for several months. The roe-deer is, I think, the prettiest animal to be seen in this country. It has a beautiful head and is so affectionate that when we approach, it comes to kiss us; it is as mild as a lamb and quite easily tamed.

As to plants and grains, the most common is Indian corn (maize), from which bread is made by mixing the meal with enough hot water to form a thick paste. This is scooped into a greased pan which has a cover, and the whole thing is pushed into the hot coals to bake. We often eat this kind of bread, which many Americans prefer to that made from wheat, which grain also grows abundantly here. There are beans, pumpkins, cantaloupes, and water-melons, and other garden products. Apples are much in use; there are white, red, yellow, and purplish varieties, and sweet ones that taste like chestnuts (which are not known in this section), but this kind cannot be stored for future use. Lentils are unknown; rice comes from Louisiana and is expensive. Besides the fruits named, the woods furnish many mulberries [evidently blackberries or raspberries] that are eaten with sugar like strawberries, which here grow wild, as does a small fruit having the name and taste of citron. One finds everywhere a herb called belldame, prepared as is spinach and resembling it in taste. Corn is eaten on the cob while it is tender. They boil it in clear water. They also make gruel out of cornmeal and water, and by mixing meal and mustard produce an effective plaster. Mercury is used a good deal in medicines. . . .

Letter 4.

To Mother d'Olivier: "From the Oak to the Olive"

Florissant, July, 1822

I have been wanting to write to you for a long time, as I learned from several people the joy and zeal you have shown in working for our mission. Among the many things that have come to me from France, either in the box brought by Mr. Mullanphy or in

Mother Lucille's luggage, I was not able to distinguish just what you sent. It would have given me real pleasure to have noted these things particularly, though I appreciate the modesty with which you offer your gifts. But please do not drop your interest in us, for if God gives us the privilege of extending our works and our houses here, we shall go only to places destitute of everything, and so we shall always have need of charitable help.

There is practically no more money in this country. Bank notes are worthless; and even when they had value, one could not purchase in the United States the things needed for liturgical worship. We have a hard time decorating our three altars, two in the church, dedicated to the Sacred Heart and the Blessed Virgin, and one in our chapel or choir, honoring St. Francis Regis, to whom we owed one. We had vowed to erect it if he obtained for us the privilege of being sent to America. When I placed on the main altar of the Sacred Heart the cross and candlesticks given by Madame de Marbeuf, there was nothing valuable left for the other two. But on solemn feasts we have Exposition of the Blessed Sacrament in our choir. . . . That is why I am so eager for a second set of candlesticks of gilded wood for the altar of the Blessed Sacrament, with some painted metal vases, or at least a quire of gold paper to cover our rough wooden vases and the boxes filled with ashes into which we put our paper flowers. The handsome lace which you most certainly sent (packed separately in a small box) did splendid service on Corpus Christi. We folded it double and put it around the throne on which the Blessed Sacrament was carried in the procession. This had been covered formerly with white cotton material that was discolored with age and stained with drops of rain water from the leaking roof and fly-specks. Four bouquets of roses at the four corners of the throne replaced the feathers—of either goose or rooster—which were formerly used. The new decoration was considered very elegant. The throne was carried by two men—an American and a Frenchman. We were nearest to the Blessed Sacrament. Four of the tallest novices carried the arch of triumph, under which we had placed our statue of the Blessed Virgin. It was decorated with all the other laces and ribbons that were in the small box.

Two of the pupils who are ribbons of merit carried the first streamers and led the singing with our nuns. The day pupils were grouped under the banner of St. Aloysius Gonzaga and the boarding pupils under that of the Sacred Heart. The women of the parish walked ahead of us, carrying the banner of the Blessed Virgin, while the men and boys at the head of the procession carried the cross and the banners of St. Ferdinand and St. Regis. These banners were made by fastening pictures of these saints, printed on paper, to pieces of taffeta. The procession went through our meadow, which is sown with oats. This was a beautiful green, and as they had cut a broad swath through it to indicate the line of march, it was like a lovely green carpet. The repository was on the highest part of the field. That procession was carried out with reverence, even on the part of the Protestants, who attended in a large group. This is a very popular kind of devotional exercise here. I regret that we had no material for prettier banners of the Blessed Virgin, St. Regis, our patron, and St. Sophie. If any of your companions are artists, they could not use their talent in a better way. I used to daub in bygone days, but here I have done nothing more than cover up some Italian immodesties. I put a fichu on St. Agatha, some swaddling bands on the Infant Jesus, and a cloud over the body of an angel. Some one gave me a picture of a nun. As it had a masculine countenance, I made of it a picture of St. Ignatius wearing a chasuble. But the lack of proper paints and skill prevents me from trying to produce a full-length figure.

The Osage Indians have promised to receive the priests who are going amongst them. This is a savage tribe that sets the example for many others. A priest is going there to establish a mission soon. He could not remain there long the first time he visited them because the hunting season was coming on. He was accompanied by some French-speaking traders and several half-breeds to act as interpreters and to help him eat, for among these people it is considered a lack of courtesy not to eat everything one is offered. This priest had to face thirty dinners that were offered him on a single day. To manage this, he just took a little out of each dish, then passed it on to the half-breeds, who eat like oxen. So do the savages, but they never store away food and so are often without anything to eat for several days.

The day this priest said Mass among the Osages he baptized a number of little children. The Frenchmen stood on one side and the savages on the other. During the instruction the Presbyterian ministers who had gone along with the party and had quantities of presents to offer in order to win the conversion of the Indians, also listened to the priest. It would be interesting to know the outcome of this. These ministers cannot get a high standing among the Indians because they have wives. Morover, the savages in this region like the French and what they bring them better than the Americans, as they call the people of the United States. They tell a story of an Indian who said to one of them: "They told us the great father of Spain had given the land to the great father of France; then the forest trees fell in a great heap and there was a great fire and dancing around it. But then they told us the great father of France had given the land to you, the Americans; then no trees fell and there was no fire and no dancing, but only the ashes of great grief."

During the Mass said by the priest, they gave two pigs and a deer to six savages to prepare for a meal. These men found the ceremony too long and ate all the meat themselves. The patience of these people is shown by the fact that the chiefs did not get angry at this; they only said, "They must have been pretty hungry."

Forty of them had come galloping up to have the honor of being the first to kiss the hand of the priest, and they returned at the same speed to the village to be the first to announce his arrival. In the council they held to decide whether or not they would admit the priest, they said to him: "We are glad to have you; we are sorry not to have had you sooner. Come and tell us the truth"—which means, "You will obtain what you ask." Traders are established in the heart of this tribe's territory. They will build a church and have two priests. It is too remote for one priest to be alone there. They told the savages the black-robed ladies would teach their girls, and I am quite sure that some of us will go there one of these days.

I recommend earnestly to your prayers several of our pupils who belong to Protestant families. Four have already received Catholic baptism, but two of them secretly. . . . Several others desire to become Catholics, and there are also some of our former pupils who wish to be admitted to the novitiate. Our Society now has at Florissant five professed religious, six novices, one postulant, twenty-five boarding pupils, fifty in the parish free school. Among the children attending this school there are ten who live with us. Five of these are orphans whom we support. The other five are from a village quite a distance from here, so they live at the school. . . . So we are carrying on three kinds of good works. We also have almost entire charge of the singing for the church services, so we have the joy of using all the voice we possess for the dear Lord. Pray that our hearts may become like unto the Heart of Jesus. In Him I am all yours,

PHILIPPINE DU CHENE *

* This is the only extant letter bearing her signature in this form.

Notes—chapter one

1. Paul Berret, *Le Dauphiné* (Paris, 1922), p. 58. "The people of Dauphiny are clever, loyal, and proud."
2. Eugene Choulet, *La Famille Casimir-Perier* (Grenoble, 1894), studies the genealogies of the several branches of the Perier family, giving short biographical accounts of its members in three or four generations. Referred to hereafter as *Choulet*.
3. Lt.-Col. Guillebon, *La Famille Duchesne*. Extrait du Bulletin de l'Academie Delphinale, 1935 (pamphlet reprint), pp. 1–2. Referred to hereafter as *Guillebon*.
4. Msgr. Louis Baunard, *Histoire de Madame Duchesne* (Paris, 1878), p. 6.
5. Louis Bergasse, *Souvenirs de Famille au XIXme Siècle* (Marseille, 1947), p. 98. Referred to hereafter as *Bergasse*.
6. For this generation of the Duchesne and Perier children see Appendix I, Tables 1–2.
7. Choulet gives 1780 as the date of the purchase of Vizille by Claude Perier and cites the deed of transfer. Augustin Perier, who inherited the property, stated that the Perier textile business had been established by his father at Vizille in 1775.
8. A. Prudhomme, *Histoire de Grenoble* (Grenoble, 1888), p. 578. Referred to hereafter as *Prudhomme*. The French word *parlement* has been retained for the sake of clarity. This name designated royal courts in France at an early date. The *Parlement* of Paris was the supreme court of justice in the kingdom; the term was also applied to courts created in provincial capitals. Grenoble, as capital of Dauphiny, had its own *parlement*, with a full hierarchy of presidents, counselors, advocates, procurators, etc., on the model of the supreme court in Paris.
9. *Ibid.*, p. 581.
10. *Ibid.*, p. 583. Also Alphonse Vernet, *Histoire Populaire et Anecdotique de Grenoble*, 3 v. (Grenoble, 1901), 3:341. Referred to hereafter as *Vernet*.
11. Cf. *Choulet*, p. 60.
12. Although Pierre-François Duchesne is named as godfather to Casimir-Pierre Perier, his signature does not appear in the baptismal register, but that of a proxy. *Choulet*, p. 93.
13. *Bergasse*, Annexe II.
14. St. Madeleine Sophie Barat to Philippine Duchesne, Poitiers, February 9, 1807. Copies of letters of St. Madeleine Sophie cited in the text are in Archives RSCJ, Maryville College of the Sacred Heart, St. Louis, Missouri.
15. Jean Delanglez, S.J., *The French Jesuits in Lower Louisiana, 1700–1763* (Catholic University of America Press, 1935), pp. 523, 526; Sister Mary Borgia Palm, *Jesuit Missions in the Illinois Country, 1673–1763* (Cleveland, 1934), *passim*.

16. *Mémoire of Philippine Duchesne to St. Madeleine Sophie*, Paris, 1818. Referred to hereafter as *Mémoire*. Shortly before his death Father Jean Delanglez, S.J., identified this Jesuit missionary for the writer as Father Jean-Baptiste Aubert. Unless otherwise indicated, original manuscripts or authenticated copies of all writings of Philippine Duchesne cited in the text are housed in Archives RSCJ, Rome. Copies are in Archives RSCJ, Maryville College of the Sacred Heart, St. Louis, Missouri.

17. Philippine Duchesne to Josephine Perier de Savoye-Rollin, Florissant, January 30, 1838.

18. Madame de Coriolis, *Histoire de la Société du Sacré Coeur* (unpublished manuscript), Archives RSCJ, Rome. Referred to hereafter as *Coriolis*.

19. Mother Duchesne noted this fact in writing several times. She received the Sacrament of confirmation sometime in 1783 before leaving the boarding school of Sainte Marie.

20. Stendhal (Henri Beyle) in his autobiographical *Vie de Henri Brulard* writes with caustic sarcasm of Abbé Raillane, who was his tutor for two or three years after the outbreak of the French Revolution. The abbé may have been as eccentric as Stendhal describes, but he had faith and courage and knew how to train students who made their mark in the world.

21. Quoted by *Vernet*, 3:290.

22. *Beatificationis et Canonizationis Servae Dei Philippinae Duchesne . . . . Positio, Responsio ad Animadversiones R.P.D. Promotoris Fidei,* p. 32. A letter written by Philippine's sister Euphrosine is quoted at length. Referred to hereafter as *Beatificationis*.

23. *Idem*.

24. *Guillebon*, pp. 2–3.

25. *Beatificationis*, Responsio, p. 32.

26. It seems pointless to document well-known events of the French Revolution; Lavisse, Sorel, and Cambridge Modern History have been relied on. With regard to Dauphiny, and Grenoble in particular, documentation is given.

27. The *parlement* of Dauphiny was composed of seventy members. The provincial courts of justice also sat in Grenoble. The city gained greatly by this, as crowds of people came from all over Dauphiny to transact business. Hence the suppression of the *parlement* would mean a considerable loss in both money and civic prestige. *Vernet*, 3:381.

28. *Ibid.*, 3:380–381. The sentence, "Justice has ceased in the city," refers to the lawyers' strike instigated by Pierre-François Duchesne.

29. *Guillebon*, p. 4.

30. From among the many deputies of the Third Estate elected in Grenoble, ten were chosen to represent the city, one of them being Pierre-Francois Duchesne. The *Remonstrance* he had prepared was not accepted by the assembly. J. A. Felix Faure, *Les Assemblées de Vizille et de Romans en Dauphiné Durant l'Année 1788* (Grenoble, 1887), pp. 165–166. Referred to hereafter as *Faure*.

31. Cf. *Cambridge Modern History* (New York, 1907–1928), 8:113.

32. *Faure*, p. 193.

33. The reference is to the well known spiritual classic, *The Practice of Perfection and Christian Virtues* by Alphonse Rodriguez, S.J.

34. *Mémoire*, Paris, 1818.

35. John Francis Regis, born in Languedoc, France, in 1597, entered the Society of Jesus at eighteen and was ordained priest fifteen years later. Until his death in 1640 he spent himself in mission work and charitable activities of many kinds. Countless were the conversions of sinners with which God blessed his zeal. In life and after death he worked many miracles, and he was canonized by Pope Clement XII in 1737.

36. *Mémoire*, Paris, 1818.

37. Marie Guyart Martin, 1599–1672, known in religion as Mother Marie of the Incarnation, entered the Ursuline convent at Tours a decade after her husband's death. A mystic and a skilful business woman, she set out for Quebec in 1639 to found the first convent and mission school for girls in Canada. Mother Duchesne had many traits in common with Mother Marie, particularly zeal for souls and devotion to the Sacred Heart, trust in Divine Providence and a relish for the *Canticle of Canticles*. References to Mother Marie occur frequently in the letters that Mother Duchesne wrote from America. Some prayers of the great Ursuline missionary are incorporated into this biography with the permission of the Mother Superior of the Ursuline Convent, Quebec, Canada.
38. *Spiritual Conferences of St. Francis de Sales* (Westminster, Md., 1945), p. 240.
39. *Abridgement of the Interior Spirit of the Religious of the Visitation of Holy Mary* (Westminster, Md., 1943), p. 132.
40. *Choulet*, p. 60.
41. *Histoire de Sainte Marie d'en Haut* par Madame Duchesne (unpublished manuscript). Referred to hereafter as *The Story of Sainte Marie*.
42. Ernest Lavisse, *Histoire de France Contemporaine* (Paris, 1920–1922), CI:187–188.
43. *Guillebon*, p. 5.
44. *Vernet*, 3:427–428.
45. Lavisse, *op. cit.*, CI:409.
46. *Journal of Mother Duchesne*, 1818–1840. Entry for December 15, 1819.
47. *Vernet*, 3:396.

Notes—chapter two

1. *Bergasse,* p. 13.
2. See Appendix I, Table 1.
3. Msgr. Henri-Charles Dulau d'Alleman, appointed to the see of Grenoble in 1788, was forced to leave France at the outbreak of the Revolution. He died in Gratz, Styria, in 1801.
4. Baunard, *op. cit.,* pp. 32–33.
5. *Choulet,* p. 38.
6. *Biographical Sketch of Mother Aloysia Jouve* (unpublished manuscript). Copy in Archives RSCJ, Maryville College.
7. *Bergasse,* p. 13.
8. *Vernet,* 3:459–460.
9. *Coriolis, loc. cit.*
10. Quoted by Baunard, *op. cit.,* p. 41.
11. *Idem.*
12. *Idem.*
13. *Ibid.,* p. 33.
14. *Bergasse,* p. 101.
15. *Ibid.,* pp. 101–103.
16. Letter undated. As Philippine mentions "our grandmothers," she had in mind both her grandmother Duchesne and her grandmother Perier. The latter died in 1799.
17. Biographical sketches of Sister Françoise-Melanie and Claire-Euphrosine Duchesne in *Année Sainte des Religieuses de la Visitation Sainte Marie* (private publication). These volumes and other Visitandine material were made available to the writer at the Georgetown monastery through the courtesy of Reverend Mother Margaret Mary Sherrin.
18. *Story of Sainte Marie.* Benedict Joseph Labre was canonized in 1881.
19. At this time Amelie de Mauduit had three children. See Appendix I, Table 1.
20. The "great misfortune" referred to may have been, as Baunard suggests, her mother's death, but from the context it seems to refer to an event that occurred before the French Revolution: "I planned to enjoy [the inheritance] by sacrificing it. . . . Now all is changed."
21. Letter undated.
22. Lillian Browne-Olf, *Their Name is Pius* (Milwaukee. 1941), pp. 49–55; *Vernet,* 3:492.
23. The Tribunate was an assembly of one hundred members whose function it was to examine all legal projects elaborated by the Council of State. Pierre-François Duchesne was named president of the body in *Messidor, An VIII,* hence it was he who announced to his colleagues the victory of Marengo. He took an active part in the compilation of the famous Code of Civil Law.

French biographical dictionaries mention at least thirty-five reports or projects from his pen that were printed at the National Printing Office. Many of these are concerned with financial questions raised by the depreciation of the *assignats*, or notes issued by the Revolutionary government with confiscated property as security. As Duchesne was an expert in the thorny problem of paper money, his proposals and advice were practically always adopted by the Council of Five Hundred. *Guillebon,* pp. 5–6.

24. Charles-François d'Aviau du Bois de Sanzay, 1736–1826, Archbishop of Vienne, France, 1790–1801, was illustrious for his courage in opposing the Civil Constitution of the Clergy. He was the first *émigré* bishop to re-enter France, May 1797. Transferred to Bordeaux, he welcomed Mother Duchesne and her companions when they reached that seaport to take ship for America in 1818.

25. The church referred to by Philippine was not the original edifice in which St. John Francis Regis ministered to the people of the Velay in 1640. That had been replaced by a more pretentious one built to enshrine the tomb of the saint, completed in 1770 and extensively repaired in 1802. The present church at La Louvesc, consecrated in 1877, was made a basilica affiliated to St. Mary Major in 1888. One of the murals decorating its sanctuary shows Blessed Thérèse Couderc, Foundress of the Society of Our Lady of the Cenacle, with Reverend Mother Marie-Aimée Lautier, a Superior General of the order, which was founded in 1826 for the spiritual welfare of women who came as pilgrims to the shrine of St. Francis Regis. A second mural portrays St. Madeleine Sophie Barat, Foundress of the Society of the Sacred Heart of Jesus, with Mother Philippine Duchesne, who was so deeply influenced by the same great Jesuit saint.

26. *Story of Sainte Marie.*

27. The house referred to is the monastery of Sainte-Marie-d'en-Haut.

28. *Story of Sainte Marie.*

29. *Coriolis, loc. cit.*

30. Unless otherwise indicated, all primary source material used in this section is taken from Mother Duchesne's *Story of Sainte Marie,* written in 1805 at the request of St. Madeleine Sophie, and from letters to her sister, Madame Jouve.

31. This was Sister Françoise-Melanie (Marie Louise Duchesne, 1738–1820), whose active apostolate during the Revolution had rivaled that of her niece Philippine, though she was thirty years older. See *Bergasse,* pp. 96–97.

32. Claude Perier died on February 6, 1801, at his home in Rue St. Honoré, Paris.

33. Philippine's relatives seem to have accepted the responsibility for this rental.

34. The Concordat had already been signed, but not proclaimed publicly.

35. Evidently she was mending the broken window panes with paper or cloth.

36. Msgr. Spina, titular Archbishop of Corinth, accompanied by Reverend Father Caselli, General of the Servites, had been sent by Pope Pius VII in 1800 to negotiate a concordat with Bonaparte. They were joined by Cardinal Consalvi, papal Secretary of State, in June, 1801, and by July 16 an agreement had been reached. The final exchange of signatures took place in September, but only on Easter Sunday, April 18, 1802, was the concordat finally published. Both Spina and Caselli were raised to the cardinalate shortly afterwards.

37. The day after the celebration at the Cathedral of Notre Dame, Paris, in honor of the concordat, the projected law regarding public education was laid before the legislative body. In the Tribunate Pierre-François Duchesne alone dared to speak out democratically. In *Lavisse,* C3:328, there is an excerpt from his speech against *La Loi du 11 Floreal, An* X (May 1, 1802).

38. *Guillebon,* p. 6.

39. Under the title *Dilette de Gesù* an order of religious women had been founded in Italy by the Archduchess Marie Anne of Austria and two of her ladies-in-waiting, Mesdames Leopoldine and Louise Naudet. Their first house was

opened in Rome in 1801, with the hope that they might carry out the idea of Father Léonor de Tournély to found an order devoted primarily to the glory of the Sacred Heart of Jesus and combining the contemplative and active lives, with education as the chief work. For a time Father Varin brought Madeleine Sophie Barat and her companions into affiliation with the *Dilette,* but in 1804 Cardinal Spina advised a separation of the two communities, as the Roman convent no longer conformed to the ideals that had inspired Tournély. Pope Pius VII ratified the decision and the separation took place in June, 1804. A few months later the community of the *Dilette* disbanded.

40. Philippine Duchesne was then thirty-three years old.
41. Marie Rivet, sister of Father Rivet, whose name occurs so frequently in the *Story of Sainte Marie,* had been a Benedictine nun before the Revolution and was well known in Grenoble for her piety and active charity.
42. Marie Balestron was born near Grenoble in 1783. According to Archives RSCJ, Rome, she joined the community at Sainte Marie in December, 1801, and took the habit on March 2, 1802, that is, before Mother de Murinais' return to the monastery. Her religious life covered half a century, as her death occurred in 1862.
43. Bishop Claude Simon was appointed to the diocese of Grenoble by Pope Pius VII and he took possession of the see in October, 1802.
44. This was the title used by the first Religious of the Sacred Heart while it was considered both unwise and unsafe for them to assume their proper title.
45. Joseph-Desiré Varin, 1769–1850, born at Besançon, France, had entered the seminary of Saint Sulpice, Paris, before the outbreak of the French Revolution. Joining the army of Condé he crossed the Belgian border and in July, 1794, at Venloo came by chance upon former seminary companions who, under the leadership of Father Léonor de Tournély, had formed an association called Fathers of the Sacred Heart. Ordained in 1796, Varin was elected to succeed Tournély, whose death occurred in 1797. In 1800 he returned to France with Father Pierre Roger (1763–1839), a zealous and courageous member of the group. Soon they were joined by Father Louis Barat and thus came to know his sister, the future St. Madeleine Sophie Barat. When the Society of Jesus was re-established in 1814, these priests and many of their companions joined that order. Through them the Society of the Sacred Heart of Jesus, founded by the saint with Father Varin's aid, was brought under Jesuit guidance and its interior life, Rule, and Constitutions were moulded under the influence of Ignatian spirituality.
46. Cardinal de Bayanne was a close friend of Pope Pius VII and accompanied the pontiff to Paris for the coronation of Napoleon. Being in touch with the religious situation in France, he was unwilling to allow his sister, now advanced in years, to risk further persecution. He was not able, however, to shield her from it in Italy later on.
47. This was Augustin Perier. He and his brother-in-law, Camille Teisseire, were members of the newly constituted municipal council of Grenoble, installed in the autumn of 1803. *Vernet,* 3:519.
48. Etienne-Joseph-Marie Gérando, later the Baron de Gérando, was a close friend of Augustin Perier.
49. Portalis was Minister of Public Worship in France under Napoleon, 1801–1807.

Notes—chapter three

1. For a brief sketch of Léonor de Tournély and his work see Louise Callan, *The Society of the Sacred Heart in North America* (New York, 1937), pp. 5–7. This book may be of interest to readers unfamiliar with the foundation and early history of the order. Some inaccuracies in its first chapters have been revealed by research during the past ten years.
2. Agnes de Beaulieu, *Léonor de Tournély et Son Oeuvre* (Vienna, 1886), p. 105.
3. Msgr. Louis Baunard, *Histoire de Madame Barat*, 2 v. (Paris, 1876), 1:105. Lyons, October 23, 1803.
4. *Ibid.*, 1:106. Lyons, August 6, 1804.
5. *Idem.* August 12, 1804.
6. Adele Cahier, *Vie de la Vénérable Mère Barat*, 2 v. (Paris, 1884). Referred to hereafter as *Cahier*.
7. *Idem.*
8. *Ibid.*, 1:88.
9. Baunard, *op. cit.*, 1:107. December 14, 1804.
10. *Cahier*, 1:88.
11. December 14, 1804.
12. *Journal de Sainte Marie, 1804–1813*, kept by Philippine Duchesne.
13. *Cahier*, 1:88.
14. *Ibid.*, 1:91.
15. *Journal de Sainte Marie* gives the names of the postulants who entered in 1805 and in succeeding years.
16. Baunard, *op. cit.*, 1:117.
17. *Cahier*, 1:95.
18. *Ibid.*, 1:92.
19. *Ibid.*, 1:94.
20. *Ibid.*, 1:97.
21. March 22, 1805.
22. *The Mystical Explanation of the Canticle of Canticles* was written by St. Francis de Sales for the Visitation nuns. The Latin text of the *Canticle* seems to have been quite as familiar to Philippine Duchesne at to St. Madeleine Sophie.
23. The reference is to night adoration before the Blessed Sacrament on Quinquagesima Sunday, 1805.
24. Canticle of Canticles, chapter 2, *passim*.
25. Madame de Vaulserre (Countess Angélique) lived at Sainte Marie for several years after it became a convent of the Sacred Heart. Ill health made it impossible for her to enter religious life. Highly esteemed in Grenoble for her generous charity and for the detachment with which she withdrew from a

prominent social position in order to help the nuns in the rehabilitation of the institution, she died at Sainte Marie in 1812.

26. *Cahier*, 1:105.

27. Cf. Achille Guidée, *Vie de R. P. Joseph Varin* (Paris, 1854), p. 178.

28. Henri Lebrument had to accept this fact nine times. See Appendix I, Table 1.

29. For the names of the Jouve children see Appendix I, Table 1.

30. The French word *dame* was used by members of several religious orders of women in the early nineteenth century instead of *soeur* (sister) to avoid attracting the notice of hostile governments. Translated as *lady* in English, it has not the same connotation and has often given an entirely false impression. The Society of the Sacred Heart uses the word *religious*, which is the title given to its members in official ecclesiastical documents. Hence the initials *R.S.C.J.*, corresponding to the Latin or to the French, *Religieuse du Sacré Coeur de Jésus.*

31. Madame de Luiset had turned over to Mother Barat her school for girls at Belley.

32. Dom Augustin de Lestrange (1754–1827) was ordained at Sainte-Sulpice, Paris, in 1778. To escape episcopal honors he entered La Trappe in 1780, became master of novices, fled with members of his community to Switzerland during the French Revolution, safeguarded the rule of his order, and is considered the savior of La Trappe. After 1804 he spent long years of travel and toil to rebuild the Trappist order in France.

33. *Mémoire*, Paris, 1818.

34. Before the French Revolution Madame Baudemont had been a Poor Clare at Rheims. By character and disposition she was fitted for responsibility, but she was authoritative and severe towards herself and others and never understood the true spirit of the Sacred Heart.

35. The term *professed* was applied at that time to all members of the Society who had made their first vows. Since 1826 the term has been used in the Society to indicate the religious who have made their perpetual vows of poverty, chastity, and obedience, along with the vow to consecrate their lives to the work of education and the fifth vow of stability in religious life until death.

36. Canticle of Canticles, 2:3, which also includes *Sedi*, "I have rested in his shadow." "Eldest daughter" is a title of affection and confidence given to Philippine by Mother Barat, though she was not as old as some other members then in the Society.

37. Blessing of incense in the liturgy of high Mass: "May you be blessed by Him in whose honor you will be consumed."

38. The rental stipulated in 1801 had been canceled through the influence of Mother Duchesne's relatives.

39. Madame Baudemont remained at Amiens as local Superior after the election of the superior general. Félicité Lefevre was a novice in whom Mother Duchesne took a very sympathetic interest.

40. Psalm 84:8: "I will listen attentively to what the Lord God speaks in my soul."

41. This phenomenon of prolonged prayer, occurring frequently in the life of Philippine Duchesne, calls for brief comment. In *The Prayer of Faith* (London, 1950), Father Leonard Boase, S.J., explains that since the supernatural activity of prayer above the level of ordinary does not of itself engage the brain, it is very restful, even when sustained for long periods. On page 92 he writes, "Then the prayer is almost as refreshing to the nervous system as is sleep." This may help to explain how so many of the saints could work strenuously all day and spend most of the night in prayer. Boase bases his explanation on A. Poulain, S.J., *Les Grâces d'Oraison (The Graces of Interior*

Prayer, translated by Leonora Yorke-Smith, St. Louis, 1928), Chapter XVI, No. 25.

42. Matthew 10:16. "Behold, I send you . . ." Her response: "I am ready to set off."
43. Cited by *Cahier*, 1:113–114.
44. Father Enfantin, one of the Fathers of the Faith and a cousin of Mother Duchesne, was then on mission work in Bordeaux. He was keenly interested in foreign missions and in Philippine's desire to devote her life to this work.
45. We know from several sources that Mother Duchesne was allowed to make repeated vows of devotion; the precise nature of the one here referred to has not been determined.
46. *Imitation of Christ*, 3:38.
47. Poitiers, May 31, 1807.
48. July 15, 1807.
49. Exodus 4:25.
50. April 6, 1808.
51. Suzanne Geoffroy was one of the first postulants in the Poitiers novitiate, 1806.
52. *Religieuses du Sacré-Coeur: Quelques Contemporaines de la Fondatrice* (Paris, 1932), p. 48 ff.
53. "Draw me: we will run after thee, following the perfume of thy ointments." Canticle of Canticles 1:3.

Notes—chapter four

1. Joseph Burnichon, *La Compagnie de Jésus en France: Histoire d'un Siècle*, 2 v. (Paris, 1914–1916), 1:17–18.
2. November, 1806.
3. May 31, 1807.
4. This was Lucille Mathevon, who pioneered in mission work with Mother Duchesne among the Potawatomi, becoming the Society's most distinguished missionary to the Indians.
5. Archives RSCJ, Rome. Copy in Archives RSCJ, Maryville College.
6. This baby was Josephine Jouve, who became a religious of Perpetual Adoration of the Chartreux in Lyons.
7. Coralie Durand, who married Hippolyte Duchesne in 1814.
8. Lise de Walter, Euphrosine Jouve, and Amelie de Mauduit.
9. Henriette Lebrument and Julie Dusaussoy.
10. A school for boys near Lyons conducted by the Fathers of the Faith.
11. Augustin and Camille Jordan.
12. The reference is to the dispersion of the Fathers of the Faith by Napoleon.
13. Melanie made her profession at the Visitation of Romans on December 13, 1808.
14. Father Noël Jordan, Curé of St. Bonaventure, Lyons.
15. February 14, 1812.
16. February 29, 1812.
17. January, 1812.
18. Letter to Madame Jouve, June 15, 1813.
19. *Bergasse*, p. 93, cites the letter of Euphrosine Jouve to her mother giving details from Amédée de Mauduit's letter.
20. Grenoble, June 15, 1813.
21. *Guillebon*, p. 6.
22. The members of the Society had not yet made a strict vow of poverty, hence they still retained the right to use any money or income they happened to possess.
23. Eugene Jouve was born in 1814.
24. Henriette Lebrument made her first Communion at Sainte Marie on November 1, 1813, and returned home shortly afterwards. *Journal de Sainte Marie.*
25. Joigny, November 16, 1813.
26. *Vernet*, 3:527.
27. April 28, 1814.
28. Forty years later Hippolyte Duchesne returned to the Church on his deathbed (1854). *Bergasse*, p. 76.

29. Father Fauvet, a Missionary Priest of the Chartreux at Lyons, was Euphrosine's confessor.
30. *Biographical Sketch of Madame Aloysia Jouve,* written at Sainte Marie. (Unpublished manuscript.) Archives RSCJ, Rome.
31. *Choulet,* p. 18.
32. *Cahier,* 1:240.
33. *Ibid.,* 1:246.
34. Mothers Paranque and Michel were among the religious who returned to Amiens from Ghent at the time of the separation of that convent from the Society.
35. On the title page of the *Constitutions and Rules of the Society of the Sacred Heart* are inscribed the letters *A.M.SS.C.J.M.G.,* the initial letters of the Latin dedication, "To the greater glory of the Sacred Hearts of Jesus and Mary," which expresses the over-all intention and purpose of the order. For many years the form, *SS.C.J.etM.,* was used in letter-writing. A shorter form, *S.C.J.M.,* was later adopted.
36. *Cahier,* 1:251.
37. *Ibid.,* 1:261.
38. William Valentine Du Bourg, 1766–1833, born in Santo Domingo and brought to France as a child, entered the Seminary of Saint-Sulpice, Paris, and was ordained in 1788. In 1792 he fled from revolutionary persecution to Spain and embarked for Baltimore in 1794. Admitted to the Sulpician community in 1795, he became president of Georgetown College in 1796, then founded a school for boys which became St. Mary's Seminary, Baltimore, and helped Mother Elizabeth Seton found the first American order of Sisters of Charity. Du Bourg was appointed Administrator Apostolic of the diocese of Louisiana and the Floridas in 1812, with residence in New Orleans. After three hectic years he returned to Europe, hoping to be relieved of the office. He was, however, appointed bishop of the diocese and consecrated in 1815. After touring Europe in search of financial aid and missionaries, he sailed for America again in June, 1817, and took up residence in St. Louis, then a frontier fur trading center. Bishop Du Bourg labored strenuously in the Mississippi Valley for nearly a decade of years. He brought several religious orders to his diocese, but frequently failed to keep to his contracts or promises in their regard. "A brilliant and learned man, but lacking in courage and firmness," he accomplished much for the Church, but wisely withdrew from his American diocese in 1826, becoming Bishop of Montauban, France, then Archbishop of Besançon in 1833, the year of his death.
39. Mother Duchesne was Assistant to Mother Barat and also her secretary.
40. In all fairness to Augustin Jordan it should be noted that he was a good friend of the Society and used his influence with government officials to obtain substantial grants of money to help the Paris convent, as Mother Barat herself attests in a letter of July 11, 1819.
41. Fathers Rauzan, Liautard, and Forbin-Janson organized the "Missions of France," working to rouse the faith and religious fervor of the country and achieving remarkable success.
42. October 21, 1816.
43. Baunard, *Histoire de Madame Duchesne,* p. 166.
44. *Cahier,* 1:281.
45. *Ibid.,* 1:282.
46. Baunard, *op. cit.,* pp. 175–176.
47. *Ibid.,* p. 176.
48. July 3, 1817.
49. These were the agreements drawn up in 1797 after the death of their mother.

50. Adrien de Mauduit became ill at school at Annonay and died in the autumn of 1817.
51. Mention of Mademoiselle de St. Pern dates this letter for us. She entered the order in Paris, June 1817, after donating her fortune to found a convent of the Sacred Heart at Quimper, France. She died in 1819.
52. *Choulet*, pp. 22–24.

Notes—chapter five

1. Charles Nicoullaud, *Casimir Perier, Deputé de L'Opposition, 1817–1830* (Paris, 1894), p. 3.
2. For the children of Augustin Perier see Appendix I, Table 2.
3. *Relation du 16 février*, Paris, 1818. Archives RSCJ, Amiens.
4. Father Bertrand Martial, born in Bordeaux in 1770, served at the St. Louis Cathedral in New Orleans and directed a school for boys until 1826, when he traveled to France with Bishop Du Bourg. Returning to Louisiana, he became chaplain at the Ursuline convent in New Orleans, where he died in July, 1832. He had served as vicar-general for both Bishop Du Bourg and Bishop Flaget of Kentucky, and held the title of honorary canon of the Cathedral of Bordeaux.
5. *Relation du 16 février*.
6. January 28, 1818. Appended to this letter is the list of notes which Mother Duchesne turned over to Madame de Rollin, amounting to 15, 212 fr., 10 c. and not including the note for 7,000 fr. from Hippolyte Duchesne. As the purchasing power of the franc in 1818 was comparable to that of the dollar today, one may estimate the contribution of the Duchesne-Perier family to the founding of the Society of the Sacred Heart in America.
7. The marriage of Louis Bergasse and Amelie Teisseire was to have a direct influence on the de Mauduit family, as the groom's older brother, Henri, aged 35, married the bride's first cousin, Amelie de Mauduit, at Grâne on September 10, 1818. The marriage agreement, drawn up the night before, stipulated about 35,000 fr. as the dowry.
8. Bishop Du Bourg's episcopal city was, strictly speaking, New Orleans. He had, however, invited the Religious of the Sacred Heart to found a convent in St. Louis and to work among the Indians of his diocese. The geography of that vast diocese was not clear to either Mother Barat or Mother Duchesne, but the agreement regarding the founding of the convent *in St. Louis* was quite clear to them both.
9. *Relation du 16 février*.
10. *Idem*.
11. Evremond Harrissart, S.J., born in Paris in 1792, was ordained by Bishop Du Bourg some months after reaching America. After a dozen years of missionary work in the Mississippi Valley he entered the Society of Jesus in Kentucky. Stationed at St. Joseph's College, Bardstown, he gave himself with unstinted devotion to students and adults alike, winning love and reverence from all who knew him. Tall, thin, ascetic-looking, serious and deliberate in manner, grave and earnest in speech, he did much good and was deeply regretted when in 1844 he returned to France, where he died a few years later.
12. Madame Vincent had given hospitality to Mother Barat in 1806 and had made

some overtures with regard to merging her community with that of the Sacred Heart. The merger actually took place in 1825. The Convent of the *Reunion* was an institution that often gave hospitality to missionaries and on this occasion had offered it to Mother Duchesne and her companions through Madame Fournier.

13. Cited by Baunard, *op. cit.*, p. 187.

14. *La Louisiane* is the geographical title given to the whole of the Mississippi Valley by the Religious of the Sacred Heart in France at this time and for many decades later.

15. Madame Morange was the sister of Mother Thérèse Maillucheau. The family was living at their country home when Mother Duchesne arrived in Bordeaux.

16. The question, "May we receive day pupils?" was a request for an innovation as at this time the Society of the Sacred Heart conducted only boarding schools in France, and it was not easy for Mother Duchesne to obtain this apparently simple permission.

17. Father Wrindts was a distinguished professor of theology when he entered the Society of Jesus in 1815. In 1826, however, he withdrew from the order, having become entangled in the meshes of the de Lamennais system. Father Nicolas Jennesseaux (1769–1842) was a follower of Léonor de Tournély, a member of the Fathers of the Faith under Father Varin, and with him entered the Society of Jesus at its re-establishment in 1814. His zealous activities and beautiful character are sketched by Achille Guidée, S.J., in his *Vie de R. P. Joseph Varin, suivie de Notices sur Quelques-uns de ses Confrères*, (Paris, 1854). Father Robert Debrosse (1768–1848) is also the subject of one of these sketches.

18. Mother Audé's account of this episode differs considerably from Mother Duchesne's. "If this had been a Spanish corsair," she wrote, "we might have been plundered, but it turned out to be an American vessel with a friendly captain." Mother Duchesne, however, repeated her account more than once.

19. Cited by *Cahier*, 1:290.

20. None of the letters mailed at the mouth of the Mississippi before the nuns actually landed seem to have reached their destination, as none are extant.

21. *Cahier*, 1:290, states that the five nuns renewed also the vow they had made in Paris to consecrate themselves to mission work among the Indians.

22. This gesture of joy and gratitude to God on reaching a new country was common among discoverers, explorers, missionaries, and pioneers. Columbus and many Spanish conquerors, Champlain and many of his compatriots, including Mother Marie of the Incarnation, even less religious-minded frontiersmen from Virginia pushing West into the great meadows of Kentucky, all kissed the ground in a rapture of joy when first they trod on it.

23. Pont-Saint-Esprit, in the department of Gard, France, famous for its magnificent bridge spanning the Rhone, lies about seventy miles southwest of the Duchesne home at Grâne.

24. Mother St. Michel Gensoul and her seven companions arrived in Philadelphia, June 10, 1810. At Baltimore they were detained for five months by Bishop John Carroll because of the peril of yellow fever. They reached New Orleans only on December 31.

25. See Letter 1, Appendix II.

26. Roger Baudier, *The Catholic Church in Louisiana* (New Orleans, 1939), pp. 265–266. Referred to hereafter as *Baudier*. Father Louis Sibourd acted as vicar-general in New Orleans for sixteen years, returning to France in 1826.

27. Mother Duchesne was misinformed on this point and many others. There were several stone houses in St. Louis in 1818, but they were not the type of building she had been accustomed to in France. The distances she quotes are sometimes wide of the mark by a hundred miles.

28. These were the Marigny girls, who spent two or three years at the Sacred Heart in Paris.
29. Father Louis Leopold Moni was for some years pastor at St. Charles Borromeo Church, Destrehan, near New Orleans. During the absence of Father Sibourd he acted as vicar-general for Bishop Du Bourg, who was residing in St. Louis. Placed in charge of the Cathedral some years later, he proved himself a staunch support of higher authority. Father Moni died in 1841.
30. Of this picture Mother Duchesne wrote: "I found a picture of St. Francis Regis so hideous and soiled that my first impulse was to burn it. But filled with the thought that always occupied me, and overcome with tender love for the saint, I promised to keep it for his sake and to have him honored by the savages, if only he would obtain for me the grace to go to them." *Mémoire,* 1818.
31. The first Convent of the Sacred Heart in New Orleans was opened only after the Civil War.
32. Father Benedict Richard, O.S.B., came to Louisiana in 1817 at Bishop Du Bourg's invitation. Sent to St. Charles, Missouri, in 1818, he later served for a time in St. Louis. Returning to Louisiana, he acted as chaplain of the Ursuline convent in New Orleans and died in the cholera epidemic of 1833. Father Richard is the only person in the Mississippi Valley who remembered Mother Duchesne with a legacy ($200).

    Michael Portier, born at Montbrison, France, in 1795, came to America in 1817, was ordained by Bishop Du Bourg in 1818, and served on the Missouri missions until 1826, when he was named Vicar Apostolic of Alabama and Florida. When the diocese of Mobile was created out of part of this territory, Father Portier became its first Bishop. Steady expansion and development marked the years that followed and a goodly harvest was being garnered for Christ in the Mobile diocese when Bishop Portier died in 1859.
33. An account of the missionary careers of Fathers John and Donatien Olivier is given in John Rothensteiner, *History of the Archdiocese of St. Louis* (St. Louis, 1928), 1:193. Referred to hereafter as *Rothensteiner.*
34. Henri Pratte was the first native-born Missourian raised to the priesthood. Born at Ste Genevieve, educated and trained by the Sulpicians at Montreal, Canada, ordained in 1815, he became pastor at Ste Genevieve. A man of simple piety and solid learning, he was quickly appreciated by his parishioners, his own people. Their grief was all the greater, then, when he died of yellow fever on September 1, 1822, at the age of thirty-four.
35. Auguste Chouteau, *Fragment of the Narrative of the Settlement of St. Louis* (St. Louis, 1858), p. 4.
36. *Glimpses of the Past* (Missouri Historical Society Publication, 1941) Vol. VIII, No. 7–9, "Earliest Picture of St. Louis."
37. Madame René (Adèle) de Perdreauville advertised and opened her "young ladies academy" in St. Louis in September, 1818, but the institution was short-lived.

Notes—chapter six

1. Bishop's Du Bourg's letter of June 24, 1818, reached Mother Duchesne in January, 1819.
2. *Missouri Gazette*, January 3, 1818.
3. *Ibid.*, March 27, 1818. Lafrenière Chauvin often befriended the nuns in later years.
4. Contract for the building of the Duquette house, Archives Missouri Historical Society, St. Louis. The house measured about 27 x 38 feet, English measure. Search for a picture of it has yielded only dim outlines in sketches of the town made in 1841 and 1850. See illustrations.
5. William S. Bryan and Robert Rose, *A History of the Pioneer Families of Missouri* (St. Louis, 1876), p. 435.
6. Timothy Flint, *Recollections of the Last Ten Years* (Boston, 1826), p. 125.
7. *Idem.*
8. John Baptist Acquaroni, C.M., born in Porto Maurizio on the Genoese Riviera, made his vows in the Congregation of the Mission in 1808, came to America with Fathers De Andreis and Rosati in 1817, and arrived in St. Louis in April, 1818. Put in charge of the parishes of La Dardenne and Portage-des-Sioux, Missouri, he worked zealously among whites, half-breeds, and Indians. In the summer of 1822 he asked to be relieved of his missions on account of ill health. Transferred to New Orleans, he became so nervous and restless, Bishop Du Bourg was greatly displeased with him, but it turned out that he was suffering intensely from what the doctors diagnosed as scurvy-leprosy, contracted at Portage-des-Sioux. On their advice he returned to Italy in 1824.
9. This may have been part of a "tall tale" that Mother Duchesne took seriously, or misinformation handed on to her as true. Her knowledge of geography was decidedly limited.
10. *Summary of the Constitutions and Rules of the Society of the Sacred Heart*, p. 52.
11. While prejudice against mixed blood was rather general, it was not shared by all the Creoles of the Mississippi Valley. Half-breed children were often well cared for and educated. Mother Duchesne had a few of these girls in the "paying day school" at St. Charles. In 1820 the little half-breed daughter of Manuel Lisa was enrolled in the convent school at Florissant.
12. Benedict Joseph Flaget, born at Contournat, Auvergne, France, in 1763, joined the Society of St. Sulpice and was ordained at Issy, near Paris, in 1787. Coming to the United States in 1792, he worked for six years in the Illinois Country, then in Havana, and later in Baltimore. Appointed Bishop of Bardstown, Kentucky, in 1808, he reached his vast diocese, embracing the Old Northwest Territory, Kentucky, and Tennessee, and stretching from the Appalachian Mountains to the Rockies, in May, 1811. During his lifetime he saw ten new

dioceses carved from his original jurisdiction and his see city moved from Bardstown to Louisville. He was a close friend of Bishop Joseph Rosati of St. Louis, on whose loyal co-operation he relied in many difficult situations. In 1847 Flaget resigned his episcopal office, and three years later he died in his eighty-seventh year. It was to Bishop Flaget that Bishop Du Bourg owed the cordial reception first accorded him when he came to Missouri in 1817.

13. Mother Duchesne had this information from Father Joseph-Marie Dunand, who wrote in much the same vein to St. Madeleine Sophie in 1822. This Trappist monk and missionary, born in Lorraine in 1774, came to America in 1805 and to the Illinois Country in 1808. Generally referred to on the frontier as "the Prior," he was in residence at Florissant from 1814 to 1821, being for several years the only missionary priest in Missouri. It was he who acted as contractor and overseer for the building of the frontier Convent of the Sacred Heart at Florissant. He was replaced as pastor there in 1820 by Father Charles De La Croix under circumstances which seem to imply some unfairness on the part of Bishop Du Bourg, and returned to the monastery of La Trappe, France, in 1822.

14. This painting is preserved at the Convent of the Sacred Heart, St. Charles, Missouri.

15. October 8, 1818.

16. The expression *école des pauvres* (school for the poor) was commonly used in France at this period to indicate a free school for children whose parents could not afford to pay for their education.

17. November 20, 1818.

18. This letter is given in Appendix II.

19. John Francis Fonsala was a general workman at Sainte Marie for several years while Mother Duchesne lived there.

20. Mother Duchesne recorded the number as *twenty*, which included five nuns and Miss Mullen, three boarding pupils, and eleven day pupils who came to spend the night.

21. *Journal*.

22. Copy in Archives RSCJ, Maryville College, St. Louis, Missouri.

23. Cited by Baunard, *op. cit.*, pp. 241–242.

24. Charles De La Croix, born in Belgium in 1792 and ordained by Bishop Du Bourg in France, came to America in 1817, being pastor first at The Barrens, Missouri, where he helped to direct the construction of the first seminary building. Sent to Florissant in 1820 to replace Father Dunand, he built a new church there, dedicating it to the Sacred Heart in 1821. Mission trips to the Osage Indians shattered his health and he was transferred to St. Michael's, Louisiana, where he built a church and convent, the latter being opened in 1825 by the Religious of the Sacred Heart. Father De La Croix went to Europe in search of health and missionary funds, returned to Louisiana against his doctor's advice, and was obliged to give up missionary life in 1834. In 1839 he became Treasurer of the Association for the Propagation of the Faith and was later appointed a canon of St. Bavon's Cathedral, Ghent, where he died in 1869.

25. The panic that swept the country in 1819 brought poverty and suffering to the West as well as to the East, and its effects were felt for nearly a decade.

26. The *Franklin*, built in 1816 at Pittsburgh, was first used on the Mississippi in 1817. Early in 1819 she struck a snag near Ste Genevieve coming upstream and sank. No passenger loss is recorded.

27. April 20, 1819. In her *Journal* Mother Duchesne added some details: "We feared the Sacred Host had been burned—but no! Though the chalice was overturned, the white Host was found intact under the charred pall and corporal. We placed It in the tabernacle, which was unharmed, as was also

the statue of the Blessed Virgin. Only the coverings were burned. We spent the night in adoration. Father Richard did the same alone in the parish church and ignorant of our catastrophe. He could not perform the ceremonies on Good Friday in our sanctuary, but with us he marveled at the goodness of God, Who had saved for us the precious things we possess—the Blessed Sacrament and the tabernacle, the statue of Our Lady, the relics, and the picture of the Sacred Heart. The floor and the partition wall were so badly burnt, they had to be removed and thrown on the wood pile; then with the aid of a carpenter we set to work to repair the damage, and all was ready in the chapel on Easter morning."

28. July 29, 1819.

29. This boat, the *Maid of Orleans*, was a schooner driven by sails at sea and a steamboat on the river. It made frequent trips from New York and Philadelphia to New Orleans and St. Louis. McCune Gill, *The St. Louis Story* (St. Louis, 1952), 1:241.

30. The first steamboats to navigate the Missouri were the *Western Engineer*, a side-wheeler, the *Expedition*, the *Thomas Jefferson*, and the *R. M. Johnson*. Along with nine keelboats, these four vessels left St. Louis on June 21, 1819, under the command of Major Stephen S. Long, to explore the Missouri River region.

31. The Abbé Dumolard was a native of La Mure, Bourg d'Oisans, a village on the Perier estate near Vizille. According to Stendhal he was a fine-looking, good-natured man who was well known in Grenoble before, during, and after the French Revolution. It was he who said Mass in Dr. Henri Gagnon's drawing room in the house on Grande Rue, Place Grenette, almost every Sunday, even during the Terror, but the "terrorists" paid no attention to the crowd of from eighty to a hundred people coming into and leaving the doctor's house. For some years after the Revolution he was chaplain at Sainte-Marie-d'en-Haut, and later he helped Madame de Savoye-Rollin with the many charitable works she established.

Notes—chapter seven

1. "New Orleans to St. Louis and Return" by Caleb Cox, in *Bulletin*, Missouri Historical Society, v. 8 (January, 1952), gives weather reports for the autumn of 1819 which include the following: September 14, cool weather at Memphis; next day, further upstream, cold enough for frost; in October, very dry but pleasant; November 3, as cold and dreary as late December; November 4, soft and pleasant as expiring summer.

2. Mathilde Hamilton, daughter of George Hamilton and Claire Fenwick, was born at Brazeau, Ste Genevieve County, Missouri, September 28, 1802. She and her sister Eulalie, born April 28, 1805, and their brother George, were reared at the home of their grandparents, Mr. and Mrs. Thomas Fenwick, who had come from Maryland via Kentucky and were related to Edward Fenwick, first Bishop of Cincinnati. The Fenwick home at Fredonia (Fenwick Settlement) was a Catholic center of hospitality where Bishop Du Bourg and his party spent Christmas Day, 1817, and announced the coming of the Religious of the Sacred Heart in the following year. Eulalie Hamilton also became a pupil at Florissant and one of Mother Duchesne's best-loved novices.

3. Emilie and Betsie were the daughters of Michael and Josephine Rolette. Virginie Labbadie was the daughter of Sylvestre Labbadie and Victoire Gratiot. She married J. A. Sire in June, 1827, and died in September of the following year.

4. The Superior of this group was Mother de Lalanne, who, with the help of Msgr. d'Aviau, had reorganized the orphanage of "The Providence" in Bordeaux after the Revolution. She and her companions joined the Society of the Sacred Heart in May, 1819.

5. Felix De Andreis, C.M., born in Piedmont, Italy, in 1778, entered the Congregation of the Mission in 1798 and was ordained in 1801. In spite of poor health he was constantly engaged in giving missions and retreats. At Bishop Du Bourg's urgent request he sailed for America with other missionaries in 1817 and was considered among them a "living saint." Reaching St. Louis in 1818, he was made vicar-general of Upper Louisiana and became director of the seminary established at the Barrens. In 1820 his health broke. His last act was to appoint Father Joseph Rosati as Superior of the American mission of the Vincentians in Missouri and Louisiana. He died on October 15, 1820. The process of his canonization was begun in St. Louis in 1900, and in 1902 the evidence was presented to the Congregation of Rites at Rome, but the cause has not been completed.

6. *Journal.*

7. *Cahier,* 1:355.

8. November 28, 1819.

9. March 1, 1820.

10. February 28, 1820.
11. *Rothensteiner*, 1:392–394.
12. March 20, 1820.
13. March 27, 1820.
14. *Idem.*
15. Philip Borgna was born in Piedmont, Italy, and came to America in 1818. As a member of the Congregation of the Mission he was raised to the priesthood by Bishop Du Bourg in St. Louis on March 19, 1820. Stationed in New Orleans, he vied with Father Andrew Ferrari in priestly devotedness during the yellow fever epidemic of 1822. The following year he went to Italy on business for Bishop Du Bourg and after the withdrawal of Du Bourg from America, he was recalled to Missouri and appointed vicar-general by Bishop Rosati. Having withdrawn from the Congregation of the Mission, he transferred to the diocese of Philadelphia after the departure of Bishop Rosati for Rome in 1840.
16. *Journal.*
17. The hostility which developed in St. Louis towards Bishop Du Bourg was due in part to the character and temperament of the prelate himself. He had, moreover, forced himself upon St. Louis, which was not his designated see city, and had imposed on the Catholics financial burdens to which they were unaccustomed. They had heretofore been independent, they did not appreciate the spiritual advantages accruing to them from the presence of the Bishop and the priests he brought from Europe, and they made things increasingly unpleasant until Du Bourg's final withdrawal from the Mississippi Valley.
18. May 8, 1820.
19. *Idem.* The postscript that follows bears this date also and was added to a letter to Mother de Lalanne, Superior in Bordeaux.
20. This was the Indian chief *Sans-Nerf.* See Gilbert Garraghan, *St. Ferdinand de Florissant* (Chicago, 1923), pp. 172–174.
21. The Constitution of the State of Missouri was drawn up in St. Louis and the first meeting of the state legislature was held there, but in 1822 the capital was fixed temporarily at St. Charles and later transferred to Jefferson City.
22. In an entry in the Baptismal Register of the church at Florissant Father De La Croix states that "the cornerstone (la première pierre) was laid by Madame Duchesne and me, the undersigned."
23. Emilie Chouteau, youngest daughter of Auguste Chouteau, co-founder of St. Louis, and Marie-Therese Cerré, was born on April 14, 1802. She made several efforts to enter the convent at Florissant but could not overcome the opposition of her parents. In 1825 she married Major Thomas Floyd Smith, an American army officer eighteen years her senior, and died in Cincinnati, Ohio, in 1843.

    Emilie Pratte, born December 25, 1806, married Ramsay Crooks, a native of Scotland in the employ of the American Fur Company, in 1825.

    Odile DeLassus of Ste Genevieve, niece of the last Spanish governor of Upper Louisiana, married Sylvestre Pratte, eldest son of General Bernard Pratte. He died in Colorado in 1828, and some years later Odile married Louis Vallé of Ste Genevieve. She died in 1842.
24. These were the Hamilton sisters, Mathilde and Eulalie.
25. This and the following excerpts are from letters dated respectively April 12 and 13, 1821.
26. Emilie St. Cyr, thirteenth child of Hyacinthe St. Cyr and Helene Herbert, born August 30, 1806, in St. Louis, made her first Communion in 1817 and counted her religious vocation from that day, though she had never seen a nun up to that time. To Mother Duchesne she felt she owed her great devo-

tion to the Sacred Heart of Jesus. She made her first vows on July 19, 1822, and her profession on June 10, 1831, having had to wait for this until she was twenty-five years of age. She filled the offices of assistant and superior and spent the last ten years of her life at Maryville, St. Louis, where she celebrated her golden jubilee of profession in 1881 and died on September 26, 1882, a few days after making a pilgrimage to the tomb of her beloved Mother Duchesne.

27. March 21, 1821.
28. *Bergasse*, Annexe II.
29. April 10–11, 1821.
30. June 12, 1821.
31. Father Louis Dusaussoy, a nephew of St. Madeleine Sophie Barat, came as a missionary to Louisiana in 1821 and spent several years in the Mississippi Valley. Aristide Anduze came to America from France in 1818, was ordained in St. Louis in 1821, taught in St. Louis College until 1823 and was then transferred to Louisiana. After a visit to France he again served in Louisiana until 1844 when with Bishop Blanc's consent he returned to France.
32. August 29, 1820.
33. Leo Deys came to America with De Andreis and Rosati. After ordination he taught in St. Louis College and served the parish under Father Niel, but missionary life was not his vocation and he returned to Europe in 1824. Father Francis Niel was the first rector of St. Louis College and became pastor of the Cathedral on the death of De Andreis in 1820. Despite his youth he suffered a stroke of apoplexy in the winter of 1823–1824 and never fully recovered. In 1825 he went to France, presumably on a begging tour, and did not return to America.
34. Gabriel Richard, born in France in 1767, joined the Society of Saint Sulpice and was ordained at Issy, near Paris, in 1791. Coming to the United States in 1792, he was sent as a missionary to the Illinois Country and in 1798 became pastor of St. Anne's Church, Detroit. His remarkable missionary, pastoral, and political career closed in 1832, when he contracted cholera while ministering to the sick and dying during the terrible epidemic that ravaged many parts of the country.
35. Father Charles Nerinckx, a native of Brabant, born in 1761, arrived in Baltimore in 1804 and traveled to Kentucky with the Trappist monks. His strenuous efforts to provide churches on the frontier gained for him the name of "Church Builder," and in 1812 he laid the foundation of a religious order, the well-known Sisters of Loretto. He made several trips back to Europe to procure missionaries and funds for his work and was very successful on these begging tours. After a life of tireless labor for Christ he died at the home of Father Dahmen, C.M., in Ste Genevieve, Missouri, August 12, 1824.

Demitrius Augustine Galitzin, referred to by Mother Duchesne as "the Russian prince," was born in 1770 and came to America in 1792. Ordained in 1795 by Bishop Carroll, the first priest to receive both minor and major orders from him, Father Galitzin went to reside with a Catholic colony in Cambria County, Pennsylvania, the place being later known as Loretto. He was frequently mentioned as a possible nominee for a bishopric, but was never so honored. After a remarkably valiant missionary career he died at Loretto in 1840. He was a distant relative of Mother Elizabeth Galitzin, R.S.C.J., who arrived in America shortly after his death.

Bishop Edward Fenwick, a native of Maryland and a member of the Dominican order, was named first Bishop of Cincinnati in 1821 and consecrated by Bishop Flaget in 1822. He built St. Peter's Cathedral in Cincinnati in 1825–1826. It was he who brought from Europe the printing press that put out the first edition of the *Catholic Telegraph* in 1831. Giving himself without counting the cost in the cholera epidemic of 1832, he contracted the disease and died on September 26.

36. December 17, 1821.
37. January 6, 1822.
38. February 18, 1822.
39. To Bishop Rosati, March 8, 1822. Father Francis Cellini had been a canon at the celebrated Hospital of the Holy Spirit in Rome before coming to Missouri in 1819. He made his novitiate in the Congregation of the Mission at the Barrens, Perry County, Missouri, but "was not built for community life," according to Bishop Rosati, so he withdrew from the order. He was an active and zealous missionary and a very capable physician, having papal permission to practice this profession after ordination. He spent some years in Louisiana, then came to St. Louis, where he died in 1849 at the age of sixty-eight years.
40. Sarah Benton was the daughter of Samuel and Mary Benton of Kentucky and a niece of the famous Missouri Senator, Thomas Hart Benton. She married Captain J. B. Brant in 1830, spent many years as an invalid, but attended Dr. Pott's Second Presbyterian Church. There is no record of her attendance at a Catholic church.
41. *Journal.* Lucille Mathevon was born at Lyons, France, on January 6, 1793, of wealthy parents whose home was a center of Catholic activity during the French Revolution. She went first to a private school in Lyons, then attended the boarding school at Sainte-Marie-d'en-Haut, Grenoble, and was received into the novitiate on July 14, 1813, by Mother Duchesne. After the departure of the first missionary band for America, Lucille was fired with one great desire—to join Mother Duchesne on the western frontier. She made her solemn religious profession on the feast of the Sacred Heart, May 29, 1818, the very day on which Mother Duchesne first set foot on American soil. Mother Mathevon became the Society's greatest missionary among the Indians, spending fifty-four years in America and thirty-four among the Potawatomi at Sugar Creek and St. Mary's, Kansas. For an account of the Potawatomi mission see Callan, *op. cit.*, Chapter IX.
42. This was Mary Radford, whose mother had married General William Clark, former territorial governor of Missouri, in 1821. Mary Radford married Stephen Watts Kearney, U. S. Army, but there is no evidence that she remained a practical Catholic. General Clark's own children had been baptized by Bishop Flaget in 1814. See J. H. Schauinger, *Cathedrals in the Wilderness* (Milwaukee, 1952), p. 116.
43. The allusion is to a number of very remarkable occurrences, perhaps miraculous, at the tomb of Aloysia Jouve, who was buried at Sainte-Marie-d'en-Haut, Grenoble.
44. See Appendix II for letter of July, 1822, describing this procession.
45. Father Hercules Brassac came to America with Bishop Du Bourg in 1817. Appointed pastor at Grand Coteau, Louisiana, in 1819, he was instrumental in obtaining from Mrs. Charles Smith the donation of land for the founding of the first Convent of the Sacred Heart in Louisiana. Father Brassac was much loved by his parishioners in both Donaldsonville and Baton Rouge. In 1837 he returned to France and for some years acted as agent in ecclesiastical affairs for the bishops of the United States.

Father Pierre Desmoulins came to America with Bishop Du Bourg's first band of missionaries. He served first at Kaskaskia, then at Baton Rouge. In 1826 he replaced Father Michael Portier in New Orleans and took charge of a boys' school that had been organized in the old Ursuline convent. His name does not appear in other records examined.

46. Herculaneum, in Jefferson County, Missouri, some thirty miles south of St. Louis, and close to the lead mines of that section.
47. Father Constantine Maenhaut came to Louisiana at the invitation of Bishop Du Bourg in 1817 and was stationed at Natchez. In 1824 he was transferred to Pensacola. After a trip to Europe with Bishop Anthony Blanc he served at the Cathedral in New Orleans, being pastor there from 1858 until his death in 1864.
48. The route traveled by Mother Duchesne and her companions from Plaquemine to Grand Coteau seems to have been by way of Bayou Tête, then up Alligator Bayou, through the forks of the Atchafalaya, and up Bayou Courtableu to Port Barré, thence overland by cart to the convent, the last lap being covered in about six hours.
49. On November 23, 1821, St. Madeleine Sophie wrote to Mother Duchesne: "If the foundation at Opelousas takes place, I put you in charge of it as Provincial." And on February 10, 1822, to Mother Audé: "I counsel you to refer all urgent questions to Mother Duchesne. She is, as it were, your Provincial. I have given her full authority, and if that title were in use among us she would certainly bear it. At least I have given her full powers. Have recourse to her in all ordinary cases and refer to me only the most difficult and those that can wait for months for an answer."

On March 2, 1822, however, Mother Audé repeated her request to be directly under the supervision of the Superior General, writing to her in characteristic fashion: "Oh, my very dear Mother, take pity on your little house of Opelousas; be its joy and its happiness—you can do so—by consenting to direct it yourself, even if it is so far away. I will not leave you in ignorance of the least thing, and a word, just one little word from you, will be the magnet which I shall use to draw all hearts to Jesus and to bind them to Him."
50. Mother Duchesne to Father Rosati, December 1, 1822. Father Borgna had recovered from yellow fever, Father Ferrari had not yet contracted it, when Mother Duchesne saw them in New Orleans.
51. To Mother de Lalanne, Bordeaux.
52. Father Desmoulins was pastor at Baton Rouge.
53. As the quarantine of steamboats at Natchez was reported in the *Missouri Republican* on November 6, 1822, along with news of the terrible epidemic raging in Pensacola and New Orleans, the religious at Florissant were aware of the danger to which Mother Duchesne and Therese Pratte were exposed, but neither they nor General Pratte could obtain information about the travelers until they reached New Madrid.
54. Jean-François de Galaup, Comte de Laperouse (1741–1788), French navigator commissioned to explore the Japan seas and waters southeast of Australia, and incidentally to attempt the Northwest Passage, sailed in August, 1785. The expedition did good work, though it ended in shipwreck. Three editions of the *Journals* sent home during the voyage were published under the title *Voyage autour du Monde* in 1797, 1799, and 1831 respectively. Mother Duchesne had come across one of the earlier editions among the books on board the *Cincinnati*.
55. The *Cincinnati* arrived at St. Louis on November 28 in such need of repair in hull and engine that it could not sail again until mid-January, 1823. Floating ice during this winter made steamboat travel extremely dangerous and at times kept all steamboats at St. Louis confined in port.
56. December 1, 1822. In a letter to Father Rosati bearing this same date Mother Duchesne repeats her plan to train noncloistered nuns to work in the villages of Missouri.
57. Captain Robert McCoy and his wife, Marie Lafond, were among the most

prominent residents of New Madrid. The Captain had commanded a galley on the Mississippi under the Spanish regime and acted as commandant of New Madrid and Tywappity Bottom. He died in 1840. His wife was the daughter of Dr. Jean-Baptiste Lafond, who with Father Pierre Gibault had guided General George Rogers Clark to the capture of Vincennes during the American Revolution.

58. Fathers Brassac and Dahmen are mentioned as two of the priest patients in the *Journal* which Mother Berthold kept up to date during Mother Duchesne's absence.

59. Hostility to Bishop Du Bourg had increased to such a pitch, it was feared he might not find a place of residence in St. Louis on his return from Baltimore.

Notes—chapter eight

1. St. Louis College, opened by Bishop Du Bourg in 1818, was never a success. It was closed in 1826 and some of its desks and benches helped to equip the first Convent of the Sacred Heart in St. Louis. Reopened under Jesuit direction, it later developed into St. Louis University.
2. Father Francis Niel was pastor in St. Louis at this time. According to *Rothensteiner*, 1:275, he bought the church property in September, 1823, then turned it over to the creditors again. An agreement with these men—Auguste and Pierre Chouteau and Bernard Pratte—was reached only in 1828, when they reconveyed the property to Bishop Rosati for about $4,750 at 6 per cent.
3. The advertisement referred to was dated January 1, 1823, and appeared in three issues of the *Missouri Republican*, January 9, 15, and 22.
4. This money had been borrowed in Paris by Mother Barat to pay Mother Duchesne's debt to Mr. Mullanphy. The Paris loan was paid off by Madame de Granville as a gift to the American mission.
5. The incident referred to took place in New Orleans on February 2, 1822, the day Mothers Lucille Mathevon and Xavier Murphy arrived from France. They were welcomed by Bishop Du Bourg himself, and it was he who disposed of the 1000 franc note on Bordeaux that was intended for Mother Duchesne at Florissant.
6. Zoë Leduc, only daughter of Marie Philip Leduc and Marguerite Papin, was born in St. Louis in 1807, left an orphan in 1810, and died at the age of sixteen years. Her closest friend was a girl named Pelagie Chouteau, called by Mother Duchesne "a cousin of the Pratte girls." Research has yielded no identification of this Pelagie Chouteau except the fact supplied by the St. Louis Cathedral Burial Register: she was interred on September 21, 1823. No record of her age or her parents was entered in the register—a very unusual procedure. The absence of her name from the Cathedral Baptismal Register lends a further bit of mystery to the memory of this girl whom Mother Duchesne wrote of as "our first and most loyal pupil."
7. This "forgetfulness" on the part of the former pupils may have been due in part to the fact that the fathers of many of them were involved in the church-property affair, and the girls may have been either forbidden or ashamed to visit the nuns.
8. The recurrence of illness in the community and school seems to have been due to the extreme seasonal changes in the weather, to a lack of provision against such changes, to poor diet, and to want of proper precautions against infection and contagion.
9. John F. Easterly, C. M., *The Life of Rt. Rev. Joseph Rosati, C.M.* (Catholic University of America Press, 1942), pp. 65–67. Joseph Rosati, born in 1789 at Sora, Naples, entered the Congregation of the Mission at Rome, where he

was ordained. He set out for America with Fathers De Andreis and Acquaroni in 1816 and spent some months in Kentucky learning English. He helped establish the seminary at the Barrens, Perry County, Missouri, and succeeded De Andreis as superior there in 1820. Appointed coadjutor to Bishop Du Bourg in 1823, he was consecrated at Donaldsonville, Louisiana, on March 25, 1824. After Du Bourg's withdrawal from Louisiana, Rosati became Bishop of St. Louis and administrator of the diocese of New Orleans until the appointment of Bishop Leo De Neckere in 1829. Under the guidance of Bishop Rosati the diocese of St. Louis made remarkable progress. In 1840 he went to Rome to report on his work. Appointed Apostolic Delegate to Haiti by Pope Gregory XVI, he asked that Father Peter Richard Kenrick be named coadjutor in St. Louis. Successful in his mission to Haiti, he returned to Europe, hoping to recover his health, but he died in Rome in September, 1843.

10. Francis Xavier Dahmen, C.M., born at Dueren on the Rhine in 1789, made his novitiate in the Congregation of the Mission under Father De Andreis and was ordained in 1819. He served for a time as pastor at Vincennes, Indiana, and also at Florissant during missionary trips made by Father De La Croix. In September, 1822, he was sent to Ste Genevieve after the death of Father Henri Pratte and there endeared himself to the people, for he was "not a grave man of learning, but alert in mind and direct in rugged speech, yet a very lovable character." He became the first pastor of St. Vincent's Parish in St. Louis, was sent to the Vincentian Motherhouse in Paris in 1852, and died there in 1866. Father Dahmen was one of the priests of the St. Louis area in whom Mother Duchesne had the greatest confidence.

11. February 20, 1823.

12. This statement applies only to the Hamilton sisters; Mary Ann Summers was bilingual when she went to live with the religious at St. Charles in 1819.

13. The revised sketch of Aloysia Jouve's life was sent to the American novices by Mother Barat in 1823.

14. *Cf.* Gilbert Garraghan, S.J., *The Jesuits of the Middle United States* (New York, 1938), 1:28–34.

15. The Sisters of Loretto, first known as "The Friends of Mary at the Foot of the Cross," were organized by Father Charles Nerinckx in Kentucky in 1812. Bishop Flaget approved of the enterprise, and God so blessed it that within twelve years there were more than one hundred Sisters in the congregation. A group of them came to Missouri in 1823.

16. Charles Felix Van Quickenborne, S.J., a native of Belgium, born in 1788, studied at the Seminary of Ghent and taught there after ordination. He entered the Society of Jesus in 1815, came to America in 1817, was appointed Master of Novices at Georgetown the following year. He moved with the novices to White Marsh, Maryland, in 1819, and came from there to Missouri in 1823. Father Van Quickenborne died in 1837.

    Peter Joseph Timmermans, S.J., born in the province of Antwerp in 1788, was twenty-nine years of age when he came to America. Archbishop Maréchal ordained him at Georgetown in 1820, and he was appointed assistant to the Master of Novices at White Marsh. Coming to Missouri in June, 1823, he died on May 31, 1824.

17. The story is given at length in Garraghan, *op. cit.*, 1:79–91.

18. Eugene Michaud, born near Le Puy, France, in 1798, reached New Orleans in 1822 and was ordained in St. Louis a few months later by Bishop Du Bourg. In 1823 he was stationed at the Cathedral in New Orleans. After the Bishop's withdrawal to France, Father Michaud returned to his native land.

    Edmund Saulnier, a native of Bordeaux, was also ordained by Bishop Du Bourg in 1822. He taught languages at the St. Louis College and later became rector of the Cathedral. It was he who administered the last sacraments to

Auguste Chouteau, co-founder of St. Louis (d. February 24, 1829). Father Saulnier was pastor at Carondelet, Missouri, for ten years, was named chancellor of the archdiocese of St. Louis in 1850, and died in March, 1864.

19. Garraghan, *op. cit.*, 1:27.
20. *Ibid.*, 1:106.
21. Therese Detchemendy was the daughter of Pascal Detchemendy of Ste Genevieve, Missouri, who was very active in the political life of the territory and is said to have been one of the richest and most influential representatives of the French element in this section of the country.
22. Garraghan, *op. cit.*, 1:101. In November, 1825, Father Theodore De Theux wrote from Florissant that all the clothing and linen used by the Jesuits were "made and repaired by the Ladies of the Sacred Heart." *Ibid.*, 1:132.
23. This is the first mention of the projected convent at Assumption in the La Fourche country, Louisiana. The Sisters of Loretto undertook the foundation in 1825. Its subsequent history appears in Chapter Nine.
24. To Mother Eugenie de Gramont, January 2, 1824.
25. Mother Barat wrote on August 7, 1823: "Madame de Rollin has just lost her husband. Her grief is difficult to describe. She sends you a thousand francs, the gift of her dead husband. He received the last sacraments and died in good dispositions."
26. Mother Duchesne is here referring to Savoye-Rollin's help in restoring Sainte Marie.
27. The efficacy of the forty-days' prayer in honor of St. Francis Regis is mentioned by Father Van Quickenborne in a letter of April 29, 1825: "I made a vow," he continues, "if they [the Indian boys] changed [their behavior], to do what I could to have that Saint the patron of our mission. The boys are entirely changed." Garraghan, *op. cit.*, 1:161–162.
28. Marie Canale left the novitiate at Florissant before the close of 1824. Later on she entered the convent of the Sisters of Loretto at the Barrens.
29. July 25, 1824.
30. Father Clorivière (Joseph-Pierre Picot de Limoleon), born in 1768, was the man who attempted to assassinate Napoleon with the famous "infernal machine." He escaped to America, spent some years in restless life, changed his name to Clorivière, after his famous Jesuit uncle, became a priest in order to pray and do penance for the many victims killed when the bomb exploded in Paris, and finally became chaplain at the Georgetown Visitation monastery in 1819. The chapel of the monastery was begun in 1820, but Clorivière and the superior, Mother Catherine, who succeeded Mother Teresa Lalor, the foundress, went so heavily into debt that in 1822 they were nearly bankrupt. The idea of dispersing the Sisters had to be faced; negotiations for merging the community with the Ursulines in Louisiana and Canada had been begun, when money came to Clorivière from France and to the Sisters from New York, and the historic monastery was saved. Prosperity was in sight before Father Clorivière's death in 1826. See David Darrah, *Conspiracy in Paris* (New York, 1953).
31. An advertisement in the *Missouri Republican*, September 13 and 20, 1824, runs as follows

YOUNG LADIES SEMINARY

Kept by the religious ladies established at St. Ferdinand
fifteen miles from St. Louis

The Religious Ladies established at St. Ferdinand give notice to the public that to yield to the desire of persons who wish to confide to them the education of their children, the price of the boarding school is now reduced to $100.

In this young ladies will be taught French and English, Reading, Grammar, Writing, Arithmetic, History, Geography, Sewing, and Embroidery.

They will, moreover, open another boarding school in a separate building for the children whose parents cannot pay the above mentioned price; for this the board is only $9 per quarter, *payable in advance,* either in cash or produce. The pupils will be taught French, English, Reading, Writing, the first rules of Arithmetic, and plain sewing.

Finally they will continue their free school for day scholars, who will be entirely separated from the boarders and will be kept from 9 o'clock in the morning until 5 in the evening.

This advertisement appeared in both French and English. It may be of interest to read, in connection with it, the "trousseau list" which Mother Duchesne sent to Father Rosati on August 27, 1823, for a prospective pupil: "We can furnish the bed for $2 a year . . . but this does not include the covers. The trousseau consists of 2 pairs of sheets, 3 bed covers, one of which is white, 6 towels, 6 chemises, 6 handkerchiefs, 6 pairs of stockings, I black dress, 1 white dress, and three or four for everyday use, 2 pairs of shoes, 1 white veil, 6 capes or white neckerchiefs, 1 knife, fork, cup, toothbrush, pins, paper, pens."

32. Father Nerinckx died at Ste Genevieve on August 12, 1824.

33. Letters of Mother Duchesne to Bishop Rosati, October 24, 1824, December 12, 1824, and February 28, 1825, exemplify this.

34. *Notes on the Life of Ven. Mother Duchesne* by Mother Amelie Jouve (unpublished manuscript). Copy in Archives RSCJ, Maryville College. Referred to hereafter as *Notes* by Mother Jouve.

35. *Ibid.* Mother Duchesne's *Journal* records many extra holidays each year, such as July 4, the last Thursday of November (Thanksgiving Day?), feast of St. Philip, May 1, of St. Mary Magdalen, July 22, and of St. Cecilia, November 22—"for those who sing." A novice of those days wrote: "The convent at Florissant was very poor and very small, but the greater our privations, the livelier our joy. A holy gaiety animated our recreations. Never was a word of complaint heard in these reunions. Their atmosphere was always that of cordial happiness and loving trust in God." *Sketch of the Life of Mother Lucille Mathevon* (unpublished manuscript). Archives RSCJ, Maryville College.

36. When questioned about the "trials" to which Mother Duchesne subjected her novices, Mother Regis Hamilton recalled as the worst she experienced the occasion on which her Mistress of Novices discovered a nest of new-born mice in the convent pantry. As Regis was in charge of that domain, she was told to kill the wee creatures. To the sensitive young novice this was an agonizing ordeal, but she determined to carry out the order in the most generous fashion, so she slew each little mouse separately instead of drowning them all in one batch. *Sketch of the Life of Mother Eulalie Regis Hamilton* (unpublished). Archives RSCJ, Maryville College.

37. "That ragged thing," however, was carefully washed and mended by Philippine and used as a coverlet for her own bed. It was dark—purple or black— with a light cross of some kind in the center, hence the somewhat gruesome tradition that Mother Duchesne's bed was at one period covered with a funeral pall.

38. John Timon, C.M., was at this time a seminarian at the Barrens. Born in Pennsylvania in 1797, he had moved with his family to St. Louis and entered the Vincentian novitiate in 1823. Ordained in June, 1825, he spent many years as a missionary in Missouri and Texas. He refused the post of Prefect

Apostolic in Texas, but accepted consecration as first Bishop of Buffalo in 1847. He at once invited the Religious of the Sacred Heart to his diocese and the present convent at Rochester, N.Y., stems from this invitation. Bishop Timon died in 1867, "utterly exhausted in the cause of Christ."

39. In a letter to Mother Audé, October 25, 1824, St. Madeleine Sophie writes with great affection of this nephew and commends him to the kindness of her communities in America. Father Dusaussoy was never very helpful to the religious because of his restless disposition, but he was always priestly and fervent.

40. Mother Duchesne was at this time in her fifty-sixth year.

41. Father Niel's European trip had as its special purpose the collecting of alms for the support of missions and missionaries in Missouri.

42. *Notes* by Mother Jouve.

43. This illness and sudden recovery are mentioned by Mother Jouve in her *Notes*.

44. Sophie McGowan, born in New York in 1811, entered the novitiate at Grand Coteau in 1825, made her first vows at St. Michael's in 1827, with her companions, Philippine and Aloysia, and died in 1836.

   Philippine Jourdain, born in St. Louis in 1812, was placed in the academy at Grand Coteau by Bishop Du Bourg in 1823. She began her novitiate there and spent her religious life at St. Michael's, where she died in 1835.

   Aloysia Hardey, born in Alexandria, Maryland, December 8, 1809, was a pupil at Grand Coteau when Mother Duchesne visited there in 1822. Entering the novitiate there, she made her final profession at St. Michael's in 1833. She became superior there, was sent as one of the foundresses of the first Convent of the Sacred Heart in New York. Later she filled the offices of local superior, Superior Vicar, and Assistant General, dying in France in 1886.

45. The General Council met only in September, 1826.

46. Pierre Ronsin, born in 1771, was admitted to the Society of the Fathers of the Faith by Father Varin in 1801, and to the Society of Jesus by Father de Clorivière in 1814. A man of deep piety and ardent zeal, he spent himself for souls, bringing devotion to the Sacred Heart into the lives of thousands of people. His book, *Instructions on Devotion to the Sacred Heart,* was published in many editions. Father Ronsin died in 1846.

47. Mother Duchesne was evidently not yet acquainted with the Association for the Propagation of the Faith which had been organized in Lyons in 1822.

48. Bishop Rosati to Mother Duchesne, March 10, 1826.

49. Father Francis Niel was still nominally pastor, though Father Edmund Saulnier had replaced him in the pastorate.

50. Archives RSCJ, St. Charles, Missouri.

51. On the night of November 9–10, 1825, fire destroyed the section of the chateau of Vizille that had housed the huge indoor tennis court where the famous political assembly of 1788 had been held.

52. Father John Rosti, C.M., came to the American mission from Milan. Ordained by Bishop Du Bourg in 1821, he was pastor at Grand Coteau, Louisiana, for several years. In 1836 he was recalled to Missouri and died as Master of Novices at the Barrens in 1839.

53. For Bishop Michael Portier, see Note 32, Chapter Five.

54. *Lettres Circulaires de Ste Madeleine Sophie,* 1:116–117.

55. Bishop Rosati to Mother Duchesne, November 20, 1826.

56. The document attesting this blessing of the Holy Father, procured by Father Philip Borgna for the Religious of the Sacred Heart in America, is in Archives RSCJ, Maryville College.

57. Bishop Rosati wrote to Mother Duchesne from Ste Genevieve on March 2,

1827: "I could not answer your letter sooner because of my trip to Kentucky, which lasted longer than I anticipated. . . . I grant you all the permissions necessary to make your will. The vow of poverty is not compromised by this, for although before the law you appear to dispose of the property, before God you make no disposition. You simply take the means necessary to assure your community of keeping what belongs to it. So be at peace."

was a diligent and zealous priest, working in parishes and on missions among the Indians. After the great flood of 1844 he contracted a slow fever from which he died in May, 1845.

39. October 23, 1828.

40. The L'Eveque sisters were Maria, Evelina, Seraphine, Amelie, Louise, and Elise.

41. Nicholas Boilvin died on a keelboat on his way to St. Louis from Wisconsin in the summer of 1824.

42. Callan, *op. cit.*, pp. 226–227.

43. *Journal.*

44. H. Castille, *Casimir Perier* (Paris, 1858), p. 21.

45. In October, 1826, Augustin Perier's eldest daughter, Camille-Josephine, wife of François-Charles, Comte de Rémusat, died at the age of 26 years, and in November, 1827, he lost his youngest daughter, Marie-Amelie, aged 21 years. A daughter of Camille and Marine Teisseire also died in 1827.

46. December 26, 1828.

47. January 18, 1829.

48. Baunard, *op. cit.*, p. 398.

49. March 15, 1829.

50. The implication is that as Mother Berthold could no longer bear the burden of superiority, Mother Duchesne thought she might need to move to Florissant.

51. Anthony Blanc, born near Lyons, France, in 1792 and ordained in 1816, came to America the following year and served as a zealous missionary in the Mississippi Valley. In 1831 Bishop De Neckere named him vicar-general, and after the death of that prelate Father Blanc was consecrated Bishop of New Orleans. In 1851 he was made first archbishop of that see, and he died there in 1860.

52. First Provincial Council of Baltimore, October, 1829.

53. Mother Eugenie Desmarquest, Assistant General and Mistress of Novices in Paris.

54. One of her steamboat letters came to light recently in the Archives of the Association for the Propagation of the Faith. A copy is now in Archives RSCJ, Rome, through the courtesy of Father W. L. Davis, S.J. Dated November 10, 1829, and addressed to Abbé Perreau, the postmark of destination bears the date of March, 1830.

55. March 3, 1830.

56. Baunard, *op. cit.*, pp. 401–402.

57. Bishop John Dubois, third bishop of New York, invited the Religious of the Sacred Heart to his see city in 1827. A year before his death in 1842, the invitation was accepted.

58. December 22, 1829.

59. By *competition places* is meant rank places in weekly tests or examinations. Report cards, or *bulletins*, as they were called, continued in use in all the academies of the Sacred Heart. Some *bulletins* dating from this period are housed in Archives RSCJ, Maryville and City House, St. Louis.

60. December 22, 1829.

61. January 20, 1830.

62. *Idem.*

63. Mother Félicité Lavy-Brun to Mother Barat, November 19, 1830.

64. *Ibid.*, December 3, 1830.

65. *Journal.* Leo Raymond De Neckere, born in Belgium, was studying philosophy at Ghent when Bishop Du Bourg accepted him for the American mission. Completing his studies with the Vincentians, he was ordained in 1822. He served as vice-rector and professor at the seminary of the Barrens and became superior of the community in 1825. Frail health took him back to

Europe for a time, but he was appointed bishop of New Orleans in August, 1829. Consecrated in 1830, he labored earnestly and with marked success. In the yellow fever epidemic of 1833 he refused to remain in the relative safety of St. Michael's, where he happened to be recuperating from an illness, and went to his see city to minister to the plague-stricken people, regardless of creed or color. Contracting the disease, he died on September 5, 1833.

66. On July 23, 1830, Bishop Rosati sent Mother Duchesne "$100 to reimburse you for the equivalent sum which you loaned to the Seminary, along with $453, or 2388 francs, on the part of the Association for the Propagation of the Faith."

67. February 14, 1830.

Notes—chapter ten

1. Peter Doutreluingne, C.M., born in Flanders in 1795, entered the Congregation of the Mission in 1825. Coming to Missouri two years later, he served at the cathedral and did mission work. In 1830 he became pastor at Cahokia, Illinois; six years later he was recalled to Missouri. He served in several Vincentian foundations until 1873, the year of his death.
2. *Journal.*
3. *Idem.*
4. There was question of the convent of Sainte-Marie-d'en-Haut, Grenoble, being closed because of municipal construction work and fortifications in the vicinity. The town council later claimed the property.
5. Mother Duchesne to Bishop Rosati, January 19, 1831.
6. March 29, 1831.
7. March 31, 1831.
8. Theodore De Theux, S.J., born at Liège in 1789, belonged to a family of Belgian nobility. Ordained in 1812, he became administrator of the diocese of Liège in 1815 and professor of Sacred Scripture and theology. He came to America in 1816 and entered the Jesuit novitiate in Maryland. In 1825 he arrived at Florissant to aid Father Van Quickenborne and in 1831 succeeded him as superior of the Missouri Mission and master of novices. His administration was marked by severity in the discharge of his duties, but also with complete uprightness of intention. In 1836 he was assigned to teaching again. In spite of some eccentricities Father De Theux was always highly esteemed and respected. He died at St. Charles, Missouri, in 1846.
9. The disturbed condition of France, following the July Revolution of 1830, accounts in part for the scant number of extant letters of Mother Duchesne to her family and to members of the Society in France during this period.
10. May 7, 1831.
11. June 3, 1831.
12. June 5, 1831.
13. *Bergasse*, p. 44.
14. August 16, 1831.
15. May 18, 1831.
16. Mother Duchesne to Bishop Rosati, December 15, 1831.
17. *St. Michel des Mines* was a name used to indicate the mining district near Fredericktown in southeastern Missouri, where the parish church was dedicated to St. Michael.
18. James Oliver Van de Velde, S.J., born in Belgium in 1795, came to America with Father Nerinckx and joined the Jesuits at Georgetown. Ordained in 1827 and sent to Missouri, he helped to build up the reputation of the Jesuit college in St. Louis by his talents and cultured education. Raised to the episcopate,

he presided first over the diocese of Chicago as its second bishop, then over that of Natchez, where he died of yellow fever in 1855.

Joseph Paquin, C.M., was the second native-born Missourian raised to the priesthood. Ordained in 1826, he was in later years president of St. Mary's College at the Barrens and superior of the Vincentian seminary in St. Louis. Having offered for the Texan missions, he went there in the summer of 1844 and was almost immediately stricken with yellow fever, dying on August 13, 1844.

19. In the ceremony of March 19, 1832, Elizabeth Missé made her first vows, and Judith Shannon received the habit and white veil.

20. Dr. Bernard G. Farrar, 1785–1849, a Virginian, practiced medicine and surgery in St. Louis from 1818 until his death in the cholera epidemic in 1849.

Dr. Samuel Merry, graduate in medicine at the University of Pennsylvania, was practicing medicine in St. Louis as early as 1820, developing a large clientele and a reputation for skill and charity.

21. *Journal*. Dr. Stephen W. Adreon, born in Baltimore in 1806, achieved remarkable success in the practice of medicine. He came to St. Louis early in 1832, and during his long career served the city in positions of responsibility, dying in 1867.

22. While authority over all the American convents of the Sacred Heart had been delegated to Mother Duchesne by the Superior General, her position had no basis in the Constitutions of the Society and the convents in Louisiana, under Mother Audé's leadership, had not felt obliged to submit their problems to her.

23. Mr. Francis H. Taylor's name appears on the masthead of *The Shepherd of the Valley*, but he seems to have been known to many as Deodat Taylor.

24. Mother Paranque was superior at Sainte-Marie-d'en-Haut, Grenoble.

25. April 23, 1831.

26. *Choulet*, p. 137.

27. July 28, 1832.

28. *Shepherd of the Valley*, August 4, 1832. Referred to hereafter as *Shepherd*.

29. According to *Choulet*, Scipion Perier "died in Casimir's arms" at the age of forty-five, in Paris on April 2, 1821.

30. *Journal*.

31. *Shepherd*, September 15, 1832.

32. *Journal*.

33. This notice was meant, evidently, to prepare the readers for the lengthy *Prospectus* which appeared in this and several other issues of *The Shepherd of the Valley* over Philippine Duchesne's name and which was copied in *The Catholic Almanac* of 1834. It is reprinted in Callan, *op. cit.*, pp. 748–750.

34. October 16 and 23, 1832.

35. *Journal. Cf.* Garraghan, *op. cit.*, 1:296n.

36. *Shepherd*, November 3, 1833.

37. Quoted by Garraghan, *op. cit.*, 1:296n.

38. *Journal*.

39. *Ibid.*

40. Irish-born Hugh O'Neil had settled at Florissant before 1820. He entered the contracting business and was the outstanding Catholic builder in St. Louis for many years.

41. One of the Louailliers girls, Isaure, became a Religious of the Sacred Heart.

42. Mother Eleanor Gray was stationed at Grand Coteau from 1828 to 1841.

43. Manuscript notes written by Mrs. Mary Ann Rourke Cartan and contributed by Mother Pauline Grindon, R.S.C.J. One of Mrs. Cartan's daughters became a Religious of the Sacred Heart.

44. Father Matthew Condamine came to St. Louis from France in 1831. He served as pastor first at Kaskaskia, then at Cahokia, Illinois, where he died in 1836.

John Mary Odin, C.M., born in the diocese of Lyons, France, in 1800, came to Missouri in 1822, entered the Congregation of the Mission, and was ordained in 1823. For many years he traveled as a frontier missionary. Going to Texas in 1840, he was appointed Vicar Apostolic and later Bishop of Galveston. In 1861 he was transferred to the archbishopric of New Orleans. He went to the Vatican Council in 1869, fell sick in Rome, withdrew to his native town of Ambierle, and died there in May, 1870.

Father Victor Paillasson, born in France in 1799, came to America as a secular priest and served the parishes of Kaskaskia and New Madrid, then entered the Society of Jesus at Florissant. He had the privilege of attending Father Van Quickenborne on his deathbed, was sent to the new college at Grand Coteau in 1839, and died there the following year.

45. The Sisters of the Visitation reached Kaskaskia in May, 1833. For eleven years they struggled there under most difficult circumstances. The great flood of 1844 forced them to move to St. Louis.

46. October 10, 1833. Mother Duchesne's several accounts of the death of Mother Berthold are almost identical and differ greatly from that given by Msgr. Baunard, who drew his material from notes written by Mother de Kersaint some thirty years after the event and by Mother Evelina L'Eveque, who was not in St. Louis in the 1830's. Neither was Father Van Quickenborne in St. Louis in September, 1833, when he was said to have been at the bedside of Mother Berthold during a terrible night of agony, September 15–16.

47. *Shepherd,* September 27, 1833.

48. To Mother Eugenie de Gramont, September 22, 1833: "I am spending the night in letterwriting, so please excuse brevity and all the stupid mistakes of an old nun, who is not sleepy, however, when chatting with you, but who is growing very weak."

49. Letter undated.

50. Bishop John Baptist Purcell was consecrated Bishop of Cincinnati in October, 1833. He invited the Religious of the Sacred Heart to his diocese several times, and when they were at last able to accept the invitation in 1869, he became a kind friend and a frequent visitor at the convent in Clifton, Cincinnati. Archbishop Purcell died in 1883.

51. June 24, 1833.

52. The Bishop of Charleston at this time was the Most Reverend John England.

53. Mother Duchesne is calculating for the years 1832–1833. Ten religious and two orphans died at St. Michael's between April, 1832, and November, 1833.

54. *Choulet,* p. 80.

55. *Ibid.,* p. 81.

56. January 26, 1834.

57. The New York Banker was Mr. James Gore King, 1791–1853, third son of Rufus King, the Federalist statesman.

58. Mother Duchesne omits her numerous duties as superior of the convent, with no religious filling the office of assistant to the superior.

59. Mother Judith Shannon, the infirmarian, was a sister of Mother Anna Stanislaus Shannon.

60. Quoted by *Cahier,* 1:601–602.

61. Mother Barat refers to Mother Audé's request in a letter to her dated October, 1833.

62. Quoted by *Cahier,* 1:602.

63. Father Rondot was a French priest who, after a short time in St. Louis, was obliged to return to his native land because of physical and mental illness.

64. On the following day, October 9, Mother Duchesne wrote to Mother Léridon at La Ferrandiére, Lyons, France: "I have received such moving details about the last days at Sainte Marie. I could forget my right hand sooner than that delightful place, and I have more right to weep over it than had Jeremias over Jerusalem. Tell my dear companions of long ago who shared the sorrow of those last days how intimately I shared their suffering and how I pray that they may enjoy a long, unbroken peace in the new home to which they have been transferred."

Notes—chapter eleven

1. This dread of hot weather seems to have been the result of an illness which Mother Duchesne described in a letter to Mother Audé, November 9, 1834. Often, she wrote, she had felt at night as if she were on fire from head to foot; sometimes she stood barefoot on the cold floor for relief, while at other times she sat on the side of her bed, unable to endure the weight of a sheet.
2. Undated.
3. November 19, 1834.
4. December, 1834.
5. December 29, 1834.
6. November 19, 1834.
7. February 17, 1835.
8. Undated.
9. February 25, 1835.
10. March 7, 1835.
11. March 14, 1835. Father Auguste Jeanjean refused the episcopal dignity several times.
12. April 17, 1835. The damage to the Cathedral did not prevent the usual services from being held, *The Shepherd of the Valley* carrying notices of "Evening services at the Cathedral at candle light" on April 18 and in the following issues.
13. Undated.
14. July 27, 1835.
15. As Mother Shannon had entered the Society at the age of fifteen, she was obliged to wait for final profession until her twenty-fifth birthday. The young religious mentioned above was Mother Mary Knapp.
16. June 5, 1835.
17. *Life of Reverend Mother Anna Josephine Shannon* (unpublished), Archives RSCJ, St. Louis, p. 43. Referred to hereafter as *Shannon*.
18. *Ibid.*, pp. 44–45. Mother Shannon lived to be eighty-five years old.
19. *Ibid.*, p. 45.
20. George Aloysius Carrell, S.J., born in Philadelphia in 1802 and educated at the Jesuit college of Georgetown, was ordained as a diocesan priest in 1829 and entered the Society of Jesus in 1835. He became President of St. Louis University in 1843, then acted as Rector of St. Xavier College, Cincinnati, from 1851 until he was named Bishop of Covington, Kentucky, in 1853. He died there in 1868.
21. Pierce Connolly and his wife, Cornelia Peacock, were converts from Protestantism. With papal permission they separated, he becoming a priest, she founding the distinguished Catholic teaching congregation of the Sisters of the Holy Child Jesus. Subsequently Connolly repudiated his priesthood

and spent the last years of his life as an Anglican, while his wife remained faithful to her religious community and died in the odor of sanctity.

22. The "opportunity" was Bishop Rosati himself, who was going to New Orleans for the consecration of Bishop Anthony Blanc. Mother Duchesne to Bishop Rosati, November 8, 1835.

23. September 2, 1835.

24. This opinion was well founded. Florissant gave six stable vocations to the novitiate between 1834 and 1840: Mary Knapp, Mary Egan, Margaret Cornelis, Anna Josephine Egan, Margaret Shannon, and Emily Regis Watts.

25. December 20, 1835.

26. Louise-Philippine Teisseire married Charles-François Rolland on July 1, 1835.

27. Hippolyte Duchesne was elected to the Chamber of Deputies, representing Saint-Marcellin, in July, 1835.

28. This school was opened by Brother Peter de Meyer, S.J., a Belgian who came to Missouri in 1823 with Father Van Quickenborne. He was the last survivor of that first missionary band, dying at St. Stanislaus Novitiate, Florissant, in 1879.

29. Mother Duchesne is referring here to her own brother, the brothers of Josephine Perier de Savoye-Rollin, and Madame Jouve's sons, who were brothers of Mothers Amelie and Constance Jouve.

30. December 25, 1835.

31. Cited by Garraghan, *op. cit.*, 1:201. Father De Theux noted in 1837, with regard to the convent school at Florissant, "Its pupils are easily distinguished from the other children by their perseverance in virtue." *Idem.*

32. February 19, 1836.

33. These grandchildren of John Mullanphy were the Chambers girls, Elizabeth and Ann, daughters of Charles Chambers and Jane Mullanphy.

34. The Destrehan girls were an interesting group, daughters of the wealthy Louisiana planter, Nicholas Noel d'Estrehan. Louise and Adele came to Florissant in 1838, transferred to the City House, St. Louis, in 1840, were joined by their sister Elisa, and remained there two or three years. Their stories are told by Harnett Kane in *The Bayous of Louisiana* and in *Plantation Parade.*

35. September 22, 1836.

36. December 2, 1836.

37. April 10, 1837.

38. June 11, 1837.

39. Camille Jordan had died in May, 1821.

40. Constans de Mauduit continued to live at Grâne until his death in 1850 at the age of ninety years. The estate at Grâne remains in the possession of descendants of Amelie Duchesne and Constans de Mauduit.

41. Casimir Perier had married Marie-Pauline Loyer in 1805. They had two sons, Auguste-Casimir and Charles-Fortunat. The older son, who used as his family name *Casimir-Perier* by way of distinction among the many Perier men, was the father of Augustin Casimir-Perier who became President of the Third French Republic in 1894.

42. Fathers Judocus F. Van Assche, Ferdinand Helias D'Huddeghem, and Peter De Vos were Belgians; Father John Lucien Gleizal was French. All four were Jesuits who served on the Missouri mission. Father De Vos was sent to the far West in 1843 and died in California.

43. Father Christian Hoecken, S.J., was a native of Upper Brabant. Arriving at Florissant in 1833, he soon began his career as an Indian missionary among the Kickapoo. His gift for languages was remarkable and enabled him to become acquainted with the Indians in a way that few missionaries enjoyed. In 1838 he founded the Catholic Mission among the Osage River Potawatomi, and in

1841 he went to Sugar Creek to work among the Southern Potawatomi. It was here that Mother Duchesne first met him. After ten years of strenuous labor Father Hoecken was stricken with cholera on a Missouri River steamboat, the *St. Ange*, while traveling with Father De Smet. Working among the sick crew and passengers in the epidemic, both priests were taken ill; each gave the other the last sacraments. Father Hoecken died on June 19, 1851, and was buried at the mouth of the Little Sioux River. On the return trip the *St. Ange* took on board the exhumed coffin and transported it to St. Louis for burial at Florissant.

44. Father Herman G. Aelen, a Belgian recruited by Father De Smet in 1834, was trained for mission work at Florissant and went as superior to the Potawatomi Mission at Sugar Creek in 1839. It was he who welcomed Mother Duchesne there in 1841. They had many things in common, among them a great devotion to St. John Francis Regis. Disagreeing with his superiors on the policy best suited to the Indian missions, Father Aelen withdrew from the Society of Jesus and took up parochial work in Kentucky.

45. January 15, 1838.

46. January 30, 1838.

47. January 25, 1838.

48. This note seems to have been written on the seventh day of the annual retreat, when the meditations center on the passion of our Blessed Lord.

49. Bishop Richard Pius Miles, first Bishop of Nashville, Tennessee, was consecrated at Bardstown on September 16, 1838. Reaching his episcopal town after a hard trip by horseback and canoe, he began a visitation of Tennessee, during which he found only three hundred Catholics in the state. In ten years the Catholic population was tripled. Bishop Miles died in 1860.

50. October 4, 1838.

51. Fathers George Hamilton and Hilary Tucker returned from Rome in 1838.

52. Pierre-Jean-Mathias Loras, born at Lyons, France, in 1792, was ordained in 1815. Coming to America in 1829, he labored in the diocese of Mobile, Alabama, until 1837, when he was consecrated Bishop of Dubuque, Iowa. By his personal example as well as his devoted service he greatly advanced the cause of Catholicism. He died in Dubuque in 1858. Where he had found one priest and a scattered little flock in 1838, he left forty-eight priests with sixty churches and 54,000 Catholics.

53. Janet Erskine Stuart, *The Society of the Sacred Heart* (Roehampton, 1914), p. 97.

54. April 26, 1840.

55. September 3, 1839.

56. Baunard, *op. cit.*, p. 476.

57. This was Father Gleizal, S.J.

Notes—chapter twelve

1. Baunard, *op. cit.*, p. 490.
2. January 29, 1832.
3. Prayer of Mother Marie of the Incarnation.
4. Baunard, *op. cit.*, p. 420. For a detailed account of the Kickapoo Mission see Garraghan, *op. cit.*, 1:404–406.
5. Paris, July 15, 1840.
6. January 15, 1841. Pierre-Jean De Smet, S.J., born in Belgium in 1801, came to the United States in 1821, and entered the Jesuit novitiate at Whitemarsh, Maryland. He belonged to the pioneer group that came to Missouri under the direction of Father Van Quickenborne, S.J., in 1823. Ordained in 1827, he ambitioned mission work among the Indians and began this in 1838 by founding a mission for the Potawatomi at Council Bluffs. His life-work really began, however, when he set out in 1840 for the Flathead country in the Rocky Mountains. The record of his missionary journeys and of the success he and his co-workers achieved is a glorious chapter in the history of Catholicity in the United States. De Smet's ascendancy over the Indians led the Government to enlist his aid many times in difficult circumstances. He died in St. Louis on May 23, 1873.
7. January 25, 1841.
8. October 9, 1872.
9. December 3, 1840. After receiving this letter, Mother Galitzin wrote to Father De Smet from St. Michael's on March 10, 1841: "After weighing our Reverend Mother General's last letter, which gives me a little opening and enables me to conceive a ray of hope for this mission among the Indians, this is what I think: I will make the sacrifice of Mother Bazire, formerly superior at Grand Coteau, whom I wished to take for the foundation in New York. I will give up Mother Lucille, whom I was anxious to send to one of the three houses that are begging for her; they have done without her up to this, they will continue to do without her. In addition to these two, I will give Mother Duchesne. If Father Verhaegen approves my plan, the foundation will be made with these three subjects; I can do no more. As to money, I have not a cent. . . . If the good God wishes this foundation, He will level all obstacles in order to finance it; if He does not wish it, who shall resist Him? I am waiting for the boat to leave this evening for St. Louis, so I cannot receive an answer from you here, but I hope to see you in St. Louis and acquaint you with final decisions and arrangements."
10. April 26, 1841.
11. Mother Mary Josephine Crawford, born in Dublin, Ireland, in 1814, entered at St. Michael's in 1840, came as a novice to St. Louis, and made her vows at the City House in 1842.

12. Mother Marie-Rose Prud'hom, born at Passavant, France, in 1802, entered in Paris, came to Louisiana in 1831, made her profession at Grand Coteau, and was transferred to St. Louis in 1838. She was treasurer at the City House at the time of her death in the cholera epidemic of 1849.

13. Mother Mathevon to Mother Galitzin; quoted by Mother Galitzin in a letter to St. Madeleine Sophie in September, 1841.

14. *Notes on the Foundation of the Sugar Creek Mission* by Mother Mathevon. Archives RSCJ, Maryville College, St. Louis. Peter Verhaegen, S.J., born in Belgium in 1800, came to America in 1821 and to Missouri in 1823, being ordained three years later. He was the first president of St. Louis University and in 1836 he was named superior of the Missouri Mission. He served in both the Maryland and Kentucky provinces in official positions and returned to the pastorate of St. Charles in 1851. In 1858 he was appointed professor of moral and dogmatic theology in St. Louis, but ill health brought him back to St. Charles, where he died on July 21, 1868.

15. Archives RSCJ, St. Charles.

16. Mother Mathevon to Mother Eleanor Gray, July, 1841, written in the form of a Journal. Archives RSCJ, Maryville College.

17. *Idem.* A full account of the mission conducted by the Religious of the Sacred Heart among the Potawatomi at Sugar Creek and later at St. Mary's, Kansas, is given in Callan, *op. cit.,* Chapter IX.

18. This letter was brought by Father Smedts from Sugar Creek to St. Charles. It is postmarked *St. Charles, Mo., July 21,* and *New York, July 31.* The date *July 21, 1841,* is inscribed on the first page of the letter in what seems to be Mother Hamilton's writing.

19. *Notes* by Mother Mathevon.

20. Baunard, *op. cit.,* p. 496.

21. Undated, 1841.

22. See Note 18.

23. Mother Marie Rivet, who had joined Mother Duchesne at Sainte-Marie-d'en Haut in 1802, died in 1841 at the age of seventy-three years.

24. February 4, 1842.

25. February 5, 1842.

26. February 4, 1842.

27. Mother Audé died in Rome on March 6, 1842.

28. Sister Marguerite Manteau died at Grand Coteau on July 4, 1841.

29. Peter Richard Kenrick, born in Ireland in 1806 and ordained there, came to the United States to aid his brother, Francis Patrick Kendrick, who filled first the see of Philadelphia and later that of Baltimore. In 1840 he was named co-adjutor to Bishop Rosati and in 1847 became first Archbishop of St. Louis. He died in the spring of 1896, one of the most highly esteemed prelates in the history of the Church in the United States.

30. *Journal of the Convent of the Sacred Heart, St. Charles.* Referred to hereafter as *Journal, St. Charles.*

31. Father De Smet had set out on his second journey to Oregon in the spring of 1841 and arrived in the Bitter Root Valley the following autumn. To obtain recruits and funds for carrying on the Indian missions established, he returned in 1842, reaching St. Louis in October.

Notes—chapter thirteen

1. Margaret Williams, *Second Sowing: Mary Aloysia Hardey*, New York, 1942, p. 196.
2. This decree was dated March 4, 1843.
3. The addition of a cloister chapel opening on the sanctuary had been planned as early as 1826 by Father Van Quickenborne, when he began the construction of the Church of St. Charles Borromeo.
4. Sister Catherine Lamarre died at Florissant on July 12, 1845.
5. *Notes* by Mother Jouve.
6. The package had been brought from France to New York the previous autumn by Mother Hardey.
7. For the story of the McSherrystown foundation, see Callan, *op. cit.*, Chapter XI.
8. Father George Hamilton, brother of Mother Regis. The church for German-speaking Catholics was built under the direction of Father John Fischer at Third Street and Gratiot and known as St. Mary of Victories.
9. The children who went to St. Louis from St. Charles in October, 1843, were: Ellen Connell, Johanna Donnellen, Agnes Lepere, Mary Lynch, Ann Mc-Laughlin, and Amanda Musick.
10. For a sketch of the life of Mother Elizabeth Galitzin see *Catholic Encyclopedia*, volume VI.
11. In April, 1844, seven Sisters of the Visitation arrived in St. Louis from Kaskaskia, opening an academy on Sixth Street near Pine. When the great flood destroyed practically the whole of the old town, the remaining Sisters were brought to St. Louis. They lived in the home of Mrs. Anne Biddle until July, 1846, when the two groups were reunited in a convent on Ninth Street which had been the archbishop's residence.
12. There is no extant letter of Mother Duchesne to Mother Barat between February, 1842, (Sugar Creek) and June, 1846 (St. Charles), and the only one to which Mother Duchesne refers in this period is that of October or November, 1843, in which she petitioned for the reopening of the academy at St. Charles and which received no direct personal answer from Mother Barat.
13. This letter is used with the permission of its present owner, Mr. Arthur C. Hoskins of St. Louis.
14. Mother Maria Cutts was Visitatrix of the convents of the Sacred Heart in the Mississippi Valley and superior at Grand Coteau; Mother Bathilde Sallion was her companion.
15. September 15, 1844. The Missouri River flood of 1844 held the record as the worst in the history of the river until the flood of 1951.
16. A perusal of the *Annals* explains their fascination for Mother Duchesne. In Volume I, published in 1842–1843, she read the story of the Louisiana Mission

to which she had come in 1818, met the names of Du Bourg, Flaget, Rosati, de Andreis, and many others she had known, traveled in spirit to Opelousas, La Fourche, New Orleans, Ste Genevieve. She also learned the progress of missions in China and many other parts of the world. As succeding volumes appeared, she found them the most satisfying reading she could desire.

17. See Note 26, Chapter Seven.
18. May 11, 1845.
19. The mayor of St. Louis at this time was Bernard Pratte, Jr.
20. May 11, 1845.
21. *Notes* by Mother Jouve.
22. The reference is to Madame Teisseire's daughters, Mesdames Amelie Bergasse, Henriette Chaper, and Louise-Philippine Rolland.
23. *Notes* by Mother Jouve.
24. Madame Jouve's son, Hippolyte, was living with his wife and children at the Jouve home in Lyons.
25. June 17, 1846.
26. Father De Smet sailed with Father John Nobili from Antwerp in January, 1844, rounded Cape Horn, and landed at Fort Vancouver in August, escorting six Sisters of Notre Dame de Namur to Oregon. Their congregation had already opened a convent in Cincinnati.
27. January 3, 1847.
28. *Notes* by Mother Jouve.
29. Letter of Father De Smet, St. Louis, October 9, 1872.
30. *Notes* by Mother Celine de Grootz, Archives RSCJ, Rome.
31. April 13, 1847.
32. *Notes* by Mother Jouve.
33. The tattered Office Book remains as a precious relic in the Society of the Sacred Heart.
34. *Notes* by Mother Jouve. This incident is not referred to by Mother Duchesne either in her *Journal* or in any of her letters.
35. *Cahier*, 2:226. It is well to recall that Mother Duchesne stated that she wrote to St. Madeleine Sophie only the two letters already mentioned or cited in the text, namely the one in the autumn of 1843, the other in June, 1846.
36. Marjory Erskine, *Mother Philippine Duchesne*, New York, 1926, p. 373.
37. *Biographical Sketch of Mother Emilie St. Cyr*. Archives RSCJ, Maryville College. For readers who expected to find here a complete unraveling of the mystery of the lost letters of Madeleine Sophie to Philippine Duchesne, the writer can offer only the solution of *a lost letter*. The uncertainty of mail in pioneer days is well known, and small wonder that letters were lost, when so many were entrusted to travelers, and others bore such vague addresses as: *Madame Duchesne, Supérieure des Dames du S.Coeur, La Louisiane*, or *A la Révérende Mère Duchesne, à Florissant par la Nouvelle Orléans, Amérique*. One other thought suggests itself: Mother Barat had continual recourse to Mother Adele Cahier's aid in her correspondence. The fact that in the spring of 1847 Mother Duchesne was writing to Mother Cahier may be the missing clue. Did Philippine fail to recognize the letters of the Secretary General as equivalent to letters from the Mother General herself? This idea is supported by a *Note* from the Superior General to all local superiors (found in Archives RSCJ, St. Michael's, now housed at Maryville), dated September 28, 1848, in which she reminds her religious that letters of the Secretary General are to be considered as letters from herself and given unopened to the persons to whom they are addressed.
38. Mother Jouve left St. Charles on September 22, 1847, with Mother Julie Bazire. The convent account book records under that date: stage fare for Mothers Jouve and Bazire, $2; ferriage, $1.

39. October, 1847. Five of the religious named here had been admitted into the Society by Mother Duchesne.
40. Latitude of Paris, 48°, 50′, 14″; of Montreal, 45°, 30′, 21″.
41. For the story of the foundation at Natchitoches (pronounced Náck-i-tosh), Louisiana, see Callan, *op. cit.*, Chapter XIV.
42. February 19, 1848.
43. *Biographical Sketch of Mother Adeline Boilvin*, Archives RSCJ, Maryville College.
44. Mother Constance Jouve was superior of the Convent of the Sacred Heart, Chambery.
45. October 24, 1848. Augustin Jordan, it will be recalled, was a cousin of Philippine and brother of Camille Jordan, of whom she was so fond. His wife, Augustine de Mauduit, had died in 1847.
46. April 29, 1849.
47. April 25, 1849.
48. The number of cholera victims in St. Louis in 1849 is usually given as 6,000.
49. September 12, 1849. Father Anthony Rey, S.J. (1807–1847), born at Lyons, France, was vice-president of Georgetown College when appointed chaplain in the U.S. Army in 1846. Heroic charity marked his conduct during the siege of Monterey and zeal for souls urged him to missionary work among the rancheros after the capture of the city. He is believed to have been killed by Mexican Indians on the way to Matamoras, as his body was found, pierced with lances, near Ceralvo in mid-January, 1847.
50. September 16, 1849.
51. January 30, 1850.
52. *Notes* by Mother Jouve.
53. February 10, 1850.
54. Father John J. Bax, S.J., a Fleming, born in 1817, came to the Missouri Mission in 1847 and worked with remarkable success among the Osage Indians at St. Francis Mission, where he contracted smallpox and died in August, 1852. Because of his boundless charity the Indians called him "Father-who-is-all-heart."

    Father John Nobili, S.J., came to the United States with Father De Smet in 1844, sailing around Cape Horn and up the Pacific to Oregon. He opened missions in New Caledonia (British Columbia) and contacted Indians as far north as the Alaskan border. Later he was assigned to the old mission of Santa Clara, California, and there founded a Jesuit college. He died in 1856.

    Father Joseph Joset, S.J., Swiss-born, reached St. Louis in 1844 and was sent out to the Rocky Mountain missions the following year, working among the Coeur d'Alenes and the Flatheads. He was placed in charge of the Mountain Missions as successor to Father De Smet, though he had neither the influence nor the personality of that great missionary. Father Joset was later transferred to California.
55. Mother Bazire eventually returned to France and withdrew from the Society.
56. Father Louis Barat had died on June 21, 1845.
57. The period of aspirantship in the Society had been lengthened in 1839 to ten years, and this regulation remained in force in America until 1851.
58. Mother Jouve's *Notes* were compiled after 1855 at the request of Mother Barat.
59. Constans de Mauduit died at Grâne on May 29, 1850, at the age of ninety years.
60. Josephine Perier de Savoye-Rollin died in Grenoble on September 23, 1850, aged eighty years.
61. February 2, 1851.
62. April 3, 1851.
63. Marine Perier Teisseire died in Grenoble on August 5, 1851.
64. November, 1851.
65. The addition at the south side of the original brick convent at St. Charles was

built in 1853, shortly after Mother Duchesne's death. It houses the library today.

66. Mother Duchesne had not understood that Mother Cutts was the Reverend Mother Vicar.

67. Mother Aimée d'Ainval was secretary to Mother Henriette Coppens, one of the Assistants General.

68. Bishop Jean-Baptiste Miège, S.J., became Vicar Apostolic of Indian Territory in 1851, arriving at St. Mary's, Kansas, in May of that year.

69. See Note 43, Chapter Eleven.

70. Summer of 1852, undated. In the account book of St. Charles for this period one finds in July, 1852, the first entry for the purchase of ice in small amounts for the sick.

71. Father Francis Xavier De Coen, S.J., a nephew of Father Charles Nerinckx, began his career as a missionary among the Potawatomi at Sugar Creek while Mother Duchesne was there. In 1846 he was recalled to St. Louis and for fifteen years did parochial and educational work. In 1861 he was sent to assist Bishop Miège at Leavenworth, Kansas, and was soon back among the Potawatomi at St. Mary's, where he died quite suddenly in July, 1864, in his fifty-fourth year. It is said that the strongest among his religious brethren wept at his death because of their deep affection for this "holy and excellent Jesuit."

72. September 4, 1852.

73. These purchases represent a very small layout of money, but they meant sacrifice for the community because the convent was so poor. The largest steady income of the house was that of Mother Duchesne's semi-annual pension from the investment made by her father for her before his death in 1814. The income varied from $60 to $175 a payment, the consul's fee being from 50¢ to $2.20, including the attestation that she was still living. At her death the convent paid at once the stipend for burial service and thirty Masses of Requiem. But her coffin, costing $5, and the cross-marker for her grave, $3, were paid for only three months later, the balance on hand in the convent treasury on December 31, 1852, being 33¢.

74. Archives RSCJ, St. Charles.

index

Acquaroni, John, C.M., 272, 282, 298, 350, 352, 354, 738, 762, n. 8

Adreon, Dr. Stephen W., 782, n. 21

Aelen, Herman G., 605, 637, 648, 658, 787, n. 44

Amyot, Louise, R.S.C.J., 632, 639, 648, 668

Andreis, Felix de, C.M., 221, 312, 315, 325, 327, 329–330, 355, 765, n. 5

Anduze, Aristide, C.M., 343, 350, 354, 767, n. 31

Ashley, General William H., 509–511

Ashley, Mrs. William H., née Eliza Christy, 509, 511

Aubert, Jean-Baptiste, S.J., 22, 112, 748, n. 16

Audé, Eugenie, R.S.C.J., novice in Paris, 191; missionary vocation, 210; voyage to America, 212, 226, 229, 231–232; in New Orleans, 242–243, 251; in St. Louis, 263; at St. Charles, 272, 274, 278, 281–282, 285–288, 290, 293, 295, 299, 303; at Florissant, 307, 309–310, 312, 316–318, 329, 331–332; foundation at Grand Coteau, La., 341, 344–348, 350–351, 358-362, 365, 369, 375–376, 378, 384, 386, 391–400, 406; attitude towards Mother Duchesne, 500–501, 769, n. 49; trip to St. Louis, 1825, 417–420; foundation at St. Michael's, La. (1825), proposed, 412–414; begun, 427, 436, 445–447, 461, 464, 466; attitude towards foundation at La Fourche, La., 467–471, 474, 476, 479–482; financial difficulties at La Fourche, 504, 515–516, 520–522; closing of convent at La Fourche, 529; illness at St. Michael's, 538, 542, 553; named Assistant General, 561–563; return to France, 563, 565–567, 579, 584, 596, 615; superior in Rome, 647; death in Rome, 789, n. 27

Balastron, Marie, R.S.C.J., 74, 90, 92, 95, 109, 752, n. 42

Barat, Louis, S.J., 89–90, 105–106, 126, 130, 166, 176, 192–193, 195–196, 212, 216–218, 223, 237, 246, 257, 276, 280–281, 294, 296, 301, 310, 318, 323, 331, 334, 339, 356, 370, 413, 426, 430, 440, 572, 606, 609, 645, 711, 737, 792, n. 56

Bax, John J., S.J., 701, 792, n. 54

Bayanne, Sister Eugenie Latier de, V.H.M., 21, 35, 37, 41, 76, 93

Bayanne, Card., Abp. of Naples, 76, 752, n. 46

Bazire, Julie, R.S.C.J., 491, 507, 515–516, 520, 525, 561, 597, 633, 662–663, 702, 792, n. 55

Berckheim, Louise de, see Madame Augustin Perier

Bergasse, Louis, 202, 759, n. 7

Bergasse, Madame Louis, née Amelie de Mauduit (niece), 61, 108, 149–150, 152, 197, 199, 207–208, 320, 759, n. 7

Bergasse, Henri, 521, 759, n. 7

Bergasse, Madame Henri, née Amelie Teisseire (cousin), 150, 152, 202, 208, 219, 587, 759, n. 7

Berthold, Octavie, R.S.C.J., postulant at Ste Marie, 179; novice in Paris, 191; missionary vocation, 209–211; voy-

795

A NOTE ON THE TYPE

IN WHICH THIS BOOK IS SET

This book is set in Janson, a Linotype face, created from the early punches of Anton Janson, who settled in Leipzig around 1670. This type is not an historic revival, but rather a letter of fine ancestry, remodeled and brought up to date to satisfy present day taste. It carries a feeling of being quite compact and sturdy. It has good color and displays a pleasing proportion of ascenders and descenders as compared to the height of the lower case letters. The book was composed and printed by The York Composition Company, Inc., of York, Pa., and bound by Moore and Company of Baltimore. The typography and design are by Howard N. King.